CORNELL STUDIES IN ENGLISH

EDITED BY

M. H. ABRAMS

FRANCIS E. MINEKA

WILLIAM M. SALE, JR.

VOLUME XLI

THE MAKING OF WALTON'S *LIVES*

BY DAVID NOVARR

The Making of
Walton's *Lives*

BY DAVID NOVARR

Cornell University Press
ITHACA, NEW YORK

For GORDY

Preface

FOR three centuries the name of Izaak Walton has been synonymous with angling. He has become the patron saint of fishermen, and fishermen have found him a most useful saint. The *Compleat Angler* has suffused its charm over the fishermen's recreation, and the veneration that Walton has ever inspired has redounded to the fishermen's credit. Walton wished to persuade men to contemplation and harmlessness and piety; *"Study to be quiet,"* he wrote. His book has served, instead, to make the Sabbath the day of greatest activity for the Leagues which bear his name.

I do not propose to wrest Walton from the fishermen. At most, they lavish their affection upon an incomplete Walton and they are unaware of the Walton who gets away. One of them said many years ago that he wanted "Walton *solus,* not Walton baited and badgered by fifty learned professors, all catechising, criticising, and cavilling at him at once." Today, Walton has become bait for the fishermen. The one hundred copies of the de luxe version of the Tricentennial Edition of the *Compleat Angler,* contrived by a fisherman, not a professor, were quickly disposed of at fifteen dollars a copy, and copy Number 1, auctioned off at the annual meeting of the Izaak Walton League, brought two thousand dollars. The fisher-editor was moved to revise Walton when four anglers of his acquaintance, eating broiled turbot with anchovy sauce at Big Ben Sea Grotto, San Francisco, confessed they had never read the *Compleat Angler* all the way through. It is an angler, not a professor, who finds (and excises) "arid" and "lifeless" passages in Walton's book; it is an angler, not a professor, who has poor Joan stroke "a syllabus or

twain" and who puts a "cock" rather than a cork on a fishing line.
The fishermen are not at home in the world of Walton's angler—a
world of peace, and patience, and calm content; a world where the
catechism was good, plain, and unperplexed; where the good old
Service Book was in use; where Kit Marlowe and Sir Walter Raleigh
were writing "old fashioned Poetry, but choicely good, . . . much
better then that now in fashion in this Critical age." Walton created
an idealized Elizabethan world in which all milkmaids sang like
nightingales and in which all fishermen had the fresh holiness of
primitive Christians, a world strange and outdated to today's
anglers. But the *Compleat Angler* was more than an ode to the good
old days, more than a hymn to retrospectual beauty. It was Walton's
subtle invitation to his contemporaries to put aside the bread,
boiled beef, and vinegar of the Puritans. Walton was much more
interested in the sharpness of his quill than in the sharpness of his
hook, but the fishermen are content with a redaction of Walton's
"recreation of a recreation." Even the *Angler "solus"* is not for
them, to say nothing of Walton's *Lives*.

My interest here is in Walton as biographer. I had originally
planned to write a critical study in biographic technique, based
largely on a structural analysis of the *Lives,* on Walton's use of his
sources, and on a collation of the editions of each *Life*. Walton's
changes and additions would clearly reveal his craftsmanship, I
thought, and, incidentally, would demonstrate the shifts of opinion
which time and new information might be expected to cause. The
results of this study are here, and something more. I soon saw that
it was not fruitful to talk of methodology apart from context, that
an understanding of Walton as biographer was often less dependent
upon his techniques than upon the comprehension of the purposes
for which he wrote a life and upon the circumstances under which
he wrote it. These matters, too, I have had to investigate.

Inevitably, I became increasingly interested in the men whose
lives Walton wrote. Since he was responsible for the first biographies of Donne and Wotton, and for the first accounts of Hooker,
Herbert, and Sanderson which were more than sketches, he, more
than anyone else, has been responsible for our conception of these
men. Walton has colored our interpretation of these men, and it is
important to see the nature of the coloration, for Walton is constantly cited in any discussion of their lives. Recently, for instance,
the validity of what has been thought to be Donne's first extant

letter has hinged in part on what Walton did or did not mean by four words and on the assumption that a small detail of language in the first edition of the *Life of Donne* has special advantages lacking in the later editions. Recently, too, the fact that Walton gave a precise date for one of Donne's poems has been used as the primary argument for the validity of the date, and we find an eminent scholar writing:

While I find it just possible to suppose that Walton might have erroneously assumed the 'Hymne to God my God' to be a death-bed poem because it looked like one, I find it quite impossible to suppose that he deliberately fabricated (I might almost say, forged) a date in support of his conjecture. He was sometimes inaccurate and his chronology was sometimes vague, but he was at least honest.

Again, the assumption that Walton was "infinitely simple" has loomed large in a discussion of the relation between Donne and Magdalen Herbert and has influenced a scholar to write in support of his opinion that Donne addressed "The Autumnall" to Mrs. Herbert:

I say that, not on the authority of our printed texts, but on the authority of Walton. That he is supported by several of our manuscripts does not much matter. Walton sometimes makes mistakes. But he never makes things up. He does not romance; there is no troubadour nonsense about him. He is bad at dates. Yet good, I think, at catching essential connexions.

I have not discussed all these specific details and many others in which what Walton says or implies is crucial. Some I have treated because they have been handled so frequently; others because they seem central to the understanding of a *Life* or because they demonstrate interesting and varied aspects of Walton at work. I have found it necessary to discuss such diverse problems as Walton's part in the editing of Donne's *Poems,* Herbert's resignation of his fellowship, Bishop Morley's attitudes toward comprehension, the authorship of *Reason and Judgement,* and Bishop Sanderson's shifts in doctrine. I have had to consider the history of the Venetians' quarrel with the Pope, the order of the printing of the versions of the *Life of Herbert* of 1670, Donne's vision, Whitgift's speeches, Hooker's stand on sovereignty, and Baxter's role at the Savoy Conference.

I could not hope to list all Walton's inaccuracies, find all his sources, or give a specific answer for every problem which he raises.

I trust that I have made a selection sufficient to show how Walton usually works and how far he may be trusted. Acquaintance with his usual methods and with his customary predispositions and knowledge of his particular purposes will allow us more confidently to revaluate and reinterpret the lives of the men he wrote about. Reinterpretation has long been under way, but it has far to go, especially for Herbert and for Walton himself. Some revaluation of Walton I hope to have made here, for to catch him at work has led to a discursive character of his mind. Gradually, I think, a new picture of Walton emerges. The traditional Walton is a displaced Elizabethan, a man who, during the interregnum and after, led the retired life of an honest and peaceable Christian and angler. The Walton who emerges here is neither so peaceable nor so honest nor so simple as has been frequently thought, but he is one who gains in stature as we see his concern for craftsmanship and his involvement in the prime issues of his time.

Walton played an active and important role, though not a central one, in the re-establishment of the High Church and of what it stood for. To define this role precisely and to examine exactly how it affected Walton as biographer, it has seemed necessary to do a detailed study. I have treated each *Life* separately in order to show distinctly its context and Walton's intents, sources, and changes. This plan has an additional advantage: it provides a consecutive and self-contained discussion for the reader interested in only one of Walton's subjects.

It has seemed sensible to quote passages as well as to cite page numbers, since some versions of the *Lives* are hard to come by. Walton's revisions are numerous. His general method of revising I have most fully illustrated in Part I, on the *Life of Donne;* the revisions which I consider in the other parts are, in the main, those which characterize the particular *Life* or those which mark important changes. The alternative was to produce a variorum edition, and this would have been more cumbersome and less useful. In referring to Walton's revisions, I compare one version with the first appearance of the previous reading. A passage in the *Life of Hooker,* 1675, for instance, will be compared with the passage in the 1665 edition if that was not altered in 1666 and in 1670. If the passage was changed in 1670, I cite that edition or indicate the progression of changes. In the quotations I have retained the spelling, punctuation, and italics of my source, changing only ∫ to *s,* *vv* to *w,* *v* to *u,* and *i* to *j* where I thought the change facilitated the reading. I do not refer to the *Life of Herbert* in *The Temple*, 1679, and to the *Life of Hooker* in Hooker's *Works*, 1676 and 1682, for these were unsupervised reprints.

This study has been under way for a longer time than I like to acknowledge. "Walton's Redaction of Hooker," by Frederic E. Pamp, Jr., appeared in *Church History*, XVII (1948), 95–116, after I had already finished writing, in its first form, my account of the *Hooker*. Our conclusions are not very far apart. I trust I shall not be thought ungenerous in not citing his fine article; since our arguments took different shapes, I preferred to leave mine intact. Professor Robert S. Bosher's magnificent book, *The Making of the Restoration Settlement* (New York, 1951), was published shortly after I had spent a number of months, through the kindness of the Fund for the Advancement of Education, in trying to piece together some of the matters which he makes so beautifully clear. The work of Professor John Butt is the foundation on which any investigation of Walton must rest, and I have been greatly helped and stimulated by it. I am indebted to Professor Alexander M. Witherspoon for his generous criticism of some parts of this book in their earlier form as chapters of my thesis at Yale, to Professor R. C. Bald for some suggestions about Part I, and to Professor Ruth Wallerstein for her careful and penetrating reading of my manuscript. The chore of verifying quotations and references was eased by the generosity of the Faculty Research Grants Committee at Cornell and the unstinting help of Mr. Husain Haddawy. I owe thanks to Dr. Arthur M. Coon for permission to quote from his unpublished Cornell dissertation, the best biography of Walton, and thanks also to the Yale Library authorities for permission to quote Walton's notes in a volume in the Albert H. Childs Memorial Collection and some notes written in a seventeenth-century hand in a copy of *Lives*, 1670. The Librarians of the Bodleian Library and of the British Museum have kindly permitted me to quote, wherever I found it necessary, from photostats and microfilms of manuscripts in their custody. I should like to acknowledge many kindnesses by the staffs of the libraries at Yale, Cornell, and the Union Theological Seminary. I have not been able to identify Walton's "the Complete woman. of a good grace"; her counterpart, for this work, as in all else, is identified on the page dedicatory.

DAVID NOVARR

February, 1957

Contents

xii

Abbreviations

Athenae Oxon.—à Wood, Anthony. *Athenae Oxonienses*. Ed. Philip Bliss. London, 1813–1820. 4 vols.

Bosher—Bosher, Robert S. *The Making of the Restoration Settlement*. New York, 1951.

Bryant—Bryant, Arthur. *King Charles II*. London, 1931.

Church Hist.—Fuller, Thomas. *The Church-History of Britain*. London, 1655.

Compleat Angler—Walton, Izaak. *The Compleat Angler or the Contemplative Man's Recreation*. Edition specified.

Compleat Walton—Keynes, Geoffrey, ed. *The Compleat Walton*. London, 1929.

Coon—Coon, Arthur Munson. "The Life of Izaak Walton." Cornell University unpublished dissertation, 1938.

DNB—*Dictionary of National Biography*.

Donne, 1640—Walton, Izaak. *The Life and Death of Dr Donne, Late Deane of St Pauls London*. In *LXXX Sermons preached by . . . John Donne*. London, 1640.

Donne, 1658—Walton, Izaak. *The Life of John Donne . . . The second impression corrected and enlarged*. London, 1658.

Fell's *Hammond*—Fell, John. *The Life of Dr. Henry Hammond*. In Nicholas Pocock, ed., *A Practical Catechism by Henry Hammond*. Oxford, 1847. (Library of Anglo-Catholic Theology.)

Gauden—Gauden, John. *The Life & Death of Mr. Richard Hooker*. In *The Works of Mr. Richard Hooker*. London, 1662.

Gosse—Gosse, Edmund. *The Life and Letters of John Donne*. London, 1899. 2 vols.

Herbert, 1674—Walton, Izaak. *The Life of Mr. George Herbert.* In *The Temple . . . By Mr George Herbert . . . The Tenth Edition.* London, 1674.

Hooker, 1665—Walton, Izaak. *The Life of Mr. Rich. Hooker.* London, 1665.

Hooker, 1666—Walton, Izaak. *The Life of Mr. Richard Hooker.* In *The Works of Mr. Richard Hooker.* London, 1666.

Houk—Houk, Raymond Aaron. *Hooker's Ecclesiastical Polity, Book VIII, with an Introduction.* New York, 1931.

Keble—Keble, John, ed. *The Works of that Learned and Judicious Divine Mr. Richard Hooker.* 7th ed., rev. by R. W. Church and F. Paget. Oxford, 1888. 3 vols.

Letters to Severall Persons—Donne, John. *Letters to Severall Persons of Honour.* London, 1651.

Lives, 1670—Walton, Izaak. *The Lives of D^r· John Donne, Sir Henry Wotton, M^r· Richard Hooker, M^r· George Herbert.* London, 1670. (Since each *Life* is paged separately, the *Life* referred to is indicated in a parenthesis.)

Lives, 1675—Walton, Izaak. *The Lives of D^r· John Donne, Sir Henry Wotton, M^r· Richard Hooker, M^r· George Herbert. The Fourth Edition.* London, 1675.

MLN—Modern Language Notes.

MLR—The Modern Language Review.

N&Q—Notes and Queries.

Nicolas—Nicolas, Sir Harris, ed. *The Complete Angler.* London, 1875.

PQ—Philological Quarterly.

Paule—Paule, Sir George. *The Life of the Most Reverend and Religious Prelate John Whitgift, Lord Archbishop of Canterbury.* London, 1612.

Polity—Hooker, Richard. *The Laws of Ecclesiastical Polity.*

"Prefatory View"—Oley, Barnabas. "A Prefatory View of the Life of Mr Geo. Herbert." In *Herbert's Remains.* London, 1652.

RES—The Review of English Studies.

Reason and Judgement—[F., D.] *Reason and Judgement: or, Special Remarques Of the Life Of the Renowned Dr. Sanderson.* Oxford, 1663.

Reliq.—Wotton, Sir Henry. *Reliquiae Wottonianae.* Edition specified.

Reliq. Bax.—Reliquiae Baxterianae: or Mr. Richard Baxter's Narrative of The most Memorable Passages of his Life and Times. Ed. Matthew Sylvester. London, 1696.

Rox. Club—*Letters and Dispatches from Sir Henry Wotton to James the First and his Ministers, in the years MDCXVII-XX.* Ed. George Tomline. London, 1850.

Sanderson, 1678—Walton, Izaak. *The Life of Dr. Sanderson, Late Bishop of Lincoln.* London, 1678.

Sanderson, 1681—Walton, Izaak. *The Life of Dr. Sanderson, Late Lord Bishop of Lincoln.* In *XXXV. Sermons . . . By . . . Robert Sanderson . . . The Seventh Edition.* London, 1681.

Sanderson, *Works*—*The Works of Robert Sanderson, D.D.* Ed. William Jacobson. Oxford, 1854. 6 vols.

Sarpi, *History*—[Sarpi, Paolo.] *The History of the Quarrels of Pope Paul V. with The State of Venice.* London, 1626.

Sisson—Sisson, C. J. *The Judicious Marriage of Mr Hooker and the Birth of The Laws of Ecclesiastical Polity.* Cambridge, 1940.

Smith—Smith, Logan Pearsall. *The Life and Letters of Sir Henry Wotton.* Oxford, 1907. 2 vols.

Sta. Reg., 1640–1708—*A Transcript of the Registers of the Worshipful Company of Stationers; From 1640–1708.* London, 1913–1914. 3 vols.

Staley—Staley, Vernon. *The Life and Times of Gilbert Sheldon.* Milwaukee, [1913].

Stoughton—Stoughton, John. *History of Religion in England.* Rev. ed. London, 1881. 4 vols.

TLS—*The Times Literary Supplement.*

Vindication—Morley, George. *The Bishop of Worcester's Letter To a Friend For Vindication of Himself from M^r· Baxter's Calumny.* London, 1662.

Wood's Life and Times—*The Life and Times of Anthony Wood.* Ed. Andrew Clark. Oxford, 1891–1900. 5 vols.

Works of Herbert—Hutchinson, F. E., ed. *The Works of George Herbert.* Oxford, 1941.

Worthies—Fuller, Thomas. *The History of the Worthies of England.* London, 1662.

Introduction

The Walton Tradition

WALTON'S *Lives* and Boswell's *Life of Johnson* have long been counted among the prose classics written in English and among the masterpieces of life-writing that belong to the literature of the world. The *Lives* have long been considered the earliest distinguished English biographies and the *Life of Johnson* the most brilliant of them all. But Walton has won affection as a sweet pietist and a great fisherman, and Boswell has gained infamy as a gossip, a fop, a drunkard, a whoremonger, a fool. Their personalities and characters, though totally different, have impeded their recognition as men of letters. The *Life of Johnson* has been frequently thought to be a happy accident: the gossip had the bad manners and the good fortune to record conversation, and it took him seven years to transcribe notes. It has been frequently thought, too, that the holiness and quietness of that aspiring artisan, "Honest Izaak," were deserving of reward, and that the angels and the wood fairies guided his pen, guided it through six books with their multitudinous revisions over forty years.

Boswell's contemporaries knew well enough his foibles as a man, but they thought that the *Life of Johnson* was a fine book and drew the seemingly inevitable conclusion that Boswell was a fine writer. For Macaulay, too, the *Life of Johnson* was the first of the world's biographies and Boswell the first of the biographers. But the number and the obviousness of Boswell's vices as a man so blinded Macaulay's judgment that he could not credit Boswell with a grain of conscious artistry. He was convinced that Boswell was a man of the meanest and feeblest intellect and he concluded that Boswell was a great writer because he was a great fool.[1] Macaulay is largely

[1] "The Life of Samuel Johnson," *Edinburgh Review,* LIV (1831), 16–18.

responsible for the separatist tradition in Boswell criticism, and, despite the impossibility of his paradox, his statements have hindered the evaluation of Boswell as a man of letters for over a hundred years.

In a sense, consideration of Walton as a man of letters has been impeded by more obstinate forces than has that of Boswell, for the impediment has been constructed by good will rather than by bad. Cognizance and evaluation of Walton's abilities have been hindered additionally because, to a large degree, he was his own Macaulay. Walton's fame has rested primarily on the *Compleat Angler,* and because he confessed to his readers, "the whole discourse is a kind of picture of my owne disposition,"[2] he has ever been associated with the pseudo-autobiographic pious philosopher, Piscator. His statement has led to a similar view of his *Lives,* and they, too, have been thought to reflect "the serenity of his well-disciplined and tranquil life" or his "negative and receptive temperament" or the "very spirit of innocence, purity, and simplicity of heart" of the *Compleat Angler.* Walton's apparent simplicity and naïveté, his sentimentality, his love for the wise apothegm have ever attracted his readers. Much of the charm of Walton is in what James Russell Lowell calls the "innocency" of his way of writing.[3] This innocency is further enhanced by his self-announced declarations of plain honesty and the reiterations of his modesty.

If Walton's innocency and honesty and modesty have largely determined traditional admiration for him, his piety has turned admiration to love and veneration. There were certainly more pious men than Walton in the seventeenth century, but piety has more frequently led to awe and respect than to love. There is a piety which offends men who are not themselves ardent lovers of all things religious. These men are repelled by a piety so extreme that it appears to be smug and self-righteous; they are embarrassed by a piety which transcends all bounds of emotional propriety. They are uncomfortable before an other-worldly piety which makes a man appear to be a demigod or a fool. But Walton's piety has seemed sweet and reasonable, gentlemanly and refined. Lowell has beautifully caught the traditional view:

[2] *The Compleat Angler* (London, 1653), sig. A5ᵛ.
[3] "Walton," in *Latest Literary Essays and Addresses* (Cambridge, Mass., 1891), p. 91.

Above all he loved the beauty of holiness and those ways of taking and of spending life that make it wholesome for ourselves and our fellows. His view of the world is not of the widest, but it is the Delectable Mountains that bound the prospect. Never surely was there a more lovable man, nor one to whom love found access by more avenues of sympathy.[4]

The veneration which has become Walton's is, as Richard Le Gallienne pointed out, one of the curious phenomena of literature. "It is not mere hero-worship," he said; "it is actually religious sentiment on the part of the Waltonian. In his loving imagination Saint Izaak is as truly a saint as any in the Calendar." And Le Gallienne saw, too, why this attitude prevented proper consideration of Walton as a man of letters: "One can hardly think of one so innocent-minded writing so well. There always seems a spice of the devil in any form of skill, and we don't readily think of the good man being clever as well. It seems a sort of wickedness in him, somehow."[5] Walton's respectable and comfortable piety and the seeming artlessness of his writing, an artlessness augmented by the ingenuousness of his self-declared modesty, have prevented serious appraisal of him. His personality has been thought so closely integrated with the qualities which seemingly pervade his books that the one was made responsible for the other. Walton has been considered a good writer because he was a good man, even as Boswell has been thought a great writer because he was a great fool.

Although Walton is himself somewhat at fault for the lack of recognition he has received as a man of letters, his ardent admirers, too, are at fault. They have been too willing to love that part of Walton which they best knew and to think at the same time that they knew him completely. But when Walton wrote that the *Compleat Angler* was "a kind of picture of my owne disposition," he qualified his statement by adding, "at least of my disposition in such daies and times as I allow my self, when honest *Nat.* and *R. R.* and I go a fishing together."[6] The Walton whose disposition admirers found pictured in the *Compleat Angler* was Walton in informal clothes. It is difficult to think of Walton with his garland and sing-

[4] *Ibid.,* p. 88.

[5] Richard Le Gallienne, Introduction to *The Compleat Angler* (London & New York, 1897), pp. lxiv, lxix.

[6] *Compleat Angler,* 1653, sig. A5ᵛ.

ing robes about him, and it is perhaps overstatement to say he wore them. But if he is no poet, soaring in the high region of his fancies, there is at least a hint of self-discipline in "such daies and times as I allow my self." Walton had ever loved the idea of fishing, but he did not himself become a fisherman until he was forty.[7] Probably he turned increasingly from passive to active angling to relieve the tedious strain of composition. The Walton who is venerated and loved is the writer on a holiday excursion. The writer at his work-bench has been largely neglected.

In his own day, Walton's name was found among those of men of letters rather than on the Saints' Calendar, and he was probably better known for the *Lives* than for the *Compleat Angler*. To be sure, Elias Ashmole said in 1672 that Walton was "a man well known, and as well beloved of all good men," but he said, too, "and will be better known to posterity, by his ingenious pen, in the lives of Doctor *Donne,* Sir *Henry Wotton,* Mr. *Richard Hooker,* and Mr. *George Herbert.*"[8] Ashmole's opinion is interesting because it was set down before the *Lives* of 1675, before Walton had written the *Life of Sanderson,* and after the *Compleat Angler* had been through four editions. Nor does it stand alone. In 1655, Fuller commended the *Life of Donne* as "no lesse truly than elegantly written."[9] John Aubrey sought information about Ben Jonson from Walton and referred to him as the author of "Dr. Donne's Life, &c."[10] Anthony à Wood knew Walton, sent queries to him,[11] and ended his sketch of Hooker in *Athenae Oxonienses* with a digression on Walton. His own insistence upon the verification of facts had caused him to become disgruntled with Walton's lack of accuracy in the *Life of Wotton,*[12] and this probably explains his reserved praise of Walton

[7] In 1662, Walton wrote in a commendatory letter for *The Experienced Angler* of Colonel Robert Venables that he had "been for thirty years past, not only a Lover but a practiser of that innocent Recreation" (printed in Geoffrey Keynes, ed., *The Compleat Walton* [London, 1929], p. 591).

[8] Elias Ashmole, *The Institution, Laws & Ceremonies Of the most Noble Order of the Garter* (London, 1672), p. 228.

[9] Thomas Fuller, *The Church-History of Britain* (London, 1655), bk. X, 112.

[10] *Compleat Walton,* pp. 603–604, 630–631.

[11] In giving his source for the date of death and place of burial of John Aylmer, Wood wrote, "as I have been informed by the letters of my sometime friendly acquaintance Mr. Isaac Walton" (*Athenae Oxonienses,* ed. Philip Bliss [London, 1813–1820], III, 957).

[12] *Ibid.,* II, 643–644.

as a biographer. Still, Wood did commend Walton, and as a biographer, for his mention of the *Compleat Angler* is an afterthought:

He hath written the lives of Dr. Joh. Donne, sir Hen. Wotton, Mr. Rich. Hooker, Mr. George Herbert, and of Dr. Rob. Sanderson sometimes B. of Lincoln: All which are well done, considering the education of the author; as also *The compleat Angler, or the contemplative Man's recreation,* &c.[13]

Higher praise than this, and again it is praise for the life-writing, was given Walton by Edward Phillips, writing in 1694. Phillips named Plutarch, Diogenes Laertius, and Cornelius Nepos as the most eminent of the ancient life-writers, and among the modern he lauded Machiavelli and Gassendus. In their company he placed three Englishmen:

Sir *Fulk Grevil,* who wrote the Life of his most intimate Friend, Sir *Philip Sidney:* Mr. *Thomas Stanly* of *Cumberlo-Green,* who made a most Elaborate improvement to the foresaid *Laertius,* by adding to what he found in him, what by diligent search and enquiry he Collected from other Authors of best Authority; *Isaac Walton,* who wrote the Lives of Sir *Henry Wotton,* Dr. *Donne;* and for his Divine Poems, the admired Mr. *George Herbert.*[14]

Although later generations were attracted to Walton the man, his own century thought of him mainly as a capable biographer.

Sentimental rather than critical appreciation of Walton began to take hold in the eighteenth century. Dr. Johnson was Walton's chief protagonist, but, despite his primary interest in the *Lives,* his contemporaries were interested in the *Compleat Angler.* When the first new edition of the *Compleat Angler* in seventy-four years appeared at mid-century, its editor, Moses Browne, said in his preface that he undertook the work *"at the Instigation of an ingenious and learned Friend"* and in a footnote named the friend as "Mr. *Samuel Johnson,* who may probably, on another Occasion, oblige the Publick with the Life of Mr. *Walton.*"[15] Unfortunately, Johnson never wrote the life, but he approved that which appeared before the *Compleat Angler* which Sir John Hawkins edited in 1760: "The

[13] *Ibid.,* I, 698.

[14] Edward Phillips, "The Life of Mr. John Milton" [prefixed to *Letters of State, written by Mr John Milton* (London, 1694)], in Helen Darbishire, ed., *The Early Lives of Milton* (London, 1932), p. 49.

[15] Moses Browne, ed., *The Compleat Angler* (London, 1750), sigs. a2ᵛ–a3ʳ.

Life of Walton has happily fallen into good hands. Sir John Hawkins has prefixed it to the late edition of the Angler, very diligently collected, and very elegantly composed."[16] Hawkins' *Compleat Angler* went through seven editions before 1800 and as many again in the first quarter of the nineteenth century, and his "Life of Walton" set a pattern within which appreciation of Walton functioned for almost 150 years. It was Hawkins who made Walton the patron saint of the angler:

> While he continued in *London* [before 1643], his favourite amusement was Angling; in which he was the greatest proficient of his time; and indeed so great were his skill and experience in that art, that there is scarce any writer on the subject since his time, who has not made the rules and practice of *Walton* his very foundation.[17]

More important, it was he who started the biographic interpretation of the *Compleat Angler* which led to the intimate association of Walton with Piscator. Hawkins argued that only a man "whose mind was the habitation of piety, prudence, humility, peace, and chearfulness, could delineate such a character as that of the principal interlocutor in this dialogue." It is to Hawkins' credit that he did not make these "moral qualities" in themselves responsible for the *Compleat Angler;* he separated the "moral qualities" from the "mental endowments" and said that Walton "formed a style so natural, intelligible and elegant, as to have had more admirers than successful imitators."[18] But despite this and despite his brief sketches of the subjects of the *Lives,* Hawkins was preoccupied with Walton's personality and with his capacity for befriending men of eminence rather than with his literary ability.

Johnson, too, observed that "it was wonderful that Walton, who was in a very low situation in life, should have been familiarly received by so many great men, and that at a time when the ranks of society were kept more separate than they are now."[19] He admired Walton, however, not for his friendships or his piety or his angling prowess, but for his craftsmanship in biography. He said of Wal-

[16] Letter of Johnson to Rev. Dr. Horne of Magdalen College, Oxford, dated April 30, 1774. *The R. B. Adam Library Relating to Dr. Samuel Johnson and His Era* (Buffalo, N.Y., 1929), I, 48.

[17] John Hawkins, ed., *The Complete Angler* (London, 1760), p. xvi.

[18] *Ibid.,* 4th ed. (1784), pp. xxi–xxii.

[19] George Birkbeck Hill and L. F. Powell, eds., *Boswell's Life of Johnson* (Oxford, 1934–1950), II, 363–364.

ton that he was a "great panegyrist."[20] Johnson commended the
Compleat Angler,[21] but the *Lives* was "one of his most favourite
books. Dr. Donne's Life, he said, was the most perfect of them."[22]
He thought that there was need for a new edition of the *Lives*,
"benoted a little,"[23] and he even proposed that the editor compile
a critical catalogue of the works of the men whose lives were written
by Walton and that he read those works carefully in preparation for
his edition.[24] On the same day (March 20, 1776) that Johnson advocated a new edition of the *Lives*, he made his celebrated comment
on biography: "It is rarely well executed. They only who live with
a man can write his life with any genuine exactness and discrimination; and few people who have lived with a man know what to remark about him."[25] In the light of his own standards, Johnson's
estimate of Walton is high praise indeed.

Johnson passed on his interest in Walton to Boswell, and he too
became an admirer. But Boswell's admiration was of another kind:
it was not the great panegyrist but the man of piety who attracted
him. On Sunday, July 17, 1774, Boswell wrote, "I had a slight conflict between what I really thought would do me most good and
the desire of being externally decent and going to Church." He
spent the morning in bed, reading Walton.

I read Sanderson's life today, all but some leaves which were awanting
in the copy which I had. I shall get the defect supplied. The simplicity
and pious spirit of Walton was, as it were, transfused into my soul. I
resolved that amidst business and every other worldly pursuit I should
still keep in mind religious duty.

He justified his stay in bed by thinking, "A man who *knows himself*
should use means to do him good which to others may seem trifling
or ridiculous," but, nevertheless, he went to church in the afternoon. Boswell had read Walton, he tells us, because he wished to
read what Johnson valued, and because he thought that he might
be able to help Dr. George Horne, the president of Magdalen College, Oxford, with his proposed edition of the *Lives*.[26] After reading
Walton, he wrote to Johnson, "If Dr. Horne will write to me, all
the attention that I can give shall be cheerfully bestowed, upon

[20] *Ibid.*, p. 364. [21] *Ibid.*, IV, 311. [22] *Ibid.*, II, 363.
[23] *Ibid.*, p. 283. [24] *Ibid.*, p. 446. [25] *Ibid.*
[26] Geoffrey Scott and Frederick A. Pottle, eds., *The Journal of James Boswell
1772–1774 (Private Papers of James Boswell from Malahide Castle,* Vol. IX;
New York, 1930), pp. 142–143.

what I think a pious work, the preservation and elucidation of Walton, by whose writings I have been most pleasingly edified."[27] Even
the greatest biographer of them all, then, loved Walton for his piety:
he looked upon Walton as a father of the Church, not as a fellow
craftsman.

Boswell had asked Johnson to get for him all the editions of the
Lives, for he thought that their republication with notes would fall
upon himself.[28] He accomplished nothing himself, but he did further Johnson's desire indirectly. An edition of the *Lives* was finally
published in 1796, and in the "Preface to the Second Edition"
(1807), its editor, Thomas Zouch, listed Boswell among "those
gentlemen whose assistance and encouragement he experienced in
the first impression of this work."[29] In his dedication, Zouch said
that the *Lives* "contain portraits of general excellence, finished by
no unskilful artist,"[30] but he, too, was anxious to explain the excellences of the book in terms of the moral excellences of the author:

Truth is never displayed to us in more grateful colours, than when she
appears, not in a garish attire, but in her own native garb, without
artifice, without pomp. In that garb Isaac Walton has arrayed her.
Deeply impressed with the excellence of those exemplary characters
which he endeavours to portray, he speaks no other language than that
of the heart, and thus imparts to the reader his own undisguised sentiments, so friendly to piety and virtue.[31]

Zouch was firmly convinced of the truth of Milton's dictum that
true eloquence consists of the serious and hearty love of truth, and
he applied it to Walton.[32] He so closely associated Walton's work
with his character that he spoke of the work only in terms of the
character. At long last, Dr. Johnson had his edition of the *Lives,*
with notes and critical catalogues, but he would have been surprised to find Walton praised for reasons other than his own. Still,
not Johnson's sentiments, but those of Hawkins and Boswell and
Zouch, were echoed in the nineteenth century.

Hazlitt called the *Compleat Angler* the best pastoral in the language, not excepting Pope's or Philips', but he thought that he perceived the piety and humanity of Walton's mind even in the de-

[27] Hill and Powell, eds., *op. cit.,* II, 284.   [28] *Ibid.,* III, 107.
[29] Thomas Zouch, ed., *The Lives of Dr. John Donne;—Sir Henry Wotton;
Mr. Richard Hooker;—Mr. George Herbert; and Dr. Robert Sanderson* (York,
1807), p. vi.
[30] *Ibid.* (York, 1796), "To the Right Honorable Sir Richard Pepper Arden."
[31] *Ibid.,* p. xlvi.   [32] *Ibid.,* note z.

scription of a fishing tackle. And while the last sentence of his short discourse on Walton shows the high place which he accorded the *Compleat Angler*—"While Tottenham Cross shall stand, and longer, thy work, amiable and happy old man, shall last"[33]—it reveals also an attitude which made assessment on a literary basis impossible. The most rapturous expression of this attitude came, as might be expected, from the pen of the poet who wished his days to be bound each to each by natural piety. Wordsworth enshrined his affection and love for Walton in two sonnets. In one entitled "Written upon a blank leaf in 'The Complete Angler,' " he called Walton "Sage benign" and "meek, thankful Soul." He found in the *Compleat Angler* an exhortation to watch each still report that Nature utters from her rural shrine, and he attributed Walton's worshipful representation of nature to the gladsome piety which flowed from every nook of his full bosom.[34] Wordsworth loved the *Lives* for the faith, the purest charity, and the mild virtues of the men whom Walton wrote about, and, as his emotion overflowed into one of his finest metaphysical flights, he created an aura about Walton which has ever glistened:

> Methinks their very Names shine still and bright,
> Apart—like glow-worms in the woods of spring,
> Or lonely tapers shooting for a light
> That guides and cheers,—or seen, like stars on high,
> Satellites burning in a lucid ring
> Around meek Walton's heavenly memory.

Nor was it merely Walton's memory which was heavenly to Wordsworth. He wrote, to explain Walton's accomplishment,

> The feather whence the pen
> Was shaped that traced the lives of these good Men,
> Dropped from an Angel's wing.[35]

The lines have been frequently cited; the explanation has ever satisfied Walton's devotees. To be sure, James Gillman knew better. He had tried to model his pious life of Coleridge on Walton's *Lives* and he had learned that mere piety was not enough to explain

[33] William Hazlitt, "On John Buncle," in *The Round Table: A Collection of Essays on Literature, Men, and Manners* (Edinburgh, 1817), I, 161–162.
[34] William Wordsworth, *Miscellaneous Poems* (London, 1820), III, 135.
[35] William Wordsworth, "Walton's Book of 'Lives,' " in *Ecclesiastical Sketches* (London, 1822), p. 85.

what Walton wrought.[36] But Walton had been impressively beati-
fied, and his innocency, his piety, his heavenly memory tempered
any estimate of his accomplishment.

At the end of the century many fine critics had acute comments to
make about Walton's art, but they offered them with sentimental
regard for Walton's memory. In the finest introduction which ever
accompanied an edition of the *Compleat Angler,* Lowell insisted
that Walton was a painstaking artist, that his persuasive simplicity
of diction was "the last and most painful achievement of conscientious self-denial," that his artlessness was not so artless as it appeared.[37] His analyses of Walton's charm and his literary originality
are perceptive and humane. Lowell, too, was sufficiently objective
to point out Walton's ignorance of Latin and his frequently leaving
his sentences in a clutter.[38] But even Lowell spoke of the *Lives* as
having endeared Walton "to all who choose that their souls should
keep good company,"[39] and his affection for the man clearly affected
the phrasing of his considered estimate of the man of letters:

In Walton's case, since a Daimon or a Genius would be too lofty for
the business, might we not take the Brownie of our own Northern
mythology for the type of such superior endowment as he clearly had?
We can fancy him ministered to by such a homely and helpful creature,
—not a genius exactly, but answering the purpose sufficiently well, and
marking a certain natural distinction in those it singles out for its
innocent and sportful companionship. And it brings a blessing also to
those who treat it kindly, as Walton did.[40]

Austin Dobson, too, wrote a fine essay on Walton, in his investigation "On Certain Quotations in Walton's 'Angler.' "[41] He demonstrated Walton's habit of using quotation marks or italics for material paraphrased or inexactly quoted from his sources, even from
sources which Walton himself names. But Dobson felt it necessary
to preface his remarks by saying that it was ungrateful to speak
censoriously or pedantically of Walton. The charm of Walton's personality, as Dobson found it charactered in the cheerful spirit and
the clean morality of the *Compleat Angler,* made him apologize for

[36] In the preface of *The Life of Samuel Taylor Coleridge* (London, 1838),
Gillman does not mention Walton's piety, but compliments his craftsmanship.
[37] Lowell, *op. cit.,* pp. 65, 71. This was originally printed as an introduction to
The Complete Angler (Boston, 1889).
[38] *Ibid.,* pp. 61–62, 90.   [39] *Ibid.,* p. 71.   [40] *Ibid.,* p. 93.
[41] Austin Dobson, *Miscellanies (Second Series)* (New York, 1901), pp. 157–169.

an examination, however delightful and commendatory, into Walton's method. Even the confident Grosart, exasperated as he was by
Walton's inaccuracies in the *Life of Herbert,* thought it wise to
mingle his criticism with deference: "It is one of those books that
must live; yet for facts and dates, none who follow 'meek Izaak' can
trust him. I name this with the profoundest veneration for his winsome memory."[42]

But Walton's winsome memory was no hindrance to Edmund
Gosse, who found frequent frustration in the facts of Walton's *Life
of Donne.* He called Walton immortal, yes, but he called him an
"immortal piscatory linen-draper."[43] "In the days of Walton," he
said, "of course, what we now call conscientious biography was un-
known." Walton's *Lives* were "too rose-coloured and too inexact
for scientific uses."[44] Leslie Stephen was even less kind to Walton
in his review of Gosse's *Life and Letters of John Donne.* "There are
two objections," he said, "to the life if taken as a record of facts. The
first is that the facts are all wrong; and the second that the por-
traiture is palpably false."[45] The bubble had burst, but only because of the combined weight of the opinions of Gosse and Stephen.
Walton might still have devotees to his winsome memory, but it
became necessary for scholars to consider Gosse's and Stephen's statements critically rather than sentimentally. Beeching's fine *defensio*[46]
showed that Gosse and Stephen had perhaps gone too far, but assessment of Walton's work was no longer determined chiefly by the
charm of his personality and the appeal of his character. Perhaps it
was wrong to criticize Walton for his nonconformity to the ideals
of the *Dictionary of National Biography,* but it was something to
have him judged by men whose primary devotion was to the history
and the principles of biography rather than to angling and saintliness.

There is today a copious lack of unanimity about Walton's accomplishment and a real confusion about Walton as biographer.
Stephen, for instance, berated Walton for not properly emphasizing the complexity of Donne's personality. To him, Walton's por-

---

[42] Alexander B. Grosart, ed., *The Complete Works in Verse and Prose of
George Herbert* (London, 1874), I, xviii.
[43] Edmund Gosse, *The Life and Letters of John Donne* (London, 1899), II, 253.
[44] *Ibid.,* I, viii.
[45] Leslie Stephen, "John Donne," *National Review,* XXXIV (1899), 595–596.
[46] H. C. Beeching, "Izaak Walton's Life of Donne," in *Religio Laici* (London,
1902), pp. 87–123.

trait of Donne had no more semblance to reality than Goldsmith's
portrait of Dr. Primrose. He saw Walton as a worthy tradesman,
dazzled by Donne's learning and rhetoric, and "offering a posthumous homage as sincere and touching as that which no doubt
engaged the condescending kindness of the great man in life."[47]
On the other hand, Harold Nicolson praises Walton for not being
blinded by reverence, for not being adulatory despite his charity, for
being absolutely sincere and charmingly modest.[48] But though he
praises Walton, too, for not being pedantic in his accuracy, he, like
Stephen, thinks that Walton fails in truth, that his portraits are incomplete and improbable. This fault he attributes, however, to the
deductive approach toward biography fostered by the character.[49]
In addition, Nicolson says that Walton had no interest in practical
activity, no sense of actuality, and he goes so far as to say that Walton had no insight into fact.[50] He finds, too, that Walton's personality and predilections intrude unduly into his work. He accuses
Walton of being interested only in those sides of character which
reflected "his own negative and receptive temperament," of imposing upon his subjects "the same qualities of scholarly and devout
complacency as he possessed, and valued, in himself," and therefore
he thinks that Walton misleads in dealing "with a singularly mundane diplomatist like Wotton, or with a tortured sensualist like
Donne."[51]

Donald Stauffer also emphasizes Walton's undue subjectivity.
He, too, holds that Walton's subjects reflect his own mind, though
he finds the key to Walton's mind not in "scholarly and devout complacency" but in pious artistry.[52] Stauffer feels that Walton became
increasingly subjective with time: "More and more in his later lives
of Herbert and Sanderson, Walton uses his subject as a vehicle to
express his own philosophy of religion and the teachings of the
Church of England."[53] Still, he would re-emphasize for those who
believe that Walton relied too much upon his own imagination and
taste the importance he attached to primary sources of information
and the great use which he made of them. But here, too, he says that

[47] Stephen, *op. cit.*, pp. 595–596.
[48] Harold Nicolson, *The Development of English Biography* (London, 1927),
p. 66.
[49] *Ibid.*, p. 41.   [50] *Ibid.*, p. 68.   [51] *Ibid.*, pp. 10, 65–66.
[52] Donald Stauffer, *English Biography before 1700* (Cambridge, Mass., 1930),
p. 92.
[53] *Ibid.*, p. 110.

with age Walton grew less concerned with rendering his narrative credible in all details.[54]

John Butt measures Walton against the two aspects of biographical truth. Of his regard for truth of fact, Butt says, "Walton's abundant revisions and his reiterated assertions that he has made no wilful mistakes and that he lacks the skill to deceive, make it quite impossible to doubt either his good intentions or his strenuous efforts to perfect the *Lives*."[55] Butt finds in Walton a certain untruth of impression, but he would largely excuse Walton for this by showing that in the *Life of Donne* and in the *Life of Herbert* irregularities are present for anyone who cares to look for them. He admits that Walton tended to emphasize sanctity and studiousness at the expense of other characteristics, but would explain and perhaps justify this by saying that "this is the personal criticism which he applied to his collected facts."[56]

Both George Herbert Palmer and R. E. Bennett think that Walton gives an impression which is generally truthful. Bennett quotes what Palmer says of the *Life of Herbert:*

In spite of some petty inaccuracies, . . . I believe that what Walton says is substantially true. But there is much which he does not say; and in general, his book should be judged rather as a piece of art than as even-handed history. In painting a glowing picture an artist selects a point of view, and to what is visible from that point subordinates all else.[57]

Bennett makes much of Walton's omissions, and says, too, that he followed an unscientific method in the combination and interpretation of the details of his portrait. But he believes that it is possible to do this and still produce truthfulness of impression; he thinks that Walton's means can be justified by his end. He says, "The portrait is remarkably accurate, but we must not try to break it down and reemploy its elements. The apparent facts which Walton used are likely to be true only with reference to the larger purpose for which he employed them."[58]

[54] *Ibid.,* pp. 97, 100.

[55] John Butt, "Izaak Walton's Methods in Biography," *Essays and Studies,* XIX (1934), 81.

[56] *Ibid.,* p. 84.

[57] George Herbert Palmer, ed., *The English Works of George Herbert* (Boston and New York, 1905), I, 45–46. Quoted in "Walton's Use of Donne's Letters," *PQ,* XVI (1937), 34.

[58] Bennett, *op. cit.,* p. 34.

It is not likely that any one of these perceptive critics is entirely wrong; yet they cannot all be right in all things. Walton has enjoyed an overabundant amount of generalization; he deserves an ample measure of documentation. Too often the generalization has been based on familiarity with one only of the *Lives,* and, too often, on familiarity with one *Life* in one only of its versions. Too often generalization about Walton has been arrived at deductively, by the same method that he has been accused of using. If we hope to generalize with validity, we must examine all the *Lives,* and examine them individually and in detail. For each was a separate work, each has its separate problems, and each needs separate assessment.

PART I

The Earliest Life
and Its Revisions

Chapter 1

The Life and Death of
Dr Donne – 1640

EARLY in 1640 there was published a volume entitled *LXXX Sermons preached by that learned and reverend divine, John Donne, D^r in Divinity, Late Deane of the Cathedrall Church of S. Pauls London.* Its 826 folio pages of sermons are preceded by a three-page dedicatory epistle, signed "Jo: Donne," and by seventeen pages headed "The Life and Death of Dr Donne, Late Deane of St Pauls London," signed by "Iz : Wa." This is the book which Richard Marriot had entered on the Stationers' Register on January 3, 1640, less than a month after the death of Sir Henry Wotton.[1] The bookseller had waited long for a life of John Donne which Wotton had intended to write, but of his projected writings—a life of Donne, a life of Martin Luther, a discourse on the art of angling, a history of England, and a survey of education—Wotton had composed only a few pages of the history and only half of Chapter I (with a few aphorisms) of the work on education. The first paragraphs of the *Life* by "Iz : Wa" tell the story of the life that is printed in the volume:

That learned Knight's [Wotton's] love followed his friends [Donne's] fame beyond the forgetfull grave, which he testified by intreating me (whom he acquainted with his designe) to inquire of certaine particulars that concerned it: Not doubting but my knowledge of the Author, and love to his memory, would make my diligence usefull. I did prepare them

---

[1] Edward Arber, ed., *A Transcript of the Registers of the Company of Stationers of London; 1554–1640* (London, 1875–1894), IV, 468.

in a readiness to be augmented, and rectified by his powerfull pen; but then death prevented his intentions.

When I heard that sad newes, and likewise that these Sermons were to be publisht without the Authors life, (which I thought was rare) indignation or griefe (I know not whether) transported me so far, that I re-viewed my forsaken Collections, and resolved the world should see the best picture of the Author that my artlesse Pensil (guided by the hand of Truth) could present to it.[2]

The life in the 1640 volume is, then, a substitute, a last-minute addition by an author who had known Wotton well enough to be familiar with his plans and who had known Donne well enough to be asked by Wotton to provide him with some biographical information.

"Iz : Wa" is first mentioned in 1619, when S. P. (Samuel Page) dedicated to him a poem called "The Love of Amos and Laura."

> To My Approved and much Respected Friend, Iz. Wa.
>
> To thee, thou more than thrice beloved friend,
>   I too unworthy of so great a bliss:
> These harsh-tun'd lines I here to thee commend
>   Thou being cause it is now as it is:
> For hadst thou held thy tongue, by silence might
> These have been buried in oblivions night.
>
> If they were pleasing, I would call them thine,
>   And disavow my title to the verse:
> But being bad, I needs must call them mine.
>   No ill thing can be clothed in thy verse.
> Accept them then, and where I have offended,
> Rase thou it out, and let it be amended.[3]

---

[2] *Donne,* 1640, sig. A5ʳ.

[3] Reprinted by Sir Harris Nicolas, ed., *The Complete Angler* (London, 1875), p. xix. Nicolas conjectures that since "The Love of Amos and Laura" of 1619 differs from the first edition of 1613 only in a single word, S. P. acknowledges alterations which Walton must have made in the original manuscript. It is more likely that Page thanks Walton for his part in the publication of the poem. Walton may have been aware that Richard Hawkins, "dwelling in Chancery Lane, neare Serjeants-Inne," was planning to reprint *Alcilia* (first printed in 1595) and Marston's *Metamorphosis of Pigmalion's Image* (first printed in 1598). Rights to these properties had been turned over to Hawkins on Oct. 11, 1613, by Edmond Mattes and Roger Barnes (*Sta. Reg., 1554–1640,* III, 478). He never registered "The Love of Amos and Laura" and "Epigrammes by Sir. J. H. and others. Never before imprinted" which he printed with his other properties, but he was probably happy to freshen his volume with new material. Walton

In 1633, an elegy by "Iz. Wa." is appended to the first edition of John Donne's poems. The second edition, in 1635, contains not only his revised elegy, but several lines of his verse under the portrait of Donne, newly engraved by William Marshall. The only other appearance of the initials before 1640 is with a commendatory poem "In praise of my friend the Author, and his Booke," prefixed to *The Merchant's Mappe of Commerce,* written by Lewes Roberts, Merchant, and printed in 1638.

"Iz : Wa" is Izaak Walton, son of a tippler of Stafford,[4] whose presence in London is first recorded late in 1618, when he was in his twenty-sixth year. On December 21, "Isack Walton" was presented to the Wardmote Inquest for defective pavement in Chancery Lane.[5] Little more than a month before, Walton had been made a member of the Ironmongers' Company. In the books of the Company is an entry for November 12 that Izaak Walton, late apprentice to Thomas Grinsell, "was now admitted and sworne a free brother of this Companie, and payd for his admittance xiii *d.,* and for default of presentment and enrollement x *s.*"[6] Had Walton's apprenticeship been a perfectly regular one, he must have been in London in 1611, but the fine exacted of him indicates irregularity. Still, it is likely that Walton had come to London in 1608, shortly after the marriage of his sister Anne to Thomas Grinsell, a middle-aged and prospering sempster of Chancery Lane who was a member of the Ironmongers' Company.[7] Walton's best biographer thinks that the slightness of the fine may be explained by the Company's knowledge that Walton had served a full apprenticeship by the time he was twenty-one or twenty-two. Their regulations set a minimum age of twenty-four for membership. After his apprenticeship Walton may have worked at his trade for a few years, perhaps with Grinsell; he applied for membership when he was ready to go

---

may have persuaded Samuel Page, now a Doctor of Divinity and Vicar of Deptford in Kent, to make public some of the romantic work of his juvenile years (see *Athenae Oxon.,* II, 486).

[4] Staffordshire Record Society, *Collections for a History of Staffordshire* (1929), p. 306, quoted by Arthur Munson Coon, "The Life of Izaak Walton" (Cornell University unpublished dissertation, 1938), p. 8. I am indebted here and elsewhere to this work, the best and fullest biography of Walton.

[5] St. Dunstan's-in-the-West, "Wardmote Inquest Presentments," I, 99b, quoted by Coon, p. 88.

[6] John Nicholl, *Some Account of the Worshipful Company of Ironmongers* (London, 1851), p. 200.

[7] See Coon's evidence, pp. 76–81, 84, 88, 97–98.

into business for himself.[8] Thus sponsored by a well-established and affluent brother-in-law, Walton found his apprenticeship and trade no burden, and he could early indulge in his taste for poets and preachers.

How he met Samuel Page and Ben Jonson ("I only knew Ben Jonson"[9]) and Michael Drayton ("my honest old friend"[10]) we do not know. Perhaps through his business as sempster and draper, perhaps through his acquaintance with sons of city families who were students at the Inns of Court in his neighborhood, perhaps through printers and booksellers who had shops near his. There is no doubt that Walton knew some of the sons of Ben, but these acquaintances were not familiar and intimate. Again, though there is no reason to think that the sempster in Chancery Lane knew very well Richard Sibbes, the eminent Puritan preacher, it is likely that his extraordinary admiration for Sibbes stemmed from having heard him preach at Gray's Inn.[11] It is likely, too, that after October, 1616, he occasionally heard the brilliant divine John Donne preach at Lincoln's Inn. There is no evidence that he knew the Divinity Reader, but he must certainly have listened as the lawyers and students discussed their Reader and his sermons.

A Lay Subsidy Roll of 1625 shows that Walton was still living in Chancery Lane in that year,[12] and the records of St. Dunstan's-in-the-West show that from 1627 through 1632 and again in 1640 he resided in Chancery Lane about the seventh or eighth house from Fleet Street.[13] By 1629, he was one of the prosperous young members of the Ironmongers' Company, destined perhaps for the livery. In that year, and again in 1635, he appeared as a bachelor in foins in the pageant honoring the new Lord Mayor.[14] In 1637, he

[8] *Ibid.*, pp. 58–59.

[9] So Walton wrote John Aubrey on Nov. 22, 1680, in a letter reprinted in *The Compleat Walton,* pp. 603–604.

[10] *Compleat Angler,* 1661, p. 136.

[11] In his will, Walton left his copy of Sibbes's *The Soul's Conflict with Itself* to his son and his copy of Sibbes's *The Bruised Reed and Smoking Flax* to his daughter (Nicolas, p. ci). Among his books now preserved in the Cathedral Library at Salisbury are three of Sibbes's works, *The Saints' Cordials, The Returning Backslider,* and *Bowels Opened (ibid.,* pp. cxlvii–cxlviii, and D. W. Wing, "Izaak Walton," *TLS,* July 13, 1951, p. 437). In the last two, Walton wrote: "Of this blest man let his just praise be given,/ Heaven was in him, before he was in heaven."

[12] Public Record Office, E179.147/537, quoted by Coon, p. 89.

[13] Nicolas, p. clii.   [14] Nicholl, *op. cit.,* pp. 224, 563.

was chosen junior warden of the yeomanry of the Company, and in the following year he duly became senior warden.[15] He apparently held no parish office until 1628, when he was nominated on the petty jury. Thereafter he was active in parish affairs, and he was elected a vestryman in February, 1640.[16] He departed from the parish about the middle of 1643.[17] The 1640 *Life of Donne* is written, then, by a respectable and prospering tradesman who for many years lived in the parish of St. Dunstan's-in-the-West, just around the corner from the church.

The popular Dr. Donne was preferred to the Vicarage of St. Dunstan's in March, 1624, some two and a half years after his appointment as Dean of St. Paul's. He must have welcomed the chance to preach again before the sophisticated lawyers and interested tradesmen, and there is ample evidence of his vigorous interest in St. Dunstan's for about four years. He preached there occasionally, encouraged a program of building and repair, and attended vestry meetings with great regularity. During his last years, however, Donne seems to have neglected St. Dunstan's. In 1631, in answer to an accusation that his interest had waned, he wrote:

My witnesse is in heaven, that I never left out S. *Dunstans*, when I was able to do them that service [preaching at Lent]; nor will now; though they that know the state of the Church well, know that I am not so bound, as the world thinks, to preach there; for, I make not a shilling profit of S. *Dunstans* as a Church-man, but as my L. of *Dorset* gave me the lease of the Impropriation, for a certain rent, and a higher rent, thē my predecessor had it at.[18]

Perhaps St. Dunstan's was not so profitable as Donne had hoped it might be. His parishioners obviously did what they could for him: they "lovingly condiscended" to give him two hundred pounds a year for the tithes of the parish, they gave him the receipts derived from the rental of some pews in the chancel, and they gave him generous presents at Christmas. Still, after the middle of 1628, Donne's energetic participation in the affairs of St. Dunstan's

[15] *Ibid.*, pp. 563–564.   [16] Nicolas, p. clii.

[17] Coon, pp. 122, 124, based on St. Dunstan's "Vestry Minutes," I, 233a–242, and Public Record Office, C54.147/577, f. 40a.

[18] "*To my Noble friend M*ris *Cokain at* Ashburne," dated "15 Jan. 1630.[31] Abrey-hatch." John Donne, *Letters to Severall Persons of Honour* (London, 1651), pp. 317–318.

lessened. He seems to have preached there only once after this time, and he attended only two or three vestry meetings.[19]

It was probably as a parishioner that Walton met Donne. If the meeting occurred in 1624, Walton was a young tradesman of thirty-one; Donne, then in his fifty-third year, was the most eminent preacher in England. Possibly the acquaintance started only after Walton's marriage in December, 1626, to Rachel Floud, whose family connections with Archbishop Cranmer and Dr. John Spenser (once president of Corpus Christi College, Oxford) might have recommended the Waltons to Donne's attention. At most, then, Walton knew Donne only for seven years, and their ages, their positions, perhaps even Donne's secondary interest in St. Dunstan's —all would seem to make the acquaintance a very casual one. Donne wrote no letters to Walton; he never mentioned him in writing. Walton wrote no part for himself in Donne's life; there is not even a "he told me," only "he often said." Still, Sir Henry Wotton, writing to Walton in 1639 about Donne, referred to "our ever memorable Friend,"[20] and Henry King thought that Walton was present at Donne's bedside three days before his death.[21] Walton possessed one of the rings of Christ on an anchor which Donne gave to his most intimate friends before his death,[22] and he also owned a book which had been in Donne's library.[23] For the last five or seven years of Donne's life, then, Walton knew him, and the

[19] The entries in the records of St. Dunstan's which refer to Donne are printed by Baird W. Whitlock in "Donne at St. Dunstan's," *TLS*, Sept. 16, 1955, p. 548, and Sept. 23, 1955, p. 564. For evidence that Donne preached at St. Dunstan's after his illness in the summer of 1628, see his letter of Nov. 18, 1628, printed in Evelyn M. Simpson and George R. Potter, eds., *The Sermons of John Donne*, VIII (Berkeley and Los Angeles, 1956), 24–25.

[20] *Reliquiae Wottonianae* (London, 1651), p. 512. The letter is undated, but refers to Dr. King "now made Dean of *Rochester*." Henry King was made Dean of Rochester on Feb. 6, 1639.

[21] "*The Copy of a Letter writ to Mr.* Walton *by Dr.* King, *Lord Bishop of* Chicester." [Izaak Walton], *The Life of Mr. Rich. Hooker* (London, 1665), sig. A2v.

[22] The impression of the ring is upon Walton's will and upon that of his son (Nicolas, pp. cii, cxix). It appears also on page 57 of a copy of *Lives*, 1675, which Walton presented to Elizabeth Chase. This copy is now at Yale.

It is possible, of course, that Walton merely copied Donne's seal. Miss Helen Gardner doubts that he received one directly from Donne (*John Donne, The Divine Poems* [Oxford, 1952], pp. 139–140, n. 3).

[23] See Geoffrey Keynes, *A Bibliography of Dr John Donne*, 2d ed. (Cambridge, 1932), p. 176.

information that the life contains during the recital of those years is presumably firsthand.

Sir Edmund Gosse introduced the speculation that Walton played Boswell to Donne's Johnson:

For some months (as I conjecture), in 1629 and 1630, he contrived to enjoy the Dean's intimacy, and beyond question to take notes of his conversation. We do not begin to understand what the early part of Walton's "Life of Donne" is until it occurs to us that it is largely Donne's own report of the incidents of his career. Replying to the enthusiastic curiosity of Walton, Donne would recount events the exact sequence of which had escaped his memory, would pass over in silence facts which seemed immaterial, and errors which he regretted, and would place his conduct in a light distinctly edifying to his listener. In short, without being in the least degree conscious that he was doing so, Donne would give a picture of his life which was neither quite accurate nor perfectly candid. Whatever the great Dean said, Walton joyfully accepted.[24]

Churchmen, it is true, found Walton's company agreeable, but it is difficult to imagine John Donne telling his life story to Walton. To hear Donne speak of himself would have been a rare treat, but it is doubtful that even the traditional placidity of Walton's nature could have tempered Donne's customarily tortured introversions into the *Life* as Walton wrote it. A close study of the *Life* shows that Walton struggled with the sequence of events, that he often knew more than he told, and that the "edifying" quality was achieved by him through innumerable carefully chosen words and literary stratagems. Walton did not joyfully accept even Donne's printed words, but he changed them to work his purpose. Much of the information which Gosse would attribute to Donne, Walton got from Henry King.

In 1658, Walton dedicated the second edition of the *Life of Donne* to Sir Robert Holt, nephew of Henry King, desiring that it be "a testimony of my gratitude to your self and Family, who descended to such a degree of humility as to admit me into their friendship in the dayes of my youth."[25] Before the *Life of Hooker* was published in 1665, Walton sent a manuscript to King, asking him for additional information or testimony and intimating that he would like to print King's letter in his book. King's reply, dated

---

[24] Gosse, I, xii.
[25] Izaak Walton, *The Life of John Donne* (London, 1658), sig. A8ᵛ.

"Nov. 13, 1664," is signed *"Your ever-faithful and affectionate old Friend"* and mentions "a Familiarity of almost Forty years continuance."[26] Walton met King, then, about the time he met Donne. Donne had known Henry King when he was a boy, for his father, John King, was chaplain to Sir Thomas Egerton when Donne was his secretary.[27] John King, then Bishop of London, had ordained Donne in 1615. Henry King was collated to the prebend of St. Pancras in the cathedral of St. Paul's in 1616, and his path merged even more closely with that of Donne when Donne was preferred to the deanship in 1621. But Henry King gave Walton more than the facts of Donne's life which he remembered and those which he had heard from his father. It is impossible to explain the source of some of the detail in the *Life of Donne* except upon the predication that Walton had access to many of Donne's papers. These he must have seen when they were in Henry King's possession. Two documents tell the story of many of Donne's manuscripts. The first is the letter from King to Walton, referred to above. In it, King says:

I shall begin with my most dear and incomparable Friend Dr. *Donne,* late Dean of S. *Pauls* Church, who not onely trusted me as his Executor, but three days before his death delivered into my hands those excellent Sermons of his now made publick: professing before Dr. *Winniff,* Dr. *Montford,* and I think your self then present at his bed-side, that it was by my restless importunity that he had prepared them for the Press; together with which (as his best Legacy) he gave me all his Sermon-Notes, and his other Papers, containing an Extract of near Fifteen hundred Authors. How these were got out of my hands, you, who were the Messenger for them, and how lost both to me and your self, is not now seasonable to complain: but, since they did miscarry, I am glad that the general Demonstration of his Worth was so fairly preserv[e]d and represented to the World by your Pen in the H[i]story of his Life.[28]

[26] *Hooker,* 1665, sigs. A6ʳ, A2ʳ. When the letter was printed the following year, "a Familiarity of almost Forty years continuance" became "a Familiarity of Forty years continuance," and the salutation *"Honest* Isaac" was added (*Hooker,* 1666, sig. *2ʳ). In the version of the letter prefixed to *Lives,* 1670, "a Familiarity of Forty years continuance" became "a Familiarity of more then Forty years continuance." The date of the letter was changed to Nov. 17. Some dozen insertions, mainly of single words, also occur. These are typical of Walton's customary revisions and were probably made by him. Bishop King died in 1669.

[27] Gosse, II, 70–71, 139, and Virgil B. Heltzel, "Sir Thomas Egerton as Patron," *Huntington Library Quarterly,* XI (1948), 111.

[28] *Hooker,* 1665, sig. A2ᵛ.

An extract from the will of John Donne, the younger, made July 21, 1657, and printed February 23, 1662, completes the story:

To Mr Isaac Walton, I give all my writings under my father's hand, which may be of some use to his son, if he makes him a scholar. To the Reverend Bishop of Chichester [Henry King], I return that cabinet that was my father's, now in my dining-room, and all those papers which are of authors analysed by my father; many of which he hath already received with his Common Place Book, which I desire may pass to Mr Walton's son.[29]

It is evident that the younger John Donne got possession of those papers which his father had entrusted to Henry King, whom he probably intended for his literary legatee. King published one of Donne's sermons in 1632, and nothing thereafter, though at least eighty sermons were ready for the press.[30] He had Donne's papers in his possession, then, for at least a year. In August, 1634, the younger Donne was tried and acquitted of a manslaughter charge, and he left England shortly thereafter. He took the degree of doctor of laws at Padua and returned to England late in 1637.[31] His interest in his father's work is obvious at this date, for, in compliance to his petition, the Archbishop of Canterbury prohibited the printing or selling of the Dean's works, subject to the son's approval.[32] If Walton did not act as messenger before August, 1634, King might well have held Donne's papers for as long as six years, and during this time Walton was able to avail himself of them.[33] It is unlikely that King possessed them after 1637, and from the time of the

[29] Nicolas, p. cxlii.

[30] In a letter dated Nov. 25, 1625, Donne wrote, "I have revised as many of my sermons as I had kept any note of, and I have written out a great many, and hope to do more. I am already come to the number of eighty, of which my son, who, I hope, will take the same profession or some other in the world of middle understanding, may hereafter make some use" (Gosse, II, 225). It would appear from this that Donne had intended the sermons for his son's use, but King's letter and the younger Donne's will point to King's possession of Donne's papers upon his death. Donne named no literary executor in his will.

[31] Gosse, II, 308–309.

[32] Herbert J. C. Grierson, *Poems of John Donne* (Oxford, 1912), II, lxvi–lxvii.

[33] If King had Donne's MSS for six years, it is possible that he did not press the publication of the sermons because the six published in 1634 by the University Press at Cambridge may have received an indifferent reception. See Gosse, II, 306–307; but see also Simpson and Potter, *op. cit.*, I (1953), 24–25, especially n. 42.

publication of *LXXX Sermons* in 1640, the younger Donne largely directed the publication of his father's work.

King did not deem it seasonable to complain of his loss in 1664, for the younger Donne had died in holy orders in 1662, but his belief that the papers miscarried and his statement that they were lost both to Walton and himself show that he did not have much use for Donne's son. If, as the younger Donne's will states, King had already received some of the papers, his letter does not mention their return, nor is there any indication that Walton's son inherited them either from his father or from King. From the conjunction of Walton's *Life* and the sermons in 1640, it would be pleasing to assume that the younger Donne made certain material available to Walton, but the inferences in King's letter would seem to minimize this possibility. It cannot be ruled out entirely, however, despite Walton's not mentioning the younger Donne in the *Life,* for had the breach between them been as wide as that between the younger Donne and King, we would be at a loss to explain the presence of the *Life* in the *LXXX Sermons.* Certain evidences of good feeling between the men exist. On June 24, 1640, Donne sent Walton a copy of *LXXX Sermons,* explaining in a letter that the book was "rather to witness my debt than to make any payment."[34] His will shows that he kept in touch with Walton, for the son of Walton's whom he mentions was not born until 1651. His preference for Richard Marriot as the publisher of his father's work is probably indicative of a friendship maintained with Walton. John Marriot and his son Richard had published none of the Dean's work during his lifetime, and the publication of Donne's poems and of an edition of *Ignatius his Conclave* by John Marriot had provoked the younger Donne's petition to the Archbishop. Walton's friendship of half a century with Richard Marriot dates from 1633, and it may well have been he who persuaded the younger Donne to allow the Marriots to publish *LXXX Sermons* in 1640, *Fifty Sermons* in 1649, and *Essayes in Divinity* and *Letters to Severall Persons of Honour* in 1651.[35] There is, then, a possibility that the materials which Henry King surrendered were not wholly lost to Walton.

In writing the life of Donne, Walton had sources of information

[34] Nicolas, p. xxix.

[35] After this date, Humphrey Moseley gradually gained control of many of Donne's works.

other than his own personal acquaintance, the remembrances of Henry King, the possible assistance of the younger Donne, and his conversations with Sir Henry Wotton. Of Donne's unpublished work, Walton saw an account book from which he quotes specifically. He had read Donne's *Biathanatos* in manuscript, for his writing that Donne "diligently survayed, and judiciously censured" the laws violated by suicide shows that he was aware of the contents, but consciously hedged on Donne's conclusion.[36] He might have seen some of the paradoxes, cases of conscience, analyses of books, and notes of English and foreign affairs that he mentions. I shall show below that he had access to a large number of Donne's letters. Of Donne's published work, Walton possessed copies of many of his sermons and he drew upon *Pseudo-Martyr* and *Devotions upon Emergent Occasions.*

Walton also used Donne's poetry in writing the *Life* that appeared in 1640. A discussion of his elegy on Dr. Donne, which first appeared with the praises suffixed to the 1633 edition of Donne's poems, is relevant here because it presents Walton's first printed impression of Donne, and because it is mixed inextricably with the problem of the editorship of Donne's poems and Walton's part in the editing. *Poems, By J. D. with Elegies on the Authors Death* was printed in 1633 by M. F. for John Marriot and sold "at his shop in St *Dunstans* Church-yard in *Fleet-street.*" The text is generally excellent, but though some attempt has been made to arrange the poems into coherent groups, the general arrangement is neither careful nor logical. The volume opens with the "Metempsychosis" and the holy sonnets; the elegies and verse letters precede the songs and sonnets, and the satires are printed at the end, followed only by "A Hymne to God the Father." Of the twelve elegies suffixed to the poems, Walton's is the sixth.

When he changed his elegy for the second time and reprinted it in the first (1670) collected edition of his *Lives*, Walton added for the first time, as the date of its composition, April 7, 1631. It appears, then, that the elegy was what Walton would call a "free-will-offering," and that it pictures Walton's estimate of Donne eight days after his death. Walton, as I shall later show, was not

---

[36] *Donne*, 1640, sig. B4^v. *Biathanatos* was not licensed for publication until Sept. 20, 1644, and was not entered on the Stationers' Register until Sept. 25, 1646. See Evelyn M. Simpson, *A Study of the Prose Works of John Donne*, 2d ed. (Oxford, 1948), pp. 163–164.

above manipulating dates, and he did so generally when a change in the date, its total deletion, or its fictitious addition would heighten and dramatize an incident or corroborate one of his statements. His tender devotion to Donne, I believe he thought, could best be demonstrated by spontaneous verses composed directly after Donne's death. Certainly the effect is highly dramatic and reflects more credit on him than would a date that would indicate that the elegy was one of many written in customary fashion for specific inclusion in a posthumous work. That the elegy was not included in *Deaths Duell* in 1632 with King's and Hyde's, and that it resembles in content the other elegies in the 1633 *Poems,* with their interest primarily in Donne's poetry, are evidence of composition later than Walton's appended date. The date is important, for if it can be trusted, we have a true delineation of Donne in the light of Walton's interest in him; if the composition took place in 1633, Walton's interest in the poetry would be natural and expected in view of the purpose for which the elegy would have been written.

The elegy indicates equal enthusiasm for Donne the poet and Donne the preacher, but the poetry is treated in greater detail. Walton speaks of Donne's graceful power of language, his great wit, and his stock of knowledge. He says that in the poetry written before his twentieth year, Donne charactered every sin in his satires and perpetuated the praise of worthy men in his funeral elegies. In mentioning the poetry of Donne's more mature years, Walton commends the "La Corona" sonnets and "The Litany." He compares the piety and wit of the hymns to those of "great grave *Prudentius.*" Donne, he says, was expert in languages, in law, in medicine, but he put them aside to visit Palestine. He returned to preach as only he could. Walton refers to Donne's friendship with him, and to the fact that he was a parishioner of Donne's. This original biographical material, wrenched from the elegiac context, represents Donne as a talented poet, with particular emphasis on the moralistic, elegiac, and religious elements of the poetry, and also, though not at such length, as a powerful preacher.

In the light of the other elegies in the 1633 *Poems,* Walton's elegy is by no means unusual in its content. The difference between Donne's early and late poetry is an element common to many of the poems, and though Walton is a good deal less frank than Thomas Browne, his recognition of the difference is obvious in the conscious selectivity of his detail and in his division of the poems into those of youth and those of maturity. The elegies in general glorify both the poet and the preacher in Donne, and here also, Walton's emphasis is not unusual. The distinction of Walton's elegy is not so much in its tone or emphasis as in the particularity of its detail.

The 1635 edition of Donne's *Poems* saw the addition of elegies by Sidney Godolphin, John Chudleigh, and Daniel Darnelly. Both Godolphin and Chudleigh pictured Donne's preaching in detail that was impressive to Walton.[37] Of the eleven elegies reprinted from 1633, Walton's was the only one to be revised. There are numerous verbal changes, the most interesting that in which Walton compares Donne's preaching to that of St. Paul. In four appended lines, Walton states that the elegy is a free-will-offering to fame and the world and regrets his inability to set forth a monument as great as Donne's matchless worth. The 1635 edition introduced a printer's error which was not corrected in the editions of 1639, 1649, 1650, 1654, and 1669. The ridiculous reading, "flowes of gratitude,"[38] for the "vowes of gratitude"[39] of 1633 persisted until 1670, when Walton revised the elegy for the *Lives*. These lines by Walton were engraved under the portrait of Donne, "Aetatis Suae 18":

> This was for youth, Strength, Mirth, and wit that Time
> Most count their golden Age; but t'was not thine.
> Thine was thy later yeares, so much refind
> From youths Drosse, Mirth & wit; as thy pure mind
> Thought (like the Angels) nothing but the Praise
> Of thy Creator, in those last, best Dayes.
>   Witnes this Booke, (thy Embleme) which begins
>   With Love; but endes, with Sighes, & Teares for sins.

Walton has been variously credited with the editing of Donne's poems of 1633 and 1635.[40] It can be shown, I think, that his part in the actual editing was negligible, although he had something to

---

[37] See pp. 76–77 and Appendix A.   [38] *Poems, By J. D.,* 1635, sig. Cc6ʳ.
[39] *Ibid.,* 1633, p. 384.
[40] The younger Donne was not concerned with his father's poetry until the edition of 1649. Despite the Archbishop's decree of 1637, John Marriot issued a third edition in 1639, but his next edition (1649) was probably taken over by the younger Donne, for only a few copies were issued (see Keynes, *op. cit.,* p. 127). The fifth edition, printed the following year from the 1649 plates, with the addition of a section of new poems, has a dedication by the younger Donne.

do with the second edition. Sir Harris Nicolas suggested that Walton might have edited the 1633 *Poems,* pointing to the inclusion there of Walton's elegy and to the fact that the volume was printed for John Marriot,[41] whose son, Richard, was Walton's friend and publisher for almost fifty years.[42] Sir Herbert Grierson proposed that Henry King might have been the editor behind Marriot.[43] There is no doubt that King was responsible for the issuance of Donne's last sermon in 1632. He had been appointed Donne's executor, his elegy made its first appearance there, and the printer's title-page advertisement echoes the elegy, "Being his last Sermon, and called by his Majesties houshold The Doctors Owne Funerall Sermon." That King was aware of the publication of the poems is obvious from the revision of his elegy, but it is doubtful that he supplied Marriot with a manuscript. In 1614, Donne, contemplating publication of his poetry, found that he did not have copies of all his verses and wrote Sir Henry Goodere, asking to borrow them.[44] Donne's plan was abandoned, probably because public acknowledgment of some of the verses would not have reflected well on a man about to enter holy orders. Marriot may have obtained Goodere's copies, for Goodere died in 1628, and most of the prose letters printed in 1633 are written to him. King, in his letter of 1664, does not mention the poetry in the catalogue of papers entrusted to him, nor does Walton in his enumeration of Donne's papers in the *Life.* But King may well have edited the manuscripts which Marriot secured. As a practicing and capable poet and as an intimate friend of Donne's, he was well equipped to produce a generally excellent text. The rather haphazard arrangement may conceivably be his, for his elegy is one of the few that do not differentiate between the secular and the religious poetry.

Walton, on the other hand, was keenly aware of the necessity of making a distinction between the early and the more religious verses. It is inconceivable that, had he edited the 1633 volume, the satires would have been printed on pages 325–349 and "La Corona" on pages 28–32. In view of the order maintained in his elegy, it would be difficult to credit him with placing the holy

[41] Nicolas, p. xxiv.

[42] Richard Marriot published almost all of Walton's work. In his will, Walton left his "old friend" £10 and a ring, and instructed his son to show kindness to Marriot if he was ever in need (*ibid.,* pp. ci–cii).

[43] *Poems of John Donne,* II, 255.

[44] *Letters to Severall Persons,* pp. 196–197.

sonnets early in the volume, before the elegies. If Walton's method of quotation is any criterion of the exactness of his editorial ability, it would be impossible to account for the competence of the 1633 text. On the other hand, there is no doubt that Walton was somehow involved with the edition of 1635. There is evidence to show that John Marriot had consulted Walton, as a neighbor and fellow tradesman interested in literature. In 1635, Marriot was issuing the *Emblemes* of Francis Quarles, and William Marshall had been making a large number of engravings for the book. It is reasonable to suppose that Marriot, considering a second edition of Donne's poems, asked Marshall to make an engraving of the picture of Donne painted in 1591 and, too, that he asked Walton, on the basis of his elegy and the closeness of his residence, for some lines to go under the picture. The mention of "emblem" in the lines is perhaps evidence that Walton was aware of Marriot's work in progress. It may be that Walton, at this time, spoke to Marriot about rearranging the poems, for the 1635 edition carries out the division suggested by Walton's elegy. The most profane poems are printed first. These are followed by the elegies and satires, and the divine poetry is printed at the end. When Marriot had seen the logic of the rearrangement, Walton wrote his lines, emphasizing the progression from love to holiness, and he took the opportunity of revising his elegy. That the 1635 text has more blemishes than the first is probably not due to Walton but to Marriot. Inaccurate as Walton was as an editor, it is reasonable to suppose that had he seen the proofs he would have been sufficiently interested in his own poem to correct the nonsensical misprint in it. Walton's quotations from Donne's poems are often unique versions, following neither the 1633 nor the 1635 text. But his writing does point to a particular interest in the second edition. In his *Life* of 1640, he made use of Donne's poem, *"To M*ʳ *Tilman after he had taken orders,"* first printed in 1635.[45] In his plans for the revised *Life* of 1658, he made note of the elegies of Chudleigh and Godolphin and of Donne's poem, *"Upon the trãslation of the Psalmes by Sir* Philip Sydney, *and the Countesse of Pembroke his Sister,"* all of them first printed in 1635.[46] The 1675 version of the *Life of Donne* shows a preoccupation with the portrait engraved by Marshall.[47]

Was Walton as early as 1635 making those notes for Wotton which in 1640 had been "forsaken" for a sufficiently long time so

[45] See p. 73.   [46] See pp. 76, 94.   [47] See pp. 118–119.

that they had to be "re-viewed"? Was he in the 1635 *Poems* already trying to point the proper manner in which Donne's life should be viewed? The particularized detail in his elegy in 1633 certainly shows his great interest in Donne's life. The words which he wrote for Donne's picture in 1635 are cautionary and directive; they indicate to the reader the proper perspective toward Donne's verse and life. There are further indications in the 1635 volume of a hand which is molding a view of Donne's life.

Sir Harris Nicolas, conjecturing that Walton had edited the 1633 *Poems,* thought it "not unlikely" that the *"Hexasticon Bibliopolae"* preceding the poems had been written by Walton, even though it is signed by John Marriot.[48] It reads:

> I see in his last preach'd, and printed booke,
> His Picture in a sheete; in *Pauls* I looke,
> And see his Statue in a sheete of stone,
> And sure his body in the grave hath one:
> Those sheetes present him dead, these if you buy,
> You have him living to Eternity.

The play on "sheets" is not typical of Walton, who had little love for conceited verse. But, in 1635, the publisher was answered in a "Hexastichon ad Bibliopolam" signed "Incerti."

> *In thy Impression of* Donnes *Poems rare,*
> *For his Eternitie thou hast ta'ne care;*
> *'Twas well, and pious; And for ever may*
> *He live: Yet shew I thee a better way;*
> *Print but his Sermons, and if those we buy,*
> *Hee, We, and Thou shall live t' Eternity.*

Gosse, in one of his many undocumented statements, suggests that this is doubtless Walton's work and that he was the revising editor of 1635.[49] His guess that Walton composed these verses is, I think, a shrewd one. If Walton did not write them, they were written by someone who is expressing a sentiment complimentary to the one in the lines inscribed under Donne's picture.

There is further evidence in the 1635 volume of a hand which is working almost counter to the intent of the volume, of someone who is trying to emphasize not Donne's verse but the holy life of Donne the divine. This evidence is in the four prose letters first printed in the 1635 *Poems,* and it is necessary to examine them

---

[48] Nicolas, p. xxiv, n. 8.   [49] Gosse, II, 307–308.

and the prose letters printed at the end of the 1633 *Poems*. Grierson considers the inclusion in 1633 of nine prose letters in a collection of poems rather odd, and he thinks they were printed because they had been transcribed into the principal manuscript used by the printer.[50] R. E. Bennett agrees that the letters came from Goodere's papers, but he thinks that they were not necessarily in the manuscript which contained Donne's poems. He thinks, too, that it is likely that all the letters to Goodere printed in *Letters to Severall Persons of Honour* (1651) were in the possession of the editor of *Poems, 1633*, and that some of them were printed in 1633 because the editor got the originals from one of Goodere's heirs (probably Sir Francis Nethersole).[51] Bennett is certainly right in believing that Donne's letters were printed with the poems as examples of epistolary elegance.[52] An examination of these letters shows that they were not haphazardly chosen, that they were carefully selected to form a manual of letter writing. Goodere himself had plagiarized Donne's letters, and both he and Sir Robert Drury had taken advantage of Donne's ability to compose lines of courtly

[50] *Poems of John Donne*, II, xci.

[51] Bennett thinks that the letters passed from the editor, by way of the publisher, to the younger Donne: "The 1633 edition of the poems was published by John Marriot, whose son and partner, Richard, published *Letters to Severall Persons*. His father did not formally sign over his rights to Donne's letters and poems until May 3, 1651, however. When he did so he listed 'Packetts of letters.' It is a safe conjecture that the Goodere letters, and possibly some of the Garrard letters, had been in the possession of the Marriots for a number of years" ("Donne's *Letters to Severall Persons of Honour*," *PMLA*, LVI [1941], 127).

Bennett's general conclusion is right, but his reasons are wrong. When John Marriot signed over his rights in "Dr DOUN'S *poems with anniversaries*" and in "*Packetts of letters*," among many other items, he merely signed them over to his son Richard (*Sta. Reg., 1640–1708*, I, 366). Richard Marriot assigned his title in the *Poems* to Humphrey Moseley on Dec. 12, 1653 (*ibid.*, p. 436). On Jan. 25, 1653, he assigned to George Badger his rights in "*Packetts of letters*," more accurately entitled in this transaction "*A Post w[i]th a Packett of mad Letters*, in two parts" (*ibid.*, p. 407). John Marriot had published Nicholas Breton's volume since 1623.

I think it likely that John Marriot, rather than his editor, procured the manuscripts of the letters and that Marriot had Goodere's letters in his possession from 1633 and Garrard's from 1635, until the younger Donne claimed them even as he claimed the papers in Henry King's possession. I think it is probable that Marriot possessed all the letters to Goodere and Garrard which were printed in 1651, because, as I shall show below, it is obvious that those printed in 1633 and in 1635 must have been very carefully selected from a much larger collection.

[52] "Donne's *Letters to Severall Persons*," p. 126.

compliment.[53] Both these men, and probably many of their contemporaries, admired in Donne something which he did not himself consider of first importance in letter writing, his polished
phrases and clever turns of expression. His own concept of what a
model letter must be is embedded in one, first printed in 1651,
which demonstrates what he means:

When Letters have a convenient handsome body of news, they are
Letters; but when they are spun out of nothing, they are nothing, or
but apparitions, and ghosts, with such hollow sounds, as he that hears
them, knows not what they said. . . . So have Letters for their principall
office, to be seals and testimonies of mutuall affection, but the materialls
and fuell of them should be a confident and mutuall communicating of
those things which we know.[54]

Donne continues, "How shall I then who know nothing write
Letters?" But he asks such a question and makes such speculations
about letters in this letter because he has a "convenient handsome
body of news" to send, and he proceeds to tell all the latest gossip
of the French court.

The letters printed in the 1633 *Poems* are not of this sort; they
are beautifully contrived little essays. They were printed not for
what they tell of Donne's life and insights, not as informal and
personal revelations of the writer; they were printed for their art
and grace. The first of them appears on the surface to contradict
my contention. It is personal; Donne tells of his projected visit to
the continent, and asks Goodere to return his Latin epigrams and
his satirical catalogue of books—if Goodere has them—so that he
may revise them. Quite obviously, however, the letter was not
printed for the information it contained, for this could only serve
to make the readers of the *Poems* conscious that the compositions
Donne mentions were missing from the book.[55] It was printed as a
fine example of cultivated correspondence in Latin. Indeed, Donne
begins his letter by comparing the worth of letters written in
the vulgar tongue with that of letters in a foreign tongue:

[53] See Stanley Johnson, "Sir Henry Goodere and Donne's Letters," *MLN*,
LXIII (1948), 38–43, and R. E. Bennett, "Donne's Letters from the Continent
in 1611–12," *PQ*, XIX (1940), 69–70, 74–75.

[54] *Letters to Severall Persons*, p. 121.

[55] The younger Donne first added the *Catalogus Librorum* to the 1650
edition of his father's poems.

Etiam vulgari linguâ scriptae testantur literae nos amicorum meminisse, sed alienâ, nos de illis meditari. In illis enim affulgent nobis de amicis cogitatiunculae, sed ut matutinae stellae transeunt, & evanescunt: In his autē haeremus, & immoramur, & amicos uti solem ipsum permanentem nobiscum degentemque contemplamur; Habes cur Latinè.

These lines are a preface to the letters which follow. Their merit lies not in their being letters, but in their being letters about letters. To search them for what has happened to Donne is to find very little. In one, Donne sends Goodere a problem and asks Goodere to return such of his problems and other papers as he may have before he makes a trip. In another, Donne writes that he has that morning come to London from Surrey, that he has received a verse letter from Goodere, and that he sends him two problems and a "ragge of verses." In still another, Donne asks the Countess of Bedford for some verses she had made in Twickenham garden. Such is the body of news in the nine letters. Formal and elegant homiletic discourses replace the "communicating of those things which we know." In the second letter, for example, Donne worries the function of letters, shows their relationship with prayer, and says that though he had intended to write a letter, it "is extended and strayed into a Homily. And whatsoever is not what it was purposed, is worse." In the third, Donne writes, "I must not give you a Homily for a letter," but only after he has made one on vice and virtue. The fourth is an elaborate thank-you for letters received, and Donne admits, "my whole letter is nothing else but a confession that I should and would write." In the fifth, Donne speaks of letters as maintaining love and friendship, and he ends by saying, "I have placed my love wisely where I need communicate nothing." The sixth is a heavily conceited letter, in which Donne uses the new astronomy to show that Goodere's life is full of variety and his own full of monotony. He is forced to communicate such thoughts, "the Sallads, and Onyons of Michin." The letter to Lady Bedford is a courtier's fair display of compliment. The eighth starts, "Because I am in a place and season where I see every thing bud forth, I must do so too, and vent some of my meditations to you," and Donne meditates on spring, vice, and vanity. In the last, Donne embroiders the theme, "we consist of three parts, a Soule, and Body, and Mind," and he ends by writing, "I meant to write a letter, and I am fallen into a discourse, and I doe not only take you from some businesse, but I make you a new businesse by drawing you into these meditations." The letters printed in 1633 are a fine prose counterpart of the poems. They are intelligent, sophisticated, introspective, clever, but they tell us no more about Donne than the poems do, nor are they intended to.

Four letters, one to *"the La. G."* and three to George Garrard, were added to the *Poems* in 1635, and we may ask why. Certainly Marriot did not go out of his way to search for new letters between 1633 and 1635, for had he wished to include more letters in the *Poems,* he could have drawn upon the store of letters to Goodere which he had. But the 1635 volume shows that Marriot was interested in printing more of Donne's poems. He added twenty-nine poems, without much questioning their authenticity. He printed two versions of the "Epitaph on himself" in different parts of the volume, either because he found it under two titles or because he found it in two manuscript collections, and he printed a number of poems quite obviously not by Donne. One of his new manuscripts Marriot probably got from George Garrard, an old friend of Donne's who had been Master of the Charterhouse since 1627. Garrard seems the most likely source for those poems printed in 1635 which Grierson attributes to Sir John Roe. Roe and Garrard were first cousins, within a year of each other in age, and had been at Oxford at about the same time. Garrard had probably kept copies of the poems of the witty, swashbuckling soldier who died in his late twenties, about the year 1608. Either the poems had got mixed with some of Donne's, or Marriot, upon receiving Garrard's manuscript, did not pay much attention to the attributions of the poems. At the same time that Marriot got the poems, he probably got Donne's letters to Garrard. It was not Marriot, however, who selected four of these letters for the 1635 volume. The very inclusion of the letters shows that they were selected by someone close to Marriot, someone who was aware of his plans to publish a second edition of Donne's poems, someone whom he trusted. But an examination of the letters shows that the immediate purpose for which they were chosen was to counteract the licentiousness of some of the poems now added for the first time and that their larger purpose runs counter to the intent of the volume itself. Marriot's purpose was to present Donne the poet, to prove that his verses "were the best in this kinde, that ever this Kingdome hath yet seene."[56] The purpose of the editor of the letters in 1635 was not precisely to belittle Donne the poet, but to show that part of Donne which was poet in its proper relation to that more distinguished part of Donne which was divine.

The first of the letters newly printed in 1635 follows almost perfectly in the pattern initiated in 1633. It is, on the whole, an artful and skillful letter of compliment addressed to a lady. Donne starts by saying, "I am not come out of England, if I remaine in the noblest part of it, your minde," and he argues that "since there is a religion in friendship, and a death in absence, to make up an intire friend,[57] there must be an heaven too: and there can be no heaven so proportionall to that religion, and that death, as your favour." The second letter is quite different. It opens conventionally enough with prettily turned sentiments on letter writing and friendship:

Neither your letters, nor sil̆ece, needs excuse; your friendship is to mee an abundant possession, though you remember me but twice in a yeare: Hee that could have two harvests in that time, might justly value his land at a high rate; but, Sir, as wee doe not onely then thanke our land, when wee gather the fruit, but acknowledge that all the yeare shee doth many motherly offices in preparing it: so is not friendship then onely to be esteemed, when shee is delivered of a letter, or any other reall office, but in her continuall propensnesse and inclination to doe it. This hath made me easie in pardoning my long silences, and in promising my selfe your forgivenesse for not answering your letter sooner.

Suddenly, however, the letter becomes highly personal, as Donne turns to justify his past actions. He tells Garrard that he has ever thought of the study of law as his best entertainment and pastime, but that he has never seriously considered it as a profession. He acknowledges his great fault in allowing his *Anniversaries* to be printed, but he defends himself from the charge of having too highly praised Elizabeth Drury by saying that, since he had never seen her, he had an ideal lady in mind, and that any lady may consider that the verses are for her if she has made herself fit for them. All this Donne writes from Paris on April 14, 1612 (N.S.), and he says that he hopes to return to England before Christmas. The third letter, dated November 2, 1630, is also highly personal, with

---

[56] "The Printer to the Understanders," *Poems, By J. D.,* 1633, sig. A^r.
[57] *Letters to Severall Persons,* p. 245, has "frame."

references to Donne's health and fortune and to the toll which he expects his preaching to exact: "If I be no worse all Spring, than now, I am much better; for I make account those Church-services which I am loath to decline, will spend somewhat; & if I can gather so much as will beare my charges, recover so much strength at *London,* as I shall spend at *London,* I shall not be loath to be left in that state I am now, after that is done." The last is even more pathetic and personal, as Donne comments on the rumors that he has died, that he has played sick to spare himself the trouble of preaching. He writes that he has ever desired to die as the result of his divine labors and that he hopes to preach at court before long.

These four letters are hardly epistolary models. They are far different from the ingenious meditations and the conceited frills of the 1633 letters. They present a miniature portrait of Donne, demonstrating chronologically his turn for dignified compliment, his avowal that he considered law a mere toy, his confession that he must wonder that he "descended to print any thing in verse," his compulsion to preach even in his illness, and his holy dying. These are odd letters to have included in a volume of poetry, and the oddness indicates careful selection.

There is further reason to believe that there was purpose in the selection. The letters were not only carefully chosen with a purpose in mind, but they were edited the better to achieve that purpose. R. E. Bennett concluded from the available evidence that when the younger Donne reprinted in 1651 the letters which had appeared in the 1633 *Poems,* he probably used the 1633 volume to provide his text. But Bennett shows quite clearly that in printing the letters which had first appeared in 1635, Donne, Jr., used not only the text of the 1635 *Poems* but also the original manuscripts.[58] How do the letters vary in 1635 and in 1651? Bennett has demonstrated that Donne's letter from Paris of April 14, 1612, is synthetic, that its pretty opening and its last sentence were in 1635 engrafted upon its body, which was taken from a letter the whole of which was printed in 1651.[59] Quite obviously, the 1635 editor was interested only in Donne's statements about the law and the *Anniversaries.* What did he omit? He substituted a graceful opening for an inventory of the letters which Donne had received from Garrard.

[58] "Donne's *Letters to Severall Persons,*" pp. 126–128.
[59] *Ibid.,* p. 128, and "Donne's Letters from the Continent," pp. 70–74.

He omitted Donne's references to his correspondence with Sir Thomas Lucy, his refutation of the rumor that Sir Robert Drury was attending churches other than Anglican, his relationship with Sir John Brooke, his description of the marriages at the French court. He was not interested, then, in Donne's activities in France or in his relations with his contemporaries. He was interested, we may assume, in what Donne had to say about the law and about the *Anniversaries*. Had he been interested solely in Donne's remarks on his poems, he would have deleted the words about the law or he might well have excerpted another letter in Marriot's possession, which Donne wrote to Goodere at just about the same time that he wrote this one to Garrard and which contains almost the same comments on the *Anniversaries*.[60] That letter, too, contains an inventory of correspondence, some indication of future travels, regards to Lady Bedford, gossip of the French court, even a worried sentence about the outcome of Mrs. Donne's pregnancy. In none of these was the editor primarily interested; his specific care was for Donne's remarks on law and poetry, and it is evident from the other letters which he printed that he was trying to point out the importance of these to Donne as compared to the greater importance to him of his clerical duties. The editor was concerned not only with the gross matter of what he quoted, but with its details, for he was so fussily busy to make sure that the sense of Donne's letter was utterly clear that in several places he changed Donne's words. For instance, Donne had written, "you may be pleased to correct that imagination where you finde it"; the editor says, ". . . wheresoever you finde it." Donne would not pardon his own stooping to print verses though he had the excuse that it had been done "even in our times, by example of men, which one would thinke should as little have done it, as I." The editor makes his thought more immediately evident: "it have excuse even in our times, by men who professe, and practise much gravitie." Donne had said, "I would not be thought to have gone about to praise any bodie in rime, except I tooke such a Person, as might be capable of all that I could say." The editor explains that Donne means that he would not have praised "her [Elizabeth Drury], or any other in rime. . . ."

The editor made just such minor changes in Donne's letter of

---

[60] *Letters to Severall Persons*, pp. 73–78. Bennett shows that this letter is to Goodere in "Donne's Letters from the Continent," pp. 71–72.

November 2, 1630, to Garrard, changes which seem sufficiently purposeful so that they are not mere errors of transcription. Donne had started, "I should not only send you an account by my servant, but bring you an account often my self." Consciously or unconsciously, the editor's sense of clarity demanded "by my selfe." Donne had written of looking for roses "at this time of the year"; the editor has "season." Donne had mentioned "Church services, which I would be very loth to decline"; the editor was bothered by the sense of possibility and futurity implied in the verb and he substituted "am" for "would be." Donne's statement "life, or health, or strength . . . enter not into my prayers for my self: for others they do" became ". . . for others they often doe." The original letter had concluded with a prayer for Garrard's servant and a platitude on the paternal affection of masters for men reared in their service, and these the editor replaced, as Bennett shows, by modifying the close of a different letter to Garrard in his possession.

The editor tampered even with the letter of compliment to Lady G., and here his changes were not dictated merely by a desire to clarify Donne's intent. Indeed, either he did not see Donne's intent, or, seeing it, he set out to change it. His first change is probably an error of transcription, but it is an error which reveals that he could not follow Donne's playful dialectic. Donne had set up a correlation between friendship and religion, and absence and death, and, in order "to make up an intire frame," that is, in order to prove his analogy complete, he says that even as religion has its heaven, so, too, must friendship have one; with a fine flourish, he announces that the heaven of his friendship is his lady's favor. The editor somewhat dulled Donne's little game by using "friend" instead of "frame." His second change shows either that he did not know the rules of such courtly sport as Donne was indulging in or that he knew them and disapproved of them. Donne had written, "Madam my best treasure, is time; and my best imployment of that, is to study good wishes for you." The editor introduced a parenthesis after "that," which reads "(next my thoughts of thankfulnesse for my redeemer)." This note harmonizes well with the religiosity of the last two letters which the editor printed, but it is completely alien in the letter of compliment in which it appears. Donne had continued, after saying that his best employment of his time is to study good wishes for his lady, "in which I am by continuall meditation so learned, that your own good Angell, when it would do you most good, might be content to come and take instructions from/ *Your humble and affectionate servant."* Apparently the editor thought such a statement sacrilege, or at least unbecoming a future dean. He spoiled Donne's magnificent hyperbole when he wrote that "any creature (except your owne good Angell) when it would doe you most good, might bee content to come and take instructions from/ *Your humble and affectionate servant."*

The care with which the editor worked to create his own picture of Donne is best seen in the letter to Garrard in which Donne wrote about the rumors of his death. The original, as printed in 1651, reads in part:

One writ unto me, that some (and he said of my friends) conceived, that I was not so ill, as I pretended, but withdrew my self, to save charges, and to live at ease, discharged of preaching. It is an unfriendly, and God knows, an ill grounded interpretation: for in these times of necessity, and multitudes of poor there is no possibility of saving to him that hath any tendernesse in him; and for affecting my ease, I have been always more sorry, when I could not preach, then any could be, that they could not hear me.

The editor omitted "to save charges" as a reason for Donne's absence, and omitted, too, Donne's defense of that particular accusation, beginning "for in these times of necessity." The implication of the omission is that while some may have accused Donne of affecting his ease, no one would accuse him of being financially dishonest. Although Donne's refutation shows his charitable nature, the editor did not want even the overtone of money to detract from his emphasis on Donne's scrupulous attendance to his duties. The original letter goes on to say:

I thank you, for keeping our *George* in in [*sic*] your memory, I hope God reserves it for so good a friend as you are, to send me the first good newes of him. For the Diamond Lady, you may safely deliver *Roper,* whatsoever belongs to me, and he will give you a discharge for the money. For my L. *Percy,* we shall speake of it, when we meet at *London;* which, as I do not much hope before Christmas, so I do not much fear at beginning of Tearm; for I have intreated one of my fellowes to preach to my Lord Maior, at *Pauls* upon Christmas day, and reserved Candlemas day to my self for that service, about which time also, will fall my Lent Sermon, except my Lord Chamberlaine beleeve me to be dead, and leave me out.

The 1635 editor's version of this reads:

Sir, I hope to see you about Candlemas, about which time also will fall my lent Sermon at Court, except my Lord Chamberlaine beleeve me to be dead, and leave me out.

It was not only a second reference to money which caused the editor to omit several sentences. The profusion of detail which indicates Donne's interest in many matters would detract from the singleness of purpose which the editor would show to preoccupy Donne's mind. Here, as in pruning Donne's letter to Garrard from France, he rigorously excludes the minutiae of Donne's immediate personal affairs to focus exclusively on the one matter that concerns him— Donne's desire to preach despite his illness. By his suppressions, he makes Donne's case stronger even than Donne had made it, and he does this also in quite another way. Donne had written that he had already procured a substitute to preach for him at Christmas, and this statement detracts greatly from the urgency to preach which he professes. The editor therefore omitted all reference to Christmas and to Donne's certainty that while he would be unable to preach at Christmas he would be perfectly able to preach five weeks later. But the editor went beyond omission here. He was so anxious to rid the letter of the compromising Christmas evidence that he added to it the date "January 7. 1630[31]." What date was on the original letter we do not know, for it is undated in 1651, but the editor's date is manifestly an impossible one.

In this letter, too, the editor makes such minute changes as he thinks will simplify Donne's diction and clarify his intent. Donne's statement "I doubt not, but amongst his many other blessings, God will adde to you some one for my prayers" becomes ". . . will adde some one to you for my prayers"; "I have been always more sorry" becomes "I have alwayes beene sorryer"; "one writ unto me" becomes "one writ to me." Donne had written, "It hath been my desire, (and God may be pleased to grant it me)"; the editor dropped the last pronoun. Oddly enough, one of the editor's changes runs counter to these. Donne's "A man would almost be content to dye" becomes "A man would be almost content to die." Donne had written that he had ever desired to die in the pulpit, "if not that, yet that I might take my death in the Pulpit, that is, die the sooner by occasion of my former labours." The editor sensed here that Donne was looking back on his career as completed, his labors finished. He changed "my former labours" to "those labours," probably to carry out the idea that the labors had not yet ended. Donne had written that he had planned to preach at St. Paul's on Candlemas Day and had added, "about which time also, will fall my Lent Sermon." The editor had omitted Donne's references to St. Paul's, and he was careful to specify where Donne would preach at Lent: "I hope to see you about Candlemas, about which time also will fall my lent Sermon at Court." The "also," which had originally referred to preaching, seems awkward in the editor's context. Donne had closed his letter, "God blesse you, and your sonne, as/ *Your poor friend and humble servant/ in Christ Jesus/* J. Donne." The editor printed, "God blesse you and your Sonne, as I wish./ *Your poor friend and servant/ in Christ Jesus,/* J. D."

This letter, as edited in 1635, Walton reproduced in the 1640 *Life of Donne* (sig. B5ᵛ), but he made such minute changes in it as, I shall demonstrate in the course of this study, are typical of his methods of revision. Some of them are apparently purposeless, but the motivation for many of them is clear enough so that we can see Walton's habitual desire to improve his copy by clarifying its intent, often by making explicit what is already clearly implied. We cannot be sure that Walton and not the printer is responsible for changing "his many other blessings" to *"his other blessings"* and "I will not oppresse you" to *"I would not willingly oppresse you."* There does not seem to be much reason for changing "I am thereby the oftner at my prayers" to *"I am so much the oftner at my Prayers."* But Walton's other changes are rather more revealing. When he changed the 1635 editor's "I hope to see you about Candlemas" to *". . . presently after Candlemas,"* he was obviously concerned to make the time reference more exact.[61] The 1635 editor had retained in his revised text the awkward "also" in "about which time also will fall my lent Sermon." This Walton dropped. Donne had written, "as long as I live, and am not speechlesse, I would not decline that service [of preaching at Lent]." Did Walton write *". . . not willingly decline"* to suggest Donne's humility?

[61] Although Donne had written that he had arranged to preach on Candlemas at St. Paul's, he probably did not do so. Walton wrote in 1640 that Donne came to London "some few dayes before his day appointed," the first Friday in Lent. In 1631, the first Friday in Lent fell on February 25. Had Donne preached on Candlemas, he would have been in London almost a month before this date.

Perhaps so, but he did not restore in the close of the letter the word *"humble"* which the 1635 version lacks. Is it possible that Walton was aware of the content of the original letter and was sufficiently troubled by Donne's words that he sought to temper their positiveness?

Walton's changes in 1640 resemble those minor changes which the editor of the letter in 1635 had made. On the basis of his changes in 1640, however, it would be reckless to assume that he was responsible for the editing of the letters in 1635. But how did he react to the publication of the letter in its original form in 1651?[62] Although the letter as published in 1651 was undated, it contained, of course, the references to Christmas. When Walton's revised *Life of Donne* appeared in 1658, it followed the corrupt text of the letter, but, though Walton still represented the letter as having been written in January 1631, he deleted the specific date, "January 7. 1630" which he had found on the letter as printed in 1635 and which he had used in 1640.[63] Did he have the *Letters to Severall Persons* of 1651 before him when in 1658 he reverted to Donne's "A man would almost be content to dye" after he had followed in 1640 the 1635 editor's "A man would be almost content to die," a surprising change by the editor in view of his habit of smoothing Donne's diction? It seems unlikely that Walton would have neglected to change the rest of the letter if he made this correction for the purpose of adhering accurately to the original. More likely, he was following his usual procedure. It is odd that the 1635 editor should have committed such a gaucherie, odder yet that Walton, who also tried to regularize Donne's diction, should have permitted the gaucherie to stand in 1640. We may be sure, however, that it was not the desire for accuracy of transcription which in 1658 dictated the reversion to the original reading. Indeed, in 1658, Walton changed "for as long as I live" (1635, 1640, 1651) to "but as long as I live"; and to "except my Lord Chamberlaine beleeve me to be dead, and leave me out" he added the redundant "of the roll."[64] Walton's treatment of the letter in 1658 shows that though he was aware of its publication in its original form in 1651 and of

[62] It is certain that he was aware of the publication of *Letters to Severall Persons*. His own copy has been preserved in the Salisbury Cathedral Library.

[63] *Donne,* 1658, pp. 100–103.

[64] Donne's meaning was clear enough in his letter, and, in the *Life* Walton had explained, just prior to reprinting the letter, that Donne had never been left out "of the Roll and number of Lent-Preachers" (*ibid.,* p. 100).

the publication's invalidating his date, he adhered on the whole to the fictitious date which he had followed in 1640 and he continued to make the sort of revisions which he had made in 1640. Certainly he had a strange attachment to the text which the 1635 editor had created.

On the basis of Walton's reaction to the publication of the original, it seems more plausible to identify him with the editing of the Christmas letter in 1635. Does his handling of the letter in the revisions of the *Life of Donne* in 1670 and in 1675 shed any additional light on the identification? The only change in 1670 is perhaps a slip of the printer's: *"I doubt not but amongst his other blessings"* becomes "I doubt not among his other blessings."[65] The only change in 1675 is a conscious one. The original letter, as printed in 1651, closes "God blesse you, and your sonne, as/ *Your poor friend and humble servant."* Did Donne mean by "as" "and may He in like fashion bless me" or did he mean "as I bless you"? That he meant the first is evident from similar closes in others of his letters. In one he says, "Our blessed Saviour multiply his blessings upon that noble family where you are, and your self, and your sonne; as upon all them that are derived from/ *Your poor friend and servant."*[66] In another he says, "God blesse you and your sonne, with the same blessings which I begge for the children, and for the person of/ *Your poor friend."*[67] Although the editor of the 1635 letters lifted this latter close from its context and engrafted it upon one of the letters which he printed, he was probably puzzled by Donne's use of "as" in the Christmas letter when he changed the close to "God bless you and your Sonne, as I wish./ *Your poore friend and servant."* We cannot tell whether the period after "wish" is his or the printer's. With the period, Donne is made to say "in the way in which I hope." Without the period (as Walton used it in 1640 and in 1658), it may perhaps mean this, but it may also mean "as I wish [He will also bless me]." In 1670, a comma replaces the period. In 1675, Walton wrote, "God so bless you and your Son as I wish, to/ *Your poor friend and servant."*[68] What Walton intended this to mean I do not know, but it is probably more than coincidental that Donne's close puzzled him even as it had puzzled the editor of 1635.

This chain of minor revisions initiated by Walton in 1640 may

[65] *Lives,* 1670 (Donne), p. 69.   [66] *Letters to Severall Persons,* p. 283.
[67] *Ibid.,* p. 287.   [68] *Lives,* 1675, p. 67.

be too slight to link him with the editor of the 1635 letters, but their methods are unusually similar. Like this editor, Walton, too, made drastic cuts and combinations in Donne's letters when he introduced them into the revised *Life* of 1670, and these will concern us later. But when we consider their similarity of method in making minor revisions in conjunction with the 1635 editor's purposeful drawing of a miniature portrait, and when we consider also Walton's directive lines under Donne's portrait in 1635, his probable regrouping of the poems themselves in 1635, and his possible authorship of the lines signed "Incerti," we can say with considerable certainty that Walton edited the letters added to the 1635 *Poems*. It is not likely that in 1635 Marriot had the help of two or three men whose inclinations were so similar as to seem identical, and Walton's certain contributions to the 1635 volume make it likely that the contributions of "Incerti" and of the editor of the letters were also his. Marriot's calling upon Walton in 1635 may have been based on more than neighborliness and his knowledge of Walton's interest in Donne. He may well have known that Walton was even then collecting material for Wotton, and, knowing this, he would have shown him the letters he had recently acquired from Garrard. In reading these, Walton saw the possibility of projecting through a judicious selection a little portrait of Donne which, placed before the divine poems, might effectively influence the impression of Donne which a reader of the first three-fourths of the volume would have. Whether Marriot was completely aware of the purpose of Walton's fit preamble we cannot tell, but Walton probably induced Marriot to add the letters to the 1635 *Poems*.

Walton's part in the 1635 volume shows that he was already by that time collecting material for a life of Donne, that he was familiar with Donne's correspondence with Goodere and Garrard,[69] and that he had already by that time arrived at rather clear conclusions about how the life ought to be written. His part in the volume shows that in 1635 his interest in Donne the poet was subsidiary to his interest in Donne the divine and makes it appear likely that his elegy on Donne was not a voluntary estimate written shortly after

[69] These letters were probably available to Walton while they were in John Marriot's possession, but not available to him after the younger Donne claimed them and had Richard Marriot print them. The guesses and emendations which Walton made in his own copy of *Letters to Severall Persons* were obviously made without the help of the originals. See J. E. Butt, "Walton's Copy of Donne's *Letters* (1651)," *RES*, VIII (1932), 72–74.

Donne's death. Its emphasis on Donne's poetry, though, to be sure, on the religious and didactic verse, was determined by Walton's knowledge that he was writing a commendatory poem for inclusion in a specific volume.

Walton knew Donne's poetry and was interested in it, but the nature of his real interest in Donne and something of the way in which he worked as a biographer may be learned from an examination of how he drew upon his elegy in writing the *Life* of 1640. He rigorously subdued the intrusion of the poetry into the *Life,* and he shaped its inclusion to his own purpose. No part of the life of Donne as it is represented by Walton can be called "the poetic period." From Walton's representation, even Donne's youth was filled with other things. The poetry is discussed in a digression, in some general observations of Donne's life as a prelude to his holy dying, and even the story of Donne the poet is told in such a way as to emphasize his piety.[70] While Walton had specifically praised the satires and funeral elegies in his poem and had stressed them as a demonstration of Donne's youthful ingenuity, all the profane poetry, despite Walton's praise of its sharp wit and high fancy, is dismissed as the recreation of Donne's youth, and the penitential Donne is pictured wishing that his early verses had not been scattered so loosely. Walton, perhaps under the influence of the elegies printed in the *Poems* of 1633, draws a sharp distinction between the early and the later poems, and he elaborates the view of the religious verses introduced in his elegy. Donne, he says, retained his love for heavenly poetry, as witnessed by "many divine Sonnets, and other high, holy, and harmonious composures." He here generalized the elegy's specific reference to Donne's weaving a crown of sacred sonnets in "harmonious-holy-numbers." He elaborates the elegy's reference to the hymns, and quotes in full "A Hymne to God the Father" to show Donne's assurance of God's favor to him in his illness. He says also that Donne composed a hymn on his deathbed. In the elegy he had been content to compare Donne's hymns to those of Prudentius. In so holy a life as is that of 1640, it is not enough that Donne's hymns are excellent poetry, and the examples of Prudentius, King David, and King Hezekiah serve as justification for the writing of divine poetry. What had been Walton's chief interest in 1633 became in 1640 a parenthesis, another illustration of the piety of Donne.

[70] *Donne,* 1640, sigs. B4r–B4v.

Donne's knowledge of languages and law is carried over from the elegy to the *Life*.[71] The elegy's reference to his proficiency in medicine is lost in a generalization,[72] for too great a diversity of interests in Donne would tend to minimize his religious inclination. Two poetical devices in the elegy receive straightforward treatment in the *Life*. In the elegy, Walton used Donne's travels to Palestine as the cause for his conversion to the religious life. Since it is the function of a large part of the first section of the *Life* to demonstrate Donne's religious tendencies, and since Walton would rather picture the conversion as inevitable, he does not need to use an incident of which he was doubtful as a sudden turning point.[73] The elegy poetically speaks of Donne as mourned by few and refers to the many who grieve in silence. The impression is remedied in the *Life,* where a literal account adds to Donne's prestige, and Walton says that, despite Donne's desire for a private burial, his funeral was voluntarily attended by an "unnumbered number," including many persons of nobility and eminency.[74] In the elegy, a personal element was necessary, and Walton mentioned Donne's affection for him and called himself, with reference to his being of the parish of St. Dunstan's, "his *Convert.*" Walton purposely excluded himself from the *Life.* For one thing, it would have been undiplomatic to have included himself in a *Life* which so carefully excluded even Donne's most intimate friends. More important, the absence of the author as a character in the *Life* lends a semblance of objectivity to the writing. Explicitly subjective biography has ever been open to the charge of bias. In not stating the extent of his acquaintance with Donne, Walton was able to cloak the working of his hand and his heart with an exterior of objectivity.

It is apparent from an examination of Walton's diversity of use of identical material in the elegy and in the *Life* of 1640 that a change of purpose determined a change in his point of view. He was, after all, writing a preface to Donne's sermons, and here, as elsewhere in the *Lives,* his consciousness of the specific occasion or purpose is reflected in the *Life.* The suitability of the information he had as prefatory material for the sermons was a major con-

71 *Ibid.,* sigs. A5ᵛ, Bʳ.

72 Walton speaks of Donne's "Learning, Languages, and other abilities" (*ibid.,* sig. A6ʳ). Grierson corroborates Donne's study of medicine (*Poems of John Donne,* II, 5).

73 See p. 70.   74 *Donne,* 1640, sig. B6ᵛ.

sideration in determining its inclusion and the method of its inclusion. He was not writing *The Life of John Donne* but *The Life and Death of Dr Donne, Late Deane of St Pauls London*. It was the venerable old Dean whom Walton knew, and it was the venerable old Dean who determined the impression that Walton gives in the *Life*. It is the reverend life of a reverend man, and the general impression is one of early religious interest, continual study, holy living, and holy dying. How deliberately Walton created this impression is evident in the pointed emphasis attained by the careful and beautiful structure of the *Life*.

Walton was concerned in 1640 with Donne as a man of God. He was interested in and wanted to stress the life and death of the Dean of St. Paul's. Still, he knew that Donne did not become Dean until ten years before his death. At his death, he had been in holy orders for only sixteen years. Walton had to narrate the story of the more than forty secular years and still emphasize the last years. It is natural that he wrenched the chronological proportions, that he devoted more than half of the *Life* to the last quarter of Donne's years, the years in which he was in orders. The secular life of Donne Walton described primarily through his elaborate account of Donne's marriage. The purpose here was twofold: first, Walton had available the detailed information which Henry King had probably received from his father; second, and at least equally important, here was an interesting series of events of a nonreligious nature which Walton could outwardly censure, which he could term the "remarkable error" of Donne's life,[75] events which demonstrated the impetuosity and passion of the secular man and which still showed him in an admirable and sympathetic light. Here is Donne breaking civil and canon law, losing his employment and his money,

[75] Donne himself, and probably his contemporaries, took this point of view of his marriage. In a letter to Lord Hay, written about 1608, Donne referred to his marriage as "that intemperate and hastie act of mine" and said, "I have been told, that when your Lordship did me that extream favour, of presenting my name, his Majestie remembred me, by the worst part of my historie, which was my disorderlie proceedings, seaven years since, in my nonage" (*A Collection of Letters, made by Sr Tobie Mathews K^t.* [London, 1660], pp. 330–331). Ten years after he had written Sir Thomas Egerton on March 1, 1602, "The sickness of which I died is that I began in your Lordship's house this love" (Gosse, I, 114), he wrote Goodere, again referring to the effect of his marriage on his fortunes: "I must confesse, that I dyed ten years ago" (*Letters to Severall Persons,* p. 122; for addressee and date, see I. A. Shapiro, "The Text of Donne's *Letters to Severall Persons,*" *RES,* VII [1931], 294–296).

forced into misery and dejection of spirit. But here, too, is Donne
fighting for the enlargement of his friends, devoted to his wife,
commended by his employer, and winning the respect of his father-
in-law. Walton's account of the circumstances attending Donne's
marriage takes up a third of the secular life story. The only other
matters which are purely of a secular nature, even in this first section, are the short accounts of Donne's ancestry and his travels. The
story of his education becomes a vehicle for the description of his
early religious consciousness, and his religious inclinations are demonstrated even before his travels and his marriage. The last section
dealing with his secular life is, in effect, a preface to his religious
life and builds a pattern of inevitability. The catalogue of Donne's
residences is a catalogue also of his studies and of his reputation for
learnedness: Pyrford and civil and canon laws; Mitcham and religious points of controversy; Whitehall and visits by men of learning and nobility; Drury Lane and Sir Robert Drury as the "daily
cherisher of his studies." Finally, Walton tells of the decisive influence in the career of Donne—King James. Donne's learning attracted the King; *Pseudo-Martyr* confirmed his belief that Donne
must become a divine. The King's persuasiveness, three additional
years of study, and considerable wrestling with his conscience and
God end the secular portion of the life on an almost ecstatic plane.

The mood in which the secular life ends affords an easy transition
into the holy life, but Walton rhetorically emphasizes the division
and change: "So now (being inspired with the apprehension of
Gods mercies)"; "Now the English Church had gained a second S.
Augustine"; "Now all his studies . . . were concentred in Divinity; Now he had a new calling. . . . Now all his earthly affections
were changed into divine love."[76] The first portion of the holy life
is a relatively straightforward recounting of Donne's ecclesiastical
career. Walton tells of his ordination, his studies in divinity, his appointment as chaplain in ordinary to the King, his preaching before the King, his honorary doctoral degree from Cambridge, his
being offered fourteen different benefices. The death of Donne's
wife interrupts the progression for only a paragraph, and Walton
continues with Donne as lecturer at Lincoln's Inn, with his visit to
Germany as chaplain to the special embassy to Bohemia, his preferment to the deanship of St. Paul's, the vicarage of St. Dunstan's,

[76] *Donne,* 1640, sigs. B⍐–B2⍐.

other ecclesiastical endowments, and his appointment as Prolocutor to Convocation. In telling of Donne's appointment as lecturer, Walton takes the opportunity of contrasting Donne the law student with Donne the preacher; in the account of the visit to Germany, he again contrasts the early and later life by telling that the Queen of Bohemia, who had known Donne as a courtier, was delighted to see him in canonical habit. His story of the King's displeasure with Donne, coming at the end of his narration of the ecclesiastical career, affords him a splendid opportunity to end the account as he had begun it—with reference to the King. It is the result of beautiful and meticulous planning and it immeasurably heightens Donne's accomplishments that the King, who solicited Donne to divinity, should say at the end of the divine career, "I was never more joyed in any thing that I have done, then in making him a Divine."[77]

The structure of the last part of the *Life* is managed as artfully as that of the first part. It was during these last years that Walton knew Donne personally, and a less artful writer might have been tempted to relate inconsequential incidents in detailed fashion. But Walton saw that there was a sameness in these years of holy devotion and high respect. Donne's holiness could better be illustrated in an elaborate account of his dying and death. The last third of the *Life* starts with Donne's illness late in 1623 and jumps immediately to his final illness. In a long digression (as he terms it), Walton sums up all that he wishes to say of Donne's life, building gradually a picture of such piety that it can be exceeded only by the extreme holiness of the death. He starts with the most profane note in the life, the marriage. His account of the poetry begins with the profane poems and develops into a praise of the devotion manifest in the divine verses. Donne's continued study and the enumeration of the visible fruits of that study give the life a highly regulated deliberateness, a note which the story of Donne's will bears out and increases. The charities of the will are followed by a particularized account of the living charities. With this pointed summary of the life out of the way, Walton is ready to concentrate on the last days. The note of studied regularity culminates in Donne's faithful attendance to his task despite his illness, his preaching of the Lent sermon. The final summing up of the life is done by Donne himself

[77] *Ibid.*, sig. B3ᵛ.

on his deathbed. Walton then proceeds to Donne's careful preparations for death, the death itself, the burial, and the monument. He ends the *Life* with a short character.

In his management of the time element in the *Life,* Walton errs in many minor details. He says, for instance, that Donne's wife died "immediately" after his return from Cambridge. In fact she died two and a half years later, during Donne's lectureship in divinity at Lincoln's Inn, but probably Walton antedated the event so that he would not have to make diffuse the emphasis which he wished to place on the difference in Donne's position when he returned to Lincoln's Inn. He misleads when he says that Donne was made Vicar of St. Dunstan's "presently after he was setled in his Deanry," for there was a space of two and a half years between the appointments. Walton probably knew when Donne came to St. Dunstan's, but his generality speeds the flow of Donne's career from high point to high point, and Walton does not have to account for the minor occurrences of two and a half years. It has been pointed out that he jumped seven years in his juxtaposing Donne's two illnesses and that he passed over the years with Sir Thomas Egerton in a few sentences. But the reader forgets to wonder what Donne did during these years at Egerton's because of the detailed story of the marriage which followed them. It is the tremendous specificity of the *Life* in some of its parts which adds credence and authority to Walton's statements and makes the reader forget the gaping lacunae. When Walton speaks of Donne's charities, he mentions seven different kinds.[78] When he describes Donne's illness, he gives the details: it was a "spotted Feaver, and ended in a Cough, that inclined him to a Consumption."[79] The numerous papers found in Donne's study after his death bear such testimony of his continued labor that the casual reader is unaware that Walton is glossing over the content of *Biathanatos.* A letter gives proof of Donne's scrupulosity in church matters;[80] a quotation from Donne's ledger book gives proof that he was a just steward of his Lord's revenue;[81] a quotation from Donne's will, though it is only of the opening and closing paragraphs, gives credence to Walton's statement that Donne was an impartial father, a lover of his friends, and an overgenerous giver of alms.[82] Sir Edmund Gosse remarked, "It is curious that the last years of Donne, when he was so celebrated and so prominent,

[78] *Ibid.,* sig. B5^r.   [79] *Ibid.,* sig. B3^v.   [80] *Ibid.,* sig. B5^v.
[81] *Ibid.,* sigs. B5^r–B5^v.   [82] *Ibid.,* sig. B5^r.

should, in spite of the evidence of Izaak Walton, be particularly obscure and empty of detail."[83] It is not so curious as it would appear. The "evidence" of Walton is restricted to the last days, and the last years are truly devoid of detail. This is an essential characteristic of Walton's technique. Prolixity of detail and documentation in some carefully chosen places hide the skipping of whole years and the omission of incidents of which Walton was aware.

Walton must have known of the high honor that came to Donne in the request of King Charles I that he preach the first sermon to him on his ascension to the throne. The incident was omitted because to mention it Walton would have had to relate at some length the death of King James. While James was important in Donne's life at one point, an account of his death merely to relate another of Donne's honors would have created an intrusion into the unity of the *Life* and would have detracted from the account of Donne's death. Many other omissions can be explained because they would entail references to the poetry which Walton was minimizing. Thus there is no mention of the Countess of Bedford despite Donne's poems to her published in the 1633 volume, none of Magdalen Herbert, though Walton had heard Donne preach a sermon of commemoration for her. Walton relates the kindnesses of Sir Robert Drury to Donne, but despite what he learned from Donne's letters he omits entirely Donne's journey to the continent with Drury. He tells of the Queen of Bohemia's acquaintance with Donne the courtier, but he omits any reference to Donne's *Epithalamion* written for her. He tells of Donne's devotion for his children, but does not digress even to state that the younger John Donne had taken orders, to say nothing of his earlier exploits and of Constance Donne's first remarkable marriage to Edward Alleyn. The spotlight is ever on John Donne the divine, and Walton does not shift it.

In the opening paragraphs of the *Life,* Walton stated that the world would see the best picture of Donne that his "artlesse Pensil (guided by the hand of Truth) could present to it." His artlessness, he said, was "much to the advantage of the beholder; who shall see the Authors picture in a naturall dresse, which ought to beget faith in what is spoken, for he that wants skill to deceive, may safely be trusted." It is the acute selection of details and the correlative omissions, creating the impression of artlessness and absolute truth, that are the touchstone of the Waltonian technique in the *Life of Donne.*

[83] Gosse, II, 263.

The apparent objectivity is an extremely real subjectivity. This subjectivity Walton carried over even into the source material that he used.

Walton did not reserve Donne's will for an appendix; he used it as an integral part of the *Life* to demonstrate the considered regularity of Donne and his charitable disposition. He said of Donne, "He did prepare to leave the world before life left him, making his Will when no facultie of his soule was dampt or defective by sicknesse, or he surprized by sudden apprehension of death."[84] The religious tone of the paragraphs which Walton selected for quotation served to accentuate the picture of devoutness and humility that he was constructing prior to his account of Donne's last days. Walton must have had a copy of the will before him to transcribe the first two paragraphs verbatim and to cite generally some of its provisions. He wanted to quote the last paragraph for the humbleness of its tone, but to quote it wholly would be to destroy the impression that he wished to create of Donne's thought of and preparedness for death. Donne's final illness, he had not long before stated, had begun in August, 1630. In order not to contradict factually the impression of preparedness that he wished to create, he consciously omitted, nor can his intent be mistaken, the final words of the will. These read, "and sealed the same [the will] and published and declared it to be my last will the thirteenth day of December 1630."[85] That Walton added the date of the will in the next edition is not reason to consider its omission in 1640 an oversight. It would be as easy to presume that its addition in 1658 was a mistake, that Walton had forgotten why he had omitted it in the first place. The addition in 1658 was probably a conscious one, and it does add finality and authenticity to the document. Walton could add it and be reasonably sure that his readers would not question the statement that Donne wrote the will out of preparedness rather than sudden fear of death, for he had put several more pages between Donne's illness and the end of the will.

Occasionally in using a source, Walton followed the method which Donne described in the "Advertisement to *the Reader*" of *Pseudo-Martyr:*

And in those places which are cited from other Authors . . . I doe not alwayes precisely and superstitiously binde my selfe to the words

---

[84] *Donne,* 1640, sig. B4ᵛ.   [85] Printed by Gosse, II, 363.

of the Authors. . . . This is the comfort which my conscience hath, and the assurance which I can give the Reader, that I have no where made any Author, speake more or lesse, in sense, then hee intended, to that purpose, for which I cite him.[86]

Walton adhered rather closely to the facts when he spoke of Donne's early religious training. He says, "They [his Catholic tutors] had almost obliged him to their faith, having for their advantage, besides their opportunity, the example of his most deare and pious Parents, which was a powerfull perswasion, and did work upon him, as he professeth in his PREFACE to his *Pseudo-Martyr*."[87] Here he merely particularized the references to the people. Donne had stated that he had had to blot out certain impressions of Catholicism *"and some anticipations early layde upon my conscience, both by Persons who by nature had a power and superiority over my will, and others who by their learning and good life, seem'd to me justly to claime an interest for the guiding, and rectifying of mine understanding in these matters."*[88]

More often Walton quoted inexactly, and he did not scruple to make a passage mean what he wished rather than what the author intended. There is little reason to doubt that Walton consciously misinterpreted a passage in the dedicatory epistle to the King of Donne's *Pseudo-Martyr*. In order to raise the reader's estimation of Donne, he desired to produce the impression that King James early took an interest in Donne and was indeed the most powerful influence in inducing him to enter orders. Walton said that the King had been impressed with Donne's learning, had valued his company, and was pleased when Donne voluntarily attended him at his meals, where Bishop Montague and Doctor Andrewes, whose presence was required, would engage in deep discourses of general learning. Of the writing of *Pseudo-Martyr*, Walton said that "his Majestie occasionally talking with M. *Donne* concerning many of those Arguments urged by the Romanists" against the Oath of Supremacy and Allegiance "apprehended such a validity and cleerenesse in his answers, that he commanded him to state the Points, and bring his Reasons to him in writing."[89] To be sure, in the dedicatory epistle of *Pseudo-Martyr*, Donne had spoken of the King's vouchsafing to descend to a conversation with his subjects and of his own con-

---

[86] John Donne, *Pseudo-Martyr* (London, 1610), sig. π2r.
[87] *Donne*, 1640, sigs. A5v–A6r.   [88] *Pseudo-Martyr*, sigs. B2v–B3r.
[89] *Donne*, 1640, sig. Bv.

ceiving an ambition to ascend to the King's presence, and the phrase "by your Majesties permission" did occur.[90] But Donne had said that the King's *books* had influenced him to write his book, that the King had conversed with his subjects *by way of his books,* and that he desired to ascend to the King's presence in the same way, that is, by way of his book. And he had asked that he might express in an exterior and, by his Majesty's permission, a public act, again referring to his book, his daily prayer to God for the King's long life. By turning a figure of speech into a personal interview, Walton did not bind himself superstitiously to Donne's words, but even made Donne's words speak not Donne's sense but his own.

In relating the early influence of the King on Donne's career, Walton followed with some accuracy Donne's own words. Donne had written in 1624 in his *Devotions upon Emergent Occasions* that

he [King James], first of any man conceiv'd a hope, that I might be of some use in thy *Church,* and descended to an intimation, to a perswasiõ, almost to a solicitatiõ, that I would embrace that calling.

When I asked, perchãce, a *stone,* he gave me *bread;* when I asked, perchãce, a *Scorpion,* he gave me a *fish;* whẽ I asked a temporall *office,* hee denied not, refused not that, but let mee see, that hee had rather I took this.[91]

Some general truth there was in Donne's words, but the King was still alive when the *Devotions* were printed, and there is little doubt that Donne was showing him in a more than favorable light.[92] The King was not the first to hope that Donne would enter orders,[93] and if he did not refuse Donne temporal preferment, certainly there was none forthcoming. Walton's picture differs from that of Donne,

[90] *Pseudo-Martyr,* sigs. A3r–A3v.

[91] John Donne, *Devotions upon Emergent Occasions* (London, 1624), pp. 192–194.

[92] Donne took particular pride in whatever part King James played in inducing him to enter orders. When, in 1621, he resigned as Reader in Divinity to Lincoln's Inn, he gave the Members of the Bench the Douai Vulgate of 1617. He inscribed the first volume with a short sketch of himself, part of which reads, "Post multos annos, agente Spiritu Sto, suadente Rege, Ad Ordines Sacros evectus" (Gosse, II, 114).
Early in 1624, in a letter to Sir Robert Ker, Donne wrote, "when I sit still, and reckon all my old Master's Royall favours to me, I return evermore to that, that he first inclined me to be a Minister" (*A Collection of Letters, made by Sr Tobie Mathews Kt.,* p. 308).
Donne's epitaph has on it "Monitu et Hortatu Regis Jacobi."

[93] See Walton's account of Bishop Morton's offer (*Donne,* 1658, pp. 24–33).

although he places the King in an equally favorable light. He changed the sequence of Donne's passages. He says that the King gave Donne some hopes of state employment because he was impressed with his general learning, but he intimates that the King changed his mind after he had read and considered *Pseudo-Martyr.* Then, he says, despite the mediation of many persons of worth, "the King denied their requests, and (having a discerning spirit) replyed, *I know M. Donne is a learned man, an excellent Divine, and will prove a powerfull Preacher.* After that, as he professeth, the King descended almost to a solicitation of him to enter into sacred Orders."[94] In Walton's hands, then, the influence of the King serves not only as the prime reason for Donne's spiritual preferment but also as an explanation for Donne's unsuccessful attempts to secure temporal employment. James's determination Walton more than justifies in the success of Donne's ecclesiastical career, but he has used that determination as the sole factor of Donne's unsuccessfulness in obtaining a state post. It may be noticed that Walton quotes the words of the King and that he has the King give the impression that Donne was already an excellent divine. He not only clarified this ambiguity in the 1658 edition, but he made the King more stubborn in his desire that Donne take orders. The 1658 edition reads:

The King gave a positive denial to all requests; and having a discerning spirit, replied, *I know Mr.* Donne *is a learned man, has the abilities of a learned Divine, and will prove a powerfull Preacher, and my desire is to prefer him that way.* After that, as he professeth, *the King descended almost to a solicitation of him to enter into sacred Orders.*[95]

By 1658, then, the King's denial had become "positive," and he desired to prefer him in a spiritual career. By 1675, Walton had forgotten completely that Donne himself had stated that the King did not refuse him temporal advancement, though he would rather recommend him in the Church. In 1658, the King says, *"my desire is to prefer him that way";* in 1675, he adds *"and in that way, I will deny you nothing for him."*[96] Walton made use of Donne's words, but they were made to fit the pattern of emphasis by which Walton was shaping the *Life.*

Another passage from the preface of *Pseudo-Martyr* and Walton's

---

[94] *Donne,* 1640, sig. B^v.   [95] *Donne,* 1658, pp. 39–40.
[96] *Lives,* 1675, p. 36.

version of it shows the meticulousness with which he scrutinized the details of his source. He selected, he regrouped, he added to make the passage his own. Donne had stated:

And although I apprehended well enough, that this irresolution [in choosing a religion] *not onely retarded my fortune, but also bred some scandall, and endangered my spirituall reputation, by laying me open to many mis-interpretations; yet all these respects did not transport me to any violent and sudden determination, till I had, to the measure of my poore wit and judgement, survayed and digested the whole body of Divinity, controverted betweene ours and the Romane Church. In which search and disquisition, that God, which awakened me then, and hath never forsaken me in that industry, as he is the Authour of that purpose, so is he a witnes of this protestation; that I behaved my selfe, and proceeded therin with humility, and diffidence in my selfe; and by that, which by his grace, I tooke to be the ordinary meanes, which is frequent praier, and equall and indifferent affections.*[97]

Walton's account reads:

He was now entred into the nineteenth yeare of his age, and being unresolved in his Religion, (though his youth and strength promised him a long life) yet he thought it necessary to rectifie all scruples which concerned that: And therefore waving the Law, and betrothing him-selfe to no art or profession, that might justly denominate him, he began to survey the body of Divinity, controverted between the Reformed and Roman Church. And *as Gods blessed Spirit did then awaken him to the search, and in that industry did never forsake him,* (they be his owne words) *So he calls the same Spirit to witness to his Protestation, that in that search and disquisition he proceeded with humility and diffidence in himselfe, by the safest way of frequent Prayers, and indifferent affection to both parties.*[98]

Although Donne had mentioned worldly considerations only to show his rejection of them, Walton was unwilling to use those words which revealed Donne's awareness that such considerations exist, and he omitted them. The sincere simplicity of Donne's *"I be-haved my selfe"* was out of place in the dignified *Life* that Walton was constructing, and he omitted it. The matter-of-fact *"ordinary meanes"* of Donne he changed to *"safest way,"* for his Donne was no ordinary man, but would choose a course with some deliberateness. Walton could permit *"indifferent affections"* at this point in Donne's life, but he would omit an equality of affection for both

[97] *Pseudo-Martyr*, sig. B3ʳ.   [98] *Donne*, 1640, sig. A6ʳ.

Catholicism and Anglicanism. He introduced a more religious tone into the passage with a typical Waltonism, *"Gods blessed Spirit."* Donne's statement that he would not be hurried into a choice is somewhat carried out in Walton's picture of deliberateness, but Walton emphasized the urgency and importance of a choice in two ways. First, he implied urgency by intimating that Donne would busy himself in a choice despite his expectation of a long life, and, secondly, he said that Donne put aside all studies that did not pertain to religion.

Sir Edmund Gosse says, in keeping with his theory that Walton was following the conversation of Donne's last years, that Donne's memory in later years was "amiably deceived when he told Izaak Walton that he continued through these years to 'proceed with humility and diffidence in disquisition and search' after religious truth."[99] Walton had indicated by a marginal note that he was here using the preface of *Pseudo-Martyr,* but Gosse neglects stating this.[100] Walton was not echoing the aged Donne, but he was relying on Donne's early printed statement. Donne's statement, however deceptive it is, has an element of frankness in it. This element Walton omitted, and though the picture which Gosse finds "amiably deceptive" is based on Donne's account, it is the work of Walton, not of Donne. Walton's method is an exceedingly painstaking one. He reproduced most of Donne's words; indeed, he retained most of the original intent. But by deft manipulation, by slight additions, by minor omissions, he changed the tone and he changed the emphasis to make them conform to the pattern he was creating. Walton has added authenticity to the *Life* by quoting Donne's words, but Donne speaks as Walton would have him do.

Walton got more than biographical details from Donne's works. Prior to writing the *Life,* he reread some of Donne's sermons, but it was not for Donne's doctrine that he turned to them. He was no more interested in Donne the theologian than in Donne the poet. He had all his life a dislike for abstruse speculation and argument about hard questions; he cared little for close exegesis; he liked plain, unspectacular, instructive preaching. But like so many of his contemporaries, he had been fascinated and magnetized by the powerful and dramatic personality of Donne as preacher, and it was to

[99] Gosse, I, 140.
[100] Furthermore, he did with Walton's words what Walton did with Donne's: he changed their order.

recapture some of Donne's dynamism and color in the pulpit that
he re-examined minutely two fine sermons which he had probably
heard Donne preach. His account of Donne's last sermon is impressive:

Many of his friends (who with sorrow saw his sicknesse had left him
onely so much flesh as did only cover his bones) doubted his strength
to performe that taske. . . . And doubtlesse many did secretly ask that
question in *Ezekiel, Doe these bones live?* Or can that soule organise
that tongue to speak so long time as the sand in that glasse will move
towards its center, and measure out an houre of this dying mans unspent
life? Doubtlesse it cannot. Yet after some faint pauses in his zealous
Prayer, his strong desires inabled his weak body to discharge his memory
of his pre-conceived Meditations which were of dying; The Text being,
To God the Lord belong the issues from death. Many that saw his teares,
and heard his hollow voice, professing they thought the Text Propheti-
cally chosen, and that D. *Donne* had preacht his owne Funerall Sermon.[101]

Walton's happy reference to Ezekiel was probably determined by
Donne's reference to Ezekiel in his sermon. In *Deaths Duell,*
Donne considers "this *posthume death,* this death after buriall";
he thinks that he must, after the manifold deaths of the world, die
again "in an *Incineration* of this *flesh,* and in a dispersion of that
dust," and he says that "even those bodies that were *the temples of
the holy Ghost,* come to this *dilapidation,* to ruine, to rubbidge, to
dust." He would show that "this death after buriall, this *dissolution*
after *dissolution,* this *death* of *corruption* and *putrefaction,* of
vermiculation and *incineration,* of *dissolution* and *dispersion* in
and *from* the *grave*" is "the most inglorious and contemptible *vili-
fication,* the most deadly and peremptory *nullification* of man, that
wee can consider." He says:

God seems to have caried the declaration of his *power* to a great height,
when hee sets the *Prophet Ezechiel* in the *valley of drye bones,* & sayes,
Sonne of man can these bones live? as though it had bene impossible,
and yet they did; The *Lord* layed *Sinewes upon them, and flesh,* and
breathed into them, and *they did live.*

But, he continues, God can perform a greater feat than the resur-
recting of visible bones. It is proof that *"unto God the Lord belong
the issues of death,"* that "by *recompacting* this *dust* into the *same
body,* & *reanimating* the *same body* with the *same soule,* hee shall in

<hr />

[101] *Donne,* 1640, sig. B6r.

a blessed and glorious *ressurection* give mee such an *issue from* this *death,* as shal never passe into any other death."[102] Walton was not interested in this demonstration of Donne's thesis, but he applied Donne's biblical illustration to the description of Donne himself. In the same fashion, at the very end of the *Life,* he transmuted Donne's terrible reflection that even those bodies that were temples of the Holy Ghost shall come to dust into a lovely description of Donne himself, and he changed Donne's argument for the greatness of God's power into a simple declaration of faith. The last words of the *Life* are *"his active body, which once was a Temple of the holy Ghost, . . . is now become a small quantity of Christian dust. But I shall see it re-inanimated."*

The epistle to the reader which prefaced *Deaths Duell* probably gave Walton the idea of calling this sermon Donne's own funeral sermon, and it gave him still another idea. The epistle starts, *"This Sermon was, by Sacred Authoritie, stiled the Authors owne funeral Sermon. Most fitly: whether wee respect the time, or the matter. It was preached not many dayes before his death; as if, having done this, there remained nothing for him to doe, but to die."* Walton took over these last words and wrote, "Now he had nothing to doe but die,"[103] but he added greatly to their original meaning. He followed them with these words:

He stood in need of no more time, for he had long studied it, and to such a perfection, that in a former sicknesse he called God to witnesse, he was that minute prepared to deliver his soule into his hands, if that minute God would accept of his dissolution. In that sicknesse he begged of his God, (the God of constancy) to be preserved in that estate for ever.[104] And his patient expectation to have his immortall soule disrobed from her garment of mortality, makes me confident he now had a modest assurance, that his prayers were then heard, and his petition granted.

When Walton wrote, "Now he had nothing to doe but die," he was not merely referring to Donne's having preached a valedictory ser-

---

[102] *Deaths Duell,* pp. 21–24.   [103] *Donne,* 1640, sig. B6ᵛ.

[104] Walton paraphrased here to cover up Donne's all too human confession. Donne had written in the *Devotions upon Emergent Occasions* (1624), pp. 628–629, *"preserve* me, O *my God* the *God* of *constancie,* and *perseverance,* in this state, from all *relapses* into those *sinnes,* which have induc'd thy *former Judgements* upon me. But because, by too lamentable *Experience,* I know how slippery my *customs* of *sinne,* have made my *wayes of sinne,* I presume to adde this *petition* too, That if my *infirmitie* overtake mee, thou *forsake* mee not."

mon, but he was paying a fine tribute to Donne for his having long regulated his life with his death in mind. His juxtaposing here again Donne's two serious illnesses intensifies Donne's eager contemplation of his dissolution. Walton had himself recapitulated Donne's life and had shown that Donne had made his will with mature deliberation. After his account of Donne's Lenten sermon, he had pictured Donne considering his life with some satisfaction, taking solemn and deliberate farewell of his friends, finishing all business yet undone. He infused with meaning the bare and uninspired statement which he copied, and pointed up its implications in 1675 by changing it to "And now he was so happy as to have nothing to do but to dye."[105]

In a magnificent passage in *Deaths Duell* which follows the exploitation of death after burial, Donne concerned himself with the manner of man's death. He says, "we have no . . . rule or art to give a *presagition* of *spirituall death* & damnation upon any such *indication* as wee see in any *dying man.*" We must draw no conclusions from a man's loathness to die; and "upon *violent deaths* inflicted, as upon malefactors," "*Christ* himselfe hath forbidden us by his owne death to make any *ill conclusion.*" Though Donne saw that we pray "for a *peaceable life* against *violent death,* & for *time* of *repentance* against *sudden death,* and for *sober* and *modest assurance* against *distemperd* and *diffident death,*" he says that we must never make "*ill conclusions* upon persons overtaken with such deaths." He holds, "Our *criticall* day is *not* the *very day* of our *death,* but the whole course of our life."[106]

Despite his reasoned approach to this problem, Donne betrays here and elsewhere the curiously morbid interest of his age in holy dying. In his *Sermon of Commemoration of the Lady Danvers* (1627), he devoted about a fourth of the space which he alloted to Magdalen Danvers to a description of her death. In a sermon of commemoration, this is not an unduly large proportion, and Donne himself shows his awareness of the occasion when he says after his summary of Lady Danvers' life, "But, I haste to an end, in consideration of some things, that appertaine more expresly to me, then these *personall,* or *civill,* or *morall* things doe."[107] He had demonstrated that "the *rule* of all her *civill Actions,* was *Religion*";

[105] *Lives,* 1675, p. 75.   [106] *Deaths Duell,* pp. 25–27.
[107] *A Sermon of Commemoration of the Lady Danvers,* in Simpson and Potter, *op. cit.,* VIII, 90.

now he turned to a consideration of her religion and her attitude toward death. Mrs. Simpson has recently sought to show that the influence of Lady Danvers' deathbed upon Donne was profound, that, indeed, the dying Donne modeled to some extent his behavior on hers.[108] This may be so, but the question is confused because our knowledge of Donne's deathbed behavior is derived largely from Walton's account, and Mrs. Simpson has herself shown Walton's indebtedness in that account to Donne's *Sermon of Commemoration.*

Walton has told us that he "saw and heard this Mr. *John Donne* (who was then Dean of St. *Pauls*) weep, and preach" this sermon in the parish church of Chelsea,[109] and we may assume that he turned to it when he was writing the *Life of Donne* because he felt it had some pertinence for the *Life.* Indeed, his aim in the *Life* coincided in part with that of Donne in his *Sermon of Commemoration.* Wherever it was possible, he tried to show that the rule of Donne's civil actions was religion. Also, he consciously made the *Life,* as a preface to Donne's own sermons, something of a sermon of commemoration for Donne, a "well meaning sacrifice to his memory."[110] Mrs. Simpson points out that in the *Life of Donne* Walton stressed a number of virtues which Donne had used to characterize Lady Danvers, and she is right in saying that, though these apply equally well to Donne, their inclusion was in part determined by their appearance in the *Sermon of Commemoration.* In both the *Sermon* and the *Life* there is emphasis upon cheerful gravity of temper, generosity to the poor, love for one's children, the enjoyment of sacred music, the eager awaiting of death. The similarity of detail is occasionally reinforced with verbal similarities. "Wee were more miserable if wee might not die" in the *Sermon* becomes *"I were miserable, if I might not die"* in the *Life.* Donne had said of Lady Danvers that she "died without any change of *countenance,* or *posture;* without any *struling,* any *disorder;* but her *Death-bed* was as quiet, as her *Grave.*" Walton wrote of Donne: "(as his soule ascended, and his last breath departed from him) he closed his owne eyes, and then disposed his hands and body into such a posture, as required no alteration by those that came to shroud him." For all of Walton's dependence upon the *Sermon of Commemoration,*

---

[108] Evelyn M. Simpson, "The Biographical Value of Donne's Sermons," *RES,* n.s., II (1951), 339–357. See pp. 347–351.

[109] *Lives,* 1670 (Herbert), p. 19.   [110] *Donne,* 1640, sig. A5ᵛ.

however, his debt is still largely in the selection of detail and in the relative emphasis of the detail.

More interesting than his debt is his rejection of the biographical portion of the *Sermon* as a model for a life, and this at the beginning of his career as a biographer, when the temptation to imitate must have been very strong. His reliance upon the *Sermon* is limited to the last part of the *Life,* when he is offering some observations of Donne's life as a preface to an account of his holy dying and when he is describing the holy death. He does not turn the *Life* into a sermon of commemoration; he writes a sermon of commemoration at the end of the *Life* as a summary of the life. Much as he may have wished to follow Donne in showing that the rule of all the civil actions of his subject's life was religion, he saw the necessity of including a major action which clearly violated the rule. Much as the sermon of commemoration must have appealed to him in its diffuseness or negligence of chronology, he saw the necessity of the chronological approach in a life, even when he had to struggle with chronology. Much as he may have been inclined to end with an explicit admonition to his readers, to follow Donne in writing, "Wake her not, with any *halfe calumnies,* with any *whisperings,"* he saw the necessity in writing a life of so coping with the calumnies in the life itself that he would not have to adjure his readers at its end. Walton was not blindly following a model. If his introduction into the last part of the *Life* of a sort of commemorative sermon and of a concluding character show that his first venture into biography is in part derivative and traditional, the manner in which he introduced his material shows his awareness of what he is doing. A self-educated man of letters, conservative by nature, he could not bring himself to conclude without a character, but even this was not mere imitation. The character approach toward biography was part of his inheritance and determined his approach toward biography during his entire career. But even here, in his first *Life,* he tried to make it evident by the very formality of the character that it was an adjunct of the *Life,* not an integral part of it, and he never again used quite so obvious a sketch. The part of the *Life* which most closely resembles a sermon of commemoration he himself termed a long digression, but even so it has a precise function in the *Life* as a substitute for the events or lack of them in Donne's last seven years. And into it, we must remember, Walton did introduce a sort of chronology, an abundance of concrete documentation, and an arrangement

which progressively intensified the holiness of Donne's life in preparation for the holiness of his death. Walton used the *Sermon of
Commemoration* as he used his other sources, not without adapting
it to his own purposes, not without originality.

Thus early in Walton's career as a biographer, then, we can see his
penchant for tampering with his sources and his real ability to
shape them so that they conform minutely to the image of his subject which he has in mind and so that they help project that image
to the reader. He shaped *The Life and Death of Dr Donne* at every
point by his careful structure, his control of the time element, and
his conscious omissions. His artful and selective use of detail covered his manipulations. Harold Nicolson is right in saying that
Walton's biography is written in the deductive manner. He is also
right in saying that Walton is a *"deliberate"* biographer. But he
underestimates the extent of Walton's deliberateness. He credits
Walton with making his digressions occur at suitable pauses in the
dramatic narrative;[111] but the long digression in the *Life of Donne*
can be considered a digression only because Walton so called it.
Actually, it advances the picture of Donne as no mere narrative
could, because the material has been so carefully chosen. Walton's
deliberateness misleads even Nicolson, for he says, "Walton, it is
true, had introduced letters into some of his biographies, but he
had done so with no very deliberate purpose." Nicolson condemns
Mason, whose purpose in introducing letters into his *Life of Gray*
was, he says, more deliberate than Walton's, for falsifying the text
of Gray's letters. "Today," he says, "we merely leave out the bits that
contradict our own thesis."[112] Walton did just this in the letter
which he edited in 1635 and used in the 1640 *Life of Donne,* and
while he did not completely falsify the will or his other sources, he
omitted, he altered ever so deftly. His writing was deliberate at
every point.

[111] *Development of English Biography,* pp. 65–67.
[112] *Ibid.,* p. 77.

Chapter 2

The Life of
John Donne – 1658

THE 1640 *Life of Donne* was Walton's first endeavor in biographical writing, but it contains many of the characteristics of his technique. Before the second edition appeared, Walton had done considerable writing and had made his name as a literary man. The *Life of Wotton* appeared in 1651, with a second edition in 1654, and the *Compleat Angler* was published in 1653 and again in 1655. Walton's statement that he thought "Time had made this relation of him [Donne] so like my self, as to become useless to the world, and content to be forgotten"[1] may be dismissed as a kind of conventional literary modesty. Even as he had not been content to be useless and forgotten, so had he not been content to forget his life of Donne, and there is evidence that he continued the collections he had started at Wotton's request.[2] In 1658, "in an Age too, in which Truth & Innocence have not beene able to defend themselves from worse then severe censures," Richard Marriot prevailed upon Walton to expose the *Life* and himself to "publick exceptions," and without the support of Donne's sermons and the late King's approbation, "which we first had and needed."[3] Walton believed that Donne's life ought to be "the example of more then that age in which he died,"[4] and this second edition of the *Life of Donne* became the first of the lives which Walton wrote to be printed independently. He regrets that the beauties and elegancies of Donne's conversations were not preserved "by the pensil of a *Tytian* or a

[1] *Donne,* 1658, sig. A4ʳ. [2] See pp. 71–72. [3] *Donne,* 1658, sigs. A4ʳ–A4ᵛ.
[4] *Ibid.,* sigs. A7ʳ–A7ᵛ.

Tentoret," but he tells Sir Robert Holt that his revision "will present you with some features not unlike your dead friend, and with fewer blemishes and more ornaments than when 'twas first made publique."[5] The second impression, "corrected and enlarged," omits mention in the title of the death of Dr. Donne; it is called *The Life of John Donne, Dr. in Divinity, and Late Dean of Saint Pauls Church London.* But the motto from Ecclesiasticus 48:14, which appears on the title page, indicates that despite expansion and revision, Walton has retained the same relative emphasis in this edition: "He did wonders in his life, and at his death his works were marvelous."

Walton's words to the reader in 1658 show his acute awareness of the materials that make for biography:

> *My desire is to inform and assure you, that shall become my Reader, that in that part of this following discourse, which is onely narration, I either speak my own knowledge, or from the testimony of such as dare do any thing, rather than speak an untruth. And for that part of it which is my own observation or opinion, if I had a power I would not use it to force any mans assent, but leave him a liberty to disbelieve what his own reason inclines him to.[6]*

Had Walton accurately followed this prescription for biography, narration plus opinion, he would have produced a type of writing popular in his day, the biography that was composed of the bare relation of facts followed by a character. It was perhaps this prescription that led Walton to append his list of generalities to the *Life of Donne* and to add to the list in 1658.[7] But, though Walton was aware of a dualism in the content of the *Life,* and though he leaves his reader at liberty to separate the narrative from the opinion, there is little of such a divorce in his writing. There are some additions to the *Life* of 1658 which may clearly be called "observations": these take the form of aphorisms and platitudes, bits of wisdom of which Walton was fond and which add a note of simple dignity to the *Life.* The additional "narrative" is no mere bare recital of facts. As in the 1640 *Life,* Walton controls the narrative superbly: his

---

[5] *Ibid.*   [6] *Ibid.,* sig. A10r.

[7] That Walton considered this section independent from the life itself is indicated by his italics. It is not likely that he would have changed "un-imitable fashion of speaking" (*Donne,* 1640, sig. B2r) to "an unexpressable addition of comelinesse" (*Donne,* 1658, p. 48), a phrase which he had already used in the "character" of 1640 and which he retained in all later editions, unless he considered the character a separate entity.

opinion is irrevocably bound with his structure and his selection of detail, and his opinion as it colors the facts can be studied in the hundreds of minor changes.

Since few of the major additions in 1658 are the result of fresh information gathered since 1640, it is doubly interesting to see what and where Walton adds when he has an opportunity to expand the life. The first two additions were included to emphasize further the early religious inclination of Donne. The first is a paragraph in which Walton tries to justify Donne's lack of decision in choosing a religion before his nineteenth year.[8] Donne was a Christian at eighteen, he says, but his reason and piety led him to believe that adherence to a particular church was not necessary. Walton would hereby show that Donne's lack of denomination was not caused by indifference but by a conscious choice. The second addition has as its subject Donne's travels. In his elegy, printed in 1633 and later, Walton implied that Donne had visited Palestine. He made no mention of the trip in 1640, for he was certain that Donne had not made such a journey. In 1658, Walton says that Donne had not intended to go to Spain after traveling in Italy, but had planned to go to the Holy Land to view Jerusalem and the sepulcher of the Saviour. That he did not specifically know what made Donne change his mind is evident in the following sentence: "But at his being in the furthest parts of *Italy,* the disappointment of company, or of a safe Convoy, or the uncertainty of returns for money into those remote parts, denied him that happiness."[9] In 1658, Walton was as certain as he had been earlier that Donne did not travel to Palestine, but he realized that it would still be to Donne's credit to have purposed such a trip. Walton included the incident in 1658 because even the desire for the journey would additionally demonstrate Donne's youthful holy tendencies.

Walton's original account of Donne's marriage had been a detailed one. He did not have a single important fact to add to this account in 1658, but he would expand this section showing the secular Donne to preserve the relative equilibrium between it and the expanded later life. He therefore rewrote it in a more leisurely fashion and added many wise saws which tend to justify the behavior of the principal actors. The impetuosity of the lovers, if not excused, is at least explained: "for love is a flattering mischief, that hath denied aged and wise men a foresight of those evils that too often prove to be the children of that blind father; a passion that

[8] *Donne,* 1658, pp. 9–10.   [9] *Ibid.,* p. 13.

carries us to commit *errors* with as much ease as whirlwinds remove feathers, and beget in us an unwearied industry to the attainment of what we desire."[10] Of Donne's behavior, he adds: "It is observed, and most truly, that silence and submission are charming qualities, and work most upon passionate men."[11] He adds an inevitability to the forgiveness of Sir George More: "(for Love and Anger are so like Agues, as to have hot and cold fits.) And love in parents, though it may be quenched, yet is easily rekindled, and expires not, till death denies mankind a naturall heat."[12]

One of the most important additions, probably the most important to Walton, was the information that he got from Thomas Morton, Bishop of Durham, before 1648. Morton (a good man and "my friend,"[13] Walton called him) told him that upon his appointment as Dean of Gloucester in 1607 he had tried to induce Donne to take orders and had offered him a benefice, but that Donne had not seen fit to accept. Sir Edmund Gosse wrote a dramatic but inaccurate account of Walton's securing this information. He assumed, because Walton wrote that Morton was in his ninety-fourth year, that the meeting between them took place in 1659 and that Morton gave Walton a document: "As the Bishop of Durham only survived a few months longer, dying in his ninty-fifth year, on the 22nd of September 1659, it is impossible to be too thankful that Walton was just in time to secure this most important document."[14] There is reason to believe that Walton must have seen Morton before 1648. Walton did not know the story of Morton's offer to Donne when he first wrote the life, for he would have been glad to include an incident of such holy significance in the early life. Morton resided in Durham from 1632 until 1640 and came to London early in 1641. He lived there until about 1649, when he removed to the home of Sir Christopher Yelverton at Easton-Maudit, and he spent the remaining years of his life on Yelverton's estate. The Parliament sought to deprive him of his canonical right to the see of Durham in 1647, and in 1648 he was driven from Durham House in London by the soldiery.[15] Walton probably had this incident in mind when he wrote, to demonstrate God's goodness in affording every age some men who are piously ambitious of doing good to mankind, "These times he did blesse with many such; some of

[10] *Ibid.*, p. 16.   [11] *Ibid.*, p. 20.   [12] *Ibid.*, p. 21.
[13] First added in *Lives*, 1675, p. 21.
[14] Gosse, I, 157. Throughout his volumes, Gosse refers to *Donne*, 1658, as the "recension of 1659."
[15] *DNB*, article "Thomas Morton."

which still live to be patterns of Apostolicall Charity, and of more than Humane Patience."[16] In the 1675 edition of the *Life*, Walton indicated by a marginal note that by "these times" he meant 1648.[17] Walton, then, aware that Morton had known Donne, probably met him during his stay in London. He did not solicit last-minute information in 1658; his interest in Donne continued through the years.

Gosse, presupposing a document, speculated that the phrasing in Walton's account of Morton's offer was neither Donne's nor Walton's and that it was probably Morton's, possibly based on notes in a diary and a précis of some of Donne's letters which he had preserved. He went on to say that Morton probably changed the reason for Donne's refusal of his offer from theological indecision to a concern with the irregularities of his early life.[18] There is no reason to assume that Walton's account is not based on Morton's oral relation of the incident, but if Walton was working from a document, he did with it what he did with similar documents—he made it his own. The cause of refusal of the offer which Gosse attributed to Morton is in fact the cause which Walton has emphasized. According to him, Donne's study in his nineteenth year had resolved for him his denomination, and Walton consciously related the story of Donne's marriage in detail to provide "irregularities" which later disturbed him. The phrasing is also Walton's. He had jotted down some notes prior to writing in 1658, and the first two of them apply to this portion of the *Life:*

At his conversion take out of Jeremy the ways of man are not in his owne powr

loke doc dones letter to Tilman[19]

---

[16] *Donne,* 1658, p. 25.

[17] *Lives,* 1675, p. 21. This note has troubled modern editors, for the printer had some faulty 6's in his box. At first glance, the date appears to be 1548; at first glance also, the marginal date referring to the fire of London in Cotton's poem prefaced to the *Lives* appears to be 1665. The dates as they apparently stand do not make sense, but an examination of a "5" in the same point type (p. 288, edition of 1675) will make it clear that defective 6's were used. George Saintsbury, in the World's Classics edition of the *Lives* (1927, 1936), used the impossible 1548 and 1665. Alfred W. Pollard, in the Library of English Classics (Macmillan) edition of *The Complete Angler & The Lives,* printed 1901, missed the point of the date completely, though he read it correctly. He has a note (p. 196) explaining that 1648 is an erroneous date and that Donne took orders in 1614.

[18] Gosse, I, 159–160.   [19] See Appendix A.

Donne's poem, "*To M^r* Tilman *after he had taken orders,*" was a favorite of Walton's, and he had in 1640 used its lines ". . . for they [preachers] doe/ As Angels out of clouds, from Pulpits speake" to describe Donne as "always preaching to himselfe, like an Angel from a cloud, though in none."[20] Walton approved of the sentiment of the poem, that any man, regardless of great riches and high birth, was fortunate to enter orders, that no function was so noble as to be "Embassadour to God and destinie."[21] In 1658, he put this sentiment in Morton's mouth: "*Remember,* Mr *Donne,* no mans education or parts make him too good for this employment, *which is to be an Ambassadour for him who by a vile death opened the gates of life to mankind.*"[22] This is Walton's phrasing, not Morton's, though Donne himself furnished the idea. Walton did not use his note out of Jeremy at Donne's conversion. He did use it directly after his relation of Morton's information to say of Donne, "This was his present resolution, but the heart of man is not in his own keeping."[23] This paraphrase of Jeremiah 10:23[24] is typical of Walton's manner of quoting from the Bible. The biblical quotation which Walton has Donne use in his account of this incident is in the same manner: "*Happy is that man whose conscience doth not accuse him for that thing which he does.*"[25] Neither Donne nor Morton, with their more exact acquaintance with Scripture, would have quoted Romans 14:22 thus.[26] The phrasing is, then, Walton's, and probably some of the drama of the passage. He revised the passage slightly in 1670 and in 1675, and he added drama in 1670 in changing the words he gave to Morton from "The King hath now made me Dean of *Glocester*"[27] to "The King hath yesterday made me Dean of *Gloucester.*"[28] Walton was indebted to Morton for his information, but his use of the passage as an early manifestation of Donne's talents in divinity, as foreshadowing what was to be, was his own.

Walton was probably aware in 1640 of Donne's relationship with

[20] *Donne,* 1640, sig. B2^r.

[21] *Poems, By J. D.,* 1635, p. 370. This idea is, indeed, the thesis of Walton's *Life of Herbert.*

[22] *Donne,* 1658, p. 29.   [23] *Ibid.,* pp. 32–33.

[24] King James Version: O Lord, I know that the way of man is not in himself: it is not in man that walketh to direct his steps.

[25] *Donne,* 1658, p. 32.

[26] King James Version: Happy is he that condemneth not himself in that thing which he alloweth.

[27] *Donne,* 1658, p. 28.   [28] *Lives,* 1670 (Donne), p. 25.

the Earl of Somerset, but he made no mention of the acquaintance. Nor did he ever mention the epithalamion (printed in 1633) which Donne wrote for Somerset in 1613. In 1658, however, he added the story of Somerset's attempt to obtain state employment for Donne. The dramatic incident points up the obstinacy of King James's desire that Donne take orders and continues the process initiated in the Morton incident of raising Donne in the readers' estimation by mentioning his powerful and learned friends. Walton added two sections to the *Life* expressly for this purpose, and Somerset is here made to say that he is aiding Donne *"To testifie the reality of my affection."*[29]

Walton describes in detail the seals or rings which, he says, Donne had made before his death. Since he had one, though perhaps not directly from Donne, and since they are mentioned in Donne's will, he was well aware of their existence in 1640, but he had not included so inconsequential a detail. He had also omitted the catalogue of Donne's friends, for in so short a preface it was necessary to keep the *dramatis personae* at a minimum. In 1658 Walton artfully recalls the names of Donne's intimate friends by telling that Sir Henry Wotton, Dr. Joseph Hall, Dr. Brian Duppa, and Henry King were given seals. It is evident that Walton is here interested in the friends, not the seals, for he says that Donne's friends Sir Henry Goodere and Sir Robert Drury were by this time dead and could therefore not be of the number who received the gifts. Again, he says, "And in this enumeration of his friends, though many must be omitted, yet that man of primitive piety Mr. *George Herbert* may not."[30] Walton dwells at some length on this long and dear friendship, for no case needed to be made for Herbert's piety, which had become proverbial, and he would emphasize Donne's piety by maintaining that there was a "Sympathy of inclinations" between the men. As testimony of the friendship, he quotes at some length from the exchange of poems which, he says, accompanied the gift of the seal. The poems had first been printed with Donne's poems in 1650, with Herbert's preceding Donne's in the volume. Walton probably used this volume, though his lines vary somewhat from those of 1650, and he has corrected the order of the poems.[31] The amount of space allocated to Donne's friendship with Herbert is disproportionately long, but there is evidence that Walton was thus early thinking about writing the life of Her-

[29] *Donne*, 1658, p. 39.   [30] *Ibid.*, p. 81.   [31] See Appendix B.

bert[32] and that the relation between Donne and Herbert received
not only separate but lengthy treatment for this reason.

The enumeration of friends is cleverly continued by Walton in
his addition in 1658 of some of the specific bequests of Donne's
will.[33] Donne's brother-in-law, Sir Thomas Grymes, Dr. Brooke,
Dr. Winniff, Paolo Sarpi, Fulgentio Micanzio, and the Earls of
Dorset and Carlisle are mentioned as friends, as is Henry King. It
will be remembered that Walton dedicated the *Life* of 1658 to
King's nephew, and King is given special consideration in addition
to being brought into the relation of the seals and of the will. Walton filled, to some degree at least, the gap in Donne's life between
his two great illnesses by relating in detail King's offer to Donne
that he accept a lease of the profits of a church estate.[34] Although
the passage shows King's solicitude toward Donne and Donne's
scrupulosity against sacrilege, even at the cost of leaving his children
a small estate, the length of the account does not proportionately
add to the stature of Donne. At least part of the reason for its inclusion was a desire on Walton's part to give King a larger role in a
book dedicated to his nephew. Walton was also anxious to contrast
Donne's attitude with the *"declining Religion"* of 1658, and while
Donne declaims against the condition of the litigious clergy of his
own day, Walton was in effect contrasting his piety with contemporary irreligion.[35]

Walton had enumerated the high points of Donne's ecclesiastical
career in 1640. He included in 1658 a short account of Donne's
regular method of composing his sermons, and added to the picture
of conscientiousness and deliberateness.[36] He also wished to elab-

[32] See pp. 307–308.   [33] *Donne*, 1658, pp. 90–92.   [34] *Ibid.*, pp. 68–72.

[35] Gosse (II, 187–189) finds fault with Walton's having King offer Donne an
ecclesiastical estate because King thought Donne's recovery doubtful, and he
thinks that the reverse must be true, that Donne was certain of recovery. He
says that it is to Donne's honor that he rejected the offer of appropriating
church income for his own use. But this custom of leases was a common one
and such leases were often long term. Walton gives credit to Donne for reject-
ing the offer *while on a sickbed*. King's offer was made to ease Donne's mind
of the financial distress in which he would leave his children, for they would
inherit the income. So great was King's solicitude for Donne. Donne did not
object entirely to the custom, for Walton has him say that he will "gladly
take the reward which the bountifull Benefactours of this Church have designed
me," if he recovers his health and can again preach. But he thought it sacrilegious to accept while there was a possibility that he could never again serve
the Church.

[36] *Donne*, 1658, pp. 86–87.

orate his account of Donne's powerful preaching and to furnish
testimony for his account. His notes for this edition give evidence
in this direction, for he wrote, "vew chidlys elligies and godolpins
[*sic*] on doc done where they are scracht."[37] The elegies of John
Chudleigh and Sidney Godolphin, which demonstrated Donne's
superb ability to combat sin from the pulpit, had appeared in the
1635 edition of Donne's *Poems.* In 1658, Walton added to his own
words and used some of Chudleigh's lines to prove that he had not
written an "immoderate commendation."[38] But both Chudleigh's
and Godolphin's poems were heavily conceited; neither furnished
Walton with a testimony straightforward enough for his taste. Walton seems to be quoting from memory here, as elsewhere, for seven
of the twelve lines which he used vary from Chudleigh's. Whenever
Walton quoted verse, he tended naturally toward direct and prosaic
expression, and his version of Chudleigh's lines is no exception.
Some of the minor changes which Walton made might be due to a
lapse of memory, but no mere lapse was responsible for his starting
his quotation with half the nineteenth line of the poem and following this with lines thirteen through sixteen and twenty-nine through
thirty-six. He omitted some of Chudleigh's elaborate conceits, and
it is likely that he purposely made the minor changes to simplify
Chudleigh's ideas. Walton could and did tailor even a poem to meet
his own precise specifications, and he regrouped Chudleigh's lines
to offer proof of his statement briefly and effectively.[39]

[37] See Appendix A.   [38] *Donne,* 1658, pp. 48–49.
[39] Lines 13–38 of Chudleigh's elegy in *Poems, By J. D.,* 1635 (sig. Cc7ᵛ) read:

> He kept his loves, but not his objects; wit
> Hee did not banish, but transplanted it,
> Taught it his place and use, and brought it home
> To Pietie, which it doth best become;
> He shew'd us how for sinnes we ought to sigh,
> And how to sing Christs Epithalamy:
> The Altars had his fires, and there hee spoke
> Incense of loves, and fancies holy smoake:
> Religion thus enrich'd, the people train'd,
> And God from dull vice had the fashion gain'd.
> The first effects sprung in the giddy minde
> Of flashy youth, and thirst of woman-kinde,
> By colours lead, and drawne to a pursuit,
> Now once againe by beautie of the fruit,
> As if their longings too must set us free,
> And tempt us now to the commanded tree.
> Tell me, had ever pleasure such a dresse,
> Have you knowne crimes so shap'd? or lovelinesse

It will be remembered that in 1640 Walton had interrupted his recital of the events of Donne's years in the church for only a paragraph to tell of the death of Anne Donne. The enduring and mutual love of Donne and his wife Walton thought to be some recompense for the irregularities of the marriage. Although he had stressed this incident as the crowning irregularity in Donne's life

> Such as his lips did cloth religion in?
> Had not reproofe a beauty passing sinne?
> Corrupted nature sorrow'd when she stood
> So neare the danger of becomming good,
> And wish'd our so inconstant eares exempt
> From piety that had such power to tempt:
> Did not his sacred flattery beguile
> Man to amendment?

Walton's version (*Donne,* 1658, pp. 48–49) reads:

> ——— —— Each Altar had his fire—— ——
> He kept his love but not his object wit,
> He did not banish, but transplanted it,
> Taught it both time & place, & brought it home
> To piety, which it doth best become.
> For say, had ever pleasure such a dresse?
> Have you seen crimes so shap't, or lovelyness
> Such as his lips did clothe Religion in?
> Had not reproof a beauty-passing sin?
> Corrupted nature sorrowed that she stood
> So neer the danger of becomming good.
> And, when he preach't she wish't her eares exempt
> From piety, that had such power to tempt.

In 1670 (*Lives,* [Donne] p. 39) Walton added,

> *How did his sacred flattery beguile*
> *Men to amend?*———

Walton had probably scratched lines 23–30 of Godolphin's poem (*Poems, By J. D.,* 1635, sigs. Cc6ᵛ–Cc7ʳ):

> Pious dissector: thy one houre did treate
> The thousand mazes of the hearts deceipt;
> Thou didst pursue our lov'd and subtill sinne,
> Through all the foldings wee had wrapt it in,
> And in thine owne large minde finding the way
> By which our selves we from our selves convey,
> Didst in us, narrow models, know the same
> Angles, though darker, in our meaner frame.

Lines 11–21 of Thomas Carew's elegy describe Donne's preaching more powerfully than the lines of Chudleigh or Godolphin, but they were obviously too strong for Walton.

and could therefore not completely justify the marriage, he would yet have the reader condone it. In 1658, then, he included, with no additional information, a highly sympathetic picture of Donne's grief at his wife's death as a manifestation of the strength of his love.[40] So powerful is the picture that Gosse called it overcharged, and, typically, he attributed it to Donne himself, finding the very language characteristic of Donne's later manner.[41] The description is Walton's own, though for part of it he relied on Donne's "A Valediction: Forbidding Mourning."[42] The parenthetical "passions may be both changed and heightned by accidents"[43] is expressive of Walton's love for the aphoristic. The many biblical phrases are quoted in the manner peculiar to Walton.[44] His love for balanced adjectives and phrases is nowhere better seen than in the sentence, "Thus he began the day, and ended the night, ended the restless night and began the weary day in *lamentations.*"[45] Walton reinforced the idea of lamentation by saying that Donne's first sermon after his wife's death was preached at St. Clement's Church, where she was buried, on the text from the Lamentations of Jeremiah, "I am the man that hath seen affliction." Perhaps Walton is right, but the only sermon by Donne on this text which has been preserved was preached at St. Dunstan's and has nothing in it which is typical of a sermon of commemoration.[46] So deep a grief does Walton depict, so pathetic a picture of holy dejection, that the marriage seems justifiable, as he really desired, although he explicitly condemned it as a "remarkable error."

In 1658, Walton also made more intense the description of Donne's holy dying. He had a great part of the added material in 1640, but did not see fit to include it at that time. He undoubtedly knew that Donne was being treated by Dr. Simeon Foxe, perhaps the foremost physician of the time, though he may not have known until Foxe's death in 1642 that he had supplied the funds for the marble monument of Donne. Though he may have been unaware in 1640 that it was Dr. Foxe who had induced Donne to pose for

[40] *Donne*, 1658, pp. 52–55.   [41] Gosse, II, 95, 101.   [42] See pp. 112–113.
[43] *Donne*, 1658, p. 52.
[44] Walton quotes and paraphrases Galatians 6:14, Psalms 102:6, Job 6:8 and 17:13, Psalms 137:1, and I Corinthians 9:16.
[45] *Donne*, 1658, p. 54.
[46] Sermon XLVIII, *"Preached at St. Dunstans,"* in John Donne, *Fifty Sermons* (London, 1649), pp. 445–455. In this collection, the last six sermons, of which this is the fourth, are represented as having been delivered at St. Dunstan's.

a picture, he was certainly aware of the picture itself, for he must have seen it when he visited Donne during his last days. The narration about Donne's picture was probably omitted in 1640 because Walton could demonstrate Donne's deliberate preparations for death without it, and he did not want any possibility of vainglory to detract from the studied and pious death. But the macabre religiosity of the incident—Donne's posing in a winding sheet, his ordering that the picture be placed at his bedside that he might hourly view it—fascinated Walton as it has all his readers, and he included it in 1658. He prefaced the account by showing Foxe as physician and friend trying to prolong Donne's life and by showing Donne unafraid of death and longing for the day of his dissolution. He says that Donne yielded easily to Foxe's persuasion that he have a monument made for him, but only after he has excused this action by relating that men who have led the severest and most mortified lives have yet not been able to kill the desire for glory and commendation, that this desire will ever exist in men and "many think it should do so," and that there are sacred examples to justify it.[47] The element of vainglory is quite forgotten in the unusual pose which Donne assumed, and the entire relation becomes a pointed example of his preoccupation with death and his fearlessness in the face of it. Walton followed this account with the epitaph which was affixed to the monument, and it becomes another example of Donne's careful preparedness for death, for Walton says that Donne himself wrote it.[48]

Walton appended four of Donne's letters to the volume of 1658, all of them reprinted from the *Letters to Severall Persons of Honour* of 1651.[49] These letters represent no random selection, but were carefully calculated to enhance the mood of the *Life* and to corroborate some of the statements in the *Life*. They are reflective and introspective in their content; only in one are there numerous topical references, and these pertain to events which show Donne in a proper light—his sickness, his composing "The Litany," and church matters. The tone is one of piety, not of wit. Walton did not choose letters full of the chattiness of the day's events; indeed, he

[47] *Donne*, 1658, p. 111.

[48] The epitaph had been printed in 1640 on the verso of the page on which Walton's *Life* ended.

[49] The *Eusebius* notes (Appendix A) contain Walton's annotation to refer to "doc dons letters." The letters, in the order printed by Walton in 1658, are on pp. 42–48, 48–53, 31–37, and 7–10.

omitted the end of the postscript of the second letter because of its
mundane detail. He purposely excluded letters of the type that
Donne wrote to Lady Bedford, letters full of ingenious, flattering
conceits. Two of the letters contain excisions, both in the 1651
volume and in Walton's. In one, the deletion consists of Donne's
remarks on the word *jollity;* in the other, of some remarks on his
composing light, witty verse. It is tempting but unprofitable to
think Walton responsible for these, as he in no way damaged the
manuscript of the letter which he printed only in part in 1635 and
in 1640. Yet, in the very selection of these letters, it is obvious that
Walton wished to stress Donne's meditative melancholy, not his
jollity, and certainly Walton was very careful not to allow the poetry
to assume dominant importance in the *Life.* There may be more
than coincidence here. Whatever letters Walton chose would have
been no great attraction in selling his book, for Donne's letters
had been printed in 1651 and again in 1654. He selected four of
them in which Donne's own words intensify and verify his picture
of Donne's life with respect to his study, his religious poetry, and his
thoughts of death.

By 1658, Walton was no longer apprehensive of his writing
ability. From the opening lines of the *Life,* he dropped the words,
"And though it may be my fortune to fall under some censures for
this undertaking."[50] The apprehensiveness was replaced by an
assumed note of modesty. In 1640, he had to declare that Wotton
thought that his knowledge of Donne "would" make his diligence
useful;[51] in 1658, his reputation assured, he could write that Wotton
thought his knowledge "might" make his diligence useful.[52] He
was more sensitive to words. He corrected ineffective repetition:
"he made a voluntary promise . . . never to bring them [his
children] under the subjection of a Step-mother: which promise he
most faithfully kept"[53] became "he gave a voluntary assurance. . . ."[54] He used adjectives increasingly to heighten a mood:
Pompey's bondsman, alone on the seashore gathering "the pieces
of an old Boat to burne the body of his dead Master"[55] became "the
scattered pieces of an old broken Boat to burn the neglected body
of his dead Master."[56] In 1640, he had written a beautiful sentence
and inserted it between the accounts of Donne's death and his

[50] *Donne,* 1640, sig. A5ʳ.   [51] *Ibid.*   [52] *Donne,* 1658, p. 2.
[53] *Donne,* 1640, sig. B2ᵛ.   [54] *Donne,* 1658, pp. 51–52.
[55] *Donne,* 1640, sig. A5ʳ.   [56] *Donne,* 1658, p. 3.

burial: "Thus *variable,* thus *vertuous* was the *life,* thus *memorable,* thus *exemplary* was the *death* of this most excellent man."[57] In 1658, he interchanged "memorable" and "excellent" and achieved an even more pointed effect through the triple alliteration.[58] Even as he had rhetorically shown the division between Donne's secular and religious life in 1640 by his use of five clauses containing the word "now," so he additionally emphasized the change in the expanded life of 1658 by two more such clauses and by inserting "now" before two others. His feeling for a scene was surer in 1658. In the original *Life* he had awkwardly described the scene in which Donne, clouded with the King's displeasure, had answered the accusation brought against him and had received the confidence of the King:

Doctor Donne protested his answer was faithfull and free from all Collusion. And therefore begged of his Majesty, that he might not rise (being then kneeling) before he had (as in like cases he alwayes had from God) some assurance that he stood cleere and faire in his Majesties opinion. The King with his own hand, did, or offered to raise him from his knees, and protested he was truly satisfied, that he was an honest man, and loved him. Presently his Majesty called some Lords of his Councell into his Chamber, and said with much earnestnesse, *My Doctor is an honest man;* And my Lords, I was never more joyed in any thing that I have done, then in making him a Divine.[59]

In 1658, Walton improved Donne's manners, having him kneel and thank the King before protesting that his answer was free from collusion. He then removed the awkward "(being then kneeling)" and merged the other parenthesis into his sentence. He removed the element of doubt in "or offered to" and the drama of the scene came to life.[60] In the original description, Walton had the King announce his opinion to the Lords of the Council in Donne's presence, as though he had to prove his opinion of Donne before witnesses. In 1658, Walton says that Donne was dismissed before the King spoke to the Council, and the logic and the force of the incident are improved. Walton was overanxious in his original account to show the King's esteem for Donne, and he made the King say that his persuasion of Donne to enter orders was the crowning point of his reign, "I was never more joyed in any thing that I have done." Such hyperbole is undignified and unconvincing, and in

[57] *Donne,* 1640, sig. B6ᵛ.
[59] *Donne,* 1640, sig. B3ᵛ.
[58] *Donne,* 1658, p. 117.
[60] *Donne,* 1658, p. 66.

1658 the King says, *"I was never better satisfied with an answer: and I alwayes rejoice when I think that by my means he became a Divine."*[61]

As Walton did not expand the *Life* merely to add "ornaments," so he did not correct it merely to patch up the "blemishes." Even as every major change served to heighten an incident or deepen an impression, so every minor change served to mingle more inextricably the "opinion" with the fact. Highly subjective as the original *Life* was, it seems quite crude in the light of the minor corrections in 1658, for Walton increased the importance of Donne through innumerable changes of word and phrase, heightened the religious mood, and raised, generally, the level of the tone.

In 1640, he had been almost insistent on the esteem which Donne commanded from noble and learned men. He tended to overwrite, as in the case of James's speech. By 1658, he had learned to create a like effect with less strain. In 1640, he wrote that

M. *Donne* tooke a house at Micham (neere unto Croydon in Surrey) where his wife and family remained constantly: and for himselfe (having occasions to be often in London) he tooke lodgings neere unto White-hall, where he was frequently visited by men of greatest learning and judgement in this Kingdome; his company being loved, and much desired by many of the Nobility of this Nation, who used him in their counsels of greatest considerations.[62]

In 1658, he added that Mitcham was "a place noted for good aire and choice company"; "(having occasions to be often in London)" was revised to "whither his friends and occasions drew him very often." Because of these almost parenthetical references to choice company and friends, Walton could temper the too obvious push in "where he was frequently visited by men of greatest learning and judgement in the Kingdome; his company being loved, and much desired" to "where he was often visited by many of the Nobility and others of this Nation."[63] Donne comes off as well, but Walton appears to work less obviously hard. Originally, Walton wrote of Donne's removal to London, "that honourable Gentleman Sir *Robert Drury* assigned him a very convenient house rent-free, next his own in Drury-lane, and was also a daily cherisher of his studies."[64] In 1658, he sought to remedy the hyperbole of "daily cherisher"

[61] *Ibid.*, p. 67.   [62] *Donne*, 1640, sig. B^r.   [63] *Donne*, 1658, p. 34.
[64] *Donne*, 1640, sig. B^r.

but to retain Drury's high esteem for Donne. He deleted "daily," but made Sir Robert, instead of an "honourable Gentleman," "a Gentleman of a very noble estate, and a more liberall mind" and changed his gift of "a very convenient house" to one that was "very choice and usefull."[65] In 1640, Walton thought it reflected sufficient credit on Donne to say, with respect to the origin of *Pseudo-Martyr,* "And his Majestie occasionally talking with M. *Donne* concerning many of those Arguments urged by the Romanists, apprehended such a validity and cleerenesse in his answers, that he commanded him to state the Points, and bring his Reasons to him in writing."[66] In 1658, even the King shows greater respect for Donne. He is shown not "occasionally talking" with Donne, but "discoursing" with him. The work itself is dignified, for the King commanded Donne "to bestow some time in drawing the Arguments into a method, and then write his Answers to them." And to emphasize the King's personal interest, Walton explicitly states the implication of "bring": Donne is "not to send but be his own messenger and bring them to him."[67]

By many such small touches did Walton weld his opinion to the narrative, and Donne is dignified by minutiae. "Gods mercies"[68] to him became "Gods particular mercy."[69] His "deare friend D. *King* the then worthy Bishop of London"[70] became also "a man famous in his generation, and no stranger to Mr. *Donnes* abilities," and not only did he receive the news that Donne had decided to enter orders with much gladness, but also with "some expressions of joy."[71] In 1640, Walton wrote that after Donne entered into his holy profession, "the King made him his Chaplaine in Ordinary";[72] in 1658, "the *King* sent for him, and made him his Chaplain in ordinary."[73] Donne's "long familiarity with persons of greatest quality"[74] became a "long familiarity with Scholars, and persons of greatest quality."[75] Originally, he was to "attend" the embassage to Bohemia under Viscount Doncaster;[76] in 1658, he was to "assist and attend" it.[77] Originally, the Viscount "had long knowne and loved him";[78] in 1658, he "had alwayes put a great value on him,

---

[65] *Donne,* 1658, pp. 35–36.

[66] *Donne,* 1640, sig. Bᵛ.

[67] *Donne,* 1658, pp. 37–38.

[68] *Donne,* 1640, sig. Bᵛ.

[69] *Donne,* 1658, p. 42.

[70] *Donne,* 1640, sig. B2ʳ.

[71] *Donne,* 1658, pp. 43–44.

[72] *Donne,* 1640, sig. B2ʳ.

[73] *Donne,* 1658, p. 46.

[74] *Donne,* 1640, sig. B2ʳ.

[75] *Donne,* 1658, p. 46.

[76] *Donne,* 1640, sig. B2ᵛ.

[77] *Donne,* 1658, p. 58.

[78] *Donne,* 1640, sig. B2ᵛ.

and taken a complacency in his conversation."[79] Donne was not only joyful "to be an eye-witnesse of the health of his honoured Mistris, the Queene of Bohemia, in a forraigne Land,"[80] but he was also joyful "to be a witness of that gladness which she expressed to see him."[81] "A person of the Nobility of great note in the Kingdome" whom Donne "loved very much"[82] became "a person of Nobility and great note, betwixt whom and Dr. *Donne,* there had been a great friendship."[83] In describing Donne's funeral, Walton had originally stated that it was attended by "many persons of Nobility and eminency."[84] To show not only Donne's social standing, but his professional as well, he added to "eminency," "for Learning."[85] He included also the statement that at the funeral "nothing was so remarkable as a publick sorrow," and where he had formerly said that Donne's grave was strewn with curious and costly flowers, he added that there was an "abundance" of them. Each of these tiny modifications and additions serves to increase the estimation in which Donne was held, each of them raises almost imperceptibly the level of his importance. And each of them is evidence of the growth of Walton's skill.

In the same manner, Walton heightened the religious tone of the *Life* and added to the dignity of its general tone. In 1640, Walton wrote that Donne returned to Lincoln's Inn, where he had been a *Saul,* that he became a *Paul,* and preached salvation to his brethren:

> Nor did he preach onely, but as S. *Paul* advised his *Corinthians* to be followers of him as he was of Christ; so he also was an ocular direction to them by a holy and harmlesse conversation.[86]

His expansion of this passage in 1658 rhetorically pointed out the change in Donne, emphasized the piety of Donne's life as well as his conversation, and accentuated the tone of holiness by his quotation, paraphrase, and exegesis of St. Paul:

> And now his life was as a *shining light* amongst his old friends; now he gave an ocular testimony of the strictnesse and regularity of it; now he might say as S. *Paul* advised his *Corinthians, Be ye followers of me, as I follow Christ, and walk as ye have me for an example;* not the ex-

[79] *Donne,* 1658, p. 58.
[81] *Donne,* 1658, p. 60.
[83] *Donne,* 1658, p. 65.
[85] *Donne,* 1658, p. 118.

[80] *Donne,* 1640, sig. B3r.
[82] *Donne,* 1640, sigs. B3r–B3v.
[84] *Donne,* 1640, sig. B6v.
[86] *Donne,* 1640, sig. B2v.

ample of a busie-body, but of a contemplative, an harmlesse, and an holy life and conversation.[87]

In 1640, Walton had summed up Donne's life through his conversation with a friend in a passage beginning:

And the next day after his Sermon, his spirits being much spent, and he indisposed to discourse, a friend asked him, Why are you sad? To whom he replyed after this manner, "I am not sad; I am in a serious contemplation of the mercies of my God to me.["][88]

In 1658, Walton added, as contrast to the seriousness and piety of Donne's reply, that the friend "had often been a witnesse of his free and facetious discourse," but he also explicitly underlined the tone of the speech by adding that Donne replied "with a countenance so full of cheerfull gravity, as gave testimony of an inward tranquillity of mind, and of a soul willing to take a farewell of this world."[89] And before Donne related his present serious contemplation, Walton prefixed several lines to indicate that Donne's preparations for death had become his nightly meditation. Originally Donne had ended his words on a note of high assurance: "but I am to be judged by a mercifull God, who hath given me (even at this time) some testimonies by his holy Spirit, that I am of the number of his Elect. I am ful of joy, and shall die in peace." In 1658, Donne is as sure of salvation, but Walton introduced a deep tone of humility by emphasizing the mercies of God rather more than the testimonies to Donne. He has Donne say that God "is not willing to see what I have done amisse. And though of my self I have nothing to present to him but sins and misery; yet I know he looks not upon me now as I am of my self, but as I am in my Saviour."[90] Donne's righteousness is further increased by Walton's having him express as they apply to him the sentiments of St. Paul and the Blessed Virgin and by Walton's identification of him with Job.[91] Walton also added references to his steady course of preaching[92] and his "sacred Ditties."[93] So intent was he on flavoring the *Life* with religious references that he even added to his statement that Donne had a servant distribute charity to all the prisons in London

---

[87] *Donne,* 1658, pp. 56–57.
[88] *Donne,* 1640, sig. B6r.
[89] *Donne,* 1658, p. 106.
[90] *Ibid.,* pp. 108–109.
[91] *Ibid.,* pp. 41, 43, 115.
[92] *Ibid.,* p. 60.
[93] *Ibid.,* p. 85.

at all the festival times of the year, "especially at the *Birth* and *Resurrection* of our Saviour."[94]

As though to harmonize with the increased importance of Donne as a person and with the heightened tone of religion, the *Life* of 1658 generally assumed a tone of more pronounced dignity and stateliness. Walton's opinion manifests itself in the more formal garb of the revision. In 1640, he had been content to compare the youthful Donne's proficiency in languages with that of boys his own age: Donne, entering Oxford, had "at that time a command of the French and Latine Tongues, when others can scarce speak their owne."[95] In 1658, Walton discarded this comparison in favor of a more formal and flattering one. He says that Donne had "a good command both of the French and Latine Tongue," and he adds, "This and some other of his remarkable abilities, made one give this censure of him, *That this age had brought forth another Picus Mirandula; of whom Story sayes, That he was rather born than made wise by study.*"[96] The added note of formality is most often evident in verbal changes. Originally Walton had been content to say of his writing the *Life*, "I re-viewed my forsaken Collections, and resolved the world should see the best picture of the Author that my artlesse Pensil (guided by the hand of Truth) could present to it."[97] In the third edition (1670) he intensified the tone of modesty by saying *"best plain Picture."*[98] But in 1658, the dignification proceeded so far that it outweighed even the traditional tone Walton used of himself, and he substituted "narration" for "picture" and "pen" for "Pensil."[99] In explaining Egerton's refusal to re-employ Donne, he changed "it stood not with his credit"[100] to *"it was inconsistent with his place and credit."*[101] "Living a most retired and solitary life"[102] became "and betake himself to a most retired and solitary life,"[103] "much trouble"[104] became "many miseries,"[105] "some good body"[106] became "some gratefull unknowne friend,"[107] *"noble pity"*[108] became *"noble compassion,"*[109] "in visiting friends"[110] became "in visitation of friends."[111] The very words that Walton

94 *Ibid.,* p. 95.   95 *Donne,* 1640, sig. A5ᵛ.   96 *Donne,* 1658, p. 6.
97 *Donne,* 1640, sig. A5ʳ.   98 *Lives,* 1670 (Donne), p. 10.
99 *Donne,* 1658, p. 3.   100 *Donne,* 1640, sig. A6ᵛ.
101 *Donne,* 1658, p. 21.   102 *Donne,* 1640, sig. B2ᵛ.
103 *Donne,* 1658, p. 52.   104 *Donne,* 1640, sig. B2ᵛ.
105 *Donne,* 1658, p. 58.   106 *Donne,* 1640, sig. Cʳ.
107 *Donne,* 1658, p. 120.   108 *Donne,* 1640, sig. Cʳ.
109 *Donne,* 1658, p. 121.   110 *Donne,* 1640, sig. B4ᵛ.
111 *Donne,* 1658, p. 87.

gave King James are dignified. In 1640, the King had said: *"Doctor Donne, I have invited you to dinner, And though you sit not downe with me, yet I will carve to you of a dish that I know you love; you love London well, I doe therefore make you Deane of Pauls, take your meate home to your study, say grace, and much good may it doe you."*[112] The King's taste was less gross in 1658, and he substituted *"beloved dish"*[113] for *"meate."* He also became increasingly aware of his regal prerogatives and told Donne to take his *"beloved dish home" "when I have dined."* Though Walton often had recourse to a stiffness of phrase to produce dignity, this was not his only method. He did not think that he was dissipating dignity when, in speaking of James's motto, *Beati Pacifici,* he replaced the formal but wooden description that it "did truly characterize his disposition"[114] with the simple but equally dignified "did truly speak the very thoughts of his heart."[115]

In 1658, then, Walton raised Donne's stature by less obvious means than he had done originally, and he omitted some of the cruder first attempts to show his importance. Other omissions in 1658 testify to Walton's conscious curb on this type of overwriting. Originally he showed Egerton's esteem for Donne by saying that he used him with much courtesy and even appointed him a place at his table. This was not enough, but he must add that Donne "continued that employment with much love and approbation."[116] His next sentence referred to Donne's acquaintance with Anne More and how his "liking" "(with her approbation) increased into a love." In 1658, Walton deleted "love and approbation," partly to avoid the repetition, partly because he realized that such consideration was already implicit in Egerton's actions, but he additionally and more subtly emphasized Donne's relationship with Egerton by saying that he continued in his employment "for the space of five years."[117] Again, after describing Donne's burial, Walton had first written, "Nor was this (though not usuall) all the honour done to his reverend ashes; for by some good body, (who, tis like thought his memory ought to be perpetuated) there was 100. marks sent . . . towards the making of a Monument for him."[118] In 1658, the added importance which he had attributed to Donne allowed him to delete "though not usuall," which betrayed his original anxiety to raise

[112] *Donne,* 1640, sig. B3r.
[114] *Donne,* 1640, sig. B2v.
[116] *Donne,* 1640, sig. A6r.
[118] *Donne,* 1640, sig. Cr.

[113] *Donne,* 1658, p. 61.
[115] *Donne,* 1658, p. 58.
[117] *Donne,* 1658, pp. 14–15.

Donne, and allowed him also to drop the reserve expressed in "tis like."[119]

Other omissions in 1658 stem from other reasons. Walton had stated that natural parental affection and Donne's own merits induced Donne's father-in-law to give his blessing to Donne's marriage. Sir George More's withholding financial aid, however, made Walton say in 1640 that he "appeared to be so far reconciled, as to wish their happinesse; (or say so)."[120] The parenthesis cast additional doubt on More's sincerity, but, indirectly, additionally limited his approbation of Donne. In 1658, Walton saw that he gained nothing by the slight slur, and he omitted it. Perhaps, too, his knowledge that More eventually settled eight hundred pounds or interest at twenty pounds per quarter on his daughter reconciled him somewhat to More.[121] Walton had made reference to Donne's financial difficulties in 1640, and he additionally emphasized them in 1658: "youth, and travell, and bounty, had brought his estate into a narrow compass";[122] "necessary and daily expences were hardly reconcilable with his uncertain and narrow estate";[123] employment in London would be welcome, "for he needed it."[124] In 1640, Walton had showed Donne's scrupulous honesty by having him say to Sir George More, after he had been appointed Dean of St. Paul's, "I am, I thanke my God, provided for, and will receive this money no longer; And not long after freely gave up his bond of eight hundred pound."[125] Whereas at this time he had found it necessary to reinform the reader of the sum that Donne received in order to emphasize the extent of his gesture in refusing it even "not long after," his added references in 1658 to Donne's financial worries made the magnanimity of the voluntary refusal obvious. He deleted the second reference to eight hundred pounds, and he magnified and dramatized Donne's gesture by omitting "not long after."[126]

To show how just a steward Donne was of his church revenues, Walton referred to a private account which he kept after he became Dean and said that he "computed first his Revenue, then his expences, then what was given to the poore and pious uses, lastly, what rested for him and for his, he blest each yeares poore remainder with a thankfull Prayer."[127] Perhaps this method of computation

---

[119] *Donne*, 1658, pp. 119–120.   [120] *Donne*, 1640, sig. A6ᵛ.

[121] *Ibid.*, sig. Bʳ.   [122] *Donne*, 1658, p. 20.   [123] *Ibid.*, p. 24.

[124] *Ibid.*, p. 51.   [125] *Donne*, 1640, sig. B3ʳ.   [126] *Donne*, 1658, p. 62.

[127] *Donne*, 1640, sig. B5ʳ.

was what Walton found in Donne's account book, but the apparent double remuneration in "expences" and "what rested for him and his," and the placing of "expences" before charities did not produce a properly disinterested and charitable picture. Walton resolved the difficulty in 1658 by omitting "then his expences."[128] In quoting "some" of Donne's "thankfull" prayers in 1640, Walton carefully preserved the dates under which the prayers were listed. The first prayer is dated 1624, 1625; the second, 1626; the third, 1628, 1629. In 1658, he omitted the dates in order to generalize the effect of the prayers and perhaps also to forestall speculation. He had intimated, probably in keeping with the impression of Donne's regularity which he would foster, that Donne made a yearly accounting; yet in two cases there are joint entries. That he wished to conceal this is evident, for while in 1640 and 1658 he wrote before the first prayer, quoting Donne perhaps, "So all is that remains of these two years," he changed the line to "So all is that remains this year" in 1670.[129] Again, he had intimated that Donne kept the account from the time of his entrance into the deanery. As the years which he listed are consecutive from 1624 to 1629 with the omission of 1627, it may be conjectured that the accounts were neither so regular nor of so long a duration as Walton would indicate. Perhaps there was an entry for 1627 which Walton omitted to further the impression that he was selecting prayers rather than quoting all of them, or perhaps there was none, but it would appear that the account covered just six of Donne's years as Dean. For though Walton removed the dates of the entries in 1658, he never deleted the line preceding the last prayer, which reads, *"In fine horum sex Annorum manet."*[130] His small Latin was less than he has generally been given credit for.

128 *Donne*, 1658, p. 98.   129 *Lives*, 1670 (Donne), p. 67.

130 Of course, Walton cites no figures, since he is interested in Donne's method of accounting, not in his accounts. But he does imply, in saying that Donne "blest each yeares poore remainder" that there was a remainder each year. This may have been true of the six years between 1624 and 1629, but it was not true of Donne's first year as Dean. On Oct. 4, 1622, Donne wrote Goodere, "I had locked my self, sealed and secured my self against all possibilities of falling into new debts, and in good faith, this year hath thrown me 400l lower then when I entred this house" (*Letters to Severall Persons*, p. 135; for addressee, see Roger E. Bennett, "Donne's *Letters to Severall Persons of Honour*," *PMLA*, LVI [1941], 123). Gosse conjectured (II, 170) that in this letter Donne is excusing himself from giving practical help to Goodere. Even if Donne, for this reason, accentuated his debt, it is not likely that he had any poor remainder this year.

Walton's omission of the dates in the account book runs counter to a general characteristic of the 1658 edition. His use of minute detail to lend authenticity to a fact or an incident has been pointed out, and 1658 saw the introduction of additional minor particularization. Many of these new details add little to the *Life* but their cumulative effect adds validity to the account. Walton had written in 1640 that Sir George More "did remove his Daughter to his owne house";[131] he added "at *Lothesley.*"[132] Christopher Brooke "of Lincolns Inne"[133] became "Mr. *Donne's* Chamberfellow in *Lincolns Inne.*"[134] To "another Ecclesiasticall Endowment"[135] he added "given to him formerly by the Earl of *Kent.*"[136] The original description of the *Devotions upon Emergent Occasions* as "Meditations in his sicknesse,"[137] Walton changed to indicate the actual structure of the book: "a composition of *Meditations, disquisitions* and *prayers.*"[138] He also added that the book was published at Donne's recovery from his illness, and that his most secret thoughts were there "Paraphrased and made publick." Walton implied that he had detailed information even when he did not give it. He said in 1640 that Donne's modesty after entering orders led him "to preach in some private Churches, in Villages neere London";[139] in 1658 he added that he was "usually accompanied with some one friend."[140] Originally he spoke of "a person of the Nobility of great note" who was discarded from Court;[141] he added, "I shall forbear his name, unless I had a fairer occasion."[142] He added the date of Donne's will,[143] and, to substantiate his statement that Donne had written "An Hymne to God, my God, in my sicknesse" on his deathbed, he added the date, *"March 23. 1630[1]."*[144] Contrary to this tendency toward particularization, he modified his original overdetailed description of Donne's illness, leaving only enough detail to indicate the nature of it. He omitted the intermediate progression, that it "turned to a spotted Feaver, and ended in a Cough,"[145] and retained only that "a dangerous sicknesse seized him, which inclined him to a Consumption."[146] Also contrary to

131 *Donne,* 1640, sig. A6ᵛ.　132 *Donne,* 1658, p. 15.
133 *Donne,* 1640, sig. A6ᵛ.　134 *Donne,* 1658, p. 19.
135 *Donne,* 1640, sig. B3ʳ.　136 *Donne,* 1658, p. 63.
137 *Donne,* 1640, sig. B3ᵛ.　138 *Donne,* 1658, p. 72.
139 *Donne,* 1640, sig. B2ʳ.　140 *Donne,* 1658, p. 46.
141 *Donne,* 1640, sig. B3ʳ.　142 *Donne,* 1658, p. 65.
143 *Ibid.,* p. 94.　144 *Ibid.,* p. 85.
145 *Donne,* 1640, sig. B3ᵛ.　146 *Donne,* 1658, p. 67.

this tendency, he omitted his parenthesis that Donne was "but forty two years of age" when he promised his children that he would not remarry.[147]

If this omission of Donne's age runs counter to the added detail of the edition of 1658, it is typical of Walton's difficulty with the exact dating of events in Donne's life. The resulting diffuseness of chronology which characterizes the *Life* abets Walton's skillful use of the time element, allows him to magnify incidents and omit whole years, to juggle dates to his own purpose and to cover up the lacunae in his information. If Walton is generally correct with regard to the progression of events in Donne's life, he is invariably wrong with respect to the exact time of a particular incident or Donne's age at the time. It would serve no end to indicate the many discrepancies of time; it is sufficient to say that Walton himself was aware of them, and that this awareness led him to omit Donne's age at the time of his wife's death. It is indicative of his method that he had inserted it in 1640, not in an attempt at accuracy of chronology, but to emphasize the extent of Donne's sacrifice in his promise to his children. In 1658, he was content that the passage could make its effect without the parenthesis and that he would be spared the necessity of a guess. For the age of Donne would have been merely a guess. Walton was not sufficiently sure even of the date of Donne's birth to include it in the *Life* until 1675, and then he was a year out of the way. At the beginning of the *Life,* he indicated the time by such phrases as "About the fourteenth yeare of his age" and "About his seventeenth yeare."[148] As the *Life* progressed, he tended to date one event by a reference to a previous one: "Immediately after his returne from Cambridge, his wife died";[149] "In this retirednesse, he was importuned by the grave Benchers of Lincolns Inne . . . to accept of their Lecture";[150] "About which time the Emperour of *Germany* died,"[151] and King James "did then" send Donne with the embassage;[152] "Within fourteen moneths he returned to his friends of Lincolnes Inne";[153] "About a yeare after his returne from Germany," the King made him Dean of St. Paul's.[154] It is evident that the exact

[147] *Donne,* 1640, sig. B2ᵛ; *Donne,* 1658, p. 52.
[148] *Donne,* 1640, sig. A5ᵛ.   [149] *Ibid.,* sig. B2ᵛ.   [150] *Ibid.*
[151] *Ibid.*   [152] *Donne,* 1658, p. 58.
[153] *Donne,* 1640, sig. B3ʳ; changed in 1658 (p. 60) to "About fourteen moneths after his departure out of *England* . . ."
[154] *Donne,* 1640, sig. B3ʳ.

chronology of Donne's life was confusing to Walton. He managed the flow of the life by such phrases as those above, and the degree of the precision of time he strove for is illustrated in his changing in 1658 the phrase "at last"[155] to the equally indefinite "after some yeares."[156]

Walton was generally content in 1658 to leave unaltered his original handling of the chronology of Donne's life, and the few changes that he made in the addition and deletion of dates were dictated by artistry, not chronology. In 1658, however, another element of time entered the *Life*. Eighteen years had passed since the first edition. Then Walton had said that the advowson of St. Dunstan's was given to Donne "by the right Honorable *Richard* Earle of Dorset a little before his death, And confirmed to him by his Brother the right Honorable *Edward* Earle of Dorset that now lives."[157] Since Edward had died in 1652, Walton wrote, in the second edition, that the advowson had been formerly given to Donne "by his honourable friend, *Richard* Earl of *Dorset*, then the Patron, and confirmed by his brother the late deceased *Edward*, both of them men of much honour."[158] The "Deane of Glouces-ter"[159] became the "then *Dean* of *Glocester* (whose name my memory hath now lost)."[160] While Walton thought in 1640 that the reason for King James's intervention in the affairs of Germany would be clear to his readers with the mere mention of the "Palsgrave,"[161] he saw fit in 1658 to add "who had lately married the Lady *Elizabeth* the Kings onely daughter."[162]

These minor changes merely reflect the passage of time. But the year 1658 represented to Walton, it will be remembered, an age "in which Truth & Innocence have not beene able to defend them-selves from worse then severe censures,"[163] and the *Life of Donne* became an advocate of the Episcopal Church. In 1640, Walton's concern with religious forces outside of Anglicanism manifested itself in a gentlemanly opposition to Catholicism. Then he had even called Cardinal Bellarmine "learned."[164] Such a concession was not to be expected in the wrangling tenseness of the Church in the days of the Protectorate, and the adjective was dropped.[165] In

[155] *Ibid.*, sig. B^r.　　[156] *Donne, 1658*, p. 35.　　[157] *Donne, 1640*, sig. B3^r.
[158] *Donne, 1658*, p. 63.　　[159] *Donne, 1640*, sig. A6^r.
[160] *Donne, 1658*, pp. 11–12.　　[161] *Donne, 1640*, sig. B2^v.
[162] *Donne, 1658*, p. 57.　　[163] *Ibid.*, sig. A4^v.　　[164] *Donne, 1640*, sig. A6^r.
[165] *Donne, 1658*, p. 11.

1640, Walton had singled out the Catholics as objecting to the Oath of Supremacy and Allegiance. In 1658, he generalized the statement "many of those Arguments urged by the Romanists"[166] to "many of the reasons which are usually urged against the taking of those Oaths."[167] He did not have to stray from the fold of Protestantism to find opposition. In 1640, it was enough to say that Donne said daily devotions to God at St. Paul's.[168] In 1658, Walton felt that he must recall the old procedure, and he added a parenthesis, "who was then served twice a day by a publick form of Prayer and Praises in that place."[169] Of the King's imprisoning a noble friend of Donne's, Walton first wrote that it "begot many rumors in the multitude."[170] He was not so kind in 1658; he was direct in his displeasure: it "begot many rumours in the common people, who in this Nation think they are not wise, unlesse they be busie about what they understand not, and especially about Religion."[171] Walton was outspoken in his comments on the sad state of the Church and the times. In his character of Bishop Morton, he wrote that he "is now (be it spoken with sorrow) reduced to a narrow estate, which he embraces without repining; and still shews the beauty of his mind by so liberall a hand, as if this were an age in which *to morrow were to care for it self*."[172] His indictment of the clergy of the time he interpolated in a generalized preface to Donne's self-questionings as to his worthiness in accepting orders: "In the first and most blessed times of Christianity, when the Clergy were look'd upon with reverence, and deserved it . . ."[173] And he had the present time of writing in mind when he had Donne say, also in contrast with the primitive church, "Our times abound with men that are busie and litigious about trifles and Church-Ceremonies; and yet so far from scrupling *Sacriledge,* that they make not so much as a quaere what it is."[174] It was to Walton a damning reflection on the times that he must write of Henry King, the "now Bishop of *Chichester,*" that as chief Residentiary of St. Paul's he was "a man

---

[166] *Donne,* 1640, sig. B^v. [167] *Donne,* 1658, p. 37.

[168] *Donne,* 1640, sig. B6^v.

[169] *Donne,* 1658, p. 118. John Evelyn wrote in his diary on Sept. 19, 1665, "On Sunday afternoon, I frequently staid at home to catechise and instruct my family, those exercises universally ceasing in the parish churches, so as people had no principles, and grew very ignorant of even the common points of Christianity" (*The Diary of John Evelyn* [Everyman's Library], I, 312).

[170] *Donne,* 1640, sig. B3^v. [171] *Donne,* 1658, p. 65. [172] *Ibid.,* p. 26.

[173] *Ibid.,* p. 40. [174] *Ibid.,* p. 70.

then generally known by the Clergy of this Nation."[175] Walton's
bitterness is manifested in the "then," which he omitted in 1670,[176]
but it is even more dramatically emphasized in another passage.

In 1640, he had included Donne's "A Hymne to God the Father"
to show Donne's preoccupation with divine poetry. The poem has
an additional function in 1658. Walton's notes for this edition
demonstrate his interest in church music. He refers to "Sʳ philip
Sidnys salms" and says also "vew the verses before Sands psalms."[177]
In his poem *"Upon the trãslation of the Psalmes by Sir* Philip
Sydney, *and the Countesse of Pembroke his Sister,"* Donne had
said that he would not consider the Church reformed until the
psalms were reformed, and he emphasized the high function of
church music:

> The Organist is hee
> Who hath tun'd God and Man, the Organ we:
> The songs are these, which heavens high holy Muse
> Whisper'd to *David, David* to the Jewes.[178]

The many verses prefatory to George Sandys's *A Paraphrase upon
the Divine Poems* (1638) are sufficient proof that Donne and Walton
were not alone in their high esteem for church music[179] and in their
belief that there was need of new versions of the psalms in the
Church. The lines of Carew, Godolphin, and Waller, among others,
echo those of Henry King:

> I must confesse, I have long wisht to see
> The Psalmes reduc'd to this Conformitie:
> Grieving the Songs of Sion should be sung
> In Phrase not diff'ring from a Barbarous Tongue.[180]

In 1658, Walton added after Donne's "Hymn" that it had been set
to music and sung by the choristers of St. Paul's, and he had Donne
comment on the power of church music. He stated that with such
music did the first Christians offer their praises to God, that St.
Augustine wept when public hymns and lauds were lost to the
Church, that many devout souls offered such acceptable sacrifices

---

[175] *Ibid.,* p. 68.   [176] *Lives,* 1670 (Donne), p. 49.   [177] See Appendix A.
[178] *Poems, By J. D.,* 1635, p. 367.

[179] Sir Thomas Browne's sentiments on church music indicate his interest
in the controversy then current. See *Religio Medici* (1643), pp. 164–165.

[180] George Sandys, *A Paraphrase upon the Divine Poems* (London, 1638),
sig. *6ᵛ.

to God. He left his bitterness at the Puritans unspoken in the broken phrase, "But now oh Lord——."[181]

Walton's remarks on the times constitute rather easily recognizable partisan opinion; they do not, however, intrude in the narrative, but rather mingle with it. This kind of opinion Walton gave the reader the liberty to disbelieve. Opinion is again easily discernible in Walton's use of platitudes, but these platitudes set a behavioristic pattern which gives an inevitability to a particular action. Why did Sir George More remove his daughter from Sir Thomas Egerton's? He knew "prevention to be a great part of wisdom."[182] Donne asked the Earl of Northumberland to inform Sir George of his marriage, "Doubt often begetting more restless thoughts then the certain knowledge of what we fear."[183] Why did Sir George endeavor in secret to reinstate Donne with Egerton? "Men do more naturally reluct for errours, than submit to put on those blemishes that attend their visible acknowledgement."[184] Why did Bishop Morton deign to notice Donne, a poor man, though one of "excellent erudition and endowments"? "It hath been observed by wise and considering men, that wealth hath seldome been the portion, and never the mark to discover good people."[185] Was Donne overgenerous in giving an impoverished friend a hundred pounds? There are some men "to whom Nature and Grace have afforded such sweet and compassionate souls, as to pity and prevent the distresses of mankind."[186] There is no questioning the truth of these platitudes, and therefore no reason to disbelieve the actions that they justify. Walton used common opinion to make the actions

---

[181] *Donne,* 1658, pp. 78–79.

How thoroughly music had been ejected from church services may be seen in the petition of John Hingston, David Mell, Wm. Howse, Rich. Hudson, and Wm. Gregory, for themselves and other professors of music to the Committee of Council for Music on Feb. 19, 1657: "By the dissolution of the choirs in cathedrals, many of us have died in want, and there being no encouragement for music, no man will breed his child in it, so that the science must die in this nation with those few professors now living, or must degenerate. We beg the erection of a college of musicians, with power to practise music publicly, to suppress obscene and scandalous songs and ballads, to reform the abuses in making of musical instruments, and in all things to regulate the profession; with power to buy lands, and have a common seal, and with restoration of such lands and revenues as have been heretofore employed for maintenance of music" (*Calendar of State Papers, Domestic Series, 1656–7,* p. 285).

[182] *Donne,* 1658, p. 15.   [183] *Ibid.,* p. 17.   [184] *Ibid.,* p. 22.
[185] *Ibid.,* p. 24.   [186] *Ibid.,* p. 96.

absolutely believable. But apart from the small body of recognizable partisan opinion and that explicit opinion which is so generally believed that it buttressed Walton's own account, the opinion is part of the very fiber of the *Life*. From the extensive catalogue of changes, it can be seen that Walton could and did register opinion in a word. Every addition raised Donne, every change imperceptibly heightened his stature or lifted the tone to a greater dignity. For all Walton's openness with his reader, the opinion can rarely be divorced from the narrative in a casual reading, so fast is Walton's grip on the whole. Walton's fine structure and careful selectivity of detail were largely responsible for the original picture of Donne. The revision of 1658 made the *Life* a work of art. The parts had been shaped in 1640. The phrases and words were shaped in 1658.

Chapter 3

The Second Revision – 1670

WALTON had originally written his lives of Donne and of Wotton as prefaces. By 1665, his stature as a biographer was sufficient to warrant the independent publication of his *Life of Hooker,* and five years later the *Life of Herbert* was separately printed. In 1670, also, Richard Marriot collected and published in one volume the four lives which Walton had written. Walton's modesty grew with his ability, and in the epistle to the reader of this volume, he wrote, *"when I look back upon my mean abilities, 'tis not without some little wonder at my self, that I am come to be publickly in print."*[1] The *Life of Donne,* which had originally served as a preface, was now graced by its own separate introduction, a revised version of the first four paragraphs of the 1658 edition. Walton here referred to himself not only as the "meanest"[2] of all Donne's friends, but he also added *"poorest."*[3] And with almost immodest modesty, he appended to the Introduction, "Before I proceed further, I am to intreat the Reader to take notice, that when *Doctor Donn's* Sermons were first printed, this was then my excuse for daring to write his life; and, I dare not now appear without it."[4] But if Walton pleaded modesty, his changes reflect his self-confidence. He expanded and dignified the figure comparing himself with Pompey's bondsman. The "neglected body of his dead Master"[5] became *"the forsaken dead body of his once glorious lord and master,"*[6] and *"Who art thou that preparest the funerals of* Pompey *the Great"*[7] became "who art thou that alone hast the honour to bury the body of

[1] *Lives,* 1670, sig. A5ʳ.   [2] *Donne,* 1640, sig. A5ᵛ.
[3] *Lives,* 1670 (Donne), p. 11.   [4] *Ibid.*   [5] *Donne,* 1658, p. 3.
[6] *Lives,* 1670 (Donne), p. 10.   [7] *Donne,* 1658, p. 3.

Pompey the great."[8] Walton had originally stated of his notes for Wotton, "I did prepare them in a readiness to be augmented, and rectified by his powerfull pen."[9] In 1670, this statement appeared lacking in dignity, and Walton, for all his modesty, did not like the connotation of "rectified." The sentence became *"I did most gladly undertake the employment, and continued it with great content 'till I had made my Collection ready to be augmented and compleated by his curious Pen."*[10] Walton was aware of his ability.

In 1670, Walton had no new information about Donne's life, but he continued to add, to change, above all, to color. It will be remembered that he appended to the edition of 1658 four letters which generally supplemented and corroborated his picture of Donne. So purposeful was Walton's selection of these letters that they may be termed an objective proof of his picture. But objectivity was no criterion of excellence for Walton in the writing of biography. In 1670, then, he omitted the appendix, but he incorporated parts of two of the letters into the body of the *Life.* From Walton's handling of the letter which appeared in the original *Life,* it would be natural to expect that he would not scruple to point up, to excise, to reword, even to add a date. R. E. Bennett has shown, in an excellent article, that he did all these.[11] Walton wished to darken the despair and dejection in which Donne lived at Mitcham, to show the utter decline of his fortunes after his marriage. To demonstrate Donne's "narrow fortune, and the perplexities of his generous minde" Walton candidly stated, "I shall present you with an extract collected out of some few of his many Letters."[12] He then quoted from what seem to be two letters by Donne. Bennett has shown that the first of these is a quotation and a paraphrase of part of a letter written in 1614, several years after Donne's residence at Mitcham,[13] and that Walton took the signature, "From my hospital at *Micham, Aug.* 10," from another letter not otherwise used by him.[14] The second and longer "letter" is made up of passages from five different letters which appeared in the 1651 *Letters to Severall Persons of Honour,* but four-fifths of it

---

[8] *Lives,* 1670 (Donne), p. 10.   [9] *Donne,* 1640, sig. A5^r.
[10] *Lives,* 1670 (Donne), p. 10.
[11] R. E. Bennett, "Walton's Use of Donne's Letters," *PQ,* XVI (1937), 30–34.
[12] *Lives,* 1670 (Donne), pp. 28–29.
[13] *Letters to Severall Persons,* pp. 151–153. Undated.
[14] *Ibid.,* pp. 207–208. *"At my* Micham *Hospitall,* Aug. 10."

is drawn from two of the letters which Walton printed in 1658.[15] The date added to it, "*Sept. 7,*" was attached, as Bennett has pointed out, "in order to create a pleasing verisimilitude."[16] Walton selected and intensified those passages in Donne's letters which unequivocally showed his melancholy. He expunged all the lighter touches, the conceits, the references to contemporary affairs. He made generalizations apply personally to Donne.[17] He consistently darkened the gloom and left out every ray of hope. It is no wonder that George Saintsbury said that the earlier part of the second letter "can scarcely be surpassed even in the Sermons, as an example of that long-drawn, echoing, melancholy music which so often lends an almost uncanny charm to its author's prose."[18] Walton's candor about his "extract" serves only to mislead the reader who assumes that the extract will be a representative and undistorted one. Walton would not let Donne's letters speak for themselves if they contained one note false to his purpose. He combined, he changed, he selected with utmost care, to produce a particular and undiminished emphasis.

In 1640, Walton had mentioned, in order to show Donne's continuing interest in divine poetry, that he "on this (which was his Death-bed) writ another Hymne which bears this Title, *A*

---

[15] *Donne,* 1658, pp. 128–134, 134–141; *Letters to Severall Persons,* pp. 48–53, 31–37.

[16] Bennett, *op. cit.,* p. 31.

[17] Bennett shows (p. 32) that Donne had written (*Letters,* 1651, p. 51): "but to be no part of any body, is to be nothing. At most, the greatest persons, are but great wens, and excrescences; men of wit and delightfull conversation, but as moales for ornament, except they be so incorporated into the body of the world, that they contribute something to the sustentation of the whole." Walton wrote: "*but to be no part of my body, is as to be nothing, and so I am, and shall so judge my self, unless I could be so incorporated into a part of the world, as by business to contribute some sustentation to the whole*" (*Lives,* 1670 [Donne], p. 30). Bennett says rightly that "Walton has caused Donne to seem to talk directly about himself instead of about himself by means of a general truth." He is too severe in calling the alteration of "any body" to "*my body*" "an egregious blunder." It is true that the edition of 1670 has "*my body*" for Donne's "any body," but the edition of 1675 correctly reads "*any body*" (p. 26). The error in 1670 was not made by Walton but by the compositor, who had trouble in distinguishing "any" and "my" in Walton's hand. In the 1670 *Life of Herbert,* the compositor printed, "*I shall compare them with any title of being a Priest*" (p. 43); Walton corrected this in 1674 (p. 32) to "*my title.*"

[18] Introduction, *Lives* (World's Classics), p. ix.

Hymne to God my God in my sicknesse."[19] In 1658, he added, as
if in verification of his statement, *"March 23. 1630[1],"* a date
which preceded that of Donne's death by only eight days.[20] In
1670, he selected and quoted those lines of the hymn which most
plainly and simply expressed religious feeling, using twelve and
one-half of the poem's thirty lines.[21] He pruned the poem in his
effort to demonstrate Donne's sincere, direct holiness; he omitted
that part which, though sacred in content, is based on an elaborate,
cosmographical conceit. Even as Walton edited the poem in 1670
in an effort to further a picture of uncomplicated piety, there is
reason to think that his attribution of the poem in 1640 to the days
when Donne was on his deathbed and his authenticating date in
1658 are additional examples of his shaping material to his own
ends. The main argument proposed in support of Walton's date
is that the poem appears in only one manuscript collection of
Donne's poems (Stowe 961). The poem appears in only one manuscript collection, it has been argued, because it was written late in
Donne's life, after most of the collections had been made. The
weakness in this position has been pointed out by Miss Helen
Gardner.[22] The best evidence for the date of the poem is in the

[19] *Donne,* 1640, sig. B4^r.

[20] *Donne,* 1658, p. 85. Sir Herbert Grierson, who supported Walton's date
in *Poems of John Donne,* II, 274, suggested that Henry King gave Walton the
exact date. But Grierson himself proposed King as editor of the 1633 *Poems.*
It is odd that King would in 1658 be so specific about the date of a poem
which he did not include twenty-five years before. (Grierson rejected Walton's
date in his *Metaphysical Lyrics & Poems of the Seventeenth Century* [1921],
p. 229.) Mrs. Simpson, who accepted Grierson's conjecture that King assisted
the printer of the 1633 *Poems,* supposed that the "Hymne" was probably included among the papers which Donne gave to King shortly before his death
("The Date of Donne's 'Hymne to God my God, in my sicknesse,'" *MLR,* XLI
[1946], 9–15; see especially pp. 12–13). If she were right, it would be even
more difficult to explain the omission of the "Hymne" from the 1633 *Poems.*

[21] *Lives,* 1670 (Donne), p. 60. Walton quoted ll. 1–7, part of l. 8, and ll.
26–30. Three of his lines contain unique readings. His use of *"thy"* in l. 2,
a reading peculiar to the 1635 edition of Donne's poems, where all the editions
from 1639 through 1669 read "the," suggests that he might have quoted by
memory from that edition. He changed the emphasis of Donne's final line by
changing the position of "therefore." Donne had written "Therfore that he
may raise the Lord throws down." Walton misquoted: *"That, he may raise;
therefore, the lord throws down."*

[22] Miss Gardner points out that though the Luttrell and O'Flaherty MSS
were made after Donne's death by compilers who collected all the poems they
could find, they do not contain the "Hymne," and she suggests that the poem

papers of Sir Julius Caesar, where a copy of the hymn bears the endorsement, "D. Dun Dene of Pauls/ his verses in his greate/ siknes./ in Deceb. 1623."[23] This date is almost certainly the correct one. Far too much reliance has been placed on Walton's statement that Donne composed the poem on his deathbed. There is good reason to believe that Walton's date was dictated by artistry rather than by accuracy. Walton was largely responsible for the ordering of Donne's *Poems* of 1635, the edition which marks the first appearance of this hymn. It is strange that he should insert it before "A Hymne to God the Father," which is the last poem in both 1633 and 1635 and which Walton says was written during Donne's former illness. Walton's detail in narrating Donne's dying is such that it suggests firsthand information, even personal observation, and he would have known the date of the poem in 1635 with as much certainty as he knew it in 1640. Yet his placement of the poem in the 1635 volume contradicts the date which he attributed to it in 1640. Also, his attribution of the poem to Donne's last days is reminiscent of his attribution of Donne's will to a time before his last illness; the dating of the poem is reminiscent of the method

is rare in manuscript because Donne did not wish it to circulate (*John Donne, The Divine Poems* [Oxford, 1952], pp. 133, 135).

Donne's poem to Mr. Tilman shows how careful we must be of the argument that the "Hymne" is a late poem because it is found in only one manuscript collection of Donne's poems. In *Poems of John Donne,* Grierson reprinted "To Mr Tilman" from the 1635 *Poems,* because it was first printed there and because he overlooked its presence in the O'Flaherty MS. Since Grierson's edition, "To Mr Tilman" has shown up in the Dobell MS (with some interesting readings, reproduced by R. E. Bennett, *Complete Poems of John Donne* [Chicago, 1942], pp. 273–274) and again in a manuscript miscellany (called *Welbeck* by Miss Gardner) probably made between 1620 and 1630, described by H. Harvey Wood in "A Seventeenth-Century Manuscript of Poems by Donne and Others," *Essays and Studies,* XVI (1931), 179–190. Mr. Wood's manuscript shows that Donne's poem was written in answer to "Mr. Tilman of Pembroke Hall in Cambridge his motives not to take orders," and Mr. Wood's subsequent findings have shown that Tilman's poem must have been written before December 20, 1618, when he was ordained deacon, and that Donne's answer was likely written shortly after that date or shortly after Tilman was ordained priest in March, 1620 ("Donne's 'Mr. Tilman': A Postscript," *TLS,* July 9, 1931, p. 547). But for his new evidence, we should have been justified in arguing, on the analogy of the infrequency of appearance in manuscript collections of the "Hymne," that "To Mr Tilman" was a late poem.

[23] Quoted in *The Divine Poems,* p. 134, where Miss Gardner convincingly suggests that the date is not that of the poem's occasion, but that of its reception by Sir Julius Caesar.

he used in dating Donne's Christmas letter in the 1635 *Poems* and in the 1640 *Life*. To transfer the date of the poem from 1623 to Donne's deathbed would corroborate as nothing else could Walton's statement that Donne did not forsake heavenly poetry, even in his declining age. Everything in Walton's biographic technique points to his using this date as he did others, to his utilization of chronology for his own purpose.

It was in 1670 that Walton first appended his own elegy to the *Life*, and at this time he added the dramatic but probably fictitious date of composition. The facts of Donne's career as they appeared in the original version of the elegy were not changed. While Walton tempered his praise of Donne's early verses to the extent of saying that they contained *"Loves Philosophy"*[24] instead of "all Philosophie,"[25] he did not alter his reference to Donne's seeing the place of Christ's nativity. Nor did he, in this, his seventy-seventh year, alter the statement that his own years "haste to *Davids* seventy," though the years which he had formerly described as "sad" now became instead *"swift."*[26] He did, however, make numerous changes and improvements in his verse.

The *Life* of 1670 continues the process of revision which Walton began in 1658. He again raised Donne's stature by means of minor additions. Where Bishop Morton had first said that his love for Donne was "begot by our long friendship and familiarity,"[27] Walton now added, "and your merits."[28] To the words of the Earl of Somerset, testifying his affection for Donne, Walton added, *"doubt not my doing this, for I know the King loves you, and will not deny me."*[29] In 1658, Walton had dealt at great length with the friendship of Donne and George Herbert; by 1670, the charm and gentility of Herbert's mother and her regard for Donne were better

---

[24] *Lives*, 1670 (Donne), p. 86.   [25] *Poems, By J. D.*, 1633, p. 382.

[26] Two statements of Walton are interesting in this connection, as showing his conception of poetry with regard to the truthfulness and accuracy of its fact. In quoting Chudleigh's verses to corroborate his own statements about Donne's powerful preaching, he prefaced them with the comment, "a known truth though it be in verse" (*Donne*, 1658, p. 48). In Chapter I of the *Compleat Angler* (1653, pp. 22–23) he wrote before some verses, "And first, what *Dubartas* sayes of a fish called the *Sargus;* which (because none can express it better then he does) I shall give you in his own words, supposing it shall not have the less credit for being Verse, for he hath gathered this, and other observations out of Authors that have been great and industrious searchers into the secrets of nature."

[27] *Donne*, 1658, p. 28.   [28] *Lives*, 1670 (Donne), p. 24.   [29] *Ibid.*, p. 34.

known to him as a result of his preparation for the *Life of Herbert,* and he added "Lady *Magdalen Herbert*" to the list of Donne's friends who had put off mortality and could therefore not be recipients of his gift of a seal.[30] Content to refer to "our Saviour" in 1658,[31] Walton could rivet attention on Donne by the expedient of referring to "his and our Saviour."[32] Originally, Walton had demonstrated Sir Thomas Egerton's esteem for Donne by saying, "The Lord Chancellor then (at M. *Donnes* dismission) protesting, he thought him a Secretary fitter for a King then a Subject."[33] In 1670, he raised Donne's stature by telling even what Egerton did *not* say:

And though the *Lord Chancellor* did not at Mr. *Donnes* dismission, give him such a Commendation as the great Emperour *Charles* the fifth, did of his Secretary *Eraso,* when he presented him to his Son and Successor *Philip* the Second; saying, *That in his* Eraso, *he gave to him a greater gift then all his Estate, and all the Kingdomes which he then resigned to him:* yet he said, *He parted with a Friend, and such a Secretary as was fitter to serve a King then a subject.*[34]

By 1670, then, Walton's technique had developed to a point where he could enhance the prestige of Donne not only by telling who of his friends had *not* received his seal, but also by relating what was *not* said of him, and even by explicitly stating that Christ was his Saviour and ours. Walton had come a long way from his original insistence on Donne's high place.

He continued also to heighten the religious feeling in the *Life.* A pronominal reference to Christ[35] became *"the God of glorie,"*[36] and Donne was made to add to his statement that his fortune was very low,[37] "as God knows it was."[38] To his account of Donne's great illness in 1623, Walton added that "it continued long and threatned him with death; which he dreaded not."[39] In 1670, Walton deepened the darkness of Donne's situation at Mitcham by his excerpts from the correspondence; correlatively he increased the fervor of Donne's religious study there. He particularized Donne's preoccupation with "some Points of Controversie"[40] by stating that these were "betwixt the *English* and *Roman Church*," and, foreshadowing his account

---

[30] *Ibid.,* p. 56.   [31] *Donne,* 1658, p. 112.   [32] *Lives,* 1670 (Donne), p. 75
[33] *Donne,* 1640, sig. A6ᵛ.   [34] *Lives,* 1670 (Donne), p. 19.
[35] *Donne,* 1658, p. 29.   [36] *Lives,* 1670 (Donne), p. 25.
[37] *Donne,* 1658, p. 107.   [38] *Lives,* 1670 (Donne), p. 73.
[39] *Ibid.,* p. 49.   [40] *Donne,* 1640, sig. Bʳ.

of the writing of *Pseudo-Martyr*, he suggested that their content was concerned with *"Supremacy* and *Allegiance."*[41] As he intensified the gloom at Mitcham, he further intensified Donne's devotion to religious matters, adding that "to that place and such studies he could willingly have wedded himself during his life."[42] And while formerly "the perswasion of friends"[43] caused him to leave Mitcham for London, in 1670 Donne's ecclesiastical tendencies more than balanced the blackness of his position, and the persuasion must be made "earnest"[44] before he would go to London.

Walton continued also to add minute, particularizing detail to authenticate his words, sometimes even needlessly, and to make changes to compensate for the passage of time. He added that Loseley and Pyrford were in Surrey.[45] In support of his statement that Donne, after taking orders, sought to preach privately in villages not far from London, he added, "his first Sermon being preached at *Paddington.*"[46] To his statement that the King appointed him to preach, he added the places where Donne had done so: "at *White-hall*"[47] and again "at St. *Paul*'s Cross, and other places."[48] The passage of time dictated slight alterations. Donne's surveying the body of divinity "as it is controverted betwixt the *Reformed* and the *Roman Church*"[49] was changed to "as it was then controverted. . . ."[50] The "then" used to describe Bishop Henry King's renown during the protectorate struggle was deleted, but the "now Bishop of *Chicester*"[51] became the "late Bishop . . ."[52] In 1658, Walton had listed Dr. Hall, "the late deceased Bishop of *Norwich,*" as one of the recipients of Donne's rings;[53] in 1670, he added an ambiguous "then" to "late deceased,"[54] a "then" which does not make sense with regard to the bestowing of the rings, but which can be accounted for by Walton's having in mind the edition of 1658. Dr. Duppa and Dr. King, who in 1658 were "both now living,"[55] became "lately deceased."[56] Walton changed in 1670 the length of time which Donne lectured at Lincoln's Inn prior to going to Germany from three[57] to two years.[58] The condition of

[41] *Lives,* 1670 (Donne), p. 32.   [42] *Ibid.*   [43] *Donne,* 1640, sig. Bʳ.
[44] *Lives,* 1670 (Donne), p. 32.   [45] *Ibid.,* pp. 17, 22.   [46] *Ibid.,* p. 38.
[47] *Ibid.*   [48] *Ibid.,* p. 47.   [49] *Donne,* 1658, p. 10.
[50] *Lives,* 1670 (Donne), p. 15.   [51] *Donne,* 1658, p. 68.
[52] *Lives,* 1670 (Donne), p. 49.   [53] *Donne,* 1658, p. 81.
[54] *Lives,* 1670 (Donne), p. 57.   [55] *Donne,* 1658, p. 81.
[56] *Lives,* 1670 (Donne), p. 57.   [57] *Donne,* 1640, sig. B2ᵛ.
[58] *Lives,* 1670 (Donne), p. 44. Here is another example of Walton's difficulty

the Church of England had been radically altered between 1658 and 1670, and Walton added the date 1656,[59] the year which marked Cromwell's severest strictures against the Episcopal Church,[60] to explain his exclamation, "But now, oh Lord."

Other additions in 1670 are foreshadowed by Walton's tendency in 1658 to state explicitly what, because of previous narration and exposition, was obvious by implication. Walton's habit of controlling and shaping his material at every point has perhaps been adequately demonstrated. In 1658, however, he accentuated the process of taking nothing for granted, of providing connections and

---

with the exact chronology of Donne's life. Donne was made Reader in Divinity at Lincoln's Inn in October, 1616, and accompanied Lord Doncaster to Germany in May, 1619 (Gosse, II, 91, 128).

[59] *Lives*, 1670 (Donne), p. 56.

[60] The conspiracies of 1654 and 1655 led to Cromwell's treating the royalists as a class apart from the body of the nation. On Sept. 21, 1655, a body of "Orders of the Protector and Council for securing the peace of the Commonwealth" was adopted, containing exactions not only against the royalists but also against their clergy (*Cal. State Papers, Domestic Series, 1655*, pp. 346–347). No immediate action was taken to enforce these orders, but on Nov. 24, 1655, Cromwell issued a declaration requiring the enforcement of the provisions concerning the clergy from Jan. 1, 1656 (see S. R. Gardiner, *History of the Commonwealth and Protectorate, 1649–1656* [London, 1903], III, 334–335). Gardiner found no evidence that enforcement was pressed and no reports alluding to the ejection of clergy from private houses (*ibid.*, p. 336). How heavily, however, the strictures lay on royalist shoulders may be seen in the following entries in Evelyn's *Diary*, and it is understandable that Walton should single out the year 1656 as a black one.

"*25th [December* 1655]. There was no more notice taken of Christmas-day in churches.

"I went to London, where Dr. Wild preached the funeral sermon of Preaching, this being the last day; after which, Cromwell's proclamation was to take place, that none of the Church of England should dare either to preach, or administer Sacraments, teach schools, &c., on pain of imprisonment, or exile. So this was the mournfullest day that in my life I had seen, or the Church of England herself, since the Reformation; to the great rejoicing of both Papist and Presbyter. So pathetic was his discourse, that it drew many tears from the auditory. Myself, wife, and some of our family, received the Communion; God make me thankful, who hath hitherto provided for us the food of our souls as well as bodies! The Lord Jesus pity our distressed Church, and bring back the captivity of Zion!

"*3rd August* [1656]. I went to London, to receive the Blessed Sacrament, the first time the Church of England was reduced to a chamber and conventicle; so sharp was the persecution" (*Diary of John Evelyn* [Everyman's Library], I, 313–314, 320. Gardiner suggests that the second paragraph should be dated Dec. 30, 1655, saying that Dr. Wilde would not have missed the opportunity of meeting his congregation on that date, the last Sunday of the year [*op. cit.*, III, 335]).

conclusions for even the minutest of ellipses, of making doubly
sure that the reader would never even slightly misinterpret his
words. Originally, Walton had written that Donne desired an employment which might "fixe" him in London.[61] In 1658, he increasingly showed Donne's impoverishment, but he added to his
statement that an employment would be welcome, "for he needed
it."[62] Originally he had written, too, that Dr. Harsnett, vice-
chancellor of Cambridge, "knowing him to be the Author of the
Pseudo-Martyr, did propose it [that Donne be made Doctor in
Divinity] to the University."[63] In 1658, he added that Harsnett
"required no other proof of his abilities."[64] In 1670, he added "that
learned Book" before *"Pseudo-Martyr."*[65] The first of these additions was previously obvious by implication; the second was obvious
because of Walton's previous discussion of the book.

This habit of stating explicitly what might normally be taken
for granted was not only an outgrowth of Walton's care in creating
a precise impression, but another manifestation of his love for
double expression, his admiration of paired adjectives and paired
nouns. "High illuminations"[66] became in 1670 "high raptures and
illuminations";[67] "hath raised"[68] became "hath Comforted and
raised."[69] The original "the mercies of my God"[70] was changed in
1658 to "the goodnesse of God,"[71] and this became in 1670 "the
providence and goodness of God."[72] When Walton changed in 1670
the ungainly phrase "a complacency in his conversation"[73] to "a
great pleasure . . . ,"[74] he could not resist the opportunity to
produce a pair, and "conversation" was coupled with "discourse."
At times he used this tendency toward word-extravagance for
rhetorical effect. Originally he had been satisfied with the alliteration in "a holy and harmlesse conversation";[75] in 1658 the phrase
became "a contemplative, an harmlesse, and an holy life and conversation";[76] in 1670, "a contemplative, a harmless, an humble
and an holy life and conversation."[77] He had written in 1640 of

[61] *Donne,* 1640, sig. B2ᵛ.
[62] *Donne,* 1658, p. 51.
[63] *Donne,* 1640, sig. B2ʳ.
[64] *Donne,* 1658, p. 50.
[65] *Lives,* 1670 (Donne), p. 40.
[66] *Donne,* 1640, sig. B4ʳ.
[67] *Lives,* 1670 (Donne), pp. 60–61.
[68] *Donne,* 1658, p. 81.
[69] *Lives,* 1670 (Donne), p. 57.
[70] *Donne,* 1640, sig. B6ʳ.
[71] *Donne,* 1658, p. 107.
[72] *Lives,* 1670 (Donne), p. 72.
[73] *Donne,* 1658, p. 58.
[74] *Lives,* 1670 (Donne), p. 44.
[75] *Donne,* 1640, sig. B2ᵛ.
[76] *Donne,* 1658, p. 57.
[77] *Lives,* 1670 (Donne), p. 43.

Donne's *"active body, which once was a Temple of the holy Ghost"*;[78] now he inserted *"that body"* before the relative.[79] But the tendency toward extravagance was more than a rhetorical idiosyncrasy; it was expressive of a state of mind. This superfluity of expression, this insistence that nothing be taken for granted, is copiously in evidence in 1670. Walton had written that Bishop Morton was "one that in his dayes of plenty used his large Revenue to the encouragement of *Learning* and *Vertue"*;[80] he must add that Morton "had so large a heart as to use his large Revenue" thus.[81] He had had Morton conclude his offer to Donne with the words, "Make me no present answer; but remember your promise, and return to me the third day with your resolution," and he had said of Donne that "he departed without returning an answer till the third day."[82] He added in 1670 that Donne "performed his promise and departed. . . ."[83] Donne had prefaced his answer to Morton with the remark that he had "an heart full of humility and thanks, though I may not accept of your offer,"[84] but Walton in 1670 added as the last words of the speech, the whole of which is a grateful refusal, "and thankfully decline your offer."[85] In 1658, the King, impressed by Donne's "clear and satisfactory" reply to accusations of infidelity, had dismissed him, called some Lords into his chamber, and said, *"My Doctor is an honest man: and my Lords, I was never better satisfied with an answer."*[86] Walton must add *"then he hath now made me."*[87] Henry King had introduced his offer of a church lease to Donne with the words, "Mr. *Dean*, I am by your favour no stranger to your temporal estate," and had concluded, "I beseech you to accept of my offer, for I know it will be a considerable addition to your present estate."[88] The reader also, by Walton's favor, is no stranger to Donne's estate, but Walton tagged King's words with the clause, "which I know needs it."[89] In the same way, Donne had made abundantly clear his refusal of the offer so long as he was on his sickbed; Walton added to his speech in 1670, "but it [the estate] shall not be augmented on my sick-bed."[90] Walton had described Donne, posing for his monument, as dressed in a winding-

[78] *Donne*, 1640, sig. C^r.
[80] *Donne*, 1658, p. 26.
[82] *Donne*, 1658, pp. 29–30.
[84] *Donne*, 1658, p. 30.
[86] *Donne*, 1658, pp. 66–67.
[88] *Donne*, 1658, pp. 68–69.
[90] *Ibid.*, p. 51.

[79] *Lives*, 1670 (Donne), p. 81.
[81] *Lives*, 1670 (Donne), p. 23.
[83] *Lives*, 1670 (Donne), p. 25.
[85] *Lives*, 1670 (Donne), p. 27.
[87] *Lives*, 1670 (Donne), p. 49.
[89] *Lives*, 1670 (Donne), p. 50.

sheet "and his hands so placed as dead bodies are usually fitted for the grave";[91] he made the obvious doubly so in saying, "as dead bodies are usually fitted to be shrowded and put into the grave."[92] Even the lines that he additionally quoted in 1670 from Chudleigh's poem, *"How did his sacred flattery beguile/ Men to amend?"* explicitly stated what the other lines already sufficiently implied.[93]

This tendency toward expressing explicitly what were the minutest of ellipses, of doubling the expression where an inevitable impression had already been adequately provided for, almost descended from redundancy to garrulity. In 1658, Walton prefaced Donne's poem to Herbert with its title, and he added as a prose continuation Donne's opening couplet ("A sheafe of Snakes . . ."), which the printer of *Poems, By J. D.,* 1650, had used as a motto or title for the poem: "To Mr. *George Herbert,* with one of my Seales of the *Anchor* and *Crest,* A sheafe of Snakes used heretofore to be my Seal, the Crest of our poor Family."[94] It is unlikely that Walton recognized, even in 1670 when he parenthesized the words following Donne's title, that he was dealing with two lines of verse, and his tendency to supply all the links, to make all the connections obvious, made him insert "which is" before the appositive "the Crest."[95] Walton had said in 1658, slightly changing his words of 1640, that even "in the most unsetled days of his youth" Donne "was employed in study" from four in the morning until past ten, pointing out as proof the "visible fruits of his labours."[96] "Unsetled" was as strong a word as Walton had used in his effort to gloss over Donne's adventurous youth. In 1670, he inserted after "All which time was employed in study" an expansion of the idea of "unsetled," "though he took great liberty after it."[97] His inclination to overexpress here led to the introduction of an almost alien note into Donne's life.

The revision of 1670 additionally demonstrates Walton's complete grasp of his materials. Here is an intensification of the process

---

[91] *Donne,* 1658, p. 112.   [92] *Lives,* 1670 (Donne), p. 75.

[93] *Ibid.,* p. 39.

[94] *Donne,* 1658, p. 83. *"Crest"* is probably a printer's error. Corrected in 1670 to *"Christ."*

[95] *Lives,* 1670 (Donne), p. 58. Here is another instance of Walton's small knowledge of Latin. He was obviously influenced by the typographical peculiarities inserted by the printer, when a glance at the Latin equivalent of the two lines, printed on the opposite page, would have told him that they were an integral part of the poem.

[96] *Donne,* 1658, pp. 87–88.   [97] *Lives,* 1670 (Donne), p. 62.

of producing a specific effect by the selection and manipulation of details, of producing a slight change of attitude by an additional phrase. Here, too, is the manifestation of an overzealousness in controlling material even to the minutest impressions it might make. Here is subjectivity stretched almost to the breaking point.

Chapter 4

The Third Revision – 1675

A SECOND edition of the four lives written by Walton was printed in 1675, and the commendatory verses by Charles Cotton, which first appeared with this edition, are a demonstration of the esteem in which the author and the *Lives* were held. In 1670, Walton had written in his dedicatory epistle to George Morley, Bishop of Winchester:

If I had been fit for this Undertaking, it would not have been by acquir'd Learning or Study, but by the advantage of forty years friendship, and thereby the hearing of and discoursing with your Lordship, which hath inabled me to make the relation of these Lives passable in an eloquent and captious age.[1]

Here is certainly modesty enough, but in 1675 Walton thought that even *"passable"* was unbecoming self-praise, and he inserted a parenthesis, "if they prove so."[2] The modesty which Walton professed is here carried to its ultimate climax. This passage in revelatory of Walton in another respect. In addition to showing what extremes he went to in producing an exact impression, it shows him disdainful of accuracy where time is concerned. He thought it worth revising the passage to enhance the note of modesty; he did not bother to change *"forty years friendship"* to forty-five.

Forty-four years had passed since Donne's death; thirty-five since Walton had written the original version of the *Life*. For the fourth edition of the *Life of Donne,* Walton had no new information, but a new edition was an opportunity for further changes and additions. This opportunity, the lapse of time since Donne's death, and Wal-

[1] *Lives,* 1670, sigs. $A3^v$–$A4^r$.

[2] *Ibid.,* 1675, sig. $A3^v$.

ton's own inclination emboldened him to relate in 1675 three apocryphal stories about Donne and to include a meditation inspired by a motto used by the youthful Donne.

The major addition to the *Life* of 1675, inserted after the details of Donne's residence in London, is the relation of his vision of his wife, *"her hair hanging about her shoulders, and a dead child in her arms."*[3] Walton gives the source of the story in one of many attempts to add to its validity. It was told to him not by Donne but *"(now long since)* by a Person of Honour, and of such intimacy with him, that he knew more of the secrets of his soul, then any person then living. . . ."[4] But Walton clouded his authority in the very same sentence, which continues, "and I think they told me the truth."

For an indication of what such a vision meant to Walton and also for a conjecture as to the identity of Walton's "Person of Honour," it is well to examine a passage in the *Life of Wotton* where Walton reveals at some length his interest in dreams and visions. In narrating Sir Henry Wotton's career at Oxford, Walton mentioned the death of his father, Thomas Wotton, and stated his wish to relate "a Circumstance or two concerning him."[5] He then digressed to the extent of relating the dream that Nicholas Wotton, Dean of Canterbury, had in 1553 about his nephew, Thomas Wotton. He went on to relate a dream of Thomas Wotton's and to tell that both Nicholas and Thomas Wotton predicted the days of their deaths. That Walton had deliberated at some length on various types of revelations is evident in his discussion of Nicholas Wotton's dream, where he imparted his own knowledge to the good Dean. The Dean knew, Walton said, that *"Dreams,* (common Dreams, that usually look the same way that our over-engaged affections, or the particular business of the day do incline us, and so are but a paraphrase on our waking thoughts) may be superstitiously considered."[6] Yet, the Dean did not disregard his dream entirely. When he had had the same dream a second time it became truly significant, for it was then a "doubled Dream, like that of *Pharaoh."* He remembered that God had revealed to Monica the conversion of her son, St. Augustine, and that God "hath even in these later times, by a certain *illumination* of the soul in sleep, discovered many things that humane wisdom could not fore-see."[7] Walton believed

---

[3] *Ibid.*, p. 30.   [4] *Ibid.*, p. 32.   [5] *Reliq.*, 1651, sig. b5ᵛ.
[6] *Ibid.*   [7] *Ibid.*, sig. b6ʳ.

that God tied himself to no rules, "either in preventing of evill, or in shewing of mercy to those, whom of his good pleasure he hath chosen to love,"[8] and he felt that the Wotton family, because of their visions, were beloved of God.[9]

It is significant that Walton, relating Donne's vision, represented it, also, as a kind of double dream.[10] He mentioned before the vision Mrs. Donne's ill health and pregnancy and her disinclination that Donne leave her, but in his desire to make Donne's dream a true vision, he neglected to introduce the possibility that it had dependence in his waking thoughts. In his argument defending the plausibility of visions, Walton mentioned, as he did in the *Life of Wotton,* Monica's dream. For Walton, the entire incident was an illustration of God's love for Donne even before he had taken orders. It was no mean and common thing that Walton was here attributing to Donne, and the nature of the incident and the awesomeness of its meaning probably detained its inclusion until 1675.

Walton stated that the story of the vision was long known to him, and he found a corollary for it in two of Donne's poems. In mustering authority to support Donne's vision, Walton argued analogously for the doctrine of sympathy of souls by pointing to the sympathetic vibration of two lutes, and this doctrine he found coupled with the theme of parting in "A Valediction: Forbidding Mourning" and in the song "Sweetest love, I do not go." There is reason to suppose that this valediction had long been a favorite of Walton's and that he had associated it with Mrs. Donne. Walton's habit of retaining a phrase or a word from his source has already been suggested. It is perhaps not too far-fetched to suggest that in relating the death of Mrs. Donne he had in his mind Donne's lines:

> Dull sublunary lovers' love
> > Whose soul is sense, cannot admit
> > Absence, because it doth remove
> > > Those things which elemented it.

In 1640, he had written of Donne's burying all his "sublunary" joys,[11] and when in 1658 he replaced "sublunary" with "earthly," he wrote of Donne that "now his very soul was elemented of nothing

---

[8] *Ibid.,* sig. b6ᵛ.　　　　　　　　[9] *Ibid.,* 1672, sig. b5ᵛ.

[10] Donne speaks of *"a dreadful Vision,"* but he says, *"I have seen my dear wife pass twice by me"* and *"at her second appearing, she stopt, and look'd me in the face, and vanisht"* (*Lives,* 1675, p. 30).

[11] *Donne,* 1640, sig. B2ᵛ.

but sadness."[12] In 1675, he quoted the poem in its entirety after the vision, saying that Donne gave it to his wife when he parted from her. It would appear that he quoted from memory, for his title, "A Valediction, forbidding to Mourn" is unique, and one-third of the poem's thirty-six lines have unique readings. The words which he attributed to Mrs. Donne, *"her divining soul boded her some ill in his absence,"*[13] were undoubtedly suggested by lines from "Sweetest love, I do not go":

> Let not thy divining heart
> Forethinke me any ill.

Although Walton was probably long aware of the story of the vision and had established in his mind the propinquity of the two poems to this apparent revelation, the vision occurred in the secular rather than in the religious part of Donne's life. This cleavage Walton had emphasized in 1640. In the second and third editions of the *Life,* he not only heightened the religious coloring of the entire work, but in 1658 he added the incident of Morton's offer to demonstrate conclusively Donne's early ecclesiastical inclinations, and in 1670 he added to these tendencies by describing Donne's studies at Mitcham. Having thus more fully developed Donne's early predisposition to things religious, Walton, who was ever disposed to credit Donne with extreme piety, felt in 1675 that it would not be unfitting to attribute a spiritual revelation to a contemporary. Whatever qualms he may have had originally the passage of decades had dissolved. Even so, in 1675, though he granted his every reader the privilege of his own opinion with regard to visions, he reinforced this particular one with his statement of his source of information and with Donne's poem, and visions in general not only with the examples of the lutes and Monica but also with reference to Brutus, Saul, the Book of Job, and the Book of Acts.

Walton stated that his "Person of Honour" told him the story "with such circumstances, and such asseveration" that he was convinced that the teller believed it true.[14] The account in the *Life* is wonderful in its specificity. The reader is told that Lord Hay was sent on an embassy to the then French king, Henry IV, that Sir Robert Drury suddenly resolved to accompany him, and that he solicited Donne to make the journey. To make Drury's request more binding on Donne, Walton, who had originally said that Drury

[12] *Donne,* 1658, pp. 52–53.   [13] *Lives,* 1675, p. 29.   [14] *Ibid.,* p. 32.

assigned Donne "a very convenient house rent-free, next his own in Drury-lane,"[15] and had in 1658 changed this to "a very choice and usefull house,"[16] now had Drury move him into "an useful apartment in his own large house in *Drewry lane.*"[17] Walton feelingly described Mrs. Donne's foreboding. His chronology of the journey was minute and particular. The journey was to take two months; the trip to Paris took twelve days; the vision occurred half an hour after dinner on the fourteenth day; the next day Drury sent a messenger to investigate Mrs. Donne's health; twelve days later the messenger returned with the information that Mrs. Donne's abortion occurred about the very same hour of the same day that Donne had his vision. The exactness of the time sequence, the precision of the detail, point to a minute knowledge of the facts.

But what are the facts? Perhaps Drury's resolution to visit France was sudden, but he was granted a license to travel on July 2, 1611, and he did not leave England until the end of November.[18] Henry IV was assassinated May 14, 1610. Lord Hay was appointed ambassador extraordinary to Paris in July, 1616. Perhaps Donne told his wife that he would be gone for two months, but it was not until the end of July, 1612, that he wrote from the continent to say that he hoped to be in London about the end of August.[19] Walton has Donne in Paris twelve days after his departure from London; the vision and abortion occur two days later; Donne was told of the tragedy and the vision was thereby corroborated within a month after he had left England. In fact, Mrs. Donne was delivered of a stillborn child two months after Donne's departure, in January, 1612. She was with her sister, Lady Oglander, on the Isle of Wight and, since there was no regular post between the island and London, had been unable to communicate with her husband.[20] At the time of her delivery, Donne was still in Amiens with Drury

---

[15] *Donne,* 1640, sig. B[r].   [16] *Donne,* 1658, p. 36.   [17] *Lives,* 1675, p. 28.

[18] See R. E. Bennett, "Donne's Letters from the Continent in 1611–12," *PQ,* XIX (1940), 67–68. I am greatly indebted to Bennett's fine article. By mustering the facts and making clear the way through Donne's correspondence from the continent, he shows the element of fiction in Walton's story of the vision. I depart from his account only in taking Walton more literally than he does when Walton says that he heard of the vision *"now long since."* Bennett does not concern himself with the significance of the vision to Walton or with his purpose in relating it, and he merely hazards the guess that Walton repeated and perhaps elaborated a good story which he did not hear until half a century or more after the events had taken place.

[19] *Letters to Severall Persons,* p. 92.   [20] Bennett, *op. cit.,* pp. 77–78.

and, from there, on February 7 (N.S.), he wrote one of his brothers-in-law, probably Sir Robert More,

When there is any way open to you to send unto Wight, I may give this letter a passage. If one could not get to that isle but by north-west discovery, I could not think the returns so difficult and dilatory, for yet I have no return from thence of any letter since my coming out of England, and this silence, especially at this time when I make account that your sister is near her painful and dangerous passage, doth somewhat more affect me than I had thought anything of this world could have done.[21]

It was probably March before Donne arrived in Paris, and at the beginning of April he still had no news about his wife. On April 9 (N.S.), he wrote Goodere from Paris that he had not received some of Goodere's letters: "I am sure I never lost any thing with more sorrow, because I am thereby left still in uncertainties, and irresolutions, of that which I desire much to know in womens businesses."[22] Later in the same week, he wrote Goodere again, saying, "I am yet in the same perplexity, which I mentioned before; which is, that I have received no syllable, neither from her self, nor by any other, how my wife hath passed her danger, nor do I know whether I be increased by a childe, or diminished by the losse of a wife."[23]

It is possible that in the many years which had passed since he had heard of Donne's vision, Walton would have forgotten the precise details. His own artistry would lead him to supply his own particulars, for they were necessary to produce a vivid and convincing episode. But there is nothing explicit in Donne's letters written from France to suggest the vision as Walton described it. Indeed, we have seen that Donne was perplexed and worried even four months after his departure from England because he had heard nothing of his wife. A vision and its prompt corroboration would have precluded the expressions of concern which are present in Donne's letters as late as April.

It is improbable that Walton trumped up the whole affair. It is more than likely that he heard about the revelations in the Wotton family from Sir Henry himself, and it is equally probable that the "Person of Honour" who related Donne's vision to him was also

---

[21] Gosse, I, 289.   [22] *Letters to Severall Persons*, pp. 127–134.
[23] *Ibid.*, p. 74. I. A. Shapiro, in "The Text of Donne's *Letters to Severall Persons*," *RES*, VII (1931), 300–301, holds that this letter is to Goodere and can be dated April 3/13, 1612. See, too, Bennett, *op. cit.*, pp. 71–72.

Sir Henry. To Walton, Wotton would well have been "of such intimacy with him [Donne], that he knew more of the secrets of his soul, then any person then living." In the first paragraph of the first version of the *Life of Donne,* Walton had written that a life of Donne was a work worthy of Wotton's efforts "and he fit to undertake it; betwixt whom and our Author [of the *LXXX Sermons*], there was such a friendship contracted in their youths, that nothing but death could force the separation." This description of Wotton certainly fits Walton's description of the "Person of Honour" who told him of Donne's vision. Gosse questioned Walton's account of the intimacy of the friendship between Donne and Wotton,[24] and, to be sure, Walton nowhere establishes the closeness of the relation between Wotton and Donne except by his statements that they were friends of Oxford and that Donne wrote a verse letter to Wotton prior to Wotton's going ambassador to Venice. Walton seems to have lacked the specific evidence necessary to prove the intimacy of Wotton and Donne, but he tried hard to persuade his readers of their intimacy. It is probable that he received his own impression of their friendship from Wotton himself. Donne's verse letters to Wotton and the fact that as late as 1623 Wotton sent a cipher from Venice to be forwarded to Donne in order to facilitate their correspondence[25] make it likely that Walton was somewhat nearer the truth than Gosse.

None of Donne's letters from the continent to Wotton survive. But on April 2/12, 1612, Donne received in Paris a packet of letters sent him from Amiens by Wotton, including a letter written by Wotton himself.[26] Wotton was on his way to Turin as a special ambassador to explore the possibilities of an alliance with the House of Savoy through a royal marriage.[27] Prior to receiving Wotton's letter, Donne had been informed generally of Wotton's embassy, either by Wotton himself or by Sir Robert Rich. Rich was one of several noblemen accompanying Wotton, and that he had com-

[24] *Gosse,* II, 314–316.

[25] See Wotton's letter to Sir Albertus Morton in Logan Pearsall Smith, *The Life and Letters of Sir Henry Wotton* (Oxford, 1907), II, 264–265.

[26] In his letter to Goodere referred to in note 23, Donne mentions "Letters that I received from Sir *H. Wotton* yesterday from *Amyens.*" In his letter to Garrard probably written April 4/14 (*Letters to Severall Persons,* pp. 253–257), Donne makes it clear that he has had a letter from Wotton himself. He tells Garrard that he received Garrard's letters of March 7 and 8 "in a letter which Sir *H. Wotton* writ to me from *Amyens.*"

[27] Smith, I, 113–123.

municated with Donne is clear from Donne's letter of April 9 (N.S.) to Goodere. Here Donne tells Goodere that he expects to be "at *Frankford* the 25 of *May,* when the election of the Emperor shall be there," and he says, "Sir *Rob. Rich* gave me his [promise], that he would divert from his way to *Italy* so much, as to be there then."[28] Before Donne had received Wotton's letter on April 2/12, then, he had thought that Wotton and Rich planned to visit Frankfort on their way to Italy. Directly after he had received Wotton's letter, he wrote Goodere again: "Presently after Easter we shall (I think) go to *Frankford* to be there at the election, where we shall meet Sir *H. Wotton* and Sir *Ro. Rich.*"[29] By this time Donne would have known from Wotton's letter that Wotton was proceeding directly to Italy. His confidence that he would see Wotton and Rich at Frankfort must come from having been informed more precisely of their itinerary; he expects to see them on their return from Italy.[30] It is possible that Donne, made newly certain of Wotton's plans, directed a letter to him at Turin, and if he did so, it is likely that he mentioned to Wotton the same worry and foreboding that he expressed to Goodere at this time. Or it is possible that Donne told Wotton of his long perplexity and final misfortune after both of them had returned to England.

To what degree of premonition did Wotton raise Donne's anxiety when he related his information to Walton some years later? Speculation here is fruitless, but that Wotton took delight in such

[28] *Letters to Severall Persons,* p. 133. Donne saw Rich in Amiens some time after the middle of January or in February. (Donne wrote Garrard, "The first of this moneth I received a Letter from you. . . . I presume, Mr *Pore,* and since, Sir *Rob. Rich* came after the writing of that Letter [*ibid.,* p. 246]. John Pory was in Amiens on or shortly before Jan. 7/17 [*ibid.,* p. 126]. Rich arrived later, probably after Jan. 14/24, when Donne wrote to Goodere without mentioning his presence [*ibid.,* pp. 120–127; for date, see Shapiro, *op. cit.,* pp. 294–296, and Bennett, *op. cit.,* p. 68, n. 16]. Donne's letter to Garrard was written after February 1, but before March 1 [see Bennett, *op. cit.,* pp. 68–70, n. 17 and 24].) Rich's promise may have been made then or by a letter written before March 28 / April 7, when he was at Amiens with Wotton (Smith, II, 1–2).

[29] *Letters to Severall Persons,* p. 75.

[30] Donne's expectations were disappointed. Rich stayed in Turin for about two weeks and suddenly returned to England (see Smith, II, 2, n. 1). Wotton visited Frankfort on his return from Italy (*ibid.,* I, 123), but probably got there after Donne had departed. After Donne had left Frankfort, he wrote from Spa on July 16/26, 1612, that he had just been told by Lady Worcester that Rich had returned to England (*Letters to Severall Persons,* p. 92). Had he met Wotton at Frankfort, he would already have known of this.

episodes is evident in his relation of the dreams of his own ancestors
to Walton. Nor would Walton himself have required an account
conforming in every respect to his conception of a true vision. Even
the hint of some slight coincidence would have been enough for
him to elaborate it into a vision, especially in view of the expression of the doctrine of sympathy of souls which he found in Donne's
poetry and of his progressively developing, in the later editions of
the *Life,* Donne's early religious bent. Walton's account of the vision demonstrates Donne's inherently holy nature more feelingly
and more vividly than even his account of Morton's offer. If he
injected drama into the information given him by Morton, he
injected both drama and imagination into that given him by Wotton. Here his artfulness reached its highest point, and he molded
from the most tenuous of circumstances the most striking passage
in the *Life.*

In 1675, Walton inserted the punning close of Donne's letter to
his wife, *"John Donne, Anne Donne, Un-done,"* informing her
that he had been dismissed by Sir Thomas Egerton.[31] The words are
used to foreshadow the misery resulting from the marriage, and
Walton commented on them, "God knows it proved too true." Also,
to increase the many honors paid to Donne at his death, he added
a eulogistic stanza written with a coal on the wall over Donne's
grave.[32] The source of these details is a puzzle, but they again demonstrate Walton's ability to heighten an impression by a small
detail, to climax a mood in the relation of a short but vivid incident.
Possibly Walton took the liberty of inserting these stories though he
had only the merest whisper of a rumor of them. It would seem
that this had been the process in the inclusion of the vision. His
method can be noticed once more in the last major addition to the
1675 volume. In 1658, Walton had described Donne's last portrait.[33]
In 1675, he dramatically summarized the development and change
in Donne's life by his reference to the early portrait engraved by
Marshall for *Poems, By J. D.,* 1635. The engraving has on it the
motto, "Antes muerto que mudado." "Sooner dead than changed"
reflects the same show of bravery that does Donne's military cos-
tume in the picture, and Donne obviously did not consider that the
motto carried any religious overtones. Walton dismissed the cos-
tume by saying that Donne was portrayed "with his sword and what

[31] *Lives,* 1675, pp. 17–18.   [32] *Ibid.,* p. 77.
[33] *Donne,* 1658, pp. 110–113.

other adornments might then suit with the present fashions of youth, and, the giddy gayeties of that age."[34] There is no evidence that Walton knew Spanish, but his translation of the motto is ingenious and artful:

> *How much shall I be chang'd,*
> *Before I am chang'd.*

He elaborated on his translation by saying that a reader, comparing the two pictures of Donne, might say, *"Lord! How much may I also, that am now in health be chang'd, before I am chang'd? before this vile, this changeable body shall put off mortality?"* and he said that Donne often commented that his most blessed change was in entering spiritual employment. Walton turned the comparison of two pictures into a recapitulation of Donne's life. He turned an audacious motto of four words into a testimonial of Donne's inherent religiosity and even into a meditation on man's journey through life.

In this edition also, Walton continued to enhance the importance of Donne's place. The vision showed the intimacy of Drury and Donne, and Walton reflected the intimacy in the change of Donne's living quarters. To his statement that many of the nobility were solicitous to the King for some secular employment for Donne, Walton added "and others that were powerful at Court."[35] He had already said that many of the nobility and others used Donne "in their counsels of greatest considerations,"[36] but he added, "and with some rewards for his better subsistence,"[37] somewhat detracting from his picture of the meanness of Donne's fortune at Mitcham in his attempt to show that people in high places not only thought Donne's counsel worth while, but that they were evidently willing to pay for it. He had written that the Earl of Somerset had "sent" for Donne to come to him;[38] he dignified the episode by specifying that the Earl "posted a messenger" for Mr. Donne.[39] In the revisions of 1658 and 1670, Walton had been exceedingly subtle in these slight changes to raise the esteem in which Donne was held. By 1675 that esteem had been so thoroughly indicated that Walton could dispense with his customary careful indirection and say, "for who speaks like him,"[40] after his statement that Donne's speech forsook

---

[34] *Lives,* 1675, p. 74. [35] *Ibid.,* p. 34. [36] *Donne,* 1640, sig. Bʳ.
[37] *Lives,* 1675, p. 25. [38] *Donne,* 1658, p. 39. [39] *Lives,* 1675, p. 36.
[40] *Ibid.,* p. 76.

him only at the last minute of his life, not to serve another master.

Ever ready to enrich the religious overtones in the *Life,* Walton, in changing his account of Donne's irresolution of denomination, added a note completely lacking in Donne's own account in the preface of *Pseudo-Martyr,* for he described Donne as "considering how much it concern'd his soul to choose the most Orthodox [religion]."[41] To his statement that Donne would often say, "Blessed be God that he is God divinely like himself,"[42] he added, descriptive of Donne's manner, *"in a kind of sacred extasie."*[43] Again he took the opportunity to interpolate holy epithets, and he added a *"blessed Jesus"* at the point of Donne's taking orders,[44] and at his going to Germany added "who is the God of all wisdom and goodness"[45] to the clause, "But God turned it to the best."[46]

Even as the 1675 edition shows Walton taking the greatest liberty with facts, it also reveals him compensating for this freedom in his attempt to lend authenticity to the *Life* by the insertion of five dates. Walton's manipulation of dates, his very invention of them, is ample evidence that he was fully aware of their value in lending an air of trustworthiness to a life, and it is no mere coincidence that he should lean heavily on them in the revision in which he was utilizing material of doubtful credibility. Possibly from his reexamination of Marshall's engraving in connection with the motto, Walton settled upon 1573 as the year of Donne's birth,[47] for the portrait bears the legend, "Anno D[omi]ni 1591. Aetatis suae. 18." Walton wished to include the date of Donne's birth for the authenticity it would add to the *Life.* It is even possible that he considered for a moment some revision of his dating of events, for in the third paragraph of the *Life* he added one year to the age at which Donne entered Oxford.[48] Still, he did not bother to change his references to Donne's fourteenth, seventeenth, and eighteenth years. When in 1675 he first gave the dates of Donne's voyages to Cadiz and to the Azores (1596 and 1597), he saw that he must alter Donne's age, which his previous chronology had placed at about twenty, but his only concession was to add several *about*'s to his

[41] *Ibid.,* p. 13.   [42] *Donne,* 1658, p. 121.   [43] *Lives,* 1675, p. 78.
[44] *Ibid.,* p. 38.   [45] *Ibid.,* p. 45.   [46] *Donne,* 1640, sig. B2v.
[47] For a summary of the evidence that Donne was born after Jan. 23 and before June 19, 1572, see I. A. Shapiro, "Donne's Birthdate," *N&Q,* CXCVII (July, 1952), 310–313.
[48] *Lives,* 1675, p. 11: "in his eleventh year"; *Donne,* 1658, p. 6: "in his tenth year."

text.[49] He may have thought about revising Donne's age in accordance with the date which he now printed, but he made no pertinent changes. The dates of the voyages only further confused his chronology, though he probably hoped that the inclusion of such documentation would convince his reader of his precise knowledge. The dates were easily accessible to him, as was the date for the printing of *Pseudo-Martyr*, which he also here included for the first time.[50] In this edition, too, he specified that he was referring to the year 1648 in his remarks preliminary to his account of Morton's offer.[51] Here also, some thirty-five years after he had written the original *Life*, he added the precise day of its completion, "*Feb.* 15. 1639[40]."[52]

It will be remembered that Walton, overcareful that his words communicated an exact impression, often appended in 1670 a phrase made redundant by an abundantly clear previous statement and that this inclination toward overexpression was in a way related to his delight in paired words. Even as he had changed his description of Donne, dressed in a winding-sheet "and his hands so placed as dead bodies are usually fitted for the grave" to "as dead bodies are usually fitted to be shrowded and put into the grave," so, in 1675, he wrote "as dead bodies are usually fitted to be shrowded and put into their Coffin, or grave."[53] He changed "survey"[54] to "seriously to survey, and consider";[55] he had said that Donne had written *Pseudo-Martyr* within six weeks,[56] but he added to the statement that he applied himself "diligently";[57] he had adequately indicated the smallness of Donne's income, but he replaced "unsetled estate"[58] with "narrow unsetled estate."[59] Again he occasionally used this tendency toward word-surplusage for rhetorical effect. In 1670, Walton had replaced a pronominal reference to the Lord by "*the God of glorie*";[60] in 1675, he added "*that God*" before the relative clause which followed.[61] This is a typical example—the indirect reference has given way not only to a direct

---

[49] "At his entrance into the nineteenth year of his age" (*Donne,* 1658, p. 10) became "About the nineteenth year of his age" (*Lives,* 1675, p. 13); "before he entred into the twentieth yeare of his age" (*Donne,* 1640, sig. A6r) became "about the twentieth year of his age" (*Lives,* 1675, p. 14); "The year following" (*Donne,* 1658, p. 12) became "About a year following" (*Lives,* 1675, p. 14).

[50] *Lives,* 1675, p. 35.   [51] *Ibid.,* p. 21.   [52] *Ibid.,* p. 79.

[53] *Ibid.,* p. 72.   [54] *Donne,* 1640, sig. A6r.   [55] *Lives,* 1675, p. 13.

[56] *Donne,* 1640, sig. Bv.   [57] *Lives,* 1675, p. 35.

[58] *Donne,* 1640, sig. B2v.   [59] *Lives,* 1675, p. 41.

[60] *Ibid.,* 1670 (Donne), p. 25.   [61] *Ibid.,* 1675, p. 22.

one, but to a direct one twice expressed. Originally he had begun
a long but logical sentence with "Nor is it hard to thinke";[62] in
1675, he repeated the sentiment in the middle of the sentence.[63]
The clarity that Walton strove for was one not only completely
lacking in ambiguity or indefiniteness, but one that left nothing to
be imagined by the reader, not a thought, not a word. He had
written that the story of Donne's marriage was purposely rumored
"that preapprehensions might make it the less enormous."[64] The
meaning appears perfectly clear. Walton must add, "when it was
known."[65] He had written, "yea even on his former sick bed, he
wrote this heavenly Hymne, expressing the great joy he then had in
the assurance of Gods mercy to him."[66] The "then" rather over-
emphasizes the time element and might almost be considered superfluous, but in 1675 Walton redoubled his emphasis and added,
"when he Composed it."[67] He had already pointed up the first of
Donne's letters from Mitcham, changing Donne's "very much sad-
nesse"[68] to *"too great a sadness"*[69] and his "afflict her much"[70] to
"afflict her too extremely."[71] But having written that Donne did
not reply to a recent letter because it found him too sad, he felt
the need to be even more explicit and changed *"found"*[72] to *"then
found."*[73] In 1670, Walton, after explaining that Mrs. Donne was
distraught over the severe illness of one of her children, followed
Donne in stating that she would have been extremely indisposed
"but that the sickness of all her children stupifies her."[74] Again,
Walton must be doubly explicit, and he specified *"all her other
children."*[75] His description of the condition of the Anglican Church
under Cromwell had ended on a broken note of despair, "But now
oh Lord ——."[76] In 1670, he showed by a marginal note that "now"
referred to the year 1656.[77] In 1675, to make doubly sure that the
unfinished ejaculation of grief would be properly interpreted, to
make certain that his reader received precisely that impression
which he wished to express, he added, "how is that place become

---

[62] *Donne*, 1658, p. 52.   [63] *Lives*, 1675, p. 42.   [64] *Donne*, 1658, p. 17.
[65] *Lives*, 1675, p. 16.
[66] *Donne*, 1640, sig. B4ʳ. *Donne*, 1658, p. 76, reads, ". . . great joy that then
possest his soul in the Assurance of Gods favour to him."
[67] *Lives*, 1675, p. 53.   [68] *Letters to Severall Persons*, p. 151.
[69] *Lives*, 1670 (Donne), p. 29.   [70] *Letters to Severall Persons*, p. 152.
[71] *Lives*, 1670 (Donne), p. 29.   [72] *Ibid.*   [73] *Ibid.*, 1675, p. 25.
[74] *Ibid.*, 1670 (Donne), p. 29. The *"all"* is Walton's addition.
[75] *Ibid.*, 1675, p. 26.   [76] *Donne*, 1658, p. 79.
[77] *Lives*, 1670 (Donne), p. 56.

desolate."[78] Again, Walton had had Donne say that he *"was so far from fearing death (which is the King of terrours) that he longed for the day of his dissolution."*[79] But, in part from a desire to place Donne more strikingly in contrast to the generality of men and in part from a desire to remove any possible ambiguity resulting from Donne's referring to death as *"the King of terrours,"* Walton in 1675 added that death was *"the King of terrors" "to others."*[80]

This tendency of taking nothing for granted persisted even after the publication of the *Life* in 1675. The 1675 volume in the Albert H. Childs Memorial Collection at Yale University contains some notes and corrections in Walton's hand. In 1675, Walton had written in the episode of Donne's vision:

And, though 'tis most certain, that two Lutes, being both strung and tun'd to an equal pitch, and then, one plaid upon, the other, that is not totcht, being laid upon a Table at a fit distance, will (like an Eccho to a trumpet) warble a faint audible harmony, in answer to the same tune: yet many will not believe there is any such thing, as a *sympathy* of *souls*.[81]

Walton had explicitly said of the doctrine of sympathetic vibration that " 'tis most certain," but he was apprehensive lest the length of his illustration of the doctrine detract from his statement of its certainty. In the Yale volume he wrote before the colon in the passage above, in reiteration of the idea of certainty, "and tho this is not t[o] be dou[bted]."[82]

The fourth edition of the *Life of Donne* is notable in that Walton shows no signs of relaxing his hold on his material. If anything, it demonstrates a further intensification of his complete control, for he shaped every detail to create an exact impression, he explicitly expressed every ellipsis of thought or word where he had formerly laid the ground for an inevitable implication.

The *Life* of 1640 was Walton's first and crudest attempt at biographical writing. Though in length and in content it was conditioned by its function as a prefatory memoir, it is still a rather impressive achievement. It is not a typical hagiography, fuzzy with conventionalized holy detail. Its detail is particularized; the main

---

[78] *Ibid.,* 1675, p. 54.　　　　　[79] *Donne,* 1658, p. 110.
[80] *Lives,* 1675, p. 71.　　　　　[81] *Ibid.,* p. 31.
[82] There is in this volume another insertion somewhat later in the vision, which, unfortunately, is not completely readable. It is worth mentioning, however, in connection with Walton's tendency toward overexpression, for he made the addition "here [or] in the . . . of word[s] follow[ing]" directly after the statement "Upon which words I will make no Comment."

events in Donne's life are chronicled; it is obviously written by a
man who knows a good deal about his subject. The holy temper of
Donne is indicated, but the claims made for the sanctity of his life
are not extraordinary. Rather, the holiness is sketched with some
hesitancy, made to evolve from the careful structure.

By 1675, the *Life,* freed from the original restriction of space,
had doubled in length. Walton amplified and particularized his
original facts somewhat, but, in the thirty-five years that had passed
since his first version, he had not discovered any vast mine of information. The only new and important information made available to him was Morton's story that he had tried to induce Donne to
enter into orders in 1607 and that Donne had refused out of scruples
of his worthiness. But it is likely that this new fact, which revealed
Morton's respect and love for Donne, influenced the revisions of
the *Life* far out of proportion to its influence upon Donne's own
life.

Walton had mentioned in 1640 Donne's study of civil and canon
law. He had indicated that some of the nobility had used Donne in
their counsels of greatest considerations. He had told that Donne
had constantly studied at Mitcham some points of church controversy. He had summarized the content of *Pseudo-Martyr.* It is
possible that in 1640 Walton knew no more about Donne's study
and work between 1605 and 1611 than he related. It is impossible,
after he had talked with Morton, that he should not know more
about Donne's working for two years or more to help Morton mus-
ter arguments against the Roman Catholic position in the matter of
allegiance to the crown. Still, Walton never mentioned Donne's
activities in the book war; he never mentioned Donne's *Ignatius
his Conclave;* and he never mentioned, in his praise of Morton,
Morton's many influential argumentative writings in the first years
of James's rule. These omissions do not stem from ignorance, but
from Walton's great disapproval of church argument. Walton hated
controversies which further rent the garment of the Church, though
he did not suppress his partisanship even in his *Lives* and in his
fishing tract. Ironically enough, he was himself forced in his later
biographies to engage in controversy by indirection, and his last
major bit of writing was to be a controversial pamphlet. Still, wherever it was possible, he avoided the analysis of knotty arguments.
The greatest compliment he could pay to a participant in a book
war was not praise for his accomplishment in debate but for his

unwillingness to enter the lists and for his mild conduct once he had been forced into them. Walton would have admired Donne for lending a hand to church and crown, but it does not necessarily follow that he would relate Donne's part in detail. It would have been troublesome for him to explore the maze of old argument and unprofitable to do so at a time when Geneva was more dangerous than Rome. And he would have had little love for the satire in *Ignatius his Conclave.*

Walton's failure to exploit Donne's activities in church controversy by recounting them in detail does not mean, then, that he was unimpressed by them. The measure of the impression they made upon him is not in his failure to provide an account of them, but in the greater confidence with which he told the story of Donne's life as a sanctified one. After all, Walton had been told by Morton of Donne's labors for the Church at a time when the Church was in new and great danger. Walton had heard from an excluded bishop that Donne, in the secular part of his life, had spent two years or more working to preserve the Church. He had heard from a venerable bishop a tale which made him aware not only of Donne's labors, but also of his scruples when he was offered a reward for those labors. The passing years had made Walton familiar with churchmen whose faith was dictated by fashion and self-interest, with churchmen who did not scruple to accept even what they did not deserve. Morton's story corroborated Walton's opinion of Donne's holiness, set forth clearly but also a little timidly in 1640, and from 1658 on he added conviction to that opinion in the *Life.* The passage of time and the times themselves made Donne appear increasingly as a saint to him, and with every revision Donne approached closer to sainthood.

The revisions of the *Life of Donne* are a cumulative monument to Walton's veneration for Donne. In them he did not care to add to the factual material which would further show Donne's activities. He was not interested even in recounting Donne's accomplishments as a theologian and preacher. After 1640, the *Life* was published without Donne's sermons, but even after 1640 there is never a summary of theological argument, never an exposition of creed, never an illustrative passage from the sermons. The changes and additions reflect not only Walton's growing veneration for Donne, but also Walton's prime interest in biography. He saw the necessity for documentation, was aware of the importance of precise authoritative information. He knew that the hagiographic generalization produced at best only a generalized effect, and he provided more events and facts than the usual seventeenth-century biographer. But once he had determined these, he was content, on the whole, to build on them, not to add to them. He buttressed them, adding a date here, a name there, but only so that there was a firm basis for his departure from them. His additions were largely character-revealing anecdotes and incidents illustrative of character which retouched the colors of the original portrait and heightened them by one shadowing.

The *Life of Donne* of 1640 is not a conventional hagiography. The *Life of Donne* became Walton's closest approach to hagiography only with the changes of thirty-five years, and it became so only because Walton increasingly became convinced as the years passed of the great sanctity of Donne's life. That conviction his growing skill as a biographer made him capable of expressing. The careful original structure gracefully bore the weight of the later additions. In 1640, Walton shaped masses of material into a pattern of his choosing, and he ended by shaping every individual phrase. Originally he took some freedom in manipulating the details of unimpeachable sources. He never lost his respect for and reliance upon fact, but believing with Sir Thomas Browne that it was right to interpret Scripture largely, he increasingly drew a wealth of impression from the vaguest hint of a fact. He trusted his own imagination, though he would guide his reader's at every point. He did not write the factual truth at all times, but he could simulate it with an artistry that outstripped truth itself in vividness of impression.

PART II

"My Honoured Friend, Sir Henry Wotton"

Chapter 5

The Life of
Sir Henry Wotton – 1651

WALTON'S friend Richard Marriot entered *"The workes of Sr Hen. Wotton never before printed"* on the Stationers' Register November 3, 1648.[1] *Reliquiae Wottonianae. or, A Collection Of Lives, Letters, Poems; With Characters of Sundry Personages: And other Incomparable Pieces of Language and Art. By The curious Pensil of the Ever Memorable Sr Henry Wotton K^t, Late, Provost of Eton Colledg* did not appear until 1651. The delay was very likely caused by the circumstances of the editor, and the editor was probably Izaak Walton. The *"curious Pensil"* of the title page foreshadows the *"curious Pen"* which Walton attributed to Wotton.[2] The description of Wotton as late Provost of Eton rather than as late ambassador to Venice coincides with Walton's prime interest in Wotton. More important, the dedication in the volume is signed "J. W."[3] After his departure from Chancery Lane, Walton had probably moved to Clerkenwell, and he was writing there in days disturbed not only by war but by the growing family of his second marriage.[4] When *Reliquiae Wottonianae* appeared, the pre-

[1] *Sta. Reg., 1640–1708,* I, 304.   [2] *Lives,* 1670 (Donne), p. 10.
[3] The younger John Donne, not Walton, wrote the dedication of *LXXX Sermons.*
[4] He carried a royal jewel, the Lesser George, from Staffordshire to London after the battle of Worcester on Sept. 3, 1651 (Ashmole, *The Institution, Laws & Ceremonies Of the most Noble Order of the Garter,* p. 228). On this basis, Coon conjectures (*op. cit.,* p. 169) that Walton may have had a headquarters in Staffordshire as well as in London and that he was engaged in some activity which made routine his travel between the two places.
He married Anne Ken in Clerkenwell on April 23, 1647 (*A True Register*

fixed *Life* and the text each started with a new gathering. This, a fresh set of signatures for each part, and the lack of pagination in the *Life* all point to a book printed in parts. That Marriot had to wait for the *Life* after the text had been printed is borne out by Walton's *"Advice to the Reader"*:

> If there shal be found some small Incongruities, either in time, or expression, in the Life of Sir *Henry Wotton;* The Reader is requested to afford him a gentle Censure, because it was by the Printer fetch'd so fast by pieces from the Relatour; that he never saw what he had writ all together, till 'twas past the Presse.

It is supported, too, in the text of the *Life* where Walton says, "But for the particulars of these and many more, that I meant to make knowne; I want a view of some papers that might informe me, and indeed I want time too; for the Printers Press stayes."[5] Moreover, the *Errata* of the *Life* contains eleven corrections for 48 pages, that of the text only nine for 540 pages.

Although Wotton had died in 1639 and Marriot had planned a commemorative volume in 1648, it was not until 1651 that Walton was rushing his *Life* toward completion. He reveals his reasons for writing the *Life* in a passage similar to the first paragraphs of the *Life of Donne:* the years have not brought forth a memorial by any one of Wotton's friends of "higher parts and imployment"; Walton wishes to show his gratitude to the memory of his friend and has been repeatedly requested by Mr. Nicholas Oudart to perform such a duty.[6] He adds, as in the *Donne,* "I am modestly con-

---

of all the Christeninges, Mariages, and Burialles in the Parishe of St. James, Clarkenwell [London, 1887], III, 80 [Registers, vol. XIII in *Publications of The Harleian Society*]). His daughter, Anne, was born March 11, 1648. A son, Izaak, was christened Feb. 10, 1650, and died June 10, 1650. Another son, Izaak, who survived Walton, was born Sept. 7, 1651 (Nicolas, p. xli).

[5] *Reliq.*, 1651, sig. c4[r].

[6] *Ibid.*, sig. b3[v] [misnumbered b2]. Nicholas Oudart was brought from Mechlin in Brabant to England by Wotton as his servant (Smith, II, 389). He was evidently in Wotton's service until Wotton died, meanwhile receiving the M.A. at Oxford in 1636. From 1641 until 1651, he served as assistant secretary to Sir Edward Nicholas, secretary of state. He was secretary to Princess Mary of Orange between 1651 and 1661 and Latin secretary to Charles II from 1666 to his death in 1681 (*DNB*, article "Nicholas Oudart").

In 1670, Walton wrote that the request that he write Wotton's biography came from Oudart "and others" (*Lives*, 1670 [Wotton], p. 9). In 1672, "the others" were identified as Sir Edward Bysshe and Mr. Charles Cotton (*Reliq.*, 1672, sig. b[v]). Bysshe was a genealogist, and, according to Wood, a great

fident my humble language shall be accepted, because I present all
Readers with a commixture of truth and his merits." In his note
to the reader of 1670, Walton says that the *Life of Donne "begot a
like necessity of writing the life of his and my honoured friend,* Sir
Henry Wotton."[7] In 1672, the theme of gratitude is re-emphasized
in a statement in the dedication: *"I have made him the best return
of my Gratitude for his Condescention, that I have been able to
express."*[8]

We may well examine the duration and the nature of the friendship between the Provost of Eton and the draper of Chancery Lane,
his junior by twenty-five years. The connections between all Walton's *Lives* are close, but the links between the *Donne* and the *Wotton* add conviction to the belief that Donne introduced Walton to
Wotton. Walton himself supplies links by his reference to Wotton
at the beginning of the *Life of Donne* and by his statement to the
reader in 1670. Still, we must remember that he nowhere establishes
the closeness of the relation between the two men except by his
suggestion of their friendship at Oxford[9] and by his inclusion in
1654 of Donne's verse letter to Wotton prior to his going ambassador
to Venice.[10] In each life he mentions his main character's voyages
with Essex, but he nowhere indicates that the men made the voyages together. The relation of the two is oblique rather than explicit. When Walton wants a frame of reference, as it were, for
what Wotton learned as the result of his jesting sentence, he refers
to Donne's "The Will." The large parallels in the two *Lives* are
many: in each, early reputation for learning is stressed; in each,
the importance of King James is evident, and both men are held
in disfavor on one occasion; the Queen of Bohemia plays a part
in each; in each, there is constant reference to pecuniary distress;
the dream element is important to both; the early indiscretion of
Donne has its parallel in Wotton's adventures with Essex and in

---

encourager of learning and learned men even during the Commonwealth
(*DNB*, article "Sir Edward Bysshe"; *Athenae Oxon.*, III, 206, 351, 1017). The
younger Cotton's poem to Walton on his *Lives* was first printed prefatory to
the 1675 *Lives*, but it is dated "Jan. 17. 1672[3]." Stanzas 9 and 10 of this poem
tell how happy the senior Cotton was to see the lives of Donne and Wotton
written. As Walton's dedication of *Reliq.*, 1672, is dated *"Feb. 27. 1672[3],"*
his mention of Charles Cotton, the Elder, of Beresford Hall, is probably part
of an exchange of compliments.

[7] *Lives*, 1670, sig. A5ᵛ.   [8] *Reliq.*, 1672, sigs. a4ʳ–a4ᵛ.
[9] *Ibid.*, 1651, sig. b7ᵛ.   [10] *Ibid.*, 1654, pp. 36–38.

his father's with Sir Thomas Wyatt.[11] Walton clearly joined the men in his own thoughts. If indeed Donne introduced Walton to Wotton, such an introduction could not have taken place before March, 1624, when Donne became vicar of St. Dunstan's-in-the-West. As Wotton was made Provost of Eton on July 19, 1624, it was the elderly Provost whom Walton knew. Wotton, aged fifty-six, had retired from the strenuous life of diplomacy; Walton, a youthful freeman of the Ironmongers' Guild, was thirty-one.

The letter which follows, one of two from Wotton to Walton which were printed in *Reliquiae Wottonianae,* shows something of Wotton's attitude toward Walton.

My worthy Friend.

Since I last saw you, I have been confin'd to my Chamber by a *quotidian* Feaver, I thank God, of more contumacie then malignitie. It had once left me, as I thought; but it was only to fetch more company, returning with a surcrew of those splenetick vapors that are call'd *Hypocondriacal:* of which most say, the cure is good company; and I desire no better Physician then your self. I have in one of those fits indeavour'd to make it more easie by composing a short *Hymn;* and since I have apparelled my best thoughts so l[i]ghtly as in Verse, I hope I shall be pardond a second vanitie, if I communicate it with such a friend as your self; to whom I wish a chearfull spirit and a thankfull heart to value it as one of the greatest blessings of our good God; in whose dear love I leave you, remaining

> *Your poor Friend to serve you,*
> H. Wotton[12]

With this letter Wotton sent a poem entitled *"A Hymn to my God in a night of my late Sicknesse."*[13] The letter obviously shows that Wotton looked upon Walton as a friend, that he enjoyed his company, had, perhaps, been visited by him, and that he knew of Walton's interest in holy verse. It may be dated with some exactness

[11] The parallels are apparent even in minor details: Donne and Wotton become deacons with all convenient speed; the Civil War figures in each life; the useful sentences which Donne uttered on his deathbed to his friends are not unlike Wotton's "dropping some choyce *Greek* or *Latine Apothegme* or sentence" whenever he left the boys at Eton (but, also like Hooker's uttering, at the customary time of procession, "some loving and effecacious observations to be remembered against the next year; especially by the boys and young people," and the elder Sanderson's "scattering short Apothegms and little pleasant Stories"). In each, the holy retirement of Emperor Charles V is mentioned, as is King James's motto. Verbal parallels are numerous.

[12] *Reliq.,* 1651, pp. 513–514. Undated.   [13] *Ibid.,* p. 515.

because of its relation to a letter which Wotton sent to his close friend and relative by marriage, Sir Edmund Bacon. The following is from a long letter to Bacon, dated "this *Ashwednesday, 1637[8]*":

> Oh my most dear Nephew . . . how have I of late, after many vexations of a fastidious infirmity, been at once rent in pieces by hearing that you were at *London:* What! said I, and must it be at a time when I cannot flie thither to have my wonted part of that conversation, wherein all that know him enjoy such infinite contentment? Thus much did suddenly break loose from the heart that doth truly honour you. And now (Sir) let me tell you both how it hath gone with me, and how I stand at the present. There is a triple health: health of Body, of Mind, and of Fortune; you shall have a short account of all three.
>
> For the first; it is now almost an whole Cycle of the Sun, since after certain fits of a Quotidian Feaver, I was assailed by that Splenetick Passion, which a Countrey good Fellow that had been a piece of a Grammarian meant, when he said he was sick of the *Flatus,* and the other hard word; for *Hypocondriacus* stuck in his Teeth: It is the very *Proteus* of all Maladies; shifting into sundry shapes, almost every night a new, and yet still the same; neither can I hope, that it will end in a solar Period, being such a Saturnine Humour; but though the Core and Root of it be remaining, yet the Symptomes (I thank my God) are well allayed: And in general, I have found it of more contumacy then malignity; only since the late cold weather, there is complicated with it a more Asthmatical straitness of respiration then heretofore: yet those about me say, I bear it well, as perchance custome hath taught me; being now familiarized and domesticated evils: In the Tragedians expression, *Jam mansueta Mala.*[14]

The two letters may well have been written on the same day. Yet that to Bacon is chatty, relaxed, informal; that to Walton is bright but lacking in levity. The one to Bacon is anecdotal, yet more learned than the other. Wotton obviously had his readers in mind as he wrote. The letter to Bacon reveals immediately that the men have been long acquainted and that they have much in common. That to Walton shows distance by the restraint of its tone, by its studied nicety of expression. The enclosure of the hymn coupled with the sententiousness in the statement that a cheerful spirit and a thankful heart are one of the greatest blessings of a good God has in it something of a pose, the studied kindliness of one man toward another who admires him. The letter helps, then, to establish the tone of the relationship between Walton and Wotton. The nature

[14] *Ibid.,* 1672, pp. 466–467.

of this relationship is revealed too in the oft-quoted letter to Walton *"In answer of a Letter, requesting him to performe his promise of Writing the Life of Dr Dunne."*[15] In the letter it is obvious that the slothful Wotton has little intention of writing a life. "My age considered," he says, it is "almost hopelesse from my Pen; yet I wil endeavour to perform my promise." That Henry King will be near him is a great spur to him and he hopes to confer with King shortly. The letter ends:

I shall write at large to you by the next Messenger (being at present a little in businesse); and then I shall set down certaine generall heads, wherein I desire information by your loving diligence; hoping shortly to injoy your own ever welcome company in this approaching time of the *Flye* and the *Corke.*

Walton has obviously been persistent in his desire to help the Provost. Wotton is too busy to indicate even generally the topics on which he needs assistance, but promises to write again. Walton does not print another letter, but the selectivity of the printed letters does not preclude his having received one. We may be sure, however, that in the letter, if it were written, Wotton again made promises and again suggested that Walton go fishing with him. Walton appears here flattered and anxious to be helpful; Wotton, whose indolence as an author was constitutional, was much more taken by Walton as a fishing companion than as a prospective research assistant.

In the *Compleat Angler,* Walton speaks of Wotton as "a man with whom I have often fish'd and convers'd."[16] Here, too, he gives Wotton's picture in miniature:

My next and last example shall be that undervaluer of money, the late Provost of *Eaton Colledg,* Sir *Henry Wotton, . . .* a man whose forraign imployments in the service of this Nation, and whose experience, learning, wit and cheerfulness, made his company to be esteemed one of the delights of mankind; this man, whose very approbation of Angling were sufficient to convince any modest Censurer of it, this man

---

[15] *Ibid.,* 1651, pp. 511–513. The reference here to Henry King's appointment as Dean of Rochester, which occurred Feb. 6, 1639, shows that the letter was written shortly after that date. Wotton says that he hopes to invite King "to a friendship with that Family [his own] where his predecessor was familiarly acquainted." It is impossible to tell from this whether King was not familiar with Wotton's family, or whether Wotton, too, did not know him. It is hard to suppose that Donne had introduced Walton but not King to Wotton.

[16] *Compleat Angler,* 1653, p. 32.

was also a most dear lover, and a frequent practicer of the Art of Angling.[17]

Walton writes here, too, of Wotton as a "Learned" man and says that he believes that "peace, and patience, and a calm content did cohabit in the cheerful heart of Sir *Henry Wotton*."[18] This picture, without its piscatorial bias, is essentially that which Walton had in mind as he wrote the life of Wotton in 1651.

The *Life* begins with a detailed account of Henry Wotton's ancestry in order to show the distinction of the Wotton family and the extent of its service to the nation:

The *Wottons* being a Family that hath brought forth many persons eminent for *Wisdome* and *Valour,* whose heroick Acts, and honorable Imployments both in *England* and in forrain parts, have adorn'd themselves, and this *Nation;* which they have served abroad *faithfully,* in discharge of their great trust, and *prudently* in their Negotiations with severall *Princes;* and also serv'd it at home with much *Honor* and *Justice,* in their wise managing a great part of the publick affairs thereof in the *Various times* both of *war* and *peace.*[19]

Walton would have his reader believe that Wotton performed actions worthy of his ancestors. The entertaining story of Thomas Wotton's second marriage serves as a transition from the ancestry to Wotton's education, his instruction by his mother and tutors, his attendance at Winchester school and at Oxford. Wotton's wisdom and ability are illustrated in his composition of a play, *Tancredo,* in his three lectures *de Oculo,* and by the high opinion which Alberico Gentili, Professor of Civil Law at Oxford, had of him. The college years are filled out not by an account of Wotton's many accomplishments, but rather by the mention of his father's death and by the relation of two dreams in which the father is involved. Here is a wide digression, yet the first of the dreams serves additionally to show the political interests of the Wotton family and the second is connected with Oxford. Walton returns to Wotton at Oxford by showing Wotton's aptitude for Italian studies in Gentili's admira-

[17] *Ibid.,* pp. 32–33.
[18] *Ibid.,* p. 33. In his dedication, Walton says that Wotton intended to write a discourse in praise of angling. He also says that he once carried a bottle of oil, supposed to tempt fish to bite, from Sir George Hastings to Wotton, "both chimical men" (pp. 226–227), and he repeats what Wotton has told him of angling for swallows and martins in Italy (p. 206).
[19] *Reliq.,* 1651, sig. b^v.

tion for his "Propensity and Conaturalnesse to the *Italian* Language."[20] Wotton's travels are treated as an extension of his education, for their purpose was "to purchase the rich treasure of forraign knowledge."[21] The travels are presented in three divisions: the first tells that Wotton spent nine years on the continent, mainly in Italy; the second prefaces an account of Wotton's employment under Essex by a description of his fine appearance and manners; the Essex episode forces Wotton to Italy, and in the third travel division the lengthy Ottavio Baldi incident serves as a link between Wotton's preparation for a diplomatic career and the career itself. A paragraph of background material on the succession at the end of Elizabeth's reign precedes the relation of Ottavio Baldi's journey and its consummation. Walton has prepared us well in noting Wotton's inclinations and experience for his career as ambassador to Venice and in demonstrating that the Baldi incident was the cause of the favor shown him by King James.

Walton then describes the knighting of Henry Wotton and the King's offer of an ambassadorship as the first steps in his account of Wotton as ambassador, the career which covered with some interruption nineteen of Wotton's seventy-one years and to which Walton devotes one quarter of his *Life*. These years are charactered rather than narrated in just four main incidents. In the first of these characters, Walton gives "for the information of Common Readers"[22] an account of the quarrel between Pope Paul V and the Venetians in the years 1603–1606. Wotton appears but twice in this history: Walton, in truth, tells us nothing of him when he says that Wotton was often in conference with the Venetian Senate and that he kept King James informed of the proceedings. Next, Walton would show the King's high esteem for Wotton, and this he accomplishes in the story of Wotton's having once fallen into disfavor with the King because of his definition of an ambassador. After a general assessment of Wotton as an ambassador, Walton characterizes Wotton's abilities and fitness in two examples. Wotton's merciful disposition is illustrated in his kind treatment of English prisoners in Venice, and the nobleness of his mind in his courteous acceptance of a jewel from Emperor Ferdinand for his diplomatic endeavors and in his immediate bestowal of the same jewel on his hostess in Vienna because he would not profit by a gift from an

20 *Ibid.*, sig. b7ᵛ.　　　　21 *Ibid.*, sig. b8ʳ.　　　　22 *Ibid.*, sig. b12ʳ.

enemy of his Royal Mistress, the Queen of Bohemia. Walton's account of the ambassadorial years is a justification of Wotton's chararacter, not a narrative of his activities.

Walton had now come to that part of Wotton's life when, it may be assumed, he knew Wotton personally. The last third of the *Life* is devoted to Wotton's final fifteen years. Walton is straightforward in his account of how Wotton received the Eton appointment. He relates at some length Wotton's money troubles and the King's promises, and he indicates that Wotton sought the position as a solution to his pecuniary distress. He gives three other reasons why Wotton wanted the position. The first is a corollary of the main reason: Wotton had "for many years (like *Siciphus*) rolled the restless stone of a state imployment."[23] The second introduces a new note: Wotton thought that a college was the fittest place to nourish holy thoughts. The third indicates that Wotton's age seemed to require that he afford rest to his body and mind. Walton again emphasizes Wotton's financial straits prior to settling at Eton and then tells that Wotton felt bound to enter orders upon his acceptance of the position. Then comes a character of the good provost in the description of Wotton's life at Eton: his devotions, his reading of the Bible and of authors of divinity, and also his love of philosophy and angling and his excellence as a good neighbor and a good educator. In this static picture of Wotton's inclinations and employment at Eton, Walton would testify that Wotton was "a great enemy to *wrangling disputes* of *Religion*"[24] and would show the readiness of his wit. He tells four short stories to demonstrate Wotton's dislike of church controversy and one about the ideal conduct of a prospective ambassador primarily to show Wotton's wit.

Walton sums up the picture of Wotton at Eton by noting that Wotton still maintained, through his friendships, "that great blessing of a chearfull heart."[25] After saying that Wotton's mirth was sometimes damped by the remembrance of his old debts, he proceeds to quote Wotton's will. His purpose is twofold: he would show that Wotton's chief design in the will was a Christian endeavor that his debts might be satisfied; and, by intruding to comment on the inscription that Wotton wanted on his gravestone, Walton gives evidence that he wanted the will to serve as further

[23] *Ibid.*, sig. c4ᵛ.   [24] *Ibid.*, sig. c6ʳ.   [25] *Ibid.*, sig. c7ᵛ.

proof of Wotton's hatred of wrangling. After indicating that the legacies were distributed and that conscionable satisfaction was made for the debts, Walton makes the *Life* proceed to a lovely close. Wotton's visiting Bocton and Oxford once a year serves as a recapitulation of his life, and his final visit to Winchester provides the foreshadowing of death and a feeling of inevitability in the "succession of boyes using the same recreations, and questionless possess'd with the same thoughts," one generation succeeding another, "both in their lives, recreations, hopes, fears, and deaths."[26] Walton recounts Wotton's final illness and surveys the circle of his life in a smaller recapitulation.

Donald Stauffer is right when he calls the *Life of Wotton* the most worldly and most entertaining of the *Lives* and when he says that in this urbane little biography Wotton is shown as "a philosopher of tolerance, an angler of a brilliant wit, a gentleman of polish."[27] Harold Nicolson, however, says that Walton misleads in dealing with a mundane diplomatist like Wotton, that he is interested only in those sides of a character which reflect his own negative and receptive temperament.[28] He believes that Walton had no insight into fact, no interest in practical activity, and that Walton, writing of Wotton as a fishing friend, was more interested in him as Provost of Eton than in his sentence about ambassadors.[29] The *Life of Wotton* is by far the most secular of Walton's *Lives*. Certainly there is not in it that stressing of holiness which pervades the *Life of Donne*. Just how secular it is becomes apparent upon comparing Walton's *Life* with that written by Logan Pearsall Smith. It is odd that Walton, admiring the quiet, learned Provost, should see Wotton as a rather secular person and should stress his charm, his good manners, his morality, but not a deep piety. It is equally strange that Smith, interested primarily in Wotton as ambassador to Venice, as an exemplar of the Italianate Englishman, and devoting five times the space to the ambassadorship that he does to the provostship, should still find study and religion, though of a proselytizing and revolutionary type, the guiding motives in Wotton's career.

Smith says that Walton gave Wotton a sanctity of character which

---

26 *Ibid.*, sig. c11ᵛ.
27 Donald Stauffer, *English Biography before 1700*, pp. 102–103.
28 Harold Nicolson, *The Development of English Biography*, p. 65.
29 *Ibid.*, p. 68.

he may have possessed in his retired old age, but which may hardly be expected to exist in a young Elizabethan courtier. However, he himself admits:

Throughout Wotton's active career we have the curious phenomenon of a man leading an unusually blameless life, in an age when great qualities were almost always associated with great faults and misdeeds, a man against whom a definite accusation was seldom or never brought, and who was yet frequently suspected of double-dealing and sinister motives.[30]

Although Smith would say that Walton's picture is somewhat over-drawn, that Wotton was not perfect, he would not refute the essential goodness of Wotton's life. Still, it is Smith, not Walton, who prepares his reader in the early Wotton for the future Provost of Eton. He pictures the ambassador in the midst of his "domestic college," made up of the cultivated young men who were in his train. He shows Wotton's delight in their philosophical speculation, their religious services, his happiness in an atmosphere of refinement and leisure.[31] In illustrating Wotton's inclination for a life of this sort, Smith makes the Eton appointment much more logical and inevitable than Walton does.

Smith demonstrates convincingly that the whole of Wotton's first ambassadorship was characterized by a preoccupation with winning the Venetians to Protestantism as the first step in bringing reformation to the religion of Italy. He shows that Wotton thought the introduction of the Anglican ritual into Italy the dearest privilege of his position and only the beginning, he hoped, of mighty changes; that he hoped for a war which should detach Venice from the papacy, that he found and made opportunities to incite Venetian defiance of the Pope; that he kept supplying secret information about the military preparations of the Pope and of the Spaniards.[32] He shows, too, that Wotton went considerably beyond his instructions in the matter of James's assistance to Venice; that he plied Venetian theologians with Calvin and many volumes of Anglican controversy, and Venetian nobles with Sir Edwin Sandys's *Europae Speculum,* translated into Italian at his instigation; that he worked with Paolo Sarpi on a plan for the advancement of the cause of religious freedom in Italy and Europe.[33] And Smith says

[30] Smith, I, 27–28.   [31] *Ibid.,* pp. 57–58.   [32] *Ibid.,* pp. 78–80.
[33] *Ibid.,* pp. 82, 90–91, 94.

that despite all Wotton's activity, his bookish abstraction led him sometimes to neglect routine duties and to forget his own interests.[34] Not mere conformity made Wotton enter orders, he says, when he became Provost of Eton.

His principal motive . . . was of a deeper nature, a desire to enter more completely into the service of the religion and Church, for which, on looking back, he felt his past life had been no unsuitable preparation. His visits to Rome, his residence in Italy, had given him much experience of the corruptions of religion, and as ambassador his efforts had had one supreme end, the advancement of the cause of a purer faith.[35]

Why, then, did Walton not make more of Wotton's religious tendencies? Certainly he, of all men, loved holy inclinations and could demonstrate them sympathetically. We need not seek far for the answer. Walton knew men whose piety made Wotton's faith seem watery, and he knew the Provost well enough to realize that not piety but politics at first and then money largely determined his holy inclination. This can readily be shown by reference to three letters which were printed in *Reliquiae Wottonianae*. Walton knew that Wotton himself thought that religion was the main subject of his employment abroad. In a letter to Charles I, Wotton wrote, in explanation of his taking orders, that his resolution "is not unsutable even to my civill imployments abroad, of which for the most part Religion was the subject."[36] Not only did Walton have this letter at hand in 1651, but in his *Advertisement to the Reader* in that volume he called attention to it by listing it as revealing "Part of the *Authors Character*."[37] Then he proceeded to neglect it. Indeed, Walton knew of Wotton's religious employment abroad, both from Wotton's letters and probably from his own lips. But would Walton—whose very motto was *"Study to be quiet,"*[38] who felt obliged, "because of a very long and very trew friendship with some of the Roman Church,"[39] to profess in his will that his faith was in all points that of the Church of England, who, indeed, would picture Wotton as an enemy of wrangling in religion—would Walton approve of the religion that Wotton practiced abroad? He knew well just how religious Wotton had been abroad, and in his very knowledge we can account for the extreme impersonality of the cold, historical account of those years in the *Life*.

In this same letter, Wotton says he has proceeded to orders out

34 *Ibid.*, p. 110.   35 *Ibid.*, p. 202.   36 *Reliq.*, 1651, p. 387.
37 *Ibid.*, sig. a3ᵛ.   38 *Compleat Angler*, 1655, p. 355.
39 Nicolas, pp. xcix–c.

of conscience and reason, not greediness and ambition, and he goes
on to say:

Perhaps I want not some perswaders, that measuring me by their affections, or by your Majesties goodnesse, and not by mine own defects
or ends, would make me think, that yet before I dye, I might become
a great Prelat. And I need no perswasion to tell me, that if I would
undertake the Pastorall Function, I could peradventure by casualty, out
of the Patronages belonging to your Royall Colledge, without further
troubling of your Majesty, cast some good Benefice upon my self, whereof
we have one, if it were vacant, that is worth more then my Provostship.[40]

If this letter written not long after Wotton entered orders but hints
at preferment, the next, written in 1629 to beg the King for money
to pay debts contracted in public service, is more outspoken, and
Wotton asks "That You will be likewise pleased to promise me,
the next good Deanry, that shall be vacant by death or remove:
whereof I also had a promise from Your blessed Father then at
Newmarket, and am now more capable thereof in my present condition."[41] The third letter, written about a year before Wotton's
death, goes so far as to mention a specific post. Wotton has heard
that Dr. Walter Balcanquhall is to be made Dean of Durham and
he supplicates for the coming vacancy of the mastership of the
Savoy. He does not think the position incompatible with his provostship, and he says:

God knows, and the value of the Thing it self may speak as much,
that I do not aime therein at any utilitie: Only, it may be some ease
of expence, and Commodity of Lodging, when I shall come (as I am
affraid shortly) to oversee certain poor things of mine own at Presse.

He confesses also that, though his fortunes are poor and his studies
private, certain sparkles of honest ambition remain in him.[42]

Had Walton wanted to mishandle the information available to
him, he might well have been able to draw a pious picture of Wotton. In his kindness, he left many things unsaid, and in so far as his
conscience permitted him, he represented Wotton as a moral, somewhat religious man. But, acquainted as he was with the secular motives of Wotton's every religious undertaking, he drew, for him, an
exceedingly secular picture.

[40] *Reliq.,* 1651, p. 385.
[41] *Ibid.,* 1672, pp. 563–564. "*Whitehall,* Feb. 12. Styl. vet., 1628[9]."
[42] *Ibid.,* 1651, pp. 429–431. For date, see Smith, II, 397.

The picture was carefully contrived. The anecdotal nature of the *Life* probably indicates Walton's large inheritance of oral material from Wotton himself and from such intimates of Wotton as Nicholas Oudart and John Hales. All the anecdote in the *Life* is delightful, most of it is made pertinent, but Walton's love for good stories led him to include some which strained his structure. Careful as he was about the proportions of the *Life,* careful as he was about the light which the detail reflected upon Wotton, he produced, by a long succession of good stories, some immediately pertinent, others not, a discursiveness which is perhaps not purposeful. Still, if these stories occasionally impede the directness of Wotton's chronicle, they add an informality, a geniality, a gentility to the *Life* which seems to corroborate those qualities in Wotton himself. A close examination of the *Life* shows that Walton had at hand, too, a vast amount of material in manuscript and in print. He shaped the *Life* not only by what he left unsaid about Wotton's motives and about his career as ambassador, but also by the way in which he utilized and integrated the sources that he was greatly dependent upon. The *Life* depends for so many details on such a patchwork of sources that it might well have been in other hands an ill-shaped grab bag of styles and of facts. But, though Walton tended to cut his material on the bias, he followed his own pattern carefully and he knew how to hide his seams. Almost always he was master of his material. At the same time, he was a sufficient craftsman to take inspiration from the particular material he was working with. Several of his deftest strokes were suggested by the material itself.

Walton had worked hard in his first version of the *Life of Donne* to show the esteem in which Donne was held. In the *Life of Wotton* he does this outside the text of the *Life;* the puffs are in the "Advertisement to the Reader." He quotes in its entirety the "Elogium Auctoris" which precedes the Latin translation of Wotton's *Elements of Architecture* printed with the *De Architectura* of Vitruvius in 1649.[43] He says that Sir Francis Bacon collected some of Wotton's sayings.[44] He then quotes Sir Richard Baker:

[43] *M. Vitruvii Pollionis De Architectura* (Amstelodami, 1649). Wotton's work has a separate title page: *Elementa Architecturae, Collecta ab Henrico Wottonio, Equite, Ex optimis Auctoribus & Exemplis, Anglico quidem Idiomate scripta & edita Londini Anno M. DC. XXIV. Nunc vero in Latinum versa A Joanne de Laet, Antwerpiano.* The "Elogium" is on p. 2.

[44] Smith (II, 461) quotes James Spedding, Robert Leslie Ellis, Douglas Denon Heath, eds., *The Works of Francis Bacon* (London, 1857–62), VII, 134,

Sir *Henry Wotton* was sent Embassador into *Italy*—and indeed the Kingdome yeelded not a fitter man to match the Capriciousnesse of the *Italian* wits. A man of so able dexterity with his pen, that he hath done himselfe much wrong and the Kingdome a great deale more, in leaving no more of his Writings behind him.[45]

The "great deale" is Walton's own contribution, but even then his source is not unbiased. Baker says that he and Wotton had been "fellow pupils, and chamber fellows in *Oxford* divers yeares together" and this may well account for his giving Wotton more lines than either Andrewes, Reinolds, Sir Edward Coke, Bacon, or Camden. That Walton was blind to what he did not wish to see is evident not only here but in Baker's account of John Donne, another old acquaintance, which precedes the account of Wotton and which Walton chose not to use. For Baker says of Donne before he had attracted the attention of King James, "leaving *Oxford,* [he] lived at the *Innes of Court,* not dissolute, but very neat; a great visiter of Ladies, a great frequenter of Playes, a great writer of conceited Verses."[46]

Baker was only one of the authorities consulted by Walton to testify that his account of Wotton's ancestry is only a part of any commendation that would be just. He utilized the accounts of Holinshed[47] and Camden,[48] quoting them, combining them, and even supplementing them from other sources. It was, indeed, in Holinshed that he found the inspiration for including the ancestors of Wotton in the *Life*. The main object of the Holinshed account is to relate something of Edward, Sir Henry Wotton's eldest brother; but, says the author,

I will . . . turne my pen to some persons of that surname, who for their singularitie of wit & lerning, for their honour and governement in

---

to show that No. 64 of Bacon's *Collection of Apophthegms* is one of Wotton's sayings.

[45] *Reliq.,* 1651, sigs. aᵛ–a2ʳ.

[46] Sir Richard Baker, *A Chronicle of the Kings of England From the Time of the Romans Goverment unto the Raigne of our Soveraigne Lord King Charles* (London, 1643), p. 156.

[47] Raphael Holinshed, *The Chronicles of England, from William the Conquerour . . . untill the yeare 1577. . . . And continued from the yeare 1577. untill this present yeare of Grace 1585. Newlie amended and inlarged* (London, 1587), pp. 1402–1403.

[48] William Camden, *Britain, Or a chorographicall description of the most flourishing Kingdomes, England, Scotland, and Ireland, and the Ilands adjoyning* (London, 1610), p. 331.

and of the realme about the prince, and elsewhere at home and abroad, deserve such commendations, that they merit *Niveo signari lapillo.*

He says at the end of his digression, "I conclude, that it is a singular blessing of God, not commonlie given to everie race, to be beautified with such great and succeeding honor in the descents of the familie." Here is the apparatus which Walton proceeded to make his own.

In neither Holinshed nor Camden did Walton find information about the great-grandfather, Sir Robert. For this and other information he had supplementary sources. For example, although in his account of the grandfather, Edward, he mentions, as does Holinshed, that Edward was a member of Henry VIII's privy council and that he refused the chancellorship, he adds from other sources the year of his birth and notices his appointment as Treasurer of Calais. He does not mention, as Holinshed does, that Edward was one of the executors of Henry VIII's will. Walton says that he quotes Camden in saying that Wotton's brother Edward was "a man remarkable for many and great Imployments in the State during her Raign, and sent severall times *Ambassadour* into Forraign Nations."[49] Camden says, to be sure, that Elizabeth approved Edward's "wisdome in waightie affaires," but it was in Holinshed that he found mention of Edward as an ambassador. Camden says, too, that Edward was Elizabeth's Controller of the Household and that he was created Baron Wotton of Marley by James. Walton used this and supplemented it by telling that Edward was knighted by Elizabeth and that he was Controller under James, of his privy council, and by him made Lord Lieutenant of Kent. He found no information in Camden and Holinshed about Wotton's other brothers and his father, Thomas, nor did he learn anything about Thomas Wotton except that he was a patron of scholars from "Master *William Lambert,* in his perambulation of *Kent.*"[50]

Walton says that his main interest is in the direct line of descent and that to look back as far as Sir Nicholas Wotton, "who lived in the raign of King *Richard* the second," might be thought tedious.

[49] *Reliq.,* 1651, sig. b2v.

[50] *Ibid.* William Lambard, *A Perambulation of Kent: Conteining the description, Hystorie, and Customes of that Shyre* (London, 1576). On sig. $\pi \pi 2^r$, "T W" signs a letter commending the book to the gentlemen of Kent. In the 1596 edition, this letter is preceded by one of dedication "To the Right woorshipfull, and vertuous, M. Thomas Wotton, Esquier" (sigs. A2r–A3r). The *Perambulation* is commonly called the earliest county history. It makes no detailed mention of Bocton, the home of the Wottons.

He finds it incumbent upon him, however, to give an account of another Nicholas, brother of Sir Henry Wotton's grandfather. Here, too, his structure follows that of Holinshed. The Holinshed account says that it will not treat the antiquity of the worshipful family and lists five names, of which the last—and the only one preceded by "Sir"—is "sir Nicholas Wootton knight, living about the daies of Richard the second." The Holinshed account, too, makes much of the two brothers, Edward and Nicholas, who served the nation with equal distinction. Although Walton preferred Camden's account of Nicholas, he got from Holinshed Nicholas' refusal of the Archbishopric of Canterbury and his appointment as one of the executors of Henry VIII's will. Holinshed reproduces in full the inscription on the tomb of Nicholas, placed there, as Walton says, by Thomas Wotton. Walton utilized the inscription, but he had trouble with its Latin. *"Utriusque juris doctor"* becomes "doctor of both lawes" in Holinshed, "Doct. of the lawes" in Camden, but "a *Doctor of Law*" in Walton.[51] The inscription reads *"ecclesiae huius primus itemque metropolitanae ecclesiae diui Petri Eboracensis decanus"*; in 1651, Walton says that Nicholas was Dean of Canterbury, and he did not add *"York"* until 1672.[52] Walton followed Camden's "sent in embassage nine times to forrain Princes, and thrise chosen a *Committee,*" instead of Holinshed's "thirteene severall times ambassador and orator to diverse princes," which is based on the enumeration of the inscription. He did rely on the inscription in his mention of Nicholas as secretary of state of Edward VI,[53] and, perhaps from the inscription but more likely from Henry Wotton himself, he got the story of Nicholas' prophesying the day of his death.[54]

Here, then, is evidence of Walton the researcher, not satisfied with Holinshed alone, or with Camden, but supplementing their information and calling even on his small Latin to help him. Here, too, is evidence that Walton recognized Holinshed's pretty structural device and utilized that device to his own ends.

Even as Walton worked to make his chronicle of the Wotton family an integral part of his structure, so he tried also to prevent his relation of two dreams from being merely a digression. I have

---

[51] *Reliq.*, 1651, sig. b3r. [52] *Ibid.*, 1672, sig. br.

[53] "Eduardi regi jam medio regni curriculo prope confecto, unus e primariis secretariis fuit."

[54] "Haec ille ante mortem & ante morbum quasi fatalem diem praesentiens, & cygneam cantionem prophetice canens, sua manu in museo scripta reliquit."

suggested that Walton was indebted to Wotton for the story of Donne's vision and for that of Nicholas Wotton's foretelling his own death. His source for the two long dreams in this *Life* was probably again Wotton. Anthony à Wood, trying to verify the second of these, could only say, "But upon my search into the university registers, records, accompts, &c. from 1584, to 1589, in which time our author Wotton was resident in Oxon, I find no such robbery committed."[55] That Walton called attention in his "Advertisement to the Reader" to the *"Dukes ominous presagements"* is proof enough of his interest and of the interest of his age in such matters.[56] Wotton's interest is shown in his saying, "I have spent some enquiry whether he [Buckingham] had any ominous presagement before his end" and in the subsequent four illustrations.[57] Although interest in dreams, not pertinence to Wotton's life, led to the inclusion of these matters, Walton yet tried to make them intrude lightly. While they interrupt Wotton's college years, Walton says that Wotton's father's death took place during those years, and not only do both dreams concern the father, but one of them has an Oxford setting. The other is political in nature and Walton would connect it to his account of the Wotton ancestry by having it demonstrate additionally God's favor to this family.

The details of the Ottavio Baldi adventure Walton also probably got from Wotton himself. Sir Henry was very fond of this story, and he made reference to it years after the incident had taken place.[58] Smith approves of the accuracy of Walton's account, and

[55] *Athenae Oxon.,* II, 644. Wotton was probably the source for the *Tancredo* and *de Oculo* stories, also, for Wood could find no evidence in the Oxford records that Wotton had proceeded M.A. (*ibid.,* p. 643).

[56] See H. W. Jones, "John Donne," *TLS,* July 20, 1946, p. 343, which suggests seventeenth-century interest. Jones is correct in saying that John Aubrey does not discuss Donne's vision in his chapter on "Ecstacy" in his *Miscellanies upon Various Subjects.* But Aubrey does use Walton's account in the chapter on "Apparitions" (ed. 1784, pp. 100–103), and he mentions, by reference to Wood, Walton's story of Wotton in his chapter on "Dreams," p. 92. He also indicates the interest in such matters of Gilbert Sheldon (p. 117), Elias Ashmole (p. 118), Sir William Dugdale (p. 111), and others.

[57] *Reliq.,* 1651, pp. 118–121. "The *Life and Death* of George Villiers, *Late Duke of* Buckingham."

[58] In a letter to Prince Henry, dated April 24, 1608, he mentions his first service to him "when a poor counterfeit Italian brought you . . . letters" (Smith, I, 426). Letters to James I, written the end of September, 1614 (*ibid.,* II, 51–53), and Dec. 2, 1622 (*ibid.,* II, 253–254; *Reliq.,* 1672, 247–249), are signed "Ottavio Baldi."

though he says that Sir Anthony Sherley introduced Wotton to the Grand Duke,[59] he mentions Wotton's friendship with the Duke's confidential secretary, Belisario Vinta. Wotton himself wrote a very short account of this incident, and Walton relied, even to the spelling of the secretary's name, on this account as a general outline and specifically for the relation between Wotton and Vinta. Wotton wrote, "It pleased him [Ferdinand, Grand Duke of Tuscany] by means of the Cavalier *Vieta,* his principal Secretary of Estate, to take some notice of my Person."[60] But Wotton's character of Ferdinand does not have the verve and liveliness, the precise detail and personal element of Walton's anecdote, and Walton imparted to it the flavor that must have come to it in Wotton's retellings of a favorite tale.

Walton's relation of the quarrel between Pope Paul V and the state of Venice well illustrates his careful research, his shaping and adapting source material, and his forming the whole into a picture consonant with his purpose. The problem of source here is somewhat confused by the multiplicity of Wotton's projected writings, some of which were concerned with Venice. It is not likely that these ventures fared better than Wotton's literary projects as a whole, and it is impossible to tell whether Walton saw them in either their incomplete or complete state. Perhaps it is significant that though Walton mentions many of Wotton's projected works, including those on angling and on Luther, of which no trace is to be found, he never refers to Wotton's Venetian manuscripts—this despite the publication of Wotton's Latin dedication of a history of Venice in the 1672 *Reliquiae Wottonianae.*

Wotton had a Venetian project in mind for some time. William Camden advised him not to publish an account of the quarrel as early as February 10, 1607, and almost five years later Sir Dudley Carleton, Wotton's successor as ambassador to Venice, said that publication would harm relations between Venice and England.[61] In 1611, Wotton may have had in his possession an English translation by William Bedell, the second of his chaplains in Venice,

[59] Smith, I, 40.

[60] *Reliq.,* 1651, p. 360. Wotton's account is on pp. 364–365 in "A Character of *Ferdinando di Medici,* Gran Duke of *Tuscany.*"

[61] Smith, I, 118, n. 3, quotes *Cl. G. Camdeni et Illustrium Virorum ad G. Camdenum Epistolae* (1691), p. 69, and *State Papers, Foreign, Venice,* Dec. 23, 1611, N.S.

of Paolo Sarpi's account of the quarrel.[62] In a letter to King James,
written December 2, 1622, Wotton, after telling His Majesty that
he is sending him melon seeds of all sorts, proposes to write a history
of Venice. He says, "I do humbly submit the death or life of this
work to your only doom" and encloses a fulsome Latin dedication
to the King. That the King did not provide the proper encourage-
ments is apparent in four extant paragraphs, a draft of the beginning
of the history of Venice, followed by *"Caetera desunt."* Walton
printed the paragraphs in *Reliquiae Wottonianae* in 1654 and again
in 1672, this time with the letter and the dedication to the King.[63]
In the 1654 *Life* Walton added to his account of Wotton as Provost
that Wotton pushed aside his life of Luther (for £500 from the
King) to write a history of England which he never finished.[64] To
have mentioned also the incomplete Venetian project would have
been to reveal something other than industry, and Walton was
quiet. Anthony à Wood lists among Wotton's works, "Journal of
his Embassies to Venice—MS. fairly written in the library of Edw.
Lord Conway."[65] The manuscript has never been found.

It is likely that nothing materialized of Wotton's Venetian
projects. A year after Sarpi's death in 1623, however, Sarpi's account
of the quarrel, written in Italian, was published.[66] In 1626, a

---

[62] Smith, I, 128.

[63] The paragraphs are part of a letter probably to Buckingham, since it is
among other letters to him (*Reliq.*, 1654, pp. 484–487). This letter, now entitled "A Letter concerning the Original of *Venice,*" the letter to the King, and
the dedication are in *Reliq.*, 1672, pp. 247–252. The letter to James is here
dated Dec. 9, 1622, and the postscript is missing. Smith found holographs of
this letter and the dedication in *S.P. Ven.*, but did not find the letter to Buckingham there (Smith, II, 253–256). We have here an indication of the materials
that Walton had copies of or access to.

[64] *Reliq.*, 1654, pp. 77–78.   [65] *Athenae Oxon.*, II, 646.

[66] *Historia particolare delle cose passate tra'l Sommo Pontefice Paolo V. e
la Serenissima Republica di Venetia. Gl' anni MDCV. MDCVI. MDCVII*
(Mirandola, 1624).

Richard Marriot entered Fulgentio Micanzio's life of Sarpi on the Stationers'
Register June 10, 1648, as *"a tract of the life & death de Padre Pauli, translated
into English"* (*Sta. Reg., 1640–1708*, I, 296). In 1651 appeared *The Life of
the Most Learned Father Paul, Of the Order of the Servie. . . . Translated
out of Italian by a person of Quality* (London, Printed for Humphrey Moseley
and Richard Marriot). That Walton knew this work is evident in his use of a
passage from "The Translator To the Reader" in his *Life of Hooker* (see p.
230, n. 28) and in his reference to the book in his *Life of Sanderson* (1678,
sig. i7v–i8r). He used nothing from it in the *Wotton,* but here is a further
indication of the extent of his research.

Latin translation by Bedell appeared,[67] and this year, too, an English translation by Christopher Potter was published.[68] Walton's account is based almost wholly on Potter's translation. It can be shown that he used this in 1651 and probably again when he added details in 1654, 1670, and 1672.

Sarpi says that the monitory of Pope Paul V drawn up against Venice on April 17, 1606, voiced four violations contrary to the authority of the Apostolic See and against ecclesiastical immunity.[69] It objected to the Venetian ordinance of 1602 which forbade ecclesiastical persons to receive or purchase immovable goods; to the prohibition of 1603 which forbade the building of churches without state permission; to the prohibition of 1605 which made subject to alienation secular immovable goods willed to the Church; and to the restraint imposed upon the Canon of Vicenza and the Abbot of Nervesa. Walton simplified the grounds of the quarrel. It is perhaps indicative of his real concern for the inviolability of church property, a concern which was instrumental in his writing the *Life of Hooker,* that in limiting his account to Sarpi's third and fourth items, he yet expanded the third. Sarpi gives a hair-raising recital of the crimes of the two clerics. Scipio Sarraceno [Saraceni], Canon of Vicenza, he says,

did his utmost endevour to seduce a *Damosell* his kinswoman; and prevailing not with her, after he had long molested and pursued her in publique, and even in the *Church,* at last in a despitefull outrage, he shamefully defiled her portall and house doores with his excrements.[70]

Count Valdemarino Brandolino, Abbot of Nervesa, was no better. He tyrannized the countryside, seized goods at his own price, committed vile rapes, poisoned among many others his brother and father, and committed incest with his sister.[71] Walton's comment, indicative of his handling the blackmailing of Hooker, tells that

complaints were justly made by the *Venetians* against two Clergy men, the Abbot of *Nervesa,* and a Canon of *Vicenza,* for committing such sins, as I think not fit to name, (nor name I these to the disgrace of any calling,

[67] *Interdicti Veneti Historia, de motu Italiae sub initia Pontificatus Pauli V. commentarius . . . Recens ex Italico conversus* (Cantabrigiae, 1626).

[68] *The History of the Quarrels of Pope Paul. V. with The State of Venice. In seven books. Faithfully translated out of the Italian, and compared with the French Copie* (London, 1626).

[69] *Ibid.,* pp. 61, 69.   [70] *Ibid.,* p. 14.   [71] *Ibid.,* p. 23.

for holiness is not tyed to Ecclesiastical Orders, and *Italy* is observ'd to breed the most vertuous, and most vicious men of any Nation).[72]

Here, then, Walton, without mentioning the monitory, for he relates the quarrel with sympathy for Venice, speaks merely of the Venetian injunctions "about the year 1603." He simplified the four objections of the monitory into two, and despite his deep-seated opinions on church property, he presented the Venetian injunction sympathetically and in detail. Again, despite a natural reluctance to vilify churchmen, he indicated that the clerics had sinned seriously, because Wotton's tie to the Venetian cause forced him to present sympathetically the Venetian point of view. Sarpi says additionally of the monitory that it threatened excommunication of the Duke, the Senate, and all their favorers, counselors, and adherents and warned that noncompliance would lead to the suspension of masses and divine services.[73] This information Walton used, too. The way in which he used the provisions of the monitory demonstrates his artistry. For he turned Sarpi's static account of the provisions of this one document into a lively historical narrative.

Walton's ability to make his source work his own ends is again evident in his catching up Sarpi's passage in which Giustinian, Venetian ambassador to England, is told to inform James I of proceedings[74] and combining it with Sarpi's account of how England (one of many countries Sarpi includes to show foreign reaction) took the news of the quarrel. Sarpi says:

The *King* then having heard the relation of the *Ambassador,* after he had shewed how well he accepted that office, and had commended the Lawes of the *Republique,* said, that he longed to see the whole *Church of God* reformed; and that to this end he desired much a Free *Councel* to determine so many Controversies, which have no other cause but the Spirituall Usurpations of the *Roman Bishops,* in which desire he thought the *King* of *France* and other *Princes* would joine with him: that perhaps *God* meant to produce this happinesse out of these troubles of the *Republique;* [t]hat he had spoken thereof to *Pope Clement,* then when hee was moved by him (when first hee came to the *Crowne* of *England*) to unite himselfe unto the *Romane Church,* but he would not heare any thing of a *Councell;* that this *Union* was much to be desired, but clearly there was no other meane to effect it, then by a free *Generall Councell.*

---

[72] *Reliq.,* 1651, sigs. b12r–b12v.   [73] Sarpi, *History,* pp. 71–72.
[74] *Ibid.,* p. 77.

The *King* added moreover that the ruine of the *Church* proceeded from this, that the *Popes* esteemed themselves as *Gods,* and further were so corrupted by flattery, that it was no marvell if they could not give eare to any reason, and if they proceeded with precipitation.[75]

Walton turned this passage so that it reflected more clearly to James's credit:

The *King's* advice . . . was the same that he gave to *Pope Clement* at his first coming to the Crown of *England* (the Pope then moving him to an Union with the *Roman Church*) namely, *To endeavour the calling of a free Councell, for the settlement, of peace in Christendom: And that hee doubted not but that the French King, and divers other Princes would joyn to assist in such a work; and in the mean time, the sin of this Breach, both with his, and the* Venetians *Dominions, must of necessity lie at the* Pope's *door.*[76]

Walton condensed, reordered, rephrased. He gave James dignity by omitting his remarks about the spiritual usurpations of the popes and their corruption by flattery, and, mindful of the function of the passage in the *Life,* he turned the whole into a demonstration that the position of the Venetians had much in common with that of the English. Even this passage, then, he planned carefully to promote sympathy for the Venetian cause.

Sarpi's detailed story of the absolution[77] Walton condensed into a few lines, even as he had crammed the essence of the 435 page book into three pages. But even for these three pages, he used additional material. His one-sentence character of Duke Donato comes from Wotton's will rather than from Sarpi's longer statement.[78] The advice which Sarpi offered to the State, "That the *Pope* was trusted to keep two Keys, one of *Prudence,* and the other of *Power;* And that if they were not both used together, Power alone is not effectuall,"[79] Walton took from another of Sarpi's books, and nowhere is his felicity of expression more apparent than in his

---

[75] *Ibid.*, pp. 117–118.   [76] *Reliq.*, 1651, sig. cʳ.

[77] Sarpi, *History*, pp. 411–426.

[78] *Reliq.*, 1651, sig. b12ʳ: "a wise and resolv'd man, and to all purposes such (Sir *Henry Wotton* would often say it) as the State of *Venice* could not then have wanted." The will refers to Donato "*in a time which needed a wise and constant man*" (ibid., sig. c9ᵛ). Sarpi says, "a Senator . . . the most eminent, for his life (full of integritie,) for his experience in Governing, and for his exquisite knowledge in all good Learning; adorned besides with all heroicall vertues, qualities rare in this age" (*History*, p. 34).

[79] *Reliq.*, 1651, sigs. b12ᵛ–cʳ.

here condensing and sharpening his source while retaining the original intent.[80] Whether Walton supplemented his account from Wotton's state dispatches cannot be determined definitely. Smith found more than a hundred letters of Wotton's from the time of his arrival at Venice on September 23, 1604, until April 21, 1607, the day that marked the termination of the quarrel, some eighty of them in the *State Papers, Venice.* There is no letter dated earlier than 1610 in the editions of *Reliquiae Wottonianae* printed during Walton's lifetime, yet in 1654 Walton quoted verbatim from a letter written in 1606.[81] It is possible that he had copies of others. From one of these he might have drawn his mention that Wotton often conferred with the Senate;[82] from another, that Bedell often conferred with Sarpi.[83] But these are minor matters and might easily have been told him by Wotton.

In this first episode illustrative of Wotton's ambassadorial years, Walton's diligent research is evident: his account is informative and generally accurate. Evident here, too, is his flair for writing of a historical nature. He well knew Wotton's active part in the proceedings he relates, but he wished to suppress Wotton's diplomatic and religious maneuvering even as he suppressed the harsher overtones of the clerics' crimes and James's statement. For this reason, he turned to the less personal, more objective kind of writing which culminated in the *Life of Hooker* and has caused it to be referred to as a life-and-times biography. Walton recognized the importance of Wotton's role as ambassador, but the older, rather more sedate Provost whom he knew dictated his picture. He wished to play down one side of Wotton's character and he contented him-

---

[80] *A Full and Satisfactorie Answer to the Late Unadvised Bull, thundred by Pope Paul the Fift, against the renowmed State of Venice: Being modestly entitled by the learned Author, Considerations Upon the Censure of Pope Paul the Fift, against the Common-wealth of Venice* (London, 1606), p. 76: "Let no man therefore be astonished, depending onely on the authoritie of a Prelate; let him remember, That not one but two keyes were given to Peter, and if they be not both used together, the effect of loosing and binding doth not ensue; the one being of power, and the other of knowledge and discretion. Christ gave not a power to be used, without due knowledge and circumspection, but with great and exquisite judgement; the which wanting, power onely takes no effect."

[81] See p. 165.

[82] Smith, I, 352. *S.P. Ven.*, holograph. "From Venice this 16 of June, 1606." To the Earl of Salisbury.

[83] *Ibid.*, p. 399. *S.P. Ven.*, holograph. "From Venice, the 13th of September, 1607. Style of the place." To the Earl of Salisbury.

self to fill these years of Wotton's life with an objective history "for the information of Common Readers" and three stories revealing the Wotton he wished to represent.

In the first of these, Walton relates how Wotton incurred King James's disfavor by his definition of an ambassador: *"An Embassadour is an honest man sent to lie abroad for the good of his Countrey."*[84] Again a document serves as the basis of his narrative. He says that Wotton wrote two apologies, one to Mark Welser of Augsburg and another to James. That to James has not survived, nor has that to Welser except as it is printed in *Reliquiae Wottonianae.*[85] Walton's account is generally accurate, but, as might be expected, he had difficulty with the Latin in the document. It states that Wotton wrote his definition of an ambassador *"in Albo Amicorum";* that Walton was troubled here is evident in his using the ablative and in his feeling compelled to define the word.[86] *"Jam ante octennium"* became "almost *eight years."* That Walton explains the pun in Wotton's definition after giving both the Latin and English versions further demonstrates his difficulty with the language. More important than this, however, is Walton's calling the letter to Welser an apology. He would show that James was so much impressed by Wotton's clarity, eloquence, and ingenuousness that he again favored him. Walton's far-fetched reference to Donne's "The Will" at this point to indicate that Wotton gained in wisdom from this experience is additional reason to suppose that the parallel situation in the *Life of Donne* was in his mind. If Walton's lack of Latin led him into small error here, it did not deter him from consciously shaping the episode by neglecting a large part of the document, for this is no letter of apology. Wotton asks that his detractor, Scioppius, be silenced, as the English translation puts it, "that your Marts may not be pester'd with the prostituted Pens of Parasites, nor the Press (the brave Invention of the *Germans*) be so miserably tormented." The letter is eloquent, indeed, but eloquent in the vituperative compliment of the day, for Wotton calls his accuser a hungry renegado, a dirty sharker,

[84] *Reliq.,* 1651, sig. c^v.

[85] *Ibid.,* pp. 400–405. "Marco Velsero *Duumviro Augustae Vindeliciae* Henricus Wottonius *S.O.*"

[86] *Ibid.,* sig. c^v: *"Albo,* a book of white paper which for that end many of the *German* Gentry usually carry about them." The English translation of the document in *Reliq.,* 1672, sigs. e8^r–f2^r, uses *"Album,"* but also interpolates a definition, which varies slightly from Walton's.

a raw pedant, the spawn of a sexton and an ammunition trull. Wotton may well have been much more confirmed in His Majesty's estimation and favor than he had formerly been, and because his letter is ingenuous and clear and choicely eloquent, but Walton was more interested in humility than in cleverness, and he slanted his material accordingly.

Little needs to be said of the other two stories by which Walton would characterize the ambassadorial days. They probably were selected and adapted from many such told him by Wotton. The first is a generalized account of Wotton's aid to English prisoners and is in accord with the right of intercession which ambassadors had. It is probable that Wotton told Walton these tales without relating that during his first embassy he also interceded for some Italian criminals, hoping for reward by way of lodging and entertainment at the hands of their relatives in cities where he was not well known.[87] An oral source can be predicated in the second story, also, for Wotton's Baroness di Gabriana became the "Countess of Sabrina" in the *Life.*

Of greater interest in showing Walton's use of his sources is his reference in the *Life* to a letter to Nicholas Pey in which Wotton explains his monetary difficulties before settling at Eton. Walton says:

To him Sir *Henry Wotton* wrote, to use all his interest at Court to procure five hundred pounds of his arrears (for lesse would not setle him in the Colledg) and the want of it wrinckled his face with care ('twas his own expression): and that being procured, he should the next day after finde him in his *Colledg,* and *Invidiae remedium* writ over his *study* door.[88]

The passage is additionally interesting because its source sheds light on the question of the editing of *Reliquiae Wottonianae* and on the authenticity of the letters printed there. The letter referred to by Walton appears, undated, in 1651, and reads:

My dear *Nic.*
More then a voluntarie motion doth now carrie me towards *Suffolk,* especially that I may confer by the way with an excellent Physician at *B.* whom I brought my self from *Venice;* where (as either I suppose or

87 Smith, I, 68, based on *Cal. S.P. Ven.,* X, 500.
88 *Reliq.,* 1651, sig. c5^r.

surmise) I first contracted my infirmitie of the Spleen; to which the very seat is generally inclined, and therefore their Physicians (who commonly studie the inclinations of places) are the likelyest to understand the best remedies.

I hope to be back by ———

It wrinckles my face to tell you, that my ——————— will cost me 500. l. that done, my thoughts are at rest, and over my studie door you shall finde written, INVIDIAE REMEDIUM. Let me end in that word, and ever rest

Your heartiest poor Friend,
H. Wotton.

Postscript.

I forbear to write further, having a World of Discourse to unload unto you; Like those that weed not a Garden till it be grown a wood.[89]

Smith points out that several phrases here occur in a letter to Mary, Lady Wotton,[90] which he dated July, 1639, on the basis of convincing internal evidence.[91] The letter reads in part:

More than a voluntary and pleasurable motion doth now carry me (since your Ladyship is out of Kent) towards Suffolck, especially that I may confer by the way with an excellent physician inhabitant in St. Edmunds Burie, whom I brought myself from Venice, where (as either I suppose or surmise) I first contracted my infirmity of the spleen, to which the very seat is generally inclined. And therefore their physicians (who commonly study the inclinations of places) are the likeliest to understand the best remedies. . . . I have a world of discourse to unlade, like those that weed not a garden till it has grown a wood.[92]

It is significant that in dedicating *Reliquiae Wottonianae,* 1651, to Mary, Lady Wotton, and her three daughters, Walton speaks of their "incouragements" to him and that in his dedication of 1672[3] to Philip, Earl of Chesterfield, he says:

Both Your Grand-mother *and* Mother *had a double Right to them* [Wotton's "Reliques"] *by a Dedication when first made Publick; as also, for their assisting me then, and since, with many Material Informations for the Writing his Life; and for giving me many of the Letters that have fallen from his curious Pen.*[93]

<hr>

[89] *Ibid.,* pp. 510–511. No MS is known.   [90] Smith, II, 285.
[91] *Ibid.,* p. 409.
[92] *Ibid.* Spelling, except that of proper names, modernized. From Corpus Christi College, Oxford, MS 318, f. 44, holograph.
[93] *Reliq.,* 1672, pp. a3r–a3v.

No letter from Wotton to Mary, Lady Wotton, other than that quoted in part above has survived. In *Reliquiae Wottonianae,* 1651, appear the only three surviving letters from Wotton to her father, Sir Arthur Throckmorton.[94] Walton did not print the letter to Lady Wotton, but that it was available to him can hardly be doubted.[95]

It would be foolhardy to think that Walton took pieces of this letter, proceeded to add to them (introducing even a Latin phrase), and so composed a letter which he then assigned to Pey—all this merely to authenticate part of a paragraph which appears in the *Life.* But an alternative suggests itself. Every man who writes two familiar letters at the same time tends to repeat himself, and Wotton was no exception.

[94] *Ibid.,* 1651, pp. 405–406, 417–419, 473–475. The last lacks an address, but is obviously to Throckmorton.

[95] It is likely that Walton was aware of Wotton's letters now in Corpus Christi 318, though he printed none of them in the *Reliquiae.* It may even be that the letters derive ultimately from the "incouragements" given to Walton by Lady Wotton and perhaps by Nicholas Pey. (Walton goes out of the way to commend Pey in a paragraph in the *Life,* 1651, sig. c5^r, and probably learned from Pey himself precisely what Wotton bequeathed to him [see p. 160].) Corpus Christi 318 contains not only the sole surviving manuscript of any letter from Wotton to Lady Wotton, but also the sole surviving manuscript of any letter from Wotton to Pey (f. 10). It contains, in addition (on ff. 45–46), a letter without address or date; Smith (II, 77) thinks it was written about May 6, 1615, and G. Knight Watson thinks it may have been written to Pey (*Archaeologia,* XL [1866], 265). This letter repeats the substance of one to King James which is printed in *Reliq.,* 1651, p. 396. No manuscript of this letter to the King exists, but we may probably assume, since only a few manuscripts survive for the letters printed in the *Reliquiae,* that Walton, whenever he could, sent manuscripts to the printer. In Corpus Christi 318, too, is a holograph letter to Sir Albertus Morton (f. 39) with which, Wotton says, he sends a letter to the Earl of Holderness. The letter to Morton was not printed in the *Reliquiae,* but that to the Earl, for which no manuscript exists, was printed in 1651, p. 407.

Corpus Christi 318 was given to the College by Richard Davis of Sandford. The Wotton materials there were obviously known to William Fulman, who helped Walton before 1670 (see pp. 285–286) and to whom Walton gave a manuscript in 1673 (see pp. 233–234, n. 51). Copies in Fulman's hand of some of Wotton's letters in Corpus Christi 318 are among Fulman's papers (in Corpus Christi 307), and, indeed, Corpus Christi 318 contains some material in Fulman's hand. Interestingly enough, the letter there to Mary, Lady Wotton, bears the notation in Fulman's hand, "v. p. 359"; in like fashion, the letter to Morton is inscribed by Fulman "v. p. 317" and the unaddressed one on ff. 45–46 "v. p. 280." On p. 359 of *Reliq.,* 1672, is the letter to Pey which is similar to the one addressed to Lady Wotton; on p. 317 is the letter to the Earl of Holderness sent with the letter to Morton; on p. 280 is the letter to King James which is similar to the unaddressed one.

Some similarity in phrasing has already been noticed in the letters on his illness that Wotton wrote at about the same time to Walton and to Sir Edmund Bacon.[96] In 1651, Walton printed a letter, without date, *"To Master ——";*[97] he indicated in 1672 that the letter was "To Mr. *Milton.*"[98] This is the letter which Wotton sent John Milton, thanking him for a copy of *Comus,* and which was first printed as a commendation in Milton's *Poems,* 1645.[99] Here the letter is dated "From the Colledge, this 13. of April, 1638." It reads in part:

> At *Siena* I was tabled in the house of one *Alberto Scipioni,* an old Roman Courtier in dangerous times, having been Steward to the *Duca di Pagliano,* who with all his familiy [*sic*] were strangled, save this only man that escap'd by foresight of the Tempest; with him I had often much chat of those affaires; into which he took pleasure to look back from his native harbour, and at my departure toward *Rome* (which had been the Center of his experience) I had won confidence enough to beg his advice, how I might carrie my self securly there, without offence of others, or of mine own conscience. *Signor Arrigo mio* (sayes he) *I Pensieri stretti, & il viso sciolto:* That is, *Your thoughts close, and your countenance loose,* will go safely over the whole World.[100]

In *Reliquiae Wottonianae,* 1651, appears another letter which starts:

> *Worthy* Sir,
> All health to your selfe, and to yours both at home and abroad. Sorrie I was not to be at *Eton* when Master B. your Nephew and my Freind came thither to visit me, being then in procinct of his travels: But I had some good while before, at an other kind visitation, together with your sons and Master S. given him a Catholick Rule which was given me long since by an old *Roman* Cou[r]tier with whom I tabled in *Siena,* and whose Counsels I begged for the goverment of my selfe at my departure from him towards the foresaid Court, where he had been so

---

[96] The similarities persist in a letter written to Dr. John Castle at this time (*Reliq.,* 1651, pp. 484–485).

[97] *Ibid.,* pp. 432–436. The deletion of Milton's name shows the degree of Walton's political partisanship. See pp. 161; 285, n. 49; 308, n. 34.

[98] *Ibid.,* 1672, p. 342.

[99] *Poems of Mr. John Milton, Both English and Latin* (London, 1645), pp. 71–73: "The Copy of a Letter Writt'n By Sir Henry Wootton, To the Author, upon the following Poem."

[100] *Reliq.,* 1651, pp. 434–435. This varies from the version in *Poems,* 1645, only in that the translation of the Italian quotation is interpolated. Naturally, Wotton would not have translated it for Milton.

well versed. *Sinor Arrigo* (saies he) There is one short remembrance will carrie you safe through the whole world. I was glad to heare such a preservative contracted into so little roome, and so besought him to honor me with it. Nothing but this (saith he) *Gli Pensiere stretti, & il viso sciolto:* That is, as I use to translate it, *Your Thoughts close, and your Countenance loose.*[101]

Smith says that *"B."* was probably Michael Branthwaite and *"S."* probably James Scudamore, and that their original visit to Wotton was probably before they journeyed to Paris in June, 1635. For want of any other indication of date, Smith tentatively placed this letter in 1636.[102] He noticed the similarity of advice here and in the letter to Milton, but he dated it too early. Since in this letter Wotton says in reference to the first visit that it was "some good while before," and since he says in the letter to Milton, "I suppose you will not blanch *Paris* in your way; therefore I have been bold to trouble you with a few Lines to Master *M. B.* whom you shall easily finde attending the young Lord *S.* as his Governor," it, too, ought probably to be dated 1638. Here, with little variation in time, is the repetition of a story, but not with absolute identity of phraseology.[103]

Walton may well have had a letter to Pey with phraseology like that to Lady Wotton, but their absolute identity in two sections makes it obvious that the letters were written at the same time, perhaps on the same day. Since the letter to Lady Wotton was written in 1639, that to Pey was also written in that year. Walton,

[101] *Ibid.,* pp. 453–454.   [102] Smith, II, 364.

[103] In a letter to the Earl of Salisbury, dated Sept. 13, 1607 (N.S.), Wotton wrote of Paolo Sarpi, "He seemeth, as in countenance so in spirit, liker to Philip Melanchton than to Luther. . . . For learning, I think I may justly call him the most deep and general scholar of the world, and above other parts of knowledge, he seemeth to have looked very far into the subtleties of the Canonists, which part of skill gave him introduction into the Senate" (*ibid.,* I, 400). When Wotton wrote to King James on Jan. 10, 1622[3] (O.S.) about the death of Sarpi, he said, "Profound almost in all kind of knowledge, but singularly versed, as his place did require, in the subtleties of the Canon Law, as the forge (for so he often said) of all the Roman corruptions. . . . And to parallel him briefly with two great instruments of light, he had surely much of the Melancthon, but little of the Luther" (*ibid.,* II, 260). Undoubtedly Wotton thought his comparison of Sarpi to the two men a particularly happy one, and it stuck in his mind; Sarpi's reputation in canon law was universal. The similarities of characterization are interesting but understandable, and that the verbal expression has changed in details after fifteen years was to be expected.

then, is doing here what he did more obviously with a letter in the
Life of Donne, but he would here have us believe that the letter
to Pey was written some fifteen years earlier than in fact it was.
It is easy to see why the letter to Pey bears no date in *Reliquiae
Wottonianae,* and the excision-indicating dashes may also be explained, for one of them obviously contained a time reference which
would have prevented Walton's crediting the letter to a different
period in Wotton's life and the other would have told that Wotton
needed five hundred pounds for a reason other than settling at
Eton. Not only does this letter show definitely that Walton edited
Reliquiae Wottonianae, but it reveals sharply something of his
method as a biographer. In order to present a seemingly authentic
account of Wotton as an undervaluer of money prior to his becoming Provost, he was willing to wrench the letter to Pey from
its context and to edit it.

Walton had quoted part of Donne's will to demonstrate the
deliberateness of his every motion in the *Life.* He says that he
quotes Wotton's will as a testimony "that his chief Designe was a
Christian Endeavour that his debts might be satisfied."[104] But the
structure of the *Life* points to another reason. Walton's main interest in the will was the way in which Wotton chose to preserve
his name through the motto he wished inscribed on his gravestone,
"Disputandi Pruritus Fit Ecclesiarum Scabies." He interrupted his
quotation of the will to give the motto, he provided a translation,
and he commented at some length on it. The will follows closely
upon Walton's account of Wotton as an enemy of wrangling in
religion and is therefore part of the character of the good provost.
In his comment, Walton says that whether or not Wotton was, as
he maintained, the first author of the motto, does not affect its
sentiment. He goes so far to justify Wotton as to say that

Sir *Henry Wottons* mind was then so fix'd on that part of the Communion of *Saints* which is above, that an holy *Lethargy* did surprize his
Memory

and that

his mind was then so fix'd on Heaven, that a holy zeal did transport
him; . . . Almighty God was pleased to make him a *Prophet* to tell
the *Church Militant,* (and particularly that part of it in this Nation)

[104] *Reliq.,* 1651, sig. c7ᵛ.

where the weeds of Controversie grow to be daily both more numerous, and more destructive to humble Piety.[105]

Walton says at the end of his comment that sad changes have proved the epitaph to be a useful caution to the English nation. Wotton's motto provided Walton in large part with the springboard for his *Life.* The motto set forth an idea which he had always cherished, and he sought to make the *Life of Wotton* conform to it by demonstrating in Wotton's every action his peaceable character and his pleasant temper. This is the message, as it were, that the *Life* was to carry, and it explains why Wotton's wrangling in Venice was suppressed. And, for the sake of conveying the message, Walton even invested the character of Wotton at this point in the *Life* with a holiness that is not in keeping with the rest of his picture.

Walton made many purposeful minor changes in the will before he included it in the *Life.*[106] Some of these serve only to smooth Wotton's diction; others were dictated by various reasons. Walton added a touch of piety when he changed "thus dispose of the poor things which I shall leave" to *"thus dispose of my selfe, and the poor things I shall leave."* Wotton had bequeathed to Nicholas Pey a chest of "Instruments and Engines of all kinds of uses: in the lower box whereof, are some fit to be bequeathed to none but so entire an honest man, as he is." In a note, Walton explained that the chest contained *"Italian* locks, pick-locks, screws to force open doors; and things of worth and rarity." To each of the fellows of Eton, Wotton had left a ring inscribed *"Amor vincit omnia."* It is impossible to tell whether Walton changed *"vincit"* to "unit" purposely or not. His faulty Latin might have caused the change, but such scraps as this probably offered him little trouble, and it is at least possible that Walton made the change intentionally to carry out, even in such a minor detail, the lesson of the epitaph.

[105] *Ibid.,* sigs. c8^v–c9^r.

[106] Smith says (I, 219, n. 1), "I give the text of this will from the original now in the P.P.C. [*sic*]. Izaak Walton prints it, with many additions and more omissions, in the first edition of the *Reliquiae.* Some of these were corrected in subsequent editions, but others were added." Subsequent to 1651, Walton made just four changes in the will. In 1654 and in the other editions of the *Life* prior to his death, he omitted "FIT" from the epitaph and changed "Audiences" to *"Audience";* in 1670, he added *"with me"* to Wotton's *"Viol di Gamba,* which hath been twice in Italy"; and in 1672 he added "many" to the "things of worth and rarity" which, his note explained, Wotton left to Pey. In 1651, Walton made about a dozen minor changes in the will in addition to those noted in the text.

In the last paragraph, Walton added a statement that a *"schedule"* might be annexed to the will and he added the name of Nicholas Oudart as a witness. Wotton, writing in 1637, had left a picture to "the Prince Charles of sweet and blessed hopes." When Walton wrote in 1651, the Prince's hopes were anything but sweet and they had apparently not been blessed very efficaciously, and he contented himself with referring to *"the most hopefull Prince."* A further change was probably indicated by the exigencies of the times. Wotton had made a bequest to the Earl of Holland. Although Holland had been beheaded in 1649 as one of the authors of the second civil war, his reputation was unsavory among the royalists. Clarendon called him "a fine gentleman in good times," but said that he "too much desired to enjoy ease and plenty when the King could have neither."[107] Although he was groom of the stole, he refused to attend Charles when he left Whitehall in January, 1642, and two months later he refused to obey a summons to York. In 1651, then, his name was distasteful to Puritans and Royalists alike, and Walton reproduced the bequest but wrote in a dash where Holland's name had appeared, for it would accomplish nothing of advantage to link his name with Wotton's. The will, then, provides a vivid demonstration of Walton at work. The great subjectivity of Walton's writing is evident in his seizing upon the epitaph as a chance to propagandize his own ideas and in his making the whole of the will function as part of the character plan which the epitaph had probably suggested. It was not enough, however, that the epitaph provided Walton with that quality in Wotton which he would emphasize above all others, not enough that the will could be used as evidence to authenticate that quality in a larger character sketch, but its details of language and content must be carefully scrutinized. Walton rid the will of every note which might be embarrassing, of any detail which would not reflect credit upon Wotton. He was as careful of the individual detail as he was of his total impression.

This care is apparent throughout the *Life* and extends even to minor points. In his attempt to add weight and dignity to the Baldi episode, Walton prefaced his account with a paragraph in

[107] Henry Rich, first Earl of Holland, 1590–1649. See *DNB*, article "Henry Rich," and Edward Hyde, Earl of Clarendon, *History of the Rebellion and Civil Wars in England*, W. Dunn Macray, ed. (Oxford, 1888), IV, 508 [bk. XI. 263].

which he sought to show the urgency and seriousness of the times. How better effect this than by authenticating the account with the work of a Catholic author who condemns the Jesuits? Walton used Watson's *A Decacordon of Ten Quodlibeticall Questions* as evidence of attempts to excommunicate and kill James of Scotland. But in order to increase in the reader's mind the importance of the role Wotton played, Walton even strengthened Watson's statements that the Jesuits endangered the life of Elizabeth and sought to influence the choice of her successor.[108] Again, when he wanted just the right sentiment with which to describe Wotton's troubles with money, one that would indicate Wotton's circumstances and still reflect to his credit, he found it in the *Elements of Architecture*. Wotton had written parenthetically of Sir Philip Sidney in citing one of his extreme views on architecture that his *"Wit* was in truth the very rule of *Congruity."*[109] Not only did Walton like the aphorism, but he liked, too, the opportunity to juxtapose the names of Sidney and Wotton. He made the quotation serve these various purposes by ingeniously comparing Sidney's wit with Wotton's lack of fortune in monetary matters: "For it may by no means be said of his providence as himself said of Sir *Philip Sidney's* wit (that it was the very measure of Congruity)."[110]

Such passages as these point up the variety of materials which went into the making of the *Life of Wotton*. Walton drew upon the chronicles of Holinshed and Camden, Lambard's county history, Sarpi's accounts of Venetian affairs, Wotton's reliques and his stories. But Walton was influenced by his sources only when they corroborated or supplemented his own views or when they suggested a way to enhance the presentation of those views. The Wotton he drew was the retired courtier whose friendship he had cherished. The Provost in all his kindliness, graciousness, good intentions, and humane urbanity cast a long shadow over Walton's *Life,* and Walton scrutinized his sources to make sure that they deepened the shadow without disturbing its outline. The motto he found in Wotton's will corroborated the impression of simple dignity

---

[108] [William Watson], *A Decacordon of Ten Quodlibeticall Questions concerning Religion and State* (1602), p. 152: "Tolleration or liberty of cōscience, wold quite have cut off two bloudy hopes, which *Parsons* hath in al his practices: to wit, aswel the indāgering of her Majesties royall person, as also the favoring, furthering, cōsenting, or any way seeking directly or indirectly the advancement of any one competitor more thē another."

[109] *Reliq.,* 1651, p. 304.   [110] *Ibid.,* sig. c4ᵛ.

and tolerant wisdom which he wished to further. It even suggested a piety altogether becoming Wotton's old age, and Walton was quick to exploit it by intruding his lengthy comment into the provisions of the will. Holinshed's digressive pedigree supplemented Walton's knowledge of the glory of Wotton's heritage, suggested to him the value of including an account of the Wotton family, and thus made it easy for him to enhance the extent of Wotton's accomplishments by saying that Wotton died "worthy of his Name and *Family*." Walton turned his sources to his own ends and made them part of his own fabric. The slight discursiveness of the *Life* does not stem from unsuccessful attempts to connect and relate variegated printed sources; it comes, rather, from Walton's self-indulgence in a surfeit of anecdote. When he relied upon a printed source, he made sure that its main emphasis was precisely his own and that its every detail conformed to the impression of Wotton he had in mind. He used printed sources cautiously, almost as though he feared they might say something other than what he thought proper. The discursiveness of the *Life* comes from the relaxation of this cautionary attitude when he deals with his oral inheritance. If he scanned his printed sources closely, almost suspiciously, he was confident that he had the sureness of touch to make an anecdote pertinent, or entertaining, or both. The liberality with which he included good stories in the *Wotton* shows the degree of trust he had in his own imagination.

Chapter 6

The Four Revisions of

the *Life of Wotton*

THREE years after the first edition of *Reliquiae Wottonianae,* a second edition appeared. The volume contained little that was new except the *Aphorisms of Education* and eight additional letters, six of them to Buckingham, this despite the phrase "with large *Additions"* on the title page. These words were more appropriate for the *Life,* for it was increased by one-sixth. Walton added to the ambassadorial years of Wotton, but two-thirds of the increase he devoted to the years as Provost. The first sections of the *Life* were refined, though Walton never added substantially in any of his four revisions to those sections treating Wotton's ancestry, education, and travels.

The first major addition in 1654 tells nothing more about Wotton the ambassador, but was obviously inserted to preserve the structural equilibrium of the *Life,* to balance the large increase in the last section, and to provide a further testimonial of the friendship between Wotton and Donne. Walton reproduced in its entirety Donne's verse letter to Wotton, "After those reverend papers"; he inserted it to show that though Donne "was not one of that number that did personally accompany him in this voyage [to Venice, 1604], yet the reading of this following Letter sent by him, to Sir *Henry Wotton,* the morning before he left *England,* may testifie he wanted not his friends best wishes to attend him."[1]

Walton's second addition also tells nothing more about Wotton, but is an attempt to improve his narrative of the quarrel between

1 *Reliq.,* 1654, p. 36.

Venice and the Pope. In 1651, he had passed from the Pope's message threatening excommunication to Sarpi's advice about the monitory to the Venetians, though he knew at that time Sarpi's passage on the Venetian countermeasure:

Proclamation was made, under paine of incurring the displeasure of the *Prince,* that whosoever had any *Copie* of a certaine *Breve* published at *Rome* against the *Republique,* should bring it unto the *Magistrates* at *Venice,* or to the Governours of Cities and other places of their *State.*[2]

When, in this more expansive account of the history of the quarrel, Walton wished to mention the Venetian proclamation for the additional sympathy and respect that would reflect to the Venetian cause, he wrote:

This act of the Popes, confirmed the *Venetians* in their resolution not to obey him; *And to that end, upon the hearing of his interdict, they presently* published by *sound of Trumpet, a Proclamation to this* effect: "That whosoever hath received from *Rome* any Copy of a Papal in[ter]dict, publish'd there, as well against the Law of God, as against the Honour of this Nation, shall presently render it to the Councel of *Ten,* up[on] pain of death.["]³

This account, considerably more specific than Sarpi's, Walton undoubtedly took from a letter written by Wotton to the Earl of Salisbury within an hour of the proclamation.[4] He preferred Wotton's on-the-spot report, vivid in its detail, to Sarpi's undramatic narrative. Although this letter, or, indeed, any other referring to the quarrel, is not among the letters in *Reliquiae Wottonianae,* Walton has followed it so closely that it must be assumed that he saw it and, therefore, that the letters which were printed represent only a selection of those available to him.

Walton added after the proclamation, "Then was the *inquisition* presently suspended by Order of the State; and the Floud-gates being thus set open, any pleasant, or scoffing wit might safely vent it self against the *Pope,* either by free speaking, or in Print."[5] This

---

[2] Sarpi, *History,* p. 78.   [3] *Reliq.,* 1654, p. 41.

[4] Smith, I, 346, from *S.P. Ven.* (dated April 28, 1606): "It may please him [James I] to know that within this hour hath been published in the chief places of this town, by sound of trumpet, a proclamation to this effect: That whosoever hath received from Rome any copy of a Papal Interdict published there, as well against the law of God, as against the honour of this Commonwealth, shall presently render it unto the Council of Ten upon pain of death." Walton's change of "Commonwealth" to "Nation" in 1654 is understandable.

[5] *Reliq.,* 1654, pp. 41–42.

addition, too, was made to emphasize the fearlessness of the Venetians, to show their righteous indignation with the Pope, to sway the reader's sympathies toward them. In making it, however, Walton seems to sacrifice a conviction dear to him, the desirability for harmony in the Church. The passage is even more perplexing because he departed here from Sarpi's account. Sarpi had written that when a paper was affixed at Vicenza and elsewhere exhorting the Venetians to break with the Roman Church and calling the Pope Antichrist, the Senate had tried to eliminate others by a very rigorous prohibition, even offering a reward for the author of the piece.[6] Walton might well have found some support for his statement in Sarpi's words that "it was not possible to retaine some lively wits, that they should not write somewhat by stealth; hence there came abroad divers Discourses on both sides, but yet onely in hand-writing."[7] But he might easily have turned his account into an illustration of the highmindedness of the Venetians and a sermon on nonwrangling, for Sarpi also wrote, "the Writings of the *Venetians,* following the intention of the *Senate,* were full of all kinds of respect unto the *Pope,* and of modestie towards them who had written in his favour; pressing the matter in hand without digressions, and without noting the faults of the *Court* of *Rome.*"[8] Walton probably differentiated wrangling in religious matters into various categories. Much as he objected to acrimonious wrangling within his own Church, he condoned the scoffing wit of the Venetians as indicative of their independence in the face of papal oppression even as in the *Life of Hooker* he condoned and praised Nashe's merry wit for dispersing the Marprelate forces which he considered unrightly antagonistic toward the Church of England. It is evident, too, that if he advocated harmony, he still enjoyed wit, provided it was used to further what he thought to be a just cause. He meant his illustrations of Wotton's dislike for wrangling in religion to serve also as demonstrations of his ready wit, and when he added an example in 1670, Wotton's wit is in evidence far more than his enmity to argument. Walton's inclinations, then, as well as his desire to show favorably the aggressiveness of the Venetian spirit, dictated the treatment of his source on this occasion.

He made only one more addition to the part of the *Life* about Wotton's career as ambassador. It will be remembered that in the

[6] Sarpi, *History,* p. 142.   [7] *Ibid.,* p. 196.   [8] *Ibid.,* p. 209.

1670 version of the *Life of Donne* Walton inserted into the text
of the *Life* parts of letters which had formed an appendix to the
edition of 1658. He had precedent for so doing, for in 1654 he added
to the *Life of Wotton* the "elogy" which had appeared in the 1651
"Advertisement to the Reader." In 1651, Wotton's years as ambassador had closed abruptly on an apologetic note: materials were
not available and time was short. The apology remained in 1654,
but Walton offered the inscription "to make up what is defective
in this place."[9] The inscription fittingly sums up Wotton's ambassadorial career, and the motto with which it closed, "Animas
fieri sapientiores quiescendo," is an admirable preface for Wotton's
life as Provost and a pretty foreshadowing of the epitaph in the
will which Walton had made so much of.

In 1654, Walton introduced into the *Life* after the passages showing dislike of wrangling an obvious digression in which he quoted
a letter and a poem written by Wotton to show his sorrow at the
death of Albertus Morton. He says that he is digressing according
to his promise to say a little of Morton and Bedell. He had made
no such promise, and the Morton passage was inserted even as that
on Nicholas Wotton had been—to show the eminence of the Wotton family. Albertus Morton, after a varied and honorable political
career, was secretary of state from February 9, 1625, until he died
on September 6 of the same year,[10] and he was related to Wotton.[11]
These facts, which Walton referred to, and Wotton's fine sentiments, account for the inclusion of the Morton material. The insertion has little pertinence to the *Life of Wotton,* and it shows
Walton indulging in his own predilections and at the same time
tampering even with sources which he himself had put into print.

The letter about Morton's death had been entirely printed in
Reliquiae Wottonianae in 1651 and was again printed in 1654,
but when Walton carried it into the *Life,* he omitted the first
six paragraphs starting "This is the account of me since you saw
me last."[12] He centered his attention wholly on the sections which
dealt with Morton. Some trivial changes appear in the letter in the
Life, most of them attempts to clarify. The last of these is particu-

[9] *Reliq.,* 1654, p. 54.   [10] Smith, II, 476.

[11] *Ibid.,* p. 474. Morton's grandfather was Robert Morton, whose widow
(Eleanor, daughter of Sir William Finch) married Thomas Wotton and was
Sir Henry Wotton's mother. Walton calls Morton Wotton's "Nephew" (*Reliq.,*
1654, p. 36) and "his Cosin" (*ibid.,* p. 67).

[12] *Reliq.,* 1651, pp. 506–507.

larly interesting. Wotton had written, "let us now, that yet remain, while our glasses shall run by the dropping away of friends, re-inforce our love to one another."[13] This Walton happily smoothed to "let us therefore that yet remain here, as our days and friends waste, re-inforce our love to each other."[14] But Wotton's sentence was sufficiently clear, and it was not for clarity that Walton made the change; the same figure appears at the end of Wotton's poem about Morton, and he would avoid duplication.

His manner of quoting in the *Life* the poem which had been printed in *Reliquiae Wottonianae,* 1651, is typical and significant, and shows how little respect Walton had for exactness of verse quotation. The poem in the 1654 *Life* has some ten changes from the version in the 1651 *Reliquiae Wottonianae,* although the ver-sions in subsequent editions of *Reliquiae Wottonianae* followed exactly that of 1651. The changes are minor, to be sure. "Will I pay" in line fourteen, for example, became "I will pay." But Wotton's last stanza read:

> Dwell thou in endlesse Light, discharged soul:
> Freed now from Natures, & from Fortunes trust:
> While on this fluent Globe, my Glasse shall role,
> And run the rest of my remaining dust.[15]

Walton, probably quoting from memory despite the printed ver-sion which he could easily have referred to, wrote:

> Dwell then in endless light, thou freed soul,
> Discharg'd from *natures,* and from *fortunes* trust;
> Whil'st on this fluid *globe* my glass shall roul,
> And run the rest of my remaining dust.[16]

When Walton revised the *Life* for inclusion in the 1670 *Lives,* he changed "I will pay" back to *"will I pay."* He realized at this time that the meter of the last stanza was awkward, but again, instead of referring to the original, he made his own changes and patched the lines to read:

> *Dwell then in endless bliss with happy souls,*
> *Discharg'd from* natures *and from* fortunes *trust:*
> *Whil'st on this fluid Globe, my Hour-glass rowls,*
> *And runs the rest of my remaining dust.*[17]

13 *Ibid.,* p. 508.   14 *Ibid.,* 1654, p. 69.   15 *Ibid.,* 1651, pp. 528–529.
16 *Ibid.,* 1654, p. 70 (misnumbered "07").
17 *Lives,* 1670 (Wotton), p. 58.

He followed this version in 1672 and in 1675. How little the accuracy of the poetic line meant to him is evident here, and his attitude reflects the lack of truthfulness which he attached to poetry in general.

Although the Morton digression has little relation to the *Life,* the Bedell material which Walton now added has a function more closely connected with it. Harold Nicolson is not quite right in saying that the introduction of Morton into the *Life* is due to mere civility; he is far from right in attributing the introduction of Bedell to the same thing: "For Walton was a kindly man, and Mr Bedell, who was difficult to fit in, would have been deeply offended had he not been fitted in at all."[18] Walton said in 1654 that Bedell died in "the late horrid Rebellion in *Ireland,*"[19] and in 1672 he added as the year of his death, "1629."[20] In fact, Bedell died in 1642, as a result of the hardships he endured in the rebellion of 1641. Walton was therefore under no obligation to fit Bedell into the *Life.* The reason for the Bedell inclusion can perhaps better be arrived at by noting where Walton inserted this "digression." He placed the Morton and Bedell additions near the close of his character of Wotton as Provost, though Morton's death took place at the end of 1625 and the Bedell material refers to events from 1605 to 1642. The Morton material precedes that about Bedell probably because it predates some of it. This crude chronology serves little purpose, for Walton had made no attempt to adhere to chronology in telling of Wotton's years at Eton. So loose was the structure of Walton's account of these years that he could have placed the additions anywhere in it without violence. Still, the additions seem to disturb the relation between the examples of Wotton as an enemy of wrangling disputes about religion and Wotton's will, which I have tried to show that Walton used as an extension and illustration of this same quality in Wotton. But Walton placed the additions where he did because he thought that some of the Bedell material was pertinent to and impinged upon this very matter. The first part of the material is concerned with the Bedell-Wadsworth-Hall letters, and Walton said, "in them their seems to be a controversie, not of Religion onely, but, who should answer each other with most love and meekness; which I mention the rather, because it seldom falls out so in a Book-War."[21]

[18] Nicolson, *Development of English Biography,* p. 67.
[19] *Reliq.,* 1654, p. 76.   [20] *Ibid.,* 1672, sig. d7ʳ.   [21] *Ibid.,* 1654, p. 72.

Walton shows the great friendship of James Wadsworth, Joseph Hall, and Bedell and relates without rancor Wadsworth's conversion to Catholicism while chaplain to the English ambassador to Spain and his subsequent monastic life. He tells that Hall tried in a letter to persuade him by sweet expressions of love to return to the Anglican fold or to show the reason for his apostasy, that Wadsworth found some expression unpleasant and wrote Bedell instead. Hall had addressed the first of his *Epistles* in 1608 to *"Jacob Wadsworth*, Lately revolted, in Spaine. . . . *Expostulating for his departure, and perswading his returne,"* and he had begun by writing:

How unhappily is my stile changed! Alas, that to a friend, to a brother, I must write as to an Apostate, to an adversary! Doth this seeme harsh? You have turned it, by being turned, your selfe. Once the same walles held us in one loving society: the same Diocesse, in one honorable function: Now, not one Land, and (which I lament) not one Church.[22]

Three years later Hall printed another letter to Wadsworth, one which Walton did not mention, a letter *"Disswading from seperation: & shortly oppugning the grounds of that errour."*[23] He confesses that in his former letter he had touched Wadsworth's conversion "with a light hand," but he would make it appear that he has had a reply from Wadsworth. The Bedell-Wadsworth letters did not appear until 1624, a year after Wadsworth's death.[24] Bedell's good will is demonstrated in his dedication to Prince Charles, where he says that he did not wish to divulge the correspondence during Wadsworth's lifetime.[25] In his first letter to Bedell, dated April 1, 1615, Wadsworth made clear enough his objection to Hall's letter:

And although for my change becomming *Catholique*, I did expect of some Revilers to be termed rather then prooved an *Apostata*, yet I never

[22] Joseph Hall, *Epistles, The First Volume: Conteining two Decads* (London, 1608), pp. 1–2.
[23] Joseph Hall, *Epistles, the Third and Last Volume. Containing two Decades* (London, 1611), p. 41. This is Epistle V of Decade VI.
[24] *The Copies of certaine letters which have passed betweene Spaine and England in matter of Religion. Concerning the generall Motives to the Romane obedience. Between Master James Wadesworth, a late Pensioner of the Holy Inquisition in Sivill, and W. Bedell a Minister of the Gospell of Jesus Christ in Suffolke* (London, 1624).
[25] *Ibid.*, sig. *4ʳ. In the dedication (sig. *3ᵛ), Bedell mentioned Wadsworth's wife and children, whom Walton chose to neglect in his effort to show that Wadsworth lived a very regular life in a monastery after his conversion.

looked for such termes from Master *Hall*, whom I esteemed either my friend, or a modester man; whose slanting Epistle I have not answered, because I would not soile my hands with a Poeticall Rayler.[26]

Walton mentioned the very word "apostasy," but he glossed over the fact that it was this word, considered in its scholastic sense, which had so hurt Wadsworth. In the same letter Wadsworth gives many reasons for his change of faith, and indicates that he does not desire further disputation about them. He asks that if Hall replies, "it may bee *directly* & *fully* to the points and in *friendly termes*" and says that on this condition, he pardons what has passed.[27] Bedell did not answer until 1619.[28] He had forwarded Wadsworth's letter to Hall and had received an answer from Hall in 1616, but had wished to conceal its contents, for while Hall had reiterated that "apostasy" was the only hard word he could be charged with, he had also said, "I pittie the *impotent malice* of the man; sure that hot Region, and *sulphurous Religion* are guiltie of this his choler. For ought I see hee is not onely turned Papist but *Spaniard* too."[29] In 1620, Bedell wrote again, and, seeking to heal the breach, he says that he is sure that Hall did not mean to charge Wadsworth with apostasy "in so horrible a sense" as Wadsworth considered the word.[30] Walton was well acquainted with these details. Hall's letters are not filled with "sweet expressions of love," and it would have been much sweeter of him to have refrained from printing the open letter which Wadsworth objected to. But Hall was the Bishop of Norwich in 1654, and out of respect for him Walton did not give an entirely truthful account. He did not, however, exaggerate or misrepresent the kindness and sweetness of the Bedell-Wadsworth correspondence. It is a remarkable exchange in an age in which argument, particularly church argument, was steeped in vituperation and malice,[31] and Walton used it to further the point of view which is at the core of the *Life of Wotton*.

Walton then included in the *Life*, with the characteristic half-

[26] *Ibid.*, p. 2.   [27] *Ibid.*, p. 15.   [28] *Ibid.*, pp. 17–23. Aug. 5, 1619.

[29] *Ibid.*, pp. 30–33. Written Jan. 10, 1615[6], but not sent "for want of carriage" until May 15, 1616.

[30] *Ibid.*, p. 40. Bedell sent a long answer to Wadsworth's first letter in a letter dated Oct. 22, 1620.

[31] On p. 59 (Wotton) of a Yale copy of *Lives*, 1670, a biased seventeenth-century reader wrote even of the Bedell-Wadsworth letters, "Mr. Wadsworths letters were mean, and meaner his motives to turn Papist."

dozen alterations, the letter Wotton had written in 1627 to Charles
I recommending Bedell's appointment as Provost of Trinity College, Dublin, a letter printed in the 1651 *Reliquiae Wottonianae*.[32]
It adequately demonstrates the relationship between Wotton and
Bedell; and a paragraph characterizing Bedell, which follows it,
reveals Walton's purpose for wishing to do this. He found in Bedell
all the primitive Christian qualities which he so greatly admired
and which were lacking in Wotton. He could not resist including
them in a *Life* where they were missing, and he would associate
Wotton with them, if only indirectly. In addition, he found Bedell's
conduct in Catholic Ireland irreproachable, and he makes much
of the respect and reverence which the Irish had for him. Again,
this mutual love and admiration which he advocated he found
lacking in Wotton's years in Venice, and he took the opportunity
to stress them when they were evident in the life of one of Wotton's
coworkers.

Walton had a further reason for wishing to associate Wotton
with Bedell. Bedell's staunch Anglicanism had not wavered during
his years in Venice with Wotton and had been recognized in his
being made a bishop. Walton probably wished to link Wotton to
Bedell's acknowledged orthodoxy in order to counteract the tinge
of Catholicism in the Wotton family. He undoubtedly knew about
Pickering Wotton's dramatic deathbed conversion to Roman
Catholicism in 1605. This young man, Sir Henry's nephew and the
eldest surviving son of Edward, Lord Wotton, had traveled to Italy
with Sir Henry at the end of 1600, had been with him in Venice
in 1603, and had succumbed to the arguments of Father Richard
Walpole at Valladolid in 1605.[33] Walton may have heard Sir Henry
himself tell the story about his nephew. He certainly knew Bedell's
version of it, for Bedell had not overlooked its similarity to Wadsworth's story and had dwelt on it in Chapter V of the long argument
he sent to Wadsworth in 1620. Walton had probably read, too, the

[32] *Reliq.*, 1651, pp. 422–423. This letter probably led Walton to believe that
Bedell was Wotton's chaplain at Venice during the quarrel. Wotton says that
Bedell "was long my Chaplain at *Venice* in the time of my first Imployment,"
and also that "his travels abroad were not obscure in the time of the Excommunication of the *Venetians*." Bedell replaced Nathaniel Fletcher, arriving
in Venice about the end of April, 1607, shortly after the settlement of the
dispute with the Pope (Smith, II, 462).

[33] Smith, I, 35–36, 38, 44; II, 481–482.

account written by Wadsworth's son in *The English Spanish Pilgrime* (London, 1629), pp. 2–3:

Meanewhile the Jesuits perceiving how little they prevailed [upon James Wadsworth], used other illusions stronger then their Arguments, even strange apparitions of miracles; amongst others, the miracle which they pretend to bee true to have hapned to the eldest sonne of the Lord *Wotton* at his death, in the city *Vallodalid* where a *Crucifix* framed him this articulate sound: *Now forsake your heresie, or else you are damn'd*, whereupon the young Lord and my Father became Proselites to their jugling Religion, the report whereof not long after became a loadstone also to the old Lord *Wotton* his Father, with many others to draw them to popish Idolatry.

Walton knew, then, that not only Pickering Wotton but also his father had died in the Roman Church. He does not mention this in the *Life of Wotton*, but he probably hoped to associate, however obliquely, Sir Henry Wotton with Bedell as against Wadsworth, Edward, Lord Wotton, and his son.

When Nicolson referred to the Morton-Bedell additions as a digression, he was perhaps accurate in evaluating the Morton material. But the Bedell passage is an oasis of religion in an otherwise secular *Life*. Walton was pleased to find such an oasis, even if it was only tangential to the life of Wotton, and its inclusion does reflect favorably to Wotton's credit. It is an inclusion, to be sure, based entirely on Walton's own inclinations and preference, but it has an important function in the *Life*.

In 1654, Walton added to his character of the Provost of Eton, showing him as an encourager of classical learning. The Morton-Bedell passages had carried Walton far from Eton, and he also inserted, prior to quoting Wotton's will, a short passage about Wotton's employments during the Eton period. His account of Wotton's proposed life of Luther is impressive and the project authenticated by reference to Dr. Duppa. Walton says that only a "perswasive loving violence" and the promise of five hundred pounds yearly from the crown forced him to lay it aside in favor of a history of England, and he points to the surviving characters (two fragments, printed in *Reliquiae Wottonianae*, 1651, pp. 163–174, 480–483) as the foundation on which Wotton was building.[34] These small addi-

[34] *Reliq.*, 1654, pp. 77–78. Smith says (I, 205) that Charles increased Wotton's pension in 1632 from two to five hundred pounds a year, and suggests that the

tions demonstrate that Walton was mindful of the structure of the
Life, but the major additions in 1654 show how intensely personal
was his conception of the art of biography. The additions were
largely dictated by personal preference rather than by the demands
of the *Life.*

The smaller changes in the 1654 *Life* are numerous, though not
so numerous as in the 1658 *Life of Donne.* The first version of the
Wotton was not so crude as that of the *Donne,* and the second appeared three years later, whereas eighteen elapsed before the second
edition of *Donne.* The changes are interesting as Walton's first
attempts at revision, and they foreshadow his future method. In
1651, he had written, in apology for the lack of fullness of Wotton's
years as ambassador, "I want a view of some papers that might informe me";[35] in 1654, he added, "his late Majesties *Letter-Office*
having suffered a strange alienation."[36] Despite the excuse,[37] one of
Walton's aims in revising was to fill in details, to lend authenticity
to what he had written. He now made explicit in marginal notes
his references to Holinshed, Camden, St. Augustine, and he added
before Wotton's will a statement that he quotes it "as it was found
writ with his own hand."[38] "Sir *William Davenant*"[39] replaced "the
Poet"[40] as the author of the lines, *"Laugh at the graver businesse of
the State,/ Which speaks men rather wise then fortunate,"* which
Walton had quoted in illustration of Wotton's new, happier life
as Provost. But additional authority was hardly the reason for
naming the poet in this edition. "The Poet" was a specific enough
reference in 1651, for at that time the poet laureate was languish-
ing in the Tower. It is probable that Walton had quoted the lines
as much to indicate his sympathy for Davenant as to express happily
Wotton's state. In 1654, Davenant was no longer confined and his
name could be used with impunity.

Walton concerned himself primarily, however, with polishing
the *Life.* The changes are perhaps best exemplified in his treatment

---

pension was never paid. This probably explains why no more of the *History*
was written.

[35] *Reliq.,* 1651, sig. c4ʳ.   [36] *Ibid.,* 1654, p. 53.

[37] That Walton used the closing of the Public Record Office as an excuse
is evident in his retaining these statements in the subsequent editions of the
Life. He even inserted "now" before "suffered a strange alienation" in 1672
(*Reliq.,* 1672, sig. c8ʳ). Smith found about five hundred of Wotton's letters
and dispatches in the Public Record Office (Smith, I, vi).

[38] *Reliq.,* 1654, p. 79.   [39] *Ibid.,* p. 59.   [40] *Ibid.,* 1651, sig. c5ᵛ.

of one passage. Walton wished to show Wotton's nobility of mind, and, after mentioning his mission to Germany on behalf of the Queen of Bohemia, he told this story in 1651:

This [attempt by Wotton to reconcile the German princes and Emperor Ferdinand to the restoration of the Queen of Bohemia and the Elector Frederick in the Palatinate] was by eight months constant Endeavours, and Attendance upon the Emperour, and his Court, brought to a probability of a successfull Conclusion, by a Treaty; But, about that time the Emperours Army fought a Battell so fortunately, as put an end to the expected Treaty, and Sir *Henry Wottons* hopes; who, when he was departing the Emperours Court, humbly advised him to use his Victory soberly; which advice the Emperour took in good part, being much pleased with his carriage; all the time he resided in his Court; saying, that though the King his Master was look'd upon as an abbettor of his Enemy, yet, he desired Sir *Henry Wotton* to accept of that Jewell, as a testimony of his good opinion of him, (which was a Jewell of Diamonds of more worth then a thousand pounds) this was received with all tearms of honour by Sir *Henry Wotton,* but the next morning at his departing from *Vienna,* at his taking leave of the Countesse of *Sabrina,* an *Italian* Lady, in whose house he was lodged; he acknowledged her merirs [*sic*], and besought her to accept of that Jewell, as a testimony of his gratitude, presenting her with the same which was given him by the Emperour; which being afterwards discover'd, was by the *Emperour* taken for an affront: but Sir *Henry Wotton* acknowledging his thankfulness, declar'd an indisposition to be the better for any gift that came from an enemy to his Royall Mistress; for so the Queen of *Bohemia* was pleas'd he should call her.[41]

The same story was somewhat amplified in 1654:

This was by his eight months constant endeavours and attendance upon the *Emperour,* his Court and Counsel; brought to a probability of a succesful Conclusion by a Treaty: but about that time, (there being then two opposite Armies in the Field) the *Emperours* Army fought a Battel so fortunately, as put an end to the expected Treaty, and Sir *Henry Wottons* Hopes: Who seeing the face of Peace altered by Victory, prepar'd for a removal from that Court; and at his departure from the *Emperour,* was so bold, *as humbly to advise him to use his Victory soberly, and still put on thoughts of Peace:* Which advice, though it seemed to be spoke with some passion, yet was taken in good part by the Emperour, who was ever much pleased with his cariage, all the time that he resided in his Court; and said, *That though the King his Master*

41 *Ibid.,* sigs. c3ᵛ–c4ʳ.

was look'd on as an Abetter of his Enemy the Palsgrave; yet, he took
him to be a Person of much *Honour* and *Merit,* and did therefore desire
him to accept of that *Jewel,* as a Testimony of his good opinion of him;
which was a *Jewel* of Diamonds, of more value then a thousand
pounds.

This was received with all Circumstances and terms of Honour, by
Sir *Henry Wotton;* but the next morning, at his departing from *Vienna,*
at his taking leave of the Countess of *Sabrina,* (an *Italian* Lady) in whose
House the Emperour had appointed him to be lodged, and honourably
entertained: *He acknowledged her Merits, and besought her to accept
of that Jewel, as a testimony of his gratitude:* presenting her with the
same that was given him by the *Emperour;* which being suddenly discovered by the *Emperour,* was by him taken for a high affront, and Sir
H. Wotton told so: To which he reply'd, *That though he received it
with thankfulness; yet, he found in himself an indisposition to be the
better for any gift that came from an Enemy of his Royal Mistress;* for
so the Queen of *Bohemia* was pleas'd he should call her.[42]

Walton was not satisfied merely with additionally explaining the
circumstances. He emphasized the daring of Wotton's advice and
made the advice more explicit. He more directly emphasized the
esteem in which the Emperor held Wotton. The final episode was
improved logically and dramatically. The entire narrative style of
the revised episode is indicative of a preoccupation with minute
detail, and in polishing detail of this kind Walton reveals his prime
interest in his revision. Nor was he yet completely satisfied with this
passage. In 1670, he explained in a more pointed manner that there
was the probability of a successful conclusion "without bloodshed,"
and he inserted, logically if perhaps unnecessarily, that "the Armies
met" between his statement that there were two armies in the field
and that the Emperor's army was superior.[43] He made use of one
of Wotton's dispatches to alter the point of view on the outcome
of the battle so that the incident is viewed through the eyes of the
Emperor's opponents: in 1654, he wrote that "the *Emperours* Army
fought a Battel so fortunately, as put an end to the expected
Treaty";[44] in 1670, "there was a battle fought, the managery whereof
was so full of miserable errours on the one side (so Sir *Henry Wotton*
expresses it in a dispatch to the King) and so advantagious to the
Emperour, as put an end to all Hopes of a succcessful [*sic*] Treaty."[45]
He continued to emphasize Wotton's boldness and had him add a

[42] *Ibid.,* 1654, pp. 51–53.   [43] *Lives,* 1670 (Wotton), p. 43.
[44] *Reliq.,* 1654, p. 51.   [45] *Lives,* 1670 (Wotton), p. 43.

pretty platitude in his advice to the Emperor: *"the Events of every Battel move on the unseen wheels of Fortune, which are this moment up, and down the next."*[46] At this time, too, implication of the most obvious sort did not please Walton when he might state his meaning explicitly. He must explain Wotton's speaking with some passion: "his dear Mistress the *Queen* of *Bohemia,* being concerned in it"; and he must explain that Wotton besought his hostess to accept the jewel as a testimony of his gratitude *"for her Civilities."*[47] Walton has here refined almost to excess, but he has carefully controlled the incident. Despite the changes, the story did not yet please him, and it was not until 1672 that it took its final form. He made it reflect additionally to Wotton's credit by saying that the battle put an end to all "present" hopes of a successful treaty, by having the Emperor go so far as to reply *"That he would consider his Advice"* and by having him comment more explicitly that Wotton's *"behaviour had been such during the manage of the Treaty"* that he believed him to be a person of honor and merit.[48] He revealed Wotton's feelings about the gift of the jewel by adding merely one word: he received it with all "outward" circumstances and terms of honor.[49] He made the entire incident more credible when he changed his words that the Emperor himself discovered Wotton's disposition of the jewel and that Wotton was merely told that he considered it an affront to "which being suddenly discovered, and told to the *Emperor,* was by him taken for a high affront, and Sir *Henry Wotton* told so by a Messenger."[50] In the final version, the story has an authentic tone, and its emphasis has been so pointed that it does substantially more credit to Wotton. If some of the changes show an overzealousness on Walton's part in making every connection for his reader, they are a further demonstration of the complete control he had over his material. This procedure of guiding his reader over the most insignificant hurdles is evident in the revisions of 1654, and the process started in 1654 continued increasingly throughout the years.

Walton's changes ranged in 1654 from the revision of entire incidents to the alteration of a single word. He coupled nouns and adjectives, as he did in the *Donne,* expanding to little purpose such a phrase as "this Age of *Controversie*"[51] to "this Age, which is made

---

[46] *Ibid.*
[49] *Ibid.*
[47] *Ibid.,* pp. 43–44.
[50] *Ibid.,* sig. c8ʳ.
[48] *Reliq.,* 1672, sig. c7ᵛ.
[51] *Ibid.,* 1651, sig. c6ᵛ.

up of opposition and *Controversie.*"[52] He explicitly characterized as one "whose earnestness exceeded his knowledg"[53] a man who railed against the papists. It was no longer enough for Wotton to draw a parallel between his own advantages in becoming Provost of Eton and those of Emperor Charles V when he betook himself to a cloistered life, but he must redefine the advantages and list in detail God's particular mercy.[54] When Walton mentioned King James's desire for the friendship of France and Spain and for an alliance with Venice, he knew that it was superfluous to show the reasons underlying the plan, but he would indicate that he knew them by adding "for divers weighty reasons."[55] In relating Nicholas Wotton's dream about his nephew and Thomas' resultant imprisonment, Walton had already said that Thomas would probably have been among those plotters who lost their lives; in 1654, he made the statement doubly obvious by adding "if he had not been confin'd."[56] He did, however, increase the logic of this story by indicating that Nicholas "returned into *England*"[57] from France before stating that he came to visit Thomas in prison. In this edition, too, he smoothed the final details of Wotton's death. He had abruptly written in 1651 that Wotton had fallen into a fever "of which he died in the tenth fit";[58] the 1654 version is far less clinical: "in the tenth fit, his better part, that part of Sir *Henry Wotton* which could not dye, put off Mortality with as much content and chearfulness, as humane frailty is capable of."[59] Even as he had increased the logic of Nicholas Wotton's dream, so he made more dramatic that of Thomas Wotton. In 1651, he had said that the letter prophesying the robbery at Oxford was written in Kent and "came to his sons hands the very morning after the night in which the Robbery was committed; (for the Dream was true, and the circumstances, though not in the exact time)."[60] He realized that the parenthesis weakened the tale, and he omitted it in the first revision. By 1670, his concern for convincing narrative so far outweighed his scruples for precise truthfulness that he added that the letter was "dated three dayes before" the robbery.[61]

The additions of 1654 do not materially affect the original picture of Wotton, for they have little bearing on Wotton's character or chronicle. The first version of the *Life* had been interlarded with

[52] *Ibid.*, 1654, p. 64.   [53] *Ibid.*   [54] *Ibid.*, pp. 60–61.
[55] *Ibid.*, p. 35.   [56] *Ibid.*, p. 19.   [57] *Ibid.*
[58] *Ibid.*, 1651, sig. c12ʳ.   [59] *Ibid.*, 1654, p. 94.
[60] *Ibid.*, 1651, sig. b7ʳ.   [61] *Lives*, 1670 (Wotton), p. 17.

anecdotes about Wotton and the Wotton family, many of which helped at least to delineate Wotton's character. The additions in the second version are all interesting in themselves, do not disturb the already informal structure of the *Life,* and affect the picture of Wotton only by vaguely associating him with capable and talented men. Walton's impression of Wotton had not changed in the three years between the first and second editions of the *Life,* nor did it ever change. His objective in 1654 was not to alter substantially the pattern of the *Life* or the character of its subject, but rather to point up and polish what he had originally written. The many changes, some of them apparently gratuitous, demonstrate that Walton was primarily interested in 1654 in refining the details of the *Life.*

Walton's revisions continued to be numerous though his additions were slight in the *Life of Wotton* which appeared in the collected *Lives* of 1670. He had mentioned Paolo Sarpi as the author of the eminent *History of the Council of Trent* in 1651,[62] and his interest in this volume is revealed anew in 1670. Formerly, he had stated that Pope Clement VIII had engaged in calm debate with the state of Venice, and he now quoted a decree from the *History of the Council of Trent* in explanation of Clement's refusal to excommunicate the Venetians. He strengthened the case for Venice by indicating that the decree of the Council was issued not many years before the quarrel. Paraphrasing part of the title page of Nathaniel Brent's English translation of the *History,*[63] Walton said that the decree was handed down "after many Politique disturbances, and delayes, and indeavours to preserve the Popes present power," and then he wrote that the Council declared

that though *Discipline,* and especial *Excommunication* be one of the chief sinews of Church government; and intended to keep men in obedience to it: for which end, it was declar'd to be very profitable; yet it was also declar'd, and advised to be used with great sobriety and care:

[62] *Reliq.,* 1651, sig. c^v.

[63] *The Historie of the Councel of Trent. Conteining eight Bookes. In which (besides the ordinarie Actes of the Councell) are declared many notable Occurrences, which happened in Christendome, during the space of fourtie yeeres and more. And, particularly, the practises of the Court of Rome, to hinder the reformation of their errors, and to maintaine their greatnesse. Written in Italian by Pietro Soave Polano, and faithfully translated into English by Nathanael Brent* (London, 1620).

because experience had informed them, that when it was pronounced unadvisedly, or rashly, it became more *contemn'd* then *fear'd*.[64]

This was taken from one of many decrees read to the Council on December 3, 1563.[65] The same paragraph of the decree from which Walton quoted goes on to say that in criminal cases "the secular Magistrate shall not prohibite the Ecclesiasticall to excommunicate, or revoke excommunication, upon pretence that the Decree hath not beene observed," but this restriction of secular power Walton omitted. As usual, he made small changes in quoting, one of them rather significant. It was not to the advantage of the Venetians to indicate that the decree specified that excommunication was not to be used "for a small cause." Since this was the real purpose of the decree, Walton substantially changed the meaning of the passage when he substituted "unadvisedly" in the place of "for a small cause." He was ready to tailor even a councillary decree, then, if in so doing he could build his own case. He slanted his source to justify the position of the Venetians.

In this version Walton also amplified his account of the end of the quarrel. Formerly, he had merely written that the Venetians had scarcely shown any acknowledgment of their absolution, and in 1670 he explained, "For they made an order, that in that day, in which they were absolv'd, there should be no publick rejoycing: nor any *Bonefires* that night; lest the Common people might judg they were absolved for committing a fault."[66] His explanation was based on Sarpi's account:

Likewise many expected in *Venice* they should make bonfires, and other signes of joy, or at least ring their bells: Notwithstanding, nothing of this was done, . . . to the end that such signes of joy might not be interpreted to signifie some absolution which they had received, or the *Republique* thereby conceived to have beene formerly in a fault; which, as an untruth and falshood, they ever abhorred.[67]

Sarpi would have it appear that there was no celebration because of some spontaneous understanding and mutual agreement on the

[64] *Lives,* 1670 (Wotton), pp. 33–34.

[65] *Historie of the Councel of Trent,* p. 809: "That, howsoever the sword of excommunication is the sinew of Ecclesiasticall discipline, profitable to keepe men in obedience, it is to be used with sobriety and circumspection, having found by experience, that it is more contemned then feared, when it is denounced rashly, for a small cause."

[66] *Lives,* 1670 (Wotton), p. 37.   [67] Sarpi, *History,* pp. 427–428.

part of the Venetians. That the celebration was banned by a state order Walton might have got from a letter of Wotton's in which he stated that the censure was revoked "without any bell ringing upon pain of death, or any other public note of gladness, or of so much as acknowledgement."[68] The Sarpi passage, if perhaps not Wotton's letter, was available to Walton in 1651. Its inclusion at this date is an indication of his general satisfaction with the *Life* as it stood, for this little addition, like the others made in this year, merely serves to round out an incident which had already been given its essential form; Walton was not interested in new material, but in perfecting what he had.

This is evident in another slight addition to the *Life*, made to illustrate further Wotton's dislike of wrangling disputes in religion and the readiness of his wit. In the first of his illustrations, Walton had written that Wotton had wittily answered a Roman priest who had asked him where his religion was to be found before Luther.[69] The additional anecdote Walton made dependent on this one, and he had Wotton ask the same priest in a note whether he really believed that the thousands of Christians, excommunicated because of the quarrel between the Pope and Venice, were damned.[70] The "honest pleasant" priest abashedly "under-writ in *French, Monsieur, excusay moy.*" Here, then, Wotton is shown drawing upon his wit to demonstrate to the priest that it is ungentlemanly to wrangle. Since, however, Wotton is provoking argument in this exchange, the added story is better illustrative of his wit than of his enmity to wrangling. In his desire to accentuate Wotton's brilliance and to introduce another pretty story, Walton somewhat diminished the strength of part of his original hypothesis.

Walton's satisfaction with the *Life* is also evident in the kind of minor revisions he made in 1670. Few are significant, and most of them indicate refinement beyond what is necessary. He probably had help with his Italian in this year, for he changed *"ocelli"*[71] to *"ocelle,"*[72] *"vertuosi"*[73] to *"Virtuosi,"*[74] and *"Guarina Baptista"*[75] to *"Baptista Guarini."*[76] Bishops Hall and Duppa had died since

---

[68] Smith, I, 387, from *S.P. Ven.* To the Earl of Salisbury, "Venice, the 27th of April, 1607. Style of the place."

[69] *Reliq.,* 1651, sig. c6ʳ.

[70] *Lives,* 1670 (Wotton), pp. 52–53.

[71] *Reliq.,* 1651, sig. b5ʳ.

[72] *Lives,* 1670 (Wotton), p. 13.

[73] *Reliq.,* 1654, p. 45. In 1651, "vertuosa" (sig. cᵛ).

[74] *Lives,* 1670 (Wotton), p. 38.

[75] *Reliq.,* 1651, sig. b4ᵛ.

[76] *Lives,* 1670 (Wotton), p. 11.

1654, and Walton changed his references to them to "late."[77] He particularized by adding that Essex' committment was "to the Tower"[78] and that Wotton glided through Kent "to *Dover.*"[79] Even as "the Queen"[80] became "Queen *Elizabeth*"[81] in 1654, so now "the Duke"[82] became *"Ferdinand* the great Duke."[83] He indicated, unnecessarily, that by "the people being charitable even to excess"[84] in giving lands or goods to the Church he meant *"the lay people being at their death charitable."*[85] He unnecessarily said that the motive of the Pope's excommunicating the Venetians was his "zeal to the *Apostolick Sea,"*[86] this after adding to his statement that Pope Paul had brought the quarrel with Venice to a much higher contention than had Pope Clement, "being a man of a much hotter temper."[87] In 1651, he had written that the King had promised Wotton the reversion of an office "which was fit to be turn'd into present money";[88] now he added, again unnecessarily, "for a supply of his present necessities."[89] Walton carried to an extreme here his desire to control every possible ambiguity, to lead the reader over every gap. Pleased with the more important aspects of the *Life,* he used the opportunity for a revision to indulge in fussing with details.

Walton's satisfaction with the *Life* is evident, too, in his disregard for much material about Wotton's career which was available to him. In revising his account of the jewel in 1670, Walton added to his description of the outcome of a crucial battle the parenthesis "so Sir *Henry Wotton* expresses it in a dispatch to the King."[90] This statement he included to give validity to his story. Walton did see Wotton's dispatch to the King, but the words which he credits to Wotton, "there was a battle fought, the managery whereof was so full of miserable errours on the one side . . . and so advantagious to the Emperour, as put an end to all Hopes of a succcessful Treaty," are not in it. The words "a sleight Battel full of miserable errours" are, however, in a letter which Wotton wrote to Sir Francis Bacon at this time and which was available to Walton at the

---

[77] *Ibid.,* pp. 59, 63.   [78] *Ibid.,* p. 22.   [79] *Ibid.*
[80] *Reliq.,* 1651, sig. b10ʳ.   [81] *Ibid.,* 1654, p. 30.
[82] *Ibid.,* 1651, sig. b10ʳ.   [83] *Lives,* 1670 (Wotton), p. 25.
[84] *Reliq.,* 1651, sig. b12ʳ.   [85] *Lives,* 1670 (Wotton), p. 32.
[86] *Ibid.,* p. 34.   [87] *Ibid.*   [88] *Reliq.,* 1651, sig. c4ʳ.
[89] *Lives,* 1670 (Wotton), p. 46. In 1672, Walton went even further and inserted "which he wanted" before the 1670 addition (*Reliq.,* 1672, sig. c8ᵛ).
[90] *Lives,* 1670 (Wotton), p. 43.

time of his original composition of the *Life,* for he included it among the letters in *Reliquiae Wottonianae,* 1651.[91] Walton's mention of the dispatch is interesting because it is indicative of the tremendous bulk of material which he had access to and which he purposely neglected to utilize for the *Life.*

The battle which Walton referred to, in which the resistance of the Bohemians was crushed, was the battle of Weisser Berg near Prague on November 8, 1620. On November 18, Wotton, then in Vienna as ambassador extraordinary to the Emperor Ferdinand, wrote a letter to Sir Robert Naunton, secretary of state, in which he said that it was rumored that Prague had been taken ten days before.[92] Four days later he again wrote to Naunton to say that corroboration of the fall of Prague was still lacking, but that he feared the rumor to be true.[93] On November 25, he wrote to verify the news. In this letter he says that he will give the King a report of the action and commentaries upon it in "an expresse dispatche *suspended til the beginning of the next weeke.*" A postscript reads, "By that Messenger which I intende to sende, his M^tie shall receave the Emperours answer touching the *declaration of his just and Royal resolution aboute the Palatinates.*"[94] Wotton sent no dispatch at the beginning of the week, and it is likely that he did not send one until a month had gone by.[95] In a letter of December 26, to Sir George Calvert, Wotton says, "By my letter to the King, your Honour will see how controversies are more easily decided by fortune than by treaty," and again, "Methinks this whole quarrel hath been like the disputation between Job and his friends, whereof the divines note that one side did carry a good cause ill, and the other an ill cause well."[96] This letter was never printed in *Reliquiae Wot-*

[91] *Reliq.,* 1651, pp. 411–416.

[92] George Tomline, ed., *Letters and Dispatches from Sir Henry Wotton to James the First and his Ministers, in the years MDCXVII–XX* (London, 1850), pp. 246–248. "Vienna this 8/18 of November 1620."

[93] Smith, II, 198–199, from *S.P. Ger. Emp.* "Vienna, the 12/22 of November, 1620." Smith says, "Almost certainly to Naunton." Not in Tomline, *op. cit.* (hereafter referred to as *Rox. Club*).

[94] *Rox. Club,* pp. 249–251. "From Vienna the 15/25 of November 1620." In the margin of this letter is written, "The Monday after ye date of this was the 20th of 9^br Style vet."

[95] Smith (II, 444) found no letter of Wotton's dated between Nov. 25 and Dec. 26, 1620.

[96] *Ibid.,* pp. 200–201, from holograph in *S.P. Ger. Emp.* "From Vienna, 16th of December, 1620. Style of England." Not in *Rox. Club.*

tonianae, though the first sentence may well have suggested the platitude on fortune which Walton included in the *Life* of 1670 and the second may have swayed him to indicate the management of the battle on both sides rather than only on the Emperor's.[97] Wotton's dispatch to the King was delayed until December 29.[98] He had received the Emperor's answer in an audience on November 28, but had waited to send the dispatch until he had been granted two further interviews.[99] It was with his dispatch of December 29 that he sent the answer of the Emperor, which he had promised a month earlier. This dispatch and the Emperor's answer were printed in *Reliquiae Wottonianae,* 1672, in a new section called "Additional Letters to Several Persons: Now first Published from the Authors own Copies," which contained some thirty letters and several state documents. Since Walton mentioned the dispatch in 1670, this material must have been available to him at that time, but he never used either the dispatch or that part of the correspondence which sheds light on Wotton as an ambassador extraordinary.

An attempt to determine where Walton may have found this material sheds light on the number of documents which he probably saw. In his will, Wotton left all his manuscripts *"not before desposed"* to the library at Eton College,[100] and Walton may well have gone to Eton to examine them. In 1850, George Tomline edited for the Roxburghe Club all the letters and dispatches of Wotton at Eton.[101] Tomline found at Eton sixty-five letters by Wotton written between August 11, 1617, and November 25, 1620,

[97] If this letter is the source of these changes in 1670, we must assume either that Walton saw a copy of the original or that, despite the protestation repeated in all the editions of the *Life,* he did make a trip to the Public Record Office. The latter does not seem so unlikely when it is remembered that he also retained in all editions his statement that the printer's press was idle in anticipation of his *Life,* though the description obtains only for the *Life* of 1651.

[98] The copy which Smith found in *S.P. Ger. Emp.* is dated "Vienna, 19/29 of December, 1620" (II, 201). *Reliq.,* 1672, p. 523, has "Decemb. 1620."

[99] *Reliq.,* 1672, p. 517: *"A Copy of the Emperors Answer to my Audience,* 28. Nov. 1620"; p. 521: *"Decemb.* 4. 1620. A Copy of the Emperours Answer to my Audience, about the Ban or Proscription intended against the *Palatine";* p. 525: "Before the going of *de Preaux,* I had one access to the Emperor, and two other while he was away."

[100] *Ibid.,* 1651, sig. c11ʳ.

[101] The completeness of the *Rox. Club* collection is shown by Smith's not finding at Eton any MS which had not been included by Tomline (Smith, II, App. I, pp. 417–454) except a MS volume of Latin poems in Wotton's honor (I, 165, n. 2).

almost all of them to Sir Thomas Lake, Sir Robert Naunton, and King James. He found, too, seventy letters from Gregorio de' Monti, Wotton's Italian secretary,[102] to Sir Robert Naunton, dated between May 17, 1619, and January 29, 1621, and several other letters and documents which were related to Wotton's diplomatic career. Walton either saw these at Eton or had copies of some of them, for, printed in *Reliquiae Wottonianae,* 1651, is a letter the manuscript of which is at Eton,[103] and in *Reliquiae Wottonianae,* 1672, is part of another letter found there.[104] But Walton also printed seven letters in *Reliquiae Wottonianae* written during the dates covered by the Wotton correspondence at Eton for which there are no manuscripts there.[105] Not only, then, did he probably see the letters at Eton, but also additional ones as well.[106]

[102] During Wotton's first embassy (1604–1610), again during 1616–1619, and in 1621 until De' Monti's death in November of that year. De' Monti was left in charge of English affairs at Venice from May, 1619, to March, 1621, when Wotton was away (Smith, II, 473–474).

[103] *Reliq.,* 1651, pp. 365–381; *Rox. Club,* pp. 198–206.

[104] *Reliq.,* 1672, pp. 498–508; *Rox. Club,* pp. 213–223.

[105] *Reliq.,* 1651, pp. 467–473, and 175–191 (part of a letter first printed entirely in *Reliq.,* 1672, pp. 253–264 [see Smith, II, 132, for full discussion]). A third letter is in *Reliq.,* 1654, pp. 472–474. There are four letters in *Reliq.,* 1672: pp. 485–486, 486–495, 509–512, and 515.

[106] Since two letters appear both in *Reliquiae Wottonianae* and in the Roxburghe Club collection, Walton, if he went to Eton, probably did not remove any letters. Where did he find the other letters printed in *Reliquiae Wottonianae* which were written during the dates covered by the correspondence at Eton? Smith (II, 180) found a holograph of the letter printed in *Reliq.,* 1654, in *Harleian* MS 1581, f. 212 (British Museum), and he found (II, 443) a transcript of that on pp. 509–512 of *Reliq.,* 1672, in *S.P. Ger. States, XVIII* (Public Record Office), but he was unable to find manuscripts for the others. Walton may have been furnished copies by one of Wotton's secretaries, Sir John Dynely or Nicholas Oudart. Dynely had accompanied Wotton to Venice in 1616 and to Vienna in 1620 and had acted as his assistant secretary in Venice from 1621 to 1623 (Smith, II, 470). Walton printed seventeen of Wotton's letters to Dynely in *Reliq.,* 1672, for none of which Smith could find manuscripts. Dynely probably left Wotton's service before Walton became acquainted with Wotton, but he was frequently in England after 1626 and Walton may have met him at Eton. Oudart's positions as assistant secretary to Sir Edward Nicholas, secretary of state, between 1641 and 1651 and as Latin Secretary to Charles II after 1666 probably made access to official papers easy for him, and he may have supplemented his request that Walton write Wotton's life by material aid. (For some indication of the scope of the papers in Oudart's hands at one time, see Francis Peck, *Desiderata Curiosa,* new ed. [London, 1779], pp. 323–324, 343–345, 387–409, 457–460 *et passim.*)

Smith found some fifty additional letters, written by Wotton during the dates of the Wotton manuscripts at Eton, which were not printed by Walton.

It has seemed useful to comment upon these matters to show how much more than he printed or mentioned was available to Walton, and to demonstrate again the selectivity of the letters in *Reliquiae Wottonianae*. In the light of the diplomatic material which was available to Walton, it is clear that the *Life of Wotton* might have been very different from what it is. Walton's purposefulness in molding the *Life* is evident in his choosing to characterize Wotton's years as ambassador extraordinary by one anecdote in which the glancing reference to a dispatch is the only indication of the wealth of factual detail upon which he might have drawn. In 1670, however, he was not greatly interested either in the materials available at the Record Office or in diplomatic materials of any kind. He had written the *Life* and had made it conform to his preconception of Wotton. In 1670 his primary interest was in shaping his original more completely to lessen the possibility of misinterpretation of what he had already written.

Walton continued this process two years later, when a third edition of *Reliquiae Wottonianae* was published. The edition of 1654 was undoubtedly exhausted by this time, and the collected *Lives* of 1670 had probably renewed the public's interest in Wotton. The letters previously mentioned and those to Sir Edmund Bacon (published separately in 1661) were included to increase the attractiveness of the volume. Walton's statement in the "Advertisement to the Reader" is far less modest than those in the *Life of Donne:* "You may be pleas'd to take notice, that in this last Relation of Sir *Henry Wotton*'s Life, 'tis both inlarg'd, and some small errors rectified; so that I may now be confident, there is no material mistakes in it."[107]

As he indicated, his interest in the revisions of 1672 was in rectifying the small errors, and he made some dozen alterations and additions in the time references. He changed the year of Sir Robert Wotton's birth from 1463[108] to "about the Year of Christ 1460"[109] and Wotton's proceeding Master of Arts from "about the nine-

---

Here is further evidence of the incompleteness of the Eton manuscripts during their dates. Most of these additional letters are in *S.P. Ven.*, in the Public Record Office, and Walton may have known of them.

[107] *Reliq.*, 1672, sig. a5^r.   [108] *Ibid.*, 1651, sig. b^v.

[109] *Ibid.*, 1672, sig. a7^v.

teenth year of his age"[110] to "about the twentieth."[111] He changed the duration of the contention between the Pope and Venice from "severall yeers"[112] to "almost two years"[113] and Wotton's mission to Emperor Ferdinand from his "second going"[114] to Venice to his "last."[115] He dated Wotton's final return to London from Venice "the year before King *James* died"[116] rather than "that yeare in which"[117] he died, and the time of his final return to Eton from Winchester became "about five Moneths before his death"[118] instead of "about 9."[119] His exactness at this time forced him to change a reference to Wotton's brother in 1603 from "the Lord *Wotton*"[120] to "Sir *Edward*, who was after Lord *Wotton*"[121] and made him add a parenthesis that Pope Paul V succeeded Pope Clement "though not immediately, yet in the same year."[122] In this year, too, he added in marginal notes the dates of Bedell's appointments as Provost of Trinity College, Dublin, and as Bishop of Kilmore,[123] and, in a parenthesis, the date of his death.[124] It is indicative of his interest in exact chronology at this time that he added that the Pope gave the Venetians only twenty-four days in which to revoke their unsatisfactory laws,[125] a bit of information which he had had at hand in 1651 but had not used.[126] In 1670, he had awkwardly and unnecessarily added "the present"[127] before the name of Pope Clement VIII, and he changed this to "the former."[128] The only alteration of time which sharpened even slightly the dramatic effect of the *Life* was Walton's changing his statement that Nicholas and Thomas Wotton foretold "the dayes of their death"[129] to "the very dayes of their own death."[130]

In this year, too, Walton filled in the blanks which had stood for the first names of Wotton's mother and her first husband[131] and that of the Provost of Eton previous to Wotton.[132] Although he did not omit the parenthetical "if I be rightly informed," he said that

[110] *Ibid.*, 1651, sig. b4ᵛ.   [111] *Ibid.*, 1672, sig. b2ᵛ.
[112] *Ibid.*, 1651, sig. cʳ.   [113] *Ibid.*, 1672, sig. c4ᵛ.
[114] *Ibid.*, 1651, sig. c3ᵛ.   [115] *Ibid.*, 1672, sig. c7ʳ.
[116] *Ibid.*, sig. c8ᵛ.   [117] *Ibid.*, 1651, sig. c4ʳ.   [118] *Ibid.*, 1672, sig. e4ʳ.
[119] *Ibid.*, 1651, sig. c12ʳ.   [120] *Ibid.*, sig. b11ʳ.   [121] *Ibid.*, 1672, sig. cʳ.
[122] *Ibid.*, sig. c3ᵛ.   [123] *Ibid.*, sig. d6ᵛ.   [124] *Ibid.*, sig. d7ʳ.
[125] *Ibid.*, sig. c3ᵛ.   [126] Sarpi, *History,* p. 72.
[127] *Lives,* 1670 (Wotton), p. 33.   [128] *Reliq.*, 1672, sig. c3ᵛ.
[129] *Ibid.*, 1651, sig. b7ʳ.
[130] *Ibid.*, 1672, sig. b5ʳ. "Own" was added in 1654 (p. 20).
[131] *Ibid.*, 1672, sig. bᵛ.   [132] *Ibid.*, sig. dʳ.

Wotton had stayed in Isaac Casaubon's house in Geneva[133] where he had before said Casaubon's father's house.[134] Walton's care for minute factual detail appears odd for a man who had previously been much more concerned with accuracy of impression than with accuracy of fact, but it is not unreasonable that his desire to shape precisely every impression should eventually lead to a corresponding desire to be precisely accurate in his facts. And he could overdo the one as well as the other. In 1672, his reference to "our late King *Charles*" was abundantly clear, and his addition of "the first"[135] is a ridiculous tautology. When, in this year, Walton expanded slightly his passage on the Venetian writings against the Pope, he added, in order to demonstrate by a fact the seriousness of the break in relations, that "*Duado* their Ambassador [was] call'd home from *Rome*."[136] Walton's source indicated that Pietro Duodo did indeed leave Rome,[137] but it stated that Duodo had been sent to Rome as ambassador extraordinary to replace Leonardo Donato when he had been elected Duke[138] and further explained:

They resolved to call home onely the extraordinarie *Ambassador*, thereby sufficiently testifying their sensiblenesse of the wrong: but to leave the Ordinary, to doe all offices of piety and reverence towards the *See Apostolique,* and to prevent an absolute rupture, which they would avoid till they were forced by an extreme violence.[139]

It is evident even at this date, when Walton was scrupulous in correcting facts, that if he had to choose between relating factual truth and changing that truth for dramatic effect, accuracy was secondary to artistry.

If Walton at this time sought to improve the *Life* factually by specifying that Wotton was the "only" child of his father's second marriage,[140] that he was a "Commoner" of New College in Oxford,[141] that in fleeing from England he reached France by liberal payment "of the Mariners,"[142] he was yet even more interested in declaring the precise significance of a passage by stating explicitly what he had sufficiently implied. He had made it clear enough that the dreams of the Wottons indicated special consideration by God, and not satisfied with adding merely that "God who in the dayes

---

133 *Ibid.,* sig. b6r.   134 *Ibid.,* 1651, sig. b8r.
135 *Ibid.,* 1672, sigs. d6r, d7v.   136 *Ibid.,* sig. c4r.
137 Sarpi, *History,* p. 79.   138 *Ibid.,* pp. 31, 36.   139 *Ibid.,* p. 77.
140 *Reliq.,* 1672, sig. b2r.   141 *Ibid.,* sig. b2v.   142 *Ibid.,* sig. b7r.

of old did use to speak to his people in visions, did seem to speak to many of this Family in dreams,"[143] he concluded by saying, "This is some account of this Family, which seemed to be beloved of God.[144] He refined his statement that the Venetians prohibited celebrations "lest the Common people might judg they were absolved for committing a fault,"[145] to "lest the Common People might judge, that they desired an Absolution, or were Absolved for committing a Fault."[146] Having already said that travellers to Venice received from Wotton "chearfull Entertainments, advice for their behaviour, and shelter,"[147] he must yet doubly point up Wotton, and he inserted before "shelter" "by his interest."[148] The revisions of 1672 indicate Walton's greater interest in factual truth, but they show no diminution in his readiness to shape fact to his own purpose or in his desire to place signposts on a road that was already clearly marked.

The enlargement in the 1672 *Life* which Walton mentioned takes the form of a conversation which Wotton had at Eton with John Hales shortly before his death, and it appears after that passage in which Wotton comments on his life in Walton's recapitulation. It contains little that is new. Wotton's first remarks, *"I have in my passage to my grave met with most of those Joys of which a discoursive soul is capable: and, being entertain'd with more inferior pleasures then the sons of men are usually made partakers of,"*[149] were merely transferred and expanded from the previous paragraph, where Wotton had been made to say in the editions previous to this one, "And though my dayes, which truly have been many, and mix'd with more pleasures then the sonns of men do usually enjoy."[150] The last remarks, in which Wotton talks of the sea of life and the harbor of death, have the same imagery which Walton had used to describe Wotton's installation as Provost. The passage adds almost nothing to the *Life*, and it was included because of Walton's interest in John Hales at this time.

Walton was well acquainted with Hales (1584–1656), who had in 1619 retired to his fellowship at Eton. In the year in which this edition of *Reliquiae Wottonianae* was published,[151] Walton was

---

143 *Ibid.*, sig. b5ʳ.   144 *Ibid.*, sig. b5ᵛ.   145 *Lives*, 1670 (Wotton), p. 37.
146 *Reliq.*, 1672, sig. c5ʳ.   147 *Ibid.*, 1651, sig. c3ʳ.
148 *Ibid.*, 1672, sig. c6ᵛ.   149 *Ibid.*, sig. e4ʳ.   150 *Ibid.*, 1651, sig. c11ᵛ.
151 *Reliq.*, 1672, was published in the first three months of 1673. The dedication is dated "Feb. 27. 1672[3]."

assisting William Fulman (1632–1688), an Oxford antiquary and
a fellow of Corpus Christi College, in collecting materials for a
life of Hales. The Hales materials are in the Fulman manuscripts
at Corpus Christi College, and the two Walton documents demonstrate his technique in biography at this time. In the first of these,
a letter written August 24, 1673, to his publisher, Richard Marriot,[152] Walton indicated that he had in his possession as much of
Hales's life as had been written by Anthony Farindon. Farindon's
fragment evidently covered Hales's early years, and Walton suggested that if Fulman occupied himself with the Oxford years, he
himself would investigate Hales's career from the time he came to
Eton. He had been to Eton, where he had made inquiries of many
people, including Mrs. Hannah Powney, the wife of Hales's servant, and Mr. Mountague, a fellow at Eton, evidently preferring their
stories to what information the Eton records might have for him.
These stories he had written down that his "memory might not
loose them," and Mr. Mountague, who knew Hales "and all his
afares best of any man," had promised to put in writing what he
remembered. The second of the documents is part of a long letter
to Fulman, written October 20, 1673,[153] made up almost entirely
of character-revealing anecdote. Here, Walton referred to conversations about Hales which he had had some time ago with Lady
Salter, the sister of Bishop Duppa; with her son; and with Lady
Anne Howe, the sister of Bishop Henry King. In labored paragraphs, full of the deletions and insertions and rephrasings which
probably characterized the first drafts of his own *Lives,* Walton told
one story which admirably reveals Hales's astuteness in matters of
religion and another interesting story of a sketch of Hales made
after his death. There is an anecdote telling that Hales lived on
bread and toast for two weeks to see how little would maintain him
if he were sequestered, and a minute revealing observation to the
effect that in his old age Hales often read without spectacles a volume of Thomas à Kempis in small print. Walton told how Hales
hid for nine weeks while he was bursar at Eton to preserve the college writings and keys from the sequestering armies, and he quoted
Hales as saying that his place of concealment was so near the college that "those that searcht for him might have smelt him if he had

[152] Fulman MS 10, f. 78^r, quoted in John Butt, "Izaak Walton's Collections
for Fulman's Life of John Hales," *MLR,* XXIX (1934), 267–268.
[153] Fulman MS 10, ff. 79, 80, quoted by Butt, *op. cit.,* pp. 270–273.

eaten garlick." In a final anecdote, Walton related that Hales, disappointed with Thomas Carew's return to the life of a libertine after he had granted him absolution, refused to absolve him a second time, though he would pray for him. These documents tell us much about Walton: his preference for interviewing and his careful reliance on notes; his preoccupation with specific idiosyncratic detail; and his relish for anecdote of a personal nature. Something of his approach to biography is revealed, too, in his desiring Mr. Mountague's remembrances of Hales not only because he knew him best of any man and because he was "like to doe it very well," but because "he will doe it affectionately."

That Walton was writing "affectionately" in the *Life of Wotton* has perhaps been sufficiently indicated. But his notes on Hales give a further illustration of this affection. In the anecdotes which he sent to Fulman, Walton wrote:

> (*he had undertaken*) he was not good at any contrivance to get or save mony for him selfe; *yet he* undertoke to doe it for *his friend* Sᵣ H. Wotton who was a neclecter of mony, and mᵣ Ha. told *me* he had got 300ˡⁱ to gether at the time of his deth a some to which Sᵣ H. had long beine a stranger an wood ever have beine if he had manag'd his owne mony-buissines. it was hapily got together to bury him, and *inable him to* doe (then) some offices of honor, and Justice and gratitude, and charitie.[154]

This passage certainly shows the extremity of Wotton's circumstances, and in the light of it may be seen the carefulness of the phrasing of the passage which Walton included in the *Life* in 1651 after his quotation of Wotton's will and which he never changed. Although he was ready to tell that Wotton was ever in need of money, he did not care to reveal that he lacked money for his very burial, and he wrote:

> I think fit to declare that every one that was nam'd in his Will, did gladly receive their legacies; by which, and his most just and passionate desires for the payment of his debts, they joyned in assisting the Overseers of his Will, & by their joynt endevours to the King (then whom none was more willing) conscionable satisfaction was given for his just debts.[155]

The Hales notes indicate clearly the trouble Walton must have gone to in his attempts at factual exactness in the revision of the

---

[154] *Ibid.,* p. 272. Walton's interlineations are italicized and his erasures put in parentheses.

[155] *Reliq.,* 1651, sig. c11ʳ.

Life of Wotton in 1672, for there is no such specificity in them. Walton wrote Fulman that Hales had died "the 19° of may," but even here he had to confess that he did not know the year, and he referred Fulman to Mrs. Powney. Even more clearly, the notes reveal that Walton's interest was far more in incident which revealed character than in the accomplishments of Hales in his career as scholar and teacher. It is indicative of this prime interest that the sole enlargement of the 1672 *Life* is not a factual elaboration of Wotton's career, but rather an incident which reveals something of his attitude before his death. Walton's struggle for expression in the notes, his continual rephrasing, is illustrative of his wish to control his material minutely. The omission in the *Life* of Hales's collection of money for Wotton is further proof that Walton did not use all the material available to him, and his emphasis on "affection" perhaps provides the main key to the intense subjectivity of his writing. The expression, "I think fit to declare," with which he introduced his statement that the provisions of Wotton's will were carried out, is the guiding sentiment in all Walton's writing.

Walton's refinements in the *Life of Wotton* in 1670 and 1672 left him little to do when he had a fourth chance to revise in 1675. He had said that Wotton had made his will "that none should be a loser by it,"[156] and he properly changed the pronoun to "him."[157] He added to the account of Wotton's willingness to leave this world and his expectancy of a better one, "and I long for it,"[158] reminiscent of his saying of Donne that *"he longed for the day of his dissolution."*[159] He strengthened Wotton's question of whether the Venetians were damned by the Pope's excommunication by adding, "even those poor Christians that knew not why they quarrel'd."[160] To bolster his argument here, Walton invoked the ignorance of the poor Christians, though in the *Donne* he was as ready to condemn the common people for their busy ignorance in matters of religion when his doing so supported Donne.[161] Just as he had mentioned in 1672 Duodo's recall from Rome to show the extent of the rupture between the Pope and Venice, so he now, for the same reason, added to his account of the Venetian proclama-

---

156 *Ibid.*, sig. c7ᵛ.   157 *Lives*, 1675, p. 138.   158 *Ibid.*, p. 148.
159 *Donne*, 1658, p. 110.   160 *Lives*, 1675, p. 128.
161 *Donne*, 1658, p. 65.

tion, *"And made it loss of Estate and Nobility, but to speak in the behalf of the* Jesuits.*"*[162] And even as he did not adhere strictly to the facts in the Duodo reference, so he here changed them, for his source indicated that the decree against the Jesuits was made almost two months after the proclamation and stated merely that the Jesuits "should never be admitted or received in any place of the *State.*"[163] From these changes it is apparent that Walton was still interested in improving the *Life,* but the smallness of their number shows that he was pleased with it.[164]

The importance of Walton's changes and additions in the later editions of the *Life of Donne* and their relative unimportance in the *Life of Wotton* cannot be accounted for merely by Walton's greater experience and skill in writing the original version of the *Wotton.* To be sure, some of the care which Walton lavished on the revisions of the *Donne* may be the result of a natural affection for the first offspring of his pen and, at the same time, of a sensitive awareness of deficiencies caused by his lack of experience. But if he filled gaps and changed dates in the *Wotton* even while he departed freely from fact in the *Donne* or used fact only to suffuse it in his wide-ranging imagination, the difference in kind of his changes was largely determined by the difference in his attitude toward his subjects. Because his veneration for Donne increased over the years, the texture of the *Life of Donne* became more lustrous and more rich. His attitude toward Wotton remained static. In his original

---

[162] *Lives,* 1675, p. 113.

[163] Sarpi, *History,* p. 139. The decree against the Jesuits is dated June 14, 1606, and the Proclamation had been issued on April 28.

[164] The changes in 1675 have been enumerated in their entirety, with two minor exceptions. Walton had written in 1651 and in the succeeding editions, "one generation succeds another, both in their lives, recreations, hopes, fears, and deaths" (*Reliq.,* 1651, sig. c11ᵛ). The dropping of the "s" from "deaths" in 1675 is probably a printer's error (*Lives,* 1675, p. 147). Although, in 1670, Walton referred to Duppa as the "late" Reverend Bishop of Salisbury, he did not change his statement that Wotton's progress with his life of Luther "is well known" to him (*Lives,* 1670 [Wotton], p. 63). In the *Errata* of the 1675 *Lives,* he changed the verb to "was."

Despite his obvious satisfaction with the *Life of Wotton,* Walton would probably have made at least one further change had he lived to see another edition. He wrote in a copy of the 1675 *Lives* that passed through his hands— and the words undoubtedly would have been included in his account of Wotton's death—"[A]nd nature being overpowrd by theise many asaults of his fever = the lamp of his life wanting oyle and burnt out" (verso of blank leaf before *Life of Wotton* in *Lives,* 1675, Albert H. Childs Memorial Collection, Yale).

picture, he had successfully caught the Wotton whom he loved by gracefully combining a multiplicity of sources and a large store of anecdote. He had no new material about Wotton's sweet and wholesome hours at Provost; indeed, even if he had it, it would only have disturbed his picture of Wotton in his garlands of repose. From the first, he had avoided the detail of Wotton's diplomatic maneuverings. He had used Wotton's ambassadorship only to point out the honor and trust which came to him, the nobility of mind which characterized the execution of his duties; of the qualities of mind that made Wotton successful in the world of intrigue, wit was the only one which Walton cared to dwell on. To make anything of the great and increasing store of diplomatic correspondence which was available to him would be to reveal a somewhat different man. He had nothing essentially new to say about Wotton. From the first, he had told the story of a gentleman, and in a gentlemanly manner. Later, he talked at somewhat greater length, elaborated his story a little, and made it surer and more convincing with each retelling.

PART III

The Judicious Life
of Mr. Hooker

Chapter 7

Background:
The Restored Clergy and
Their Adopted Champion

The Life of Mr. Rich. Hooker, the first of Walton's lives to be published separately on its original appearance, was indirectly connected with a chain of events in the history of the Church of England which had begun at least as early as 1593 with the publication of *The Laws of Ecclesiastical Polity* and was directly connected with the policies of the Church of England at the Restoration.

Charles's entrance into London on May 29, 1660, "the ways strewed with flowers, the bells ringing, the streets hung with tapestry, fountains flowing with wine,"[1] signified not only the restoration of the crown but also the restoration of the Laudian Church.[2] The Book of Common Prayer of 1604 was at once reintroduced in the King's chapel[3] and in the House of Lords,[4] and on July 8, John Evelyn recorded in his diary, "From henceforth, was the Liturgy publicly used in our churches, whence it had been for so many years banished."[5] While the King and the Lord Chancellor sparred with the Convention Parliament, they quietly assisted the High Church clergy in recapturing the Establishment. In Ireland, where the King possessed absolute power of nomination,[6] it was rumored

[1] *The Diary of John Evelyn* (Everyman's Library), I, 341. Entry for May 29, 1660.

[2] See Robert S. Bosher, *The Making of the Restoration Settlement: The Influence of the Laudians 1649–1662* (New York, 1951).

[3] Vernon Staley, *The Life and Times of Gilbert Sheldon* (Milwaukee, [1913]), p. 71.

[4] Bosher, p. 163.   [5] Evelyn's *Diary*, I, 344.   [6] Bosher, p. 91.

even before the end of June that nominations to the vacant sees had been made, and by July 7 John Bramhall had been appointed Archbishop of Armagh.[7] In England and Wales, where eighteen of the twenty-seven sees were vacant,[8] the dean and cathedral chapter must formally elect the candidate nominated by the King,[9] and by the end of August the filling of the cathedral chapters had been largely accomplished.[10] On the last day of August, the King ordered Parliament to recess from September 8 to November 6,[11] and it is clear that the interim was to be used for re-establishing episcopacy. As early as August 28, Brian Duppa, Bishop of Salisbury, was nominated to Winchester. On September 2, the aged and ailing Bishop of London, William Juxon, an obvious symbol of the old order though he was completely out of touch with church affairs, was nominated to Canterbury, vacant since the death of Laud in 1645. On the same day, the Bishop of Lichfield, Accepted Frewen, was nominated to York. On September 13, the actual day of the adjournment of Parliament, Juxon's election took place at Canterbury, and a week later the appointment of new prelates began with the nomination of George Morley to Worcester and of Gilbert Sheldon to London.[12] On October 28, just two weeks after the execution of six of the regicides,[13] Morley and Sheldon were consecrated in King Henry VII's chapel in the Abbey. At the same service, the first of its kind since 1644, Humphrey Henchman was consecrated Bishop of Salisbury; Robert Sanderson, Bishop of Lincoln; and George Griffith, Bishop of St. Asaph. Canon John Sudbury preached the sermon, appropriately taking as his text I Timothy 3:1: "This is a true saying, If a man desire the office of a bishop, he desireth a good work." In dedicating his printed sermon to Edward, Lord Hyde, he wrote, "I hope at least some will lay aside that envy with which they look upon the Bishops for the height and dignity of their Office, and *esteem them very highly in love for their Work sake.*"[14]

By January 13, 1661, all but two of the sees were filled,[15] and the

---

[7] *Ibid.*, pp. 157–158.   [8] *Ibid.*, p. 92.   [9] *Ibid.*, p. 91.
[10] *Ibid.*, p. 161.   [11] *Ibid.*, p. 176.   [12] *Ibid.*, p. 180.
[13] Evelyn's *Diary*, I, 346. Entry for Oct. 14, 1660.
[14] John Sudbury, *A Sermon Preached At the Consecration of the Right Reverend Fathers in God, Gilbert Lord Bishop of London, Humphry Lord Bishop of Sarum, George Lord Bishop of Worcester, Robert Lord Bishop of Lincolne, George Lord Bishop of St. Asaph* (London, 1660).
[15] Bosher, p. 182.

bishops lost little time in getting to work. The King issued his warrant for the Savoy Conference on March 25, 1661,[16] and limited to four months the duration of his gesture of tolerance to nonconformity. The commissioners did not assemble for the first time until April 15.[17] There was no conferring among the twelve bishops and the twelve nonconformist ministers. The ministers were forced to submit a copy of their proposals for the change of the Book of Common Prayer to the bishops, and they, newly restored to power with their ceremonies and the Book of Common Prayer of 1604, were unwilling to make any major concessions. Indeed, by the very terms of the royal commission, the current Book was to be the basis for any revision.[18] It was inevitable that nothing was accomplished. Before the Savoy Conference had even opened, the King had ordered a writ of summons for Convocation,[19] and on May 8, concurrently with the opening ceremony of the Cavalier Parliament, the opening service of Convocation was held.[20] Some weeks were spent in drawing up forms of prayer for January 30 and May 29, to commemorate the martyrdom of Charles I and the restoration of Charles II.[21] During the summer adjournment, several bishops worked to revise the Book of Common Prayer,[22] and it is no surprise to find that on November 21, at the first session of Convocation held after the close of the Savoy Conference, eight bishops were formally asked to prepare the Book of Common Prayer for revision.[23] Within a month, the Book had been revised and the revisions approved by the Convocation.[24] By the Act of Uniformity, which received royal assent on May 19, 1662,[25] all ministers were required to assent to "all and everything contained and prescribed" in the Book of Common Prayer, to subscribe to all the Thirty-nine Articles, and to be in episcopal orders.[26] They were given but three months to choose between conformity or expulsion from their benefices.[27] The nonconformist laity had been legislated against even before its clergy felt the restored power of the parliament and the bishops: in 1661, the Corporation Act required that all civil officeholders take the oath of supremacy and allegiance to the crown and that they receive

---

[16] *Ibid.*, p. 211.   [17] *Ibid.*, p. 226.   [18] Staley, p. 73.

[19] Bosher, p. 213.   [20] *Ibid.*, p. 219.   [21] *Ibid.*, p. 230.

[22] *Ibid.*, p. 244.   [23] Staley, p. 92.

[24] *Ibid.*, p. 99. Approval and subscription by the members of both houses of Convocation took place on Dec. 20, 1661.

[25] Bosher, p. 254.   [26] *Ibid.*, p. 250.   [27] *Ibid.*, p. 254.

the Holy Communion according to the Prayer Book Rite.[28] The concessions made to religious dissentients in the King's Declaration of Indulgence on December 26, 1662, were short lived, for the bill to implement them was opposed by Clarendon, denounced by the Commons, and defeated in the House of Lords.[29] Charles's very overture produced further restrictions on nonconformity. The Conventicle Act of 1664 prohibited assemblies of nonconformists for religious purposes, and went so far as to state that when more than four persons in addition to the household were present at family prayers, all were liable to punishment.[30] The Five-Mile Act, passed a year later, specified that any minister who had not assented to the Act of Uniformity could not reside within five miles of any city or corporate borough.[31]

In all this legislation of conformity, and, indeed, in the filling of the episcopal vacancies, the power of one man was largely influential. That man was Gilbert Sheldon, Bishop of London, who was upon Juxon's death made Archbishop of Canterbury on August 31, 1663. Although Sheldon was not an eminent theologian or a great preacher, he was precisely what the Church of England needed at this time—a capable administrator and a shrewd politician, perhaps the most powerful man in England, a man jealous of the prerogatives and privileges of the Church. His picture has been ingenuously drawn by Pepys. On September 3, 1662, Pepys wrote:

Dr. Fairbrother tells me, what I heard confirmed since, that it was fully resolved by the King's new Council that an Indulgence should be granted the Presbyters; but upon the Bishop of London's speech (who is now one of the most powerful men in England with the King,) their minds were wholly turned.[32]

At the same time Pepys noted that Sheldon forestalled controversy and opposition to his policies by filling the places of the ejected ministers with very good and able men.[33] Somewhat later he wrote that though some of Charles II's present favorites were violently antiepiscopal, "the Bishop of London keeps as great with the King

[28] Staley, p. 81.

[29] Richard Lodge, *The History of England from the Restoration to the Death of William III* (*The Political History of England,* Vol. VIII; London, 1910), pp. 67–68.

[30] Staley, p. 82.   [31] *Ibid.*

[32] *The Diary of Samuel Pepys* (Everyman's Library), I, 283.

[33] *Ibid.*

as ever, is got into favour, so much that, being a man of great business and yet of pleasure; and, drolling, too, he, it is thought, will be made Lord Treasurer."[34] He called Sheldon "a mighty stout man, and a man of a brave, high spirit" for censuring the King's relations with the Duchess of Richmond,[35] but he was somewhat shocked when, after a dinner at Lambeth, Sheldon sanctioned and enjoyed behind locked doors a mock Presbyterian sermon, preached "with all the possible imitation in grimaces and voice."[36] Pepys clearly indicated Sheldon's influence, his zealousness for the Church, his capacity for independent thinking, and, withal, his worldliness.

Sheldon's capacities had been recognized by Charles I, and about 1634 he had been made chaplain-in-ordinary to the King.[37] In 1644 he was sent, as the King's chaplain, to attend his commissioners at the Treaty of Uxbridge.[38] In 1647, the King called him to the Isle of Wight to discuss the demands of Parliament and to determine just how much he could concede.[39] Sheldon's career during the War and the Commonwealth was an honorable one from the view of the Church, for on April 13, 1648, he was ejected from the wardenship of All Souls College, Oxford,[40] to which he had been elected thirteen years before.[41] He was probably not closely confined, however, since there are entries in his hand in the parish register of St. Nicholas' Church, Ickford (where he was rector from May 8, 1636) shortly after his ejection from All Souls.[42] He was probably not ejected from Ickford until the end of 1650.[43] He did not join the court in exile, probably because the King and Edward Hyde had an important role for him to play in England. Already in 1649, Hyde was writing him, "You are one of those few by whose advice and example I shall most absolutely guide myself, and upon whose friendship I have an entire and absolute dependence."[44] From that time it is clear that Sheldon had unofficially succeeded Laud. To be sure, it was not Sheldon but Henry Hammond who led and directed the intellectual defense of the High Anglican position. Sheldon added no word to the tremendous output of apologetic and propaganda of the fifties, though Hammond asked him to do so and even suggested specific chores.[45] Thus early Sheldon was more

[34] *Ibid.*, p. 368. Entry for May 15, 1663.
[35] *Ibid.*, II, 412. Entry for Dec. 27, 1667.
[36] *Ibid.*, p. 690. Entry for May 14, 1669.
[37] Staley, p. 10.
[38] *Ibid.*, p. 38.   [39] *Ibid.*, p. 39.   [40] *Ibid.*, p. 15.
[41] *Ibid.*, p. 10.   [42] *Ibid.*, pp. 16–17.   [43] *Ibid.*, p. 21.
[44] Bosher, p. 55.   [45] *Ibid.*, p. 36.

completely concerned with discipline than with doctrine. On a host of matters, the ousted clergy sought his advice, obviously because he was known to be Hyde's spokesman in England.

Hyde had written Sheldon in October, 1659, "When you meet, as meet you will, I think you will be satisfied with [the King], and nobody is like to do so much good upon him as you are, for sure he reverences nobody more."[46] On the evening of May 26, 1660, the King received at Canterbury his first visit since his return from an Anglican clergyman.[47] The visitor was not one of the old bishops, but Gilbert Sheldon. Sheldon's appointment in 1660 as Dean of the Chapel Royal[48] does not reveal his real part in the early weeks of the Restoration. Into his hands, and those of George Morley and John Earle, Hyde placed control of the presentation of the bulk of the crown benefices.[49] Sheldon endorsed more certificates attesting the orthodoxy of petitioners than any other divine.[50] In addition, he was made, according to Walton, "a chief Trustee to commend to him [the King] fit men to supply the then vacant Bishopricks."[51] As Dean of the Chapel Royal and as Bishop of London, Sheldon assumed, in the ailing Juxon's stead, the responsibility of controlling the Savoy Conference, and it was he who made sure that Convocation would be solidly Anglican by overriding, in accordance with his rights as Bishop of London, the election of Richard Baxter and Edward Calamy by the London clergy.[52]

It is wrong to think of Sheldon as the mere instrument of Hyde and the King. As Bishop of London and later as Archbishop of Canterbury, he was deeply involved in political maneuvers, but he approached them single-mindedly: how did they affect the Church? Pepys's reference to Sheldon's turning the King's council against an indulgence to Presbyterians shows Sheldon's independence. The King and the Lord Chancellor, worried about uprisings when the Act of Uniformity was to take effect, prepared at the last minute an indulgence which would have allowed those who did not subscribe to retain their livings and to continue preaching if they secured readers to officiate at Common Prayer.[53] That Sheldon had to play his own game is shown not only in his defeating single-handedly this move to subvert an Act of Parliament beneficial to the Church, but also in his letter to Hyde: "give me leave to complain of your

---

46 *Ibid.,* p. 136.   47 *Ibid.*   48 Staley, p. 66.   49 Bosher, p. 159.
50 *Ibid.,* p. 160.   51 *Sanderson,* 1678, sigs. k7ᵛ–k8ʳ.   52 Bosher, p. 215.
53 *Ibid.,* p. 269.

great unkindness upon Thursday in offering to expose me to certain ruin by the Parliament, or the extreme hatred of that malicious party in whose jaws I must live, and never giving me the least notice of it. You cannot blame me if it be sadly resented."[54] Upon this occasion and again later, when Charles issued his Declaration of Indulgence in 1662, Sheldon was willing to threaten to desert the King and throw in his lot with Parliament. In January, 1663, he wrote the King:

By your Act you labour to set up that damnable and heretical doctrine of the Church of Rome, whore of Babylon. . . . Besides, this Toleration . . . cannot be done without a Parliament, unless your Majesty will let your subjects see that you will take unto yourself liberty to throw down the laws of the land at your pleasure.[55]

These are not isolated instances. Long before, Sheldon had become accustomed to bargaining with the King.

On August 11, 1660, Brian Duppa, then Bishop of Salisbury, wrote to Sheldon, expressing his anxiety about the state of affairs of the Church, and he concluded:

You are the only person about His Majesty that I have confidence in, and I persuade myself that as none hath his ear more, so none is likely to prevail on his heart more, and there was never more need of it; for all the professed enemies of our Church look upon this as the critical time to use their dernier resort to shake His Majesty's constancy. But I hope by this time you have recovered those buried papers which can't but have a powerful influence upon so dutiful a soul as his. I shall wait upon you so soon as I hear that my coming may be any way useful. In the mean time I am the more at ease because I know you stand ready upon the place to lay hold upon all opportunities, and are diligently upon your watch *ne ecclesia aliquid detrimenti capiat.*[56]

The buried papers refer to a vow which Charles I had made at Oxford on April 13, 1646, shortly before his imprisonment, in which he promised, should he be re-established on his throne, to give back to the Church

all those Impropriations wh^ch are now held by the Crowne; and what lands soever I now doe or shall enjoy which have been taken away either from any Episcopall See or any Cathedrall or Collegiate Church, from any Abbey or other Religious House. I likewise promise for here-

54 *Ibid.*, p. 262.   55 *Ibid.*, pp. 264–265.
56 Staley, p. 45, from Tanner MSS, vol. xlix, f. 17.

after to hold them from the Church under such reasonable Fines and
Rents as shall be set downe by some conscientious persons, whome I promise to chose wth all uprightnes of Heart to direct me in this particular.[57]

Sheldon had attended Charles at Oxford in April, 1646, as his
chaplain and Clerk of the Closet,[58] and Sheldon brought the vow to
light. The document bears this postscript, dated August 21, 1660,

> This is a true copye of the King's Vow wch was perserved thirteene
> yeares under ground by mee.
>
> Gilbert Sheldon.[59]

Regardless of the motivation which caused Charles I to write or
sign such a document, there is little doubt that Sheldon and the
Church were using it as a guarantee for their privileges and lands,
and they had much to offer Charles II in return. The idea of the
social contract was becoming popular, and the official view of the
Church was antagonistic to it. Bishop Overall's *Convocation Book*
(1606) stated that any man who believes in the idea of social contract
and the contract of submission "and that consequently all civil
Power, Jurisdiction, and Authority was first derived from the people, and disorder'd multitude; or either is originally still in them,
or else is deduced by their consents naturally from them; and is
not God's Ordinance originally descending from him, and depending upon him, he doth greatly Erre."[60] In return for Charles's adherence to the vow of his father, Sheldon and his colleagues could
offer much support to the King by upholding the traditional position of the Church on kingship.

Shortly after the Restoration, the churchmen went to the print-
shop to provide ammunition for the establishment of their opinions
about episcopal government, liturgy and ceremonies, church lands,
and kingship. In the many battles of books and pamphlets, Sheldon's
hand, as before, is conspicuously absent, but, quite involuntarily, he
became involved in the controversy on kingship as that controversy
tended to revolve about the opinions of Richard Hooker. The terms
of controversy had changed but little since the 1640's, and both the
High Church and the nonconformists reprinted a large number of
pre-Civil War pamphlets.[61] This was more than a labor-saving de-

[57] *Ibid.*, p. 42, from *Clarendon State Papers* (2176 Bodleian Library).
[58] *Ibid.*, p. 38.   [59] *Ibid.*, p. 43.
[60] *Bishop Overall's Convocation-Book, MDCVI* (London, 1690), pp. 3–4.
[61] Bosher, p. 165.

vice. Both sides hoped to demonstrate a continuity of tradition and to ground their argument in authority, and both sides looked for support from past champions of the Church, even from those whose position was not precisely theirs. The High Church, for instance, adopted as one of its champions Archbishop Ussher, who had died in 1656. Ussher was a moderate Anglican who had been on friendly terms with Cromwell, and, indeed, Cromwell had contributed two hundred pounds toward his burial in Westminster Abbey.[62] In the year of his death there had been published his proposal for limited episcopacy, *The Reduction of Episcopacy unto the Form of Synodical Government*. At the Restoration, Ussher's name had a far more pleasant ring in nonconformist ears than Laud's, and many Presbyterian divines were more than ready to use Ussher's reduction as the basis for an accommodation. The High Church used Ussher's name in an attempt to win popular support, but at the same time it allied his name with those causes about which Ussher spoke as the Restored Church wished him to speak. Early in 1661 appeared *The Power Communicated by God to the Prince, and the Obedience Required of the Subject. Briefly laid down, and Confirmed out of The Holy Scriptures, The Testimony of the Primitive Church. The Dictates of right Reason, and The Opinion of the Wisest among the Heathen Writers. By the most Reverend Father in God, James, late Lord Archbishop of Armagh, and Primate of all Ireland*. The volume has a dedication to Charles II, and Robert Sanderson, Bishop of Lincoln, emphasized in his Preface to the Reader the authenticity of the work[63] and said that it was written by Ussher at the special command of Charles I when *"unhappy distempers . . .* did first begin to appear openly in our Land."[64] In the preface, too, Sanderson would demolish Hobbes's Leviathan, and he maintained that the social contract was never proved, nor will ever be, from scripture, reason, or history: *"Jus gladii*, the right and power of the Sword (which is really the Sovereign Power) belongeth we know to Kings, but it is . . . *by the Ordinance of God*, not the donation of the People."[65]

Somewhat later the same year appeared more ammunition, this time entitled, *Clavi Trabales; or, Nailes Fastned by some Great*

---

[62] S. R. Gardiner, *History of the Commonwealth and Protectorate, 1649–1656* (London, 1903), III, 335.

[63] James Ussher, *The Power Communicated* (London, 1661), sigs. a^r–b2^r. The Preface is dated Dec. 31, 1660.

[64] *Ibid.,* sig. a^r.   [65] *Ibid.,* sig. d^r.

Masters of Assemblyes. Confirming The Kings Supremacy. The Subjects Duty. Church Government by Bishops. The Particulars of which are as followeth I. Two Speeches of the late Lord Primate Ushers. The one of the Kings Supremacy, The other of the Duty of Subjects to supply the Kings Necessities. II. His Judgment and Practice in Point of Loyalty, Episcopacy, Liturgy and Constitutions of the Church of England, III. Mr. Hookers Judgment of the Kings Power in matters of Religion, advancement of Bishops &c. IV. Bishop Andrews of Church-Government &c. both confirmed and enlarged by the said Primate. V. A Letter of Dr Hadrianus Saravia of the like Subjects. Unto which is added a Sermon of Regal Power, and the Novelty of the Doctrine of Resistance.[66] Again, Bishop Sanderson did the Preface to the Reader, stressing the legitimacy of the contents of the volume, and saying of the authors that they were *"men of exquisite* learning, *sober* undertakings, *and of exemplary* piety *and* gravity, *all concurring in the same* judgment, *as concerning those points* (Factious Spirits *in these latter times so much opposed*) of Regal *Soveraignty,* Episcopal *Government, and* Obedience in Ceremonialls."[67] Thus did Ussher speak again for the Church, and also Lancelot Andrewes, who died Bishop of Winchester in 1626; Hadrian Saravia (died 1613), an exile from Holland who, despite his presbyterian ordination on the continent,[68] became a firm advocate of episcopacy and of the apostolic succession in the Church of England; and Richard Hooker, who had died in 1600. The editor of the volume had not always conformed to the discipline of the High Church, and he was himself probably using the book to ingratiate himself with the new powers in the Church. Nicholas Bernard had been ordained by Ussher in 1626 and was the Archbishop's librarian from 1635 to 1641. Like Ussher, Bernard was a moderate Episcopalian, and it was he who had published and written the preface for Ussher's *Reduction.* Bernard left Ireland soon after the rebellion and was appointed Rector of Whitechurch, in Shropshire, and Preacher to the Society of Grey's Inn. He was later appointed chaplain and almoner to Cromwell, but on the Restoration, he continued to hold his living at Whitechurch.[69] The

[66] The Preface to the Reader is dated Aug. 10, 1661 (sig. d4^v).

[67] *Clavi Trabales,* sigs. c2^r–c2^v.

[68] Raymond Aaron Houk, *Hooker's Ecclesiastical Polity, Book VIII, with an Introduction* (New York, 1931), p. 102.

[69] Charles Richard Elrington, *The Life of James Ussher (The Whole Works of the Most Rev. James Ussher,* Vol. I; Dublin, 1864), p. 115, note z.

Laudian Church was relying on every proponent, living or dead, regardless of previous sectarian preference, in its fight for the supremacy of the King, the high place of episcopacy, the retention of traditional ceremony, and respect for the rights of the Church.

There is reason to believe that the Church considered Richard Hooker the foremost of its champions and looked especially to his writings for support in its search to authorize the favored doctrines. Thomas Fuller wrote of Hooker's *Polity* in 1662, "True it is, his Book in our late Times was beheld as an *Old-Almanack* grown out of date; but blessed be God, there is now a Revolution, which may bring his Works again into reputation."[70] The parallel between the situation of the Church with regard to nonconformity after the defeat of the Armada and after the Commonwealth was an obvious one, and Bishop Henry King pointed to it and Hooker's role when he called Hooker *"Schismaticorum Malleus"* and said that he was

so great a Champion for the Church of *Englands* Rights against the Factious Torrent of Separatists, that then ran high against Church-Discipline, and in his unanswerable Books continues to be so against the unquiet Disciples of their Schism; which now under other Names still carry on their Design, and who (as the proper Heirs of their Irrational Zele) would again rake into the scarce-closed Wounds of a newly bleeding State and Church.[71]

At this time, too, the *Polity* was being turned into Latin. John Earle had probably started his translation even before he became Charles II's personal chaplain on the continent, and after the Restoration, when he became Bishop of Worcester and later of Salisbury, he worked on it until his death.[72] But in its champion

[70] Thomas Fuller, *The History of the Worthies of England* (London, 1662), p. 264.

[71] *Hooker*, 1665. "The Copy of a Letter writ to Mr. Walton by Dr. King, Lord Bishop of Chichester," sig. A3v.

[72] Earle was made Dean of Westminster in June, 1660; Bishop of Worcester on Nov. 30, 1662; and Bishop of Salisbury on Sept. 28, 1663; he died in 1665 (*DNB*, article "John Earle"). Walton thought that his translation of the *Polity* had been "lately finisht" (*Hooker*, 1665, p. 122). In the margin of p. 95 (Hooker) of a presentation copy of *Lives*, 1670, in the Yale Library, is the following comment (not in Walton's hand): "at Bishop Earl's death this work unperfect & deficient came to the hands of Bishop Morley of Winton, who comãnded dr Adam Littleton to finish it. but the Doctor on perusal found the stile so un-imitable, that he said, if he should proceed upon it, the translation would not look all of a piece, and that it were better for some one person of leisure & ability to begin the work a new, which none, I think, hath undertaken to this time 1697." Littleton (1627–1694) was the author of *Linguae Latinae Liber*

Hooker, too, the Restoration Church found a man who was not wholly in accord with its every doctrine, and the previous experience of the Church with Hooker should have led to caution.

The story of the printing of the *Polity* and the history of Hooker's manuscripts have been admirably related by Mr. C. J. Sisson.[73] He has shown that when the first four of the proposed eight Books were ready for press, there was no market for books dealing with church discipline, particularly for those presenting the views of the established Church.[74] Publication of the *Polity* was, therefore, financed by Edwin Sandys, Hooker's pupil and friend, and one of his advisers with regard to the *Polity*. The contract for printing was signed on January 26, 1593, the book entered on the Stationers' Register three days later,[75] and the printing finished before March 13 of the same year.[76] More than friendship prompted Sandys to back the *Polity*. The haste in its printing may be accounted for by his desire to use it as support for the point of view which he presented in Parliament on March 13, 1593, advocating the inclusion of the Brownists and Barrowists in a bill which would extend the enforcement of conformity over dissenters as well as Catholics.[77] Thus early, then, was the *Polity* thrown into the battle against nonconformity. Book V, longer than the first four, was published in December, 1597, and was again paid for by Sandys.[78] The *Polity* sold slowly; Books I–IV were not disposed of until 1604.[79] In this year, new sheets of Books I–IV were added to the old sheets of the 1597 Book V to produce a new "edition," an indication that Book V had not sold out by 1604.[80]

Upon Hooker's death in 1600, his father-in-law, John Churchman, took custody of his numerous manuscripts.[81] Within a year, he turned them over for examination to Sandys; Dr. John Spenser, a trustee under Hooker's will; and Dr. Henry Parry, later Bishop of Worcester.[82] Among the many manuscripts were Books VI and

---

Dictionarius quadripartitus. A Latin Dictionary in four parts, published in 1673. A letter from Smith to Hearne, dated Sept. 13, 1705 (in the Bodleian Library) says that Earle's translation was "utterly destroyed by prodigious heedlessness and carelessness" (*DNB,* article "Adam Littleton").

[73] C. J. Sisson, *The Judicious Marriage of Mr Hooker and the Birth of The Laws of Ecclesiastical Polity* (Cambridge, 1940).

[74] *Ibid.,* pp. 50–51.   [75] *Ibid.,* p. 60.   [76] *Ibid.,* p. 64.

[77] *Ibid.*   [78] *Ibid.,* p. 68.   [79] *Ibid.,* p. 72.

[80] *Ibid.,* pp. 72–73.   [81] *Ibid.,* pp. 92, 149, 152.

[82] *Ibid.,* pp. 92–93, 133, 151–152.

VII of the *Polity,* not in finished shape but rather complete, and some sections and fragments of Book VIII;[83] these were given to Dr. Spenser to prepare for the press.[84] When Spenser wrote his address "To the Reader," prefixed to the 1604 edition of Books I–V of the *Polity,* he said of the last three Books:

[Hooker] *lived till he sawe them perfected. . . . But some evill disposed mindes, whether of malice, or covetousnesse, or wicked blinde Zeale, it is uncerteine, . . . as soone as they were borne, and their father dead, smothered them, and by conveying away the perfect Copies, left unto us nothing but certaine olde unperfect and mangled draughts, dismembred into peeces.*

He also said, with regard to publication, *"it is intended that they* [many great and worthy persons] *shall see them as they are."*[85] Still, when the *Polity* appeared in 1611, newly set by William Stansby, successor to the original publisher, John Windet, it again contained only Books I–V.[86] When Spenser gave evidence in Chancery on January 27, 1613, on the manuscripts he had helped to examine, he stated parenthetically, "the Choyse writings of the s[ai]d M[r] Hooker w[ch] were most desyred being kept away from this dep[onen]t and the rest or utterly perished." [87] On February 9, 1613, he testified that Sandys had told him that he supposed that "the perfect coppies of those 3 latter books weare concealed" from him so that he could not profit by their printing.[88] On the same day, Spenser reiterated that it had been planned to print the last three books, and he said that he

hathe taken some paynes in the fittinge & perfectinge of those 3 last bookes and hathe brought two of them viz[t] the 6th & the 7th to some reasonable perfection. though not yet thought fitt for the presse, for some causes w[ch] because he thinckethe they doe not concerne the matter nowe in question under favour of this hon[ored] court he forbearethe nowe to sett downe.[89]

Spenser, then, not only gave confusing evidence on the last three Books, but he was unwilling to give evidence on a question which was put to him. The question intimated that the printing of the

---

[83] *Ibid.,* pp. 93, 152.   [84] *Ibid.,* pp. 94, 152.
[85] Richard Hooker, *Of the Lawes of Ecclesiasticall Politie, Eight bookes* (London, 1604), sig. A2[v].
[86] Sisson, p. 73.   [87] *Ibid.,* p. 133.   [88] *Ibid.,* p. 153.
[89] *Ibid.*

Books had been suppressed because of a difference of opinion between Sandys and Bishop Andrewes (who had early joined the
group editing Hooker's manuscripts)[90] which arose over "the in-
sertinge of a tracte of confession . . . into the said bookes."[91] Sisson holds that the part of Book VI which has survived is the tract
of confession[92] and that while Andrewes favored Hooker's emphasis
here on the pastoral and sacramental functions of the Church,
Sandys, more interested in the place of the Church in an ordered
commonwealth, wished additional compromise with Geneva and
additional argument against Rome.[93] Doctrinal, rather than editorial, policy, then, was responsible for the withholding of the last
Books, and they did not appear even in the 1632 issue of the *Polity*.

In 1648, the year when monarchy and episcopacy were falling,
Books VI and VIII were finally printed.[94] The epistle "To the
Reader" by the printer, Richard Bishop, says:

> *Here is presented unto thee, Two of the Three so long expected and*
> *much desired Books of Learned Mr Hookers Ecclesiasticall Policy; viz.*
> *the Sixth and the Eighth, as they were preserved in the hands of those*
> *Mirrours of Learning, Dr Andrewes late Lord Bishop of Winchester,*
> *and the present Dr Usher Lord Archbishop of Armagh, with great hopes*
> *the Seventh would have been recovered, that they might have been pub-*
> *lished to the Worlds view at once: but endevours used to that purpose*
> *have hitherto proved fruitlesse. And now hearing that some erronious,*
> *if not counterfeit Copies are abroad, hath occasioned the Publishing of*
> *these, to prevent as much as may be any addition of abuses to the abused*
> *Author; and also that he which so much desired the Unity of the Church,*
> *might have the divided members of his Labours united.*[95]

Despite Bishop's listing "The severall Copies compared before
Publication,"[96] Book VI contains only the tract of confession, and

---

90 *Ibid.*, p. 94.   91 *Ibid.*, p. 144.

92 *Ibid.*, p. 101. That part of Book VI is missing is indicated by the existence
of a manuscript which contains extensive notes by George Cranmer and
Edwin Sandys referring to eighty-five pages of fair copy in their hands (*ibid.*,
pp. 101–102). Sandys's last note refers, too, to material as yet unhandled. The
notes are printed in *The Works of that Learned and Judicious Divine
Mr. Richard Hooker*, ed. John Keble, 7th ed., rev. by R. W. Church and
F. Paget (Oxford, 1888), III, 108–139.

93 Sisson, pp. 100–101, 106.

94 *Of the Lawes of Ecclesiasticall Politie; The Sixth and Eighth Books.
A work long expected, and now published according to the most Authentique
Copies* (London, 1648).

95 *Ibid.*, sig. A2r.   96 *Ibid.*, sig. A2v.

Book VIII is incomplete. It has been suggested that Ussher was responsible for this volume, hoping thereby to influence the King toward a more moderate view of his power and to influence the people to a reasonable allegiance to the King.[97] Neither the remainder of Book VI, which dealt with lay elders, nor Book VII, which dealt with episcopacy, would have served to unite the royalists and the nonconformists, and perhaps for this reason they were omitted.

Church interest in the *Polity* continued, then, for a half-century after Hooker's death, but the changing position of the Church during that time made it inevitable that the *Polity* did not always coincide with the current fashion. And though the *Polity* and Hooker were looked upon as champions of the Church, it is doubtful if the *Polity* completely reflected at any time the views of anybody but Hooker, and those only as they had been tempered in discussions with Sandys and George Cranmer. As a young man, Hooker had been exposed to Puritan doctrines[98] and had even been expelled from Oxford for advocating them.[99] But his battle in his prime was against Geneva, for fears of Rome had somewhat abated with the destruction of the Spanish Armada. Hooker was the very antithesis of the Biblical literalist; he had a keen historical sense, was acutely aware of classical and Christian tradition, and was well grounded in political philosophy. Mr. E. T. Davies has recently said of him:

The fact is that Hooker's historical sense was far too strong to allow him to commit himself to any one particular theory of the origin of civil power. . . . So far from containing one theory of power, his *Laws* contain many. Thus, the theory of the Divine Right of Kings is present here, and it is obvious that this is inconsistent with the Contract theory. . . . But historical truth must prevail over a theory, and, however inconsistent it might appear to the doctrinaire, Hooker knew that the complex events of history can supply ammunition for every philosophical armoury.[100]

Hooker's historical bias in the *Polity* led him to encompass in his discussions all the historical variations. Though he warned that "over-nice and curious speculations become not the earnestness of

[97] Houk, pp. 117–118.

[98] His tutor, John Reinolds, has been called "the last Oxford puritan advocate of the Cartwright school" (Samuel E. Morison, *The Founding of Harvard College* [Cambridge, Mass., 1935], p. 117).

[99] See pp. 285–286.

[100] E. T. Davies, *The Political Ideas of Richard Hooker* (London, [1946]), p. 68.

holy things,"[101] the scope of his examinations and the minuteness
of his discriminations show that he, too, had to contend with By-
path Meadow and the Hill Difficulty. The *via media* which he is so
frequently supposed to have taken is hardly straight and narrow.
His large view is generally sympathetic toward episcopacy, church
prerogatives, and constitutionally limited monarchy, but his is no
clear-cut system, and in his reservations and, even, contradictions,
the High Churchmen found cause for perplexity. Hooker was their
champion, but phrases and sentences could be plucked from the
Polity to demonstrate opinions which differed radically from theirs.
The objection was not so much to the five Books which Hooker
had finished; the others, however, were yet rough—Book VIII even
disjointed—and Hooker's materials had not been smoothed and
had not been given proper emphasis and connection. Thus, in these
the contradictions were even more evident and they invited varying interpretations. Hooker himself had accused the Puritans of
citing Scripture to their own purpose, and he had written, with
Calvin in mind, "Nature worketh in us all a love to our own counsels. . . . Wherefore a marvel it were if a man of so great capacity
. . . could espy in the whole Scripture of God nothing which
might breed at the least a probable opinion of likelihood, that divine authority itself was the same way somewhat inclinable."[102]
Ironically, the *Polity* itself has ever been subject to this kind of
reading.

Because Hooker's treatment of kingship is historical, he provides support for people of varying views who wish to cite him regardless of context. This treatment is complicated additionally by
the specific and practical handling of the subject in Book VIII as
opposed to the theoretical approach in Book I. Richard Baxter insisted in 1673, however, with much justification, that "if any (cause-
lesly) question whether the eighth (imperfect) Book be in those
passages his own, let them remember that the sum of all that I confute, is in his first Book."[103] Still, it is possible to cite the *Polity* on
kingship to one's own purpose: Hooker says, "That the Christian
world should be ordered by kingly regiment, the law of God doth

[101] *Polity,* V. lxxix. 8 (Keble, II, 489).
[102] *Ibid.,* Preface, ii. 7 (Keble, I, 138).
[103] Epistle to the reader prior to "Christian Politicks," pt. IV of *A Christian Directory: Or, A Summ of Practical Theologie, and Cases of Conscience* (London, 1673).

not any where command,"[104] and, again, "to live by one man's will
became the cause of all men's misery,"[105] but he also says, "If it
should be at this day a controversy whether kingly regiment were
lawful or no, peradventure in defence thereof, the long continuance
which it hath had sithence the first beginning might be alleged."[106]
These are but snippets excised from their historical context, and
Hooker's approach to kingship is thoroughly historical:

> In power of dominion, all kings have not an equal latitude. Kings
> by conquest make their own charter: so that how large their power,
> either civil or spiritual, is, we cannot with any certainty define, further
> than only to set them in general the law of God and nature for bounds.
> Kings by God's own special appointment have also that largeness of
> power, which he doth assign or permit with approbation. Touching
> kings which were first instituted by agreement and composition made
> with them over whom they reign, how far their power may lawfully
> extend, the articles of compact between them must shew: not the articles
> only of compact at the first beginning, which for the most part are either
> clean worn out of knowledge, or else known unto very few, but what-
> soever hath been after in free and voluntary manner condescended unto,
> whether by express consent, whereof positive laws are witnesses, or else
> by silent allowance famously notified through custom reaching beyond
> the memory of man.[107]

Davies concludes that the nearest approach to a definite basis for
political authority in the *Polity* lies in Hooker's teaching that the
force of law is based on the consent of the governed.[108] He quotes as
central to this concept, "the lawful power of making laws to command whole politic societies of men belongeth so properly unto the
same entire societies"[109] and grounds the concept in an earlier statement, "The general and perpetual voice of men is as the sentence of
God himself."[110] Although the contractual idea is basic to much of
Hooker, he does not develop it or rely on it in all its ramifications.
With regard to limiting the King's power and making him practi-
cally accountable for usurpation of power, for instance, Hooker
says:

It must be presumed, that supreme governors will not in such case oppose themselves, and be stiff in detaining that, the use whereof is with

[104] *Polity*, VIII. ii. 6 (Keble, III, 346).   [105] *Ibid.*, I. x. 5 (Keble, I, 243).
[106] *Ibid.*, VII. ii. 1 (Keble, III, 145).
[107] *Ibid.*, VIII. ii. 11 (Keble, III, 350–351).
[108] Davies, *op. cit.*, p. 69.   [109] *Polity*, I. x. 8 (Keble, I, 245).
[110] *Ibid.*, I. viii. 3 (Keble, I, 227).

public detriment: but surely without their consent I see not how the body should be able by any just means to help itself, saving when dominion doth escheat. Such things therefore must be thought upon beforehand, that power may be limited ere it be granted.[111]

Davies, who warns that too much may be read into Hooker's contractarianism,[112] despite his finding in it the idea most nearly basic to Hooker's feelings on political authority, says of this passage, "Even in theory, Hooker comes perilously near a doctrine of royal absolutism, and when we test whether there be any practical checks on this power, we find that, in practice, royal power is absolute."[113] The Rev. Norman Sykes says of the same passage, "This answer can scarcely be called a solution. Hooker, not unlike the harassed Pilate, had raised a question of acute complexity, and had sought rather to evade than to answer it. His words could afford no guidance in case of practical urgency."[114] Still, Sykes holds that "Hooker was a convinced advocate of constitutional monarchy,"[115] and his view is essentially confirmed by A. P. d'Entrèves[116] and Peter Munz.[117] But Hooker's treatment of sovereignty is not free of ambiguity, and if modern commentators seem to agree essentially on Hooker's position, the High Church of the Restoration determinedly interpreted that position as one of royal absolutism.

[111] *Ibid.,* VIII. ii. 10 (Keble, III, 350).

[112] Davies, *op. cit.,* p. 66: "We have seen that the *pactum unionis* [the social contract proper: a number of people, living in a state of nature, decide to form an organized society] does not exist in his writings, but there are traces of the *pactum subjectionis* [the contract of submission: social units yield power to a chosen authority], although this aspect of the Contract theory by no means occupies a key position in Hooker's political thought." Here Davies substantially agrees with Alexander Passerin d'Entrèves, *The Medieval Contribution to Political Thought* (Oxford, 1939), pp. 128–131.

[113] Davies, *op. cit.,* p. 78.

[114] Norman Sykes, "Richard Hooker," p. 81, in *The Social & Political Ideas of Some Great Thinkers of the Sixteenth and Seventeenth Centuries,* ed. F. J. C. Hearnshaw (London, [1926]).

[115] *Ibid.,* p. 80. Sykes says of Hooker (p. 80), "In his view the normal manner of instituting kingship was by the Social Contract, which expressed the desire of an ungoverned multitude to enter into organised social life." Again (p. 82), "The two principles upon which he insisted were the necessity of the consent of the whole people to legislation, and the subordination of the king to the laws of the nation."

[116] D'Entrèves, *op. cit.,* pp. 132–135.

[117] Peter Munz, *The Place of Hooker in the History of Thought* (London, 1952), pp. 101–105.

Even as the question of kingship in the *Polity* has provoked disagreement, Hooker's position on the apostolic succession has called forth varying interpretations, though his approval of the episcopal institution cannot be doubted. It is significant that Hooker's views on episcopacy are mainly set forth in Book VII of the *Polity,* the last of the Books to be printed. John Keble, in his Preface to the *Polity,* tries at great length to prove that Hooker has demonstrated the apostolic succession in the Church of England,[118] and he cites much evidence in an attempt to show that Hooker's views reflect the thought of his time as it appears in the writings of Hadrian Saravia, Richard Bancroft, and Thomas Bilson.[119] To support his proposition, he quotes the strongest statement in the *Polity* on the subject: "Wherefore let us not fear to be herein bold and peremptory, that if any thing in the Church's government, surely the first institution of bishops was from heaven, was even of God, the Holy Ghost was the author of it."[120] This, Keble holds, is Hooker's final view on the question, and he again cites the *Polity* to show that Hooker himself says that he did not always think thus:

Myself did sometimes judge a great deal more probable than now I do, merely that after the Apostles were deceased, churches did agree amongst themselves for preservation of peace and order, to make one presbyter in each city chief over the rest, and to translate into him that power by force and virtue whereof the Apostles . . . did preserve and uphold order in the Church.[121]

But even so High Church a man as Keble must say, that "if (as many will be ready to assert) they [these passages] are expressly or virtually contradicted by other passages of the same author, the utmost effect of such contradiction must be to neutralize him in this controversy, and make him unfit to be quoted on either side."[122] He tries to explain away such a statement as "there may be sometimes very just and sufficient reason to allow ordination made without a bishop,"[123] but he must admit in the end that there is a marked difference between Hooker and such orthodox churchmen as Laud, Hammond, and Leslie.[124]

[118] Keble, I, lxvi–lxxxv.   [119] *Ibid.,* pp. lxxiii–lxxviii.
[120] *Polity,* VII. v. 10 (Keble, III, 168), quoted in Keble, I, lxxix.
[121] *Ibid.,* VII. xi. 8 (Keble, III, 209–211), quoted in Keble, I, lxxx.
[122] Keble, I, lxxx.
[123] *Polity,* VII. xiv. 11 (Keble, III, 231), quoted in Keble, I, lxxxiv.
[124] Keble, I, lxxxv.

More recently, Davies has stated that by quoting the words of the *Polity* beyond their context, Hooker could be regarded as the fountainhead of diverse theological theories.[125] But, he holds, there is no doubt about the general character of the *Polity:* "the standpoint is that of a reformed Catholicism."[126] He points, as does Keble, to Book VII. v. 10, to show that Hooker's final judgment on episcopacy is consistent with his general doctrine.[127] Still, Davies must note as "surprising"[128] Hooker's belief that the Church has the authority to abolish episcopacy and his statement that the basis of episcopal power is traditional rather than prescribed:

Bishops, albeit they may avouch with conformity of truth that their authority hath thus descended even from the very apostles themselves, yet the absolute and everlasting continuance of it they cannot say that any commandment of the Lord doth enjoin; and therefore must acknowledge that the Church hath power by universal consent upon urgent cause to take it away, if thereunto she be constrained through the proud, tyrannical, and unreformable dealings of her bishops. . . . Wherefore lest bishops forget themselves, as if none on earth had authority to touch their states, let them continually bear in mind, that it is rather the force of custom, whereby the Church having so long found it good to continue under the regiment of her virtuous bishops, doth still uphold, maintain, and honour them in that respect, than that any such true and heavenly law can be shewed, by the evidence whereof it may of a truth appear that the Lord himself hath appointed presbyters for ever to be under the regiment of bishops, in what sort soever they behave themselves. Let this consideration be a bridle unto them, let it teach them not to disdain the advice of their presbyters.[129]

Keble and Davies, then, find in the *Polity* a fundamental advocacy of the apostolic succession, though both are aware of some contradictions. Sisson says, however, "There is nothing in Hooker to serve as a foundation for an episcopacy by apostolic succession and divine institution; indeed his reservations upon this matter might furnish ammunition for an opposition."[130] Houk, too, says that Hooker's defense of episcopacy is not based on divine right, but rather on long use and proven expedience.[131] He considers the idea of the social contract and the sovereignty of the people behind all of Hooker's thinking, and this is incompatible with apostolic suc-

[125] Davies, p. 88.   [126] *Ibid.*   [127] *Ibid.*   [128] *Ibid.*
[129] *Polity*, VII. v. 8 (Keble, III, 165–166).
[130] Sisson, pp. 107–108.   [131] Houk, p. 75.

cession.[132] He would additionally explain the absence of the doctrine of divine right by saying that Hooker desired in the *Polity* to win the Puritans to conformity with the usages of the Church of England, and that "it would have been one thing to persuade the Presbyterians to tolerate episcopacy as in accord with the law of the land and another thing to impose it upon them as of divine right."[133] But it is needless to multiply examples. Hooker's stand on episcopacy and particularly the apostolic succession has ever provoked and is still provoking argument and counterargument.[134]

On the subject of church property, Hooker reflects almost completely the stand of the Church: it is inalienable. He grounds his argument in Scripture,[135] and he condemns the contemporary situation: "For as those ancient nursing Fathers thought they did never bestow enough; even so in the eye of this present age, as long as any thing remaineth, it seemeth to be too much."[136] He speaks of Elizabeth's respect for the rights of the Church, though his tone is almost one of hope and advice rather than praise,[137] and he even suggests the greatness and certainty of the revenue which the crown receives from the Church.[138] To strengthen his case, he is even willing to admit that the Church has upon occasion been guilty of abuse of its privileges and that God is righteous in taking away what men abuse, but he holds that occasional abuse does not excuse the violence of thieves and robbers.[139] But here, too, Hooker's sense of history led him into difficulty, for he chose to refer to the days of Henry VIII. In considering the policy of Henry VIII in alienating church property, Hooker purposely deals almost exclusively with the alienation of monastic property. About all he says of Henry's abuse of property other than monastic is, "My meaning is not hereby to make the state of bishoprick and of those dissolved companies alike, the one no less unlawful to be removed than the other."[140] Keble has aptly indicated Hooker's dilemma: "He must either expressly condemn a principal part of the settlement at the reformation in England, confirmed and carried on as it

---

[132] *Ibid.*   [133] *Ibid.*

[134] The best statement of Hooker's position is in Peter Munz, *op. cit.,* pp. 59–62.

[135] *Polity,* VII. xxiv. 20–21 (Keble, III, 317–319).

[136] *Ibid.,* VII. xxiv. 22 (Keble, III, 319).

[137] *Ibid.* (Keble, III, 320).   [138] *Ibid.,* VII. xxiv. 23 (Keble, III, 321).

[139] *Ibid.,* VII. xxiv. 24 (Keble, III, 322).

[140] *Ibid.,* VII. xxiv. 23 (Keble, III, 321).

had been by subsequent monarchs; or else (which he chose to do) must deny the sacredness of the confiscated property."[141] Hooker chose to treat the monasteries as lay corporate bodies and property forfeited by abuse, but his qualifications are evidence of his embarrassment. When he says of monastic personnel that "they were properly no portion of God's clergy," he must yet add, "(only such amongst them excepted as were also priests)."[142] When he says of monastic goods that they "may in part seem to be of the nature of civil possessions," he must except "(that . . . which they unjustly held through the pope's usurped power of appropriating ecclesiastical livings unto them)."[143] Hooker, then, justifies Henry VIII in order to uphold the settlement at the reformation, but it is a forced justification; he pleads special circumstances; his favor is reticent and burdened with qualifications. But even his half-hearted endorsement of a particular case where alienation was involved might provide fuel for controversy, and it is perhaps significant that his main discussion of church property was centered in the yet suppressed Book VII. Although Hooker had completely justified the inalienability of such property in Book V, he had not locked the door: "I will not absolutely say concerning the goods of the Church that they may in no case be seized on by men, or that no obligation, commerce and bargain made between man and man can ever be of force to alienate the property which God hath in them."[144]

Book VII finally appeared in 1662, in an edition of Hooker's works, prefaced by a *Life*. It is easy to see why the newly restored Church should want the support of its champion in this year. But if it had been inopportune to print Book VII in 1648 because it contained Hooker's ambiguous position on the apostolic succession and on the divine right of bishops and his apparent sanctioning of the alienation of church property in cases of abuse and superstition, why was 1662, a time when the Church was even less willing to compromise and was supremely preoccupied with the firm establishment of its position, more opportune? Here was gratuitous ammunition for nonconformity.

The author of the *Life* and the man responsible for the edition of 1661–1662 was John Gauden. Gauden was, indeed, Bishop of Exeter, but it is odd that the Church entrusted Hooker to him.

---

141 Keble, I, cvi–cvii.   142 *Polity*, VII. xxiv. 23 (Keble, III, 321).
143 *Ibid.*   144 *Ibid.*, V. lxxix. 16 (Keble, II, 498).

Undoubtedly, the edition and the *Life* were his own idea, and he probably started without official sanction. Gauden had made his peace with the parliamentary party and had retained his preferments during the interregnum, though, to be sure, he did publish occasionally in behalf of the Church of England.[145] He was a moderate, if not a temporizing, Anglican, one of those who in 1656 had welcomed the proposals for limited episcopacy in Ussher's *Reduction*.[146] It appears that before the Restoration he took special pains to reinstate himself with the King and the High Church. He published a remonstrance which, he said, he had presented to Cromwell on behalf of the Church of England clergy suffering from the Declaration of 1655. S. R. Gardiner is convinced that the remonstrance is a fraud,[147] but Gauden certainly used it as he used the *Eikon Basilike* to vouch for his continued efforts for the Church. It was probably on the basis of the remonstrance and the *Eikon Basilike* that Gauden was on the Restoration made chaplain to the King and, in November, 1660, Bishop of Exeter. It is probable, too, that he owed his bishopric to the King, that, in fact, Sheldon and Morley opposed him.[148] At the Restoration, he had placed his faith in Morley as an intermediary to get his claims before Hyde, and Morley and Sheldon had misled him on the revenues of the diocese of Exeter. His appointment to so poor a see showed him that the promises of favor made to him by the High Churchmen were merely promises, and he later addressed his pleas for money and translation directly to Hyde.[149] His *Life of Hooker* and his edition of Hooker's works were a further attempt to ingratiate himself not only with the King, to whom he dedicated the volume, but with the High Church.

Gauden's original intention, it may be suggested, was merely to add a *Life* to those parts of the *Polity* which had already been published. Perhaps because *Clavi Trabales*, published sometime after August, 1661, contained some Book VIII material not in the 1648

[145] *DNB*, article "John Gauden." [146] Bosher, p. 46.
[147] Gardiner, *op. cit.*, III, 336, n. 2.
[148] See Burnet's *History of My Own Time*, ed. Osmund Airy (Oxford, 1897), I, 87, 324.
[149] Gauden complained to Hyde of the poverty of Exeter several times, and in a letter dated Jan. 21, 1660[1], openly based his claims for better preferment on his authorship of the *Eikon* (*State Papers Collected by Edward, Earl of Clarendon* [Oxford, 1767–1786], III, supp., xxvi–xxxii, and app., xcv–xcvi).

edition which Gauden used as the source for Book VI and Book VIII,[150] publication of the 1661–1662 volume was delayed until Gauden could uncover additional text for the last Book. That he was successful is evident, for the 1661–1662 Book VIII follows that of 1648 but has additional text, though it still does not contain everything published in the Book VIII selections of *Clavi Trabales*. It is likely that the search for a supplement to Book VIII led to the discovery of a manuscript for Book VII. This conjecture is supported by the way in which the 1661–1662 volume is put together. The frontispiece, which is dated 1661, is engraved, and therefore its date remained unchanged, though a delay in publication is evidenced by the "1662" on the title page. The *Life* is separately paged; Books I–V of the *Polity* are on pages 1–345. Book VI starts, strangely, on page 137[151] and ends on page 183; Book VIII begins on page 184 and goes to page 224; Book VII, paged 1–75, is inserted between pages 183 and 184.[152] Gauden's dedication to Charles II, which is dated January 1, 1661[2], mentions Book VII, an indication that though the contents were fixed by that time, the printing of Book VII probably caused the delay which the date of the title page points to.

Gauden does not state where the manuscript for Book VII came from. In his *Life of Hooker*, however, in referring to the new edition of the *Polity*, he says that

by the care of some Learned men, especially of the Right Reverend Father in God, *Gilbert* now Lord Bishop of *London*, those genuine additions are now made of the *three last Books*, promised and performed

---

[150] Houk, p. 121.   [151] See Appendix C.

[152] The signatures, as well as the pagination, show that Book VII was inserted. Book VI ends on sig. Zz4r (p. 183). Zz4v is blank (the second blank side in the text of the *Polity*). Book VII starts on sig. *Ar (p. 1) and ends on sig. [*]K2r (p. 75). Book VIII starts on sig. *K2v, but with p. 184, and p. 185, instead of being sig. *K3r, is Aaar, showing that p. 184 was originally to have been printed on the blank sig. Zz4v.

It can also be shown that an addition to Book VIII was made after the originally planned volume had been printed. That part of Book VIII which Gauden reprinted from the 1648 edition ends with "to give judgement" on p. 216. Following the *Polity*, several treatises by or concerning Hooker were printed. These start on p. 217. The pagination is regular through p. 220, though irregular thereafter. The material which Gauden added to that of Book VIII in the 1648 volume repeats these numbers, being paged 217–224. Book VIII (in fours) is regular through sig. Ddd3v (p. 214). We should expect p. 215 to be Ddd4r; it is, instead, Ee[e]. The first signature for the treatise material is also Eee.

by him [Hooker], but long concealed from publique view, not without great injury to the publique good.[153]

It may well have been Sheldon who gave the manuscript for Book VII to Gauden, whose confidence in his sources points to his trust in the giver:

But Providence in time, hath not onely confuted those mens [Hooker's antagonists'] projects and confidences, but also brought forth those esteemed *Abortives*, the three last Books, with such *lineaments* of their Fathers Vertue and Vigor on them, that they may be easily and justly owned for *genuine;* although (perhaps) they had not the last politure of their Parents hands: Their strength shews them to be a *legitimate Progeny*, however they may seem to want *something* of that *beauty* and *lustre* which always attended Mr. *Hookers consummations.*[154]

The Venerable *Author of these eight Books,* had formerly given the world an account of *his design in each of them:* Of which, five have many year been *extant in publique;* the last three were thought to have been *never finished,* and to be sure, they have been for many ages *suppressed;* which are now come to light, after our late long troubles. . . . Such as they are, it is thought meet to present them to the *Reader;* each of them is by *learned Criticks* judged to be *genuine,* or *Authentick,* though possibly not so compleat and exact as the curious Author intended: The seventh book, by comparing the writing of it with *other indisputable Papers,* or known *Manuscripts* of Mr. *Hookers,* is undoubtedly his *own hand* throughout: The eighth is written by *another hand* (as a Copy) but interlined in many places with Mr. *Hookers own characters,* as owned by him.[155]

Houk says that Gauden "probably welcomed the witness of the Seventh Book because of its moderate positions on the question of the offices of the ministry."[156] But Houk himself says that the Restoration Church was "in no mood for moderate preachments; the reaction had already set in."[157] Why then should Sheldon, and the evidence points to him as the donor, have given Gauden access to the manuscript of Book VII? It has been shown that, though Hooker's stand on the question of the apostolic succession does not conform with that of the High Church, his statements are capable of being interpreted variously. It may be supposed that Sheldon, in

---

[153] John Gauden, *The Life & Death of Mr. Richard Hooker* in *The Works of Mr. Richard Hooker* (London, 1662), p. 1.
[154] *Ibid.,* p. 24.   [155] *Ibid.,* p. 26.   [156] Houk, p. 122.
[157] *Ibid.*

the rush to get the 1661–1662 volume to press, did not carefully examine every word in Book VII and that he thought that Hooker's sentiments confirmed the apostolic succession. Gauden, despite his general Low Church positions, was now, after all, a bishop, and one who was still in the process of ingratiating himself with the Church. There can be no doubt in what light he considered Book VII. The title page of 1661–1662 describes Book VII as "touching *Episcopacy,* as the Primitive, Catholick and Apostolick Government of the Church." In summarizing Book VII in the *Life,* Gauden says nothing which might detract from a favorable view of episcopacy,[158] and he describes that Book in a light which would be acceptable to the High Church, even as he insists in his summary of Book VIII that Hooker asserts the *"Supremacy* of *Soveraign Princes."*[159] Gauden was going along with the High Church.

It may well be, then, that Book VII appeared in 1662 because Gauden was anxious to demonstrate his good will toward the High Church and because Sheldon was not completely aware of what he had given Gauden. Bishop Burnet was a little harsh when he wrote of Sheldon, "He seemed not to have a deep sense of religion, if any at all: and spoke of it most commonly as of an engine of government, and a matter of policy," but Burnet was fair enough when he said, "Sheldon was esteemed a learned man before the wars: but he was then engaged so deep in the politics, that scarce any prints of what he had been remained."[160] Sheldon's disposition to leave the intellectual defense of the Church to others finally caught up with him. He must have been greatly displeased when the ambiguity of Book VII was made known to him after its publication. Nor was his displeasure limited only to this aspect of the volume. In the *Life* Gauden had indulged his Low Church propensities by placing the blame for the fall of the Church during the interregnum not only on the fury of the nonconformists, but also on the too close adherence to forms, rites, and ceremonies of the Church itself.[161] Again, though the title page of the volume read

---

[158] Gauden, pp. 24–25.   [159] *Ibid.,* p. 25.   [160] Burnet, *op. cit.,* I, 313.
[161] Gauden, pp. 3–5. "The strength of the Church of *England* was much decayed and undermined, before it was openly battered; partly by some superfluous, illegal and unauthorized innovations in point of Ceremony, which some men affected to use in publique, and impose upon others, which provoked people to jealousie and fury, even against things lawful, every man judging truly, that the measure of all *publique obedience* ought to be *publique Laws;* partly by a supine *neglect* in others of the main matters in which the

that the *Polity* was "Now compleated," it must inevitably have been brought to Sheldon's attention that Book VIII did not contain everything published in *Clavi Trabales*. Moreover, despite Gauden's statement that Hooker asserts the supremacy of sovereign princes, he had attached to the close of Book VIII an addition which infelicitously suggested that "such usurpers . . . as in the exercise of their power do more than they have been authorized to do, cannot in Conscience binde any man unto obedience." His addition ended with these words:

Disobedience therefore unto Laws, which are made by men, is not a thing of so small account as some would make it.

Howbeit, too rigorous it were, that the breach of every Humane Law should be held a deadly sin: A mean there is between those extremities, if so be we can find it out.[162]

Such statements might be used to urge resistance of superiors, and Sheldon must have writhed when he was informed that Gauden had authenticated Books VI–VIII "notwithstanding those poysonous assertions against the regal power, which are to be found in them."[163] To cap the climax, the *Life* itself was enough to turn Sheldon's displeasure into active dislike. It is hardly flattering and extremely inaccurate; its forty folio pages are written in a style that is lumbering, extravagant, utterly without charm, and full of sententious comment.

Gauden announces the pattern of the *Life* only after six pages on Hooker as a bulwark against nonconformity; on the distress of the Church, caused, despite Hooker, by nonconformists and over-ceremonial churchmen; and on the final restoration of peace in the Church. Of his six parts, the first, on Hooker's birth and education, consists of two paragraphs. His second part he announces as *"His genius and temper* of body and minde, with the most critical *instances* of his *life* and *actions;* his Person also, and outward Mine, or Aspect, which is no small indication of mens *mindes* and *man-*

Kingdom of God, the peace of *Conscience,* and of the *Churches* happiness do chiefly consist, while they were immoderately intent upon meer *Formalities,* and more zealous for an *outward conformity* to those shadows, then for that inward or outward conformity with Christ, in *holy hearts,* and *unblameable lives,* which most adorn true Religion" (p. 4). See also Gauden's last paragraph, p. 40.

[162] *Ibid.,* p. 224.

[163] The words are Anthony à Wood's, *Athenae Oxon.,* I, 696.

ners."[164] For some seven pages, he speaks rather generally of Hooker's garb, deportment, conversation, and academic proficiency. The picture of Hooker at college and shortly after is hardly a flattering one:

> While Mr. *Hooker* continued in *Corpus Christi Colledge,* few men of any note in either University, but promised more then he did, as to any great and publique undertaking: Not that he wanted a publique spirit, or excellent abilities in Nature and Education; but he was so locked up and reserved by a natural modesty, and *self-deficiency* or distrust.[165]

> *Hooker* . . . seemed not to have been to any great *conspicuity* or *expectance,* while he continued in the *Colledge,* if we may take an *estimate* of the opinion had of him by the first *offer of preferment,* or rather imployment, made to him, yea and accepted by him, as to those small obscure livings; one of which was first given him by the Colledge, and *leaving* that, another was conferred on him by some private Patron, each of them being thought *competent* entertainments.[166]

> Mr. *Hooker* looked more to his employment and retirement then his *Preferment:* hence I finde him *aground* as soon as *lanched* out, and as it were buried so soon as he parted from his *Mother the University,* still shut up for many years in *Countrey obscurities.*[167]

Section three is a summary of the manner and matter of the *Polity,* covering a third of the pages in the *Life.* In dealing next with Hooker's "*Sufferings* and *Tryals,*" Gauden juxtaposes two incongruous episodes. The first of the trials is Hooker's controversy with Walter Travers, and his story of its outcome points almost to the chastisement of Hooker as well as of Travers:

> When the *conflagration* grew too flaming and publique . . . both of them were brought *before the Queen* and *Council.* . . .

> At last prudent *Applications* and time . . . cooled the *calentures* on *both sides;* chiefly by parting the *Antagonists,* and placing them in *several stations:* Mr. *Hooker* was by his worthy and deserving Patron *Archbishop Whitgifts* means, removed to another place of less *envy,* and more privacy in *Kent,* being loth to have so excellent a light too much *wasted,* by its standing too long in *the blaze* and *wind.*[168]

Then, in all its particulars, follows an account of the blackmailing of Hooker. After this tabloid tale, Gauden pauses to comment on

[164] Gauden, p. 6.   [165] *Ibid.,* p. 10 [misnumbered "12"].
[166] *Ibid.,* p. 11 [misnumbered "9"].   [167] *Ibid.,* p. 13.
[168] *Ibid.,* p. 31.

the paucity of the factual material available to him. He spends just two paragraphs on Hooker's particular rewards and preferments, and a half-dozen pages on his death and burial and on the monuments and testimonials in his honor. Here, obviously, was no *Life* befitting the champion of the Restoration Church.

Sheldon's displeasure was made evident even within the short time which Gauden lived after his publication of 1661–1662. Gauden, it will be remembered, had tried to persuade Hyde to translate him from Exeter. How certain he was of a change is made clear in an entry by Pepys for July 25, 1663, telling of a visit to the home of Dennis Gauden, brother of the bishop:

When I come there, the first thing was to show me his house, which is almost built. I find it very regular and finely contrived, and the gardens and offices about it as convenient and as full of good variety as ever I saw in my life. It is true, he hath been censured for laying out so much money; but he tells me that he built it for his brother, who is since dead, (the Bishop) who, when he should come to be Bishop of Winchester, which he was promised, to which bishopricke at present there is no house, he did intend to dwell there.[169]

Sheldon saw that Gauden did not get to Winchester. His own friend, George Morley, was translated from Worcester to Winchester in 1662, and, on June 10, Gauden replaced Morley at Worcester. "It is said that vexation at having missed the aim of his ambition brought on a violent attack. . . . He died on 20 Sept."[170]

[169] Pepys's *Diary*, I, 396.   [170] *DNB*, article "John Gauden."

Chapter 8

The Authorized *Life*

of Hooker – 1665

SHELDON could not be satisfied merely with castigating Gauden; the damage done by the volume of 1661–1662 had to be repaired. When, in 1666, the next edition of the *Polity* appeared, it was just a reprint of Gauden's text, and though the Restoration Church sought to discredit the authenticity of the last three Books, it was never able to produce alternative versions. Here is implicit proof that Sheldon and the Church had provided Gauden with what manuscripts they had available. The damage could be repaired, however, by an alternative life of Hooker which would show the inaccuracies in Gauden's *Life* and would thereby discredit his statements about the *Polity*. For this task Sheldon had to seek out a reputable biographer whose religious views accorded with his own. Nor did he have to go far afield. Walton's *Life of Donne* and his *Life of Wotton* had both, by this time, gone through two editions (the *Compleat Angler* was in its third), and in these his High Church position was clear. Moreover, Walton was at this time in Sheldon's back yard. In 1661 and 1662, he acted as Bishop Morley's personal steward at Worcester.[1] His second wife died on April 17, 1662,[2] leaving him with two young children, and, this same April, Morley was translated to Winchester and soon moved there.[3] Walton probably lived for almost the whole of the remainder of his life

---

[1] Canon Clement Price showed this by reproducing entries in the chapter accounts of Worcester Cathedral (*TLS*, Aug. 14, 1919, p. 437).

[2] So recorded in Walton's prayer book (*Compleat Walton*, p. 584).

[3] Nicolas, p. lxx.

with Morley at Winchester, in the episcopal residence at Farnham Castle, or in the London episcopal headquarters in Chelsea.[4] In dedicating his *Life of Hooker* to Morley, Walton says that it was written under his roof,[5] and in dedicating to Morley also the *Lives* of 1670 and 1675, he repeats this statement and adds that the *Life of Herbert,* too, was there written.[6] He reveals his debt to Morley in saying that if he was fit to undertake not only these but also the *Life of Donne* and the *Life of Wotton* "*it would not have been by acquir'd Learning or Study, but by the advantage of forty years friendship, and thereby the hearing of and discoursing with your Lordship, which hath inabled me to make the relation of these Lives passable in an eloquent and captious age.*"[7]

There is reason to believe that Sheldon had known Walton for some time. Walton said of him in 1655, "And if you would know more of fishing for the *Umber* or *Barbel,* get into favour with Doctor *Sh.* whose skil is above others; and of that the poor that dwell about him have a comfortable experience."[8] The particularity of this points to personal acquaintance. From Walton himself, though not until 1670, comes the story of how Sheldon persuaded him to write the *Life of Hooker:*

Doct. Ga. (*then Lo. B. of* Exeter) *publisht* the Life of Mr. Ric. Hooker, (*so he called it*) *with so many dangerous mistakes, both of him and* his Books: *that discoursing of them with his* Grace, Gilbert *that now is Lord Arch bishop of* Canterbury, *he injoyned me to examine some Circumstances, and then rectifie the Bishops mistakes, by giving the World a truer account* [9] *of Mr.* Hooker *and his* Books. . . . *And, indeed, till* his Grace *had laid this injunction upon me, I could not admit a thought of any fitness in me to undertake it: but when he had twice injoyn'd me to it, I then trusted his judgment, and submitted to his Commands; considering that if I did not, I could not forbear accusing my self of disobedience: And, indeed of* Ingratitude *for his many favours.*[10]

If Walton had resisted before December, 1662, he could hardly have done so after. In that month Sheldon gave Walton a lease of

[4] *Ibid.,* pp. lxx, ci. Samuel Woodforde says in the "Ritornata" of his commendatory poem to Walton, printed before the *Life of Hooker* in *Lives,* 1670, "*To* Chelsea, *Song.*"
[5] *Hooker,* 1665, verso of 4th unsigned leaf.
[6] *Lives,* 1670, sig. A3^v; *ibid.,* 1675, sig. A3^v.
[7] *Ibid.,* 1670, sig. A3^v–A4^r.
[8] *Compleat Angler,* 1655, p. 279; *ibid.,* 1661, p. 201, has "Sheldon."
[9] *Lives,* 1675, sig. A5^r: "*a fuller and truer account.*"
[10] *Ibid.,* 1670, "To the Reader," sigs. A5^v–A6^r.

a newly erected building, adjoining a house called the Cross Keys in Paternoster Row, for forty years, at the yearly rent of forty shillings.[11] Sheldon *"injoyn'd"* Walton by means more substantial than words.

Walton's resistance, as he tells of it, is probably exaggerated. He most certainly would have been willing to perform a service for the Church, encouraged as he was by Sheldon and Morley. He had himself been interested in Hooker for many years, and may even have started collecting notes for a *Life* long before Sheldon broached the subject.

In the epistle to the reader prefixed to the *Life of Hooker* in 1665, Walton said of Gauden's omissions, *"I suppose his more weighty Business and Want of Time, made him pass over many things without that due Examination, which my better Leisure, my Diligence, and my accidental Advantages, have made known unto me."*[12] He does not refer merely to the sanction and help of the Church. The *"accidental Advantages"* are revealed in his Introduction to the *Life of Hooker:*

> *About forty years past . . . I began a happy affinity with* William Cranmer, *(now with God) grand Nephew unto the great Archbishop of that name; a Family of noted prudence and resolution; with him and two of his Sisters I had an entire and free friendship: one of them was the Wife of Dr.* Spencer, *a Bosom-friend, and sometime Com-pupil with Mr.* Hooker *in* Corpus-Christi College *in* Oxford, *and after President of the same.*[13]

He says that William Cranmer and his sisters were friends of Hooker's, indeed, that they had even studied under his direction.

[11] Nicolas, p. lxxi. This was a profitable transaction for Walton. The building was destroyed in the Great Fire, and in 1670 Walton petitioned the "Court of Judicature for determination of differences touching houses burnt in London." He was willing to rebuild if he received an abatement of rent and an increase in the term of the lease. It was to Walton's advantage to rebuild the premises when the court extended his lease to sixty years, even though the rent was to remain the same and even though he had to pay the arrears then due (*ibid.*, pp. lxxviii–lxxix, from Add. MS 5088, f. 142 in British Museum). In his will, Walton wrote, "I give my son-in-law Doc^r Hawkins and to his Wife, to them I give all my tytell and right of or in a part of a howse and shop in Pater-noster-rowe in London: which I hold by lease from the Lord Bishop of London for about fifty years to come" (Nicolas, p. c). Walton, unlike Donne in his illness, had no qualms about accepting a profitable lease on Church-owned property in return for his service to the Church, and just as Henry King had suggested to Donne that such a transaction would benefit his children, so Walton looked upon it as a fine inheritance for his children.

[12] *Hooker,* 1665, sig. A6^v.   [13] *Ibid.*, p. 3.

Walton mentions his own *"happy Cohabitation"* with the Cranmers and says:

Having some years before read part of Mr. Hookers Works with great liking and satisfaction, my affection to them made me a diligent Inquisitor into many things that concerned him; as namely, of his Person, his Nature, the Management of his Time, his Wife, his Family, and the Fortune of him and his. Which hath given me much advantage in the knowledge of what is now under my consideration.[14]

Walton's first wife, whom he had married on December 27, 1626, was Rachel Floud.[15] Her mother was Susannah Cranmer Floud, sister of George Cranmer (1563–1600), the pupil and friend of Hooker, and consulted by him about the *Polity*. Mrs. Floud became a widow in 1623,[16] and it is likely that she lived in London with Walton and his wife after their marriage.[17] Her sister Dorothy probably lived with the Waltons, also, and doubtless she could relate many things about Hooker. Dorothy had first married John Spenser, who must have known Hooker at Corpus Christi College, Oxford, and who was one of Hooker's literary executors. Spenser died on April 3, 1614,[18] and his widow married, probably in October, 1616, Richard Field, Dean of Gloucester.[19] Field had been friendly with Spenser, and was by him probably introduced to Hooker, whom he knew during the last two years of Hooker's life.[20] Dorothy was a widow for the second time in two years by Field's death on November 21, 1616.[21] She and Mrs. Floud, living with Walton eight years or more, are probably the source of many of the *"Little things"* which Walton says he *"received by Tradition."*[22]

Walton's statement that he did not consider himself fit for the task of writing Hooker's life before Sheldon requested him to do so[23] perhaps indicates that he was projecting such a life. He had quoted from the *Polity* in the 1651 *Life of Wotton*[24] and in his "Advertisement to the Reader"[25] had called attention to Wotton's

---

[14] *Ibid.*, pp. 4–5.   [15] Nicolas, p. xxi.

[16] *N&Q*, 4th ser., XII (Nov. 15, 1873), p. 384.

[17] Walton's phrase, *"happy Cohabitation"* points to this. Also, she describes herself in her will, dated April 20, 1635, as of the parish of St. Dunstan's-in-the-West (Nicolas, p. xxx).

[18] *Athenae Oxon.*, II, 146.   [19] *DNB*, article "Richard Field."

[20] *Athenae Oxon.*, II, 182.   [21] *DNB*, article "Richard Field."

[22] *Hooker*, 1665, sig. A6ᵛ.   [23] *Lives*, 1670, "To the Reader," sig. A6ʳ.

[24] *Reliq.*, 1651, sig. c9ʳ. The edited quotation is from IV. i. 1 (Keble, I, 417).

[25] *Ibid.*, sig. a3ʳ.

character of Whitgift,[26] which he quoted in the *Life of Hooker*.[27] That Walton may even have been collecting materials for a life of Hooker as early as 1651 is perhaps shown in his quoting in 1665 from the "Translator To the Reader" of Fulgentio Micanzio's *Life of Sarpi*, which had been published in 1651 by Walton's friend Marriot.[28] Walton says in the Introduction to the *Life of Hooker*:

> *I had also a friendship with the Reverend Dr.* Usher, *the late learned Archbishop of* Armagh; *and with Dr.* Morton, *the late learned and charitable Bishop of* Durham; *as also with the learned* John Hales *of* Eaton College; *and with them also (who loved the very Name of Mr.* Hooker) *I have had many discourses concerning him: and from them, and many others that have now put off Mortality, I might have had more Informations, if I could then have admitted a thought of any fitness for what by persuasion I have now undertaken. But, though that full harvest be irrecoverably lost, yet my Memory hath preserved some gleanings.*[29]

Ussher and Hales died in 1656 and Morton in 1659, and Walton's conversations with them may indeed have come before he seriously considered writing Hooker's life. But there is additional evidence to indicate more than interest in Hooker before 1658. It will be remembered that Walton jotted down some notes on the inside of the cover of his copy of the 1636 *Eusebius*. Among these are found:

vew hookers preface: and hooker—226 & 229
vew the verses before Sands psalms and Sʳ Tho. Haukins his horrace.[30]

These notes were probably written with reference to the church music addition in the 1658 *Donne*,[31] but George Sandys is mentioned in the *Life of Hooker*,[32] and one of the two only references to Horace in the *Lives* is in the *Hooker*.[33] In the *Eusebius* notes appears also:

[26] *Ibid.*, p. 19, in "Of Robert Devereux, *Earl of* Essex; *and George Villiers, Duke of* Buckingham."
[27] *Hooker,* 1665, p. 63.
[28] *The Life of the Most Learned Father Paul:* "The Translator To the Reader," sig. A2ᵛ: "*I may say of him* [Sarpi], *as twas said of* Adryanus Turnebus, *that he not onely knew more then others, but what he knew he knew better; (he knowing by* causes *by* definitions *by* relations *and* practise)." *Hooker,* 1665, p. 24: "*He* [Hooker] *did not onely know more, but what he knew he knew better than other men.*" Changed to "*He did not onely know more of Causes and Effects . . .*" in *Hooker,* 1666, p. 5.
[29] *Hooker,* 1665, pp. 5–6.　　　[30] See Appendix A.　　　[31] See pp. 94–95.
[32] *Hooker,* 1665, pp. 30–31.　　　[33] *Ibid.*, p. 43.

make his discription that he was 1º for his complexion. then his
behaviour   then his stature. then his discourse minesterd grace to the
herer

that he was like the dove wᵗh out gall.

Except for the reference to complexion, which contradicts what
Walton actually says of Hooker,[34] the rest of this note might well
refer to Hooker,[35] and the last line surely refers to him. Spenser,[36]
Fuller,[37] and Gauden[38] had referred to Hooker's dovelike temper,
and Walton himself uses the expression on two occasions.[39] It is
possible, then, that more than Walton's reputation as a biographer,
his known Church affiliation, and the convenience of his situation
led to his choice as the author of the semiofficial *Life of Hooker*.
Sheldon undoubtedly knew that Walton was connected with the
Cranmer family and that the connection would lend authenticity
to what Walton would write, and he may very well have known
that for some time Walton had projected a life.

It was imperative that the semiofficial *Life* be authoritative and
that it appear at the earliest date consonant with accuracy of writing.
Despite Walton's statement in 1665 that he will not undertake to
justify the traditional content of the *Life*,[40] it is not surprising
to find him saying, *"And now for my self, I can say I hope, or rather
know, there are no Material Mistakes in what I here present to him
that shall become my Reader."*[41] He asks every lover of truth and
the memory of Hooker to make known to him any material omissions, and he promises *"to acknowledge and rectifie any such Mistake in a second Impression, which the Printer says he hopes for."*[42]
But, in marked contrast to his attitude in the *Life of Donne* and the
Life of Wotton, Walton was confident of the authoritativeness of
this *Life*, and his subsequent revisions bear out his confidence, for
the only material additions came about in 1670, as the result of

[34] *Ibid.*, p. 128: *"his face full of Heat-Pimples."*
[35] See *Hooker*, 1665, pp. 128–129, 133.
[36] ". . . *as if he like the bird of the holy Ghost, the Dove, had wanted gall"*
("To the Reader," *Polity*, 1604, sig. A2ᵛ).
[37] "His innocency survived to triumph over those aspersions which the malice
of others (advantaged by his own *dove-like simplicity*) had cast upon him"
(Thomas Fuller, *The Church-History of Britain* [London, 1655], bk. IX,
235).
[38] ". . . a Dove-like *innocency* in his manners" (Gauden, p. 16).
[39] ". . . the Dove-like temper of this meek, this matchlesse man" (*Hooker*,
1665, p. 107). Walton also quotes Spenser's words (*ibid.*, p. 111).
[40] *Hooker*, 1665, sigs. A6ᵛ–A7ʳ.   [41] *Ibid.*, sig. A6ᵛ.   [42] *Ibid.*, sig. A7ʳ.

new material made available to him. The paucity of the number of important changes points to the care which went into the *Life*.

This care is also evident in the time which Walton needed to complete the *Life*. Walton himself indicated that he wrote the *Life of Donne* in two months.[43] To be sure, he had known Donne personally, his collections for the *Life* must have been reasonably complete, and the original *Life of Donne* was less than half the length of the original *Life of Hooker*. But even these things do not account for the tremendous difference in the time spent on the two lives. Gauden's *Life* was printed early in 1662, but it was not until early in 1665 that Walton's *Life* appeared. He spent at least two years on the *Hooker* despite the rush to get it into print. For Walton to have indicated haste in his prefatory material would have been to invalidate his claim of authenticity, but the circumstances leading to his project and the specific circumstance of the publication of his *Life* show how anxious the Church was for the book. The date of Sheldon's lease to Walton may reasonably serve as evidence that Walton was at work by the end of 1662. Despite his early interest in Hooker, and perhaps his notes for the *Life,* despite the availability of Gauden's *Life* and Fuller's sketches of Hooker, even despite his access to advice and help from the Church, Walton had not done until late in 1664. The imprimatur by Archbishop Sheldon is dated October 29, 1664,[44] Walton's dedication to Morley is dated November 28, 1664,[45] and the *Life* was entered on the Stationers' Register on December 12, 1664.[46] The haste is best shown by reference to the letter of November 13, 1664, by Bishop Henry King, which is prefixed to the 1665 *Life of Hooker*. King's letter indicates, by its specific reference to Walton's text, that Walton had sent him a manuscript of the *Life* for comment.[47] It is true that Walton

[43] He started after Wotton's death, Dec. 5, 1639; in 1675, he added to the *Life of Donne* the date of its completion, Feb. 15, 1639[40]. To be sure, this date may be inaccurate, but *LXXX Sermons* was published before June 24, 1640 (the date of the younger Donne's letter to Walton).

[44] *Hooker*, 1665, verso of 2d preliminary leaf.

[45] *Ibid.*, sig. A^r.   [46] *Sta. Reg., 1640–1708*, II, 350.

[47] *Hooker*, 1665, sig. A2^r: "Though a Familiarity of almost Forty years continuance, and the constant experience of your Love even in the worst times, be sufficient to indear our Friendship; yet I must confess my Affection much improved, not onely by Evidences of private Respect to many that know and love you, but by your new Demonstration of a Publick Spirit, testified in a diligent, true, and useful Collection of so many Material Passages as you have now afforded me in the Life of *Venerable* Mr. *Hooker*. Of which, since desired

would have wanted to print so commendatory a letter, and he could not have done this and at the same time have incorporated into his text all of King's suggestions. King said, for instance, "You have done much for Sir *Henry Savile,* his [Hooker's] Contemporary and familiar Friend; amongst the surviving Monuments of whose Learning (give me leave to tell you so) two are omitted, his Edition of *Euclid,* but especially his Translation of *King James his Apology for the Oath of Allegeance* into elegant Latine."[48] It would have been awkward for Walton to revise his passage on Savile and still print this part of the letter. But one change indicated by King, Walton might have made without embarrassment. He had written that Dr. Spenser had on his deathbed told his wife to deliver the manuscript of the last three Books of the *Polity* to Dr. Abbot, the Archbishop of Canterbury. King's letter stated that Spenser "bequeathed them as a precious Legacy to my Father, then Bishop of *London;* after whose Death they rested in my hand, till Dr. *Abbot,* then Archbishop of *Canterbury,* commanded them out of my Custody, authorizing Dr. *John Barkeham* to require and bring them to him to *Lambeth.*"[49] That Walton wished to make his story comply with King's, and that he could easily have done so, is evident in the 1666 *Life,* where he added after the name of Abbot *"or unto Doctor* King, *Bishop of* London."[50] By the time Walton had received King's letter, however, it was too late for him to change his manuscript. The *Life* was probably at the printer's, and Walton was forced to include "or the Bishop of London" with his *Errata.*[51]

---

by such a Friend as your self, I shall not deny to give the Testimony of what I know concerning him and his learned Books."

[48] *Ibid.,* sig. A5ᵛ.   [49] *Ibid.,* sig. A4ᵛ.   [50] *Hooker,* 1666, p. 29.

[51] King's letter says in part (*Hooker,* 1665, sigs. A5ʳ–A5ᵛ), "Lastly, I must again congratulate this Undertaking of yours, as now more proper to you than any other person, by reason of your long Knowledge and Alliance to the worthy Family of the *Cranmers,* (my old Friends also) who have been Men of noted Wisdom, especially Mr. *George Cranmer,* whose Prudence added to that of Sir *Edwin Sandys,* proved very useful in the Completing of Mr. *Hookers* matchless Books; one of their Letters I herewith send you, to make use of, if you think fit."

"One of their Letters" points to a joint communication by Sandys and Cranmer to Hooker. It is quite likely that the "letter" which King sent to Walton contained Sandys and Cranmer's Notes on Book VI of the *Polity.* The Notes are among the Fulman MSS in Corpus Christi College, Oxford. The friendship of Fulman and Walton has already been touched on with regard to Walton's collections for Fulman's proposed life of Hales. Sandys and Cranmer's Notes bear this inscription in Fulman's hand: "Written with their

That Henry King was aware of the nature of Walton's task is evident not only in his account of the history of Hooker's manuscripts, which concludes with their falling into the hands of Hugh Peter,[52] but in his statement that "there wanted not other Endeavours to corrupt and make them speak that Language for which the Faction then fought, which was *To subject the Soveraign Power to the People.*"[53] He says, too,

> I need not strive to vindicate Mr. *Hooker* in this particular, his known Loyalty to his Prince whilest he lived, the Sorrow expressed by K. *James* at his Death, the Value our late Soveraign (of ever-blessed Memory) put upon his Works, and now, the singular Character of his Worth by you given in the passages of his Life, especially in your *Appendix* to it, do sufficiently clear him from that Imputation.[54]

In the last paragraph of his Appendix, Walton says, in about the same language that he later uses in relating the vision of Donne, "In this relation concerning these three doubtful Books of Mr. *Hookers,* my purpose was to enquire, then set down what I observ'd and know, which I have done, not as an ingaged Person, but indifferently, and now leave my Reader to give Sentence, for their Legitimation, as to himself."[55] To what degree was Walton actually "ingaged" in the *Life of Hooker?* It is not likely that he was taken completely into confidence by the Churchmen or that the many ramifications of their purposes were explained to him. This would not have been necessary, for it is obvious from everything that Walton says about the behavior of the lay member of the Church that he would go along with the bishops if they merely told him that the last three Books were suspect and implanted doubt in his mind by producing even slight evidence to prove their point. As a pious

own hands and given me by my friend M. Isaac Walton 1673" (Keble, III, 108, n. 1).

King probably retained the Notes when he surrendered other materials to Barkeham. That Walton did not make use of them is perhaps another indication of the desire to get his *Life of Hooker* into print quickly. Investigation would have shown Walton that here was absolute proof of the incompleteness of Book VI as it was printed in 1648 and in 1661–1662, irrefutable testimony for the argument he presented in the Appendix of the *Life.* Nor did he use the Notes in subsequent revisions. Either he never realized their importance, or the Church, confident that his Appendix as written implanted sufficient doubt about the completeness of Books VI–VIII, did not care to have the document made public.

[52] *Hooker,* 1665, sig. A4ᵛ. [53] *Ibid.* [54] *Ibid.,* sig. A5ʳ.
[55] *Ibid.,* p. 173.

member of the Church, he would have been offended by Gauden's dislike of ceremony. The documentary evidence which he had about Hooker's college career and the more accurate material which he had about Hooker's career after the debates with Travers would have convinced him of Gauden's inaccuracies. The extent of Gauden's error would have been evident to him by his noting in Hooker's will (the very existence of which Gauden doubted) that Hooker was not a bachelor, as Gauden had made him out to be. In the light of these circumstances, it might be expected that Walton would work doubly hard to shape his material so that it would clearly correct Gauden's picture of Hooker's mediocrity at college; that he would point up sharply whatever material would engender distrust of the last three Books of the *Polity;* that he would, to counteract the ambiguity of these Books, state clearly Hooker's position or, more accurately, what the bishops thought Hooker's position was or should have been on those questions which primarily interested them. And, indeed, this is almost precisely what he does in the *Life.*

Walton indicated one aspect of his task in the first sentence of the Introduction of the *Life:* "*I have been persuaded, by a Friend that I ought to obey, to write* The Life of Richard Hooker, *the happy Author of Five (if not more) of the eight learned Books of* The Laws of Ecclesiastical Polity."[56] In the Introduction he speaks of the difficulties which the *Life* presents—"*For I knew him not in his Life, and must therefore not onely look back to his Death, now* 64 *years past; but almost* 50 *years beyond that, even to his Childhood and Youth*"[57]—and he advances as evidence of his fitness for the task his association with the Cranmers and his conversations with Ussher, Morton, and Hales. The first large section of his *Life* concerns Hooker's birth and education. Walton says that Hooker was born at Exeter, and because that city fathered Sir Thomas Bodley, Bishop John Jewel, Sir Francis Drake, and Sir Walter Raleigh, he takes the opportunity to join their names with Hooker's. He tells of the virtue and industry of Hooker's parents and of their inclination to educate their children despite their lack of riches. In the first of many characters, he presents a picture of Hooker as a youth, admitting frankly that it is conjectural and based on Hooker as he was at forty, and he shows him as a child of humble gravity, an early questioner of remarkable modesty, and a wonderful scholar.

[56] *Ibid.,* p. 1.   [57] *Ibid.,* p. 2.

The extent of Hooker's scholarly talents Walton makes clear in relating that his schoolmaster not only instructed him without payment but even induced his uncle, John Hooker, to provide for him during his first year at Oxford. A short account of the career of John Jewel, Bishop of Salisbury, is inserted here prior to Walton's revealing that Jewel found Hooker to be a talented youth. By Walton's telling of Jewel's exile in Mary's reign and his subsequent favor under Elizabeth, not only is Jewel's prestige enhanced but his becoming Hooker's patron is made doubly impressive. The extent of Jewel's kindness to Hooker is directly demonstrated on the occasion of Hooker's visit to him, and the significance of Jewel's patronage is enhanced indirectly by Walton's accounts of Jewel's piety and of his holy death. Respect for Hooker's learning is again shown by the story in which Dr. Cole, the President of Corpus Christi College, tells Hooker not to fear for his future subsistence and says that he will himself become his patron. The crowning compliment to Hooker's learning, however, is in the incident next related. Upon Bishop Jewel's recommendation, the Archbishop of York, Edwin Sandys, himself a Cambridge man, sent his son Edwin to Oxford to study under Hooker. Walton, not satisfied even with such evidence, comments explicitly on Hooker's learning, reason, and industry and on the superb method of demonstration which made him an excellent teacher. Then follows a short character of the perfect student: Hooker's behavior toward God is demonstrated by his missing chapel prayers but twice in four years; in his behavior toward men, says Walton, he was never angry or passionate, but ever grave and innocent, the strictness of his behavior begetting an early reverence for his person.

As though to counteract Gauden's impression that Hooker was hardly brilliant at college, Walton's next section deals with Hooker's honors and friendships at Oxford. His mentioning that Hooker was in 1573 admitted as one of the scholars of the foundation at Corpus Christi College allows him to join Hooker's name with those of Bishop Jewel, Dr. John Reinolds, and Dr. Thomas Jackson, all great and learned churchmen and the first two renowned for their defense of the Church. Mention of Hooker's being Inceptor of Arts in 1576 serves to link him with Dr. Herbert Westphaling, the vice-chancellor of the university. Mention of his being made Master of Arts in 1577 again links him with his patron Dr. Cole, then vice-chancellor, and with Henry Savile, then one of the proctors. The recital of some facts of Savile's academic career and of the titles of his eminent works serves as a prelude to the statement, " 'Twas this Sir *Hen: Savill,* that had the happinesse to be a Contemporary, and familiar friend to Mr. *Hooker,* and let Posterity know it."[58] Hooker's being chosen a fellow of Corpus Christi College in 1577 serves to associate him with other contemporaries and friends, Reinolds and Dr. John Spenser, both men of learning and later presidents of Corpus Christi. The prestige of Hooker as a teacher is augmented by the enumeration of the works of his pupil, Edwin Sandys, and those of Sandys's brother, George; by reference to the testimonies of the "learned Mr. *Cambden,* the Lord *Tottenes, Fines,* [sic] *Morison*" about another pupil, George Cranmer; and by a paragraph of explicit comment on Hooker's sacred friendship with Sandys and Cranmer. This section of the *Life* concludes with a character of Hooker the scholar and his study of philosophy, casuistry, the schoolmen, sacred and civil law, scripture, music, and poetry.

After saying that Hooker entered orders, Walton shows at some length the effect of Hooker's marriage on his career in the Church. The story of Hooker's appointment to preach in London in 1581 serves to introduce Hooker's future father-in-law, and John Churchman is shown as a destitute draper who is forced to run a boarding-house, but who is yet a man of virtue, a trait which, Walton says, was lacking in his wife. Walton foreshadows Hooker's controversies by telling that in this, his first public appearance, Hooker crossed an opinion of Calvin, and he enhances Hooker's point of view by relating that it was later supported by Dr. Jackson, Dr. Hammond, and Bishop Aylmer, who was then Bishop of London and one of Hooker's auditors. Walton indicates that gratitude for Mrs. Churchman's hospitality on this occasion prompted Hooker to allow her to choose a wife for him, and he says that in marrying her daughter Joan, Hooker got neither beauty nor portion. He cites the marriages of Job and Moses and discourses on affliction as a divine diet before he tells that because of his marriage, Hooker was forced to leave in 1584[59] the peace of Oxford for the activity of the country living at Drayton Beauchamp. A visit to this place by Cranmer and Sandys emphasizes strongly Hooker's "corroding cares": he is shown tending sheep and rocking a cradle. The same visit, Walton says, produced a change in Hooker's fortunes. Sandys told his father of

---

[58] *Ibid.,* p. 29.   [59] "1594" in *Hooker,* 1665, p. 43.

Hooker's condition, and, on the death of the learned and venerable Father Alvie, when a like man was wanted to succeed him as Master of the Temple, the Archbishop recommended Hooker. Walton says that Hooker had to be persuaded to accept the post, because he would have preferred a better country living "where he might *see Gods blessings spring out of the Earth, and be free from Noise*."[60] So ends almost the first third of the *Life,* in which Walton covers thirty-two of the forty-seven years which Hooker lived.

The next section, only a little smaller than this, Walton devotes to "a Character of the Times, and Temper of the people of this Nation, when Mr. *Hooker* had his admission into this Place [the Temple]."[61] This part of the *Life,* containing Walton's most forceful and most impassioned writing, is, in effect, a brief history of Elizabethan nonconformity and an account of Archbishop Whitgift as the champion of the Church of England. Walton says that in Elizabeth's reign animosity, envy, and oppositions had made for three parties, "The active Romanists, The restless Non-conformists . . . and The passive peaceable Protestant."[62] His interest is in the nonconformists, with whom Hooker engaged in a book war. He tells of their spiritual wickedness, their pride, malice, and their opposition to government; he lashes those whose tender consciences prevented their taking an oath before a lawful magistrate, but who covenanted and swore to each other in their zeal to set up the Presbyterian discipline; he relates their progression from tender petitions to admonitions and satirical remonstrances, their threatening the bishops, the Queen, and Parliament, and their encouragement by Leicester, who sought to discredit the bishops and to alienate their lands. He would show the English nonconformists as confederates of the Scotch clergy, whom he characterizes by telling of Edward Dering's insult to Elizabeth and the clergy's disrespect for King James. By the device of a letter from an Italian observer, he ridicules the common people, the women and shopkeepers who believed themselves expert in church government, who sought a "*Super-* or *Re-reformation* of Religion."[63] He indicates that even atheism was rampant, and, having drawn a powerful picture of the irregularity of the times, he introduces Whitgift. A short factual account of his life follows the citation of Wotton's character of Whitgift. Walton tells of the confidence which the Queen placed in him,

[60] *Hooker,* 1665, p. 47.   [61] *Ibid.,* p. 48.   [62] *Ibid.,* p. 51.
[63] *Ibid.,* p. 60.

and he is willing to let one example serve as testimony of Whitgift's interest with the Queen and his care for the rights of the Church. This testimony is a long speech made by Whitgift to Elizabeth, proving that the alienation of church property is sacrilege, that it is, in addition, a begetter of sinfulness; and Whitgift cautions the Queen of the necessity of adhering to her vows to preserve such property. Walton then demonstrates the Queen's reliance upon Whitgift by saying that he was able to preserve the remaining church lands, that he managed Elizabeth's church affairs and advised her in temporal matters, and that he was her personal religious adviser until her death. Whitgift's charity and humility are shown in his building an almshouse and a free school, and King James's visit to him on his deathbed is turned into a demonstration of his care for the Church. An account of Whitgift's controversy with Thomas Cartwright and the statement that Hooker's controversy with Travers at the Temple was a continuation of this serve to get Walton back into the narration of the life itself.

After this forceful conjunction of Whitgift and Hooker, Walton pauses for a moment to say that, despite the conclusion of the Whitgift-Cartwright battle, a new generation of restless men had sprung up who were positive in asserting that *"a Papist cannot be saved,"*[64] and he notes that they became as gods "so far as to set limits to his Mercies."[65] He also mentions the Marprelate tracts and the witty pamphlets of Tom Nashe that stopped them. Walter Travers, lecturer for the evening sermons at the Temple, is described as a man of learning whose life was blameless, but also as a man who was ordained at Antwerp and who wished to institute the presbyterian church government in England. The forenoon sermon at the Temple spoke Canterbury and the afternoon Geneva, Walton says, until Whitgift prohibited Travers' preaching. He explains the friendship of Whitgift and Hooker as based on Hooker's voluntary and reasonable answer to Travers' supplication for reinstatement. Two main points of controversy characterize the contentions between Hooker and Travers. Walton says that Travers opposed Hooker's statements that *"the assurance of what we believe by the Word of God, is not to us so certain as that which we perceive by sense"*[66] and that *"God was merciful to many of our fore-fathers living in Popish Superstition, for as much as they Sinned ignorantly."*[67] Walton justifies Hooker by quoting and paraphrasing

[64] *Ibid.,* p. 87.   [65] *Ibid.*   [66] *Ibid.,* p. 93.   [67] *Ibid.,* p. 98.

at some length Hooker's two sermons on Habakkuk 1:4. The controversy illustrates, he says, Hooker's dovelike temper and the pertinacious zeal of the dissenters, and he again shows what he considers to be the place of the lay church member when he says that peace and piety will not flourish until God blesses the common people with a belief that laws are not made for private men to dispute but to obey. Not only does Walton make the Hooker-Travers controversy an illustration of Hooker's wisdom, humility, and mild temper, but he says that Hooker formulated the plan for the *Polity* to undeceive Travers' advocates.

The following tenth of the *Life* deals with the *Polity,* not with its content or style, but with Hooker's situation during its composition, with the circumstances of its printing, and with the esteem in which it was held. Walton says that Hooker voluntarily petitioned Whitgift for a quiet place in which to write the *Polity* and that he was given the living at Boscombe in 1591 and the same year made a minor prebendary of Salisbury. At Boscombe, Walton says, Hooker completed four of his proposed eight Books. These were not printed until 1594, he says, though they had been entered on the Stationers' Register on March 9, 1592. Hooker continued his work at Bishopsbourne, the living which the Queen presented to him on July 7, 1595, and Book V was printed in 1597. The esteem in which the book was held is illustrated in several ways: Cardinal Allen and Dr. Stapleton recommended it to Pope Clement VIII, who praised its learning; King James praised it extravagantly to Whitgift; Charles I enjoined his son to read it; Camden wished that it might be translated into Latin, and Bishop Earle, so similar to Hooker in wisdom, learning, and "pious, peaceable, primitive Temper,"[68] had just completed such a translation.

Walton's long account of Hooker at Bishopsbourne has two purposes: he would indicate Hooker's orthodoxy in church matters and would show his excellence as a country priest. At Bishopsbourne, Walton says, Hadrian Saravia sought Hooker's friendship. A long account of Saravia's service to the Church, particularly on the question of episcopacy, leads to the statement that "these two excellent persons began a Holy Friendship, increasing dayly to so high and mutual affections, that their two wills seemed to be but one, still assisting and improving each others vertues, and the desired comforts of a peaceable Piety."[69] There follows a detailed character of Hooker's person: his poor clothes, his mean stature, his

[68] *Ibid.,* p. 123.   [69] *Ibid.,* p. 127.

body worn with study and mortification, his face covered with heat pimples. In still another character, his bashful disposition and humble behavior are illustrated in the statement that *"his poor Parish Clark and he did never talk but with both their Hats on, or both off at the same time,"*[70] and his shortsightedness is made responsible for his method of reading his sermons. Both his modesty and his dim sight, Walton says, may explain why Hooker trusted Mrs. Churchman to choose a wife for him. But Walton did not introduce Hooker's parish clerk into the *Life* merely to exemplify his humility. The same man is artfully used to show Hooker's point of view in church matters. Walton says that in the third or fourth year of the Long Parliament, this parish clerk saw the parson at Bishopsbourne sequestered, and he has the clerk say that *"they had sequestered so many good men that he doubted if his good Master Mr. Hooker had lived till now they would have Sequestred him too."*[71] He quotes the clerk again to show how greatly disturbed he was by the Genevan sacrament: *"all men will say my Master Hooker was a good Man and a good Scholar, and I am sure it was not used to be thus in his days,"*[72] and, he says, the old man went home and died. A third character, this of the good country priest, follows, and Hooker's convincing sermons, his fasting and piety on Ember days and weeks, his processions, his visiting the sick and the distressed, his prevention of lawsuits—all make him a pattern for posterity to imitate. Having thus demonstrated the excellences of Hooker, Walton inserts, before getting on to the details of Hooker's last days and death, an account of how he was abused at Bishopsbourne. The details of the blackmail are entirely lacking, but Walton compares Hooker with Jesus and Susannah, suggests that the plot was contrived by a dissenting brother who hated church ceremonies and Hooker's books, and emphasizes Hooker's praise to God for his deliverance, his attempted kindness to the culprits, and his prayers for them.

The *Polity* hovers over Walton's recital of Hooker's last months. He says that Hooker begged God not for long life, but only for time to finish the last three Books, that Hooker hastened his death in giving life to the Books, and that God heard his prayers though he denied the Church the benefit of those Books "as completed by himself."[73] He shows Hooker's concern for the Books when his house was robbed not many days before his death. Walton reports that

[70] *Ibid.,* p. 129.   [71] *Ibid.,* p. 131.   [72] *Ibid.,* p. 132.
[73] *Ibid.,* p. 146.

"his Question was, *Are my Books and written Papers safe?* and being answered *that they were;* his Reply was, *then it matters not, for no other loss can trouble me.*"[74] The *Life* ends on a note of lofty piety. On the day before his death, Hooker was given absolution and the sacrament by Saravia, and on the very day of his death, Walton says, he spoke to Saravia about God's forgiveness of sin. Walton describes his inward joy and final sleep and ends with a prayer: *"Let Glory be to God on high, let Peace be upon Earth, and Good-will to Mankind. Amen, Amen."*[75]

But Walton had not yet finished. The *Life* itself is Walton's personal conception of Hooker, tempered by those ideas of the bishops which he had made his own. Perhaps he would not have been so insistent on Hooker's brilliance at the university had he not been correcting Gauden's account, but his attempts to shed a luster on his main character by showing him to have enjoyed the friendship of others more popularly acknowledged to be great have parallels in the *Life of Donne* and in the *Life of Wotton.* The controversy with Travers, central as it was in Hooker's career, was given its just due. Hooker's life as a pastor of souls received proper emphasis, particularly in view of Walton's own interests in pastoral duties. The long digression on nonconformity and Whitgift is not unlike the lesser digression in the *Life of Wotton,* nor is it here without purpose. It is not necessary to predicate the hand of Morley or Sheldon behind the passage. Walton's expression of his Church sympathies in the *Donne* and in the *Wotton* had perhaps been more guarded, but even in those lives the desire to express himself on the times had not been completely restrained, and Walton commented upon the slightest provocation. Now, with the Restoration, there was no necessity to be quiet; there was, moreover, real reason to comment upon the nonconformity which had so great an influence on Hooker's life, and Walton took full advantage of this opportunity. The passage on Whitgift has its parallel in the Bedell passage, for Whitgift becomes Hooker's *alter ego* even as Bedell had been Wotton's. Walton found in Whitgift's life that singularity of purpose, expressed in deeds, which was at most implied in the words of Richard Hooker, and Whitgift is his idealized Hooker even as Bedell represented those things which Walton had wanted to find in Wotton. When Whitgift speaks to the Queen about church property, we have not merely what the bishops were most anxious

<hr>

[74] *Ibid.,* pp. 147–148.   [75] *Ibid.,* p. 152.

to hear in 1665, but what Walton would have Hooker say on the subject. Undoubtedly the subject itself is included because of dictation—the bishops were desirous of counteracting the ambiguity of Book VII—but Walton found no such utterance by Hooker, and to have attributed it to him would have been folly. There was nothing, however, to prevent his allocating such a speech to Whitgift; indeed, everything in his career pointed to the logic of attributing it to him. Walton would have its sentiments reflect on Hooker by emphasizing his closeness to Whitgift. It was even so in the *Life* with the matter of episcopacy. Again, in the light of Book VII, it would have been folly to insist that Hooker unequivocally supported the divine right of bishops. And again, though the idea that episcopacy must be brought into the *Life* may well have come from the bishops, Walton's treatment reveals his consummate artistry. If it was not proper in the *Life* to discourse at length on the question of episcopacy, especially in view of Hooker's ambivalent attitude, it was proper to relate one of Hooker's important friendships. By emphasizing Hooker's friendship with Saravia, by explicitly indicating the very oneness of their minds, Walton would, by suggestion, attribute to Hooker Saravia's favorable and well-determined stand on the apostolic succession. Throughout the *Life*, then, Walton tempered the bishops' arguments and controlled them by his own comprehension of his function as a biographer and of what he considered proper in life-writing.

It was so with Walton's treatment of the *Polity* in the *Life*. As the greatest of Hooker's achievements, it receives due emphasis—but no more. When Walton merely remarked on the incomplete state of the last three Books, his mention was fitting. His conception of his task as biographer made him aware that it would spoil the already forced unity of the *Life* to digress at length on the *Polity*, and when he mentioned in the *Life* Hooker's efforts to complete it, he inserted a parenthesis: "of all which more properly hereafter."[76] His discussion of the validity of the last three Books was reserved for an Appendix, where it would not destroy the structure of the *Life* by turning narrative into argument and where, by separation, it would gain additional emphasis and unity unto itself. At the beginning of the Appendix, Walton explains that he has given the reader "the true relation of Mr. *Hookers* Life,"[77] and it is possible that by "relation" he means not only narration but

---

[76] *Ibid.*, p. 114. [77] *Ibid.*, p. 155.

also that the parts of the life are so proportioned as not to create a misleading emphasis or impression. And he says again that he wishes to acquaint the reader with some observations that relate to Hooker's life "which could not properly fall to be spoken till after his Death."[78]

Before speaking of the *Polity,* "which is chiefly intended in this Appendix,"[79] Walton discusses the date of Hooker's death, showing by reference to his will that it occurred in 1600. From the will also, he shows the provisions that Hooker made for his four daughters, and he says that Hooker's estate of £1,092, which was more than he thought himself worth, was secured by the care of his servant, Thomas Lane, rather than by the frugality of his wife. Walton then tells what he knows of the daughters and says that he has recently spoken with two children of one of them. Of Mrs. Hooker, he says that "she staid not a comely time to bewail her Widdowhood; nor liv'd long enough to repent her second Marriage, for which doubtless she would have found cause, if there had [not] been but four months betwixt Mr. *Hookers* and her death."[80]

Walton's attitude toward Mrs. Hooker is the least kindly in the *Lives,* and the reason for his attitude is apparent even in the first paragraph of the Appendix that deals with the *Polity.* He says that Hooker lived to finish the last three Books, "but whether we have the last three as finisht by himself, is a just and Material Question."[81] He then tells a story related to him some forty years past. About a month after Hooker's death, Archbishop Whitgift sent one of his chaplains to Mrs. Hooker to inquire about the Books, and she would not or could not give any account of them. Three months later Whitgift summoned her to London, and the day before she was to have been examined by some of the Queen's council she told him at Lambeth that *"one Mr. Charke and another Minister that dwelt near* Canterbury, *came to her, and desired that they might go into her Husbands Study, and look upon some of his writings; and that there they two burnt and tore many of them, assuring her that they were writings not fit to be seen."*[82] But this, while it explains Walton's attitude toward Mrs. Hooker, is only the first of his arguments to indicate reason for distrusting the last three Books. He quotes from John Spenser's epistle to the reader which prefaced the *Polity* of 1604 and says that, though it has usually been printed before the

78 *Ibid.*   79 *Ibid.,* p. 160.   80 *Ibid.,* p. 159.   81 *Ibid.,* p. 160.
82 *Ibid.,* p. 162.

various editions of the *Polity,* it is "omitted, I know not why, in the last impression of the eight Printed together in *Anno* 1662. in which the Publishers seem to impose the three doubtful as the undoubted Books of Mr. *Hooker.*"[83] To support his story of the mutilation of the manuscripts, he says that Dr. Spenser's wife told him forty years ago that her husband *"made up or finisht Mr.* Hookers *last three Books";*[84] he says that the many manuscripts which survive, most of them pretending to be in Hooker's hand and largely disagreeing, are merely transcripts of Spenser's version, which his wife, in compliance with his request on his deathbed, delivered to Archbishop Abbot. Walton takes for granted the authenticity of *Clavi Trabales* and offers it as testimony that men have tried to make Hooker's judgment suit their fancies in order to give authority to their own designs. Bernard, he says, "found the three written Books which were supposed the 6. 7. and 8. of Mr. *Hookers* Books of Ecclesiastical Polity, and that in the said three Books (now printed as Mr. *Hookers*) there are so many omissions that they amount to many paragraphs, and which cause many incoherencies."[85] Quoting from *Clavi Trabales* a selection from Book VIII, Walton joins forces with the Church to show that sovereign power is not derived from the people and that kings cannot be held accountable in this world, but only before a heavenly tribunal. For further support, he appends an attestation by Fabian Philipps to the effect that Bishop Sanderson affirmed that in a manuscript in Hooker's hand he had found *"no mention made of the King or Supreme Governors being accomptable to the People."*[86] Walton then draws the conclusion that there appear to be both omissions and additions in the last three Books, and he crowns his argument by stating that Charles I was doubtful that the last three Books were Hooker's and that he would consent to what Lord Saye proposed to prove out of the doubtful Books only *"if he would but consent to the Judgement of Mr.* Hooker *in the other five that were the undoubted Books of* Mr. Hooker."[87] Only after making an extremely convincing case for the illegitimacy of the last three Books does Walton say that he is not an engaged person and that the reader may draw his own conclusions.

Walton's engagement influenced the *Life* itself only indirectly: the view of the *Polity* which he was asked to present was in part

[83] *Ibid.,* p. 163.   [84] *Ibid.,* p. 167.   [85] *Ibid.,* pp. 168–169.
[86] *Ibid.,* p. 171.   [87] *Ibid.,* p. 173.

responsible for the peculiar stressing of the Whitgift and Saravia materials, and the role which Mrs. Hooker played in the disposition of the *Polity* determined in part her portrait in the *Life*. But Walton's engagement in the Appendix cannot be doubted. At the same time that he casts doubt on the authority of Books VI–VIII of the *Polity,* he demonstrates Hooker's advocacy of royal supremacy. He follows precisely the line of the restored Church, which considered absolutism an effective cure for nonconformity. The Appendix is another of the Church's briefs on the absolute power of the sovereign in the tradition of *The Power Communicated by God to the Prince* and *Clavi Trabales.* We may be sure that in the Appendix Walton was writing expressly to demonstrate the views of the Church, and we may be sure that the Church considered the Appendix rather than the *Life* as Walton's major contribution to its cause. Bishop King singled out the Appendix for special commendation, and further evidence points to the Church's interest in it.

Walton's innumerable revisions in the *Life of Donne* and in the *Life of Wotton* have been described at some length, and those in the *Life of Hooker* are no less frequent. Although Walton's care in the writing of this *Life* led to only one major addition, there are a number of minute changes. But it is not so in the Appendix. The Appendix is no slight postscript; it is one-eighth the length of the *Life.* Yet, despite numerous changes in the *Life* in its first revision (1666), the *only* changes made in the Appendix are the incorporation of the reference to Bishop King which had in 1665 been put with the *Errata* and the correction of the spelling of *"Trabales"* from the original *"Trebales."* In 1670, Walton merely added to the Appendix a long marginal footnote to show the very day of Hooker's death. Not until 1675 did he make changes of the type which characterizes all his writing, and in this edition there are nine slight changes of a word or two to make more explicit what was previously sufficiently clear.[88] To be sure, Walton would have been extremely careful in composing the Appendix, but his hesitancy to alter it for ten years, despite the opportunities, probably points to the bishops' part in it. It is not necessary to picture Morley sitting at Walton's elbow as he wrote, but the bishops probably helped

[88] There is also one typical addition made to lend authority to the conversation between Charles I and Lord Saye. Walton says that this took place "in the time of the *Long Parliament"* (*Lives,* 1675, p. 238). This change and the nine mentioned are the only ones made.

make the case and approved the passage, and Walton undoubtedly feared to tamper with a single word lest the argument go awry. It is possible to envision a minimum of interference in the *Life*, but the Appendix shows evidences of intimate consultation, if not more.[89]

The Appendix is not, however, the last item in Walton's volume. It is followed by a letter written in February, 1598, by George Cranmer to Hooker. Keble suggests, quite rightly, that the letter is an answer to a request by Hooker after the publication of Book V of the *Polity* for such hints as Cranmer might have for concluding the work.[90] Cranmer starts by alluding to the sympathy with which the Presbyterian discipline was originally greeted in England. He tells of Whitgift's forceful opposition to it, of the gradual disenchantment of others when they noted Presbyterian practices. He shows that the Presbyterians started by peaceably stressing small differences and that they proceeded to admonitions and open raillery. He mentions at some length the men who directly or indirectly

---

[89] Bernard says nowhere in *Clavi Trabales* that he found Books VI–VIII of the *Polity*, nor could he, in speaking of omissions, be referring to Gauden's edition, which appeared after *Clavi Trabales*. Walton implies that Bernard printed omissions from Books VI, VII, and VIII, but all his selections are from Book VIII. Walton's misspelling of *Trabales* (he used *Trebales*) may be due to his faulty Latin, but the inaccuracy of his comment upon the book may indicate that he did not see it. True, he corrected his spelling in 1666 (though he reverted to *Trebales* in 1670 and 1675), but neither at that time nor later did he change his misquotation of "*Kings therefore, or no man can have lawful power to Judge*" (Hooker, 1665, p. 170) to agree with Bernard's "*Kings therefore no man can have lawfull power and Authority to judge*" (*Clavi Trabales*, p. 94).

In the "Preface to the Reader" of *Clavi Trabales*, Bishop Sanderson identified as in Ussher's hand the annotations on the Hooker MSS which Bernard used. He relied on Bernard's authority, referring (sig. c^v) to Bernard's words on "pag. 47" (actually pp. 49–50). Fabian Philipps' statement that Sanderson saw a manuscript of Hooker written in his own hand seems like a misreading and dramatization of Sanderson's words. Philipps, a barrister, was an outspoken royalist who in 1660 wrote *Veritas Inconcussa, or, a most certain truth asserted, that King Charles the first was no man of blood, but a Martyr for his people*. His fondness for repeating tales favorable to the crown is evident in Aubrey's crediting him with such a tale (*Miscellanies*, 1784, p. 162). Walton probably quoted Philipps' attestation accurately, since Philipps did not disclaim it (he lived until 1690), but there is no doubt that Philipps would have been glad to attest to this statement since it perfectly supported his own views.

It is possible that in the comment on *Clavi Trabales* and in the securing of Philipps' attestation, we have evidence of the guiding hands behind Walton's Appendix.

[90] Keble, II, 598, n. 2.

got strength and encouragement from the Puritans: Hacket and Coppinger, the Brownists and Barrowists, godless politicians, atheists, and papists. Cranmer would have Hooker show that the quintessence of Presbyterianism lies solely in its program to overthrow episcopacy and to establish the authority of presbyters. He suggests that the Presbyterians complain not to amend, but to innovate, that they have no wish to cure a part but to destroy the whole. Their complaints deserve to be censured for being bitter and reproachful, for being aimed at the common people, who are insufficient and incompetent judges. Their exceptions are frivolous and impertinent. Cranmer's last point ("a Point in my Opinion of great regard, and which I am desirous to have enlarg'd") is that the Presbyterians strike not only at the ecclesiastical order, but also at the civil state.

Why did Walton append this letter, which Falconer Madan calls "a dull discourse in favour of the existing state of things"?[91] The letter *Concerning the New Church Discipline* was first printed in February, 1642, at Oxford, undoubtedly to bolster the episcopal and royalist cause by associating Hooker with it.[92] Walton reprinted it partly for its polemical value in 1665, but for other reasons, too. In introducing the letter, he wrote:

Tis observable, that as Mr. *Hooker* advis'd with Doctor *Spencer,* in the design and manage of these Books, so also, and chiefly with his dear Pupils [*sic*] George *Cranmer* (whose Sister was the Wife of Doctor *Spencer*) of which this following Letter may be a Testimony, and doth also give authority to some things mentioned both in this Appendix and in the Life of Mr. *Hooker,* and is therefore added.[93]

The letter provides verification for almost nothing in Hooker's life, but it does serve, by association, to verify certain of Hooker's views. Its outline of nonconformity serves as a verification or, at least, as a repetition of Walton's account in the *Life.* But there is little doubt that Walton used it to "give authority," and it does add authorita-

[91] *Oxford Books* (Oxford, 1912), II, 157.

[92] Keble suggests that Walton was not aware of its publication in 1642 because his collation of the 1642 edition with the text in *Lives,* 1675, showed "remarkable differences" (Keble, I, xxviii). The differences are not remarkable; moreover, the differences increase with each revision. Walton made some minor changes to clarify diction when he first used the letter, and then he made additional small changes in his usual fashion for each new edition.

[93] *Hooker,* 1665, p. 174.

tiveness to Walton's book. It serves to demonstrate Cranmer's friendship with Hooker, even his aid to Hooker, and it serves, therefore, to raise Cranmer in the reader's esteem. The esteem with which it endows Cranmer carries over to Cranmer's sister and her husband, and since the sister was Walton's informant for much that is in the *Life*, the same esteem carries over to the author of the *Life* and to the *Life* itself. The details of the letter authorize little, but Walton used it because he knew it would work upon the reader to increase the authority of the *Life*.

Thus did Walton fulfill his chore. The 1666 edition of the *Polity* is proof that the bishops were satisfied with Walton's performance, for his *Life*, the Appendix, and Cranmer's letter appear before an unchanged text.

Walton's method of handling in and out of the *Life* the problems which specifically interested the bishops shows his awareness that there is a limit to the amount of argumentative freight that a life can bear and still remain a life. The artificial organization of Gauden's *Life* must have made him doubly conscious of structure as he planned his own work, and even as he avoided Gauden's example, so he avoided turning his biography into a partisan tract. Other aspects of Walton's concept of his chore as biographer are made clear when we examine the materials that went into the *Life*.

How greatly Walton's *Life* differs from Gauden's in impression and content has already been suggested. Gauden's *Life* was invaluable, if only as a spur to opposition, for its vagueness made Walton search for facts, and the very facts permitted him to see relationships and connections of which Gauden was ignorant. Gauden's account of Hooker's rewards and preferments reads in part:

The uneasiness of his small maintenance [at Oxford], and his willingness to go out to the wider World, invited him to accept the offer of a small Living called *Buscomb*, in the West; thence *Anno* 1584. he was removed to *Drayton Beauchamp* in *Lincolnshire*, no very great Benefice; *Anno* 1592. he had the Dignities of a *Prebendary* in *Salisbury*, and the *Subdeanry* bestowed on him; and by the Queen he was preferred to be *Master of the Temple*; . . . hence *Anno* 1594. he was removed to his last station, at *Bishopsbourn* in *Kent*, and was made also Prebend of *Canterbury*.[94]

This passage accounts for the tremendous specificity of Walton in his references to Hooker's career. He says of Drayton Beauchamp

[94] Gauden, p. 35.

that it is "in *Buckingham-shire,* not far from *Alesbury,* and in the Diocese of *Lincoln*"[95] and that Hooker was presented to the living there by "*John Cheny* Esquire, then Patron of it, the 9. of *December,* 1594."[96] He says that Hooker was "by Patent for Life made Master of the Temple the 17. of *March,* 1585" and in a marginal note he reproduces the pertinent part of the Temple records as verification.[97] He goes into great detail to prove how faulty Gauden's reference to Boscombe was:

About this time the Parsonage or Rectory of *Boscum,* in the Diocess of *Sarum,* and six miles from that City, became void. The Bishop of *Sarum* is Patron of it, but in the vacancy of that Sea (which was three years betwixt the death of Bishop *Peirce* and Bishop *Caldwells* admission into it) the disposal of that and all Benefices belonging to that Sea, during this said vacancy, came to be disposed of by the Archbishop of *Canterbury,* and he presented *Richard Hooker* to it in the year 1591. And *Richard Hooker* was also in the said year Instituted, *July* 17. to be a minor Prebend of *Salisbury,* the Corps to it being *nether-Havin,* about ten miles from that City.[98]

The particularity of his reference to Hooker's appointment to Bishopsbourne, too, can be explained by his desire to point up the inaccuracy of Gauden.[99] It is not hard to see why it was impossible for Gauden's *Life* to have any narrative continuity, and why, on the other hand, Walton could proceed on firm ground and could see relationships which Gauden could not possibly establish. Gauden's lack of facts drove him into inaccuracies beyond those of chronology. His scanty research was probably responsible for his saying that Hooker's "Friends or *Confidents* were few, but choise,"[100] and, indeed, he names none. Walton would counteract this impression by the almost gratuitous enumeration in his *Life.* Where Gauden,

[95] *Hooker,* 1665, p. 42.
[96] *Ibid.,* p. 43. "1594" changed to "1584" in *Hooker,* 1666, p. 8.
[97] *Ibid.,* p. 47.   [98] *Ibid.,* p. 113.
[99] *Ibid.,* pp. 114–115. "He left *Boscum* in the year 1595. by a surrender of it into the hands of Bishop *Caldwell,* and he presented *Benjamin Russel,* who was Instituted into it 23. of *June* in the same year.
"The Parsonage of *Bishops Borne* in *Kent,* three miles from *Canterbury,* is in that Archbishops gift, but in the latter end of the year 1594. Doctor *William Redman* the Rector of it was made *Bishop of Norwich,* by which means the power of presenting to it was *pro ea vice* in the Queen; and she presented *Richard Hooker,* whom she loved well, to this good living of *Borne* the 7. of *July* 1595."
[100] Gauden, p. 9.

laboring under the misapprehension that Hooker "ever lived a single and *unspotted life*,"[101] could only speculate at great length on the reasons for his leaving Oxford,[102] Walton's knowledge of Hooker's marriage allowed him to point directly to a reason (though, to be sure, a wrong one). Gauden's disjointed relation permitted him to discourse at some length on Hooker's style;[103] for Walton, biography was no place for a critique of style, and when he mentions Hooker's manner, it is only in conjunction with his matter,[104] and both are mentioned only as the basis of the praise given the *Polity* by Pope Clement VIII and King James when Walton wishes to show the esteem in which the *Polity* was generally held.

Both Gauden and Fuller had written about the Travers-Hooker controversy. Fuller passed by the lesser differences which the two expressed on the subject of predestination and gave as the main argument:

> *Hooker* maintained.
> The Church of *Rome,* though not a pure and perfect, yet is a true Church, so that such who live and die therein[105] upon their repentance of all their sins of ignorance may be saved.
> *Travers* defended.
> The Church of *Rome* is no true Church at all, so that such as live and die therein, holding Justification in part by works, cannot be said by the Scriptures to be saved.[106]

Gauden, too, concerned himself with presenting rather objectively the views of both men on Rome as the central point of the controversy, though his interpretation of Hooker's stand is somewhat more sympathetic. Of other matters of dispute he merely said, "This one *Capital Controversie,* drew after it a long tail of all Controversies *between the Reformed* and *Roman parties.*"[107] Hooker's position was a bold one in his day when the Puritans were already convinced that Canterbury looked too much like Rome, and Walton was not one to leave such a position unjustified or improperly defended. He sways the sympathies of his readers even before he treats the Travers-Hooker controversy by ridiculing those men who

[101] *Ibid.,* p. 12. He was following Fuller, *Church Hist.,* bk. IX, 235.
[102] *Ibid.,* pp. 11–12.　　　　[103] *Ibid.,* p. 14.
[104] *Hooker,* 1665, pp. 118, 120–121.
[105] Fuller's marginal note here reads, "Being *weak, ignorant,* and *seduced.*"
[106] *Church Hist.,* bk. IX, 216.　　　　[107] Gauden, p. 31.

set limits to the mercies of God. In dealing with the controversy itself, he does not place the full force of the disagreement on the single question of Rome, but he first demonstrates Hooker's argument on a totally different question. Only then does he introduce Rome into the controversy, and even at this place he presents Hooker's position within the larger frame of the subject of justification and works, and he traces at some length Hooker's entire argument and quotes substantially from it. There is no word on the reasons for Travers' opposition. By introducing and ridiculing the point of view on Rome antagonistic to Hooker in a different context, by splitting the emphasis of the controversy, by showing Hooker's views on Rome as they are related to a larger problem, Walton deals admirably with a difficult question. In indicating the breadth of the Travers-Hooker controversy and in de-emphasizing what had been represented to be the only important point of contention, Walton all the more completely justifies the position of Hooker on the question of Rome. Gauden, it will be remembered, had related that the controversy ceased when Whitgift parted the antagonists and placed them "in *several stations*"; he did not mention Travers' fate but said that Hooker was removed to Kent. Walton shows Hooker in an entirely different light here. He says that it was Travers who was prohibited from preaching and that Hooker voluntarily sought a quieter place. He contrasts Travers' supplication to remain and the noise of his followers in protesting his ouster with Hooker's desire to leave the fury of the public scene in order to reconsider the issues of the controversy and to disabuse the nonconformists, and the contrast is much to Hooker's advantage. Gauden treated the controversy as an isolated incident; it was one of Hooker's "sufferings." His ignorance of the facts of Hooker's life, here specifically the date of Hooker's appointment to the mastership of the Temple, kept him from perceiving any connection between the controversy and the composition of the *Polity*. Attempting to account for the origin of the *Polity,* he could merely say that Hooker laid out the design of the *Polity* in his eight years of country obscurities because he heard "Those unseasonable and tedious noises which *some Non-conformists made*."[108] Walton, confident of his facts, was able to show cause and effect and to indicate the relationships of the incidents in Hooker's life.

Although the chief value of Gauden's *Life* to Walton was the

108 *Ibid.,* p. 14.

negative one of what to avoid and what to contradict, Walton did avail himself of some little things in Gauden's attempt. Gauden's statement on Hooker's birth, "God oft raiseth as noble *Plants* out of *small beds,* as out of the *stateliest Gardens,*"[109] was probably the source of Walton's platitude on the same subject: "Nature is not so partial, as always to give the great blessings of Wisdom and Learning, and with them the greater blessings of Virtue and Government, to those onely that are of a more high and honourable Birth."[110] Not in 1665, but the next year, Walton expanded slightly Gauden's reference to Athanasius in referring to Hooker's blackmail.[111] Walton knew, to be sure, as Gauden did not, that Hooker had left a will, but when he was hard pressed to explain Hooker's comparative wealth, he fell back on Gauden's statement, "onely his excellent *Library* was his Treasury,"[112] and he said of Hooker's estate "a great part of it being in Books."[113] The amount of misinformation in Gauden's *Life* did not discourage Walton from using what he found there when it suited his purpose.

Walton also availed himself of many bits of information which he found in Thomas Fuller's *The Church-History of Britain* (1655). Fuller had said of Bishop Jewel, "It is hard to say, whether his *soul,* or his *Ejaculations* arrived first in *Heaven,* seeing he prayed dying, and died praying,"[114] and Walton neatly used the statement in his relation of Jewel's death.[115] In telling of the alienation of church property, Fuller had said:

Indeed *Liecester* cast a covetous eye on *Lambeth-House,* alledging as good arguments for his obtaining thereof, as ever were urged by *Ahab* for *Naboths-Vineyard.* Now *Grindall,* though generally condemned for remisness in this kinde, (parting with more from his *See,* then ever his successors thanked him for) stoutly opposed the alienating of this his principal Palace, and made the *Liecestrian* Party to malice him.[116]

This information about Leicester and Lambeth Walton turned to his own use to show the motive behind Leicester's support of the nonconformists.[117] It was not to his purpose to indicate Grindal's opposition to Leicester, and he therefore omitted this information, but he used the reference to Grindal's remissness when he wished

---

[109] *Ibid.,* p. 7.

[110] *Hooker,* 1665, p. 7.

[111] Gauden, p. 32; *Hooker,* 1666, p. 24.

[112] Gauden, p. 35.

[113] *Hooker,* 1665, p. 157.

[114] *Church Hist.,* bk. IX, 102.

[115] *Hooker,* 1665, p. 21.

[116] *Church Hist.,* bk. IX, 130.

[117] *Hooker,* 1665, pp. 56–57.

to enumerate the oppositions which confronted Whitgift on his becoming Archbishop.[118] Fuller, in recounting the death of Edward Dering, had told how Dering referred to Elizabeth in preaching before her as an "untamed Heifer";[119] Walton used this episode to emphasize the boldness of the Scotch clergy, whom he would represent as confederates of the English nonconformists.[120] In his relation of the death of Mary, Queen of Scotland, Fuller had said, "She was buried in the *Quire* of *Peterborough,* and *Doctor Wickham Bishop* of *Lincolne* preached her *funeral sermon;* causelessly carped at by the *Martin Mar-Prelate,* as too favourable concerning her *final condition,* though he uttered nothing inconsistent with *Charity* and *Christian discretion.*"[121] Walton artfully used this story to illustrate the fanaticism of the men who asserted that a papist could not be saved.[122] He apparently tried to verify it, for he changed the name of the preacher;[123] and to make it conform to his purpose more precisely, he made much stronger Fuller's statement that the Bishop was "causelessly carped at" by saying that he "was reviled for not being positive for her Damnation."[124]

In Fuller's factual and objective account of Travers' career was a document which stated that Travers had been ordained minister by the Presbytery at Antwerp.[125] Walton revealed in 1670 how he used this manner of Travers' taking orders, when he wrote that Travers got with them "some opinions, that could never be eradicated."[126] Fuller had compared the manner in which Hooker and Travers delivered their sermons in the *Church-History*[127] and had

---

[118] *Ibid.,* p. 66.

[119] *Church Hist.,* bk. IX, 109.

[120] *Hooker,* 1665, p. 57.

[121] *Church Hist.,* bk. IX, 181.

[122] *Hooker,* 1665, p. 87.

[123] *Ibid.:* "Dr. *Dove,* then Bishop of *Peterborough*"; changed in 1666 to "Dr. *Howland*" (p. 15). Walton probably confused the funeral sermon, preached six months after Mary's execution, with the prayers offered for her by the Dean of Peterborough while she was on the scaffold. He had read about Mary's execution in John Spottiswoode's *History of the Church of Scotland* (London, 1655), pp. 355–357. Thomas Zouch in his edition of the *Lives* (York, 1796) shows that Fuller was undoubtedly right (note a, pp. 251–252).

[124] *Hooker,* 1665, p. 87.

[125] *Church Hist.,* bk. IX, 214.

[126] *Lives,* 1670 (Hooker), p. 77.

[127] *Church Hist.,* bk. IX, 216: "Where his [Hooker's] eye was left fixed at the beginning, it was found fixed at the end of his Sermon: In a word, the doctrine he delivered, had nothing but it self to garnish it. . . .

"Mr *Travers* his utterance was gracefull, gesture plausible, matter profitable, method plain, and his stile carried in it *indolem pietatis a Genius of grace* flowing from his sanctified heart."

even compared the popularity of the men: "Some say, that the congregation in the Temple, *ebb'd in the fore noon, and flowed in the afternoon*, and that the auditory of Mr *Travers* was far the more numerous."[128] When he spoke of Hooker in his *History of the Worthies of England*, he said that "the pulpit spake pure *Canterbury* in the *Morning*, and *Geneva* in the *Afternoon*," and he again described Hooker's plain and colorless manner of sermonizing.[129] Gauden, in his comparison of Hooker and Travers, was even more outspoken on Travers' greater brilliance as a preacher and his greater popularity.[130] Walton availed himself of Fuller's fine statement which summed up so nicely the points of view of the contestants,[131] but, zealous as he was of Hooker's reputation in every particular, he preferred, understandably, to concern himself with the matter rather than the manner of the sermons. He reserved his discussion of Hooker's manner of preaching until he could describe Hooker in front of his country congregation, where earnestness and plainness were to be preferred to brilliance.[132] Although Fuller had given three specific reasons why Whitgift prohibited Travers from preaching,[133] Walton merely indicated that Whitgift silenced him. He saw no need to justify Whitgift other than to state that "the Oppositions became so visible, and the Consequences so dangerous" that prudence made the prohibition necessary.[134] Walton took for granted the wisdom of this measure, since it redounded to Hooker's credit, and he was interested not in the details of the silencing but rather in what it led to—the friendship of Whitgift and Hooker and the writing of the *Polity*. Fuller had shown that Travers, despite the controversy, held Hooker in reverend esteem and had said, "And when an unworthy aspersion (some years after) was cast on *Hooker*, . . . Mr *Travers* being asked of a private friend, what he thought of the truth of that accusation, *In truth*,

[128] *Ibid.*

[129] *Worthies*, p. 264. "He may be said to have made good *Musick* with his *fiddle* and *stick* alone, without any *Rosin;* having neither *Pronunciation* nor gesture to grace his matter."

[130] Gauden, p. 29. "Mr. *Hooker* meekly suffered himself to be *eclipsed* and *undervalued* in comparison of Mr. *Travers:* If the paucity of vulgar *hearers* when Mr. *Hooker* preached, and the frequency or crowd when Mr. *Travers*, were the *competent Judge* and discrimination of their worth, Mr. *Hookers* Sermons were as some rougher *coyn*, good gold, and full weight, but not of so fair and smooth a stamp to vulgar eyes and hands as Mr. *Travers*."

[131] *Hooker*, 1665, p. 90.   [132] *Ibid.*, pp. 133–134.
[133] *Church Hist.*, bk. IX, 217.   [134] *Hooker*, 1665, p. 91.

(said he) *I take Mr Hooker to be a holy man.*"[135] Gauden, too, had echoed this attitude, and had even represented the esteem and affection as mutual.[136] It was not to Walton's purpose to ascribe such sentiments to Travers after his account of the controversy. He permitted himself to say of Travers before the account that he was "a man of competent Learning, of a winning Behaviour, and of a blamelesse Life,"[137] but after it, he wished to emphasize Hooker's dovelike temper in a book war and to contrast it to the zeal for argument of the nonconformists.[138] Fuller had wisely stated of Hooker and Travers that "we behold their actions not as the deeds of private persons, but the publick Champions of their *Party*,"[139] and this attitude Walton implicitly made his own by stating that the controversy was a continuation of that between Whitgift and Cartwright. Fuller had said in the *Worthies* that "no inclination of his [Hooker's] own, but obedience to others, put him on so publick a place,"[140] and Walton made much of this point of view, showing that Hooker had to be persuaded to accept the mastership of the Temple when he would have preferred only a better country living.[141] Fuller had in the *Church-History* anticipated his sentence in the *Worthies;* he had said that conscience, not covetousness, had made Hooker engage in controversy, and that he never got nor cared to get any eminent dignity in the Church of England.[142] Again this attitude is implied by Walton, but he explicitly emphasized Hooker's voluntary interest in the life of a country pastor.

In his account of the Whitgift-Cartwright controversy, Fuller had enumerated the writings of the men and had said that Whitgift's last pamphlet remained unanswered.[143] He had listed five reasons assigned to Cartwright's silence: he had spent his ammunition; he had felt that he had sufficiently refuted Whitgift's arguments; he

---

[135] *Church Hist.,* bk. IX, 217–218.

[136] Gauden, p. 31. "*At distance* they grew nearer *to each* other in their mutual good esteem and *affections;* each of them, as occasion offered, *professing* an high value of the other."

[137] *Hooker,* 1665, p. 89.

[138] *Ibid.,* p. 107.

[139] *Church Hist.,* bk. IX, 213–214.

[140] *Worthies,* p. 264.

[141] *Hooker,* 1665, p. 47.

[142] *Church Hist.,* bk. IX, 214.

[143] *Ibid.,* 103.

"1. The *Admonition, first,* and *second,* made by Mr. *Cartwright.*

2. The *Answer* to the *Admonition* by Dr. *John Whitgift.*

3. The *reply to the answer* of the *Admonition* by Mr. *Tho. Cartwright.*

4. The *defence* of the *answer* by Dr. *John Whitgift.* This last kept the field, and (for ought I can finde) received no solemn refutation."

had not wished to multiply replies; his party had turned from serious books to satirical pamphlets; he had considered himself vanquished.[144] Walton followed Fuller's bibliography, and merely said of Cartwright's silence that "he wrote no more, but left the Reader to be judge which had maintained their Cause with most Charity and Reason."[145] Fuller had cited Sir George Paule's *Life of Whitgift* (1612) as the source of his picture of Cartwright upon his retirement: "we finde him at this time growing rich in the Towne of *Warwick,* (there Master of an Hospitall) by the Benevolence and Bounty of his Followers, where he preached very temperately, according to his Promise made to the Arch-bishop."[146] Walton used this information,[147] but instead of emphasizing that Cartwright lived up to his promise, he rather stressed the extent of the kindness shown him by Whitgift.[148] For this attitude and other material, Walton went directly to Paule's *Life of Whitgift.* To show the degree of Whitgift's kindness, Paule had even stated that the Queen had been offended by Whitgift's permitting Cartwright to preach without subscription;[149] to such lengths Walton was unwilling to go, and he merely said that "the Bishop gave him a Licence to Preach, upon promise not to meddle with Controversies, but incline his Hearers to Piety and Moderation."[150] While Walton was willing to fashion his attitude after Paule's in this instance, he preferred to consider Fuller's recent bibliography of the Whitgift-Cartwright controversy more authoritative than Paule's. Paule's account had more accurately given the last word to Cartwright,[151] but Paule then

---

[144] *Ibid.*   [145] *Hooker,* 1665, p. 85.

[146] *Church Hist.,* bk. X, 2; Sir George Paule, *The Life of the Most Reverend and Religious Prelate John Whitgift, Lord Archbishop of Canterbury* (London, 1612), p. 54. Fuller's parenthesis is based on Paule, p. 17.

[147] Walton did not use Fuller's parenthesis, however, until 1666 (*Hooker,* 1666, p. 15).

[148] *Hooker,* 1665, p. 85: "After some silence, Mr. *Cartwright* received from the Bishop many personal Favours."

[149] Paule, p. 54.   [150] *Hooker,* 1665, pp. 85–86.

[151] Paule, p. 15. After saying that Whitgift wrote his *"Defence of the answere to the Admonition, against the Reply"* in answer to Cartwright's *Reply,* Paule says, "But Maister *Cartwright* (glorying belike to have the last word) published a second Reply."

A fine account of the exchange between Cartwright and Whitgift is in A. F. Scott Pearson's *Thomas Cartwright and Elizabethan Puritanism 1535–1603* (Cambridge, 1925), ch. ii. Whitgift's *The Defense of the Aunswere to the Admonition* (1574) was followed by Cartwright's *The Second Replie agaynst Maister Whitgiftes Second Answere* (1575) and his *The Rest of the Second Replie* (1577).

had to explain that Whitgift "was by the advise of some, (whose judgements he much esteemed,) disswaded from troubling himselfe, in refuting that which he had alreadie overthrowne."[152] Fuller's account had, by giving Whitgift the last word, forced the reader to speculate about Cartwright's silence, and Walton, zealous of Whitgift's esteem, preferred to leave any question about the last word of the controversy in Cartwright's lap.

From Paule, Walton got not only the information that he needed about Whitgift's career, but also many revealing details. Paule had said that the Queen, in making Whitgift Bishop of Worcester, had shown her favor "in forgiving him his first fruits . . . as also in bestowing on him . . . the disposing of all the Prebends of that Church of Worcester, during his continuance there."[153] Walton, despite the conciseness of his summation of Whitgift's career, still found room to mention the first of these favors.[154] He followed Paule, too, in showing that Whitgift managed with prudence and piety the many ecclesiastical duties which the Queen voluntarily entrusted to him,[155] and he repeated, with some small changes, Paule's story of James I's last visit to Whitgift.[156] But Walton did far more than copy Paule's facts. His awareness of the connotations of every fact transmuted a fact into a revealing impression, so that it was endowed with emotional rather than informational value. Paule had said, in telling of Whitgift's burial:

Doctor *Babbington*, Bishop of Worcester, made his Funeral Sermon; who likewise was his Pupill in Cambridge, and performed that duty . . . with very great commendation, choosing for his text a portion of Scripture most fitting the worthynes of his person. *But* Jehoida *waxed olde, and was full of daies and died. An hundred and thirtie yeares olde was hee when hee died. And they buried him in the Citie of* David, *with the Kings, because hee had done good in Israell, and toward God and his house.*[157]

In Walton's short summary of Whitgift's life, it would have been superfluous to include this information. But Walton transformed the fact here, and Paule's statements became the source of the fine last sentence of his account of Whitgift's career: "In all which Removes he was like the Ark, which left a blessing upon the place

[152] Paule, p. 15.   [153] *Ibid.*, p. 20.   [154] *Hooker*, 1665, p. 65.
[155] *Ibid.*, p. 67; Paule, p. 59.   [156] *Hooker*, 1665, pp. 82–83; Paule, p. 90.
[157] Paule, p. 93.

where it rested; and in all his Imployments was like *Jehoida*,[158] that did good unto *Israel*."[159]

Walton's insight into fact and his ability to create something more than was implied in his source is better illustrated in his use of two unrelated passages in Paule's *Life*. In order to show Whitgift's liberal hand and his favor with the Queen, Paule had said:

Every yeere hee entertained the Queene at one of his houses, so long as he was Archbishop: and some yeeres twice or thrice, where all things were performed in so seemely an order, that shee went thence alwayes exceedingly well pleased. And beside many publique, and gracious favours done unto him, she would salute him, and bid him farewell by the name of *blacke husband;* calling also his men her servants,[160] as a token of her good contentment with their attendance and paines.[161]

In listing Whitgift's good works later in his *Life,* Paule had referred to "his hospitall of the blessed Trinitie in Croydon, which he built very faire, and colledge-wise, for a warden, and eight and twenty Brothers, and sisters,"[162] and had said:

And albeit the Archbishop had ever a great affection to lie at his mansion house at Croydon, . . . yet, after he had builded his hospitall, . . . he was farther in love with the place, then before. The chiefe comfort of repose, or solace that he tooke, was in often dyning at the hospitall among his poore bretheren, as hee called them.[163]

Walton combined these two passages to produce a moving picture:

He built a large Almes-house near to his own House at *Croydon* in *Surrey,* and endowed it with Maintenance for a Master and twenty eight poor Men and Women; which he visited so often, that he knew their Names and Dispositions, and was so truly humble, that he called them Brothers and Sisters: and whensoever the Queen descended to that lowliness to dine with him at his Palace at *Lambeth,* (which was very often) he would usually the next day shew the like lowliness to his poor Brothers and Sisters at *Croydon,* and dine with them at his Hospital; at which time, you may believe, there was Joy at the Table.[164]

158 Walton's spelling here follows Paule's and probably indicates that he had Paule's passage before him as he wrote. He did not use the more conventional form, "*Jehoiada,*" until 1675 (p. 188).

159 *Hooker,* 1665, p. 65.

160 *Ibid.,* p. 67: "His Merits to the Queen, and her Favours to him were such, that *she called him her little black Husband,* and *called his Servants her Servants.*"

161 Paule, p. 78.   162 *Ibid.,* p. 83.   163 *Ibid.,* p. 84.

164 *Hooker,* 1665, pp. 81–82.

Walton's artistry is truly catalytic here, for he made a highly complimentary picture of Whitgift by reading into Paule's passages a relationship which was totally lacking. And Walton's version reveals not only his artistry, but also the intensive subjectivity of his approach toward biography. He took two fine stories and made one finer one of them. He handled the facts freely to produce a new implication. Paule's stories show us that Whitgift was equally at home with the great and with the humble. Walton's story is an unforgettable demonstration of Whitgift's charity and humility. But it is a demonstration produced by manipulating the facts. The facts themselves are not much violated, but they have become charged with new value in their new conformation.

The nature of Walton's approach to biography is seen also in the passage which follows the one just mentioned. Paule had linked the almshouse to Whitgift's building a free school and had then said:

After the finishing of this hospitall, among many other his good deeds, the French lieger Embassadour in England, called *Boys Sisi*, enquired what workes the Archbishop had published, for that he would willingly reade his bookes, who was reputed *The Peerelesse Prelate for Pietie and Learning in our dayes,* and whom in conference, hee found so grave, godly, and judicious; when it was answered that hee onely published certaine bookes in the English tongue, in defence of the Ecclesiasticall government (although it be very well knowne to many, who were neere unto him, that he left divers learned Treatises in written hand, well worthy the printing) and that it was, thereupon incidently tould the Embassadour that he had founded an Hospitall, and a Schoole, he used these words; *Profectô Hospitale, ad sublevandam paupertatem, et schola, ad instruendam juventutem, sunt optimi libri, quos Archiepiscopus conscribere potuit;* Truely an Hospitall to sustaine the poore, and a schoole to trayne up youth, are the worthiest bookes that an Archbishop could set forth.[165]

This pretty story appealed to Walton, but, while he liked the words of the French ambassador[166] as a reflection on Whitgift's piety, he did not like what the passage implied of Whitgift's written works. He therefore so altered the passage that it demonstrated high regard for both Whitgift's scholarship and charity; he had *"Boyse Sisi"* say, *"The Bishop had published many learned Books, but a Free-*

[165] Paule, pp. 83–84.
[166] Jean de Thumery de Boissise. See Keble, I, 45, n. 2.

school to train up Youth, and an Hospital to lodge and maintain aged and poor People, were the best Evidences of Christian Learning that a Bishop could leave to Posterity."[167]

In the first part of the *Life of Whitgift,* Paule had emphasized Whitgift's enforcement of uniformity in the Church, and he had also shown in two detailed incidents Whitgift's zeal for the preservation of church property. Describing the first incident, Paule had said:

He found the Bishoprick [of Worcester] at his first comming much impaired by his Predecessours, granting away in long Leases, divers Manours, Parks, and Mansion houses: But that which much troubled him, and wherein he most of all stirred, was the letting to Maister *Abington,* cofferer to the late Queene, the Rent corne of his two best Manours, *Hollow* and *Grimley.* . . . This Lease being let to Maister *Abington* (a great man then to contend withall; his wife also being sometimes the Queenes bed-fellow) the Bishop notwithstanding did call it in question. . . . Maister *Abington* by his wifes greatnesse, procured her Majesties gracious Letters, written very earnestly in his behalfe.[168]

But, Paule had gone on to say, Whitgift informed the Queen how prejudicial such a lease was to the bishopric, and she exerted her influence for him. Abington was willing to surrender the lease for the duration of Whitgift's stay at Worcester, but Whitgift refused and voluntarily paid Abington three hundred pounds out of his own purse for its permanent surrender. Describing the second incident, Paule had said that shortly after Whitgift's elevation to the primacy he

recovered from the Queene, as part of the possessions of the Archbishoprick, long Beachwood in Kent, contayning above a thousand acres of land, which had beene many yeeres detained from his predecessor, by Sir *James Croft,* then Comptroller of her Majesties houshold, farmer thereof to her Majestie.[169]

These two incidents provided ample demonstration of Whitgift's concern for church property. The concern of the Restoration Church in such matters has perhaps been sufficiently shown, and it may well be that Walton saw in these passages an opportunity to counteract in behalf of the Church the ambiguity of Hooker's Book VII by emphasizing Whitgift's determined and more orthodox point of view. Here, then, is probably the seed for the dramatic

[167] *Hooker,* 1665, p. 82.   [168] Paule, pp. 20–21.   [169] *Ibid.,* pp. 28–29.

speech which Walton would have his reader believe was made by Whitgift to Elizabeth.[170] In Paule's *Life*, however, Whitgift had been shown preoccupied with his diocesan lands in Worcester and Kent. Walton's speech generalizes his interest in church property, and, as might be expected in view of Walton's purpose, especially stresses the sovereign's obligations to the Church. John Strype had Walton's speech in hand when he said in his *Life of Whitgift* that in 1578 some of the Queen's *"Concelers"* had their eyes on Hartlebury, the chief seat and manor of the see of Worcester, upon coming into Worcestershire commissioned to search for lands and possessions forfeited to the crown.[171] Strype quoted from Whitgift's correspondence to the Lord Treasurer in order to show that Whitgift was being unjustly molested about his lands,[172] and he said:

And here I cannot but take Notice (though perhaps it fall within the Compass of some other Year afterwards) of the earnest, bold Speech of our Prelate spoken to the Queen, (yet with a due Deference to her Majesty) concerning these Commissions. It is set down in the Life of Mr. *Richard Hooker;* and was occasioned by some hot Speeches in her Presence between him and the Earl of *Leicester.* . . .

I do not know where the abovesaid Writer met with this memorable Speech of our Bishop.[173]

Walton probably met with the inspiration for this speech in Paule's *Life*, but it is of his own making. He does not cite a documentary source, saying only that Whitgift "spake to her [Majesty] . . . to this purpose."[174] Whitgift would hardly have dared express himself so strongly before the Queen. In the speech, according to Walton, Whitgift cautioned the Queen that it was sacrilege to deprive the Church of its rights and reminded her of rulers who had given land and immunities to the Church and who had, indeed, put a curse upon alienators. He stated that at her coronation she had sworn, in obligation to Magna Carta and many modern statutes, to maintain church lands and rights, and he begged her not to punish posterity

---

[170] *Hooker*, 1665, pp. 70–77.

[171] John Strype, *The Life and Acts of the Most Reverend Father in God, John Whitgift* (London, 1718), bk. II, ch. i (Anno 1578), p. 85.

[172] *Ibid.*

[173] *Ibid.*, p. 86. The Rev. John Ayre, following Strype's account, also accepted as apparently genuine Whitgift's speech in the *Life of Hooker* (*The Works of John Whitgift, D.D., . . . The Third Portion* [Cambridge, 1853]. See p. xiii of the "Biographical Memoir").

[174] *Hooker,* 1665, p. 70.

for the misdeeds of a few contemporary clergymen. He cited the case of her own father to show that the addition of church lands to justly inherited property leads to the unavoidable loss of both, and he said of Henry VIII, "God did so far deny him his Restraining Grace, that he fell into greater sins than I am willing to mention." He warned her that a poor clergy leads to the decay of religion and reminded her that sovereigns, too, have a day of judgment. At the end, he asked her pardon for his "affectionate plainnness," and well he might have. Not only do the tone and content of the speech point to Walton rather than to Whitgift, but there is further evidence indicative of Walton's hand. The changes in the speech in later editions are many more than Walton normally makes when he is quoting a document, and the interpolations are lengthier. In 1670, for instance, he said additionally of the curse leveled upon those who do not uphold the Magna Carta, *"A Curse like the* Leprosie, *that was intail'd on the* Jews; *for, as that, so these Curses have and will cleave to the very stones of those buildings that have been consecrated to God; and, the fathers sin of* Sacriledge, *will prove to be intail'd on his Son and Family."*[175] The power of this simile appealed to Walton, and he used it in the speech a second time in 1675.[176] In 1670, he also added a comparison of King Henry VIII and King Saul.[177] In these and in many other changes[178] Walton's pen can be recognized, and the number of the additions makes it certain that he was responsible for the original version.

[175] *Lives*, 1670 (Hooker), p. 49.

[176] *Ibid.*, 1675, p. 191 [misnumbered "171"]. The words in capitals are the addition: *"God prevent Your Majesty AND YOUR SUCCESSORS from being liable to that Curse WHICH WILL CLEAVE UNTO CHURCH-LANDS, AS THE LEPROSIE TO THE JEWS."*

[177] *Ibid.*, 1670 (Hooker), p. 50.

[178] The following passage may be quoted because it represents Walton's typical fashion of improving his own writing. The changes are in excess of any he makes on a document, particularly in excess of changes he makes after he has quoted it in the first version of a *Life*.

1. "And consider that S. *Paul* said to those Christians of his time that were offended with Idolatry" (*Hooker*, 1665, p. 72).

2. *"And consider that it was S.* Paul *that said to those Christians of his time that were offended with Idolatry"* (*Hooker*, 1666, p. 13).

3. *"And consider that it was St.* Paul *that said to those Christians of his time that were offended with Idolatry, yet committed* Sacriledge" (*Lives*, 1670 [Hooker], pp. 47–48).

4. *"And I beseech you to consider that it was St.* Paul *that said to those Christians of his time that were offended with Idolatry, and yet committed* Sacriledge" (*Lives*, 1675, p. 191 [misnumbered "171"]).

Walton was certain of the orthodoxy of the speech, for he had constructed it in large part from an authoritative tract on the rights of the Church. Sir Henry Spelman's *De non temerandis Ecclesiis* had been published in 1613 and again in 1616. In 1646, it was thrown into the lists of controversy by his son Clement, who had the book published at Oxford with a long epistle to the reader in which he recounted the misfortunes attendant upon sacrilegious persons in all ages. From this volume Walton drew his statements that the inheritance of confiscated church lands leads to distress,[179] that there are such sins as sacrilege and prophaneness,[180] that Henry VIII fell from one sin to another,[181] that Christ whipped prophaners out of the Temple and overthrew the tables of the money-changers.[182] Spelman's suggestion that kings were anointed with the oil of priesthood at their coronations led to Walton's particularization of the obligations which the Queen undertook at her coronation,[183] and his statement that "none will apply themselves . . . to the study of Divinity, when after long and painful study, they shall have nothing whereupon to live" was probably the root of Walton's idea that "when they that serve at Gods Altar shall be exposed to Poverty, then Religion it self will be exposed to Scorn, and become contemptible."[184] Walton reread Spelman prior to 1670 (probably because another edition of his work appeared at Oxford in 1668), and he incorporated into Whitgift's speech Clement Spelman's statement that "as the leprosy with the Jews, with us the curse of sacrilege, cleaves to the consecrated stone."[185] He added also Spelman's comparison of Henry VIII and Saul,[186] and he used, not very felicitously, Spelman's reference to "God's and the Levite's portion."[187]

Walton went to still another Civil War tract for this speech. He had written, *"Church-land added to an ancient Inheritance, hath proved like a Moth fretting a Garment, and secretly consume[d] both: Or like the Eagle that stole a coale from the Altar, and thereby*

---

[179] Henry Spelman, *De non temerandis Ecclesiis* (Oxford, 1841), p. 37 ff.; *Hooker,* 1665, pp. 75–76.

[180] Spelman, p. 26; *Hooker,* 1665, p. 71.

[181] Spelman, p. 61; *Hooker,* 1665, p. 76.

[182] Spelman, pp. 130–131; *Hooker,* 1665, pp. 71–72.

[183] Spelman, p. 152; *Hooker,* 1665, pp. 73–75.

[184] Spelman, pp. 157–158; *Hooker,* 1665, pp. 76–77.

[185] Spelman, p. 67.   [186] *Ibid.,* p. 61.

[187] *Ibid.,* p. 81; *Lives,* 1670 (Hooker), p. 50.

set her Nest on fire, which consumed both her young Eagles, and her selfe that stole it."[188] His story of the eagle is not just a recollection of Aesop. It shows that he had read Ephraim Udall's *Noli Me Tangere Is A Thinge to be thought On* (London, 1642). Udall holds that alienation of church lands is sinful even when accomplished by a parliament,[189] and he suggests that the restoration of tithes to their proper owners would be "a worthy work and fitting a Parliamentary Reformation."[190] He quotes Hosea 5:12, "Therefore will I be unto Ephraim as a moth, and to the house of Judah as rottenness"[191] and makes the following suggestion to the gentry to preserve them from the sin of sacrilege:

That they would have a Tablet hang up alwaies in the Dining-Roome, where they ordinarily take their repast; in which should be drawn an Altar, with Flesh and Fire on it, for Sacrifice, with an Eagle ready to take wing, having in her Talons a piece of Flesh, with a burning coale at it, and something beside it; and higher than the Altar, a tall Tree, with an Eagles Nest in it, and the Heads of the young ones discovered above the Nest, and the Nest flaming with a light fire about them, with this Inscription over the Altar, *Noli me Tangere, ne te & tuos perdam:* For things belonging to the Altar, will certainly prove a snare to the devourers of [t]hem.[192]

The title page of *Noli Me Tangere* is just such a "Tablet," and the striking picture must have impressed itself on Walton's mind.

When Walton wrote that Whitgift "spake to her [Majesty] . . . to this purpose," he expected his readers to accept the words of the speech as Whitgift's, or, at least, as a paraphrase of what Whitgift said, and he used quotation marks to further the impression of precise citation. Walton misleads his readers here. As we have seen, he constructed the speech largely by elaborating and generalizing a hint in Paule's *Life* and by dipping into two tracts written after Whitgift's death. How detrimental to the writing of biography is this sort of misrepresentation and what does it show of Walton as a biographer? There is no question that Walton included the speech to support a thesis close to his heart, that when he had Whitgift speak "to this purpose" he meant his own purpose. After the Restoration, Walton, like the restored churchmen, was peculiarly sensitive to matters of sequestration and confiscation; re-establishment

[188] *Hooker*, 1665, pp. 75–76.
[190] *Ibid.*, p. 15.
[192] *Ibid.*, p. 27 [misnumbered "19"].

[189] *Noli Me Tangere*, p. 10.
[191] *Ibid.*, p. 12.

meant more than doctrine and discipline: it meant physical re-habilitation. Walton was well aware of the needs of the Church. As Morley's steward at Worcester, he had seen the bishop expend six thousand pounds within a year on cathedral repairs alone.[193] It is understandable that he should wish to sustain the Church's belief in the inviolability of its property. He wrote the impassioned speech for the *Life* because it showed Whitgift's attitude directly and Hooker's by suggestion, and therefore gave forceful support to the Church. Our judgment of what Walton does here must depend not merely on an examination of his motives, not merely on the presence of his thesis. It must be based on the area of coincidence between Walton's thesis as expressed by Whitgift and the real sentiments of Whitgift and Hooker. If Walton does not give us what Whitgift said, he does give us what Whitgift would have wanted to say. Walton, then, does not falsify Whitgift's views. His misrepresentation lies in his writing the boldest speech he can (and stressing its "great humility and reverence"), in endowing Whitgift with an ingenuousness and forthrightness which falsifies the relationship between Whitgift and the Queen. The Whitgift of the speech is not the man whom the Queen called her little black husband. Again, though the speech associates Hooker indirectly with a position which was essentially his, it deceives in its omission of Hooker's subtleties and qualifications. In its broad outline, there is perhaps a sufficient area of coincidence between thesis and fact to allow us to condone the speech, but we boggle at the details.

The danger in Walton's method of making the wish or thesis the father of the fact is evident in the *Life of Hooker*. Thesis and fact clash in the black-and-white approach to nonconformity, in the one-sided picture of the Cartwright and the Travers controversies. Thesis and fact are not sufficiently coincidental in the representation of Saravia's views as Hooker's, and even in such a minor detail as Hooker's manner of preaching. We must grant Walton's real artistry in creating a pattern in the *Life* and in molding the details to fit his pattern. But Walton's usual tendency was to follow his own predisposition, to bend facts to support his predisposition, to abide by his thesis despite the facts, to make insufficient concession to the facts, to temper the facts to comply with doubtful oral information from people he trusted, and this tendency is a detriment to biographical writing. It was to be a great pitfall in the *Life of Hooker*.

[193] Bosher, p. 235.

C. J. Sisson has shown that Walton's *"accidental Advantages"* led to his inheritance of a mass of misinformation. The principal new documents that Sisson has found consist of a series of records of lawsuits brought in the Court of Chancery, arising out of the claims of Hooker's daughters as legatees under his will. Six lawsuits, running their course in Chancery from January, 1610, to April, 1624, bear upon the legacies to Hooker's daughters and upon the manuscripts, including those of the last three Books of the *Polity,* which were part of the estate left to his widow and, upon her death, to his daughters. The facts which the Chancery records contain led Sisson to other materials. He says that Edwin Sandys probably introduced Hooker to his friends and neighbors, the Churchmans, in 1581,[194] and he found the precise date of Hooker's marriage to Joan Churchman, February 13, 1588, in an entry in the parish register of St. Augustine's, Watling Street.[195] Joan's dowry amounted to seven hundred pounds.[196] Her father, the records of the Merchant Taylors' Company show, was in 1581 elected Third Warden of the Company, and became First Warden in 1589 and Master of the Company in 1594.[197] Sisson found no evidence of Hooker's residing at Drayton Beauchamp, to which he was presented December 9, 1584, and is quite certain that he was an absentee parson; he considers this a stop-gap appointment pending Hooker's becoming Master of the Temple in February, 1585, and he cites evidence to show that Hooker was already in London early in December, 1584.[198] He found no evidence that Hooker had ever lived at Boscombe or at Salisbury, to which he had been appointed after he left the Temple in 1591,[199] and he says:

We may fairly assume a reasonable certainty that Hooker continued to live in London with John Churchman, in Watling Street and at

[194] Sisson, pp. 25–26.

[195] *Ibid.,* p. 21. Walton says that Hooker came to London "in or about the year 1581" (*Hooker,* 1665, p. 38), and he does not attempt to date the marriage, saying merely that Hooker promised "upon a fair summons to return to *London,* and accept of her [Mrs. Churchman's] choice. And he did so" (*ibid.,* p. 40). He indicates that Hooker was married before he was presented to the living at Drayton Beauchamp on Dec. 9, 1584 (*ibid.,* pp. 42–43). In 1666, he tried to date the marriage more exactly and wrote that Hooker carried out his promise to return to London and marry "in that, or the year following" (*Hooker,* 1666, p. 7). Walton thought, then, that the marriage took place about 1581–1582.

[196] Sisson, p. 24.   [197] *Ibid.*   [198] *Ibid.,* pp. 20–21.

[199] *Ibid.,* p. 45.

Enfield, and gave his whole time to the writing of the *Ecclesiastical Polity,* freed from the duties of an active cure and from the preoccupations of his controversy with Travers, until he removed to Bishopsbourne in January 1595 and became at last, and for the first time, a country parson with a cure of souls.[200]

Sisson uncovered, too, in the parish register of Bishopsbourne, a record of Mrs. Hooker's marriage on March 23, 1601, to Edward Nethersole,[201] who had been Mayor of Canterbury in 1590.[202] Mrs. Hooker's solicitude for her children is obvious in the marriage contract which bound her new husband to double the legacy left them by their father, and she saw to it that more than half of her dowry was assured them.[203] She was buried in Canterbury on February 18, 1603.[204] At the time of her death, her husband was an alderman of the city,[205] and the next year he became mayor a second time.[206] Sisson has shown conclusively, then, the good fortune which was Hooker's in his marriage, the prosperity and kindness of his father-in-law, the love that his wife had for his children even after his death and her choice of a respectable stepfather for them, and he has shown, too, that Hooker did not become an active country parson until five years before his death.

How are we to account for Walton's wholesale inaccuracies in these matters and especially for his so blackening the character of Mrs. Hooker? It is true that he had a predecessor in painting thus dark a picture of Hooker's marriage. Fuller corrected in 1662 his reference in the *Church-History* to Hooker's single life and said that "he had Wife and Children, though indeed such as were neither to his comfort, when living, nor credit when Dead. But Parents cannot stamp their Children from their *Head* or *Hearts.*"[207] In the light of Sisson's discoveries, we can see the origin of Walton's misinformation and its traditional perpetuation. Mrs. Hooker's second marriage, just five months after Hooker's death, might well provide to a certain kind of mind evidence of lack of devotion to her first husband. Her second husband, despite his apparent respectability,

---

[200] *Ibid.,* p. 46.   [201] *Ibid.,* pp. 14–15.   [202] *Ibid.,* p. 42.
[203] *Ibid.,* p. 37.   [204] *Ibid.,* p. 15.   [205] *Ibid.*
[206] *Ibid.,* p. 42.
[207] *Worthies,* p. 264. In a note, Fuller explained that he received this information "From the mouth of his [Hooker's] Sister lately living at *Hogsden* nigh *London.*" Perhaps this was Elizabeth Harvey, who, Walton says, "liv'd to the Age of 121. years, and died in the moneth of *September,* 1623" (*Hooker,* 1665, p. 159). The year was corrected in *Hooker,* 1666 (p. 28), to "1663."

had, Sisson shows, probably married Mrs. Hooker for her money, and the marriage was probably not a happy one. Indeed, not long after her death, the former mayor of Canterbury was imprisoned on a charge of forgery and perjury.[208] Here, then, was more grain for the rumor mills; nor was this all. Hooker's father-in-law, eminently successful while Hooker was alive, had, after his death, financed shipments of goods consigned to Irish merchants, and he lost heavily in the anarchic conditions of trade which followed Mountjoy's campaign in Ireland.[209] In December, 1604, he was forced to sell his shop and house to meet urgent debts; in February, 1605, he was adjudged bankrupt.[210] The former Master of the Merchant Taylors' Company had to become a pensioner of his guild.[211] In these many unfortunate happenings probably lies the seed for the story of Hooker's unfortunate marriage. The lawsuits of some fourteen years also served to create ill will in Hooker's family and in his friends. For example, Sir Edwin Sandys was accused by Hooker's heirs of failure to pay to them their share of profits from the *Polity* and was asked to justify his actions as Hooker's literary executor.[212] John Spenser, torn between his loyalty to Sandys and to Hooker, was troubled to give evidence on several occasions. Bitterness was bound to result from accusations and questionings, and this bitterness was undoubtedly perpetuated in the memory of Sandys's friends and Spenser's relations, the Cranmers. And the Cranmers, particularly Dorothy, the wife of Dr. Spenser, Walton cites as his informants. Their stories, slanted in their telling after many years, and further clouded and exaggerated by the passage of the decades, Walton incorporated in his *Life*. Fuller's statement corroborated the tenor of the misinformation, and wishful thinking, particularly with regard to Mrs. Hooker's connection with the manuscripts which the Church wished to make suspect, caused Walton to tell some false and damaging tales.

Walton tells us that he was told about the destruction of Hooker's manuscripts "almost 40. years past by one that very well knew Mr. *Hooker* and the affairs of his Family."[213] The date, coinciding with that of his marriage and of his acquaintance with the Cranmer family, is the same one he offers for other information given him by Dorothy Spenser, and Mrs. Spenser would appear to be his in-

208 Sisson, p. 41. 209 *Ibid.*, p. 34. 210 *Ibid.*, p. 35.
211 *Ibid.*, p. 36. 212 *Ibid.*, p. 16.
213 *Hooker*, 1665, p. 161.

formant here. Mrs. Spenser was reporting events which had taken place a quarter-century before, and her recollection was confused. The story about the tearing and burning of Hooker's manuscripts by Mr. Charke and another minister who lived near Canterbury seems so close to the story which Walton tells about Hooker's house being broken into a few days before his death that it seems likely that Mrs. Spenser's memory was fuzzy. Still, she remembered the name of *"one Mr. Charke."* Her very remembrance of Charke's name is, however, another indication of her confusion. Almost certainly, her unpleasant association with Charke's name came from events connected not with Dr. Spenser or with Hooker, but with her second husband, Dr. Field. When Richard Field became Reader in Divinity at Lincoln's Inn in 1594,[214] he took over the post held previously by William Charke. Charke was a Puritan; he had, in fact, been expelled from his fellowship at Peterhouse in 1572 for declaring in a sermon that the episcopal system was introduced by Satan.[215] At the end of 1581, he was invited to be the first Reader in Divinity at Lincoln's Inn.[216] He stayed in this position until early in 1593, when he was suspended for puritanism by Archbishop Whitgift.[217] Charke's post at Lincoln's Inn was analogous to that which Hooker had at the Temple from 1585 to 1591; the doctrine he preached must have been similar to Travers'. Perhaps Field had mentioned Hooker and Charke to his wife of a few months in 1616. It would seem that ten years later, when pressed for a name to circumstantiate her story of the destruction of Hooker's manuscripts, she picked the name of a Puritan whom she vaguely associated with Hooker. Just how detailed Mrs. Spenser's information was, we cannot, of course, know, but it is likely that even precise details would have escaped Walton after forty years and that the precision of his own account stems from his desire to offer a convincing and persuasive story.

Perhaps we can see better the degree of particularity in Mrs. Spenser's stories if we examine another which Walton got from her. Walton cites no source for his wonderful story of George Cranmer and Edwin Sandys's visit to Hooker at Drayton Beau-

[214] See W. P. Baildon, ed., *The Records of the Honorable Society of Lincoln's Inn. The Black Books* (London, 1897–1902), II, 35, 39, and *Athenae Oxon.*, II, 182.

[215] *DNB*, article "William Charke."   [216] *Black Books*, I, 424.
[217] *Ibid.*, II, 28.

champ, but there is little doubt that he heard its outlines from Mrs. Spenser. His story reads:

And in this condition he [Hooker] continued about a year, in which time his two Pupils, *Edwin Sandys* and *George Cranmer,* were returned from Travel, and took a journey to see their Tutor, where they found him with a Book in his hand, (it was the *Odes* of *Horace*) he being then tending his small allotment of Sheep in a common Field, which he told his Pupils he was forced to do, for that his Servant was gone home to dine, and assist his Wife to do some necessary houshold business. When his Servant returned and released him, his two Pupils attended him unto his House, where their best Entertainment was his Company, which was presently denied them, for *Richard* was call'd to rock the Cradle; and the rest of their Welcom was so like this, that they staid but till next morning, which was time enough to discover and pitty their Tutors condition; and having given him as much present comfort as they were able, they were forced to leave him to the company of his Wife *Joan,* and seek themselves a quieter Lodging.[218]

Some such story was going the rounds at Oxford in 1661. It is preserved in a note made by Anthony à Wood:

Hooker, somtimes fellow of C. C. C. Oxon, rector of Bourn in Kent where he died. He was very unhappy in a wife who by all was reputed an imperious whore. She would make him rock the cradle purposely to hinder his study but whilest he did that office with one hand he would hold the book in the other. She would not allow him paper to write upon, etc. He dying, she afterwards married a captaine who turned his [Hooker's] children out of doores, soe that in a short time they either begged their bread or died in the streets with hunger.[219]

Wood's informant was Mrs. Martha Iles.[220] Mrs. Iles must have had a large fund of church lore at her fingertips. Wood says that in her younger days she had been the mistress of Dr. John Williams, who was afterward Archbishop of York, and when Wood knew her she was the widow of Dr. Thomas Iles, a canon of Christ Church. She had first married Dr. Thomas Anyan, who had succeeded Dr. John Spenser as president of Corpus Christi College, Oxford. It would seem that Mrs. Iles inherited not only the house which Spenser had built for his Dorothy, but also Dorothy's story.[221] The tenor of

[218] *Hooker,* 1665, pp. 43–44.
[219] Andrew Clark, *The Life and Times of Anthony Wood* (Oxford, 1891–1900), I, 425.
[220] *Ibid.,* II, viii.
[221] *Ibid.,* I, 154.

Mrs. Iles's version is the same as that of Walton's, but it lacks the precise circumstances of Walton's account. I would suggest that Walton got from Dorothy Spenser a story like Mrs. Iles's, an un-particularized bit of gossip. I would suggest that she told him, too, that a visit by her brother George and by Sandys led to Hooker's appointment to the mastership of the Temple. The circumstantiality and resolution of the two stories are Walton's.

Walton found it troublesome to construct a persuasive narrative here. Since he dated Hooker's residence at Drayton Beauchamp from December, 1584, and his appointment as Master of the Temple in March, 1585, he seems to have Hooker tending sheep in a Buckinghamshire field in the middle of winter. As we envision the scene, the hand that holds the *Odes* gets chillier every minute. But this particular detail did not trouble Walton, for his statement that Hooker continued at Drayton Beauchamp "about a year" shows that he misinterpreted the Temple records and thought that Hooker became master of the Temple not in March, 1595, but in 1595/6.[222] Trouble arose, however, because Walton had to date Cranmer and Sandys's visit during Hooker's residence at Drayton Beauchamp if he was to show that the visit led indirectly to Hooker's appointment at the Temple. But Camden's account of Cranmer seemed to preclude such a visit at this time. Camden says that Cranmer "continued Master of Arts of six yeeres standing" before he left Oxford to serve under Secretary Davison and then under Sir Henry Killigrew and that he traveled abroad with Sandys for three years prior to serving under Mountjoy in Ireland, where he died in 1600.[223] Camden erred in saying that Cranmer started on his travels after the death of Sir Henry Killigrew, for Killigrew did not die until 1603. In this error Walton followed him. But Camden's account of Cranmer was accurate in its general outline, and Walton could not reconcile so long a period of residence at Oxford and so late a date for the travels with a visit to Buckinghamshire by Cranmer and Sandys about 1585. Rather than change his own story, he

[222] Walton dates Hooker's birth in 1553 (*Hooker*, 1665, p. 7). In 1666, he added to the date of Hooker's being made Master of the Temple, "He being then in the 34th year of his Age" (*Hooker,* 1666, p. 9).

[223] A detailed account of George Cranmer first appears in the 1635 edition of Camden's *Annals*, p. 517. Walton may have got it there, but his reference at the close of his account to a battle against the rebels near Carlingford follows a departure from Camden made by the editor of Cranmer's *Concerning the New Church Discipline* (1642), sig. A2ᵛ.

changed Camden's: he says only that Cranmer continued Master of Arts "for many years" before he left Oxford, and he says that Cranmer and Sandys traveled abroad for three years *before* Cranmer went into Davison's service.[224] The inheritance from Mrs. Spenser, freely shaped into a coherent pattern by Walton, won out over Camden.

Walton revised his account of the visit for the version of the *Life* which appeared with Hooker's *Works* in 1666. He had originally concluded his story somewhat abruptly, but effectively, with the departure of Cranmer and Sandys to seek a quiet lodging. In 1666, he made more explicit his intent in the passage by adding Cranmer's words of consolation to Hooker on his unfortunate marriage and Hooker's philosophic reply, which is an admission of the miseries which the marriage entailed.[225] The addition is another indication of the imagination which Walton brought to bear upon his oral inheritance and of his freedom in developing it. Some time before 1670, Walton learned once more that something was wrong with his story. We have seen that in 1673 he was helping William Fulman collect materials for his *Life of Hales*. But Walton and Fulman were helping each other before 1670, for Walton's most substantial additions to the *Life of Hooker* in 1670 stem from material made available to him by Fulman.[226] Fulman knew definitely that Cranmer had not been made Master of Arts until July 13, 1589,[227] and he must have made this information, too, available to Walton. Walton had followed Camden in stating that Cranmer had stayed at Oxford long after he had been made Master of Arts; he had changed Camden to read that Cranmer had traveled for three years after his residence at Oxford; he had put the visit to Drayton Beauchamp after the travels. Fulman's information made this sequence of events untenable; it moved the visit which Walton had made responsible for Hooker's appointment to the Temple to a time when Hooker had already retired from the Temple. It is to Walton's credit that he made a concession to his new material, but the nature of his concession shows the strength of his attachment to the pattern which he had constructed on the basis of his interpretation of oral testimony. He merely omitted from his account of the

---

[224] *Hooker,* 1665, pp. 31–32.   [225] *Hooker,* 1666, p. 8.
[226] See pp. 285–286.
[227] Keble, I, 25, n. 2: "Now it appears from Fulman's papers, vol. VIII. that Sandys was made regent M.A. July 8, 1583; Cranmer, not till July 13, 1589."

visit the words stating that it had been made when Cranmer and Sandys "were returned from Travel."

Walton must have known from his own experience that domestic felicity is not incompatible with rocking the cradle. He knew, too, Fuller's character of the faithful minister in *The Holy State:*[228]

He is carefull in the discreet ordering of his own family. A good Minister and a good father may well agree together. When a certain Frenchman came to visit Melanchthon, he found him in his stove with one hand dandling his child in the swadling-clouts, and in the other hand holding a book and reading it.[229]

But Walton was less interested in showing Hooker as a good father than he was in showing Mrs. Hooker as a bad mother and wife. His inherited impression led him consistently to blacken Mrs. Hooker, and the deliberateness with which he developed in the *Life* the impression that he considered accurate makes entirely believable his story of the disposition of Hooker's manuscripts. His inherited impression led him also to endow Hooker with such traits as might explain his marriage. The story of how Hooker became or thought he became obligated to Mrs. Churchman, Walton made convincing in its detail, and we are the more willing to accept Hooker's behavior when Walton informs us, in connection with Hooker's manner of reading his sermons, that "though he was not purblind, yet he was short or weak sighted."[230] The bashfulness which Walton attributed to Hooker upon the occasion of his choosing a wife he used also to explain that Hooker's unworldliness made him an easy subject for blackmail. Knowledge of Hooker's appointment to Drayton Beauchamp became fused in Walton's mind with Fuller's comment on Hooker's disinclination to be in a public place and provided him with further evidences of unworldliness. He therefore again developed this trait in Hooker by ascribing his resistance to the eminence of the mastership of the Temple to his preference for a country parsonage, and, indeed, by portraying him at Bishopsbourne as the prototype of the excellent country parson. Walton's misapprehensions about Mrs. Hooker and his taking for granted Hooker's residence at Drayton Beauchamp permitted him to dramatize the nature and extent of Hooker's affliction in the incident of Sandys and Cranmer's visit. The story is false in every detail. But

228 See p. 336.   229 *The Holy State* (Cambridge, 1642), p. 86.
230 *Hooker,* 1665, p. 129.

every false and magnificent detail, especially that of Hooker's reading Horace's *Odes* as he tended his flock, is a tribute to Walton's ability to construct a picture powerful in its appeal and beautifully integrated to the *Life* as a whole in its revelation of Hooker's character and in its bearing on Hooker's career as Walton saw them.

The *Life of Hooker* of 1665 is a crucial experience in Walton's development as a biographer. The circumstances leading to its composition point to Walton's firm grasp of the difference between a biography and a treatise. Moreover, Gauden's dismal *Life* and the necessity of counteracting it seem to have made Walton increasingly aware of the importance of proper documentation. There seems to be in the *Life of Hooker* a respect for records which is different from Walton's rather cavalier use of them in the *Donne* and in the *Wotton*. Walton cites the Stationers' Register and the Temple records; the specificity of his dates when he writes about Hooker at Oxford shows that he consulted university records; the particularity of his accounts of Hooker's benefices shows the kind of knowledge derivable only from diocesan records; he cites an attestation by Fabian Philipps and another by William Somner; he cites the best authorities—Archbishop Spottiswoode and William Camden.

But the date which Walton gives for the entering of the *Polity* on the Stationers' Register is incorrect. He misinterpreted the Temple records with regard to the year of Richard Alvie's death and the year of Hooker's becoming Master.[231] He wrongly takes Hooker's presentation to the benefice of Drayton Beauchamp as certain evidence of his residence there. He is wrong when he states that Thomas Cranmer witnessed Hooker's will, and his statement when he seems to be citing the will that the great part of Hooker's estate was in books is an interpolation inspired by Gauden. His treatment of the will makes it seem that he did not see a copy of it, but rather an attestation by William Somner to some of its provisions. He does not authenticate his account by quoting the will but by calling Somner "the Archbishops Register for the Province of *Canterbury*."[232] Somner had been Laud's registrar of ecclesiastical courts of

[231] Walton says that Alvie died in 1585 (*ibid.*, p. 45), "27 *Eliz.*" (*ibid.*, p. 47). Keble follows Strype in saying that he died in August, 1584 (I, 26, n. 2), and he is called "deceased" in Inner Temple records for Nov. 3, 1584 (F. A. Inderwick, *A Calendar of the Inner Temple Records* [London, 1896], I, 330–331). The same records refer to Hooker as "now appointed to be master of the Temple" on Feb. 7, 1585 (*ibid.*, p. 333).

[232] *Hooker*, 1665, p. 157.

the diocese of Canterbury, but after the Restoration, when he probably made his attestation for Walton, he had other preferments in Canterbury.[233]

The use which Walton made of Spottiswoode's *History of the Church of Scotland* must also make us chary of saying that Walton saw the value of authoritative history. His note *"Vide Bishop* Spotswoods *Hist. of the Church of Scotl."* refers to one long sentence in the *Life:*

And in *Scotland* they were more confident, for there they declared her [Queen Elizabeth] an *Atheist,* and grew to such an height, as not to be accountable for any thing spoken against her, *nor for Treason against their own King, if spoken in the Pulpit;* shewing at last such a disobedience to him, that his Mother being in *England,* and then in distress, and in prison, and in danger of Death, the Church denied the King their prayers for her: and at another time, when he had appointed a Day of Feasting, the Church declared for a general Fast, in opposition to his Authority.[234]

Walton selected four gaudy, isolated instances from the context of Spottiswoode's account of thirteen years to show the opposition of the kirk to monarchy; he did not go to Spottiswoode to gain an understanding of the history of Scotland but rather to find specific evidence to support his own contention that there was a confederacy between nonconformists in England and Scotland. Spottiswoode had specified that late in 1596 one of the ministers of St. Andrews, David Blake, had called Queen Elizabeth an atheist; he had also said that King James "did not think much of that matter" but desired Blake to appear before his council in order to pacify the English ambassador.[235] He had shown that here and elsewhere the Scots were not insistent upon their unaccountability; they held that *"speeches delivered in pulpit, albeit alledged to be treasonable, could not be judged by the King till the Church took first cognition thereof."*[236] Walton refuses to see that the main question here is the one of what matters come under civil and what under ecclesiastical jurisdiction. In the instance of the Church's declaring a fast when the King wished to hold a feast, he hides the fact that

---

[233] *DNB,* article "William Somner."   [234] *Hooker,* 1665, pp. 57–58.
[235] Spottiswoode, *op. cit.,* p. 420.
[236] *Ibid.,* p. 421. Blake insisted that he must be judged by the Church *"In prima instantia";* he was following the advice of Andrew Melville, almost the very words Melville had used in the winter of 1583. See *ibid.,* p. 330.

the feast was to honor two suspect French ambassadors shortly after the King's detention at Ruthven.[237] Walton plucked his illustrations out of context. He did not go to Spottiswoode for authentic history; he cited him to authenticate his own history.

In the same way, Walton cited Camden only to refute him on the date of Hooker's death and to show his own more accurate information. He used Camden's sentence that the *Polity* deserved to be translated into Latin to add to his catalogue of praises for the work and to mention Bishop Earle and his translation. He used Camden's "very words" to show that Whitgift consecrated his life and labors to God and the Church, but he later gave the wrong volume of Camden as his source.[238] The changes he made in Camden's account of George Cranmer have already been examined. In 1670, he deleted Camden's reference there to Secretary Davison; Davison's name had questionable overtones which Walton did not care to have associated with Cranmer, and he substituted for the name "a Privy Counsellour of note, for an unhappy undertaking."[239] In 1675, he replaced Davison's name, but only after he had added that Davison "became clouded and pitied."[240] Walton did not go to Camden for an authentic account, but, to use his own words, for *"a more Authentick Testimony than my Pen can purchase."*[241]

In writing of Cranmer, Walton had pointed also to the testimony of the Earl of Totnes and of Fynes Moryson. Walton must have assumed or have been told that some mention of Cranmer appeared in *Pacata Hibernia; or, A History of the Wars in Ireland* (1633), which was frequently thought to have been written by George Carew, Earl of Totnes; but there is none. After the *Life* of 1666, the reference to the Earl of Totnes is missing. Walton must have looked at the volume prior to 1670, and he corrected his obvious error. But he retained his reference to the testimony of Fynes Moryson, though he never quoted it. Moryson mentioned Cranmer just twice in the *Itinerary*. He recorded Cranmer's death in a sentence somewhat less than memorable: "Master George Cranmer was killed, betweene Sir William Godolphin and Mast. Henrie Barkely, Master Ram his Lord[ps]. Chaplaines horse was killed, and a Gentle-

---

[237] *Ibid.*, p. 324.

[238] Walton cited "his *Annals*" in *Hooker*, 1666, p. 12; in 1675, he added "of Queen *Elizabeth* (*Lives*, p. 188). The words about Whitgift are in Camden's *Britain* (1610), p. 338.

[239] *Lives,* 1670 (Hooker), p. 23.   [240] *Ibid.*, 1675, pp. 169–170.

[241] *Hooker,* 1665, p. 4.

man of his Lordships chamber, called Master Done (that carried his cloake) shot through the leg." Then he stated that he took Cranmer's place as secretary.[242] It is obvious that Walton referred to the Earl of Totnes and to Fynes Moryson only to establish through them the impression that George Cranmer was highly regarded in high places.

Throughout the *Life,* Walton worked hard to emphasize the closeness of the relationship between Cranmer and Hooker. He took pains to stress their "sacred Friendship" at Oxford; he described Hooker's miseries at Drayton Beauchamp through Cranmer's eyes; he pointed to Cranmer's part in exposing Hooker's blackmailers; he even made Thomas Cranmer, George's father, Hooker's "dear Friend" and a witness of his will; his last words in the Appendix were that Cranmer was Hooker's chief consultant for the *Polity.* Walton did not thus belabor the intimacy of Cranmer and Hooker merely to pay tribute to the deceased uncle of his deceased first wife. He was himself convinced of this intimacy and he thought that his primary qualification in writing the *Life of Hooker* was his inheritance from the Cranmer family. His reliance on Cranmer in the *Life* is evident not only in his frequent mention of him, but also in the use he made of Cranmer's letter. If he cursorily skimmed Spottiswoode's *History,* he thoroughly absorbed Cranmer's letter. His account of nonconformity stems directly from the letter: he followed Cranmer in mentioning Hacket and Coppinger, in speaking of admonitions and satires, in referring to the common people and to the atheists. Even the seed for the passage on Whitgift is in the letter. Walton followed its structure, strengthened its tone, and elaborated its references. And then he printed the letter to "give authority to some things mentioned." When in his Introduction he spoke of his happy affinity with the Cranmer family, he adventitiously mentioned brother George. In the Appendix, he vouched for the authority of Dorothy Spenser's statements and, by indirection, the authority of his *Life* by referring to her as "my Aunt and Sister to George *Cranmer.*"[243]

The difference in Walton's attitude toward the material which was his oral inheritance and that which was authoritatively historical or definitively documented indicates their relative importance to him. The *Life* seems to show Walton's greater respect for

[242] *The Itinerary of Fynes Moryson* (Glasgow, 1907), II, 341, 344.
[243] *Hooker,* 1665, p. 166.

records, a greater reliance upon detailed documentation. It is likely that the increased documentation of the *Life* was an accidental advantage; the sponsors of the *Life* must have spared no effort to make available to Walton all the materials which they thought he needed. It is likely, too, that Walton was far more impressed by the utility of the materials than by their real value and necessary application. Though he used them to enrich the texture of the *Life,* even to shape in places the structure of the *Life,* his primary and fundamental dependence is on materials of another sort. Still, the documentary evidence available to him was important beyond its utility in counteracting Gauden's mistakes and vaguenesses; it made him more conscious than he had hitherto been of the utility of facts. This additional consciousness is not readily apparent in his next venture in biography, the *Life of Herbert* of 1670, but at least Walton made some effort to get the key dates in Herbert's life. And the revisions of the *Lives* in 1670 are factual to an extraordinary degree.

But, in the *Life of Hooker,* as elsewhere, Walton did not basically rely on the facts to lead him to impressions; he used the facts to bolster his own impressions as they had been shaped by oral testimony. Walton was undoubtedly sincere when he wrote that he conceived *"writing to be both a safer and truer preserver of mens Vertuous actions, then tradition,"*[244] but he was ever inclined to put his trust in the *"Little things"* that he *"received by Tradition (to which there may be too much and too little Faith given)."*[245] In the *Life of Hooker,* Walton's too great faith in the little things of tradition led him farthest astray from the truth, but to distrust them would have been to suspect the motives and memories of trusted relations, to disregard Fuller, to reject information which seemed to corroborate what the bishops must have told him of the last three books of the *Polity.* Walton erred greatly in the *Life of Hooker,* and the nature of his error points to his greatest shortcoming as a biographer. But we must not allow the deficiency, serious as it is, to blind us to the artistic effectiveness of Walton's accomplishment. Walton so pointed and so developed his material that his *Life* became a closely integrated and beautifully articulated whole. When, in 1682, Dryden set out to describe the rise of nonconformity in his preface to *Religio Laici,* he went to Walton's *Life of Hooker* and to Cranmer's letter. Anthony à Wood constructed his memoir of

[244] *Lives,* 1670, sigs. A6r–A6v. [245] *Hooker,* 1665, sigs. A6v–A7r.

Hooker for *Athenae Oxonienses* largely from Walton's *Life,* and he paid homage to Walton's labors by appending a sketch of Walton's life to that of Hooker. It is more than coincidence that his memoir of Hooker is directly followed by one of Cranmer. Walton not only accomplished all that the restored churchmen could hope for, but he also created a persuasive picture of Hooker which was on the whole unchallenged for almost three centuries. If Archbishop Sheldon found time to read Walton's book, he must have been mightily pleased.

Chapter 9

The Revisions –
1666, 1670, 1675

THE nature of Walton's chore in the *Life of Hooker* was undoubt-edly responsible for the care which made the *Life* approach com-pleteness in its first version in 1665. When it appeared a second time, as a preface to an edition of Hooker's works in 1666, the *Life* contained no substantial additions and merely a slight change or two of fact.[1] However, Walton made a number of his customary changes to state more precisely what he intended. Some of the changes are extraneous. He had said of the youthful Hooker that "he seemed to be filled with the Holy Ghost even from his Mothers womb";[2] now he added that he seemed "like St. *John Baptist,* to be sanctified" from his mother's womb.[3] He had been content in 1665 to say that Hooker bore the burden of the day "by a quiet gentle submission";[4] he must now add "and resignation of his will to the Wisdom of his Creator."[5] But most of the changes in 1666 are im-provements and serve to convey Walton's meaning more minutely and more exactly. In 1665, he had praised Bishop Jewel by saying that there was in him "a willingness to oblige his Friends."[6] The statement was to Jewel's credit, but it did not reflect well on Hooker to account for Jewel's patronage merely on the basis of Jewel's friendship with Hooker's uncle. Walton remedied this im-pression by saying in 1666 that there was in Jewel a willingness "to do good and oblige his Friends."[7] He had effectively associated

---

[1] See p. 254, n. 123; and p. 257, with n. 147.   [2] *Hooker,* 1665, p. 17.
[3] *Hooker, 1666,* p. 4.   [4] *Hooker,* 1665, p. 25.   [5] *Hooker, 1666,* p. 5.
[6] *Hooker,* 1665, pp. 14–15.   [7] *Hooker,* 1666, p. 3.

Hooker and Saravia in the original version by saying that "their two wills seemed to be but one."[8] In 1666, he went one step farther, for he wished to associate not only the men, but their views on church matters, and he suggested that their wills were "one and the same" with regard to their "designs both for the glory of God, and peace of the Church."[9] His original description of Hooker's bashfulness had been effective, to be sure, in establishing Hooker's real humility,[10] but, lest any reader mistake the significance of his passage, he interpolated, "God and Nature blest him with so blessed a bashfulness,"[11] and there could then be no misunderstanding his point of view. In 1665, he had been content to end the *Life* with a prayer. In 1666, even the prayer, now enlarged, served a more immediate function, for Walton held up Hooker as a pattern for the clergy when he added:

Bless, O Lord, Lord bless his Brethren, the Clergy of this Nation with ardent desires, and effectual endeavors to attain, if not to his great Learning, yet to his remarkable meekness, his godly simplicity, and his Christian moderation: For these are praise-worthy; these bring peace at the last.[12]

And, not satisfied merely to repeat the original prayer, *"Let Glory be to God on high, let Peace be upon Earth, and Good-will to Mankind,"*[13] he said that the glory of God and the desire for peace and good will had been Hooker's design in writing his books, and he asked that God bless this design.[14]

The shortness of the interval between the first and second editions of the *Life of Hooker* had not allowed Walton to verify minor details of a factual kind. When he included the *Life* in the *Lives* of 1670, he tried to rectify minor inaccuracies, and his changes in this year are primarily factual. The degree of his concern for accuracy on this occasion is demonstrated in his willingness even to change his statement that Edwin Sandys was "then almost of the same Age"[15] as Hooker to "not then much yonger"[16] and to add to his statement that Archbishop Sandys entrusted his son to Hooker's tutelage "about twelve moneths"[17] after his resolution to do so,

---

8 *Hooker,* 1665, p. 127.
10 *Hooker,* 1665, pp. 128–129.
12 *Ibid.,* p. 26.
14 *Hooker,* 1666, p. 26.
16 *Lives,* 1670 (Hooker), p. 19.

9 *Hooker,* 1666, p. 22.
11 *Hooker,* 1666, p. 22.
13 *Hooker,* 1665, p. 152.
15 *Hooker,* 1665, p. 23.
17 *Hooker,* 1665, p. 23.

"or not much longer."[18] Walton had said in his original Introduction, *"I am now in the seventieth of my Age,"*[19] and since his seventieth year was in 1662–1663, he was probably writing with some precision. He let this statement stand in 1666, but in 1670 he changed it to *"I am now past the Seventy of my Age."*[20] His particular concern for accuracy in 1670 is demonstrated, too, in his not bothering to change the *"Seventy"* to "eighty" in 1675.[21]

He was meticulous enough in 1670 to say that the Cranmers had only *"a part of their Education"*[22] with Hooker, deleting the *"great"* which had preceded *"part"* in the previous versions.[23] Now, too, he incorporated a fact which had been available to him in Fuller's *Worthies*[24] from the time he composed his first version of the *Life*. He made more precise the place of Hooker's birth, changing "within the Precincts, or in the City, of *Exeter*"[25] to "at *Heavy-tree* near or within the Precincts, or in the City of *Exeter*."[26] He had originally said that Jewel was made Bishop of Salisbury "In the third year"[27] of Elizabeth's reign; despite his specificity here, he was not certain, and in 1670 he wrote "In the second or third Year."[28] He did specify at this time, however, that Jewel died "in *September*," 1571.[29] Walton had stated that Hooker was admitted as one of the twenty scholars of the Foundation of Corpus Christi College, Oxford, "being elected and admitted as born in *Devon-shire*."[30] In 1670, he added "or *Hantshire*"[31] to his statement, perhaps because it glorified Hooker's appointment to make more extensive the field of selection, but also because in this year every additional fact was important to him. This preoccupation with fact is evident in his adding now Cardinal Pole to the list of eminent men who were of the Foundation. Reginald Pole had been created a cardinal in the Roman Catholic Church in 1536, had been appointed Archbishop of Canterbury by Queen Mary in 1556, and had as the single purpose of his life the restoration of the ecclesiastical system shattered by Henry VIII.[32] In 1675, Walton realized how far his concern with fact

[18] *Lives,* 1670 (Hooker), p. 19.

[19] *Hooker,* 1665, p. 3.

[20] *Lives,* 1670 (Hooker), p. 8.

[21] *Ibid.,* 1675, p. 156.

[22] *Ibid.,* 1670 (Hooker), p. 9.

[23] *Hooker,* 1665, p. 4; *Hooker,* 1666, p. 1.

[24] *Worthies,* p. 264. "Richard Hooker was born at *Heavy-tree* nigh *Exeter*."

[25] *Hooker,* 1665, p. 6.

[26] *Lives,* 1670 (Hooker), p. 10.

[27] *Hooker,* 1665, p. 14.

[28] *Lives,* 1670 (Hooker), p. 14.

[29] *Ibid.,* p. 18.

[30] *Hooker,* 1665, pp. 26–27.

[31] *Lives,* 1670 (Hooker), p. 21.

[32] *DNB,* article "Reginald Pole."

five years before had led him, and, though he was willing to retain his statement that Corpus Christi "may glory, that it had Cardinal *Poole*,"[33] he added "but more, that it had"[34] Jewel, Reinolds, and Jackson.

Walton must have scrutinized every fact in the *Life* in preparation for the 1670 edition, and none was too small to merit attention. In the original *Life,* he had explained Hooker's appointment to Boscombe by the Archbishop of Canterbury as taking place during the vacancy of the see of Salisbury "(which was three years betwixt the death of Bishop *Peirce* and Bishop *Caldwells* admission into it)."[35] In 1670, Walton did not overlook even the accuracy of his parentheses, and Bishop Pierce's "death" gave way to his "Translation . . . to the See of *York*."[36] Although he had said in the original *Life* that Hooker was born "about the year of our Redemption 1553,"[37] he had said, too, that Hooker went to Oxford "about the fourteenth year of his age, which was *Anno* 1567."[38] In 1670, "fourteenth" became "Fifteenth."[39] Walton had originally written, concerning the promise made by Hooker's uncle to his schoolmaster that he would make himself responsible for Hooker's education, "This promise was made about the fourth year of the Reign of Queen *Mary*."[40] In 1670, Walton must have seen the improbability that Hooker's schoolmaster had recognized his pupil's talents before he was five years old, and he no longer gave a date for the uncle's promise.[41] But for all his care, Walton did not check his facts systematically or consistently. He never changed his statement that Hooker was, in December, 1573, in the "nineteenth year of his age,"[42] nor, despite his precise knowledge about the time of Hooker's death, did he ever change the information which Whitgift gave King James "that he dyed a year before Queen *Elizabeth*."[43] Nor, as we have already seen in his treatment of the date of Cranmer's travels, was Walton ready to sacrifice an impressive effect for strict accuracy. In 1665, he had stated that a happy marriage was denied "to patient *Job,* and (as some think) to meek *Moses,* and to our as meek and patient Mr. *Hooker*."[44] In 1670, Walton omitted

33 *Lives,* 1670 (Hooker), p. 21.

34 *Ibid.,* 1675, p. 167.

35 *Hooker,* 1665, p. 113.

36 *Lives,* 1670 (Hooker), p. 90.

37 *Hooker,* 1665, p. 7.

38 *Ibid.,* p. 16.

39 *Lives,* 1670 (Hooker), p. 15.

40 *Hooker,* 1665, p. 13.

41 *Lives,* 1670 (Hooker), p. 13.

42 *Hooker,* 1665, p. 26.

43 *Ibid.,* p. 120.

44 *Ibid.,* pp. 41–42.

the parenthesis.[45] To gain a more effective parallel, he blackened Moses' wife as he had Hooker's.

For the only major additions to the *Life*, Walton was indebted to William Fulman. In the original Appendix of the *Life*, Walton had discussed the confusion about the date of Hooker's death and had shown by reference to Hooker's will that his death had taken place between October 26 and December 3 in 1600.[46] Before 1670, Fulman showed him, he says, the inscription which Archbishop Laud had made on the title page of his copy of the *Polity*, and he was able to state not only the exact day, "Novemb. 2." but almost the exact hour, *"circiter horam secundam postmeridianam."*[47] From Fulman, too, Walton received information which he used as the climax of his account of Hooker's eminence at Oxford.[48] He added that Hooker read the Hebrew Lecture at Oxford from 1579 until he left, upon the recommendation of the "Chancellor of the University"[49] that he was excellently qualified to substitute for the indisposed incumbent.[50] Walton then tells for the first time the story of Hooker's expulsion from Oxford, and he reproduces a letter from John Reinolds to Sir Francis Knolles, telling of the expulsion. Walton was willing to include the episode because Reinolds' letter says that he and Hooker and others were expelled *"for doing that which by Oath we were bound to do"* and that *"our Cause is so good, that I am sure we shall prevail by it."*[51] Not only does the letter indicate that injustice has been done, but Reinolds names only Hooker of the four men expelled with him and shows the importance of the case by saying that it is to be heard before the Bishop of Winchester. The episode dramatically demonstrates to what degree Hooker would support what he thought right and shows also that he was considered of some importance in the university. Walton made doubly sure that the expulsion would reflect to Hooker's credit by saying that the men were reinstated within a

---

[45] *Lives,* 1670 (Hooker), p. 31.   [46] *Hooker,* 1665, p. 157.

[47] *Lives,* 1670 (Hooker), p. 113.

[48] Fulman extracted from the convocation register, July 14, 1579, the Chancellor's letter which contains the information related by Walton. (Fulman MSS VIII. 183; noted by Keble, I, 19, n. 1.)

[49] The Chancellor was the Earl of Leicester, and the reason for Walton's suppression of his name is obvious in the light of his treatment of Leicester in the *Life*.

[50] *Lives,* 1670 (Hooker), p. 26.   [51] *Ibid.,* pp. 26–27.

month and by saying that its cause, of which he professed ignorance, was a "pretended" one.[52] He says only that the expulsion was effected by Dr. John Barfoote, chaplain to the Earl of Warwick and vice-president of Corpus Christi. There is, however, reason to believe that Walton knew more than he wished to tell. He received the Reinolds letter, which he dated *"Octob.* 9. 1579"[53] from William Fulman. Fulman commented on the letter, "It should seem that in October 1580, J. B. took occasion to expel J. R. and others: though I once thought it to be in 1579, and so told Mr. Walton, who thereupon added the year, which was not in the copy, but in the margin."[54] Not only did Fulman give the letter to Walton, then, but the men also discussed the matter of its date. It is likely that they discussed, too, the circumstances leading to the expulsion and that Fulman sufficiently enlightened Walton on these matters, for he had in his possession at least fourteen letters relating to them.[55] He probably told Walton that Reinolds, Hooker, and others remonstrated against the appointment of Dr. Barfoote to succeed Cole in the headship of Corpus Christi, and that there was a group, supported even by Sir Francis Walsingham, which wished Reinolds himself installed as head in case of a vacancy. Reinolds was willing enough to give up his own aspirations, but objected to Barfoote because he was an orthodox Church disciplinarian. Hooker's expulsion, then, points directly to his early Calvinist leanings. Not for nothing was Walton silent on the cause. He was happy to include the episode for what it revealed of Hooker's importance at Oxford, but he did not wish to jeopardize his picture of Hooker as the champion of conformity by indicating his youthful nonconformist tendencies. Despite Walton's desire to be accurate in all the facts which he included in the *Life,* he did not feel compelled to include those which did not serve his purpose. The oneness of the *Life of Hooker,* like that of the *Life of Donne* and the *Life of Wotton,* is dependent upon the omission of all material in opposition to or not relevant to Walton's predetermined view of the men about whom he wrote.

But not all the changes in 1670 are of a factual kind. Despite the emphasis on fact, Walton continued to rework the *Life* for nicety

[52] *Ibid.,* p. 27.   [53] *Ibid.*
[54] Fulman MSS IX. 182. The letter itself is in Fulman MSS IX. 180. Noted in Keble, I, 20, n. 1.
[55] In Fulman MSS IX, briefly calendared by Keble, I, 114–116.

of expression and impression, and some of his changes apparently show an inclination to revise even more thoroughly than before. To be sure, most of the changes are typical; they could be made by inserting a caret: nouns are coupled, Biblical allusions and small platitudes added, and phrases expanded for increased smoothness of diction and definiteness of impression. There are, however, revisions of a less typical kind here; there appears to be a willingness, unusual in Walton, to revise drastically.

The original passage in which Hooker asks Whitgift for a transfer from the Temple to a quiet place for the purpose of writing the *Polity* had been straightforward and appealing:

The foundation of these Books were laid in the Temple; but he found it no fit place to finish what he had there designed; and therefore solicited the Arch Bishop for a remove, saying, *When I lost the freedom of my Cell, which was my College, yet I found some degree of it in my quiet Country Parsonage: but I am weary of the noise and oppositions of this place; And indeed God and Nature did not intend me for Contentions, but for Study and quietness: I have begun a work in which I intend the Justification of our Laws of Church-Government, and I shall never be able to finish it, but where I may Study, and pray for Gods blessing upon my indeavours, and keep my self in Peace and Privacy, and behold Gods blessing spring out of my Mother Earth, and eat my own bread without oppositions; and therefore if your Grace can Judge me worthy such a favour, let me beg it, that I may perfect what I have begun.*[56]

In 1666, Walton added very substantially to the passage: he related the writing of the *Polity* much more closely to the controversy with Travers; he indicated something of Hooker's preparations; he defined more exactly the questions in which Hooker was interested:

My Lord, my particular Contests here with Mr. Travers, *have prov'd the more unpleasant to me, because I believe him to be a good Man; and that belief hath occasioned me to examine mine own Conscience concerning his opinions; and, to satisfie that, I have consulted the holy Scripture, and other Laws, both Humane and Divine, Whether the the [sic] Conscience of him, and others of his Judgment, ought to be so far complied with us, as to alter our Frame of Church-Government, our manner of Gods worship, our praising and praying to him, and, our establisht Ceremonies, as often as their tender Consciences shall require us.*[57]

In his typical manner, he expanded what Hooker intended in the *Polity*, referred specifically to Cartwright and Travers as reasonable

[56] *Hooker*, 1665, pp. 111–112.   [57] *Hooker*, 1666, p. 19.

adversaries, and emphasized Hooker's preparations by mentioning them a second time:

And, in this Examination, I have not onely satisfied my self; but have begun a Treatise, in which I intend the satisfaction of others, by a demonstration of the reasonableness of our Laws of Ecclesiastical Polity; *and therein laid a hopeful foundation for the Churches Peace; and, so as not to provoke your Adversarie Mr.* Cartwright, *nor Mr.* Travers, *whom I take to be mine (but not my enemy) God knows this to be my meaning. To which end, I have searched many Books, and spent many thoughtful hours; and I hope not in vain; for I write to reasonable men.*[58]

Ever wishing to make what was clear doubly so, he specified in this version that Hooker's request was for *"some quiet Countrey Parsonage."* He added one of his common sentiments of piety as a further reason for the request:

A place where I may without disturbance, Meditate my approaching Mortality, and that great account, which all flesh must at the last great day, give to the God of all Spirits.   this is my design; and, as these are the desires of my heart, so they shall by Gods assistance be the constant indevors of the uncertain remainder of my life.[59]

In his normal fashion, he changed the end of the speech to make even more explicit Hooker's plea to Whitgift:

And therefore if your Grace can think me and my poor labors, worthy such a favour? Let me beg it, that I may perfect what I have begun: which is a blessing I cannot hope for in this place.[60]

When Walton was revising this part of the *Life* in 1670, he followed his version of 1666, only omitting the *"holy"* before *"Scripture,"* to the point at which he has Hooker state what he intends; at that point he reverted abruptly to the 1665 version.[61] The large omission which resulted had not been, to be sure, brilliant writing, but it contained changes which were completely in accord with Walton's tendencies in revising. Why were these omitted? Is it possible that in 1670 Walton thought that he had sufficiently indicated Travers to be the spur which instigated the *Polity* and that it was therefore unnecessary to refer again to him and to introduce Cartwright into the passage? Is it possible that he thought that his account of Hooker's studies sufficiently implied the extent of

---

[58] *Ibid.*   [59] *Ibid.*, pp. 19–20.   [60] *Ibid.*, p. 20.
[61] *Lives,* 1670 (Hooker), p. 89.

Hooker's labors? Did he see on this occasion that his platitude added piety without sufficiently pointing to Hooker's purpose, that it was perhaps to Hooker's greater credit to be granted a favor on his own merit and without reference to his *"poor labors,"* that his last clause was entirely superfluous? The omissions may well be thought to improve the passage, but to admit Walton's purposefulness in making them is to admit at this point that he consciously changed his habits of revision. Still, if the omissions were accidental, Walton might have included them in 1675. This he did not do. Indeed, he substituted for them a passage which explicitly mentioned in connection with Hooker's purpose in writing, as did that of 1666, the words "Ecclesiastical Polity," and which piously iterated his statement made in the preceding passage that Hooker's wish was to satisfy, not provoke, the nonconformists.[62] The piety of this statement he emphasized by using, even as he had in 1666, a reference to *"the last great day."*[63] The compensation in 1675 for the omissions made in 1670 might, then, indicate that the omissions were purposeful, for had they been accidental, we should expect the 1675 passage to contain more than echoes of 1666.

Another passage, however, may shed light on this problem, for its history closely parallels that of this one. In 1665, Walton had said in his account of the opinions and activities of the nonconformists:

In which number of Non-conformists, though some might be sincere and well-meaning men, yet of this Party there were many that were possest with an high degree of Spiritual wickedness; I mean with an innate radical Pride and Malice; I mean not those lesser sins that are more visible and more properly carnal, as Gluttony, & Drunkenness, and the like, (from which good Lord deliver us;) but sins of an higher nature, more unlike to the nature of God, which is Love, and Mercy, and Peace; and more like the Devil, (who cannot be drunk, and yet is a Devil) those wickednesses of Malice, and Revenge, and Opposition, and a Complacence in working and beholding Confusion, which are more properly his work, and greater sins, though many will not believe it; Men

[62] *Hooker,* 1665, p. 110: "intending therein to shew such Arguments as should force an assent from all men, if Reason, delivered in sweet Language, and voyd of any provocation, were able to doe it."

[63] *Lives,* 1675, p. 210: *"I intend a Justification of the Laws of our Ecclesiastical Polity: in which design God and his holy Angels shall at the last great day bear me that witness which my Conscience now does; that my meaning is not to provoke any, but rather to satisfie all tender Consciences, and I shall never be able to do this, but where I may Study."*

whom a furious Zele and Prejudice had blinded, and made incapable
of hearing Reason, or adhering to the ways of Peace; Men whom Pride
and a Self-conceit had made to overvalue their own Wisdom, and become
pertinacious, and dispute against those Laws which they ought to obey;
Men that labour'd and joyed to speak evil of Government, and then to
be the Authors of Confusion; whom Company, and Conversation, and
Custom had blinded, and made insensible that these were Errours; and
at last became so hardened, that they died without repenting these
spiritual wickednesses.

And in these times which tended thus to Confusion, there were also
many others that pretended a Tenderness of Conscience, refusing to
take an Oath before a lawful Magistrate; and yet in their secret Conventicles did covenant and swear to each other, to be faithful in using
their best endeavours to set up the Presbyterian Discipline. To which
end there were many that wandered up and down, and were active in
sowing Discontents and Sedition, by venemous and secret Murmurings,
and a Dispersion of scurrilous Pamphlets and Libels against the Church
and State, but especially against the Bishops: by which means, together
with indiscreet Sermons, the Common people became so Phanatick, as
to believe *the Bishops to be Antichrist,* and the onely Obstructers of
Gods Discipline; and then given over to such a desperate delusion, as
to find out a Text in the *Revelation of S. John,* that *Antichrist was to
be overcome by the sword.* So that those very men, that began with
tender and *meek Petitions,* proceeded to *Admonitions,* then to *Satyrical
Remonstrances,* and at last, having numbered who was not, and who was,
for their Cause, they got a supposed Certainty of so great a Party, that
they durst threaten *first the Bishops,* then *the Queen and Parliament;*
to all which they were secretly encouraged by the *Earl of Leicester,* then
in great favour with her, and the reputed Cherisher and Patron general
of these pretenders to Tenderness of Conscience; his Design being by
their means to bring such an *odium* upon the *Bishops,* as to procure an
Alienation of their Lands, and a large proportion of them for himself:
which Avaritious desire had so blinded his Reason, that his ambitious
and greedy Hopes had almost put him into present possession of *Lambeth-
house.*[64]

Walton's changes in 1666 had been typical: there are more than a
score of them, varying in kind and importance from the addition of
a rather lengthy scriptural allusion to a more definite reference to
an already clear subject, from the coupling of adjectives to the
artful pointing up of a meaningful contradiction:

[64] *Hooker,* 1665, pp. 52–57.

In which number of Non-conformists, though some might be sincere and well-meaning men, whose indiscreet zeal might be so like Charity, as thereby to cover a multitude of Errors, yet of this Party there were many that were possest with an high degree of Spiritual wickedness; I mean with an innate restles radical Pride and Malice; I mean not those lesser sins that are more visible and more properly Carnal, and sins against a mans self, as Gluttony, and Drunkenness, and the like, (from which good Lord deliver us;) but sins of an higher nature; because more unlike to the nature of God, which is *Love*, and *Mercy*, and *Peace;* and more like the Devil: (who is not a glutton nor can be drunk; and yet, is a Devil:) those wickednesses of Malice, and Revenge, and Opposition, and a Complacence in working and beholding Confusion (which are more properly his work, who is the Enemy and disturber of mankind, and greater sins, though many will not believe it) Men whom a furious Zeal and Prejudice had blinded, and made incapable of hearing Reason, or adhearing to the ways of Peace; Men whom Pride and Self-conceit had made to overvalue their own Wisdom, and become pertinacious, and to hold foolish and unmannerly disputes against those Men which they ought to Reverence, and those Laws which they ought to obey; Men that laboured and joyed to *speak evil of Government,* and then to be the Authors of Confusion (of Confusion as it is Confusion:) whom Company, and Conversation, and Custom had blinded, and made insensible that these were Errours: and at last became so restless, and so hardened in their opinions, that like those which perisht in the gain-saying of *Core,* so these dyed without repenting these spiritual wickednesses, of which *Coppinger* and *Hacket,* and their adherents are too sad testimonies.

And in these times which tended thus to Confusion, there were also many others that pretended a Tenderness of Conscience, refusing to submit to Ceremonies, or to take an Oath before a lawful Magistrate: and yet these very Men did in their secret Conventicles, Covenant and Swear to each other, to be assiduous and faithful in using their best endeavours to set up a Church Government that they had not agreed on. To which end, there was many Select parties that wandered up and down, and were active in sowing Discontents and Sedition, by venemous and secret Murmurings, and a Dispersion of scurrilous Pamphlets and Libels against the Church and State; but especially against the Bishops: by which means, together with very bold, and as indiscreet Sermons, the Common people became so Phanatick, as St. *Peter* observed, there were in his time, *some that wrested the Scripture to their own destruction:* so by these men, and this means many came to believe *the Bishops to be Antichrist,* and the onely Obstructers of Gods Discipline; and many of them were at last given over to such desperate delusions, as to find

out a Text in the *Revelation of* St. *John, that Antichrist was to be overcome by the sword,* which they were very ready to take into their hands.
So that those very men, that began with tender *meek Petitions,* proceeded to print publick *Admonitions;* and then to *Satyrical Remonstrances;* and at last, (having like *David* numbred who was not, and who
was, for their Cause,) they got a supposed Certainty of so great a Party,
that they durst threaten *first the Bishops,* and not long after, both *the
Queen and Parliament;* to all which they were secretly encouraged by
the *Earl of Leicester,* then in great favour with her Majestie, and the
reputed Cherisher and Patron-general of these Pretenders to Tenderness of Conscience; whom he used as a sacreligious snare to further his
Design, which was by their means to bring such an *odium* upon the
Bishops, as to procure an Alienation of their Lands, and a large proportion of them for himself: which Avaritious desire had at last so blinded
his Reason, that his ambitious and greedy Hopes had almost flattered
him into present possession of *Lambeth-house.*[65]

In 1670, Walton continued to make changes in his normal fashion.
He added to God's qualities of love, mercy, and peace that of order,[66]
and thereby further emphasized the ungodliness of the nonconformists. Men who had "a Complacence in working and beholding
Confusion" were more sharply characterized by being called instead "Men that joyed to be the Authors of misery."[67] Men whom
"Pride and *Self-conceit,* had made to overvalue their own pitiful,
crooked wisdom"[68] were additionally called "the dregs of Mankind."[69] The reference to Coppinger and Hacket was expanded.[70]
In the first paragraph, too, there are three meaningful omissions.
The reference to "the nature of God, which is *Love"* was made more
concrete in "God, who is the God of *love."*[71] The meaningless parenthesis, "of Confusion as it is Confusion," was dropped.[72] Walton
had already sufficiently characterized the nonconformists as men
whom "Company, and Conversation, and Custom had blinded,"
and his addition to his sentence here made it much too unwieldly.
He therefore omitted calling them also "so restless, and so hardened
in their opinions," and compensated for the omission by referring
to their "sins" instead of their "Errours."[73]

Although Walton's revisions in the first paragraph are in keeping

[65] *Hooker,* 1666, p. 10.   [66] *Lives,* 1670 (Hooker), p. 37.
[67] *Ibid.*
[68] *Ibid.,* pp. 37–38. The adjectives are not in the sentence in 1666.
[69] *Ibid.,* p. 37.   [70] *Ibid.,* p. 38.   [71] *Ibid.,* p. 37.   [72] *Ibid.,* p. 38.
[73] *Ibid.*

with his usual method, his handling of the second paragraph is almost completely atypical. In the first change here, he strangely omitted that the nonconformists refused "to submit to Ceremonies," which he had added in 1666, coupling it with their refusal to take an oath. Why he should want to drop it in 1670 is unexplainable. His second change is highly artful. He had written in 1665 that despite the nonconformists' refusal to take an oath, "yet in their secret Conventicles [they] did covenant and swear to each other, to be faithful in using their best endeavours to set up the Presbyterian Discipline." In 1666, he had made the nonconformists even more ridiculous by further indicating their contradictory behavior in saying that they swore "to be assiduous and faithful in using their best endeavours to set up a Church Government that they had not agreed on." In 1670, he retained the additional ridicule while specifying, as he had in 1665, their goal: "assiduous and faithful in using their best endeavours to set up the *Presbyterian Doctrine* and *Discipline;* and, both in such a manner as they themselves had not yet agreed on."[74] But with this fine change, the revisions cease, and the rest of the paragraph reverts to the original version, omitting all the changes and additions made in 1666. Why should Walton wish to drop his pointed comment on the nonconformists' literal interpretation of the sword that was to overcome Antichrist in St. John, "which they were very ready to take into their hands"? Why should he wish to delete his description of Leicester's design as a "sacreligious snare," or change his statement that Leicester's hopes had almost "flattered" him into present possession of Lambeth-house back to the flat "put" of the first version?

Although Walton's omissions in the first paragraph are meaningful and can be accounted for, those in the second paragraph cannot easily be explained. Why, if they are accidental, did Walton not include them in 1675? It can be shown that he had probably forgotten about them. When he revised this passage in 1675, he made only his customary slight changes. He smoothed the syntax of his sentence, "Men that joyed to be the Authors of misery, which is properly his work that is *the enemy and disturber of Mankind;* and, greater sins than *Gluttony* or *Drunkenness,* though some will not believe it"[75] by ending it "and thereby, greater sinners then the *glutton* or *drunkard,* though some will not believe it."[76] In typical fashion, "the dregs of Mankind" became "the very dregs and pest of

74 *Ibid.*   75 *Ibid.,* p. 37.   76 *Ibid.,* 1675, p. 182.

Mankind." In his desire to be eminently clear, Walton imposed a redundant logic on his statement, "Men, that labour'd and joyed to find out the faults, and to speak evil of Government," and it became "Men, that labour'd and joyed first to find out the faults, and then to speak evil of Government." He made even more obvious his belief in the insincerity of the nonconformists by calling them "scruple-mongers."[77] The three other changes made in this passage in 1675 are doubly interesting because not only are they typical revisions, but they all echo, as it were, revisions which had been made in 1666 and omitted in 1670. It is as though Walton, having forgotten the changes of 1666, vaguely recovered ideas which had occurred to him nine years before; as though certain objects on a once familiar, but now forgotten road, produced in him semblances of impressions which he had experienced before. In 1666, Walton had referred to the "very bold, and as indiscreet Sermons" of the nonconformists. In 1670, he went back to the original "indiscreet Sermons."[78] But in 1675, he used "venomous and indiscreet Sermons."[79] After quoting in 1666 the belief of the nonconformists that *"Antichrist was to be overcome by the sword,"* he had stated "which they were very ready to take into their hands." In 1670, he omitted this comment, but it reappeared in different form in 1675. He had introduced the text from St. John by saying that some nonconformists were given over to such a desperate delusion as to find it; in 1675, the echo of the omission came to him and he wrote that some of them were given over to "so bloody a Zeal"[80] and such other desperate delusions as to find the text. Walton's last change is the most interesting. It reveals more clearly that the omissions in 1670 were accidental; it reveals that Walton forgot that he had once added to the passages and that only a kind of residuum remained in his mind. In 1666, he had compared the nonconformists, numbering "who was not, and who was, for their Cause," to David. He had in mind the story of Absalom's revolt against David in II Samuel 13–19. Chapter 18:1 reads, "And David numbered the people that were with him, and set captains of thousands and captains of hundreds over them." Although Walton's reference was accurate, it was not a very apt one, for he compared opposites in the nonconformists and David. He omitted the simile in 1670, but he recollected the numbering for the cause in 1675. In this year, how-

[77] *Ibid.*   [78] *Ibid.*, 1670 (Hooker), p. 39; *Hooker,* 1665, p. 55.
[79] *Lives,* 1675, p. 183.   [80] *Ibid.*

ever, the precise Biblical passage had escaped him and the artist in him led him to connect the rebel of the story with the nonconformists. He erred technically in attributing the numbering for the cause to Absalom,[81] but his blunder was on the side of art.

We need not merely assume that Walton normally used the last printed version of a *Life* as the basis of a revision. An examination of his changes shows that most of those in any *Life* were made by the insertion of carets in the preceding version. The changes in the *Life of Hooker* of 1675, then, stem from the 1670 version. Had Walton been aware that he had in 1670 reverted for two passages to the 1665 *Life of Hooker,* we would almost certainly have had in 1675 the reproduction of the many changes of 1666 and an additional number of refinements on them and extensions of them. Since the two passages contain in 1675 only what appear to be the recollected overtones of some of the changes of 1666, it is likely that Walton had in 1675 forgotten the changes of 1666. That some overtones do appear in 1675 points to accidental omission in 1670. It is possible that in 1670 Walton had occasion to refer to the 1665 version in addition to that of 1666. Indeed, we have noticed that he incorporated the words, "Presbyterian Discipline," which were in the 1665 *Life,* into the 1670 version, joining them effectively with his 1666 passage. Since the wholesale omissions in 1670 begin in the sentence following that in which this joining was made, it may be that Walton accidentally copied the rest of the passage from the 1665 *Life.* A like error may perhaps be presumed for the second passage in which a large omission occurred in 1670.

These passages, then, are probably not indicative of any purposeful willingness on Walton's part to revise drastically in 1670. The revisions that Walton made in the first paragraph of his account of nonconformity and many like them do indicate, however, that he was in this year interested in making more than changes of fact. His preoccupation with factual accuracy in this year overshadowed but did not suppress his effort to shape his meaning more precisely.

By 1675, Walton was almost completely satisfied with both his fact and his expression. His revisions and additions when the *Life of Hooker* was to appear a second time in the collected *Lives* are picayune and, in the main, unnecessary. The attention which he now paid to mere trifles shows that he thought that more important matters had been adequately treated. His reference to "the Mother

[81] *Ibid.*

of S. *Augustine*"[82] was preceded in this year by her name, "*Monica*."[83] He had said of Bishop Jewel that he "changed this for a better Life. Which may be believed, for that as he lived, so he died, in devout meditation and prayer."[84] In 1675, he was hardly satisfied to let a pronoun do the work of a noun, and even less satisfied with an indefinite relative; he therefore inserted "happy change"[85] after "Which." He was not content to say merely that Archbishop Sandys resolved that his son Edwin was to be "Pupil to Mr. *Hooker, though his Son Edwin* was not then much yonger,"[86] but he must clarify: "*Edwin* was not much younger then Mr. *Hooker* then was."[87] Walton was anxious not only to extend a comparison that was abundantly clear but even to cite a source that was obvious. He had said that Hooker gave Mrs. Churchman "such a power as *Eleazar* was trusted with when he was sent to chuse a Wife for *Isaac*";[88] now he added, "(you may read it in the book of *Genesis*)."[89] It is typical of him that he was not willing to assume his reader's knowledge or understanding even of Genesis, but he must here, too, point the way for him. He had written that the severities of Elizabeth's church and state would have been inexcusable "if it had not been to prevent Confusion, and the perillous consequences of it; which, without such prevention, would have been Ruine and Misery to this numerous Nation."[90] In 1675, he felicitously elaborated the character of the confusion, but he wished to make even more clear his argument that confusion was at the root of ruin and misery. His desire to lead the reader from step to step caused him to state ineptly that the first consequence of confusion is confusion: "if it had not been to prevent the gangrene of Confusion,[91] and the perillous consequences of it; which, without such prevention, would have been first Confusion, and then Ruine and Misery to this numerous Nation."[92] It would appear for a moment that Walton was aware of his restless tendency to pile

---

[82] *Hooker*, 1665, p. 17.

[83] *Lives*, 1675, p. 163.

[84] *Hooker*, 1665, p. 20.

[85] *Lives*, 1675, p. 164.

[86] *Ibid.*, 1670 (Hooker), pp. 18–19.

[87] *Ibid.*, 1675, p. 165.

[88] *Hooker*, 1665, p. 40.

[89] *Lives*, 1675, p. 175.

[90] *Ibid.*, 1670 (Hooker), p. 40.

[91] Gauden, writing of Hooker's design in the *Polity*, had said that "he collects and applies what he thinketh most proper to stop the Gangreen of Faction" (Gauden, p. 17).

[92] *Lives*, 1675, p. 185.

phrase on phrase and that he tried to counteract it. He had made Hooker say in his thankful prayer of deliverance from his black-mailers:

When false witnesses were risen up against me, when shame was ready to cover my face, when I was bowed down with an horrible Dread, and went mourning all the day long, when my nights were restless, and my Sleeps broken with a fear worse than Death, when my Soul thirsted for a deliverance, as the Heart panteth after the rivers of waters, then thou Lord didst hear my Complaints.[93]

Lovely as the passage is, Walton probably saw that he was out-psalming the psalms, and in 1675 he omitted, "when I was bowed down with an horrible Dread, and went mourning all the day long" and "and my Sleeps broken with a fear worse than Death."[94] But the usual inclination was too strong in him, and he made the customary elaboration later in the passage. After "I will . . . mag-nifie thy mercies, who didst not give me over as a prey to mine enemies"[95] he added, *"the net is broken and they are taken in it."*[96]

These revisions and others even less significant show again Walton's desire to make all transitions for his reader, to provide every link. No detail was too minute, no statement too clear to merit his attention. If Walton's satisfaction with the *Life of Hooker* is evident in 1670, when the minuteness of the factual changes reveals anew the care that went into the original version, it is doubly evident in 1675, when there remained little for him to do but refine to such a degree that he overwrote. Walton was never one to rely on under-statement, but the redundant changes in 1675, which go beyond the substitution of explicit statements for eminently clear implied ones, are an index to his realization that he had performed his chore well. Certainly, any great errors in the *Life* would have been corrected before it was allowed to stand as a preface to Hooker's works in 1666, but, indeed, such had been Walton's care that great changes were not necessary. Despite, then, the Church's pleasure with the *Life* in 1666, Walton continued to revise in 1670 and in 1675, for artistic considerations were no less important to him than his considerations for the Church. In writing the *Life of Hooker*, Walton was, to be sure, a semiofficial biographer, and as such he

---

[93] *Hooker*, 1665, p. 142.
[95] *Hooker*, 1665, pp. 142–143.
[94] *Lives*, 1675, p. 223.
[96] *Lives*, 1675, p. 224.

fulfilled his obligations, but his incessant changes indicate that he never considered his artistic obligations completely satisfied.[97]

[97] The Yale copy of the 1675 *Lives* with corrections and alterations in Walton's hand has two interesting annotations by Walton in the *Life of Hooker*. The first of these, on the verso of the blank leaf before the *Life* reads, "whipt them out of the temple with a divine indignation." It probably shows Walton's dissatisfaction with his awkward statement in Whitgift's speech that Christ "himself made the Whip to drive the Prophaners out of the Temple" (*Hooker*, 1665, p. 72). In the second change Walton substituted a precise word for an inexact one. He had written in 1665, "For in that [the time of Hooker's youth], Children were less pregnant, less confident, and more malleable, than in this wiser, but not better, Age" (*ibid.*, p. 9). There is no reason to believe that Thomas Zouch, who edited the *Lives* in 1796, ever saw the Albert H. Childs-Yale copy of the 1675 *Lives,* but his edition has this note (p. 207, n. q) on the sentence, "The age was, perhaps, not wiser, though it might be more knowing in some respects." It would have pleased Zouch had he known that though the sentence remained unchanged throughout the editions of the *Life,* Walton, in the Yale copy, scratched out "wiser" and wrote in its place "more [kn]o[w]ing" (*Lives,* 1675, p. 159).

PART IV

The Compleat Parson, or,
The Religious Man's Occupation

Chapter 10

The "Almost Incredible Story" of George Herbert

THE *Life of Herbert,* perhaps even more than the *Life of Donne,* was a labor of love. The *Life of Hooker* was in many ways Walton's most arduous biographical task; the *Life of Herbert* conformed most closely to the desires of his heart. It appeared early in 1670, and, like the *Life of Hooker,* it was published independently. Within two months and without textual changes by Walton, it was printed a second time in the collected *Lives.*[1]

Its appearance was the culmination of Walton's long interest in Herbert. He had quoted from Herbert's verses as early as the *Compleat Angler* of 1653. Piscator would give a sweet conclusion to his discourse on the active and contemplative merits of angling and to his short contemplation of rivers by citing some lines from "that holy Poet Mr. *George Herbert* his Divine Contemplation on Gods providence."[2] Piscator's twelve lines are a pretty, self-contained unit, made by citing three of Herbert's thirty-eight stanzas called "Providence" with the alteration of their order and with some minor verbal changes.[3] Piscator also quotes in its entirety with a few variations Herbert's "Vertue," to show what "holy Mr. *Herbert*

---

[1] Citations to the *Life of Herbert,* 1670, will be made from *Lives,* 1670, because it is more readily available, though it can be shown that the independent version appeared first. See Appendix D.

[2] *Compleat Angler,* 1653, p. 19.

[3] Walton uses lines 141–144, 29–32, and 25–28. His l. 1 has *"Lord"* for "But," l. 3 has *"they"* for "which," l. 7 has *"does"* for "dost" and *"strangely"* for "strongly," and l. 8 has *"Whilst"* for "While" and *"end"* for "will."

saies of such dayes and Flowers as these."[4] In citing both these poems, Walton referred to Herbert as "holy." He reveals his affection for Herbert when he has Viator add to his speech of thanks to Piscator for reciting "Vertue" that he believes Herbert loved angling "because he had a spirit sutable to Anglers, and to those Primitive Christians that you love, and have so much commended."[5]

There is further indication of Walton's early interest in Herbert in his acquaintance with Christopher Harvey, vicar of Clifton in Warwickshire from 1639 to 1663. The second edition of the *Compleat Angler* (1655) contains commendatory verses signed "C. H., Master of Arts";[6] the fifth edition (1676) identifies the poet as *"Ch. Harvie."*[7] In the second edition, too, Piscator said, after being thanked for his rendition of "Vertue,"

> And since you like these Verses of Mr. *Herberts* so well, let mee tell you what a Reverend and Learned Divine, that professes to imitate him, (and has done so most excellently) hath writ of our *Service Book,* which I know you will like the better, because he is a friend of mine, and I am sure no enemy to *Angling.*[8]

Piscator then quoted in full Harvey's poem, "The Book of Common Prayer."[9] Even as Walton has Piscator call Harvey "friend" here, so Harvey referred to Walton as "friend" in his commendatory poem. That the friendship arose from Walton's admiration of Harvey's *The Synagogue,* which was frequently bound with *The Temple,* is made clear in Walton's commendatory verses for the third edition of *The Synagogue* (1657).[10] Walton's interest in Herbert led to interest in his imitator, and the verses themselves furnished Walton with the sentiment thrice revised on the inside cover of his *Eusebius* which probably represents his first jottings for the *Life of Herbert,* some dozen years before he wrote it.

Walton had quoted Herbert's verses in 1653 and had eulogized Herbert in his verses to Harvey in 1657. In 1658, his interest in Herbert poured over into the revised *Life of Donne.* His immediate purpose was to add to the piety of his picture of Donne by indicating a sympathy of inclination between him and Herbert, whose piety,

---

[4] *Compleat Angler,* 1653, p. 119.   [5] *Ibid.,* p. 120.
[6] *Ibid.,* 1655, sig. A9^v.   [7] *Ibid.,* 1676, sig. A8^r.   [8] *Ibid.,* 1655, p. 158.
[9] The inclusion of verses which justified the Book of Common Prayer was a measure of partisan daring during the Commonwealth. Walton even mangled one of Harvey's lines to take an even more positive position: he changed "Should choose to do it so" to *"Should do it so."*
[10] See Appendix A.

it will be shown, was more popularly acknowledged. The Herbert portrayed here is the holy man pictured in the *Compleat Angler,* and here, too, Walton's love for *The Temple* is clear:

And in this enumeration of his friends, though many must be omitted, yet that man of primitive piety Mr. *George Herbert* may not, I mean that *George Herbert,* who was the Author of the *Temple* or *Sacred Poems and Ejaculations.* (*A book,* in which by declaring his own spirituall Conflicts he hath raised many a dejected and discomposed soul, and charmed them into sweet and quiet thoughts: *A book,* by the frequent reading whereof, and the assistance of that Spirit that seemed to inspire the Author, the Reader may attain habits of *peace* and *piety,* and all the gifts of the *Holy Ghost* and *Heaven;* and by still reading, still keep those sacred fires burning upon the Altar of so pure a heart, as shall be freed from the anxieties of this world, and fixt upon things that are above).[11]

This image of Herbert corroborates that of 1653; both reveal Walton's essential conception of Herbert and are printed proof of his interest in Herbert.

But it is likely that Walton's interest in Herbert was previous to these proofs in print. In 1651, Walton had in the *Life of Wotton* made Wotton liken his position upon being made deacon to that of Emperor Charles V:

I thank *God* and the *King,* by whose goodness I now am in this condition: a condition, which that great Emperour *Charls* the fifth, seem'd to approve: who, after so many remarkable Victories, when his glory was great in the eyes of all men, freely gave his *Crown* and the cares that attended it, to *Philip* his son, making a holy retreat to a cloysterall life, where he might by devout *meditations* consult with *God* (which the rich or busie men seldome doe) and have leasure both to examine the errors of his life, and prepare for that great day, wherein all flesh must make an account of their actions.[12]

The *Compleat Angler* of 1661 makes a reference in passing to Charles V,[13] and the revised *Life of Donne* of 1670 also refers gratuitously to him.[14] Walton's most extended account of Charles V

[11] *Donne,* 1658, pp. 81–82.   [12] *Reliq.,* 1651, sig. c5ᵛ.
[13] *Compleat Angler,* 1661, p. 118.
[14] *Lives,* 1670 (Donne), p. 19: "And though the *Lord Chancellor* did not at Mr. *Donnes* dismission, give him such a Commendation as the great Emperour *Charles* the fifth, did of his Secretary *Eraso,* when he presented him to his Son and Successor *Philip* the Second. . . ."

appears in the *Life of Herbert,* and here Walton refers also to his Cavalier Valdesso, the author of *The Hundred and Ten Considerations.* He says that he is indebted for his account of Valdesso to "a Friend, that had it from the mouth of Mr. *Farrer.*"[15] The story of the abdication of Charles V and of his entering a monastery does not appear only in Walton,[16] but it is odd to find him mentioning Charles V in three of the *Lives* and in the *Compleat Angler.* His statement that he received his account of Valdesso from a friend who got it from Nicholas Ferrar probably reveals the source of his information about Charles V and of much of his information about Herbert and shows that a great deal of the material which appeared in the *Life of Herbert* was gathered prior to 1650. The Ferrars, it is known, were particularly fascinated by Charles V, in whose renunciation of the world they probably saw an early parallel of their own situation. The *Story Books* of Little Gidding refer occasionally to him,[17] and one of these five volumes, yet unprinted, is entitled *Charles V his Relinquishment of this World.*[18] In translating *The Hundred and Ten Considerations,* Ferrar included the address to the reader of Coelius Secundus Curio, who was responsible for the Italian translation. Ferrar therefore believed that "John Valdesso *was by Natiõ a Spaniard of noble kindred of an honourable degree, and a resplendent Chevalier of the Emperour*" who became a resplendent Chevalier of Christ.[19] Walton, following the account related by Ferrar's friend, also calls Valdesso "a

[15] *Ibid.* (Herbert), p. 73.

[16] Herbert certainly has Charles V in mind in the fourth stanza of "Content," and Barnabas Oley uses an ancedote about him in his "A Prefatory View of the Life of Mr Geo. Herbert" prefixed to *Herbert's Remains,* 1652, sigs. a7v–a8r.

[17] See E. Cruwys Sharland, ed., *The Story Books of Little Gidding* (New York, 1899), pp. 15–16, and B. Blackstone, ed., *The Ferrar Papers* (Cambridge, 1938), pp. 150, 174, 187.

[18] Sharland, *op. cit.,* p. vii; Blackstone, *op. cit.,* p. xxi. An extract appears in Mansfield D. Forbes, "Nicholas Ferrar: America & Little Gidding," ch. ix of *Clare College 1326–1926* (Cambridge, 1928–1930), II, 523–533.

[19] [Juán de Valdés], *The Hundred and Ten Considerations of Signior John Valdesso: treating of those things which are most profitable, most necessary, and most perfect in our Christian Profession. Written in Spanish, Brought out of Italy by Vergerius, and first set forth in Italian at Basil by Coelius Secundus Curio, Anno 1550, Afterward translated into French, and Printed at Lions 1563, and again at Paris 1565. And now translated out of the Italian Copy into English, with notes. Whereunto is added an Epistle of the Authors, or a Preface to his Divine Commentary upon the Romans* (Oxford, 1638), sig.***r.

Cavalier."[20] The Italian translator, Ferrar, and Walton fall into the error of confusing Juán de Valdés with his brother Alonso, who was knighted in the service of Charles V.[21] But there is further reason to suppose that Walton relied on the oral account of "a Friend" for his knowledge of Valdesso and Charles V. Walton says that Ferrar translated Valdesso's book "out of *Spanish*";[22] Ferrar's title page says that he used the Italian translation. Also, Walton has Valdesso and the Emperor renounce the world simultaneously. Charles V resigned the Netherlands and Spain to his son Philip in 1555–1556 and abdicated in favor of his brother Ferdinand in 1557. Curio's address to the reader says that Valdesso died in Naples about the year 1540.[23] It is highly probable, then, that Walton did not consult the Valdesso volume in 1670 and that his account is based on the blurred recollection of his friend's words.[24]

The friend was unquestionably Ferrar's first cousin and the executor of Herbert's will, Arthur Woodnoth, although Walton does not name him. How Walton became acquainted with him is not known, but he was a goldsmith in Foster Lane when Walton was practicing his trade at Fleet Street and Chancery Lane. Woodnoth, like Walton, had a greater than normal interest in the paths of sanctity, and his intimacy with the Ferrars was probably responsible for his wish at one point to enter orders.[25] Not only their status as men of business but also their holy inclinations would have made Walton and Woodnoth congenial to each other. Woodnoth was strongly attached to his aunt Mary Woodnoth Ferrar and to his cousins, and, indeed, had arranged the purchase of Little Gidding for Mrs. Ferrar in 1625.[26] The Ferrars had long been in-

---

[20] *Lives,* 1670 (Herbert), p. 72.   [21] *Works of Herbert,* p. 566.

[22] *Lives,* 1670 (Herbert), p. 72.

[23] In fact, Juán de Valdés died in 1541, his brother Alonso in 1532. *Works of Herbert,* p. 567.

[24] Peter Peckard's version of the renunciation of Valdesso and Charles V in his *Memoirs of the Life of Mr. Nicholas Ferrar* (Cambridge, 1790), pp. 215–216, is without doubt a paraphrase of Walton's account. Peckard does not cite Walton's *Life of Herbert,* but his statement, "This account stands upon the authority, and is nearly in the words of Mr. Nich. Ferrar," is merely a strengthening of Walton's own words about his source.

[25] Woodnoth wrote to Ferrar on Oct. 13, 1631, "[Herbert] told me we were much troubled about words for the Name of a Divine wold satisfy all when in truth I might doo the office tho I wanted the tytle" (Blackstone, *op. cit.,* p. 267; see also p. 77).

[26] See *DNB,* article "Arthur Wodenote." In recounting events of the year

terested in the Virginia Company,[27] and Woodnoth probably became a member through them before 1623.[28] One of the members of the Company, Sir John Danvers, was certainly well known to the Ferrars by 1619,[29] and he may have met Woodnoth about this time. There is no reason to believe that Woodnoth knew Danvers' stepson, George Herbert, this early, but it is likely that he knew him from 1626 on. Woodnoth was frequently at Little Gidding, and Herbert apparently delegated to him some of the responsibility for rebuilding Leighton Church, six or seven miles away.[30] Before October, 1631, Woodnoth was employed by Danvers, probably as a

---

1625, John Ferrar writes about Little Gidding as "a Lordship that his Mother had bought a year before" (Blackstone, *op. cit.,* p. 24), but H. P. K. Skipton writes that "it is certain that the formalities were not completed until May 30, 1625, when the indentures of sale were signed by Thomas Sheppard, Arthur Woodnoth, and Nicholas Ferrar" (*Life and Times of Nicholas Ferrar* [London, 1907], p. 82).

[27] The elder Nicholas Ferrar was one of the incorporators of the second Virginia Charter in 1609. See Alexander Brown, *The Genesis of the United States* (Boston and New York, 1890), I, 221. John Ferrar joined the Virginia Company after 1612 and was the deputy treasurer from April 28, 1619, to May 22, 1622. Nicholas Ferrar bought shares in the Company in March, 1619, and was deputy treasurer from May 22, 1622, to July, 1624 (*ibid.,* II, 890).

[28] Woodnoth was not connected with the Virginia Company prior to 1612 since he is not one of the incorporators of the third Virginia Charter of that year. A "Mr Woodnutt" was present at an Extraordinary Court of the Company on Oct. 20, 1623. See Susan Myra Kingsbury, ed., *The Records of The Virginia Company of London* (Washington, 1906–1935), IV, 290–291.

[29] Danvers first subscribed to the Virginia Company in 1611 (Brown, *op. cit.,* I, 466) and was a member of His Majesty's Council for the Company prior to 1617 (*ibid.,* II, 796). On June 14, 1619, he and John Ferrar were appointed to a "Comittie of choice Gentlemen" to consider the founding of a college in Virginia for "the trayning and bringing up of Infidells children to the true knowledge of God & understanding of righteousness" (Kingsbury, *op. cit.,* I, 231, 220).

[30] Nicholas Ferrar promised to assist Herbert by having his brother John supervise the workmen thrice weekly and provide them with materials (Blackstone, *op. cit.,* p. 58). Woodnoth was probably in charge of finances. In an unprinted letter (in the library of Magdalene College, Cambridge) to Nicholas Ferrar, received on March 25, 1632, Woodnoth writes that he and Sir Henry Herbert have secured from the Duchess of Lennox £100 for the repair of Leighton Church (*Works of Herbert,* p. 584). In a letter written the same month to Ferrar, Herbert concludes, "you write very lovingly that all your things are mine, If so, Let this of Leighton Church the care, be amongst the chiefest also, so also have I required Mr W. for his part" (Blackstone, *op. cit.,* p. 78). In his will, Herbert bequeathed £20 to Woodnoth, "whereof fifteene pound shalbe bestowed uppon Leighton Church" (*Works of Herbert,* p. 382).

steward.[31] Although Walton never credits Woodnoth with providing information for the *Life of Herbert,* his many references to
Woodnoth and the large part Woodnoth is made to play in the *Life*
make it evident that Woodnoth furnished him with substantial
knowledge of Herbert.[32]

The crucial moments of Herbert's life are told through the
medium of Woodnoth. Walton praises Woodnoth highly, for,
"having attain'd so much [wealth] as to be able to shew some
mercy to the Poor, and preserve a competence for himself, he
dedicated the remaining part of his life to the service of God,"[33]
and he says that Woodnoth was a useful friend to Herbert and his
parents. Woodnoth appears actively as a character in the *Life* as
one of the benefactors of Leighton Church, and again in time to
accompany Herbert to Bemerton not long after his marriage. Woodnoth, Walton says, saw Herbert prostrate before the altar at his
induction into Bemerton; he says that Herbert told Woodnoth that
he made rules for himself before the altar, and Walton relates
Herbert's resolutions as they were told to Woodnoth that very night.
Walton says that the *Country Parson* fell into Woodnoth's hands
at Herbert's death and that he gave it to Barnabas Oley, who
published it. Woodnoth enters the *Life* actively again three weeks
before Herbert's death, and he becomes the eye-witness through
whom the last words and last moments of Herbert are related. Walton's debt to Woodnoth is implicit in the extent to which Woodnoth
hovers over the second half of the *Life*. Woodnoth was dead by
1651; Walton's reliance upon him in the *Life* is indicative of particular interest in Herbert twenty or more years before his *Life*.[34]

[31] Danvers came into possession of the estate of Lavington, Wiltshire, through
his second marriage on July 10, 1628, to Elizabeth Dauntsey (*DNB,* article
"Sir John Danvers") and probably employed Woodnoth to help him straighten
out his finances. Woodnoth maintained his trade and attempted to restrain
Danvers' extravagances. His lack of success apparently bothered him, and he
sought Herbert's advice about his future career: should he give up trade, should
he devote all his time to Danvers' problems, should he enter the church? See
Woodnoth's letter to Nicholas Ferrar, Oct. 13, 1631, with "Mr Herberts reasons
for Arth. Woodenoths Living wth Sr Jhon Da[n]vers" in Blackstone, *op. cit.,*
pp. 266–270. Woodnoth is called "a true friend and Servant to Sir John Danvers" on page 1 of his pamphlet, *A Short Collection of the Most Remarkable
Passages from the originall to the dissolution of the Virginia Company* (London, 1651).

[32] See Appendix E.   [33] *Lives,* 1670 (Herbert), p. 35.

[34] It is quite likely that Walton talked to Woodnoth before the outbreak of

That interest may have stemmed from his interest in Donne. He had, indeed, heard Donne preach his sermon of commemoration for Lady Danvers on July 1, 1627, and the letters of "amity" between Donne and Magdalen Herbert (of which he said he had many[35]) probably whetted his interest in the Herbert family. His high esteem for Magdalen Herbert is evident in the *Life of Herbert*. But it is not necessary to predicate his interest in Herbert upon either Donne or Mrs. Herbert. As a lover of verse, particularly holy verse, he must have been fascinated by *The Temple* when it was published in 1633. Although he did not care for the abstruse conceits of the metaphysical poets, he was undoubtedly attracted by the seeming simplicity of Herbert's verse. He would have been attracted, too, by Herbert's emphasis on ritual and ceremony and by his nonquestioning of fundamentals. The intensity of feeling in the poems coupled with the resignation and obedience and quiet of their endings would have appealed to the man who advised his readers to study to be quiet, and these were doubtless the qualities that he equated with primitive piety. Walton's interest in Herbert must have increased with the growing popularity of his verse, and it must have been fired by the contemporary view of Herbert

---

the Civil War. Woodnoth was deputy to the governor of the Bermuda Company in 1644 (J. H. Lefroy, *Memorials of the Discovery and Early Settlement of the Bermudas or Somers Islands 1515–1685* [London, 1877], I, 590). His pamphlet on the Virginia Company was published in 1651, the year that Sir John Danvers was made Governor of the Bermuda Company. His defense of Danvers' conduct in the concerns of the Virginia Company and the general tone of the pamphlet support the statement of its publisher that Woodnoth was a Parliamentarian. Walton knew that Sir John Danvers was a regicide, and he never mentions Danvers by name in the *Life;* Danvers is "a Noble Gentleman, the brother and Heir of the Lord *Danvers* Earl of *Danby*" *(Lives,* 1670 [Herbert], p. 13). Walton left London in May, 1643, was probably out of the city during most of 1644, and until the Restoration probably lived as frequently out of London as in it (Arthur Munson Coon, "The Life of Izaak Walton" [Cornell University unpublished dissertation], pp. 122, 124, and ch. vi). Since he was never an investor in the Bermuda Company, and since he was out of London, he probably never knew of Woodnoth's deputy governorship. He may never have seen Woodnoth's pamphlet nor have known that Woodnoth was a Parliament sympathizer, for in the *Life* he praises Woodnoth for his retirement from trade and for his service to God. That his relationship with Woodnoth was only casual is suggested by his giving Woodnoth's name as "John" in the *Life* of 1670. That the relationship existed prior to the war seems apparent in the sympathetic portrayal, for Walton is hardly so kind to those whom he knew to be on the other side.

[35] *Lives,* 1670 (Herbert), pp. 18–19.

as a man. Nicholas Ferrar's statement in his preface to *The Temple* strikes the note of the contemporary estimate; he says that Herbert's faithful discharge of God's service was such "as may make him justly a companion to the primitive Saints, and a pattern or more for the age he lived in."[36] Not only was George Herbert's name a byword for the holy life in his last years and after his death, but so at a time when the priesthood as a profession was looked down upon.[37]

Had Walton written the *Life of Herbert* in 1650, he would probably have been content merely to portray Herbert as a pattern of primitive piety. But during the Civil War and the Commonwealth, he had had to be satisfied with only occasional reference to opinions dear to him, with such expressions of his beliefs as he could insert covertly in the *Life of Wotton* of 1651 and in the *Life of Donne* of 1658; in the *Compleat Angler* he had been forced to content himself with reminiscence of the good old days, to make his brief for the Book of Common Prayer within the covers of a fishing tract. His conception of Herbert had not changed by 1670, but the intervening years caused the *Life* to be more than the narration of Herbert's holy life. It was to carry additional freight. Walton had been able to express his Anglicanism fervently and openly in the *Life of Hooker,* but he was yet restricted by the nature of his task. Not until the *Life of Herbert* was he able to give the widest latitude to the expression of his own ideas and beliefs. This *Life* amongst all of them is a labor of love, and that Walton considered it so is clear in his calling it a free-will offering. The *Life of Herbert* represents the full flowering of ideas that had been stunted for twenty years. Those ideas were in part reinforced by Oley's Preface to the *Country Parson.* Oley's Preface was carefully conceived, if badly written, and it was an attempt to recall the clergy to their sense of duty. The appearance of the Preface was probably influential in making Walton unsatisfied with portraying Herbert only as a model and led him to indicate in detail how the model could be followed. The purpose of Oley's Preface mingled with Walton's proclivities to give the *Life of Herbert* the slant it has.

In many ways the *Life of Herbert* is the highly personalized han-

---

[36] *Works of Herbert,* p. 3. See also Hutchinson's discussion, pp. xxxix–xliv.
[37] See Oley's "Prefatory View," sigs. a11ᵛ–a12ʳ; H. C. Beeching, ed., *George Herbert's Country Parson* (Oxford, 1898), pp. xvi–xvii, and Herbert's chapter, "The Parson in Contempt."

dling of ideas which had attracted Walton earlier. The slightest
acquaintance with Walton is sufficient to reveal his interest in the
Church. Of the five men whose lives he wrote, four had entered
orders, and the other had considered doing so and had been made
deacon. His family life was tied up with the Church: his first wife
numbered an archbishop among her ancestors; through his influence his brother-in-law Thomas Ken became interested in the
Church and had a fine career;[38] he intended his only son who
reached manhood for the Church and saw him become in 1678
domestic chaplain to Seth Ward, Bishop of Salisbury;[39] his only
daughter married about 1670 Dr. William Hawkins, a prebendary
of Winchester and rector of Droxford in Hampshire.[40] A list of his
clerical friends would contain many names, a number of them distinguished. Apart from his interest in Herbert engendered by his
poetry and his friendship with Donne, Walton's interest is the logical outcome of his preoccupation with church matters.

For all his interest in the Church, Walton was all his life a layman, and one of his most lively interests was the relationship between the churchman and the laity for whom he was responsible.
It was not enough to say that Donne was a brilliant preacher; Walton must indicate the effect of Donne's sermons on his listeners. It
was not enough to tell that Wotton was a deacon; Walton must
show the deacon influencing the boys of Eton with his apothegms.
This interest led to the detailed account of Hooker's relationship
with his parishioners, for it was in the country parson that Walton
found the most direct manifestation of the relationship between
church and laity. Walton's interest in the country parson was dual
in nature: he was interested in the influence which the parson exerted on his parish from the pulpit and in the influence which he
had more directly in the community because of his position, his
rather more personal relationship with his parishioners. Walton
concerned himself with both these aspects in the *Life of Hooker*.
He says that Hooker's sermons were "neither long nor earnest, but
uttered with a Grave zeal, and an humble voyce" and that

the design of his Sermons . . . was to shew Reasons for what he spake;
and with these Reasons such a kind of Rhetorick as did rather convince

[38] Ken, Bishop of Bath and Wells from 1685 to 1691, was half-brother to
Anne Ken, Walton's second wife. He was a youngster of ten when his sister
married. He was at one time chaplain to Bishop Morley of Winchester
[39] Wiltshire *Notes and Queries*, IV (1902–1904), 293–294.
[40] *Compleat Walton*, pp. 591–592.

and perswade, than frighten men into Piety; Studying not so much for matter (which he never wanted) as for apt Illustrations to inform and teach his unlearned hearers by familiar Examples, and then make them better by Convincing Applications; never laboring by hard words, and then by needless Distinctions and sub-distinctions to *amuse* his hearers, and get glory to himself: But glory only to God.[41]

On the other hand, he quotes Hooker to the effect that *"the Life of a pious Clergy man was visible Rhetorick,"* and he tells of his visits to the sick and to the distressed, his diligence to prevent lawsuits.[42] In the last of the *Lives,* that of Sanderson, Walton again concerned himself with the twin duties of the country parson. He says that Sanderson did not trouble his parishioners "by preaching high and useless notions, but such plain truths as were necessary to be known, believed, and practised, in order to their salvation."[43] And, in speaking of Sanderson, he explicitly indicated that he did not think that the parson's duties were circumscribed by the chapel:

And this excellent man did not think his duty discharged by only reading the Church Prayers, Catechizing, Preaching, and administring the Sacraments seasonably; but thought (if the Law or the Canons may seem to injoyn no more, yet) that God would require more than the defective Laws of man's making, can or does injoyn; the performance of that inward Law, which Almighty God hath imprinted in the Conscience of all good Christians, and inclines those whom he loves to perform. He considering this, did therefore become a law to himself, practising what his Conscience told him was his duty, in reconciling differences, and preventing Law-suits, both in his Parish and in the Neighborhood. To which may be added his often visiting sick and disconsolate Families, perswading them to patience, and raising them from dejection by his advice and chearful discourse, and by adding his own Alms, if there were any so poor as to need it.[44]

In both the *Life of Hooker* and the *Life of Sanderson,* Walton was concerned mainly with other things, with Hooker as apologist of the Church of England and with Sanderson as ideal and representative bishop, but his preoccupation with the relationships of church and laity affected both the *Lives.* The preoccupation was able to be developed fully in the *Life of Herbert,* for Herbert, of all the men whom Walton wrote about, was exclusively a country parson. The views which were put forth summarily in the *Life of Hooker* were

[41] *Hooker,* 1665, pp. 133–134.   [42] *Ibid.,* pp. 134–137.
[43] *Sanderson,* 1678, sig. c8^v.   [44] *Ibid.,* sigs. c8^v–d^v.

fully elaborated in the *Life of Herbert* and spilled over into the
Life of Sanderson.

But Walton's ideas on the ideal country parson were not the only
personal freight that the *Life of Herbert* was made to carry. Even
as Herbert served to illustrate Walton's views here, he was to illustrate another persistent idea which Walton had expressed long before but which he was now to develop fully. Walton would ask with
Donne:

> What function is so noble, as to bee
> Embassadour to God and destinie?
> To open life, to give kingdomes to more
> Than Kings give dignities; to keepe heavens doore?[45]

In his poem to Mr. Tilman after he had taken orders, Donne takes
cognizance of the disrepute of the clergy and has no sympathy for
the view that orders are beneath the dignity of a gentleman:

> Why doth the foolish world scorne that profession,
> Whose joyes passe speech? Why do they think unfit
> That Gentry should joyne families with it?
> As if their day were onely to be spent
> In dressing, Mistressing and complement;
> Alas poore joyes, but poorer men, whose trust
> Seemes richly placed in sublimed dust;
> (For, such are cloathes and beauty, which though gay,
> Are, at the best, but of sublimed clay)
> Let then the world thy calling disrespect,
> But goe thou on, and pitty their neglect.

Walton's admiration for this poem has already been mentioned, and
it will be remembered that in the *Life of Donne* (1658) he had
Thomas Morton say to Donne in order to induce him to enter the
Church, "*Remember,* Mr. *Donne,* no mans education or parts make
him too good for this employment, *which is to be an Ambassadour
for him who by a vile death opened the gates of life to mankind.*"[46]
He had Donne say, too, "my refusall is not for that I think my self
too good for that calling, for which Kings, if they think so, are not
good enough."[47] But Walton's first statement on this subject is
earlier than 1658; his interest and his attitude are well defined in
the *Life of Wotton.* Indeed, it may be that Walton's interest in

---

[45] "*To* Mr Tilman *after he had taken orders," Poems, By J. D.,* 1635, p. 370.
[46] *Donne,* 1658, p. 29.　　　　[47] *Ibid.,* p. 30.

Wotton was occasioned by his being a man of worldly reputation and excellent antecedents who had joined the Church. Certainly the digression on Nicholas Wotton in the *Life* was determined to a large degree by this interest, for Nicholas was simultaneously eminent churchman and eminent statesman. Sir Henry Wotton was himself aware of the attitude of his day toward churchmen, and at his becoming deacon he wrote to King James, "I comfort my self also with this Christian hope, That Gentlemen and Knights Sons, who are trained up with us in a Seminary of Church-men, (which was the will of the holy Founder), will by my example, (without vanity be it spoken) not be ashamed, after the sight of Courtly Weeds, to put on a Surplice." Walton printed this letter in its entirety in *Reliquiae Wottonianae,* 1651 (pp. 384–388), and it undoubtedly inspired the passage in the *Life of Wotton* in which Walton made Wotton justify his action by drawing a parallel between himself and Emperor Charles V. This passage is not only indicative of Walton's interest in men of nobility and affairs who joined the Church, but it demonstrates that his interest in Charles V was stirred because he provided a most efficacious example. In George Herbert, Walton found a man who came from a noble line connected to the powerful Pembroke family, a man of education who was prominent in his university, a man who was early in life of the courtly circle, and, withal, a man who became a country parson. The *Life of Herbert,* then, became among other things an illustration of the thesis that the Church was a profession not below the dignity of men of talent and education and family.

That the propagation of this idea was one of Walton's purposes (if not the main one) in the *Life of Herbert* is not only evident in the *Life* itself but enforced by its peripheral adjuncts. Walton chose as a motto for the *Life* words from the Wisdom of Solomon, *"He pleased God, and was beloved of him: so that whereas he lived among sinners, he translated him."* Because he looked upon the clerical profession as the highest attainment possible for a man regardless of his birth and ability, he saw in Herbert's ultimate choice a translation from sin to blessedness. The attitude which accounts for the motto also accounts in part for the Introduction to the *Life,* in which Walton cites the story of the change in Mary Magdalene. He justifies his use of the story with the explanation that even as Christ rewarded Mary by preserving her memory through a record of her deeds, so he has endeavored to preserve the

memory of Donne and Wotton, and now Herbert. But there is little
doubt that his reason for citing the story was that in his own mind
he saw a parallel between it and the story of George Herbert: and
what they have in common is the translation from the worldly to
the spiritual life. The motto and the introduction, then, illustrate
Walton's belief in the high place of devotees of piety; all others are
sinners whether they be prostitutes or well-born university orators
who move in courtly circles. But there is more external evidence that
Walton was in the *Life of Herbert* making a brief not only for the
dignity of the clerical profession, but also more specifically a brief
that it was not beneath the dignity of the well born and the talented.
Charles Cotton's commendatory poem prefixed to the collected
Lives of 1675 contains his impression of what Walton demonstrates
in the *Life of Herbert:*

> *And* Herbert: *he, whose education,*
> *Manners, and parts, by high applauses blown,*
> *Was deeply tainted with Ambition;*
>
> *And fitted for a Court, made that his aim:*
> *At last, without regard to Birth or Name,*
> *For a poor Country-Cure, does all disclaim.*

Cotton's stressing in his précis of the *Life of Herbert* the extent of
Herbert's renunciation of his worldly advantages when he entered
the Church indicates an awareness of the nature of the point that
Walton sought to make.

Walton's point of view is probably reflected, too, in Oley's new
Preface to *Herbert's Remains,* 1671. Even as Oley's second paragraph was a correction of Walton's history of the manuscript of the
Country Parson, so his fifth section is a more vehement statement
of Walton's purpose. There Oley deals with a book entitled *The
Grounds and Occasions of the Contempt of the Clergie* by T. B.[48] He
admits that T. B. has rightly censured *"divers things worthy of
Reproof,"* but he thinks that T. B. has overreached his intent in
drawing so vivid a picture of the contempt of the clergy. He would
chastize T. B. if his book *"shall (by Accident only) deterr but one
Ingenuous youth, one Hopeful Gentleman, one Noble man of good
and great Endowments, from Entring into Holy Orders."* This
quotation shows the kind of man that Oley had in mind, and he

---

[48] Grosart ascribes the book, published in 1670, to John Eachard (*Complete
Works of George Herbert,* III, 259).

seeks to counteract T. B.'s book by a compliment to the nobility for their discernment: *"Though the vulgar, ordinarily do not, yet The Nobility and Gentry do distinguish and abstract the Errors of the man, from the Holy Calling, and not think their dear Relations degraded by Receiving H. Orders."* Oley goes far beyond Walton in his argument that nobility is compatible with taking orders. He lists contemporary men of good birth who entered orders or were inclined to orders, saying even that Henry VIII was designed by his father to be Archbishop of Canterbury if his brother Arthur had lived to succeed to the crown. He says that such men as he mentions have cast a luster upon the clergy, that height of birth gives a nobleman or a gentleman considerable advantage over a clerk of lower parentage in doing God's service, for his influence on the people is more powerful. But Oley goes beyond this in his propagandizing; he is not jesting when he holds out to the nobility his crowning inducement to look favorably upon the Church as a profession: *"Our Laws give that privilege to Higher Birth, which a man of meaner descent must stay, and Study, and perform divers Exercises for, by the space of Fourteen years. To be a Knights son, born in Wedlock, is as good a Qualification for some preferments, as to be a Batchelor in Divinity."* He states in his *"Address to the Nobles"* that his first two purposes are to persuade them "1. To think the Priesthood a Function not unworthy of them, or their Relations. 2. To Look upon the Patrimony of the Church, as a Good provision for their own dear Children." Walton's *Life of Herbert* of 1670 probably led to the inclusion of the new preface in *Herbert's Remains* of 1671, and there is little doubt that its fifth section is an explicit statement of what Walton would do by implication.

The structure of the *Life of Herbert* makes it evident that Walton was interested in more than writing of Herbert as a pattern for posterity to imitate, that he was interested not merely in telling the story of Herbert's life, but, by his use of Herbert as the prototype of the good parson, in making abundantly clear what he considered the function and practices of the parson to be, and, by his relation of Herbert's birth and capacities and his entrance into orders, in providing support for his feeling that the Church was a worthy profession for men of the highest station, education, and abilities. These two theses dominate the gross design of the *Life*. Its first third is devoted to showing the eminence of Herbert's family, his brilliance in the university and great promise of success in the temporal world as they are climaxed in his oratorship and in the King's favor; and in a minor key Walton plays upon the strain of Herbert's virtue and holiness which is to culminate in his choice of the religious life. The last half of the *Life* covers only the last three years of Herbert's life and is in part a character of the good country parson, based on Herbert's *Country Parson,* and in part a more highly particularized account of Herbert himself as the good country parson.

Walton shows that Herbert was of a family "that hath been blest with men of remarkable wisdom, and with a willingness to serve their Countrey, and indeed, to do good to all Mankind; for which, they were eminent."[49] He demonstrates the temporal brilliance of the family, devoting (as might be expected) as much space to Edward, Lord Herbert of Cherbury, as to all the others of Herbert's brothers and sisters. In George Herbert's early education Walton emphasizes his pretty behavior and wit and says that "he seem'd to be marked out for piety, and to become the care of Heaven, and of a particular Angel to guard and guide him."[50] He tells of the care that Herbert's mother took to select for him at Trinity College, Cambridge, a tutor who would see that he retained "that virtue and innocence which her advice and example had planted in his mind."[51] Before resuming his account of Herbert's years at Cambridge, Walton tells of Herbert's mother, in a section larger than the part of the *Life* that precedes. This digression was probably dictated by Walton's interest in her and in her relations with Donne rather than by any wish to show the illustriousness of Herbert's parentage. After telling of her widowhood and remarriage, Walton concentrates on her residence in Oxford. His statement that there her wit, cheerful gravity, and obliging behavior led her into acquaintance with most people of eminent worth or learning about the university ends "and particularly, with Mr. *John Donne.*"[52] The rest of this section, in which Walton quotes from "The Autumnall" and presents a letter and a sonnet from Donne to Mrs. Herbert, describes their friendship. Walton returns to Herbert, giving some account "of his disposition, and of the employment of his time, till he was Master of Arts, which was *Anno* 1615."[53] To show that Herbert consecrated the first fruits of his early age to virtue and the serious study of learning, Walton quotes from Herbert's New Year's

49 *Lives,* 1670 (Herbert), p. 9.   50 *Ibid.,* p. 12.   51 *Ibid.,* p. 13.
52 *Ibid.,* p. 15.   53 *Ibid.,* p. 22.

gift to his mother on first going to Cambridge, a letter in which he reproves love poetry and consecrates his abilities in poetry to God's glory, and two sonnets in testimony of his sentiment. Walton offers explicit comment at this point to fortify his account of Herbert's inclinations:

In this morning of that short day of his life, he seem'd to be mark'd out for vertue, and to become the care of Heaven; for God still kept his soul in so holy a frame, that he may, and ought to be a pattern of vertue to all posterity; and especially, to his Brethren of the Clergy, of which the Reader may expect a more exact account in what will follow.[54]

Briefly, he lists Herbert's scholastic achievements and tells of his love for music. He is then sufficiently ingenuous to note Herbert's faults:

If during this time he exprest any Error, it was, that he kept himself too much retir'd, and at too great a distance with all his inferiours; and, his cloaths seem'd to prove, that he put too great a value on his parts and parentage.[55]

Walton probably felt that he could thus emphasize Herbert's consciousness of his station because he had already underlined his holy propensities; he knew, too, that he must emphasize Herbert's expression of his inheritance if Herbert was to serve as an example to the nobility that the church was a fit occupation for them.

Walton then relates the story of Herbert as University Orator, the high point in his temporal career. He stresses the importance of the position by telling of the careers of Herbert's predecessors: Sir Robert Naunton became secretary of state and Sir Francis Nethersole secretary to Queen Elizabeth of Bohemia. Herbert's qualifications for the office, Walton says, were great learning, high fancy, civil and sharp wit, and natural elegance, and he expresses his intention of giving three illustrations of these traits, his real purpose being to associate Herbert with the most eminent members of the courtly circle. He tells of Herbert's letter of thanks to King James upon the presentation of his *Opera Latina* to the university and of the resulting commendations by the King and by William, Earl of Pembroke. His next illustrations not only demonstrate Herbert's eminence as Orator, but were doubtless chosen because they prove, too, Herbert's interest in church affairs and in churchmen. In one, Walton tells of Herbert's showing his great abilities and

[54] *Ibid.*, p. 21. [55] *Ibid.*, p. 22.

also "his great affection to that Church in which he received his *Baptism*" in his answering the satirical poetry of Andrew Melville against the traditional liturgy, ceremonies, and church government. In the other, he shows again Herbert's favor in the eyes of the King through the King's request that Herbert attend him at Royston, and he shows, too, Herbert's friendship with Bacon and Andrewes. Bacon, Walton says, usually desired Herbert's approbation before he sent his books to press, and he dedicated his verse translation of the Psalms to Herbert as the best judge of divine poetry; Andrewes talked with him about predestination and the sanctity of life and treasured all his life a long letter written in Greek by Herbert. Sir Henry Wotton and John Donne are mentioned as Herbert's friends, and the story of the seal Donne sent to Herbert is retold. Walton paints a glowing picture of the promise of Herbert's career as a courtier. Herbert, he says, had at this time learned the Romance languages in preparation for a place as a secretary of state, and his friendship with the King and nobility, his love of court conversation, and his ambition drew him from Cambridge to attend the King. Herbert's favor with the King is shown in the gift of a sinecure, and the favor is magnified by identifying the sinecure with that which Queen Elizabeth had given to her favorite, Sir Philip Sidney. How decidedly temporal Herbert's desires were Walton demonstrates by saying that the sinecure and other income allowed Herbert to enjoy his genteel humour for clothes and courtly company and also that Herbert turned over to a proxy all his oratorical duties at Cambridge unless the King himself was present. Except for his mother's insistence, Walton says, Herbert would have severed his university ties, for he thought that study injured his health; Walton quotes from "Affliction I" to prove what Herbert thought his own inclination to be. He says that Herbert's court hopes died with the deaths of the Duke of Richmond, the Marquis of Hamilton, and King James, but he shows, nevertheless, that Herbert's renunciation of the painted pleasures of court life was not compulsory, that he carefully weighed at this time the courtly life and the holy one. How intense the conflict was Walton indicates only by indirection: "These were such Conflicts, as they only can know, that have endur'd them; for, ambitious Desires, and the outward Glory of this World, are not easily laid aside; but, at last, God inclin'd him to put on a resolution to serve at his Altar."[56]

[56] *Ibid.,* p. 31.

Walton's next section is transitional, linking the brilliant and worldly courtier with the holy country parson. It starts as Herbert, voicing Walton's own sentiments, answers a friend whom he had acquainted with his resolution to enter sacred orders and who had told Herbert that it was "too mean an employment, and too much below his birth, and the excellent abilities and endowments of his mind":

It hath been formerly judg'd, that the Domestick Servants of the King of Heaven, should be of the noblest Families on Earth: and, though the Iniquity of the late Times have made Clergy-men meanly valued, and the sacred name of Priest contemptible; yet, I will labour to make it honourable, by consecrating all my learning, and all my poor abilities, to advance the glory of that God that gave them; knowing, that I can never do too much for him, that hath done so much for me, as to make me a Christian. And I will labour to be like my Saviour, by making Humility lovely in the eyes of all men, and by following the merciful and meek example of my dear Jesus.[57]

Herbert's first step on the road to becoming a man of God was to be made deacon; his next was his acceptance of the prebend of Leighton Ecclesia and his resolution to repair the church at Leighton Bromswold. His earnestness at this time is demonstrated in his disobeying his mother when she objected to his undertaking the reconstruction of a church with his weak body and empty purse. Walton names Herbert's benefactors and devotes much space to Arthur Woodnoth as a man of the world who set limits to his wealth and devoted the remainder of his life to the service of God. Herbert's behavior during a long illness in his thirty-fourth year showed, Walton says, that "he was inclinable to bear the sweet yoke of *Christian Discipline*,"[58] and at his recovery Herbert declared his resolution both to marry and to enter orders. His resignation of the oratorship gives Walton another opportunity to show not only the eminence of the position but also that another incumbent turned to the church instead of the state, for he points out that Herbert's successor was Robert Creighton, who became Dean of Wells. The account of Herbert's marriage is prefaced by a short view of his person in which Walton says that Herbert's speech and motion declared him to be a gentleman, but a meek and obliging one. Walton tells that Herbert and Jane Danvers were married three days after they first met and he feels obliged to show in some detail that

[57] *Ibid.*, pp. 31–32.   [58] *Ibid.*, p. 36.

the match was not a *"Love-phrensie,* or worse." He then relates the circumstances of the offer to bestow Bemerton upon Herbert and of his subsequent induction. Perhaps with one eye on the rush of the marriage, Walton says that apprehension of the responsibility of a cure of souls made Herbert fast and pray and consider for not less than a month. Again he indicates only by indirection the intensity of Herbert's struggle, which resolved him to decline the offer: *"He endur'd* (as he would often say) *such spiritual Conflicts, as none can think, but only those that have endur'd them."*[59] But he makes Herbert's induction inevitable: one evening the Earl of Pembroke talked to Bishop Laud about Herbert; the next day Laud told Herbert it was a sin to refuse the offer;[60] by the following day a tailor had finished the necessary ceremonial clothes; and the same day, April 26, 1630, Davenant, Bishop of Salisbury, gave Herbert institution.

Walton stops at this important moment to prepare (in italics) his reader for *"an almost incredible story, of the great sanctity"* of the remainder of Herbert's holy life. If St. Chrysostom, he says, could have written the story, *"there would then be no need for this Age to look back into times past for the examples of primitive piety; for they might be all found in the life of* George Herbert." Not only does he here state explicitly his hagiographic intent, but he also reveals, not too obliquely, the motivation of the *Life:* "[I] *profess my self amaz'd, when I consider how few of the Clergy liv'd like him then; and, how many live so unlike him now."*[61] After informing the reader in his typical fashion of his own lack of eloquence, but of his diligence, truthfulness, and sincerity, Walton returns to Herbert's induction and says that he spent longer than the ordinary time alone in the church to toll the bell in order to set some rules for the management of his life. Herbert's intent, related through a conversation with Woodnoth, Walton makes the key speech of the *Life.* It underlines the superiority of the holy over the courtly life, the necessity of the virtue of the clergyman's life to provide a living example to his parish, and reiterates the eminence of the title *priest* over eminence of birth or conferred dignities:

59 *Ibid.,* p. 40.
60 The improbability of Laud's intervention is discussed by Hutchinson, *Works of Herbert,* p. xxxiv, and by Joseph H. Summers, *George Herbert, His Religion and Art* (London, 1954), p. 35.
61 *Lives,* 1670 (Herbert), p. 41.

I now look back upon my aspiring thoughts, and think my self more happy than if I had attain'd what I so ambitiously thirsted for: And, I can now behold the Court with an impartial Eye, and see plainly, that it is made up of Fraud, and Titles, and Flattery, and many other such empty, imaginary painted Pleasures. Pleasures, that are so empty, as not to satisfie when they are enjoy'd; but, in God and his service, is a fulness of all joy and pleasure, and no satiety: And I will now use all my endeavours to bring my Relations and Dependants to a love and reliance on him, who never fails those that trust him. But above all, I will be sure to live well, because the vertuous life of a Clergy-man, is the most powerful eloquence to perswade all that see it, to reverence and love, and at least to desire to live like him. And this I will do, because I know we live in an Age that hath more need of good examples, than precepts. And I beseech that God, who hath honour'd me so much as to call me to serve at his Altar: that, as by his special grace he hath put into my heart these good desires, and resolutions: so, he will by his assisting grace enable me to bring the same to good effect; and, that my humble and charitable life, may so win upon others, as to bring glory to my Jesus, whom I have this day taken to be my Master and Governour; and am so proud of his service, that I will alwayes observe, and obey, and do his Will, and alwayes call him Jesus my Master: and I will alwayes contemn my birth, or any title or dignity that can be conferr'd upon me, when I shall compare them with any title of being a Priest, and serving at the Altar of Jesus my Master.[62]

That Herbert carried out his intentions is demonstrated in various ways. Walton introduces a paraphrase of "The Odour" and a paraphrase and quotation of "The Pearl" as evidence. He says that Herbert quickly exchanged his sword and silk clothes for a canonical coat, that he advised his wife of her functions as a minister's wife. He relates the story of Herbert's first experience with a member of his parish, a poor old woman of necessitous condition, in such a manner that Herbert's conscious humility and condescension almost embarrass the reader, and he makes general the effect of the incident by saying, "There be many such passages both of him and his Wife." He says that Herbert repaired the church, beautified the chapel, and rebuilt the parsonage at his own cost. "An account of the rest of his behaviour" starts with Herbert's impatience for ordination, and the story of his entrance into holy orders is made pathetic by quoting Humphrey Henchman, Bishop of London: *"He laid his hand on Mr. Herberts Head, and (alas!) within less than*

[62] *Ibid.*, pp. 42–43.

three Years, lent his Shoulder to carry his dear Friend to his Grave."[63] The account goes from this specific detail to a generalization when Walton says that Herbert wrote down the rules he had set for himself in the *Country Parson* and that "his behavior toward God and man, may be said to be a practical Comment on these."[64] It becomes digressive, but necessarily so in view of Walton's purpose, when Walton calls the *Country Parson* a book "so full of plain, prudent and useful Rules, that, that *Countrey Parson,* that can spare 12*d.* and yet wants [it], is scarce excusable; because it will both direct him what he is to do, and convince him for not having done it."[65] The account becomes specific again when Walton relates the story of the publication of the *Country Parson* and tells of Herbert's first sermon. He says that Herbert delivered his sermon in a most florid manner, with great learning and eloquence, but that he told his parishioners that *"for their sakes, his language and his expressions should be more plain and practical in his future Sermons."*[66] With this last detail, Walton's account of Herbert in the pulpit becomes general; Herbert becomes fused with the ideal in the *Country Parson* to such an extent in the following 10 per cent of the *Life* that Walton himself must indicate in a parenthesis that by the "he" of the account he means Herbert.[67]

This section of the *Life* is, indeed, a character of the good country parson in the church though Walton calls it an account of Herbert's diligence "to make his Parishioners understand what, and why they pray'd, and prais'd, and ador'd their Creator";[68] it is a practical summary of the logic of the Anglican service for the education and edification of prospective clerical and lay readers. It is Izaak Walton's "The Compleat Parson, or, the Religious Man's Occupation." Walton comments on such matters as the singing of hymns, the encumbrances of "that Law which our Fore-fathers groan'd under," the Lord's prayer, kneeling and standing, holy days and Ember weeks, catechizing, and he shows his own feelings when he says that if Herbert were at any time too zealous in his sermons it was to reprove the behavior of the congregation at divine service and to criticize ministers that "hudled up the Church-prayers."[69]

Walton's picture of Herbert carrying out those duties to his congregation which must be performed in church is a highly idealized

63 *Ibid.,* p. 48.   64 *Ibid.,* p. 49.   65 *Ibid.*   66 *Ibid.,* p. 50.
67 *Ibid.,* p. 56.   68 *Ibid.,* p. 58.   69 *Ibid.*

one. The picture of "the excellencies of the active part of his life" is as lengthy, but much more particular in its selected representative anecdote. Herbert's regular practice of public devotion and its influence upon the parish is followed by an account of his private devotions and his care for the spiritual well-being of his own family. Walton justifies Herbert's love for and practice of divine music, and his statement that Herbert went twice a week to the cathedral church in Salisbury to enjoy music, *"his Heaven upon Earth,"* allows him to relate some of the happy accidents of Herbert's walks. Walton uses three stories to prove that Herbert "did daily take any fair occasion to instruct the ignorant, or comfort any that were in affliction."[70] He tells first of a gentleman still living in Salisbury whom Herbert gave "such Rules for the tryal of his sincerity, and for a practical piety" that he would often contrive to meet him on his walks. He tells next of Herbert's conversation with a neighboring minister about the wickedness of the time and the contempt of the clergy. Herbert's suggested remedies for the decay of piety Walton again turns into a lesson for the clergy. The clergy themselves must keep Ember weeks strictly and beg their parishioners to join them in fasting and prayer for a more religious clergy. Catechizing must be restored. But it is most important that

the Clergy themselves would be sure to live unblameably; and that the dignified Clergy especially, which preach Temperance, would avoid Surfeting, and take all occasions to express a visible humility, and charity in their lives; for this would force a love and an imitation, and an unfeigned reverence from all that knew them: . . . This, (said Mr. Herbert) *would be a Cure for the wickedness and growing Atheism of our Age. And,* my dear Brother, *till this be done by us, and done in earnest, let no man expect a reformation of the manners of the* Laity: *for 'tis not learning, but this, this only, that must do it; and till then, the fault must lie at our doors.*[71]

The third anecdote shows Herbert helping the distressed as well as praying for them in the justly famous story of his aiding the poor man with a poorer horse that had fallen under its load. A passage which points up Herbert's charities by means of his reply to a friend who advised him to be more frugal concludes the story of Herbert's life as an active pastor.

It is not surprising that Walton spends 10 per cent of the *Life* on Herbert's holy dying; it is surprising to find him introducing a

[70] *Ibid.,* p. 63. [71] *Ibid.,* p. 62.

digression of equal length into its midst. He shows Herbert weakened by consumption, appointing his curate of the church at Ful-
ston, Mr. Bostock, to read prayers for him, and he tells of the visit
which Edmund Duncon made to Herbert at the instance of Nicholas
Ferrar one month before his death. Walton uses Duncon as a witness still living to show the majesty and humility reconciled in
Herbert's appearance and behavior, to show the awful reverence
which he inspired. Duncon's departure with a promise to return
in five days provides Walton the chance to give an account of Nicholas Ferrar, which he had promised his reader when he included
Ferrar among Herbert's benefactors in the rebuilding of Leighton
Church. This digression has the same function as similar ones in the
other *Lives*. Ferrar stands in the same relation to Herbert as Herbert himself stood to Donne in the 1658 edition, as Bedell stood
to Wotton, and Whitgift and Saravia to Hooker. Here, in a concentrated capsule, is a résumé and a repetition of the thesis of the *Life
of Herbert*. Walton's factual knowledge of Ferrar is slight, nor is he
much interested in the details of his life. He is more interested in
the man who was, he says, called St. Nicholas at the age of six, in
the man of learning and wealth who condemned the manners and
vanities of the world and resolved to live a life of mortification,
devotion, and charity. Most of the passage about Ferrar, therefore,
consists of a description of the constant and methodical service of
God at Little Gidding. Walton makes his intention here abundantly
clear when he concludes by saying, "And 'tis fit to tell the Reader,
that many of the Clergy that were more inclin'd to practical piety,
and devotion, then to doubtful and needless Disputations, did often
come to *Gidden Hall,* and make themselves a part of that happy Society."[72] He explicitly links "Mr. *Farrers,* and Mr. *Herberts* devout
lives" by telling that their new holy friendship was maintained only
by letters, and he cites Herbert's letter to Ferrar about Valdesso's
The Hundred and Ten Considerations as testimony of their friendship and pious designs. But Walton's purpose in mentioning this
letter is hardly to produce evidence for the relationship between
the two men. He describes Valdesso as a cavalier much valued and
loved by Emperor Charles V, and he uses Valdesso and the Emperor to further his thesis that the holy life is to be preferred to the
courtly. In some detail he tells how they forsook the world for a
contemplative life, and he thus bolsters additionally the value of

[72] *Ibid.,* p. 71.

the choice made by Herbert and Ferrar. The Ferrar and Valdesso passages must be considered almost wholly digressive in their relation to the life of Herbert, but they must as surely be considered integral to the thesis which Walton's *Life* is made to present.

Although Walton succeeded in reinjecting this late in the *Life* his contention that the holy life was honorable and dignified for men of birth, learning, and affairs, he was not yet satisfied to proceed smoothly to Herbert's holy dying. The reappearance of Duncon is used to relate how Herbert sent his poems to Ferrar, and Walton praises *The Temple* and shows its popularity. He then tells of the licensing of the book for printing, that the vice-chancellor of Cambridge objected to the verses, "Religion stands on tip-toe in our land,/ Readie to passe to the *American* strand," and that he finally allowed them to be printed, saying, "*I knew Mr.* Herbert *well, and know that he had many heavenly Speculations, and was a Divine Poet; but, I hope the World will not take him to be an inspired Prophet, and therefore I License the whole Book.*"[73] Walton was not merely interested in giving the vice-chancellor's opinion of Herbert. Here, at the very end of the *Life,* he is issuing a warning to the clergy, this time in Herbert's own words. Only after this does he finally relate the details of Herbert's holy death: the prayers of all the clergy for him; his own anticipation of death; his rising from his bed the Sunday before his death to sing his divine verses; his evaluation of his works; his calm, upset only by the grief of his family; and the presentation of his will to his executor, Woodnoth. Walton ends the *Life* on a truly hagiographic note, saying that Herbert lived and died like a saint. Following his example in the *Life of Hooker,* he disposes of Mrs. Herbert in an appendix, telling of the continued esteem in which she held her husband, her remarriage, her death, and her assiduity in preserving Herbert's private writings. The appendix is followed by eight of Herbert's letters, most of them selected to show his high place at Cambridge and his holy inclinations even at the moment of his appointment as orator. Three letters from Donne to Magdalen Herbert testify to their relationship, which Walton had indicated in the *Life.*

The proportions of the *Life,* particularly the large development of Herbert's last three years, reveal Walton's interest in the function of country parsons in general and in Herbert as a pattern for imitation. The particular emphasis on Herbert as orator and the

[73] *Ibid.,* p. 75.

inclusion of digressions on Ferrar and Emperor Charles V show
Walton's preoccupation with proselytizing the gospel of the fitness
of the holy life for men of worldly attainment. Such wrenching of
proportion suggests that Walton's view of Herbert was preconceived, that he knew exactly what he wanted to say about Herbert
before he had precise knowledge of Herbert's life. But even to
shape the life of Herbert according to his own desires, Walton would
have needed detailed materials on several subjects: the eminence
of Herbert's birth and family, the extent of his secular attainments,
the culmination of his holy inclinations, his general character and
specific practices at Bemerton. Some information was immediately
accessible to him, and his craftsmanship may be examined in his
utilization of what was quickly available. Other information he
needed to search for to supply deficiencies, and his methods here also
show his approach to biographical writing.

Directly at hand he had Nicholas Ferrar's introductory notice to
The Temple (1633); Oley's "A Prefatory View of the Life," prefixed to the *Country Parson* in 1652; his recollection of his conversations with Arthur Woodnoth; Herbert's printed works; Donne's
sermon of commemoration for Lady Danvers (1627); and probably
some of the correspondence between Donne and Lady Danvers. The
last two sources would be of value only indirectly in showing
something of the eminence of the Herbert family. The others would
be most useful in supplying information about the last part of
Herbert's life. In his short preface Ferrar was content "to make
the common Reader privie to some few particularities of the condition and disposition of the Person" of George Herbert.[74] Slight
as his remarks are, they were undoubtedly important in a general
way in their influence upon the outlines of the life Walton was
planning. Ferrar's second paragraph contains the germ of the ideas
which Walton developed:

> Being nobly born, and as eminently endued with gifts of the minde,
> and having by industrie and happy education perfected them to that
> great height of excellencie, whereof his fellowship of Trinitie Colledge
> in Cambridge, and his Orator-ship in the Universitie, together with
> that knowledge which the Kings Court had taken of him, could make
> relation farre above ordinarie. Quitting both his deserts and all the
> opportunities that he had for worldly preferment, he betook himself
> to the Sanctuarie and Temple of God, choosing rather to serve at Gods

---

74 "The Printers to the Reader," *Works of Herbert,* p. 3.

Altar, then to seek the honour of State-employments. . . . As God had enabled him, so he accounted him meet not onely to be called, but to be compelled to this service: Wherein his faithfull discharge was such, as may make him justly a companion to the primitive Saints, and a pattern or more for the age he lived in.

His fifth paragraph, which just mentions Herbert's remarkable obedience and conformity to the Church and the effect of his example on his parish, again probably provided the impulse for Walton's elaboration. The few minor details in Ferrar's introduction were carried over into Walton's *Life*. Ferrar's statement that when Herbert mentioned the name of Jesus he added *"My Master"* was taken over by Walton[75] and illustrated in Herbert's conversation several times.[76] His story of Herbert's reference on his deathbed to Leighton Church as *"a good work, if it be sprinkled with the bloud of Christ"* Walton made to redound even more to Herbert's credit by making *"work"* plural.[77] Ferrar's interpretation of the poems in *The Temple* as mirrors of Herbert's "inward enforcements" in leaving the world for the holy life led to Walton's like interpretation. He has Herbert say:

Sir, I pray deliver this little Book to my dear brother Farrer, *and tell him, he shall find in it a picture of the many Spiritual Conflicts that have past betwixt God and my Soul, before I could subject mine to the will of Jesus my Master, in whose service I have now found perfect freedom; desire him to read it, and then if he can think it may turn to the advantage of any dejected poor Soul, let it be made publick; if not, let him burn it, for I and it, are less than the least of Gods mercies.*[78]

Even the last clause here was probably taken over from the last line of Ferrar's account. Walton used Ferrar's preface, then, both generally and specifically. On one point he is even more honest than Ferrar. While Ferrar stated that there were no "outward" enforcements upon Herbert to enter the church, Walton demonstrated not only the influence of Herbert's mother but also the effect of the deaths of the supporters of his court hopes, though, to be sure, he makes Herbert's choice a voluntary one. In view of the almost complete utilization of Ferrar's account by Walton, the two omissions which he made stand out strongly. He did not see fit to follow Ferrar's words: "Next God, he loved that which God himself hath

[75] *Lives*, 1670 (Herbert), p. 43.
[77] *Ibid.*, p. 78.
[76] *Ibid.*, pp. 58, 77, 78.
[78] *Ibid.*, pp. 74–75.

magnified above all things, that is, his Word: so as he hath been heard to make solemne protestation, that he would not part with one leaf thereof for the whole world, if it were offered him in exchange." Nor did he follow Ferrar's words that Herbert "did earnestly endeavour the resignation of an Ecclesiasticall dignitie, which he was possessour of."

This is doubly strange since Oley followed Ferrar here and even identified the "Ecclesiasticall dignitie" as Leighton. The omissions serve to point up the high individuality of Walton as a biographer. They are additional evidence that though Walton was greatly indebted to Ferrar and Oley for items in their accounts which suggested to him the pattern and structure of his *Life* and some of the details for supporting the pattern, he made the pattern and structure of the *Life* his own, and his own structure rather than the accounts he drew upon determined the inclusion and exclusion of details. Ferrar's account is only an assemblage of remarks. Oley's structure is an impossible one for a biography, and, indeed, he did not intend his account to be a life but a hortatory and didactic preface. His introduction to *Herbert's Remains* is about half as long as Walton's *Life,* and though it is entitled "A Prefatory View of the Life of Mr Geo. Herbert," it is addressed *"To* the *Christian,* more designedly, to the *Clergy*-reader of the same Time, and Rank, and Mind, and in like Condition with the Epistler. Grace, &c. and Recovery, and Profit by the ensuing Tract."[79] The book was printed in 1652, and the first quarter of Oley's introduction was dictated by the circumstances of the clergy. He says that he refuses to call the ousted clergy companions in tribulation, that their present condition is just punishment for their deficiencies. Nor does he think this confession gives advantage to the Presbyterian clergy, for he advocates the confession of sins as an efficacious method of giving glory to God. To show that there have been good men of God in the Episcopal Church, he devotes one-third of the introduction to a view of three primitive, holy, and heavenly souls, *"vessels chosen and fitted for the service of the Sanctuary."* He gives a *"briefe of some confrontments"* common to Thomas Jackson, Nicholas Ferrar, and George Herbert, proving by example that each of the men was subject to censure and antagonism, each was a defender of the Protestant religion established in the Church of England, and each had the spirit of prophecy. Here he gives more space to Ferrar and

[79] "Prefatory View," sig. a^r.

Jackson than to Herbert, but the last 40 per cent of the account is a demonstration of the *"proper excellencies"* of Herbert. Oley quickly mentions Herbert's family (giving over most of his remarks to the praise of Magdalen Herbert), his oratorship, his re-edifying the church at Leighton. He devotes three paragraphs to Herbert's *"right managing of the* Fraternall duty of reproof," one to the friendship of Herbert and Ferrar, one to a comparison of the mental endowments of Herbert, Ferrar, and Jackson, and one to a demonstration of their essential unity of souls, despite their varied gifts, as it appears in their interest in Valdesso's *The Hundred and Ten Considerations.* In cursory fashion he mentions Herbert's industry, temperance, and frugality; his observation of holy days; his devotion to the liturgy of the Church and to Scripture; his fondness for church music. In conclusion, he states that he has wished only to show the lineaments of Herbert's mind, that he has not wasted a stroke of his pencil on Herbert's person or his domestic life.

Oley's Preface provided Walton with some details and reaffirmed others for him. It mentioned the possibility of secular honors beyond the oratorship, it dwelt on the friendship of Herbert and Ferrar maintained without interviews, it told of Ferrar's mastery of foreign tongues and of attempts made in Italy to convert him to Catholicism. Donne's verses to Herbert and Bacon's dedication of his translation of the Psalms to Herbert were here mentioned. Walton found here, too, a reference to Valdesso, a long passage on Herbert's devotion to the church liturgy, and the statement that Herbert was *"so great a Lover of* Church-Musick; *That he usually called it* Heaven upon earth, *and attended it a few days before his death."*[80] But if Oley's Preface was only occasionally helpful for its details, it was more important in providing ideas which Walton modified and developed. Oley's explicit purpose of recalling the clergy to their duties in 1652 became the implicit thesis of the *Life of Herbert* in 1670. Oley's linking of Herbert and Ferrar and his information about Ferrar are probably the source of the Ferrar digression in the *Life.* Oley's statement about criticism of Herbert, *"I have heard sober men censure him as a man that did not manage his brave parts to his best advantage and preferment, but lost himself in an humble way,"*[81] is probably the direct source of Walton's story about Herbert's court friend who tried to persuade him to alter his resolution to enter orders "as too mean an employment,

[80] *Ibid.,* sig. c4[r].   [81] *Ibid.,* sigs. a11[v]–a12[r].

and too much below his birth, and the excellent abilities and endowments of his mind." If it is not the precise inspiration of Walton's concern in the *Life* with this idea, it must at least have powerfully forwarded Walton's design. The spirit of prophecy which Oley
attributed to Herbert he illustrated with those lines which Walton speaks of as holding up the licensing of *The Temple,* and Walton's use of the story was undoubtedly suggested by the context of
the lines in Oley's Preface.

Oley's account, then, provided Walton not only with some specific
details, but even influenced the structure of Walton's *Life* by suggesting or re-enforcing those ideas which Walton stressed. But if it
influenced Walton's structure, that structure itself determined the
rejection of some of the details in Oley's account. Oley had specified
that the ecclesiastical dignity, mentioned by Ferrar, which Herbert
sought to resign was Leighton. He added, too, that Herbert would
have resigned it to Ferrar, but that Ferrar refused and diverted
Herbert to the rebuilding of the church.[82] Walton, however, had
already indicated, by the time he came to tell the Leighton episode,
that Herbert had resolved to enter the Church, and he wished to
use the episode as a demonstration of the constancy of Herbert's
resolution after he had been made deacon. This he did by showing
that Herbert's resolve to rebuild the church was so great that it
forced him even to be undutiful to his mother for the first time in
his life. He neglected the account of Ferrar and Oley here, for its
inclusion would have vitiated the pattern he was creating. For a
like reason he neglected Oley's repetition of Ferrar's statement that
Herbert professed that he would not part with one leaf of Scripture
though he might have the whole world in exchange.[83] Walton had
no sympathy for the particular delight which the clergy of the
Commonwealth had taken in breaking set forms in the church service, in overthrowing traditional practice, in relying on their own
interpretation of Scripture. He knew that Herbert himself had
called the Scriptures "the chief and top" of the parson's knowledge,
"the storehouse and magazene of life and comfort," and that he had
condoned the use of "Commenters and Fathers" in understanding
Scripture, but only as a fourth means, after the living of a holy life,
prayer, and collation of passages.[84] But he hesitated to put so much
emphasis on Scripture, so much reliance on the inner light avail-

---

[82] *Ibid.,* sigs. b8v–b9r.   [83] *Ibid.,* sigs. c4r–c4v.
[84] "The Parsons Knowledg," *Works of Herbert,* pp. 228–229.

able to an individual, to the exclusion of liturgy, preaching, and catechizing which he considered fully as essential to religion. He therefore would not give one element priority over the others, would not emphasize Scripture, but would rather show that Herbert labored to point out to his parishioners that *"the whole Service of the Church*, was a reasonable, and therefore an acceptable Sacrifice to God."[85] Oley's catalogue of confrontments had forced him to seek evidence that Herbert was a staunch defender of the Church of England, and he had illustrated this by stating that *The Temple* contained not only metrical versions of passages in Scripture and in the Fathers but also poems which strongly refuted the doctrine of Rome. Walton's view of Herbert as a defender of protestantism was a larger one, embracing the whole life as Herbert lived it, particularly in his service to his parishioners, and he went along with Ferrar in conceiving of *The Temple* as the reflection of Herbert's inner struggle and acceptance of the holy life. Oley had referred at some length to Herbert's *Parentalia,* and it is conceivable that his calling these poems *"dull or dead in comparison of his* Temple Poems"[86] may have caused Walton to omit mentioning them. Nothing in Walton's structure would have precluded their inclusion, but it is likely that he could not read the Greek and Latin and that he therefore sought to demonstrate the relationship between son and mother in other ways.

The omissions in Oley's account acted even as Gauden's had when Walton was writing his *Life of Hooker,* and Walton felt it incumbent upon himself to remedy Oley's deficiencies. The description of Herbert's person and dress and the large part which Jane Herbert plays in the *Life* have their source in Oley's avowed silence on these matters, and the detail and anecdote which make Herbert live as a parson compensate for Oley's vapid account of Herbert's excellences. The enumeration of excellences was no more a life than Gauden's enumeration of Hooker's sufferings and trials, and the example before him probably reinforced in Walton's mind the necessity of a design which would show development, a chronological pattern that would compensate for Oley's complete disregard for dates.

To what extent was Walton indebted to Arthur Woodnoth? Three stringent limitations may be suggested. First, there is no reason to assume either from Walton's account of the relationship

[85] *Lives,* 1670 (Herbert), p. 50.   [86] "Prefatory View," sig. b7ʳ.

between Herbert and Woodnoth or from other sources that Woodnoth was acquainted with Herbert before the middle of 1626 or
that he knew him well before 1630. Woodnoth could have related
at first hand only the story of Herbert's life after Herbert had decided upon the holy life. Second, there was probably only a casual
familiarity between Woodnoth and Walton. Walton knew that
Woodnoth was a goldsmith in Foster Lane and he knew Woodnoth's general disposition, but he was troubled to remember Woodnoth's given name. He probably knew nothing of Woodnoth's
activities after 1642, and it is likely that had he known of them,
he would not after this time have associated with him. Third, although it has been conjectured that Walton kept a diary, because
he reported in detail a conversation with Sanderson in 1655 and he
remembered in 1675 the very day he completed his first version of
the *Life of Donne,* Walton himself wrote in 1665 that he did not
remember the details of his conversations about Hooker with John
Hales, Archbishop Ussher, and Bishop Morton. "My Memory hath
preserved some gleanings,"[87] he wrote, and it is likely that only
gleanings remained of his conversations with Woodnoth after a lapse
of almost thirty years. Walton probably heard from Woodnoth,
and remembered generally, the stories of the rebuilding of Leighton
Church, Herbert's induction into Bemerton, and his relationship
with Little Gidding. He probably remembered in somewhat more
detail what Woodnoth told him of Herbert's death. The years had
blurred for him the details of the Valdesso episode, perhaps even
the story of the manuscript of the *Country Parson.* He had remembered that Woodnoth had been a useful friend to Herbert's stepfather, and it was natural for him to add "to his Mother," but it is
more likely that Woodnoth knew only Sir John Danvers' second
wife. Walton probably reconstructed himself Herbert's remarks to
Woodnoth the night of his induction into Bemerton, to his wife
upon his return to Baynton House, and to Woodnoth while he was
on his deathbed. Walton never explicitly says "Mr. Woodnoth told
me," only that Herbert would speak "to this purpose," and the
speeches are general and derivative. It may be that Woodnoth, as
Herbert's executor, was able to make available to Walton the correspondence and new poems which he printed,[88] but on the whole,

---

[87] *Hooker,* 1665, p. 6.
[88] I find no other reasonable way of accounting for Walton's having them.

despite the kind of role that he plays in the *Life,* Woodnoth's detailed contributions to the *Life* are not many.

It is surprising how much that Walton obliquely suggests that he received from Woodnoth he probably got instead from Herbert's own works. The *Life of Herbert* provides an innovation in Walton's technique in biography in the extent to which he was willing to utilize the works of his subject as the basis for biographical information. In the *Life of Donne* he had, to be sure, paraphrased and quoted from the autobiographical *Devotions* and had interpreted rather too literally a passage in the preface of *Pseudo-Martyr.* He had for the most part neglected Donne's poetry as revealing something of Donne, probably because he thought it revealed aspects of Donne's character which he did not care to disclose, but also because of his customary skepticism of the truthfulness inherent in verse.[89] Probably because Herbert's verse so nearly reflected his preconceived image of Herbert, Walton was willing to draw upon it profusely. The seeming use of the poetry is to authenticate a generalization which Walton has made; in fact, particular verses are frequently used as evidence for generalizations which the verses themselves must originally have suggested.

Walton prepares for Herbert's transition from orator to deacon by stating that Herbert had frequently thought about leaving the university because study impaired his already poor health. He adduces as evidence the fact that Herbert frequently said, *"He had a Wit, like a Pen-knife in a narrow sheath, too sharp for his Body."*[90] This is an obvious reworking of "Affliction IV," "My thoughts are all a case of knives,/ Wounding my heart," and it is likely that the lines themselves suggested Walton's statement which he uses the paraphrase to support. Walton further develops his thesis by stating that Herbert's mother "would by no means allow him to leave the University, or to travel" and that he always submitted to her wisdom.[91] Walton then quotes as evidence the last five stanzas of "Affliction I," though he is himself aware that his deduction may only "partly appear" there and he feels compelled to justify his quotation

---

Perhaps, too, George Herbert had in his possession at his death Donne's letters to his mother, and Woodnoth may have shown these to Walton. They may have been, however, among the Donne papers which Walton saw when they were in Henry King's possession.

[89] See p. 102, n. 26.   [90] *Lives,* 1670 (Herbert), p. 28.   [91] *Ibid.,* p. 29.

further by calling it "a pious reflection on Gods providence, and some passages of his life."[92] This poem was undoubtedly the inspiration for Walton's entire idea here, for in it Herbert writes of his sicknesses and consuming agues, and his reference to "a blunted knife" mingled with the "case of knives" in "Affliction IV" to produce Walton's variation. Herbert's statement "my friends die" may even have suggested to Walton the passage which follows immediately his quotation of the poem, in which the deaths of the Duke of Richmond, the Marquis of Hamilton, and King James are made to spell the end of Herbert's court hopes. If Walton was willing to place a biographical interpretation on these matters in the poem, he was not willing to do so for the poem as a whole. Oley had interpreted its military imagery as literal evidence that Herbert had to suppress a desire for *"Martiall Atchievements,"*[93] and Walton rightly saw fit to disregard this theory. More important, Herbert makes reference to his "sudden soul" and to his "fiercenesse," to the hasty disposition and excitability which are supported by Edward Herbert's statement that his brother was "not exempt from passion and choler,"[94] but Walton maintains a discreet silence here. Although Walton's dependency upon his subject's works is greater in this *Life,* there is nothing new in his method of using that source. His idiosyncratic selectivity is as obvious here as elsewhere.

How large his debt was to Herbert's writings can readily be shown. The speech which Walton says that Herbert made to Woodnoth on the night of his induction to Bemerton, starting *"I now look back upon my aspiring thoughts,"* seems like an imaginative reconstruction, suggested perhaps by Herbert's "Content" and liberally supported by "The Pearl." "The Pearl" was undoubtedly attractive to Walton because it clearly reveals Herbert's intimate knowledge of the pleasures of the court and the university and his voluntary choice of the holy life. The speech is supported by a paraphrase of "The Odour," which both Ferrar and Oley had drawn upon, and Walton then paraphrases and quotes from "The Pearl" to show that Herbert arrived at the conclusions of "The Odour" through an "unforc'd choice." It is even possible that Walton's statement immediately after this that Herbert exchanged his sword and silk clothes for a canonical coat after he was made rector of

[92] *Ibid.*   [93] "Prefatory View," sig. b7v.
[94] Sidney L. Lee, ed., *The Autobiography of Edward, Lord Herbert of Cherbury* (London, 1886), p. 22.

Bemerton was occasioned by Herbert's lines that he wished to exchange his "lay-sword/ For that of th' holy Word" in "The Priesthood," one of the poems which Oley had used in order to show that Herbert *"knew full well what he did when he received Holy orders."*[95]

The impulse for the first of Herbert's deathbed speeches to Woodnoth also derives from a poem, and Walton wrenched the meaning of the poem to his own purpose. He has Herbert say, *"I now look back upon the pleasures of my life past, and see the content I have taken in beauty, in wit, in musick, and pleasant Conversation, how they are now all past by me, as a shadow that returns not, and are all become dead to me, or I to them."*[96] Nothing in "The Quip" points to Herbert's content with these things; the poem shows cognizance of their appeals and the poet's belief that God's love is more than adequate compensation for their absence in his life. Not only did Walton interpret the poem loosely, but he omitted money and "brave Glorie" from Herbert's catalogue. Herbert had not included music in his list, though, to be sure, he had shown the appeal of money in terms of musical imagery. But Walton had made very evident Herbert's taste for music, and he probably added it to show the degree of Herbert's mortification prior to his death. His willingness to shape Herbert's verse to his own end, however, led him into mild contradiction at this point, for he immediately shows that music, at least holy music, had not lost its attraction for Herbert. Walton has Herbert rise from his bed the Sunday before his death, call for an instrument, and say:

> *My God, my God,*
> *My Musick shall find thee,*
> *And every string*
> *shall have his attribute to sing.*

The first line is Walton's own contribution; the remainder he plucked from "The Thanksgiving." He then has Herbert play and sing the fifth stanza of "Sunday." Here is a dramatic deathbed scene, one that effectively demonstrates Herbert's reverence for the Sabbath, but which demonstrates, too, that Herbert was alive to the beauty of holy music even as he died.

Precisely where the indebtedness of the *Life* to *The Temple* ends it is difficult to say, but even the description of Herbert's delivery of

---

[95] "Prefatory View," sigs. b8r–b8v. [96] *Lives,* 1670 (Herbert), p. 76.

his first sermon at Bemerton may stem from the verse. Walton makes the same distinction between the florid manner, great learning, and eloquence of the first sermon and the plainness and practicality of the rest that Herbert makes in "Jordan (II)" between his early and late verse. His reliance upon the verse is clear in his constant allusion to it. Ferrar's scorn for worldly pleasures is expressed in Herbert's words: they are a "nothing between two dishes."[97] The line from "The Posie" which Ferrar and Oley had quoted as Herbert's motto, Walton worked into Herbert's conversation with Duncon about the manuscript of *The Temple: "I and it, are less than the least of Gods mercies."*[98] He quoted Herbert's youthful sonnets to his mother as testimony that Herbert consecrated the first fruits of his early age to virtue and a serious study of learning, a liberal inter-pretation of the quoted part of Herbert's letter which says, *"my poor Abilities in* Poetry, *shall be all, and ever consecrated to Gods glory."*[99] He mentions Herbert's *Musae Responsoriae* to illustrate his youthful affection for the Church. Walton's propensity for utilizing poetry freely in the *Life* makes it likely, though positive evidence is lacking, that he even went so far as to attribute to Herbert an adaptation of some lines printed in 1642 as part of Fuller's character of "The faithfull Minister," and it is likely, too, that the verses themselves suggested to him the tale that Herbert had them engraved on the chimney mantel in the Bemerton parsonage.[100]

The importance that Walton was attaching to verse as a source of biographical information in the *Life* is further demonstrated by his quoting four lines from Donne's "The Autumnall." The extent of his dependency upon the lines is evident in the degree of the inconsistencies they led him into. He wished to use them not only to show Donne's estimate of Magdalen Herbert's beauties of body and mind, but also as evidence of Donne's meeting her at Oxford and as evidence of the kind of friendship between them. He therefore says that Donne wrote the poem upon leaving Oxford at the time that Mrs. Herbert was making a home there for her son Edward.

[97] "Dotage," l. 5. [98] *Lives,* 1670 (Herbert), pp. 74–75.
[99] *Ibid.,* p. 20.
[100] Fuller's version is in *The Holy State* (London, 1642), p. 87. Hutchinson quotes from F. Warre, *A Collection of Papers relating to Bemerton* (Salisbury, 1893), to the effect that in a modern restoration of the Bemerton parsonage to its previous state, no indication of any inscription on the chimney mantel was found (*Works of Herbert,* p. 550).

He says too that their amity was not one which "polluted their Souls; but, an *Amity* made up of a chain of sutable inclinations and vertues," for both were "then past the meridian of mans life"; indeed, he says, Donne was about forty and had a wife and seven children.[101] Mrs. Herbert was at Oxford for two years, not four as Walton states, and she moved to London some time before February, 1601.[102] Donne was married in December, 1601, and he was not a father for the seventh time until 1611.[103] All the correspondence which Walton prints between Donne and Mrs. Herbert dates from 1607, and probably this was the time he vaguely had in mind.[104] Walton's story of the Oxford meeting may not be totally inaccurate, for it is indeed possible that Donne did meet Mrs. Herbert at Oxford in 1599,[105] but his attempt to ascribe "The Autumnall" to the first meeting made his account highly inconsistent, for it was probably sent to her shortly before her second

---

[101] *Lives,* 1670 (Herbert), p. 16. [102] Lee, *op. cit.,* pp. 42, 81.
[103] Gosse, II, 5.

[104] Anthony à Wood points out the probable reason for Walton's confusion about the date of Mrs. Herbert's stay at Oxford. Walton had written that Mrs. Herbert had "entred *Edward* into *Queens Colledge.*" Wood says (*Athenae Oxon.,* III, 242), "The reader is to know, that one Edward Herbert an esquire's son of the county of Mountgomery, was matriculated in the university as a member of Qu. coll. in the beginning of July 1608, aged 17 years, but he is not to be taken to be the same with the former who was lord Herbert, tho' Isaac Walton in the *Life of Mr. George Herbert* doth, and from him the society of the said coll." Walton may have confused Edward Herbert, who had matriculated in May, 1596, from University College, with a younger first cousin of the same name, son of Charles Herbert of Aston.

H. W. Garrod (in "Donne and Mrs. Herbert," *RES,* XXI [1945], 161–173) would identify as Magdalen Herbert's third son the William Herbert who matriculated from Queen's College on the same day in 1608 as had Edward Herbert, and he then suggests that William's matriculation brought Mrs. Herbert to Oxford a second time. He suggests, too, that she knew Donne prior to this visit, but that at his accidental coming to Oxford (also conjectured), their friendship deepened. He suggests, too, that Mrs. Herbert would have stayed in Oxford to superintend William's education had she not married again in "1608." This, of course, would mean that she was willing to leave to shift for himself her son George, younger than William by a couple of years, who was at this time resident at Westminster School.

[105] Mario M. Rossi conjectures that Donne visited at Oxford in 1599, when he was Sir Thomas Egerton's secretary, to attend the graduation of Egerton's stepson, Sir Francis Wooley. Donne and Wooley had met on the Azores expedition, and Wooley resumed his studies in October, 1597. Wooley and Edward Herbert were known to each other, and Wooley may have introduced Donne to Herbert and his mother (*La Vita, le opere, i tempi di Edoardo Herbert di Chirbury* [Florence, 1947], I, 39).

marriage in the spring of 1609.[106] Walton's trouble here stems from his allowing the poem to determine for him not only the nature of the relationship between Donne and Magdalen Herbert but also the date of the beginning of that relationship. The poem was not used to support a body of authenticated fact, but whatever factual information Walton may have had was made to reflect the content of the poem. From his large dependency upon Donne's verse here, it was only a short step to his reconstruction in 1675 of Donne's vision largely on the basis of hearsay evidence and of the verse.

In the same way that he drew upon *The Temple* for suggestions, Walton drew upon the *Country Parson,* and it is likely that he treated it as an autobiography. Herbert's note to the reader says, "I have resolved to set down the Form and Character of a true Pastour, that I may have a Mark to aim at,"[107] and this was possibly the basis for Walton's story of Herbert's unduly long stay in Bemerton Church upon his induction: "he set some Rules to himself, for the future manage of his life; and then and there made a vow, to labour to keep them."[108] Walton says parenthetically of this statement "as he after told Mr. *Woodnot,*" but he had made Woodnoth, too, the source of conversations which he reconstructed from *The Temple.* He refers again to these rules before telling of Herbert's ordination, says even that Herbert had doubtless made "Rules to himself for his Christian carriage both to God and man before he enter'd into *Holy Orders,*"[109] and then he proceeds to relate these rules to those that Herbert wrote down in the *Country Parson.* Herbert's chapter "The Parson praying" is undoubtedly the seed from which sprang Walton's long account of Herbert as the prototype of the good parson in the pulpit. Herbert's words on the parson's manner of speaking, "his voyce is humble, his words treatable, and slow," are the likely source of Walton's saying that Herbert was too zealous in his sermons only when he reproved "those Ministers that hudled up the Church-prayers." Walton coupled with this Herbert's reproof of the indecencies of the people's behavior at divine service, and in the *Country Parson,* too, the passage following that on the parson's delivery is followed by a detailed account of the parson's instructing his people how to conduct themselves

106 See *The Poems of John Donne,* II, 62–63.
107 *Works of Herbert,* p. 224.　　108 *Lives,* 1670 (Herbert), p. 42.
109 *Ibid.,* p. 47.

in divine service. Herbert then emphasized the necessity for the congregation to meditate as they made answer to the parson: "This is that which the Apostle cals a reasonable service, *Rom.* 12. when we speak not as Parrats, . . . but when we use our reason, and apply our powers to the service of him, that gives them." This is likely the basis of Walton's saying that Herbert made it appear to his parishioners "that, *the whole Service of the Church,* was a reasonable, and therefore an acceptable Sacrifice to God." More important, it probably inspired Walton's subsequent demonstration of the reasonableness of the whole church service, which takes up 10 per cent of the *Life.* There are other evidences of Walton's dependence on the *Country Parson.* Herbert's statement that the people *"labour profanely, when they set themselves to work like brute beasts, never raising their thoughts to God, nor sanctifying their labour with daily prayer"*[110] is probably the basis for Walton's saying that "some of the meaner sort of his Parish, did so love and reverence Mr. *Herbert,* that they would let their Plow rest when Mr. *Herberts Saints-Bell* rung to Prayers, that they might also offer their devotions to God with him, and would then return back to their Plow."[111] Herbert's words in "The Parson in Journey"—"The Countrey Parson . . . leaveth not his Ministry behind him; but is himselfe where ever he is. Therefore those he meets on the way he blesseth audibly, and with those he overtakes or that overtake him, hee begins good discourses, such as may edify"—doubtless suggested to Walton the use of the "happy accidents" of Herbert's walks to Salisbury, and the chapters "The Parson Catechizing" and "The Parson's Library" ("The Countrey Parson's Library is a holy Life") may even have suggested the actual content of one of the accidents. Walton's specific debt to the *Country Parson* is great; the largeness of the dependency can be calculated accurately only by the extent to which Walton captures in the *Life* the very tone of sweetness and reasonableness of piety that distinguishes the *Country Parson.*

One further source is worthy of mention, for it shows that Walton relied on that material which was immediately available to him, however tangential it might seem. Walton had heard Donne preach his sermon of commemoration for Lady Danvers. That he went to the printed sermon in writing the *Life of Herbert* is evident in his

---

[110] "The Parson in Circuit," *Works of Herbert,* pp. 247–248.
[111] *Lives,* 1670 (Herbert), p. 59.

reference to Mrs. Herbert's children as *"Job's number,* and [in the revision of the *Life* in 1674] *Job's distribution,"*[112] following the sermon rather than Oley, who had printed "Job's *distinction."*[113] Donne's sermon furnished Walton with the information that Mrs. Herbert befriended at Oxford "divers reverend persons, of eminency, and estimation," that she was a widow twelve years, and that her second husband was attracted by her *"personall* and *naturall endowments."*[114] Walton quietly passed over the large difference in the ages of Danvers and Mrs. Herbert—he was younger than her eldest son—although Donne had dwelt on this detail as evidence of her attractiveness. Walton's use of this sermon reveals his tendency in the *Life of Herbert* to draw upon material which was readily accessible. To be sure, the unduly large part of the *Life* devoted to Magdalen Herbert and to her relationship with Donne was in part dictated by Walton's interest in Donne. But, too, he wished to demonstrate the nobility and capability of the entire Herbert family. The material which concerned Herbert's mother was quickly available to him, and in view of the paucity of his information about the remainder of the family, he took advantage of what was accessible.[115]

[112] *Ibid.,* p. 10; *Herbert,* 1674, p. 2.   [113] "Prefatory View," sig. b6[v].

[114] John Donne, *A Sermon of Commemoration of the Lady Danvers,* in Simpson and Potter, eds., *The Sermons of John Donne,* VIII, 88.

In the sermon Donne says that he "had the favour to be admitted" into Lady Danvers' family during the plague in 1625. Prior to this, he says of Lady Danvers that "from that *Worthy family,* whence shee had her originall extraction, and birth, she suckt that love of *hospitality* . . . which dwelt in her, to her end." Walton seems to have thought that Donne was here, too, making an autobiographical reference, for he writes that Mrs. Herbert "prov'd one of his most bountiful Benefactors," and he prints as testimony Donne's letter, *"Your Favours to me are every where. . . ."* Donne's statement in the sermon that "in the *Universitie"* Mrs. Herbert "contracted a friendship, with divers reverend persons, of eminency, and estimation there; which continued to their ends" is obviously the basis for Walton's statement that Mrs. Herbert was acquainted with men of eminent worth or learning in or near Oxford, and, since Walton added "and particularly, with Mr. *John Donne,"* he seems to have thought that Donne was once more speaking of himself. This may have led him to try to interpret "The Autumnall" as testimony that the friendship of Donne and Mrs. Herbert began at Oxford.

[115] It has been conjectured from Walton's telling nothing about Herbert's immediate family that does not appear in Lord Herbert of Cherbury's *Autobiography* that Walton may have seen a copy in manuscript. Walton does not avail himself, however, of all of Herbert's little detail, and this is strange in view of his obvious desire to stress the eminence of the family. The *Autobiography* would have afforded him no information about George Herbert

The accessible material, it can be seen, was for the most part general in its content, more useful for its suggestiveness than its fact, more helpful with Herbert's character than his chronicle, and most of it pertained to Herbert's last years. If Walton was to write a biography rather than a character sketch, he needed specific information about Herbert's career at Cambridge of the kind which university records and Herbert's university acquaintances might furnish. In order to understand Herbert's experience with Leighton Church, he needed to consult the records of the diocese of Lincoln and to visit Leighton Bromswold. To write in accurate detail an account of Herbert's short life and death at Bemerton, he had to examine documents at Bemerton and Salisbury and talk with surviving inhabitants who would have known Herbert. Walton's concept of his function as a biographer in the *Life of Herbert* may be understood and evaluated by a consideration of his attempts to supplement the material which was his inheritance.

Walton knew when he wrote the *Life* that Sir Henry Herbert, George's younger brother, was still living. It is conceivable that he had even met Sir Henry during his stewardship under Bishop Morley at Worcester, for after 1627 Herbert's residence was at Ribbesford in Worcestershire.[116] Sir Henry might have illuminated for Walton many dark places in Herbert's life. Walton had little information about Herbert's thirty-fourth year, but he knew that Herbert had spent it at Sir Henry's estate at Woodford in Essex. Sir Henry could assuredly have supplied particulars here, and might even have shed light on the following two years of his brother's life, about which Walton tells almost nothing. But there is no evidence that Walton sought out Sir Henry Herbert. There is no evidence, too, that he troubled Herbert Thorndike for information. He knew that Thorndike was in 1670 Prebendary of

---

except Edward's statements of George's saintliness and his not being exempt from choler. It is difficult to see why Walton would say Mrs. Herbert entered Edward at Queen's College (*Lives*, 1670 [Herbert], p. 14), when Edward himself says that he was sent to University College before his father's death (Lee, *op. cit.*, p. 39). Had he read the *Autobiography*, Walton would have known, too, that Mrs. Herbert spent two, not four, years at Oxford. Upon Lord Herbert's death in 1648, two copies of the MS of the *Autobiography* remained in the Herbert family, one with his brother Sir Henry, the other with his grandson Edward, later 3rd Lord Herbert (*ibid.*, unpaged leaf before p. 1). There is no evidence that Walton consulted either of them in writing the *Life of Herbert*.

[116] *DNB*, article "Sir Henry Herbert."

Westminster. He knew, too, that Thorndike had frequently substituted for Herbert as University Orator. Thorndike no doubt
possessed invaluable information not only about Herbert's university career, but also about his activities as Prebendary of Leighton Ecclesia, for he succeeded Herbert in that place.[117] The inaccuracy of Walton's account of Leighton Church makes it obvious
that he never spoke to Thorndike.

Walton did examine or had someone examine the Lincoln Chapter Acts, which informed him that Herbert was already deacon
when he was made Prebendary of Leighton Ecclesia on July 5,
1626.[118] The rest of his account is a patchwork of what he found
in Ferrar and Oley and what Woodnoth told him. Ferrar's preface is the source of Walton's saying that the church had been in
ruins for almost twenty years and that attempts to rebuild it by a
public collection had failed. Woodnoth probably supplied the list
of contributors. Walton himself obviously never saw the church
which Herbert re-edified. It is probable that he did not even know
quite where it was. He speaks of *"Layton Ecclesia . . .* a Village
near to *Spalden* in the County of *Huntington."*[119] The church itself and the landed property which endowed the prebend of Leighton Ecclesia in Lincoln Cathedral were at Leighton Bromswold.
Walton's first editor pointed out that Spalden, or Spalding, is a
town in Lincolnshire, and that Walton has mistaken that town for
Spaldwick in Huntingdonshire.[120] When Walton referred to the
church as "for the workmanship, a costly *Mosaick,"*[121] he was misreading Oley, who spoke of the church and in the same sentence
called *The Temple* a *"costly piece (of Mosaick or Solomonick
work)."*[122] Walton says that the church was "so Wainscoated, as to
be exceeded by none." Zouch wrote in 1796 that no traces of wains-
coating were discoverable.[123] Walton is wrong, too, in saying that
Herbert "became restless, till he saw it [the church] finisht as it now
stands." A letter by Herbert to his brother Sir Henry shows that

---

[117] *Works of Herbert,* p. 607.

[118] *Lives,* 1670 (Herbert), p. 32: "I find by the Records of *Lincoln. . . .*"
Walton says *"July* 15. 1626," and he does not reveal that Herbert was instituted by proxy, one Peter Walter, clerk, standing in his place. See *Works of
Herbert,* p. xxxi, and John J. Daniell, *The Life of George Herbert of Bemerton* (London, 1902), p. 103.

[119] *Lives,* 1670 (Herbert), p. 32.

[120] Thomas Zouch, ed., *Lives,* 1796, p. 346, note u.

[121] *Lives,* 1670 (Herbert), p. 33.   [122] "Prefatory View," sig. b9[r].

[123] Zouch, *op. cit.,* p. 346, note x.

funds were still being solicited in March, 1632.[124] Walton's statement reveals the motivation underlying his account of Herbert's activity at Leighton. By stating that Herbert lived to see the church rebuilt, by calling it "the most remarkable Parish-Church, that this Nation affords," he thought to demonstrate the degree of Herbert's piety, for his interest in the episode lay in its representing the transition of Herbert from the courtly to the holy life, in its revealing concretely the result of Herbert's determination to embrace the holy life. No doubt he drew upon the Lincoln records because it was extremely important for him to know the exact date that Herbert became deacon; this step Walton considered the most obvious manifestation of Herbert's inclination toward piety, the turning point in his life. Failing to find this information, he emphasized the first important event which followed Herbert's becoming deacon, his being awarded the prebend of Leighton Ecclesia. But these were the matters in which he was primarily interested. He did not think it important or essential to verify in detail the information about Leighton which he had inherited or to examine Leighton himself.

Walton's entire account of Herbert's university career shows that he was aware of the importance of chronology in biography, but if he struggled to maintain some semblance of chronology, he was content with some approximation of the truth. He was primarily interested in demonstrating Herbert's brilliance, particularly as Orator, and he was more concerned with suitable illustration than with accuracy of fact. If he consulted the university records, he did so only haphazardly. To be sure, he attempted in 1675 to correct obvious errors in chronology, but his prime purpose was to establish the eminence of Herbert in courtly and scholarly circles, and he was only secondarily interested in removing discrepancies in time which might detract from the conviction his account would carry. He worked from his thesis to his chronology, and not from the record of events to a generalization. After stating that Herbert was "transplanted" to Trinity College, Cambridge, "about the year 1608," Walton summarily dismissed all of Herbert's stay until he became Orator in 1619[20], contenting himself with the chronicle that Herbert was made *"Minor Fellow* in the year 1609. *Batchelor of Art* in the year 1611. *Major Fellow* of the *Colledge, March* 15. 1615[16]. And that in that year, he was also made *Master of Arts.*"[125]

[124] *Works of Herbert,* p. 377.   [125] *Lives,* 1670 (Herbert), p. 21.

The particularity of the date that Herbert became Major Fellow seems to indicate specific reference to the university records, yet they state, too, that Herbert became Minor Fellow on October 3, 1614, and that he became Bachelor of Arts in 1612[13].[126] It is doubtful, then, that Walton actually consulted the university records. His omission in 1675 of the reference that Herbert became a Minor Fellow in 1609 seems to bear this out. Grosart would explain the omission by saying that the words were accidentally dropped out.[127] More likely Walton was made aware of the impossibility of his date, and he cut the reference.[128] But his secondary interest in chronology is in evidence here. He did not keep a date which was manifestly incorrect, but he did not feel compelled to search for the correct one. Walton makes no mention either of Herbert's appointment in 1617 as Sublector quartae classis or of his appointment in 1618 as Praelector or Reader in Rhetoric. Both offices might have shown the additional honors which came to Herbert, and both would have served to show the path that Herbert traveled to the oratorship. Either he was ignorant of Herbert's holding these positions, or he omitted them to concentrate on the oratorship. He correctly states that Herbert became Orator in 1619[20] and that his first notable duty was the composition of a letter of thanks to King James for his gift to the university. But the other occasions by which he would illustrate Herbert's fitness for his position he had to force into his preconceived pattern.

[126] Grosart, *op. cit.,* I, xliv.

[127] *Ibid.,* III, 105. Grosart's note is misleading, for it implies that the reference was dropped from the *Life* in 1674. It was not omitted until 1675.

[128] There is further evidence that Walton's omission of *"Minor Fellow* in the year 1609" was a conscious one. In 1670, he had written that Herbert's mother had died in 1627 and that Herbert had "kept his Fellowship in *Cambridge,* and his Orators place, till after her death; and then, declin'd both: And, the last, the more willingly, that he might be succeeded by his friend *Robert Creighton"* (*Lives* [Herbert], p. 37). In 1675, he wrote instead that Herbert "kept his Orators place, till after her death; and then presently declin'd it: And, the more willingly . . ." (*ibid.,* p. 289). This change is hardly accidental; it is apparent that between 1674 and 1675 Walton had tried to learn something more about Herbert as a fellow of Trinity. (See Appendix F.) His investigation must have pointed up the impossibility of the date he had assigned to Herbert's becoming Minor Fellow.

Walton probably retained "1611" as the year in which Herbert was made B.A. because he thought that Herbert had been matriculated from Trinity in "1608." Herbert was not appointed King's Scholar at Trinity until May 5, 1609, and was not matriculated pensioner at Trinity until Dec. 18, 1609 (Grosart, *op. cit.,* I, xliv).

The second of these occasions was intended to demonstrate that Herbert even as Orator was a defender of the Established Church. Walton tells that Andrew Melville (Walton uses "Melvin," perhaps following Fuller's version of the Latin "Melvinus"[129]), a gentleman of Scotland averse to the Established Church, returned to England from travel in France and Geneva "some short time before, or immediately after" Herbert was made Orator. He says that Melville "writ and scattered in Latin, many pieces of his wit against our *Altars,* our *Prayers,* and our *Publick Worship* of God," and he would shed glory on Herbert by saying that his answers to Melville were "to the satisfaction of all un-ingaged persons."[130] He says further that Melville was "at last so bold" in his raillery that he wrote himself into the Tower, but that he does not care to trouble his reader with an account of Melville's enlargement from prison. The last sentence of Walton's appendix says of Herbert *"He dyed without an Enemy, if* Andrew Melvin *dyed before him?"*[131] His question mark here is well chosen and revealing. He kept it when he rephrased the sentence in moving it into the *Life* proper in 1674, and dropped it in 1675,[132] but in neither year did he offer further information about Melville's enlargement and death. He seems never to have learned that Melville was in the Tower between 1607 and 1611 and that after his release he lived abroad until his death in 1622.[133] By 1675 Walton had learned, however, that Melville had been imprisoned three years, that he was a minister, rector of St. Andrews, and that he had scattered the verses which caused his arrest when he attended a conference at Hampton Court called by King James in "the second year after his Coronation in *England.*"[134] He was faced with the problem of explaining how Herbert came to reply when he was Orator to verses written when he was a child.

Walton seems always to have believed that Herbert had replied to the verses for which Melville had in fact been imprisoned. Herbert's *Musae Responsoriae* is a reply not to these, but to Melville's *Anti-Tami-Cami-Categoria.* This poem was first published in 1620, and its publication brought forth several replies, Herbert's among

---

[129] *Church Hist.,* bk. X, 70.   [130] *Lives,* 1670 (Herbert), p. 24.
[131] *Ibid.,* p. 82.   [132] *Herbert,* 1674, p. 59; *Lives,* 1675, p. 326.
[133] See Thomas McCrie, *Life of Andrew Melville* (Edinburgh, 1899), pp. 270–272, 319, 339.
[134] *Lives,* 1675, pp. 274–275.

them.[135] But Melville had written it in 1603/4 to attack the hostile resolutions of Oxford and Cambridge against the Millenary Petition, and the manuscript had provoked replies at this time.[136] Since Walton was confused about the particular poem of Melville which Herbert had answered and since the date of the composition of *Anti-Tami-Cami-Categoria* was close to that of the verses for which Melville was imprisoned, Walton was content to write in 1675 that Melville's verses were "brought into *Westminster-School,* where Mr. *George Herbert* then, and often after, made . . . answers to them."[137] It is to Walton's credit that he made some effort at revision in the light of his new knowledge.[138] The nature of his revision

[135] Herbert's epigrams were first published by James Duport in his *Ecclesiastes Solomonis,* 1662. Walton referred to Duport's "honourable memorial" of Herbert in 1670 (*Lives* [Herbert], p. 25). Duport wrote commendatory verses which are prefixed to the *Life of Herbert* in *Lives,* 1675, and others for the fifth edition of the *Compleat Angler,* 1676.

[136] See *Works of Herbert,* pp. 587–588.　　　　　[137] *Lives,* 1675, p. 275.

[138] It is hard to determine Walton's sources of information about Melville and Herbert's relationship with him. From his use of the form "Melvin," it appears that he must have known Fuller's passage in *Church Hist.,* bk. X, 70–71. Fuller mentions Melville's release from the Tower under the year 1615 and suggests that after he had procured his liberty and had gone to France he wrote "a *scroule* of *Saphicks,* entituled *TAMI-CHAMI-CATEGERIA.*" Perhaps this chronology misled Walton in 1670. Fuller calls Melville "an excellent Poet (but inferiour to *Buchanan* his Master)," and Walton in 1670, in a sentence dropped in 1675, referred to Melville's wit as "exceeded, I think, by none of that Nation, but their *Bucanen.*" But Fuller gives a different version of the couplet of Melville's which Walton printed to "give the Reader a taste of his others" and rightly says that it was addressed to Sir William Seymour; Walton says that it was addressed to his wife, Lady Arabella. Fuller rightly says, too, that Melville had been imprisoned not for his *Anti-Tami-Cami-Categoria* but "for writing some *satyrical Verses* against the *Ornaments* on the *Altar* (or *Communion-Table*) in the *Kings Chappell.*" He gives one version of the verses and says that Herbert made a most ingenious retort to them. Walton may have had Fuller's account in mind when he wrote in 1670 that Melville wrote "against our *Altars,* our *Prayers,* and our *Publick Worship* of God," but he changed these words in 1675 to "against our *Liturgy,* our *Ceremonies,* and, our *Church-government.*" Fuller makes no mention of Melville's presence at Hampton Court.

Walton's attitude toward Melville is similar to that of Archbishop John Spottiswoode in his *History of the Church of Scotland,* 1655. Walton owned a copy of this history (see the Finding List of the Exhibition of Waltoniana at the Rowfant Club, Cleveland, Oct. 26, 1896) and referred to it in a marginal note in the *Life of Hooker.* Spottiswoode had written, "Mr. *Andrew Melvill* that would not be idle, and was still speaking against the Orders of the *English* Church, having dispersed some bitter and scornfull verses against the Rites used in his Majesties Chappell, which was brought to the King by one of the Chaplains, was called before the Councell of *England,* and charged with the

shows, however, that though he wished, within bounds, to make his details accurate, he was not going to lose his story because of a matter of detail. He did not investigate all the details carefully; he was content to hit upon a scheme that allowed him to use the episode, as he had originally done, in order to bolster his argument that Herbert as Orator was zealous in his attack on the Church of Scotland. It is perhaps fortunate that he had no real understanding of Melville's eminence as a theologian or he might have further inflated and elaborated his tale.[139]

Walton kept up the show of chronology both in 1670 and in the later editions of the *Life* in introducing his next example of Herbert's brilliance as Orator by saying that

About this time King *James* came very often to hunt at *New-market* and *Royston;* and was almost as often invited to *Cambridge,* where his entertainment was suted to his pleasant humor*, and where Mr. *George Herbert* was to welcome him with *Gratulations,* and the *Applauses* of an *Orator;* which he alwayes perform'd so well, that he still grew more into the Kings favour.[140]

His marginal note identified the entertainment as *"Albumizer"* and *"Ignoramus."* "The year following" is the phrase which Walton uses to date the next visit of James to Cambridge and to introduce the story of Herbert's friendship with Francis Bacon and Lancelot Andrewes. The King did go to Cambridge just twice while Herbert was Orator, and these visits, the third and the fourth made during his reign, are those which Walton had in mind as he wrote. On the

---

injuring of the State and Church: where in stead of acknowledging his offence, he behaved himself insolently; and more like a mad man, then Divine; for which he was committed in the Tower of *London.* There he remained three years and more, and afterwards upon the Duke of *Bulloign* his request, was sent to *Sedan,* where he lived in no great respect, and contracting the Gout lay almost bedfast to his death" (p. 500). Spottiswoode mentions Melville's presence at Hampton Court, but makes it plain that Melville was there from Sept. 22, 1606 (p. 497)

[139] Grosart's patience with Walton exploded at the point of his account of Melville. He wrote, "Dear as are 'meek' Walton's name and memory, the truth must at long-last be told, and this mingle-mangle of unhistoric statement and mendacious zeal exposed. There are nearly as many blunders as sentences in the Narrative, and the *animus* is as base as the supercilious ignorance is discreditable. Alas that I must say these 'hard things' of anything from the pen of one I so revere (substantially)! Alas that they should be true!" (*op. cit.,* II, li).

[140] *Lives,* 1670 (Herbert), pp. 25–26.

first of these Herbert did make an oration, but it was a farewell speech, not one of welcome.[141] But Walton confused the King's visit of March 12, 1623, with his first triumphal progress to Cambridge on March 7, 1615. In 1615, the King had been entertained by four plays, Thomas Tomkis' *Albumazar* and George Ruggle's *Ignoramus* among them, and was so delighted that he could hardly wait to see them again.[142] He probably failed in his attempt to get the university players to perform at court, and went to Cambridge again in May to see *Ignoramus*.[143] James's approval must have given the plays a certain notoriety, and Walton, unsure of the chronology of the King's visits, and remembering details vaguely or relying on the blurred reminiscences of others, used the names of the plays to document his account. Evidently he was informed in 1675 that he had attributed to the third visit of the King the plays he had seen on his first trip. In 1675, then, he wrote that the King was entertained by "Comedies," and he omitted the titles.[144] But this was the extent of his concession to accuracy of detail. He did not care to seek out the title of the play that was performed in 1623; more important, he did not try to make more accurate the rest of his account of the King's visits. He was sufficiently mindful of the truth to delete an obviously inaccurate detail, but did not trouble himself to verify other details which he considered only as pegs on which to hang his story of the esteem which Bacon and Andrewes had for Herbert.

But if he provided pegs—albeit somewhat shaky ones—for this account, he did not do so for those which follow. He bolstered Herbert's courtly position by indicating his "long and intire friendship" with Sir Henry Wotton,[145] a friendship which rests entirely on his statement of it. And for the high point of the King's affection for Herbert, he reserves the story that the King gave him a sinecure, "the same, that Queen *Elizabeth* had formerly given to her Favourite Sir *Philip Sidney;* and valued to be worth an hundred and twenty pound *per Annum.*"[146] The high degree of honor that this held for Walton can be estimated only by the lengths to which

---

[141] *"Oratio in Discessum Regis ab Academiâ Cantabrigiae habita* 12° *die Martii* 1622," *Works of Herbert,* pp. 443–444.

[142] See John Chamberlain's letters of March 16 and *ca.* 30, 1615, to Sir Dudley Carleton. Norman Egbert McClure, ed., *The Letters of John Chamberlain* (Philadelphia, 1939), I, 586–592.

[143] *Ibid.,* p. 597.

[144] *Lives,* 1675, p. 276.

[145] *Ibid.,* 1670 (Herbert), p. 27.

[146] *Ibid.,* p. 28.

he went to squeeze a reference to Sidney into the *Life of Wotton*. That the story makes its point, and strongly, is undeniable. But it, too, rests only on Walton's authority.[147]

Although the material available immediately to Walton emphasized Herbert's days at Bemerton, nowhere in it did he find three facts necessary to him if he was to produce more than a generalized character. These minimum essentials were the date of Herbert's induction into Bemerton, the date of his entering holy orders, and the date of his death. The *Life* furnishes just one of these dates: it states that Herbert was inducted into Bemerton on April 26, 1630.[148] The other two are given only in a general way. Walton intimates that Herbert was ordained during the Ember week following his induction into Bemerton when he says that Herbert "long'd for the next *Ember-week, that he might be ordain'd Priest.*"[149] This he may have assumed because of the information which he had about the date of Herbert's death, for he dates the death only with reference to the ordination. He says that Bishop Henchman told him, *"He laid his hand on Mr. Herberts Head, and (alas!) within less than three Years, lent his Shoulder to carry his dear Friend to his Grave."* On the surface, it would appear that Walton was satisfied to fill three important gaps with one precise date and two approximations, perhaps volunteered by Henchman. But it would surely be odd for Henchman to have given Walton a precise date for Herbert's induction into Bemerton, though there is no evidence that he was present, and approximations for two events which he witnessed. Woodnoth, however, was present at Herbert's induction into Bemerton. Did he give the date to Walton? Woodnoth may have told Walton that Herbert was inducted into Bemerton on April 26, 1630, may even have told him that Herbert died on March 1, 1633, for he was present at his death and wrote Ferrar that Herbert died "Uppon friday about foure a Clock" and that "His will He made but Uppon munday before hee dyed."[150] Although Walton's account of Herbert's years at Bemerton shows heavy reliance upon Woodnoth, especially for some of the death-bed details, Walton probably did not remember precisely any dates which Woodnoth might have mentioned. The text of the *Life* shows that Walton found it necessary to supplement what he got from Woodnoth, that he did so perhaps by interviewing in Salisbury

---

[147] See *Works of Herbert*, p. xxxii. [148] *Lives*, 1670 (Herbert), p. 41.
[149] *Ibid.*, p. 48. [150] Blackstone, *op. cit.*, pp. 276–277.

and certainly by talking to Bishop Henchman and Edmund Duncon. Duncon was a qualified informant, but it is unlikely that
he was present at Herbert's institution and even less likely that he
could remember the precise date after forty years. Henchman, to
whom Walton had probably been introduced by Bishop Morley,
was admirably well qualified to know about Herbert. He had been
a contemporary of Herbert's at Cambridge and early in 1623 was
appointed precentor and a prebendary of Salisbury Cathedral. His
ties to Salisbury were strengthened by his marriage in 1630 to the
niece of John Davenant, then Bishop of Salisbury, and he was
himself Bishop of Salisbury for three years after the Restoration.[151]
When he told Walton that he had taken part in Herbert's ordination and that he had been present at Herbert's burial, Walton must
have asked him to date these events. Almost certainly Henchman
referred Walton to the records of the diocese of Salisbury.

There Walton found or had found the exact date of Herbert's
induction into Bemerton, for the register of institutions by Bishop
Davenant is perfect up to 1640.[152] The register of Davenant's ordinations, however, ceases with the year 1625.[153] Still, if Walton
had known definitely that Herbert had waited impatiently for the
Ember week after his induction to be ordained, he would have been
able to write that Herbert's ordination took place on Trinity
Sunday, May 23, 1630. But Walton had no such definite information; his account of Herbert's urgency to enter holy orders as soon
as possible after he had become a parson is an attempt to demonstrate Herbert's piety by letting his readers infer that Herbert
could hardly wait for a month to pass. His refusal to be more
specific may even stem from his knowledge that Herbert was not
ordained until the autumn Ember week. Henchman may not have
remembered the precise day of Herbert's ordination; he may well
have remembered the season. Did he tell Walton that Bishop
Davenant did not normally ordain at the summer Ember season?[154]

---

[151] *DNB*, article "Humphrey Henchman."   [152] Daniell, *op. cit.*, p. 183.

[153] *Ibid.* Daniell says (p. 184) that when the Diocesan Registry at Salisbury
was searched in April, 1893, some old rolls were discovered which proved to
be subscriptions to the articles of candidates for ordination in 1630. Here were
found Herbert's subscription before his institution to Bemerton on April 26
and his subscription before ordination on September 19. These are reproduced
by George Herbert Palmer in *The English Works of George Herbert* (Boston
and New York, 1895), III, opposite pp. 6 and 64.

[154] See Daniell, *op. cit.*, p. 183.

Walton's mere hint of a date may be due to his desire to save himself such an explanation; it may stem, however, from the fact that no such explanation was vouchsafed him.

If Walton did not let his lack of Latin deter him from examining the Salisbury records himself, he probably would have examined the parish register at Bemerton, little more than a mile distant, where his lack of Latin would have been no hindrance. There he would have found the date of Herbert's burial.[155] Perhaps his not reproducing this date is evidence that he did not himself make a journey to Bemerton, that he had only the Salisbury records searched. But it is possible that the date of Herbert's burial was available to him and that his failure to use it reflects something of his own concept of himself as biographer. To give the precise date of Herbert's burial without the date of his death would be to point up a deficiency in his knowledge. Better to omit the date which would so clearly reveal the absence of another date, and to indicate the time only generally.

Apparently, then, Walton went to some trouble to ascertain the three dates so essential to him. But these were crucial dates, and even here Walton's success was only partial. Reference to a few other places in the *Life* will help to show the extent to which Walton troubled himself to search for accurate fact. He did not know the date of Herbert's marriage (March 5, 1629) and therefore placed it about four months before his induction into Bemerton instead of thirteen, so that he could show Herbert swiftly carrying out "his resolution both to marry, and to enter into the Sacred Orders of Priesthood."[156] He felt that it was *"a Debt justly due to the memory of Mr.* Herberts *vertuous Wife"* to give a very short account of the remainder of her life,[157] but, though he wrestled with his facts, he did not care that they were inconsistent: his main desire was to show that in her widowhood, her remarriage, and her second widowhood she ever commended the excellences of Herbert. In 1670, he wrote that she was a widow five years, the wife of Sir Robert Cooke of Highnam for eight, and Cooke's widow for nine years, and then he said that she died in 1663.[158] In 1674, he revised her periods of widowhood to *"about six"* and *"about fifteen,"* but retained 1663

---

[155] Zouch, *op. cit.,* p. 391, note t: "Mr. George Herbert, Esq. Parson of Fugleston and Bemerton, was buried 3d day of March, 1632[3]."

[156] *Lives,* 1670 (Herbert), pp. 36–37.   [157] *Ibid.,* p. 81.

[158] *Ibid.,* pp. 81–82.

as the year of her death.[159] In fact, she died on November 27, 1661, outliving her second husband by eighteen years.[160] If Walton was only vaguely interested in Mrs. Herbert's chronology, he cared less for that of the three nieces who made their home with the Herberts. To be sure, he is not to be condemned here, but he would not have said that the three nieces were present at Herbert's deathbed had he searched out and read Herbert's will. Half of that document is devoted to the legacies of one of the nieces, Dorothy Vaughan. Walton's account of Ferrar, too, shows that he did not concern himself unduly with fact where it was not absolutely essential to his purpose. He says that Ferrar "doubtless had good education,"[161] but he gives no particulars, and when in 1674 he improved his statement that Ferrar "was at a fit age made Fellow of *Clare-Hall* in *Cambridge*," he merely changed "fit" to "early."[162] He dates the beginning of Ferrar's travel "About the 26*th* year of his Age," and says that "not long after his return into *England,* he had by the death of his father, or an elder brother, an Estate left him, that enabled him to buy Land to the value of 500 *l.* a year, the greatest part of which Land was at *Little Gidden,* four or six miles from *Huntington,* and about 18 from *Cambridge*."[163] In fact, Ferrar was twenty when he began his travels in 1613, and he returned to England in 1618, two years before the death of his father.[164] His mother purchased Little Gidding in 1625. Walton's interest in introducing Ferrar into the *Life* is evident, as has been pointed out, in his telling that he was called St. Nicholas when he was six years old and that he maintained his obedience to the Church of England despite attempts to persuade him to embrace Catholicism. Even these details are merely prefatory, for Walton's prime purpose was to illustrate in detail Ferrar's "constant and methodical service of God" at Little Gidding. He was obviously less concerned with the Ferrar chronicle, and he did not bother to supply more than a haphazard and unverified guide.

The *Life of Herbert* is like the others of Walton's *Lives* in that here, too, his own interest and purpose determined the structure of

---

[159] *Herbert,* 1674, p. 60.   [160] *Works of Herbert,* p. 586.

[161] *Lives,* 1670 (Herbert), p. 67.   [162] *Herbert,* 1674, p. 50.

[163] *Lives,* 1670 (Herbert), p. 68. Walton's lack of knowledge here is evident in his indecisive changes. In 1674, he put the value of the land at "4 or 500 *l.* a year" (p. 51), and in 1675 he wrote that Ferrar had his legacy by the death of "his father, or an elder brother, or both" (p. 316).

[164] Blackstone, *op. cit.,* pp. 9, 13, 20–21.

the *Life*. It is like the others, also, in that materials readily available determined the inclusion of some of the details, but Walton's preconceived plan determined the utilization and emphasis of the details. The slight didacticism of the *Life of Wotton* and the covert argumentation in the *Life of Hooker* blossomed into explicit preaching in the *Life of Herbert*. Walton's inclination to stress in the youth of his subjects those characteristics which he wished to display in their maturity, evident in the *Life of Donne* and in the *Life of Hooker,* is obvious in the *Life of Herbert*. This *Life,* moreover, shows how deeply ingrained this propensity was in Walton. His thesis in the *Life of Herbert* turns to a large extent on his ability to demonstrate two sides of Herbert. He must prove him to be noble and brilliant and worldly in order to show that even so noble and brilliant and worldly a man can see fit to renounce the worldly life for the holy one, and he must then show his particular piety to hold him up as an example for the clergy. This thesis is not incompatible with Herbert's life; it provides a clue, an insight, in terms of which Herbert's life can perhaps be best understood. To be sure, it seems to have been chosen independently. It seems that Walton did not arrive at it as the best explanation of Herbert's life, but that it was conceived apart from the life and grafted upon the life. It intrudes too much into the *Life* because Walton was interested in demonstrating it for its own sake, in proving its independent validity. Still, it might have provided a rationale for Herbert's life had it been properly illustrated in terms of Herbert's life. But even in the *Life of Herbert,* where if Walton was to argue convincingly that his thesis was valid he must present a convincing picture of Herbert in his secular brilliance and glory, he was so continually engrossed in finding evidences of the later, saintly Herbert in the earlier courtly man that he succeeds in demonstrating that piety may be present in high places instead of demonstrating that the life of piety has sufficient appeal to attract the class in a best position to be content with worldly toys. To demonstrate his thesis convincingly, Walton needed to present a dramatic conflict in Herbert, or, at least to lay clearly open an important disharmony or ambivalence in his temperament. It is likely that Walton could not represent real struggle in his subjects because he had no experience with it, and he was forced in the *Life of Herbert,* where he felt it necessary to indicate such struggle, to say, "These were such Conflicts, as they only can know, that have endur'd them," and, again, *"He endur'd . . . such spiritual Conflicts, as none can think, but only those that have endur'd them."*[165] Though his thesis cried out for the representation of this struggle, Walton could not show it. So strongly committed was he to the conception of a simple, single, inevitable unity in the life of every man that he must always show the man in the child.[166]

The *Life of Herbert* shows, even as does the *Life of Hooker*, Walton's faith in the reliability of the testimony of others when it fitted his own purpose. His heavy reliance on his conversations with Woodnoth and Duncon indicates his preference for material come by easily and discursively rather than laboriously through the sifting of records. And for the *Life of Herbert* he not only indulged in this method but did not trouble himself to seek out the best informants. His large dependency in this *Life* on the works of his subject, which differentiates it so clearly from the others, shows that he was particularly willing here to lean upon ready material, that he did not feel compelled to search out factual details except in rare instances because the available material itself supported adequately the impression he wished to communicate. The *Life of Herbert* supports the other *Lives* in demonstrating that Walton was sensitively aware of the difference between a character and a biography, but it reveals more clearly than the others that he approached

---

[165] *Lives*, 1670 (Herbert), pp. 31, 40.

[166] In the best recent interpretation of Herbert's life (ch. ii of *George Herbert, His Religion and Art* [London, 1954]), Joseph H. Summers says that there is a central core of truth in Walton's remarks about Herbert's worldly ambition and its frustration, but, he says, Walton's "dramatization" is misleading. He suggests that the transformation from the Cambridge orator to the parson-poet of Bemerton was perhaps not so great as it seemed to Walton and even to Herbert in retrospect. Summers thinks that Walton has too radically dichotomized Herbert. I am suggesting that Walton has not made the dichotomy which he would present sufficiently convincing and persuasive to support his thesis.

The sheer amount of holy material in the secular part of Herbert's life as drawn by Walton fits Summers' interpretation better than it fits Walton's. Summers holds that Herbert's change was no sudden conversion, that Herbert was devoted to religion from his seventeenth year, that for a long time he saw no necessary contradiction in his desire to combine divinity with a high place in civil affairs, and that his enormous disappointment at not advancing on the courtly ladder disillusioned him and made him condemn what he had once thought feasible. His treatment of Herbert as an Elizabethan idealist who would be both statesman and divine seems satisfactory until we ask why Herbert felt it essential to press so exclusively and so long for earthly preferment. It would seem that Herbert envisioned himself as a statesman with religious interests rather than as a divine who might wield civil influence.

biography with a far more avid interest in character than in events. He saw the necessity for the chronological approach in biography, and followed it even if he had to invent the chronology. But in this respect the *Life of Herbert,* which came after the *Life of Hooker,* represents a reversion to the *Life of Donne.* In the light of the *Life of Herbert* the factual particularity of the *Life of Hooker* stands out afresh, and it is possible to see in its detail the extent to which Walton's *Life* was determined by the necessity of correcting Gauden's *Life.* His purpose there, supplemented probably by documents made available to him by the bishops, was far different from the free-will offering which the *Life of Herbert* is. In the *Life of Hooker,* factual detail, handled freely to be sure, was essential to his thesis and purpose. But in the *Life of Herbert* Walton was again satisfied to produce a quasi-chronological life. His purpose could be fulfilled with vague chronology, and he was more interested in elaborating a portrait by anecdote and in teaching lessons that were timeless. Walton's particularity of detail in illustrating character sets him apart from the other biographers of his time. But it would be wrong to equate this quality in the *Life of Herbert* with detailed research, accuracy of fact, or even reliable authentication.

The *Life of Herbert* was twice revised, first in 1674 when it was added to "The Tenth Edition" of Herbert's *The Temple* and again in the following year when it appeared in the second edition of the *Lives.* It has already been suggested that in both revisions Walton did alter such details as might detract from the general reliability of the *Life* as a whole. Even if he was frequently satisfied with less than precise accuracy of fact, he did attempt to approach the truth more closely in 1674 by correcting Woodnoth's given name and by revising his data about Herbert's widow and in 1675 by changing his account of Melville and by omitting his reference to Herbert's minor fellowship. In 1674, too, he dropped his story about the destruction of Herbert's library in Montgomery Castle[167] and he revised his estimate of the number of copies which *The Temple*

---

[167] *Lives,* 1670 (Herbert), p. 82: The *"late Rebels,"* Walton said, *"burnt or destroyed a choice Library, which Mr.* Herbert *had fastned with Chains, in a fit room in* Mountgomery *Castle, being by him dedicated to the succeeding* Herberts, *that should become the owners of it."* Daniell conjectured that Walton "had received some intimations that the Library was not destroyed" (*op. cit.,* pp. 308–309).

had sold from "Ten thousand"[168] to "more then Twenty thousand."[169] This estimate, however, probably shows again that Walton frequently left fact behind in lieu of a proper impression. To
be sure, he may have had more accurate figures in 1674, but it is
more likely that he felt it necessary to increase the number of
copies sold because four years had elapsed since his first estimate.
There was no new printing of *The Temple* between 1667 and
1674. Walton was sufficiently interested in factual accuracy to
change in 1675 his reference to Laud at the time of Herbert's induction into Bemerton from "the Archbishop of *Canterbury*"[170] to
"then Bishop of *London,* and after Archbishop of *Canterbury,*"[171]
but he still referred to Sir Henry Herbert and Herbert Thorndike
as living, though the one had died in 1673 and the other in 1672.
How erratic Walton was with detail which might be considered
adventitious is evident in his taking note in 1674 of Robert
Creighton's advancement (in 1670) from Dean to Bishop of Bath
and Wells, but in never altering his reference to Creighton, who
died in 1672, to the past tense.[172]

Since Walton indicated in 1670 that his *Life of Herbert* was not
"writ in haste,"[173] it was hardly to be expected that in four years
he would have any large additions to make. Still, he added to the
body of the *Life* in 1674 another letter from Herbert to his
mother.[174] Long, full of scriptural consolation to his mother in her
sickness, Herbert's letter is dated *"Trin.* Col. *May* 29. 1622," and
obviously belongs to the oratorship period of Herbert's life. Walton did not put it there, but after the Leighton episode. He probably saw that in the Melville and Bacon and Andrewes passages he
had more than sufficiently stressed Herbert's holy inclinations at
the time of his greatest temporal glory; the fulsome piety of the
letter would have thoroughly diffused Walton's emphasis on Herbert's worldly attainments. Placed where it is, the letter foreshadows
Herbert's illness and his mother's death and, coming just after the
Leighton episode, is further evidence of his holiness. Also, coming
just after the brief sketch of Woodnoth, the letter fitted easily into
the text; Walton was able to say that Woodnoth delivered it, for
he had written immediately before that Woodnoth was a useful

---

[168] *Lives,* 1670 (Herbert), p. 75.   [169] *Herbert,* 1674, p. 56.
[170] *Lives,* 1670 (Herbert), p. 40.   [171] *Ibid.,* 1675, p. 292.
[172] *Ibid.,* 1670 (Herbert), p. 37; *Herbert,* 1674, p. 27.
[173] *Lives,* 1670, sig. A6ᵛ.   [174] *Herbert,* 1674, pp. 22–25.

friend to Herbert's father and mother and that there was a holy friendship between him and Herbert. It has been shown that Woodnoth probably did not know Herbert as early as 1622, but here as elsewhere in Walton's writing the exigencies of fact gave way before the exigencies of impression.

This letter constitutes Walton's major addition to the *Life*. The extent of his care in the revisions may be estimated in the light of his own apology in 1670 that he had intended to "review" the *Life* before it was made public but had not been in London when it was being printed, *"so that the Reader may finde in it, some double expressions, and some not very proper, and some that might have been contracted, and, some faults that are not justly chargable upon me but the Printer."*[175] The Errata which appear in 1670 bear out Walton's statement, and these changes were incorporated into the revised text. In 1674, Walton corrected another printer's error when he changed, in a speech attributed to Herbert, the nonsensical *"any title of being a Priest"*[176] to *"my title"*;[177] but he never corrected an even more obvious mistake. His copy in 1670 probably read, "About the year 1626. and the 34*th* of his Age, Mr. *Herbert . . . ,"* and the printer had inverted a six and produced "1629."[178] In Walton's failure to pick up this error, we may find again his subsidiary interest in chronology.

By *"double expressions"* Walton probably meant expressions which he had used more than once without intending to do so. For example, he had written in 1670, "And now his care was to recover from his Consumption by a change, from *Woodford* into such an air as was most proper to that end. And his remove was from *Woodford* to *Dantsey* in *Wiltshire*."[179] In 1675, he omitted the second "from *Woodford*."[180] *"Double expressions"* may have been intended to cover also those which led him into inconsistencies. He had written of Herbert before his marriage that his speech and motion *"were all so meek and oblieging, that both then, and at his death, he was said to have no Enemy,"*[181] but the last sentence of the appendix had read, *"He dyed without an Enemy, if Andrew Melvin dyed before him?"*[182] In 1674, he changed the first of these statements to *"were all so meek and obliging, that they purchased love*

[175] *Lives,* 1670, sig. A6ᵛ.
[176] *Ibid.* (Herbert), p. 43.
[177] *Herbert,* 1674, p. 32.
[178] *Lives,* 1670 (Herbert), p. 35.
[179] *Ibid.,* p. 36.
[180] *Ibid.,* 1675, p. 289.
[181] *Ibid.,* 1670 (Herbert), p. 37.
[182] *Ibid.,* p. 82.

and respect from all that knew him."[183] It is possible to see purpose in Walton's never altering the double expression that Herbert's conflicts were such as only they can know "that have endur'd them," for the restatement not only saves him the analysis in each case but serves to set Herbert apart from ordinary men. It is possible to see purpose, too, in his failure to strike out the repetition about Herbert's being made deacon,[184] for the repetition partly compensates for his not being able to give an important date. There may be conscious reiteration in Walton's saying of Herbert when he was at Westminster school that "the beauties of his pretty behaviour and wit, shin'd and became so eminent and lovely in this his innocent age, that he seem'd to be marked out for piety, and to become the care of Heaven,"[185] and in his saying that Herbert at sixteen "seem'd to be mark'd out for vertue, and to become the care of Heaven,"[186] for he wished to indicate strongly the pious strain in Herbert before he showed him in the temporal glory of the oratorship. It is not likely, however, that his triple play upon the hymns and anthems sung in heaven, first by Donne and Mrs. Herbert, next by the blessed saints, and then by Herbert and Ferrar,[187] is intentional, but the triple expression went unaltered. Nor was there any reason to state twice that the chapel at Bemerton was adjoining to the parsonage, but this, too, was never changed.[188] Walton had said of Herbert's personal devotions that he appeared "constantly with his Wife, and three Neeces (the daughters of a deceased Sister),"[189] and his later mention of Herbert's three nieces as "then a part of his Family"[190] is unnecessary, but he never omitted his second explanation. That Walton's changes are only partial probably indicates less than a consuming interest in his revisions for the *Life of Herbert.*[191]

Changes of expression are frequent in 1674, and there are some

---

[183] *Herbert*, 1674, p. 27.

[184] *Lives*, 1670 (Herbert), p. 32: "within that year he was made Deacon, but the day when, or by whom, I cannot learn; but that he was about that time made Deacon, is most certain"; *ibid.*, p. 41: "and he gave him Institution immediately (for Mr. *Herbert* had been made Deacon some years before)."

[185] *Ibid.*, p. 12.   [186] *Ibid.*, p. 21.   [187] *Ibid.*, pp. 18, 52, 77.

[188] *Ibid.*, pp. 46, 58.   [189] *Ibid.*, p. 58.   [190] *Ibid.*, p. 76.

[191] In the copy of *Lives*, 1675, in the Albert H. Childs Memorial Collection at Yale, Walton crossed out on p. 261 the tautological "*blessed blessing*" of Mary Magdalene's having her sins pardoned, and substituted "*machles mercie.*" His attempt to delete the double expressions was a continuing one if a haphazard one.

in 1675, but again it is difficult to be certain of what Walton meant by *"some not very proper"* expressions. Perhaps his substituting in 1674 a plural pronoun referring to "clergy" for the original *"him"*[192] was the correction of such an expression, though it may be the correction of a printer's error. His description of a conversation between Duncon and Herbert as "some discourse"[193] seems more proper than the original "a conference."[194] Walton was dissatisfied with the looseness of the construction of one of Herbert's speeches, which started:

I now look back upon the pleasures of my life past, and see the content I have taken in beauty, in wit, in musick, and pleasant Conversation, how they are now all past by me, as a shadow that returns not, and are all become dead to me, or I to them; that as my father and generation hath done before me, so I shall now suddenly (with Job) *make my Bed also in the dark; and, I praise God, I am prepar'd for it; and, that I am not to learn patience, now I stand in such need of it.*[195]

But his revision is hardly more proper:

I now look back upon the pleasures of my life past, and see the content I have taken in beauty, in wit, in musick, and pleasant Conversation, are now all past by me, like a dream, or as a shadow that returns not, and are now all become dead to me, or I to them; and I see that as my father and generation hath done before me, so I also shall now suddenly (with Job) *make my Bed also in the dark; and, I praise God I am prepared for it; and I praise him, that I am not to learn patience, now I stand in such need of it.*[196]

Walton's reference to expressions which he might have contracted is an intriguing one, for his tendency was certainly in the other direction. The revision of 1674 shows that to a minute degree Walton did make some effort to check his normal impulse. "An *Anchor,* which is the emblem of hope"[197] became "an *Anchor* (the emblem of hope),"[198] and *"a kind of Vow to God"*[199] became "a Vow to God."[200] Walton had written of Ferrar that "he did so contemn the World";[201] both his subject and his object were repetitive, and he omitted the subject and referred to his object pronomi-

[192] *Lives,* 1670 (Herbert), p. 61; *Herbert,* 1674, p. 46.
[193] *Herbert,* 1674, p. 49.　　　　　[194] *Lives,* 1670 (Herbert), p. 66.
[195] *Ibid.,* p. 76.　　　　　　　　　[196] *Herbert,* 1674, p. 57.
[197] *Lives,* 1670 (Herbert), p. 27.　　[198] *Herbert,* 1674, p. 15.
[199] *Lives,* 1670 (Herbert), p. 34.　　[200] *Herbert,* 1674, p. 21.
[201] *Lives,* 1670 (Herbert), p. 68.

nally.[202] He had originally written of Valdesso's *The Hundred and Ten Considerations,* "which Book, Mr. *Herbert* did read, and return back with many marginal Notes, as they be now printed with that excellent Book."[203] In 1674, he replaced the last three words by "it," but he inserted the adjective before "Book."[204] This "saving" characteristic of Walton is in keeping with his customary method, and it is no surprise that for every contraction, there are several unnecessary expansions. In 1674, a reference to Donne and Magdalen Herbert as "them"[205] was, for the sake of an adjective, changed to "these two worthy persons."[206] "Who had sent"[207] became "upon the occasion of his sending,"[208] and "being then high"[209] became "he being at that time very high."[210] "Mutual affections"[211] turned into "mutual and equal affections";[212] "decayed"[213] was coupled with "fall'n down";[214] "weak"[215] was added to show why Duncon found the ill Herbert on his bed. Although he had already stated that Duncon "betook himself to a Journey to *Bath,*"[216] Walton added that his return was "from the Bath."[217] In 1675, prior to quoting from Donne's "The Autumnall," Walton inserted that Donne wrote "in verse";[218] and to Herbert's words to his mother, *"my poor Abilities in* Poetry, *shall be all, and ever consecrated to Gods glory,"*[219] he added, "and I beg you to receive this as one testimony."[220] He had said that Donne had closed a letter to Magdalen Herbert with the words, "Your unworthiest Servant, unless your accepting him, have mended him";[221] he now elucidated, *"unless, your accepting him to be so, have mended him."*[222] Nor did the Herbert letter inserted in 1674 escape untouched. Herbert had written, "Your last Letter gave me Earthly preferment, and kept

---

[202] *Herbert,* 1674, p. 51.

[203] *Lives,* 1670 (Herbert), p. 72.

[204] *Herbert,* 1674, p. 54.

[205] *Lives,* 1670 (Herbert), p. 16.

[206] *Herbert,* 1674, p. 7.

[207] *Lives,* 1670 (Herbert), p. 23.

[208] *Herbert,* 1674, p. 12.

[209] *Lives,* 1670 (Herbert), p. 28.

[210] *Herbert,* 1674, p. 16.

[211] *Lives,* 1670 (Herbert), p. 39.

[212] *Herbert,* 1674, p. 28.

[213] *Ibid.,* p. 33.

[214] *Lives,* 1670 (Herbert), p. 45.

[215] *Herbert,* 1674, p. 49; *Lives,* 1670 (Herbert), p. 66.

[216] *Lives,* 1670 (Herbert), p. 67.

[217] *Herbert,* 1674, p. 55.

[218] *Lives,* 1675, p. 267.

[219] *Ibid.,* 1670 (Herbert), p. 20.

[220] *Ibid.,* 1675, p. 271.

[221] *Ibid.,* 1670 (Herbert), p. 17. Walton himself was responsible for these words, which are a paraphrase of the close of Donne's letter of July 11, 1607, to Mrs. Herbert, printed in the appendix to the *Life of Herbert.* See "The Dating of Donne's *La Corona,*" *PQ,* XXXVI (1957), 259–265.

[222] *Ibid.,* 1675, p. 269.

Heavenly for your self."[223] Walton inserted *"I hope"* after the conjunction.[224] He meddled unnecessarily in 1674 with Herbert's speeches to insert in one place a reference to Matthew, *"though my spirit be willing yet my flesh is weak";*[225] in another place "[I] *do not repine at my want of health"*[226] was expanded to *"I do not repine but am pleas'd with my want of health."*[227] Only in 1675 is a more artful emphasis added, when Walton followed *"thus lowly, was Mr.* George Herbert *in his own eyes"*[228] with the words "and thus lovely in the eyes of others."[229]

Measured even against the apology of 1670, Walton's revisions are only partial. That the apology was dictated by his peculiar modesty rather than by any serious doubts about his work is clear in his adding to the apology in 1675, after the most obvious errors had been rectified, *"some mistakes"*[230] before his original list of faults. Walton had carried out his intent well in 1670, so well that there was little that he could make more explicit in the revisions. He had put a halo about Herbert's head, had made his case that the halo glorified even noble and learned heads, and had shown the clergy precisely how they, too, could obtain like halos. His revisions serve only to show that he was himself pleased by his accomplishment.

---

[223] *Herbert,* 1674, p. 23.

[224] *Lives,* 1675, p. 285.

[225] *Herbert,* 1674, p. 49.

[226] *Lives,* 1670 (Herbert), p. 74.

[227] *Herbert,* 1674, p. 55.

[228] *Lives,* 1670 (Herbert), p. 46.

[229] *Ibid.,* 1675, p. 297. When he made an addition to the *Life of Herbert* in the copy of the 1675 *Lives* now in the Childs Collection at Yale, Walton followed his usual bent. The second paragraph of the Introduction had started by making an adequate reference to the first, *"Upon occasion of which fair example . . ."* Walton now inserted gratuitously after these words, "of our saviours perpetuating, the n[ame] of th[is] hapi[e] wo[man]."

[230] *Lives,* 1675, sig. A5[v].

PART V

The Diocesan and the Dissenters:

History and Augury

Chapter 11

The Remarkable *Life* of Dr. Sanderson

IN 1678 was published *The Life of Dr. Sanderson, Late Bishop of Lincoln. Written by Izaak Walton. To which is added, Some short Tracts or Cases of Conscience, written by the said Bishop.* The title page is an indication of how far Walton had come since 1640. Then the few folio pages of the *Life of Donne* had served as a prefatory memoir to the vast bulk of Donne's sermons. In 1651, his *Life of Wotton* was introductory to Wotton's scattered papers. When the *Life of Donne* was independently printed in 1658, Walton apologized for its appearing without its original bulwark. But no such apology was necessary for the *Life of Hooker* in 1665, and Marriot's exploitation of the *Life of Herbert* in 1670 is evidence that Walton's repute was well established. In 1674, the printers of the tenth edition of Herbert's *The Temple* thought that Walton's *Life* would add to the attractiveness of their volume. The following year a second edition of the collected *Lives* was called for, and the next year saw the appearance of the fifth edition of *The Compleat Angler.* In 1678, the *Life of Sanderson* is no prefatory memoir to some of Sanderson's tracts. On the contrary, the cases of conscience by the Bishop of Lincoln, one of the most highly esteemed of Anglican casuists, and a sermon by the great Hooker are an appendix to Walton's *Life,* the by-product of his research.

If the *Life* was not written to introduce Robert Sanderson's remains, why was it written? Walton himself suggests that at eighty-five his age might have procured him a "Writ of Ease,"[1] and we

1 *Sanderson*, 1678, sig. A6r.

must agree with him despite our knowledge that his was a late-flourishing talent. In his Preface, he tells his readers that he undertook the *Life* because he wondered that no one had seen fit, in the fifteen years since Sanderson's death, to preserve his memory, and because he met "with such perswasions to begin, and so many willing Informers since, and from them and others, such helps and incouragements to proceed."[2] It is likely that he had thought about writing the *Life* for some time. George Morley had introduced him to Sanderson, perhaps at Great Tew, about 1638,[3] and his admiration of Sanderson is obvious in the words that he wrote at the end of the Preface (1655) of Sanderson's *Sermons* which he had purchased on June 25, 1658: "This Preface is an humble and bold challenge to the dissenting brethren of the Clergy of England: And was writ by that humble and good man the author, in the times of persecution and danger."[4] His respect for Sanderson is obvious in his citation of Sanderson's opinion on Hooker in 1665, and some intimacy of knowledge is there displayed in his reference to Sanderson's prohibiting the publication after his death of his previously unprinted manuscripts.[5] In his epistle to the reader of the *Lives* (1670), he expresses his confidence that the next age will continue to admire the learning and clear reason in Sanderson's works, and he reveals not only his desire that Sanderson's life be written but also what it is in Sanderson that he admires when he asks:

Who, if they love vertue, would not rejoyce to know that this good man was as remarkable for the meekness and innocence of his life, *as for his great learning; and as remarkable for his* Fortitude, *in his long and* patient *suffering (under them, that then call'd themselves the Godly Party) [as] for that* Doctrine, *which he had* preach'd and printed, *in the happy daies of the Nations and the Churches peace?*[6]

If, in the epistle of 1670, Walton wishes that someone else would write the life of Sanderson, he shows at the same time that he has sufficiently considered such a life that he can sketch the lines which ought to be followed. He must have felt a deep desire to write the life of a diocesan. Although not consciously at first, perhaps, he had dedicated his pen to the Church. He had memorialized a

[2] *Ibid.,* sigs. A6r–A6v.

[3] *Ibid.,* sigs. A3v–A4r. See also my article "Izaak Walton, Bishop Morley, and *Love and Truth," RES,* n.s. II (1951), 34–35.

[4] Nicolas, p. xciii.   [5] *Hooker,* 1665, pp. 171–172.

[6] *Lives* (1670), sig. A7r.

preacher, an evangelist, a champion, and a parson. Still, he had ever been an ardent advocate of episcopacy and he had long been intimately acquainted with many bishops. It must have seemed to him, as it does to us, that the writing of the life of a bishop would be the logical culmination of his endeavors. But why Sanderson? Since the Restoration, the Church had lost such good sons and fathers as Brian Duppa, William Juxon, John Bramhall, John Earle, Jeremy Taylor, and Henry King. Walton's choice probably reveals again his long friendship and great love for Bishop Morley.

There is little doubt that Walton wished to write Morley's life. His admiration for Morley is evident in the indebtedness he so freely emphasizes in his dedications in the *Lives* and in the *Sanderson*. And he cannot resist introducing a digressive encomium of Morley in the *Sanderson*. But while Morley lived, Walton would not write his life. He wrote instead the life of Morley's great friend. Morley had known Sanderson at Oxford and at Great Tew; together they had attended the unhappy King on the Isle of Wight in 1648; together they had been ejected from their stalls at Christ Church; together they had been consecrated at Westminster; and together they had labored at the Savoy Conference. Morley's high regard for Sanderson is evident in his singling him out for mention when he wishes to refer to a churchman known for piety, learning, and fortitude:

Many *Livings* were so poor, that the haughty *Presbyterians* disdained to stoop to them, and therefore suffered those that were owners of them to continue in them, though they read the *Liturgy*, and professed and Preached for *Loyalty*: and of these I know and can name divers, as I can some others likewise, whose interest and reputation for Piety and Learning was so great in the Countries wherein they lived, that their Enemies thought it better to expect their Deaths, than by depriving them of their *Benefices*, to contract so much hatred, as they should have done unto themselves. And of these I will name but one for all, *viz.* the Reverend, Learned, and Pious Dr. *Sanderson*, (now Bishop of *Lincoln*) who notwithstanding he was for the aforesaid reason suffered to keep his *Benefice*, yet I think no man will be so impudently malicious as to say, that he renounced either his *Religion* or his *Loyalty* by so doing. For he never took the *Covenant*, nor *Ingagement*, nor ever used the *Directory*, but officiated always as he ought to do; and always maintained both the *Doctrine* and *Discipline* of our *Church*, as well publickly in *Print*, as privately in his *Pulpit*; witness his *Judicium Oxoniense*, his *Lectures* touching the *Obligation of Oaths*, and that excellent Volume of *Sermons,* all Printed, or Reprinted, and owned by him, during the time of the *Rebellion,* together with that Learned, Judicious, and Resolute *Preface* (before his Book of *Sermons*) wherein the *Authority, Government* and *Discipline* of the *Church of England* is unanswerably asserted against the *Presbyterians* and all other *Sects* and *Sectaries,* who then domineered in and over the whole Kingdom.[7]

It is likely, too, that Morley had another motive, a more immediate provocation, for wishing Walton to write Sanderson's life. In 1663, the very year of Sanderson's death, there was published a pamphlet entitled *Reason and Judgement: or, Special Remarques Of the Life Of the Renowned Dr. Sanderson, Late Lord Bishop of Lincoln.* Since it appeared with both Oxford and London imprints, it is almost inconceivable that Morley should not know it. If he and Walton were unaware of it in 1670, it is hardly likely that they were ignorant of it after that time, for certainly readers of Walton's plea for a life of Sanderson would have made *Reason and Judgement* known to him. Still, Walton reiterated his plea in 1675,[8] and again in 1678 he wrote that no one had undertaken to write the life.[9] Here is neither ignorance nor inadvertence, but conscious omission. *Reason and Judgement* seems to be an inoffensive character, inadequate and undistinguished, unworthy of mention. But even if it were only the harmless, well-meaning tribute it has always been thought to be, we may surmise that Morley would have liked to see a more impressive memorial erected.

Neither his own inclinations nor Morley's desire for a corrective to *Reason and Judgement* was strong enough to disrupt Walton's ease. The impetus was more pressing and more challenging. Even the casual reader is quickly aware that the *Life of Sanderson* is not just a biography but also an illustration and a lesson. It is Walton's concern for his lesson which causes him in places to use a magnifying glass instead of a microscope, to write history rather than biography. John Butt rightly says that the *Life of Sanderson* is a return to life-and-times biography: "Just as Hooker became synonymous with the Puritan struggles in Elizabeth's reign, so Sanderson became synonymous with the Puritan struggles in Charles I's reign and the Church's evil days in the Commonwealth period."[10] But

---

[7] *A Letter from Father Cressey . . . with The Bishops Answer to it,* pp. 14–15, in Morley's *Several Treatises, Written upon Several Occasions* (1683).

[8] *Lives,* 1675, sig. A6r.   [9] *Sanderson,* 1678, sig. A5v.

[10] John Butt, "Izaak Walton's Methods in Biography," *Essays and Studies,* XIX (1934), 72.

Walton's interest in history was hardly antiquarian; for him history was a teacher. The story of Elizabethan nonconformity was pertinent to Walton because he felt that it had contemporary parallels; it was included not to provide the background of Hooker's "times" but because it was relevant to the state of church affairs in 1665. It was an integral part of Walton's attempt to aid the re-establishment of the High Church at the Restoration, an aggressive, well-bolstered argument at a time when insecure churchmen felt they could not make the Church secured by law secure enough. In a way it is possible to view the *Life of Sanderson* as a continuation of the *Life of Hooker*. The lives of Hooker and Sanderson overlap for only thirteen years; the history of the times they lived in covers over a century. More important, the *Life of Hooker* was written to help re-establish the High Church, and it is possible to show that the *Life of Sanderson* was an attempt to preserve the re-establishment and maintain the *status quo*. One is an aggressive attack on a citadel, the other a fight to hold the fort. One is an argument, the other a justification. Both reflect the dominant issues which Walton felt were stirring the Church at the time he was writing.

The problem which so agitated Walton prior to 1678 that he was willing to dispense with his writ of ease is an aspect of the chief problem of the century, that of a Church Established and its relation with nonconformity. The problem is broadly that of religious toleration. In our day, we are so entranced by the development of an idea, especially of an idea we cherish, that in our hot pursuit of its development we forget or minimize the pressures, political, religious, economic, which may have affected it and we divorce it from the context of history. This is peculiarly true of the idea of religious toleration. The admirable and persuasive works of John Tulloch and W. K. Jordan, with their pictures of the almost inevitable development and growth of the idea, have obscured for us, whatever their authors' intentions, the motivations of the idea and resistance to the idea. We become so greatly interested in Latitudinarian thought that we attribute to pure philosophical speculation what may have been dictated in part by more mundane considerations, and we look on the maturity of Falkland and Chillingworth—if we look on it at all—as disappointing and anticlimactic. We become so fascinated in the ideas of the Cambridge Platonists that we overestimate their immediate influence. In order

to show precisely what led Walton to sharpen his quill once more
and to explain also his point of view, it is necessary to take the idea
of toleration into the political and religious arena, to see not only
what the High Church and, more specifically, Bishop Morley
thought, but also what they did.

Jordan sums up his four volumes on the development of religious
toleration in England by stating, "The evidence which this work
has examined suggests that in 1660 the mass of men in England—
what might be described as the centre of gravity of opinion—had
conceded the case for religious toleration with very few reservations."[11] He thinks that Cromwell and the Puritans grossly over-
estimated the strength which the Laudian extremists possessed in
the Church of England. He points out that between 1640 and 1660
those who wrote as Anglican extremists were men whose philosophy
stemmed from politics rather than from religion, who were royalists
rather than churchmen, and he says that he has not found a single
theological defense of the Anglo-Catholic position.[12] It is hard to
believe that Cromwell was to a large degree misinformed. Even if
we were to accept Jordan's statistics or lack of them with regard to
treatises defending the Anglo-Catholic position, we must remember
that there is no necessary correlation between Laudian strength and
Laudian articulateness; the paucity of Sheldon's words is no measure
of the violence of his belief. Laudians in general appear to have
been far more interested in the enforcement of their discipline than
in the justification of their doctrine.

Jordan develops at length the thesis that there was during these
years a great body of moderate Anglican thought. He says that "at
no other time in its history has the Church of England ever attained
so large and magnanimous a conception of its mission, so rich and
tolerant a charity, and so reasonable and thoughtful a definition of
the sources of its strength as during the period of its greatest physical weakness."[13] He says that the Anglican thinkers of this moderate
group did not "at any time plead for particular ends while conceal-
ing general convictions that lay at variance with their announced
aspirations."[14] The group which he mentions is a remarkably motley
assortment: John Davenant and Thomas Fuller, Jeremy Taylor and
Bramhall, Thorndike and Gauden, Edward Reynolds, Sanderson,

[11] W. K. Jordan, *The Development of Religious Toleration in England*
(Cambridge, Mass., 1932–1940), IV, 467.
[12] *Ibid.*, pp. 361–362.   [13] *Ibid.*, p. 434.   [14] *Ibid.*, p. 435.

and Hammond. Such a conglomeration explains in part why Jordan could find no treatises defending the Anglo-Catholic position. By calling Hammond and Thorndike moderate Anglicans, Jordan gives extremity a new name and admirably supports Hammond's words "that as far as he knoweth, all that owned the same Cause with him against the Presbyterians, were come to be of his mind herein" and Baxter's contention that Hammond's "new singular way of Pleading for Episcopacy," his Laudian approach to Church structure, became identified with orthodox Anglicanism.[15] Also, it may not be unreasonable to question the honesty of a deposed group, to think, even if we do not question it, that the honesty was conditioned by special circumstances and that different circumstances might lead to a different honesty. The intentions of all these men are not open to equal suspicion, but we may wonder about those of the men who were most closely affiliated with the High Church. There is an ambiguity which Jordan does not intend in his statement that "the peculiar strength and quality of his [Jeremy Taylor's] moderation is to be found in the fact that he framed the magnificent architecture of his conception in an age when the Church which he loved lay in ruins."[16] Where do we find Taylor's real attitude in 1647? In *The Liberty of Prophesying* he devotes Section XVI to *"Whether it be lawfull for a Prince to give toleration to severall Religions"* and he concludes that

it concernes the duty of a Prince because it concernes the Honour of God, that all vices and every part of ill life be discountenanced and restrain'd: And therefore in relation to that, opinions are to be dealt with. . . . In all other cases it is not onely lawfull to permit them, but it is also necessary, that Princes and all in authority should not persecute discrepant opinions.[17]

In the same year Taylor signed, with Sanderson, Duppa, Sheldon, Brian Walton, Hammond, and others, a paper in Hammond's hand:

Qu: Whither upon any necessity or exigence of state it bee lawfull for a Christian Prince, beside the Religion established, so to tolerate the exercise of other religions in his Kingdome, as to oblige himself not to punish any subject for the exercise of any of them?

[15] *Reliquiae Baxterianae: or, Mr. Richard Baxter's Narrative of The most Memorable Passages of his Life and Times,* ed. Matthew Sylvester (London, 1696), Appendix VIII, p. 124.

[16] Jordan, *op. cit.,* IV, 409.

[17] *A Discourse of The Liberty of Prophesying* (London, 1647), pp. 216–217.

Answe[r]:
That

Although every Christian Prince bee obliged by all just and Christian wayes to maintein and promote to his power the Christian religion in the truth and purity of it, yet in case of such exigence and concernment of Church and state as that they cannot in humane reason probably be preserv'd otherwise, We cannot say that in conscience it is unlawfull, but that a Christian Prince hath in such exigents a latitude alowd him, the bounding whereof is by God left to him.[18]

Is Taylor's real attitude in his published statement that latitude is not only lawful but necessary, or in the unpublished begrudging and hedged response that latitude is not unlawful if the existence of Church and State is threatened?

We are willing to agree with Jordan that the *theory* of religious toleration was complete in 1660; we may even be willing to agree that *on paper* the case for religious toleration had been won by 1660. But Jordan himself is aware of the difficulty of accommodating institutions to the fact of historical change and he is aware of a "reaction" which entered England with the Restoration. It is conventional to charge this "reaction" to royalist and episcopal extremists, but such a group does not spring to life in a day. Laud's disciples had not been beheaded with Laud, and his beheading brought him new disciples. For fifteen years, a learned, energetic group of them had worked together in England, while an equally devoted and talented group had clung together on the continent. If we are surprised to find in 1647 so begrudging a commitment to toleration from Hammond and Sheldon and Sanderson, all of whom consorted earlier with the Falkland group at Great Tew, we shall be even more surprised to find that among the firmer advocates of the prerogatives of the crown and the mitre at the Restoration were not only Sheldon and Sanderson, but also their friends at Great Tew, Morley and Hyde. But the Latitudinarian group of the thirties was socially conservative, strongly royalist, and addicted at least to an Erastian episcopacy, and it is not difficult to believe that twenty unpleasant years had hardened them. The wars had forced them to side with extremity; at the Restoration, they saw new champions waving their old banners with the enlightenment which springs from exigency and expediency. They did not care to look

[18] Tanner MSS, LVIII, pt. 2, f. 454, printed in *The Works of Robert Sanderson, D.D.,* ed. William Jacobson (Oxford, 1854), VI, 459–460.

upon the interregnum as a scourge for their sins; Walton does not follow the text of Oley and of Gauden in self-chastisement. They did not think, "What did we do that was wrong?"; they thought only that they must not concede anything that would in the least impair their power restored. Walton was typical of most men in that whatever he thought and wrote in the Restoration was written with the outcast years in mind. These years had identified in many minds heresy and treason; nonconformity was disloyal and insurrectionary. As late as 1714, John Walker quotes on the title page of his *Sufferings of the Clergy* Bramhall's words:

Let Mr. Baxter sum up into one Catalogue *all the Nonconformists throughout the Kingdom of* England, *ever since the Beginning of the Reformation, who have been* Cast aside, *or* Driven away—I *dare abate him* all the rest of the Kingdom, *and only exhibit the Martyrologies of* London *and the* Two Universities; *or a List of those, who in these Late Intestine Wars have been* Haled away to Prisons, *or* Chased away into Banishment *by his* own Party, *in* these Three Places alone, *or left to the Merciless World to* Beg their Bread, *for* no other Crime *than* Loyalty, *and because they* stood affected to the Ancient Rites and Ceremonies of the Church of *England, and they shall* Double them for Number; *and for* Learning, Piety, Industry, *and the* Love of Peace, *Exceed them incomparably, so as his* PARTY, *which he* glorieth so much in, *will scarcely* deserve to be named in the same Day. *And if he compare their* Persecutions, *the* Sufferings *of his* supposed Confessors *will appear to be but* Flea-bitings, *in comparison of theirs. But after all this, the* Greatest Disparity *remaineth yet untouch'd; that is, in the* CAUSE *of their Sufferings, the One suffer'd for* FAITH, *and the Other for* FACTION.[19]

If it is true that by 1660 the mass of men in England had conceded the case for religious toleration with very few reservations, it is equally true that in 1660 the sects who had shared the army's domination were discredited and unpopular. Bryant would go so far as to say that in 1660 toleration meant freedom for the blasphemies of fanatics and the idolatry of papists and that it was the most hated word in the language.[20] Of one thing we may be sure.

[19] *Bishop Bramhall's Vindication of himself and the Episcopal Clergy, from the Presbyterian Charge of Popery, As it is managed by Mr. Baxter in his Treatise of the Grotian Religion* (London, 1672), pp. 166–167.

[20] Arthur Bryant, *King Charles II* (London, 1931), p. 126.

In October, 1660, just prior to the publication of the King's Declaration, Hyde suggested to a group of eminent Episcopal and Presbyterian divines, because of petitions made by the Independents and Anabaptists, that there be

By 1660, the bulk of the people had had enough of clerical preten-
sions and clerical quibbling. Powicke is probably close to the heart
of the matter when he says that most people wanted an easy religion
about which they would have no need to trouble themselves once
they had performed the required ritual. They liked the Book of
Common Prayer because it told them precisely what form of worship, what fasts and feasts, were required of them. They were ready
for the easy way and wanted to get on with the real business of making money and enjoying themselves.[21] But the absolutisms of
Charles I and Laud rose again in 1660—with this difference, as
Powicke says, "that Charles II had to hide his absolutism as best he
could, while the Bishops got theirs assured to them by law."[22]
Sheldon was quick to pick up the reins and whip which had fallen
from Laud's hands. His Church provided no shelter for toleration
in 1660. At most it dreamed wistfully of a limited comprehension
for the more tractable Presbyterians, and then only as an aftermath
of papist-nightmares. If it occasionally mouthed concessions, "No
Abatement" was written on its heart. If it argued points of doctrine,
it would abide always by its own discipline, and even comprehension meant comprehension on its own terms.

But the High Church did not always have its own way between
1660 and 1678. It was only one of many factions which played politics with toleration and comprehension. The King and Clarendon,

---

added to the Declaration the words, *"others also be permitted to meet for Religious Worship, so be it, they do it not to the disturbance of the Peace: and
that no Justice of Peace or Officer disturb them."* Although Dr. Gunning had
previously spoken against the papists and the Socinians, he and the other
Episcopal divines remained silent. Richard Baxter saw that the Presbyterians
were caught: to be silent was to consent, and to consent was to take the blame
for opening the gates to the papists and the sects; to speak against the proposal was to set the sects against the Presbyterians as the causers of their
sufferings. He finally said, *"this Reverend Brother Dr. Gunning even now speaking against Sects, had named the Papists and the Socinians: For our parts we
desired not favour to our selves alone, and rigorous Severity we desired against
none! As we humbly thanked his Majesty for his Indulgence to our selves, so
we distinguish the tolerable Parties from the intolerable: For the former, we
humbly crave just lenity and favour; but for the latter, such as the two sorts
named before by that Reverend Brother, for our parts we cannot make their
Toleration our request"* (*Reliq. Bax.,* II, 277 [¶ 110]).

[21] Frederick J. Powicke, *The Reverend Richard Baxter under the Cross* (London, 1927), pp. 260–261.

[22] *Ibid.,* p. 221.

Shaftesbury and Parliament, all had a hand in the game. The moves were dictated by Charles's political ends, Clarendon's ambivalent ties, Shaftesbury's wind-blown desires, Parliament's hold on the purse strings, by Danby's royalism and Sheldon's Laudianism, and the Duke of York's popery. The Clarendon Code was probably severer than Clarendon wished, but the King's desires for toleration had led Parliament and the bishops to force a quickening of restraints, and the code was in full swing after the passage of the Five-Mile Act in October, 1665. The King had waited until Parliament was prorogued and Clarendon incapacitated with the gout, and then he had published on December 26, 1662, his Christmas greeting to the nation, his first Declaration of Indulgence. He stated that out of his mercy he would dispense with the execution of penal laws against all religious dissentients (including Catholics) who should live peaceably until a bill could be laid before Parliament.[23] The holiday lasted only until Clarendon had recovered and Parliament had reconvened in February. The King waited until after Clarendon's fall to make his next move.

Clarendon's fall was a signal for the temporary eclipse of the bishops in the favor of the King and for the printing presses to buzz with tracts on comprehension and toleration. Late in 1667, a bill for comprehension was drawn up; it was never printed or brought into Commons. But in January, 1668, Sir Orlando Bridgeman, Clarendon's successor, proposed a plan for the comprehension of moderate dissenters, and a bill for that purpose was drawn up by Sir Matthew Hale. On February 10 the King himself advocated the bill in the House of Lords. The Commons reacted by moving that people who had a mind to bring new laws about religion into the House should come with ropes about their necks, and carried a vote for the enforcement of the Act of Uniformity.[24] At the beginning of March, Commons proceeded in a body to Whitehall to request the King to enforce his laws against nonconformists.[25] This was the year that had started with the Anglo-Dutch Alliance; it was the year of the Triple Alliance, and the people rejoiced in the thought of Charles II intimidating France and Spain as the champion of Protestantism. The signs for conciliation were propitious, but if the bishops' stars were clouded, the heat of the parliamentary sun was increasingly violent.

[23] Bryant, pp. 154–155. [24] See Pepys's *Diary,* entry for Feb. 10, 1668.
[25] Bryant, p. 199.

It was clear that Parliament had not overthrown Clarendon to weaken the Clarendon Code, and it was soon clear, too, that if the bishops had fallen into disfavor they had not fallen into oblivion. To be sure, the years between the demise of Clarendon and the results of the passage of the Test Act in March, 1673, were hard ones for them. The King was prone to listen not to them but to the Cabal which soon succeeded to the powers vacated by Clarendon, and which did not have a sound Anglican in it. The bishops may have lost Charles's sympathy, their desires may have been impeded, but they were not to be deterred. The Conventicle Act of 1664 had lapsed; its operation had been limited to the end of the next session of Parliament after the expiration of three years. From the spring of 1668, the nonconformists enjoyed a temporary respite, labored under one restriction less. Sheldon was not content that he might still proceed against them through the Five-Mile Act. For two years he contended with the Cabal, with prorogations of Parliament, with the deviating desires of the King, and after much debate and amendment, a new bill against conventicles was passed in the spring of 1670.[26]

The next move was the King's. By the secret treaty of Dover, signed in May, 1670, and the sham treaty of the next year (for the benefit of the Protestant members of the Cabal, who were unaware that its real purpose was the establishment of Catholicism in England), he agreed that England was to be subsidized by France, and Holland destroyed. The English provoked an incident on March 13, 1672, and declared war on the Dutch four days later. Just before the declaration of war, on March 15, Charles issued a second Declaration of Indulgence. By it, penal laws were suspended, places of public worship were promised to Protestant nonconformists, and freedom of worship in their own houses was assured to Catholics.[27] Charles wished to unite the nation, and, at the same time, to exalt himself and his authority by founding indulgence upon royal power and not upon an act of Parliament. It did not bother him that Lord Keeper Bridgeman refused to affix the Great Seal to the declaration because he thought it unconstitutional. The Seal was transferred to Ashley, and as Lord High Chancellor, under the title of Earl of Shaftesbury, he affixed it. Such indiscriminate latitude

[26] See John Stoughton, *History of Religion in England,* rev. ed. (London, 1881), III, 381–389.
[27] Bryant, p. 224.

hardly appealed to the Anglicans, and even the Presbyterians disliked it.[28] They thought that Charles had opened the gates too wide; they wished to be comprehended into the Church, but they thought that toleration was an invitation to popery. They did not wish to be classed with other sectaries and they certainly did not wish to be taunted with recriminations that their zeal for self-profit had allowed equal profit to papists. But for a year they profited while Parliament remained prorogued. It was a suspicious and enraged Commons, one that had not convened for almost two years, that Charles's empty purse called back on February 4, 1673. The French Alliance made the Dutch War smell badly. The Commons scented arbitrary government in the declaration and popish schemes in every act. The war was going poorly. In one breath Charles demanded supplies for the fleet; in another he stated his intention to stick to his declaration. Within two days he had his answer. Parliament voted a resolution that penal statutes in matters ecclesiastical could not be suspended save by act of Parliament.[29] For a month Charles stewed, and on March 8 he informed the Houses that he would withdraw both his declaration and the right claimed in it.

But Parliament was not yet finished with Charles. He got his Subsidies bill coupled with a Test Act. This famous Test of 1673 forbade anyone to hold civil or military office under the crown who would not subscribe a declaration against transubstantiation, take the Oath of Supremacy, and publicly receive the sacrament according to the rites of the Church of England. The bishops were delighted with the antipopish test. The Catholics were in no position to object violently, and in the House of Lords the Catholic Earl of Bristol went so far as to defend the test on the ground that it would quiet a popular panic by the simple removal of a few Catholics from office without enacting any new penalties against Catholic worship. (But he managed to get a clause inserted which secured to him and to his wife a royal pension and exemption from the test).[30] The Presbyterians were obliged to support so obvious an antipopish measure even though it struck the most scrupulous of them. Despite the cancellation of the Declaration of Indulgence, they were not much disturbed, since their licenses for worship remained individually unwithdrawn.[31] Moreover, the Commons was so terrified of popery and so appreciative of Presbyterian opposition to the un-

[28] Stoughton, III, 396.
[30] Stoughton, III, 417–418.
[29] Bryant, p. 226.
[31] *Ibid.,* p. 425.

constitutionality of the declaration and of Presbyterian support of the test that it passed a bill for the Ease of Protestant Dissenters— which was stopped in the House of Lords by the bishops.[32] Shaftes- bury was shrewd enough to see the way the wind was blowing; he bowed to the storm and spoke for the test. If Charles wanted funds, he must take the test with them; at the end of March he reluctantly consented.

The black charter of English Protestantism provoked a sharp turn of fortunes. It forced the Cabal to crumble in 1673. Clifford's Catholicism was smoked out, as was the Duke of York's. On No- vember 9, the seals were taken from Shaftesbury. Charles aban- doned his idea of a Catholic monarchy. But he would still rule absolutely, and he knew where to look for support. Between the end of 1673 and 1678, he allied himself with Anglicanism. He made a Yorkshire Cavalier, Sir Thomas Osborne, first minister of the crown, and Osborne lost no time in building up the new Tory party by appealing to the old Cavalier principles of royal prerogative and intolerant Anglicanism. Almost immediately he called to his councils on church affairs two prelates whom the nonconformists disliked, Morley and Ward. The nonconformists did not have to be fearful immediately. The bishops must deal with Rome before looking to Geneva. Before the end of November, 1673, a proclama- tion was issued forbidding Catholics at court and putting the laws against recusants into execution.[33] It did not go unnoticed by Shaftesbury. Shaftesbury had lost his office; he had not lost his touch with reality. To be sure, he and Sacheverell were busy in both Houses building up the Whig party on the principles of par- liamentary supremacy and toleration, but he was not to be out- maneuvered on the popery question. He would show that his vehemence against Catholics surpassed even Osborne's, and he so terrified the Lords with his stories of armed Catholics that they petitioned that all papists should be banished from London.[34] It was clear that popery was to be the whipping-horse while the par- ties measured their strength.

The King kept Parliament prorogued from February 24, 1674, until April 13, 1675. Just prior to the prorogation, he had con- cluded peace with the Dutch; England was prosperous and seemed

[32] G. M. Trevelyan, *England under the Stuarts,* 9th ed. (London, 1920), p. 378.
[33] Bryant, p. 234.   [34] *Ibid.*

quiet. But Osborne (now Earl of Danby) was consolidating his forces, and Shaftesbury, when not pressing for the removal of Lauderdale and Essex from Scotland and Ireland in the hope of reproducing rebellion, was trying to force a dissolution of Parliament in the hope of a reversal of the electoral decision of 1661. When Parliament met, after the issuance of the government's proclamations against Catholic priests and dissenters,[35] Shaftesbury again cried "Popery" and demanded the recall of British volunteers in the army of France. Danby was ready. He could outcry the Whigs in his hatred for popery and in his demands for a war with France because he knew that Parliament would never vote supplies for an army while it suspected that Charles might use it to establish absolute monarchy. Danby was ready for Shaftesbury's cry, and ready to stifle it at the same time. There was proposed in the House of Lords the Non-Resisting bill, a test to be imposed upon every member of Parliament and upon all persons holding office under the crown. The bill is proof of the intimacy of Danby's workings with the bishops, and it is proof, too, that if the bishops occasionally felt obliged to justify their position by appeals to Scripture and tradition they were quick to see the more immediately practical value of justification by Parliament. Even in modified form the bill read, "I do swear that I will not endeavour an alteration of the Protestant religion now established by law in the Church of England; nor will I endeavour any alteration in the Government of this kingdom in Church or State, as it is by law established."[36] The autocratic boldness of the measure is breathtaking. Danby knew that it would have filled the Houses exclusively with ardent Anglicans and Cavaliers; it would have excluded the future Whig party by law from political life; it would have concentrated all political power in the Anglican party. The bishops knew that it would have invested their Church with infallibility. Shaftesbury knew that everything was at stake. His attack was oblique; he defeated the bill by precipitating between the Houses a violent quarrel about the judicial powers of the Lords.

Charles once more prorogued Parliament, this time for fifteen months (from November 22, 1675, to February 15, 1677). The little bubble of economic prosperity had burst; Danby more desperately mustered his strength and Shaftesbury's words became more inflammatory. When at the opening of Parliament, Buckingham relied

[35] *Ibid.*, p. 242.   [36] Stoughton, III, 426; *Reliq. Bax.*, III, 167–168.

on an obsolete statute enjoining annual Parliaments to move in the
Lords that the present Parliament was no longer a lawful assembly,
the Lords cried "insult." Buckingham and his supporters, Salisbury,
Wharton, and Shaftesbury, were committed to the Tower. All but
Shaftesbury recanted in June, 1677, and were released; Shaftesbury
did not win his liberty until he asked the pardon of the Lords in
February, 1678. Even though its leaders had been jailed, the opposition had not lost its power, especially in the Commons. The bishops
were to learn quickly that if Parliament had so often supported
their restrictive measures against popery, it had been motivated by
its dread of popery, not by its love for or faith in the bishops. Within
a week after Parliament had met, Danby introduced, with the concurrence of the bishops, two measures as additional bulwarks against
papal aggression. That the measures should even have been introduced is evidence of the immense influence of the bishops on
Danby. But they reveal, too, the basic insecurity of the High
Churchmen, their desire to make their position invulnerable, to
provide for every contingency. The first measure was dictated by
the possibility that a Catholic prince might occupy the throne, and
it made three provisions in the event of his refusing a severe test
in the form of a denial of the doctrine of transubstantiation: 1.
Upon the occurrence of a vacant see, the bishops should name three
persons, one of whom the sovereign might select. If he did not do
so within thirty days, the person first named should take possession.
2. The two archbishops should present to all livings in the royal gift.
3. The children of the sovereign, between seven and fourteen years,
should be under the joint guardianship of the two archbishops and
the bishops of London, Durham, and Winchester. The second
measure was to provide for the more effectual prosecution and conviction of popish recusants. Among other things, it would exempt
from penalties—other than ineligibility to hold civil and military
office and to perform the office of guardians and executors—those
papists who registered and paid a yearly fine of 5 per cent of their
incomes to a fund for the support of poor converts to Protestantism.
That both measures passed in the Lords is an indication of the
power of the bishops. But the Commons opposed the first on the
ground that it would not prevent popery but would convey more
power to the bishops and unanimously defeated the second on the
ground that it gave liberty to papists who could pay for it and was
therefore virtual toleration. They proposed in its place a stronger

antipopery measure, one that would not cede to the Church 5 per cent of the Catholic income, but this was not noticed by the Lords. On three acts the Houses finally agreed, one for the better observance of the Lord's Day, another on the improvement of small livings, and a third on the repeal of the law *de Haeretico Comburendo*. But the third act showed that the bishops still had the power to preserve their prerogatives. In the Lords, a proviso was added which perpetuated the jurisdiction of the Ecclesiastical Courts in cases of atheism, blasphemy, heresy, or schism, and which sanctioned excommunication and other ecclesiastical penalties, including that of death.[37]

In 1677, then, the High Church seemed to be riding high. It had Danby's support and Charles's favor. Still, it was aware of the King's papist inclinations and it knew that his seeming favor was only expediency prompted by his desire to ally himself with an absolutism which endorsed his own ideas of monarchy. For some time the High Church had not felt the necessity of making concessions to nonconformity, but the intensity of its campaign against popery is evidence not only of its knowledge of Charles's propensities but also of its wish to appear pure and beyond reproach in nonconformist eyes. It would have been glad to have additional support. If the introduction of the Non-Resisting bill and the measures to provide against the succession of a Catholic prince appear to show the influence the bishops wielded, their very conception shows basic insecurity and the fate they met shows the degree of the antagonism they provoked. Despite the imprisonment of Shaftesbury, the bishops were worried by the power of the opposition in the Commons. Indeed, the very act that had led to the imprisonment of the Lords was a measure of the increasing desperation of the Whigs. The bishops had plenty of cause for worry, not only in Charles's ambiguous favor, in the Duke of York's religion, but also in the possibility of the dissolution of Parliament and new elections, and in the armed bands and godly preachers who were once more roving over Ireland and Scotland. Such was their troubled peace when Walton was writing the *Life of Sanderson,* and even as he was writing a further blow fell. On November 9, 1677, Sheldon died. Danby's, and probably the bishops', candidate for Canterbury was Henry Compton, the young Bishop of London whose rise had been so quick that it is evident that he was being groomed. In

[37] Stoughton, III, 451–455.

December, Charles chose William Sancroft, the humble Dean of St. Paul's, who would happily have remained at his chore of rebuilding his cathedral, a man so gentle that he cared not to persecute and was even rumored to be the choice of the Duke of York.[38] The High Church had reason to be disappointed and afraid.

In what way, we may ask, did these jockeyings for place and power affect Walton? After all, most laymen have not time to follow parliamentary debates and are but vaguely aware of behind-the-scenes politicking. The conventional picture of Walton represents him as a peaceable Protestant, a devout Anglican, a man who loved the good old days, the good old traditions, and the Book of Common Prayer. But Walton's efforts in the *Life of Hooker* and the *Life of Herbert* have prepared us for a different picture, a Walton peculiarly sensitive in church matters both by inclination and by opportunity. His inclinations were encouraged and his opportunities multiplied as his relationship with Bishop Morley became more familiar. In 1678, their friendship was almost half a century old; for almost two decades they had lived under the same roof. Morley gave Walton more than a home. He watched over the careers of Walton's son and his young brother-in-law. Thomas Ken became Morley's chaplain about 1665; in 1669 he was appointed a prebendary of Winchester; in 1679 he was appointed chaplain to Princess Mary of Orange, granddaughter of Morley's friend Clarendon and daughter of Anne, whose religious upbringing had been in Morley's hands.[39] Young Izaak was in 1678 made domestic chaplain to Morley's friend, Seth Ward, Bishop of Salisbury.[40] Walton was grateful not only for this patronage but also for the chance for learning and study which he himself had under so expert a tutor and for the chance to know the most eminent divines of two generations. The long relationship of the two men places their compatibility beyond doubt; we need not question Morley's kindness to Walton and Walton's reverence for Morley. If Walton was predisposed to revere men of religion, he was ready to love and to follow the diocesan who had done so much for him. His dedication of the *Lives* (1670) to Morley reads like the words of a pupil to his teacher, though Walton was seventy-seven at the time and Morley four years

---

38 *DNB*, article "Henry Compton," and *Wood's Life and Times*, II, 396–397.
39 E. H. Plumptre, *The Life of Thomas Ken* (London, 1890), I, 82–84, 89, 125–129.
40 See p. 310, n. 39.

younger. Also, we should expect most men to be humble of opinion in matters of religion before a learned bishop, especially a man of Walton's background and education. Walton was ever inclined to feel that the road to Heaven was not paved with hard questions, but he knew, too, that hard questions existed. He was ready to accept on faith Morley's answers. If Walton was not himself a prime actor in church affairs of the Restoration, Morley was. If we examine Morley's activities and points of view, we shall come close to seeing how matters affected Walton. We need not think that Walton merely holds a mirror up to Morley, but everything points to a fairly accurate reflection. And if we need more evidence, we shall soon see that Morley was not much inclined to tolerate about him such men as disagreed with his points of view.

In our day Morley is remembered, if at all, as Walton's patron or, perhaps, for his statement, when asked what it was the Arminians held, "that *They held all the best Bishopricks and Deaneries in England*."[41] His statement is used to show his Calvinist leanings and his wit, but it is not noticed that its very wit is dependent upon a certain Laudian dogmatism and practicality. He is remembered vaguely, too, as the Bishop of Worcester who refused to permit Richard Baxter to return to his flock at Kidderminster. This action is used to show him as an ardent proponent of Anglo-Catholicism. Sometimes both the sentence and the action are remembered simultaneously, and then it is said that Morley was customarily moderate in dealing with dissenters. The quality of Morley's moderation as it reveals itself in his activities needs to be critically examined.

Some of the luster of tolerance usually associated with Great Tew has shone on Morley. In the thirties he did make his way occasion-

[41] *The Life of Edward Earl of Clarendon* (Oxford, 1759), p. 26. Clarendon's account of Morley's theology is a confusing one. In reporting Morley's definition of the Arminian tenets, he suggests that it was a harmless and jocular saying made in accidental discourse out of high facetiousness. But he then says that Morley's doctrine lost him the favor of those who had the greatest power in ecclesiastical promotions and caused Laud to entertain some prejudice toward him. He says, too, that Morley had no sympathy for ecclesiastical and political Calvinism and opposed its advocates "both in private, and in publick; which had the more Effect to the Benefit of the Church." In a parenthesis, he suggests that Laud "lived to change his Mind, and to have a just Esteem of him." It is likely that Laud esteemed Morley when he found out how ardently Morley supported Laudian discipline, and it is likely, too, that Laud never bothered to change Morley's theology. Wood probably reflects popular opinion of Morley when he says, "He was a great Calvinist, and esteemed one of the main patrons of those of that persuasion" (*Athenae Oxon.*, IV, 154).

ally to Falkland's circle where from time to time he saw Chillingworth, Sheldon, Hammond, Earle, Hyde, Barlow, and Sanderson.
Obviously his visits to Tew need not constitute an endorsement by
him of the tenets of Falkland and Chillingworth; they do show that
he found Tew congenial and that Tew found him so. The latitude
in which Tew was suffused need not have stemmed in equal proportion from each of its habitués; indeed, some of the habitués may
have been tolerated because of the latitude of some of the others.[42]
The master of Tew may have frowned on doctrinal disputation and
censured theological and ecclesiastical systematology; he hated the
bitterness engendered by quarrels and the self-interest which motivated power-thirsty churchmen. But his guests were not high in the
hierarchy, and if they differed in their opinions they were gentlemanly in their differences. Besides, they were all good royalists,
their well-being dependent upon the preservation of society as it was
then constituted. The atmosphere of Tew affected each of them
differently, and each, as he took a more active part in church and
state, was affected by new places and new friends.

In 1641, Morley was made a canon of Christ Church, Oxford.
Here, in addition to Hammond and Sanderson, his associates were
such stiff Anglicans as Samuel Fell, Richard Gardiner, Thomas Iles,
Robert Payne, Edward Pocock, and John Wall. Of these, the only
one to make his peace at the end of 1647 and in 1648 with the parliamentary visitors was Wall. Morley's orthodoxy was unquestioned,
and when the King wanted solace and advice at Newport at the
end of 1648, Morley was amongst the dozen distinguished divines
whom he requested to attend him.[43] There is no question about
Morley's motives and loyalties during the war and the interregnum.
He left England for the Hague in 1649, and then went to Antwerp,
where he spent a year with Sir Charles Cotterell and three years
with Lady Frances Hyde, whose husband was the King's ambassador

---

[42] Clarendon says of Falkland, "He had so dispassioned a Consideration,
such a Candour in his Nature, and so profound a Charity in his Conscience,
that in those Points, in which He was in his own Judgment most clear, He
never thought the worse, or in any Degree declined the Familiarity, of those
who were of another Mind; which, without Question, is an excellent Temper
for the Propagation, and Advancement of Christianity" (*Life,* 1759, pp. 22–23).

[43] See Fell's *Life of Hammond,* pp. xlv–xlvi, note u, prefixed to Nicholas
Pocock's edition of *A Practical Catechism by Henry Hammond* (Library of
Anglo-Catholic Theology; Oxford, 1847).

to Spain. He left the service of Hyde for two years and a half to serve in the Hague as chaplain to the Queen of Bohemia, and then for four years he attended Lady Hyde at Breda.[44] His years of exile with the court were passed in an atmosphere far removed from the comfortable and invigorating air of Tew. Genial disputation had been replaced by blasted hopes and heavy responsibility. The abundant hospitality of the country manor had been replaced by the stringent generosity of foreign cities; Falkland had been replaced by Hyde; the relaxed energy of middle age had been replaced by the nervous vigor of age.

It is a little surprising to find Morley writing from Breda in a letter to John Cosin on February 10, 1660, "I am very glad the King was at the Protestant Churches, which gives great satisfaction to those Ministers here to whom I have told it. I wish there were not some of our Clergy too rigid in that particular."[45] Had Tew so influenced him that he could at such a distance yet condemn the Anglican clergy for their narrowness? His latitude here is more easily explained. His sentiment was dictated in part by his awareness of Cosin's point of view. In exile, Cosin had joined in the worship of the French Protestants and had permitted his children to do so.[46] Even after the Restoration, he had accepted the validity of Presbyterian orders when they had been taken where Episcopacy was not established.[47] His temper was more genuinely moderate than that of most Anglican churchmen. At the Savoy Conference, he was the only representative of the Established clergy whom Baxter singled out for his affability and familiarity,[48] and at the Convocation which followed he went further than most in suggesting changes in the Book of Common Prayer.[49] Also, although Morley here says that he approves the King's actions, he did not himself so act. In 1683, he wrote:

When I was in France, *I did at* Paris *assist Doctor* Cozins, *late Bishop of* Durham, *in preaching to the* English Protestants *there at Sir* Richard Brown's *House, then* Resident *there for our* King, *but never went to*

[44] *Athenae Oxon.*, IV, 151.

[45] *The Correspondence of John Cosin, D.D.* (pt. I, 1869), p. 292 (vol. LII of the Publications of the Surtees Society).

[46] *Ibid.*, p. xxxvii.

[47] *Ibid.* (pt. II, 1872), pp. xliii–xlv (vol. LV of the Publications of the Surtees Society).

[48] *Reliq. Bax.*, II, 363. [49] *Correspondence of Cosin* (pt. II), pp. xi–xv.

the French Presbyterian Church *at* Charenton, *no more than I did after-wards to that of* Caen *in* Normandy, *whilst I was there.*[50]

He justified himself in that year by citing the reasons he had given in 1649 to Samuel Bouchard, chief pastor of the Huguenot church at Paris: the French churches lacked the set liturgy of his own Church; his inability to cope with spoken French made it impossible for him to be edified by the service; the Huguenots had not publicly or privately condemned the rebellious proceedings of the Presbyterians in England against the King and the Church.[51] There is further evidence that Morley's approbation of the King's behavior was not founded on principle but on expediency. His letter to Cosin is largely concerned with the possibility of a change of government in England, and if Morley was not himself chiefly responsible for the policy of reinstituting the Church, he was at least Hyde's chief agent in effecting the policies he had helped determine.

Hyde had met Morley at Great Tew and had for seven years put into the hands of him whom he called "the best man alive"[52] the religious welfare of his family. Their feelings in the matter about which Morley wrote Cosin were identical. Although Hyde had advised others at the end of 1646 and in 1647 to join in communion with the French Protestants, he had changed his mind by the middle of 1648.[53] Apparently provoked by the Huguenots' attitude toward English affairs, he concurred with Charles I and the high Anglicans in the view that Huguenot ministrations were invalid since their Church lacked bishops. But the very letter which informs us that Morley was sent by Hyde to England at the end of March, 1660, tells us also the policy which Hyde's agents deemed necessary. One of them wrote, "I beseech God he [Morley] may proceed with more than ordinary coolness, lest it exasperate our Presbyterians to their accustomed insolence, who are now apt for good impressions,

---

[50] Preface to *Several Treatises, Written upon Several Occasions* (1683), p. viii.

[51] Morley's letter provoked in the following year a reply from Bouchard, *Epistola qua repondetur ad tres Quaestiones: De Presbyteratu & Episcopatu,* in which Bouchard justified episcopacy in England and condemned rebellion against sovereignty in defense of religion or for any other reason, but there is no evidence that Morley changed his habits.

[52] In a letter to Nicholas, dated Nov. 7, 1653, *Calendar of the Clarendon State Papers* (Oxford, 1869), II, 271.

[53] See B. H. G. Wormald, *Clarendon, Politics, History & Religion, 1640–1660* (Cambridge, 1951), pp. 310–311.

if gently applied."[54] Morley had been given directions to tread circumspectly. Hyde reassured his imploring agent on April 16, 1660: "I am heartily glad, that Dr. *Morley* is with you, whom you will find a very worthy and discreet Person, and fit to keep you Company, in allaying the too much Heat and Distemper, which some of our Friends are in this unseasonable Conjuncture very much accus'd of."[55] He could write confidently because he had already received Morley's letter of April 13, which states:

> I have both before and since done what I can in order to the business I came for, particularly by endeavouring to allay the indiscreet and unseasonable zeal of some Divines of our party, by representing unto them the ill effects of it in general, and the offence and troublesome carriage of theirs will, I am sure, give unto the King in particular.[56]

In this letter Morley candidly reveals his inmost disposition and temper:

> By what is told me by those that converse with them, I find that my being here is acceptable enough to the Presbyterian party, as being thought by them to be somewhat more moderate than others of our clergy are, and than those perhaps I am.

He reveals, too, his inmost feelings about the status of episcopacy:

> Those [Presbyterians] that are the chief, and have most power amongst them, are content to admit of the name Bishop, but not with the power, which we think to be inseparable from his office, viz. a negative voice in such things as he thinks fit not to be done, and an affirmative for the doing of such as he thinks fit to be done, though not without the advice, yet without consent, of his Clergy, if he cannot have it.

And he reveals that his job was to pour oil on the waters, to ensure the reinstatement of episcopacy without definite commitments:

> At my first coming, and since, there hath been much talk of a friendly conference to be had betwixt some of the Episcopal and some of the Presbyterian persuasion . . . ; but I think there will be no meeting, Easter being so near, and the Parliament so soon after Easter; and besides, as they do not press it, so have we no reason to desire it; partly, because we have no command, nor leave from the King for it; and

---

[54] Brodrick to Hyde, March 30, 1660, *Clarendon S.P.* (Oxford, 1786), III, 714.

[55] In Peter Barwick, *The Life Of the Reverend Dr. John Barwick, D.D.* (London, 1724), p. 517.

[56] *Clarendon S.P.*, III, 727.

partly, because there is little or no fruit to be expected from it; neither can any thing to oblige either of the parties be concluded in it. And therefore (as we tell them) we think it best for both parties to refer all the differences betwixt us to be disputed there, where they may be decided, viz. in a Synod and a free Parliament.

But a conference did take place, and how well Morley managed it is evident in Baxter's words: "Dr. *Morley,* and other of the Divines on that side, did privately meet with several Persons of Honour, and some Ministers, and professed Resolutions for great Moderation and Lenity."[57] The Presbyterians received only professions; Morley's accomplishment was more considerable. He wrote Hyde on May 4:

I have been since my coming to town with divers of the chief of the Presbyterian Ministers, and have reason (as I think) to hope they will be persuaded to admit of and submit to Episcopal government, and to the practice of the Liturgy in publick, so they may be permitted before and after their sermons, and upon occasional emergencies, to use such arbitrary forms as they themselves shall think fit, without mixing of any thing prejudicial to the government of the Church and State, as they shall be settled.[58]

In addition Morley had sounded out their sentiments on the possibility of some of their own number receiving bishoprics and had estimated their strength:

If three or four of the leading men might be gratified with such other preferments as they may hold with their charges here in the City, . . . they would be a great means to bring over their whole party; which, though I hope it be not so powerful as absolutely to hinder, yet it is strong enough I fear to give the King much trouble.

One passage in his letter shows that Morley's policy was hardly dictated by earnest desires for toleration, that it was a policy of seeing how little he could cede and how much he could get, a policy not of moderation but of begrudging concession:

I foresee the main difficulty will be touching their ordinations by Presbyters, without Bishops, which we cannot acknowledge to be lawful, nor will they, I am afraid, be brought to acknowledge to be unlawful, and much less to be mere nullities. In this case I have thought of two expedients; the one, that no notice be taken whether there have been any such ordinations or no. The other, that there may be an hypothetical

[57] *Reliq. Bax.,* II, 217.   [58] *Clarendon S.P.,* III, 738.

re-ordination by Bishops of such as were so ordained, which re-ordination, as it will be a provision against the nullity of such ordinations, so it will not conclude them to be nullities, but only irregular and uncertain. And this is much the better *salvo* of the two, if they can be brought to it.

There is little doubt that Morley's professed resolutions for great moderation and lenity were vapid and ambiguous: "I was bold to tell them the King was sensible of what they had done already, and did not doubt but they would do much more yet for him, and that I was sure they would have no cause to repent of it." Morley had done his job well. On May 9, Lord Mordaunt wrote to the King that Morley wished the King would not cede should Parliament ask for a synod of the three nations and the assistance of foreign divines. He had received the assurances of the Scots that they would cause no trouble, and he had prevailed with Reynolds and Calamy to comply with episcopacy and the liturgy with little alteration, though they could not yet vouch for their brethren.[59]

Morley's attitude toward nonconformists did not change after the Restoration. Because the Church could never be sufficiently strong for him, he yearned to bring at least the moderate Presbyterian flock within the established fold. He cast longing eyes at their shepherds and wooed them with words of love, but when they approached and asked for part of his loaf, he saw '41 carved on their foreheads. Ever he walked toward them, and ever he withdrew. He professed to love them; he loved the established prerogatives more. About the time of the Restoration, John Gauden promised Baxter to effect a meeting between him and other Presbyterians and Morley and other Episcopal divines. Morley did not appear, perhaps because he did not care to meet Baxter under Gauden's aegis. Baxter had heard that Morley was "a Moderate Orthodox Man," that he had encouraged other Presbyterians with "Pacificatory Professions," and again he sought an hour's discourse with Morley to know whether he really inclined to concord. His disappointment in Morley is evident in his report of the meeting: Morley "spake of Moderation in the general, but came to no particular Terms."[60] At the Savoy Conference, Morley, now Bishop of Worcester, was not conciliatory but contentious; in Baxter's words, "the greatest Interrupter of us; vehemently going on with what he thought serviceable to his end, and bearing down Answers by the said fervour and

[59] *Ibid.,* pp. 743–744.   [60] *Reliq. Bax.,* II, 218 (¶81).

interruptions."[61] And under no circumstances could his refusal to grant Baxter a license to preach at Kidderminster be termed conciliatory. Morley had promised to permit Baxter to preach there, even as Sheldon, now Bishop of London, had licensed him to preach in his diocese. To be sure, the impatient Baxter had preached there before receiving Morley's long-delayed permission, and Morley could then accuse him of presumption (and add that he was factious in preaching and rebellious of civil authority).[62] Morley talked of moderation, part of his heart may even have desired conciliation; always, though, despite his words, despite the vague stirrings in his heart, he adhered literally to Anglican discipline. There is nothing in his actions in the attempts at abatement in 1668, 1670, 1673–1674, and 1675 to indicate a change of view.

If the Presbyterians were in doubt about Morley's stand on toleration, Charles II was not. He knew that Clarendon's fall would hardly make Morley more lenient and that he must still listen to Clarendon's strictures while Morley was close to the Court. On February 4, 1668, just prior to his advocacy of Sir Orlando Bridgeman's plea for dissenters in the Lords, he dismissed Morley as Dean of the Chapel Royal, though Morley was scheduled to preach an Ash-Wednesday sermon the next day.[63] On February 8, he replaced him with Herbert Croft, Bishop of Hereford, whom he thought more sympathetic to the bill of comprehension and limited indulgence.

At the end of 1670, some of the bishops, among them Morley, Ward, and Dolben, made known their fear of popery and indicated their desire for abatements and leniencies which might lead to comprehension. Publicly they lamented that the Duchess of York had turned papist; privately they may have heard of Charles's deal with Louis. There was long talk. Nothing was done. The slur which Baxter reports, that some people thought the bishops made overtures only to divert odium from themselves while what they professed to fear was accomplished, is unfair. But we must sympathize with him when he says that "if they are yet truly willing of any healing, they will shew it by more than their discourses," and we

[61] *Ibid.*, p. 363 (¶236).

[62] *The Bishop of Worcester's Letter To a Friend For Vindication of Himself from M*r. *Baxter's Calumny* (London, 1662), pp. 6–9.

[63] See Pepys's *Diary,* entry for Feb. 6, 1668, and *Poems and Letters of Andrew Marvell,* ed. H. M. Margoliouth (Oxford, 1927), II, 63–64.

must agree with him when he says, "it's strange that those same Men that so easily led the Parliament to what is done (when they had given the King thanks for his Declaration about Ecclesiastical Affairs) can do nothing to bring them to moderate abatements, and the healing of our Breaches, if they are truly willing."[64] Baxter over-emphasizes the influence of the bishops on legislation, particularly at this time when they were out of favor, but there is no question that Morley and the High Church bishops did nothing to influence Parliament toward moderation when they were rather more able to, and there is no question that they would do nothing while they believed that comprehension must be synonymous with conformity. There is no question, either, that each of the moves for comprehension in which Morley was involved was provoked not by further softening of his heart, but by his fears that popery was on the increase.

Thus, late in 1673, as a result of the inclinations which the King had demonstrated in his Declaration of Indulgence, the discovery of the Duke of York's popery and his marriage to Mary of Modena (an Italian papist, and kin to the Pope), and the successes of the French with the aid of English troops over the Dutch, Sir Thomas Osborne and Morley, who was now on the inner council of church affairs, proposed through the Earl of Orrery that Baxter should draw up in brief the terms and means which might so satisfy the nonconformists that the Protestant Church of England might stand united against popery. Even though Baxter was temperamentally impatient, we can only sympathize with his forebearance and endurance when he writes, "I wisht them all to tell him [Morley] from me, that he had done so much to the contrary, and never any thing this way since his Professions of this sort, that till his real Endeavours convinced Men, it would not be believed that he was serious."[65] Morley met Baxter's list of terms and means with strictures and animadversions and, shortly after, showed his inability to make a concession of any sort. The Commons had passed a bill for the ease of Protestant dissenters; Morley countered it by introducing an empty act of his own which repealed certain strictures which other legislation would yet enforce. Baxter says that when other bishops objected to "this ensnaring shew of abatement," Morley told them "that had it been but to abate us a Ceremony, he would not

[64] *Reliq. Bax.*, III, 84–85 (¶179).   [65] *Ibid.*, p. 109 (¶256).

have spoken in it: But he knew that we were bound to the same things still, by other Clauses or Obligations, if these were Repealed."[66]

Still Morley represented himself as an ardent proponent of moderation, spoke so repeatedly in Parliament on the dangers of popery and the need for abatements which would unite the Church that he was known as the "forwardest desirer" of comprehension.[67] In April, 1675, he set upon his old course again, and he and Bishop Ward were "famed to be the two Bishops that were for Comprehension and Concord, none so forward as they."[68] The year before, Baxter had concluded his letter of terms and means by expressing confidence that could he consult with such moderate men as Stillingfleet and Tillotson, they might agree in a week.[69] Now he and other nonconformist divines met with Tillotson and Stillingfleet and reached agreement. Baxter tried to get Bishops Ward and Pearson to meet with him, thinking that the chance for concurrence was better while Morley was out of town. But no meeting took place and negotiations were dropped. Morley's part in this attempt is hazy. We do not know whether Morley purposely absented himself to see how far things might proceed without him; whether this was an effort by the more liberal faction of the High Church to try for agreement and then to see how far Morley would be willing to go (though Ward, certainly, was aware of their attempt); or whether Tillotson and Stillingfleet were innocent decoys to hide the bishops' real intentions. On April 11, 1675, Tillotson wrote Baxter that after talking to Ward he "plainly perceived several things could not be obtained" and that Ward had never set a time for a meeting. Also, in answer to Baxter's request that he might make public the names of the participants in the attempt and the nature of their agreement in order to promote concord, Tillotson wrote:

I am unwilling my Name should be used in this Matter; not but that I do most heartily desire an Accommodation, and shall always endeavour it: But I am sure it will be a prejudice to me, and signify nothing to the effecting of the thing, which as Circumstances are cannot pass in either House, without the Concurrence of a considerable part of the Bishops, and the Countenance of His Majesty; which at present I see little reason to expect.[70]

[66] *Ibid.*, pp. 140–141 (¶257).   [67] *Ibid.*, p. 156 (¶285).
[68] *Ibid.* (¶286).   [69] *Ibid.*, p. 110.   [70] *Ibid.*, p. 157.

Tillotson's reason for expecting little became clear in just two days. Parliament met on April 13, and there was introduced not legislation for comprehension but the Non-Resisting bill. Many of the Lords "spake vehemently against it, as destructive to the Privileges of their House, which was to Vote freely, and not to be preobliged by an Oath to the Prelates."[71] Who were the great speakers for it? Danby, Finch, Ward, and Morley. When the story of the debate on the Non-Resisting bill was secretly printed, the nonconformists were alienated from Morley. The publication of Bishop Croft's *The Naked Truth* and the animadversions and annotations of the animadversions which followed showed them who their real friends were. Morley was silent.

Hyde had picked the ideal man for his job in 1660. If Morley's royalism and his obvious adherence in matters ecclesiastical and sacerdotal made him unimpeachable to the High Church, his Calvinism gave him a doctrinal tie with nonconformists. Burnet wrote, not quite correctly, that Morley "was a Calvinist with relation to the Arminian points, and was thought a friend of the puritans, before the wars: but he took care after his promotion to free himself from all suspicions of that kind."[72] Morley was so free from suspicion in the eyes of the High Church that he could presume on his tie with the nonconformists. Still, it may well be that his variance from orthodox High Church doctrine made him doubly meticulous in demonstrating his adherence to High Church discipline. His doctrine was close to that of Hooker and Bilson; his discipline was that of Laud. Morley could safely assert Calvinist doctrine after the Restoration because he had adequately shown his dislike for the political and ecclesiastical forms that Calvinism had assumed. His doctrine was a survival from his youth; he accepted his inheritance and was comfortable in it. His unbending and unreasoned fealty in doctrinal matters is indicative of his resistance to change, and it is this same stiffness which may explain, too, his fanatic loyalty to the King and to the discipline of the Established Church. The whole question of comprehension was for Morley not one of doctrine but of discipline. His attitude toward church ceremonies accurately mirrors the extent of the concessions he was willing to make. He

---

[71] *Ibid.*, p. 167 (¶295).

[72] *Burnet's History Of My Own Time,* ed. Osmund Airy (Oxford, 1897–1900), I, 314.

interpreted the thirty-fourth of the Thirty-nine Articles agreed upon in the Convocation in 1563[73] not in the spirit of vagueness and compromise in which it was written, but as Laud had interpreted it in making it his charter against the Puritans. A statement of his belief which he issued in 1662 and considered valid in 1683 shows his unwillingness to abate a tittle and explains why. He refused to admit that the penalty of withholding the sacrament from those who would not kneel in receiving it was incomparably greater than the offense, "for the greatness of the offence in such cases, and as it stands in relation to such or such a penalty appointed for it, is not to be measured by the Quality of the Act considered in it self, but by the more or less mischievous consequences it is likely to produce, if men be not restrain'd from such an Act by such a penalty."[74] He cited with utter seriousness an analogy which he was sure would prove his point:

When a Souldier is hang'd for stealing of a Hen, or for taking away any thing of never so little a value, without paying for it, no wise man will blame the *General* for such a severity; because if he did not do so, every one would take what he pleased, which would discourage the Countrey from bringing in provisions, and consequently the whole army would be ruin'd. And as the Martial, so the Civil and Ecclesiastical Laws likewise in commanding or forbidding any thing under such or such a penalty, have an eye not so much to the merit of the Action it self, as to the more or less danger of the Publick in the consequences of it.[75]

Morley's intolerance toward diversity, his finding in every slight

---

[73] "It is not necessary that traditions and ceremonies be in all places one or utterly like, for at all times they have been divers, and may be changed, according to the diversity of countries, times, and men's manners, so that nothing be ordained against God's word. Whosoever through his private judgment, willingly and purposely doth openly break the traditions and ceremonies of the Church, which be not repugnant to the word of God, and be ordained and approved by common authority, ought to be rebuked openly (that other[s] may fear to do the like) as he that offendeth against the common order of the Church, and hurteth the authority of the Magistrate, and woundeth the consciences of the weak brethren.

"Every particular or national Church, hath authority to ordain, change, and abolish ceremonies or rites of the Church ordained only by man's authority, so that all things be done to edifying" (cited by Helen C. White, *English Devotional Literature [Prose] 1600–1640* [Madison, Wis., 1931], p. 32, from *The Text of the Thirty-Nine Articles of 1553, 1563, 1571,* ed. W. M. M[eredith] [London, 1889]).

[74] *Vindication,* pp. 16–17.   [75] *Ibid.,* p. 17.

difference an invitation to heresy and treason, is obvious in his argument:

The whole is not to be endangered out of tenderness and indulgence to some particulars. . . . he that worshippeth God one way, will either judge or condemn him that worshippeth God another way; he that *Kneeleth* at the Sacrament, will be thought to be Idolatrous or Superstitious by him that *Kneeleth not,* and him [*sic*] that kneeleth not will be thought wilful, or weak, by him that kneeleth. And thus from diversity grows dislike, from dislike enmity, from enmity opposition, and from opposition, first Separation and Schism in the *Church,* and then Faction, Sedition and Rebellion in the State; which is a progress very natural, and I would we had not found it to be so by our own experience; for as the safety of a State depends upon the safety of the Church, so the safety of the Church depends upon Unity, and Unity it self depends upon Uniformity, and Uniformity there cannot be, as long as there is diversity or divers wayes of worship in the same Church, which will be alwaies, unless it be lawful for publick Authority to oblige all particulars to one way of publick worship, and that under such penalties, as the Law-givers shall think necessary to prevent the disturbing of the publick Peace and safety; . . . And surely when there is a necessity of the yeilding of the one or of the other, it is much more reasonable that a part should yield unto the whole, then the whole unto a part, especially when the whole cannot yield without endangering it self, and with it self even those themselves also, that, will they nill they, must be involved in the ruine of it; as the *Presbyterians* have found by their own experience also, who by their groundless and needless separation from us, have given example and ground enough for others to separate from them, till by dividing and subdividing from one another, there was nothing of Uniformity, or unity, or order, or decency left in that *Church,* which was formerly (and I hope by the Prudence and Piety of Publick Authority will be now again) the Glory and Pattern of all other Protestant and *Reformed* Churches in the world.[76]

For Morley, the order and decency of the Church depended upon Church unity, and therefore he professed comprehension. But unity depended upon uniformity, and that is why he would concede nothing. He believed that the Church could not yield to a minority without endangering itself, and he was happy when the prudence and piety of public authority supported his point of view.

In the late 1670's, Morley's happiness was mixed with fear. From

[76] *Ibid.,* pp. 18–20.

his high place on Danby's councils on religious matters he could help shape official policy, but that policy, despite Shaftesbury's imprisonment, was meeting increasing resistance in Parliament. The prudence of public authority had vitiated his attempts in the Non-Resisting bill and in the legislation to provide for Episcopal power should a Catholic succeed to the throne. For twenty years Morley had fretted over the papist inclinations of the royal family. As early as 1659 he had told the Duke of York that his and the King's tendencies toward popery were endangering the possibility of their return. Even then he had written Hyde, "All the fruits I expect from this discourse, is but the comfort I shall find in having discharged mine own conscience."[77] Since then Anne Hyde, for whose religious education he had been responsible, had died a papist, and the Duke's Catholicism was public knowledge. If the public was still in doubt about the King's religion, Morley was not. His hatred of popery forced him to look for support to dissent. He saw clearly the necessity for the Church to be united to maintain its position, to ensure that no matter what happened the Church might remain secure in its prerogatives and powerful in the political arena. Conciliation with dissent meant insurance, but conciliation meant concession, too, and Morley, in his distrust of dissent, was willing to cede nothing. So convinced was he that dissent was unreasonable, so sure was he that reason was on his side and that others were blind not to see it, that all he could do was try to strengthen the position of his own party, try to justify the maintenance of the *status quo*.

Morley's life and disposition are not Walton's. Walton did not experience at first hand Morley's happiness and Morley's fears. But he lived in their reflection, and if Morley's sentiments were not his, they yet directed and colored his. His relation with Morley made Walton's interest in the contemporary situation more acute than that of the ordinary layman, his knowledge of it more immediate, his response to it more intimate. The contemporary situation caused him to create in Sanderson an ideal bishop even as the situation in 1670 had caused him to create in Herbert the ideal parson. He would represent Sanderson's experience with nonconformity as typical; he would show that his hardships and those of his fellow churchmen were surpassed only by their fortitude; he

[77] *Clarendon S.P.*, III, 458–459.

would indicate Sanderson's moderation to be that which characterized the Anglican Church. The life of Sanderson became almost synonymous with the condition of the Church during the wars and the Protectorate in order to justify the Church's stand on comprehension and to warn of evils which would again beset the Church in 1678 if dissent were to get into the saddle. But if in the *Life of Herbert* Walton could without too much presumption write a prospectus for the life of the Church and a manual for the country parson, he would not have presumed in the *Life of Sanderson* to the extent of writing a handbook for bishops. He rather sought to present such a picture of a son and father of the Church as would win from the general reader sympathy and support for the High Church and the Episcopal position. He would rectify the stereotype of the dogmatic diocesan, remote in demean and resplendent in luxury, would set in its place the long-suffering, temperate, mild, and humble overseer of the realm of God. Conversely, he would reveal the dissenter of tender conscience to be a temporizing zealot, an unscrupulous schismatic governed only by self-interest.

The title page of the *Life of Sanderson* bears the motto, *"Mysteries are revealed to the meek,"* and the last words of the *Life* are *"Blessed is the man in whose Spirit there is no guile."* These words provide an accurate index to what Walton would tell of Sanderson's life, and they are the motif of the *Life of Sanderson*. But in order to show a great casuist of the Anglican Church as a meek and mild Christian, Walton counterpoints his theme with a hymn of hate for nonconformity. Sanderson is the representative Anglican churchman, humble and reasonable, peaceable in his desire to avoid quarrels. Walton would demonstrate the real concessions he —and his fellows—made in his ardor for the unity and catholicity of the Church and what impossible demands he would not concede to. He would show the extent of Sanderson's sacrifices, what the commotions of the Covenanters inflicted in pain and in penury upon him and upon the nation. He would make vivid what happened to such a divine during the interregnum, would show that he was one of many who suffered equally. Walton may originally have had in mind to portray Sanderson as a model bishop; he was soon justifying not only Sanderson but the episcopacy of his own day. He may originally have had in mind to show the harshness of the treatment that Sanderson was exposed to when dissent was in the saddle, but Sanderson merged in places with the generality which was in like fashion exposed, and Walton was soon writing not biography or history, but augury. The chronicle of Sanderson's life became in part a chronicle representative of the Church, and Walton, with an eye on the contemporary arena, was soon writing not hagiography but prophecy. He may have begun to justify one man and the Church of bygone decades; the justification became a contemporary one, and when it became contemporary, it became, too, admonitory.

Although the structure of the *Life of Sanderson* is looser than that of the other *Lives,* it still reveals Walton's interests and intents. Walton sought to use a chronological approach, and the *Life* abounds in dates, but his chronology is frequently diffuse and erratic. In some degree this is due to Walton's attempt to fasten Sanderson's life by two geographical pegs, Oxford and Boothby Pagnol. Walton managed to create some sort of equilibrium between the two places, though from 1619 to 1660 Sanderson was in the main at Boothby Pagnol except for the two years (1646–1648) during which he lectured at Oxford. Walton did not wish to emphasize Sanderson's role as a country parson; he indicated that Sanderson fulfilled that role admirably, but it did not preoccupy his interest as it had in the *Life of Herbert.* He wished to show above all else Sanderson's mild temper, his open-mindedness in religious matters, his willingness to make reasonable concessions. Merely to demonstrate Sanderson's devotion to pastoral duties and his moderate behavior in the country would not be to demonstrate the significant qualities of his moderation or to reveal the breadth of his activities. Sanderson's sixteen years as student and fellow at Oxford receive fair treatment in pre-empting about one-sixth of the *Life.* The twenty years which follow—at Boothby Pagnol—are covered in shorter measure (about one-tenth of the *Life*). At the end of this section, in the account of the gradual recognition of Sanderson's abilities, chronology and geography become blurred as Walton sought to emphasize Sanderson's activities at the outbreak of trouble in 1639 by hanging on a thin and devious Oxford thread his part in the tumultuous times until 1648. To these nine years are allocated almost one-fifth of the *Life,* as Walton frequently took the spotlight off Sanderson to focus on university affairs and off both to shift to the Covenanters and London. These were years of confusion for Sanderson, but Walton's impressionistic picture of the general confusion is at Sanderson's expense. To Sanderson's years at Boothby Pagnol from 1648 to 1660 Walton devoted some three-tenths of the *Life,* but only half the material here is a chronicle of Sanderson's life. The rest is a repository for other matters. The structure of the *Life* shows, then, despite its diffuseness, or, perhaps, by its looseness, that Walton's interest in Sanderson as a country parson was minor. Walton's major interest is revealed in a larger view of the structure: the last third of Sanderson's life, that part which starts about 1640, gets more than two-thirds of the *Life.* To the last three of these years, Sanderson's years as a bishop and the days of his holy dying, Walton devoted about a fifth of the *Life,* a large proportion but one easily accounted for since the bishopric caps the climax of Sanderson's life and since Walton ever felt obliged to give a detailed deathbed account. The years prior to these are the years of the interregnum, and here lay Walton's greatest interest. About half the *Life* is devoted to these years, and here the Covenanters and the clergy as a whole share the spotlight with Sanderson.

Walton must have sensed a certain lack of firmness in the structure of the *Life,* and in his effort to compensate for it he plainly revealed his hand. He overcame the structural deficiency by his use of the first person. If Walton had subjectively intruded into the other *Lives,* he had taken some pains to hide his presence. Now, with a less formal structure, he personally entered the *Life,* occasionally to lead and direct his reader from place to place, more frequently to register comments, even to report his own relationship with Sanderson and to relate their conversations. When the structure of the *Life* does not clarify Walton's intent, his pointed comment does.

The opening section of the *Life* tells of Sanderson's family, his youthful temperament, and his early education at the grammar school at Rotherham. Walton merely indicates that Sanderson was of honorable descent and spares the reader details by moralizing on inherited titles. He stresses Sanderson's unwearied diligence to attain learning, his seriousness, and his uncommon modesty. He states that Sanderson "began in his Youth to make the Laws of God, and Obedience to his Parents, the rules of his life,"[78] that even then he dedicated himself to piety and virtue, and that his calm, quiet, and happy temper of mind made the whole course of his life "easie and grateful" both to himself and to others. He tells that "the Master and whole number of Scholars lov'd him, as

[78] *Sanderson,* 1678, sig. a3ᵛ.

one man,"[79] shows in a pretty story that Sanderson was an excellent grammarian at twelve, and quickly gets him to Oxford.

Walton's account of Sanderson's career at Oxford is detailed and documented; its importance for him is evident in its careful construction. He makes it clear that he has consulted the college records to provide an authentic report of Sanderson's activities and honors, but he is hardly content with a factual report. He merely mentions Sanderson's matriculation on July 1, 1603, and his being chosen fellow on May 3, 1606, before he tells that when Sanderson took his Bachelor of Arts his tutor told his friend and counselor, Dr. Kilbie, Rector of Lincoln College, that *"his Pupil Sanderson had a metaphysical brain, and a matchless memory: and that he thought he had improv'd, or made the last so by an Art of his own invention."*[80] He underlines the words by adding, "And all the future imployments of his life prov'd that his Tutor was not mistaken." But at this point he says, "I must here stop my Reader," to relate an incident which occurred after 1611. It is the story of Sanderson's accompanying Kilbie on a journey to Derbyshire, where they heard a young preacher find fault in his sermon with several words in the new translation of the Bible, unaware that Kilbie was one of the translators. Walton tells it to report Kilbie's words that the young man *"might have preach'd more useful Doctrine"*[81] and Sanderson's wish that he would not himself ever prove guilty of such indiscretion. Having demonstrated Sanderson's early lesson in the proper function of preaching and in the unworthiness of quibbling, Walton returns to Oxford to tell of Sanderson's appointments as Reader in Logic and Subrector of Lincoln College. These offices procured him love and reverence from the whole society, but there was general sorrow for his "happy infirmities," his timorousness and his bashfulness. Walton promises "more hereafter" about these qualities, and he makes his promise abundantly good, for he never for a moment lets his reader forget them. Here they are prefatory to his account of Sanderson's unsuccessful candidacy for the office of proctor for the university in 1614, to show that he was not satisfying any ambition of his own but complying with the desires of his college, which had not had one of its members elected in sixty years. In 1615, he was persuaded to lay aside his modesty to methodize and have printed his lectures on logic. Walton stresses Sanderson's achievement here, "For Logick may be said to be an *Art*

[79] *Ibid.,* sig. a5^r.   [80] *Ibid.,* sig. a6^v.   [81] *Ibid.,* sig. a7^v.

of right reasoning,"[82] and he shows Sanderson's mastery of the art by telling that his *Logic* was still used as a text and that over ten thousand copies had been sold. He explains that the *Logic* was evidence to the university of Sanderson's learning and prudence, that those who had maneuvered his defeat at his running for the proctorship repented, that Sanderson overcame his "inward unwillingness" to run a second time. On April 10, 1616, he was chosen Senior Proctor. Walton devotes almost half of his account of Sanderson's years at Oxford to the year of his proctorship, more than 7 per cent of the total space of the *Life*. It is not hard to see why. He is able to demonstrate Sanderson's unselfishness of motive, his lack of ambition for high office, the universal opinion of his worthiness for office. He is able to show his capability in coping with high office, that he was less interested in the allurements for self-aggrandizement which it offered than in the quiet performance of his arduous responsibilities. The account of the proctorship is divided into two parts. In the first Walton recounts in detail the "many memorable accidents" of the year of the proctorship. These he tells to show, in the second part, that there was much that Sanderson could have dwelt upon in his valedictory speech as proctor, but that "though his Office seem'd, according to Statute and Custome, to require him to do so at his leaving it; yet he chose rather to pass them over with some very short Observations, and present the Governours, and his other Hearers, with rules to keep up Discipline and Order in the University."[83] He goes beyond this proof of Sanderson's unselfish devotion to his duty to show that he effectually enforced a multiplicity of new and confusing statutes, that his behavior in unsettled times was unreproachable, that he was "so happy as to lay down this dangerous imployment, as but very few, if any have done, even *without an Enemy*."[84] After a pretty little incident in the proctorship, told because it commemorates the friendship of Sanderson and Sheldon, Walton hastily summarizes Sanderson's career to the resignation of his fellowship and his appointment to the cure of Boothby Pagnol.

Walton does not relate in any detail Sanderson's "contented obscurity" at Boothby Pagnol. He quickly tells that Sanderson's careful considerations of marriage "turn'd his faint purpose into a positive resolution" and that Anne Nelson brought him years of joy. He is content merely to state that Sanderson lived with his

---

[82] *Ibid.*, sig. b3ʳ.   [83] *Ibid.*, sigs. b7ᵛ–b8ʳ.   [84] *Ibid.*, sig. cʳ.

parish and his patron "in a religious love, and a contented quietness. He not troubling their thoughts by preaching high and useless notions, but such plain truths as were necessary to be known,
believed, and practised, in order to their salvation."[85] To show
that Sanderson had no narrow interpretation of the parson's function, Walton cites just one long example as typical of his concern
for his parish: he tells how Sanderson rather violently persuaded
a landlord to forgive a poor, dejected neighbor the rent for a field
which had been flooded. Content that the one incident will prove
Sanderson's worth, Walton lists the honors which his growing fame
brought him. In telling that the bishops asked him to preach many
visitation sermons and that the gentry asked him to preach at
assizes, Walton plays again on Sanderson's shyness: despite his extraordinary memory, he had such an innate invincible fear and
bashfulness that he could not memorize his sermons and was forced
to read them. Walton tells of Laud's recommending Sanderson to
the King, of the King's appointing him his chaplain in ordinary in
November, 1631, and of his great satisfaction in Sanderson's sermons and his cases of conscience. In an almost parenthetical paragraph, Walton takes his reader back to 1625 to tell of the honor
conferred upon Sanderson as a representative from Lincoln to the
Convocation. He justifies his slight interruption of the chronological sequence of Sanderson's honors "because about that time
did arise many disputes about Predestination, and the many Critical
Points that depend upon, or are interwoven in it," and he says that
Sanderson "then drew up for his own satisfaction such a Scheme
(he call'd it *Pax Ecclesia*[*e*]) as then gave himself, and hath since
given others such satisfaction, that it still remains to be of great
estimation among the most learned."[86] He forewarns his reader that
he will have occasion to mention the Convocation of 1640 and the
later debates of the predestinarian points by Sanderson, Hammond,
and Pierce, and then he brings the list of Sanderson's honors to a
climax by telling that at the King's progress to Oxford in 1636
Sanderson was created Doctor of Divinity.

In the following section of the *Life,* Walton would show the
effect of the war years upon Sanderson. Since Sanderson was appointed Regius Professor of Divinity in 1642 and took up his post
at the end of 1646, Walton shifts his scene to Oxford. Walton's
memories of these years were so highly charged with personal feel-

[85] *Ibid.,* sigs. c8r–c8v.   [86] *Ibid.,* sig. d7v.

ing, so deeply impressed with the violent effect of the times upon so many people, that he cannot tell his story from Sanderson's point of view alone. Sanderson's experience had parallels with his own, and he cannot keep himself out of the account. Sanderson's experience was that of many at Oxford, and Walton was soon writing about Oxford in general. The disruptions at Oxford were the disruptions of the country as a whole, and Walton was soon writing about neither Sanderson nor Oxford, but about London and all of England. His first sentence in this section is painted on a historical canvas: "Some years before the unhappy long Parliament, this Nation being then happy and in peace (though inwardly sick of being well) namely in the year 1639 . . ."[87] Then he tells of the invasion of the Scots in that year and again in 1643, when they marched into England carrying the Covenant high. Immediately, he gives his own response: "This I saw, and suffer'd by it." Only after praising God that he was not a Covenanter does he remember Sanderson: "And I have been the bolder to say this of my self, because in a sad discourse with Dr. *Sanderson* I heard him make the like grateful acknowledgment." And only after the historical and personal outburst does he recollect himself to say, "This digression is intended for the better information of the Reader in what will follow concerning Dr. *Sanderson*."[88] The same lack of control and intensity of feeling characterizes all of this section.

Walton tells how, in 1641, Sanderson altered, at Laud's request, the Book of Common Prayer to abate ceremonies that troubled the tender consciences of the Covenanters, and he mentions the uselessness of his effort in the confusion which followed. He shows the esteem in which Parliament held Sanderson in naming him to settle church controversies, his refusal to heed a summons which lacked royal authority, and his acceptance of the King's appointment to the chair in divinity at Oxford. He praises Sanderson's courage in lecturing on the true obligations of oaths "in a degenerate Age, when men had made perjury a main part of their Religion,"[89] and he praises the wisdom of his lectures *De Obligatione Conscientiae*. He then tells that Parliament sent the Covenant and the Negative Oath to be subscribed at Oxford and describes Sanderson's part in drawing up the manifesto which showed that the oaths violated consciences. But he leaves the story of Oxford's resistance to Parliament temporarily incomplete to enlarge upon

[87] *Ibid.*, sig. e[r].   [88] *Ibid.*, sigs. e2[v]–e3[r].   [89] *Ibid.*, sig. e5[r].

Sanderson's service to the King. The King's esteem for Sanderson is demonstrated by his conferring with Sanderson about parliamentary proposals, by his asking him to consider the relationship of episcopacy and monarchy and to write more cases of conscience, by his confessing to Sanderson his errors in consenting to Strafford's death and in abolishing episcopacy in Scotland, and by his translating into English Sanderson's lectures on oaths. Walton then returns to his Oxford story to tell of Sanderson's fortitude in continuing to read his lectures and of his expulsion in 1648, and he broadens his canvas to tell in some detail about Morley's brave efforts in 1647 to plead the case for the university before a parliamentary committee. He leaves Oxford to the "self-loving Reformers" and "Scruple-mongers" who filled the university, to "make an account of the then present affairs of *London.*"[90] He does not write a reasoned history but a highly slanted memoir which mentions the suffering of the deposed clergy and concentrates on the covetousness, malice, and villainy of the men who hurried into their places and on the madness and ignorance of the common people who supported them. From the filling of prisons with divines in 1648, he turns to Laud's execution in 1645 and to the revival of Thomas Brightman's revelations after 1641, when the bishops were excluded from Parliament. He bitterly attacks the common people for dictating doctrine and their ministers for engaging "their hearers to contend furiously for truths which they understood not."[91] He shows the temporizing of the Covenanters and the Independents, who agreed only "to preach down *Common Prayer,* and get into the best sequestred Livings,"[92] and he indicts the Presbyterians in a damning, barely veiled parable: he tells of a Scot who began to reform his new churchyard by cutting down trees which ornamented it, and he says, "I have hear'd (but do not affirm it) That no Action lies against him that is so wicked as to steal the winding sheet of a dead body after 'tis buried; and have heard the reason to be, because none were supposed to be so void of humanity, and that such a Law would vilifie that Nation that would but suppose so vile a man to be born in it."[93] The story is an accurate index of Walton's contempt for and fear of nonconformists, and the note of the license and the contentiousness of dissent which it sounds is ever in the reader's mind as he reads the rest of the *Life,* coloring

[90] *Ibid.,* sigs. f5v–f6r.   [91] *Ibid.,* sigs. f8r–f8v.   [92] *Ibid.,* sig. gr.
[93] *Ibid.,* sigs. g2r–g2v.

his attitude toward dissent and providing a contrast for the reasonableness and honesty of Sanderson and Conformity.

Walton finally takes his reader to Boothby Pagnol, where Sanderson lived until the Restoration, but his account of these years includes more than a continuous chronicle. It is artfully constructed to allow Walton to show Sanderson's ideas on doctrine and liturgy. It starts, however, with a continuation of the story of the ravages of the Covenanters, now in the country; Walton says that "all corners of the Nation were fill'd with Covenanters, Confusion, Comittee-men and Soldiers, serving each other to their several ends, of revenge, or power, or profit."[94] He tells how soldiers disturbed Sanderson in church, tearing his prayer book, and he shows the slightness of the alteration that Sanderson, to secure his place, made in his service by quoting the form of confession which he used. He quotes approvingly Sanderson's words to justify his course during these years and clinches the matter of his loyalty by telling that he started to translate into Latin the *Eikon Basilike*. Artfully, he continues his chronicle by starting his account of Henry Hammond's visit to Boothby Pagnol with a delightful story about Sanderson's unsuccessful attempt to deliver a sermon from memory. But Hammond's visit is merely an excuse to introduce the knotty points of the Quinquarticular Controversy and to consider Sanderson's doctrinal beliefs. Walton gives a short summary of the matters which they and Thomas Pierce discussed and of the circumstances which led to the discussion, primarily to show that it was a "charitable disquisition" into which Sanderson was unwillingly drawn and to prove Sanderson's willingness to change his mind. He points his lesson explicitly: "And let me here tell the Reader also, that if the rest of mankind would, as *Dr. Sanderson*, not conceal their alteration of Judgment, but confess it to the honour of God and themselves, then our Nation would become freer from pertinacious Disputes, and fuller of Recantations."[95] And if this does not make his point clearly enough, he contrasts Sanderson's reasonable attitude with the obstinacy and personal bias of the nonconformists by referring to Laud's sermon on the scaffold and his words of warning when he was accused of endeavoring to introduce popery:

He declar'd with sadness, *That the several Sects and Divisions then in* England (which he had laboured to prevent) *were like to bring the Pope a far greater harvest, than he could ever have expected without*

[94] *Ibid.,* sigs. g2ᵛ–g3ʳ.   [95] *Ibid.,* sig. h3ʳ.

them. And said, *these Sects and Divisions introduce prophaneness under the cloak of an imaginary Religion;* and *that we have lost the substance of Religion by changing it into Opinion;* and *that by these means this Church, which all the Jesuits machinations could not ruine, was fall'n into apparent danger by those which were his Accusers.*[96]

Sanderson, he says, expressed the same sentiments in the Preface to his *Sermons* (1655) and in his will, and "these Covenanters ought to take notice of it"[97] and to think about the remarkable body of casuistry which they lost for the nation by ejecting Sanderson from Oxford.

Walton shows his awareness of his departure from chronicle by saying, "I should now return to *Boothby Pannel* where we left Dr. *Hammond* and Dr. *Sanderson* together, but neither can be found there."[98] He picks up his chronicle by telling about Sanderson's imprisonment, the special provision made for him, and, despite this, his "being several times plundered, and once wounded in three places."[99] He shows Sanderson's "peaceful moderation" in these times by pointing to the satisfaction which his cases of conscience gave to many and his fortitude by pointing to his hazarding his safety to make public his sentiments in the Preface of 1655, at a time "when the common people were amaz'd & grown giddy by the many falshoods and misapplications of Truths frequently vented in Sermons; when they wrested the Scripture by challenging God to be of their party, and call'd upon him in their prayers to patronize their Sacriledge & zealous Frenzies."[100] Walton carefully gives the impression of continuing his chronicle by relating the details of his accidental meeting with Sanderson at this time. But this meeting and a later one are the means by which he communicates his own and Sanderson's "useful observations." Sanderson's commendation of the Book of Common Prayer and of the Psalter is followed by his sorrow that the pulpits rang with needless debates because "every man preach'd and pray'd what seem'd best in his own eyes,"[101] and Walton has him say:

That the way to restore this Nation to a more meek and Christian temper, was to have the Body of Divinity (or so much of it as was needful to be known) to be put into 52 Homilies or Sermons, of such a length as not to exceed a third or fourth part of an hours reading; and these needful Points to be made so clear and plain, that those of a mean

---

96 *Ibid.,* sig. h4ᵛ.   97 *Ibid.,* sig. h5ʳ.   98 *Ibid.,* sig. h5ᵛ.
99 *Ibid.,* sigs. h7ʳ–h7ᵛ.   100 *Ibid.,* sigs. iᵛ–i2ʳ.   101 *Ibid.,* sig. i6ᵛ.

capacity might know what was necessary to be believed, and what God requires to be done; and then some applications of trial and conviction: and these to be read every Sunday of the year, as infallibly as the blood circulates the body; and then as certainly begun again, and continued the year following.[102]

Walton shows what additional objections he had to the nonconformists in having Sanderson lament their refusal to fill mean livings and their denial of the sacrament to their parishioners "unless upon such conditions, and in such a manner as they could not take it."[103] He had had Sanderson mention his *"unmanly bashfulness"* in his commentary on the times, and he now gives a detailed character of Sanderson's person and temper. He stresses Sanderson's "plain comliness" of behavior, that had only just enough "ceremony or courtship" in it; the useful matter and clear distinctions in his preaching; his firm and matchless memory, overcome only by his bashfulness; his humility, gained by his having conquered "all repining and ambitious thoughts."[104] His account of Robert Boyle's admiration of Sanderson's character and his casuistry and Boyle's kindness in sending money to the poverty-stricken Sanderson serves to restore some semblance of chronicle to the *Life* but does not hide the fact that Walton's detailed and selective character is an announcement of the traits which so well qualified Sanderson for a bishopric when God at the Restoration made "ready to pay them [the wretched nonconformists] such wages as he does always reward *Witches* with."[105]

After telling that Sanderson, at seventy-three years of age, approximated the ideal bishop of the primitive church and that he was recommended to the King by Sheldon, Walton reveals Sanderson's part in the Restoration settlement. He mentions Sanderson's mildness, patience, and reason at the Savoy Conference and contrasts his behavior with the illogic and perversity of Baxter, illustrating their "friendly debate" with the quotation of the argument about the lawfulness of a command given by a lawful superior. He then enumerates in detail Sanderson's share at the Convocation in giving the dissenters satisfaction by "alteration, explanation, and addition" to the Book of Common Prayer. There follows "a part of his behaviour" as Bishop of Lincoln, which stresses his obligingness to the meanest of the clergy and to his parishioners and the un-

---

[102] *Ibid.,* sigs. i6ᵛ–i7ʳ.   [103] *Ibid.,* sig. i8ᵛ.   [104] *Ibid.,* sig. k4ʳ.
[105] *Ibid.,* sig. k6ʳ.

selfish expenditure of his income to repair his episcopal residence and to augment the revenue of small vicarages. Walton completes his picture of the good bishop by having Sanderson reveal that the foundation of his great and clear learning was in his having by heart Aristotle's *Rhetoric*, Aquinas' *Secunda Secundae* (the second part of the *Summa*), Cicero's *De Officiis*, and Zouch's *Elementa Jurisprudentiae*.

Before giving an account of Sanderson's last sickness, his death, and burial, Walton quotes at some length from Sanderson's will, "for confirmation of what hath been said, and what I think convenient to be known."[106] The will serves to underline sentiments which Walton heartily approved of. Sanderson, in professing his belief in the Church Established, says that he was

led so to do, not so much from the force of custom and education . . . as upon the clear evidence of truth and reason, after a serious and unpartial examination of the grounds, as well of Popery as Puritanism, according to that measure of understanding, and those opportunities which God hath afforded me: and herein I am abundantly satisfied, that the Schism which the Papists on the one hand, and the Superstition which the Puritan on the other hand, lay to our charge, are very justly chargeable upon themselves respectively.[107]

And he humbly beseeches God

that it would please him to give unto our gracious Sovereign, the Reverend Bishops, and the Parliament, timely to consider the great danger that visibly threatens this Church in point of Religion by the late great increase of Popery, and in point of Revenue by sacrilegious enclosures; and to provide such wholesome and effectual remedies as may prevent the same before it be too late.[108]

Walton then quotes at length Sanderson's desire to be buried *"with as little noise, pomp, and charge as may be"* as "a further manifestation of his humble thoughts and desires."[109] His detailed story of Sanderson's last days shows again Sanderson's great care for his clergy, the careful regularity of his private worship, the part of the Psalms in his devotions. The story is particularized by Sanderson's own words and by the details of his receiving the sacrament and absolution from his chaplain, Mr. Pullen. Walton ends the *Life* with a prayer that his own death may be like Sanderson's.

106 *Ibid.*, sig. m⁵.   107 *Ibid.*, sigs. m2ᵛ–m3ʳ.   108 *Ibid.*, sigs. m3ᵛ–m4ʳ.
109 *Ibid.*, sig. m4ʳ.

Walton's accomplishment in the *Life of Sanderson* is a major one. It has been minimized or overlooked because after the middle of the seventeenth century the western world found heroes who replaced clergymen and casuists. Carlyle's *Life of Sterling* is a great biography, but it is taken off the shelf today for the chapter on Coleridge. Prying interest in the papal laundry has led readers to Strachey's "Cardinal Manning," but it is his "Florence Nightingale" which is acclaimed or damned. In our day the minutest dictum of a minor political officeholder is relished; the very name of the Archbishop of Canterbury is not known. We need not regret that hundreds of bloodless hagiographies yellow in the storage vaults of libraries; their luminous generalities and vapid holinesses are well forgotten by a world which has a different fashion in stereotypes. Walton's *Sanderson* suffers the fate of these, though it is not of them.

The *Life of Sanderson* is a remarkably individualized picture, despite the generalized function it is made to serve. Walton has so managed the *Life* that Sanderson comes to life. He is represented as a man of activity in the midst of the activities of his environment, and from the contrast which emerges his qualities stand out. Walton has produced a bishop who is extremely attractive, thoroughly likable, and worthy of esteem. He has shown us a man who is reasonable and temperate, forthright and honest in his opinions, but not dogmatic in holding them or enforcing them; a trimmer whose integrity is unquestionable and whose fortitude is unquestioned. And withal, a shy and bashful man whose humility is dignified. His virtues are intensified by the vices of the nonconformists. Walton has stressed the violence of their activity, their disregard for persons, their forceful irreverence for sanctified things. He has underlined the temporality of their motivation, their desire for place and money, their wish to rule. He has made the anarchy they instituted dependent upon the anarchy of their opinion, their perverseness and disputatiousness dependent upon their illogic. He does not credit them with interest in or consistency of doctrine of any kind, and he condemns them for their eccentric rationalizations. On the other hand, he continually praises Sanderson's learning and doctrine. But, oddly, these are talked about, not demonstrated. The lucidity of Sanderson's judgments in *De Juramenti Promissorii Obligatione* and in *De Obligatione Conscientiae* is commended; the works are not summarized. The cases of conscience are extolled and their titles listed; their doctrine is not discussed. Even Walton's account of the Quinquarticular Controversy is largely concerned, not with doctrine, but with Sanderson's aversion to debate on difficult questions and with his willingness to change his mind. Throughout the *Life,* Sanderson's doctrinal beliefs are subordinated to emphasize Walton's idea that it was Sanderson's fundamental belief that the road to salvation is easy and can be followed with few directions. Walton talks about the difficulty of writing cases of conscience and about Sanderson's expenditure of effort on his work, but he never reveals the result of that work. His picture of Sanderson omits the subtlety of Sanderson's mind.

We may say that Walton took for granted the distinction of Sanderson's learning and his doctrine. Did he not intimate in 1670 that the function of a life of Sanderson was to show that the meekness and innocence of Sanderson's life, his fortitude and suffering under Nonconformity, were equally remarkable with these?[110] Still, there are other general reasons for the mere mention they get in the *Life.* Walton himself had long believed in the simplicity of saving doctrine. Note his commendation of Alexander Nowell in the *Compleat Angler* for making a catechism that is "good, plain, unperplext": "though he was very learned, yet knowing that God leads us not to heaven by hard questions."[111] His own slight education precluded the detailed knowledge and intellectual subtlety needed for the understanding of doctrinal intricacies. His own interest in church matters was ever ecclesiastical and sacerdotal, not theological. He reflected the interest of his times, for the battleground of religion was far more often that of discipline than of doctrine. But even if Walton had had any interest in or great knowledge of doctrine, it is likely that he would have minimized it in the *Life.* For to have discussed Sanderson's doctrine in detail would have been to create a different picture of Sanderson. Some intimation of Sanderson's doctrine it was necessary for him to give, but to have exploited it would have been to temper Sanderson's attractive simplicity and mildness with intellectual complexity and subtlety, to have traded sympathy and love for the distance of respect and the coldness of awe. He wished to avoid this, and, too, aware of his incapacity to do justice to doctrine, he continually sought to postpone his discussion of it. His embarrass-

[110] *Lives,* 1670, sig. A7ʳ.   [111] *Compleat Angler* (1653), p. 31.

ment is evident in his insistence on the sufficiency of plain truths and in his lack of confidence in his ability to define precisely Sanderson's positions.

How important it was to Walton to show that Sanderson was early impressed with the necessity of right preaching we have seen in the digressive story of Sanderson's accompanying Kilbie to Derbyshire. If the lesson is there stated in terms of what is bad, Walton makes his point positively in his account of Sanderson's preaching at Boothby Pagnol, where he stresses Sanderson's belief that it is essential to preach not high and useless notions but such plain truths as must be known, and where he indicates that only the love which a parson inspires in his parishioners makes the doctrine which he preaches effectual.[112] Again, in his account of his meeting with Sanderson, he has Sanderson say that we may safely be ignorant of knotty doctrinal points "because Almighty God intends not to lead us to Heaven by hard Questions, but by meekness and charity, and a frequent practice of Devotion."[113] These passages make Walton's reader believe that his many confessions of his inability to discuss matters of doctrine reflect his humility and his sentiment that such matters are unessential. But they do not hide his constant avoidance of doctrine and his insecurity in talking about it. When he mentions the letter which King James sent to Oxford in 1617 to regulate studies, he says that his only purpose is to acquaint his reader with its "occasion"; he merely speculates whether the King objected to Calvin's doctrine or to Calvin's interpreters, saying, "I pretend not to have an ability to judge."[114] When in telling of the honor that came to Sanderson in 1625 he mentions the many critical points of the Quinquarticular Controversy, it is only to announce that he will "hereafter have occasion to mention" them.[115] He has occasion to mention them when he talks about the Covenanters' strange observations on election, reprobation, and free will, but he merely says that these matters are "such as the wisest of the common people were not fit to judge of: I am sure I am not," and again he says, "I must mention some of them historically in a more proper place, when I have brought my Reader with me to Dr. *Sanderson* at *Boothby Pannel*."[116] Finally, at Boothby Pagnol, he says of the controversy, "I

112 *Sanderson,* 1678, sig. c8ᵛ.   113 *Ibid.,* sig. i5ᵛ.   114 *Ibid.,* sig. b7ᵛ.
115 *Ibid.,* sig. d8ʳ.   116 *Ibid.,* sig. gᵛ.

shall proceed, not to give any Judgment (I pretend not to that) but
some short Historical account which shall follow."[117] He cites three
opinions about predestination and summarizes them as "truths, or
untruths, or both, be they which they will."[118] Instead of showing
the particulars of Sanderson's position, he rather emphasizes his
dislike of debate, his willingness to change his mind, and he lets
the matter drop by quoting Hammond's words, *"God can reconcile
his own contradictions, and therefore advises all men, as the Apostle
does, to study mortification, and be wise to sobriety."*[119] In 1678,
Walton apparently thought that *Pax Ecclesiae,* which he dates
1625, represented Sanderson's final judgment on several points of
doctrine, and he said that it gave Sanderson and others such satisfaction "that it still remains to be of great estimation among the
most learned."[120] In 1681, he thought differently; he dropped
"among the most learned" and added, "And here the Reader may
note, that in letters writ to the said Dean [Pierce, of Salisbury], Dr.
Sanderson seems to have alter'd his Judgment in some Points, since
he writ his Scheme called *Pax Ecclesia[e],* which he seems to say in
his last Will, besides other reasons to think so."[121] In 1678, Walton
had in the Preface of the *Life* told of Sanderson's injunction against
printing his unpublished work after his death, for *"he might have
chang'd his opinion since he first writ it."*[122] In 1681, he added "as
'tis thought he has since he writ his *Pax Ecclesiae."*[123] If these
passages reveal Walton's confusion and unsureness as well as his
disinclination, they show, too, that he was aware of the necessity
of facing the problem of Sanderson's doctrine. But because it was
tangled and knotty and because it would blur the picture he wanted,
he reserved larger discussion of it for an appendix, and he probably
hoped to have the appendix written for him. He went to the best
authorities, but he found them somewhat disappointing.

Walton knew that Dr. Thomas Pierce had corresponded at
length with Sanderson, and he applied to him for information about
the change in Sanderson's doctrine on the points controverted
between the Calvinists and the Arminians. Pierce's temperament
and mind were hardly congenial to Walton. Wood calls him "a
person more for the pulpit then government" and says that during
the years he *"raigned* (for he use to stile himself 'prince')" as

[117] *Ibid.,* sigs. g7^v–g8^r.   [118] *Ibid.,* sig. h^r.   [119] *Ibid.,* sig. h2^v.
[120] *Ibid.,* sig. d7^v.   [121] *Ibid.,* 1681, p. 16.   [122] *Ibid.,* 1678, sig. A6^v.
[123] *Ibid.,* 1681, sig. (b)^v.

president of Magdalen, "the College was continually in faction and faction he fostered. High, proud, and somtimes little better than mad. But at last they got him out for the deanery of Salisbury."[124] In 1663, Clarendon had chided him for his "too rigid and severe actions in his college."[125] In the same year, his college was forced to submit to a visitation of the Bishop of Winchester, statutably responsible for Magdalen, and Morley found it necessary to vindicate himself from the aspersions cast upon him by Pierce.[126] Still, Wood names him, Hammond, and Heylyn the "chiefest champions among the old, regular and conformable clergy," and a long catalogue of works testifies that he was "very well read and exercis'd in the quinquarticular controversies."[127] Though Pierce had originally been a Calvinist, he was "a zealous son of the ch. of England"[128] and he "preached up Arminianism."[129] He was exceptionally well qualified to tell Walton about Sanderson's doctrine, and Walton's desire for authoritative information overcame even his predisposition to seek help largely from people he liked.

Not only did Pierce comply with Walton's request but he also permitted Walton to use his letter as he wished and to use his name as warranty for statements it made. Walton reproduced it completely after the *Life,* though part of it puzzled him. His own evidence in 1678 led him to believe that Sanderson's doctrinal judgments had been modified by his correspondence with Pierce and Hammond after 1648. Indeed, he wrote:

I think the Judgment of *Dr. Sanderson* was by these Debates altered from what it was at his entrance into them; for in the year 1632. when his excellent Sermons were first printed in 4°. the Reader may on the Margent find some accusation of *Arminius* for false Doctrine; and find, that upon a review and reprinting those Sermons in folio in the year 1657. that accusation of *Arminius* is omitted.[130]

124 *Wood's Life and Times,* I, 420.   125 *Ibid.,* p. 491.
126 See *ibid.,* pp. 473–474, n. 4, and *ibid.,* II, 16.
127 *Athenae Oxon.,* IV, 301–302.   128 *Ibid.*
129 *Wood's Life and Times,* I, 465.

130 *Sanderson,* 1678, sigs. h2ʳ–h2ᵛ. Walton has in mind Sanderson's first sermon ad Clerum, preached on April 17, 1619. This was first printed in 1621, and then in the collected editions of 1627, 1632, 1637, and 1657. Not until 1657 did Sanderson delete from ¶27 his marginal note, "Of late our *English Arminians* have got the trick to fetch in within the compasse of this Title of *Puritanes,* all orthodox Divines that oppose against their *Semi-pelagian* subtilties; of purpose to make sound truth odious, & their owne corrupt novelties more passable, and plausible." In 1657, too, he deleted his reference to Ar-

But in his next sentence, Walton deferred to Pierce's authority, and he wrote, "And the change of his judgment seems more fully to appear in his said Letter to *Dr. Pierce.*" Pierce's paraphrase of Sanderson's letter misled Walton into thinking, despite his own evidence, that *Pax Ecclesiae* represented Sanderson's settled judgment. Pierce had written that Sanderson had in 1625 "reduced the *Quinquarticular Controversie* into *five Schemes or Tables;* and thereupon *discerned a necessity of quitting the Sublapsarian way*" and that Walton would find Sanderson's "happy *change of Judgment* to have been ever since the year 1625, even 34 years before the World either *knew,* or (at least) *took notice of it.*"[131] If Walton was confused, still he did not question Pierce's authority; in 1678, his account of Sanderson's doctrine was ambiguous, and he repaired the damage only slightly in 1681 by his hesitant alterations.

Sanderson's doctrine is not easy to define. He accepted no ready-made garment but cut one to his own specifications. Even in his letter to Pierce he wrote that he was confirmed in the opinion that *"we must acknowledge the work of both (Grace and Freewill) in the conversion of a sinner. And so likewise in all other events, the Consistency of the Infallibility of God's foreknowledge at least (though not with any absolute, but conditional Predestination) with the liberty of man's will, and the contingency of inferiour causes and effects."*[132] He had originally been inclined toward Calvinism, and he gradually and gently shifted closer to Arminianism. *Pax Ecclesiae* indicates his first wanderings from Calvin. This is the "happy *change of Judgment*" that Pierce refers to; as an ardent Arminian, he was aware that *Pax Ecclesiae* was Sanderson's crucial judgment. But his statement that the world was unaware of Sanderson's change for thirty-four years led Walton to believe that the doctrine of *Pax Ecclesiae* did not differ from Sanderson's doctrine in 1660. Walton, then, praised *Pax Ecclesiae* extravagantly in 1678 despite his own evidence, and, though it is likely that Sanderson specifically had it in mind when in his will he tried to suppress his hitherto unpublished work, Walton printed it amongst the tracts at the end of the *Life.*

---

minianism from the marginal note to ¶29: "So *Pelagius,* from whose root *Popery* (in that branch) & *Arminianisme* sprouted . . ." In the text of ¶29, "wee see *Arminius* his corrupt doctrine in our dayes have spred," became, in 1657, "we see in our days not only the suspected tenets of Arminius, but even the bold heresies of Faustus Socinus have spread. . . ."

131 *Sanderson,* 1678, sig. n6r.   132 *Ibid.,* sig. n7v.

There is no doubt that in *Pax Ecclesiae* Sanderson attempted to encompass Arminianism within a modified Calvinist doctrine and that his bias is anti-Arminian. He admits that he is forced to cope with Arminianism because it has passed in England from private discussion to the public stage, and dangerous schism is likely to ensue unless it is speedily prevented.[133] He is forced to consider Arminianism because of the advantages the Arminian party has. He lists among these

The plausibleness of *Arminianism,* and the congruity it hath in sundry Points with the Principles of corrupt Nature, and of carnal Reason. For it is a wonderful tickling to flesh and blood, to have the powers of Nature magnified, and to hear it self flattered, as if she carried the greatest stroke in the work of Salvation; especially when these soothings are conveyed under the pretence of vindicating the dispensations of God's Providence from the Imputation of Injustice.[134]

Also among these advantages he lists the "manifold cunning of the *Arminians* to advance their own party,"[135] and he cites as their most unjust, most uncharitable, and most powerful recourse their "seeking to draw the persons of those that dissent from them into dislike with the S[t]ate, as if they were Puritans, or Disciplinarians, or at least that way affected."[136] Although he says that in his scheme for ordering God's decrees concerning man's salvation "no impeachment is done to grace by magnifying nature, or to the efficacy of grace, by enlarging the powers of Free-will,"[137] he is yet strenuous in his assertion of the doctrine of the elect and he thinks that the "inconveniencies, which either do ensue, or seem to ensue upon that Opinion [which Calvin and Beza are said to have held], may be fairly waved another way, and yet without Arminianism."[138] And in his very last sentence he shows that his purpose has been

to keep our understandings within some competent bounds of sobriety and truth, that we neither lose our selves in curious Enquiries to little purpose, nor suffer our judgments to be envenomed with the Poison either of rank *Pelagian* heresie, or *Semi-Pelagian* popery, or quarter-*Pelagian* and *Arminian* novelty.[139]

Sanderson's position in *Pax Ecclesiae* is in part a conciliatory one, and the fact of his concessions to Arminianism is important. He

[133] *Ibid.,* p. 58.   [134] *Ibid.,* p. 60.   [135] *Ibid.,* p. 61.
[136] *Ibid.,* p. 63. Compare with the marginal note which Sanderson omitted in 1657 (p. 413, n. 130).
[137] *Ibid.,* p. 76.   [138] *Ibid.,* p. 61.   [139] *Ibid.,* pp. 83–84.

took his step to preserve the quiet of the Church; he was willing
to make concessions in doctrine to preserve the ecclesiastical structure. As the Arminians became identified as the champions for the
Church Established in the political events which followed, Sanderson became more closely bound to them because his ecclesiastical
ends were similar to theirs and he became slightly more amenable
to the Arminian position. But *Pax Ecclesiae* is begrudging toward
Arminianism; only later did Sanderson become somewhat more
conformable.

So firmly convinced was Christopher Wordsworth of the sublapsarian bias of *Pax Ecclesiae* that he thought it must not be identified
with the "tables" which Pierce says were written in 1625. But the
"tables" and *Pax Ecclesiae* were written in 1625, and the "tables"
were the schematic guide upon which *Pax Ecclesiae* was based.[140]
Why did Pierce intimate in his letter to Walton that Sanderson's
change of judgment had occurred in 1625 when he knew that Sanderson had in that year taken only a first step away from Calvinism?
The story is not without interest, for it reveals how Pierce and
Hammond tried before the Restoration to bring Sanderson's doctrine into conformity with the prevailing High Church orthodoxy.
Pierce referred Walton to two published accounts of Sanderson's
riper judgments, one in the Appendix of his own *Impartial Inquiry
into the Nature of Sin* (1660) and the other in Hammond's Χάρις
καὶ Εἰρήνη, or *A Pacifick Discourse of Gods Grace and Decrees: In
a Letter, of full Accordance written to the Reverend, and most
learned, Dr. Robert Sanderson* (1660). In his own book, Pierce cites

---

140 In his *Ecclesiastical Biography*, 4th ed. (London, 1853), IV, 432, Wordsworth wrote, "It may be worth observing that this collection of schemes or
tables must not be confounded with the tract published by Isaac Walton under
the title *Pax Ecclesiae,* which Walton attributes to the year 1625. In that tract
it is plain, that he still retains the *Sub-lapsarian* opinion: and there are other
reasons to prove that the tracts are not the same. In truth, the *Pax Ecclesiae*
can hardly be considered as the work of Dr. Sanderson at all." In his last
sentence, Wordsworth does not mean to deny Sanderson's authorship of
Pax Ecclesiae; he means that its views bear little resemblance to those which
Sanderson later professed. That *Pax Ecclesiae* was not written prior to 1625
is evident in Sanderson's reference there to Richard Montagu's *Appello
Caesarem,* which was printed in 1625. That the "tables" which Sanderson
drew up in 1625 provided the basis for *Pax Ecclesiae* is evident in the five
manuscripts where the "tables" ("Series Decretorum Dei") are conjoined to
the text of *Pax Ecclesiae* (the third and fourth parts of which are entitled
"Series Decretorum Dei" and "Utilitas huius Seriei"). See Sanderson, *Works,*
V, 278.

Sanderson's letters, changing the pronoun from "I" to "he," to refute the printed statements of Henry Hickman that he had found support against Pierce's view of sin in Sanderson's Fifth Sermon ad Populum. Sanderson, he says, is

not unwilling the world should know, *that having from his younger years (as his Genius led him) addicted himself mostly to the study of the moral and practical part of Divinity; but especially having (for fear of approaching too neare to the Ark of Gods secret counsels) kept a loof off from medling (more then needs must) with those more nice and intricate disputes concerning Gods eternal decrees,* the cooperation *of Gods* free Grace, *and* mans free-will, *&c. He contented himself for* sundry years *to follow on (as most others did) by a kinde of* implicit credulity, *in the* Sublapsarian way, *as the then most troden path; until having a just occasion, (A.D.* 1628.) *to make a little farther inquiry after the truth in those questions,* upon due search *he saw a necessity of receding from that way in some things: a more particular account whereof is given in a* narrative *lately printed with* his consent, *which if well considered,* ought *(he thinketh) in reason and charity to excuse him from the necessity of justifying every syllable or phrase that might slip from his tongue or pen, in any thing by him spoken or written before that year, and whilst he was very* little *(or rather* nothing at all) *versed in the study of those Questions.*[141]

In his book Pierce writes, "I have the leave and consent of that most learned and pious person [Sanderson], to *communicate* as much of his *Letters* to me on this occasion, as I conceive may tend to his *vindication,* and with all to the *advantage of peace and truth,*"[142] and he writes Walton, too, that the letters were printed with Sanderson's consent.[143] Sanderson's consent was not readily given. Pierce wrote Sheldon on November 21, 1659, that "Dr. Sanderson hath at last consented," but he had written him on October 8 that

the liberty which he [Sanderson] gave me, before Dr. Hammond writ to him, he hath since thought fit to take away. For whereas he gave me leave to publish his departure from the Sublapsarians, together with his grounds and motives to it, he is now resolved, as Dr. H[ammond] lately writ me word, that I shall either print his whole Letter, (which will not be to my advantage, much less to his, whilst he condemns or doubts in some places the very things which he allowed and affirms in others,) or lose the advantage which I expected in printing any part of it.[144]

Pierce did not think it expedient to let Sanderson speak for himself.

Pierce had sent Sanderson's account of his change of judgment to Hammond.[145] In *A Pacifick Discourse,* Hammond says that he saw fit to publish Sanderson's opinions because

it seemed not improper, to offer at this time to publick view the present Sentiments of the Judicious Dr. Sanderson, *the* Regius Professor *of the* University *of* Oxford, *(and the rather, because some manuscript Tables of his former thoughts,*[146] *and some passages from his Sermons, long since preached, and now republished, have been made use of, to gain authority to those Doctrines which he is now far from owning:) and briefly and perspicuously to annex unto, and compare with them, those* Amicable *and* Pacifick *Reflexions, which may hope to gain the unanimous consent of all true Sons of our Venerable Mother, the* Church of England, *whose chiefe aime it hath alwayes been to discountenance divisions and fractions, and occasions and fomenters of those, especially* singular Doctrines *and* Novell Articles *of* Faith.[147]

Hammond, the prime builder of an intellectual defense for the High Church during the interregnum,[148] wished to pull Sanderson's doctrine within the bounds of High Church orthodoxy, but he could no more easily do so by allowing Sanderson to speak for himself than could Pierce. He, too, wrote Sheldon of Sanderson's perversity: "I have again returnd the Papers to D^r Sa: I hope in such a forme as he will approove, & am sure more for his interest then it would be, if (as he desires) all his letter were publisht."[149] Ap-

---

[144] Letters in Tanner MSS, II, f. 158, printed in Sanderson, *Works,* VI, 355, note †.

[145] *Sanderson,* 1678, sig. n5ᵛ.

[146] These were referred to in Edward Reynolds' epistolary preface (sig. d3ʳ) for William Barlee's *Praedestination, As before privately, so now at last openly defended against Post-Destination. In a Correptorie Correction* (1656), written to refute Pierce's *A Correct Copy of Some Notes Concerning Gods Decrees, Especially Of Reprobation* (1655). The weight which Sanderson's opinion had is clear in Reynolds' calling him "a learned writer" and in his seeking to discredit a posthumously printed tract of Bishop Andrewes' by arguing that Sanderson did not refer to it in his "tables." Pierce shows his awareness of the importance of Sanderson's opinion by copying with Reynolds' argument in his *The Divine Purity Defended* (1657), where he says (p. 124) that "Dr. *Sandersons* making *no mention* of it is but a *negative Argument,* and therefore signifies very *little* to an *intelligent* Reader."

[147] *A Pacifick Discourse,* Preface, ¶7.   [148] See Bosher, p. 36.

[149] Letter in Harleian MS 6942, f. 66ᵛ, printed in Sanderson, *Works,* V, 289 (corrected from photostat).

parently Sanderson approved, for his opinions are in *A Pacifick Discourse,* interspersed with longer opinions by Hammond in which he interprets Sanderson's statements and makes them conformable to the party line. He cites at some length Sanderson's history of the development of his thought, from which I excerpt those passages which correspond to the personal account which Pierce printed in his *Impartial Inquiry:*

But as for the questions of Election, Reprobation, Effectuall Grace, Perseverance &c. I took as little notice of the two first, as of any other thing contained in the book [Calvin's Institutes]; both because I was alwayes affraid to pry much into those secrets, and because I could not certainly inform my self from his own writings, whether he were a Supralapsarian (as most speak him, and he seemeth often to incline much that way) or a Sublapsarian, as sundry passages in the book seem to import. But giving my self mostly still to the study of Moral Divinity, (and taking most other things upon trust, as they were in a manner generally taught both in the Schools and Pulpits in both Universities) I did for many years together acquiesce without troubling my self any farther about them, in the more commonly received opinions concerning both these two, and the other points depending thereupon. Yet in the Sublapsarian way ever, which seemed to me of the two, the more moderate, rationall and agreeable to the goodness, and justice of God: for the rigid Supralapsarian doctrine could never find any entertainment in my thoughts from first to last. But MDCXXV . . . I made it my first business to take a survey of the severall different opinions concerning the ordering of Gods Decrees, as to the salvation or damnation of men. . . . Which opinions, the better to represent their differences to the eye . . . I reduced into five Schemes or Tables. . . . Having all these Schemes before my eyes at once, so as I might with ease compare them one with another, and having considered of the conveniences and inconveniences of each, as well as I could, I soon discerned a necessity of quitting the Sublapsarian way of which I had a better liking before, as well as the Supralapsarian, which I could never fancy.[150]

According to Hammond, Sanderson *"discerned a necessity of quitting the Sublapsarian way"* in 1625. According to Pierce's account of Sanderson's letter in 1660, Sanderson had occasion in 1628 to inquire further into the decrees of God and "upon due search *he saw a necessity of receding from that way* [sublapsarian] *in some things.*" It seems likely that when Pierce refuted Hickman in 1660, he had before him the manuscripts of Sanderson's letters. Although he refers Hickman to Sanderson's "narrative *lately printed with*

[150] *A Pacifick Discourse,* pp. 9–12.

his consent" in Hammond's book, he did not himself have Hammond's book before him as he wrote. When he wrote Walton that he would find Sanderson's "happy *change of Judgment* to have been ever since the year 1625, even 34 years before the World either *knew,* or (at least) *took notice of it,"* he was not quoting Sanderson's letter but paraphrasing one of Hammond's interpolations, *"these have been your thoughts, ever since the year* 1625, *i.e.* 34. years since."[151] Hammond could not maintain that Sanderson's change of judgment had taken place prior to 1625, because Sanderson's "tables" of that year had been widely circulated, but he thought he could safely represent Sanderson's change as having taken place in that year though he knew that some things in Sanderson's sermons published after 1625 refuted his statement.[152] Pierce, as determined as Hammond to show Sanderson's early orthodoxy, went along with Hammond's story.

In 1678, Walton carefully refrained from printing the unorthodox "tables" of 1625, but he willingly accepted Pierce's words (and Hammond's) on the orthodox position which the "tables" had led

151 *Ibid.,* p. 16.

152 In a letter to Sheldon, Hammond wrote, "I am very sorry he [Sanderson] hath been so negligent to omit the altering of those things in his Sermons, which have done so much hurt; for, that opportunity being past, I fear he will never take any other, to set himself and the Truth right in that matter" (Sanderson, *Works,* I, v). This letter is undated, but must have been written either after the publication in 1656 of twenty of Sanderson's sermons which had not been previously printed or after the reprinting in 1657 of the fourteen sermons collected in 1637. If Hammond wrote before 1657, it may well be that Sanderson's marginal changes, referred to by Walton, were concessions to him. In addition to the marginal changes, Sanderson made such slight alterations as the substitution of "Pelagianism" for "Arminianism" in his reference (¶26 of Sermon I ad Populum) to "that rotten principle and foundation of the whole frame of Arminianism," and again in his description of the conclusions which Conrad Vorstius drew from blasphemous principles (¶9 of Sermon II ad Populum). If Hammond wrote after 1657, it is obvious that he did not consider Sanderson's slight concessions sufficient. Even Jacobson, the sympathetic editor of Sanderson's *Works*—who tried to accept literally Hammond's and Pierce's statements that Sanderson changed his views in 1625 and who covered up Sanderson's retention in 1632 and 1637 of the marginal note in the First Sermon ad Clerum in order to explain its appearance in 1627 "by an oversight" of Sanderson's (*Works,* II, 32, note*)—was forced to say of Sanderson's Sixth Sermon ad Populum (preached in April, 1627, and reprinted essentially without change in 1637 and 1657), "The change in Sanderson's Theological Views, which dates from 1625, . . . cannot, in the first instance, have been absolute and entire. The language in the close of this Sermon is, once and again, more in keeping with the tone of the Lambeth Articles than with the teaching of Holy Scripture and the Church of England" (*ibid.,* III, 267, note*).

Sanderson to adopt. If the "tables" represented Sanderson's last unorthodoxy, the tract attached to them must represent his new-found orthodoxy. Also, despite his difficulties with the detail of doctrine, Walton must have been impressed by Sanderson's advocating in *Pax Ecclesiae* a moderate position. [153] Sanderson's liberal sentiments introductory to his ordering of God's decrees in *Pax Ecclesiae* were the sort which appealed to Walton and which gave support to the picture of temperance which he had drawn. Sanderson advocates that churches be as tender as possible in such points as predestination and reprobation, the power of free will, the necessity, efficacy, and extent of divine grace, especially where latitude is not prejudicial "to the Substance of the Catholick Faith, or to the Tranquillity of the Church, or to the Salvation of the Dissenter."[154] He would not require men to subscribe by oath to minor points, would permit private opinions so long as the Church was not disquieted.[155] Catechisms, he believes, "should not be farced with School-points and private Tenets."[156] Arminians, he says, should not brand Calvinists with Puritanism, and Calvinists should not charge Arminians with popery; the Church of England can embrace both parties, if they will subscribe to the articles of the Book of Common Prayer and if they will not disturb the peace of the Church by their differences.[157] These prefatory exhortations, and also Sanderson's plea that men acknowledge freely their errors in judgment,[158] predisposed Walton to accept the orthodoxy of the doctrine of *Pax Ecclesiae,* and he took Pierce's and Hammond's words at their face value. Their too enthusiastic attempt to show that Sanderson held in 1625 views which the High Church considered orthodox in 1660 backfired when Walton ingenuously printed the tract which, to be sure, Pierce and Hammond had not named, but which they doubtless had in mind as representing an important change in Sanderson's doctrine. Walton probably saw *Pax Ecclesiae* as a bid for moderation and comprehension based on the Book of Common Prayer; he may even have hoped that in 1678 its latitude and its deference to Calvin might win over some of the moderate Pres-

[153] Walton must have consulted Bishop Morley about the doctrine of *Pax Ecclesiae*. It is likely that Morley, whose Calvinism was not so heavily subjected to pressure as was Sanderson's, saw reflected in Sanderson's statement of 1625 his own convictions in 1678. He would have approved it.
[154] *Sanderson, 1678,* pp. 51–52.   [155] *Ibid.,* p. 53.   [156] *Ibid.*
[157] *Ibid.,* pp. 57–58.
[158] *Ibid.,* p. 56.

byterians. By 1681, Walton had learned, sadly, that *Pax Ecclesiae* was not Sanderson's final judgment, that its bias was not flattering to the contemporary Church, and he modified his statements about it. But its printing in 1678 reflects his confusion about Sanderson's doctrine and shows, too, his willingness to accede to authority in such matters.

Pierce's letter is dated March 5, 1678, and Walton had ample time to make use of it in the *Life*, though his publisher was anxious to get under way. Marriot's impatience and Walton's reliance on Pierce are evident in Marriot's entering on the Stationers' Register on March 30 only Sanderson's tracts, a sermon of Hooker's, and Pierce's letter.[159] Apparently Walton's confusion with matters of doctrine made him consider the *Life* incomplete, and there is probably further evidence of his reluctance to consider doctrinal matters completely settled even after he had received Pierce's letter in the five-week interval between the tracts' being entered on the Stationers' Register and the date of the imprimatur on Walton's book. Walton had applied for information to Thomas Barlow and he hesitated to call the *Life* finished until he had received Barlow's opinions. The imprimatur, dated May 7, 1678, is a license for the printing of the *Life* "with the Letters and Tracts at the end thereof, and Mr. *Hooker*'s Sermon."[160] Since the only letters printed at the end of the *Life* are those by Pierce and Barlow, and since Barlow's letter is dated May 10, 1678, we must assume, if the dates of the imprimatur and of Barlow's letter are accurate, that the licenser approved the book before Walton had received Barlow's letter, but that Walton had informed him that he expected such a letter. That Walton considered his chore complete with the reception and inclusion of Barlow's letter is clear in Marriot's entering the *Life* with the *"letters"* and tracts on the Stationers' Register on May 30, 1678.[161]

Walton had good reason to make inquiries of Barlow. He probably knew that Barlow had been acquainted with Sanderson and had corresponded with him.[162] He must have been aware of the eminence of Barlow's reputation in casuistical matters. Moreover, Barlow

---

[159] *Sta. Reg., 1640–1708*, III, 59.   [160] *Sanderson, 1678*, sig. A8v.

[161] *Sta. Reg., 1640–1708*, III, 65. The book was advertised in the Term Catalogues on June 22, 1678 (*The Term Catalogues, 1668–1709*, ed. Edward Arber [London, 1903–1906], I, 318).

[162] Barlow writes, "I confess I had the happiness to be particularly known to him [Sanderson] for about the space of 20 years, and (in *Oxon*) to injoy his conversation, and his learned and pious Instructions while he was *Regius*

was the incumbent of the see of Lincoln, which Sanderson had once held. Also, he had lived most of his life at Oxford, was for many years head keeper at the Bodleian, and had acquired manuscripts not only for the library but for himself. With such varied qualifications, Barlow should have been for Walton a mine of information, and Walton doubtless expected much aid from him, particularly in matters of doctrine.[163] But Barlow's qualifications were brilliant only on the surface. Always interested in casuistry and content to be known as a renowned casuist, he yet used his casuistry to justify many changes of opinion obviously motivated by self-interest. In 1648, he had ridiculed (anonymously) the parliamentary visitors to Oxford in his pamphlet, *Pegasus, or the Flying Horse from Oxford. Bringing the Proceedings of the Visitours and other Bedlamites there, by Command of the Earle of Mongomery.* Still, he used his influence with Thomas Kelsey, deputy governor of the garrison at Oxford, and John Owen, his former pupil and vice-chancellor of the university, to remain at Oxford, and he rose to be head keeper of the Bodleian and provost of Queen's College. At the Restoration, he was himself one of the commissioners appointed for restoring members of the university unjustly ejected in 1648 and was made Lady Margaret Professor in Divinity.[164] He had been a seeming friend of the papists prior to September, 1678, but in December, 1678, his *Letter concerning Invocation to Saints* appeared, "to kick them further when they were falling."[165] Cordial to James when he was proclaimed king, he took oaths to William and Mary when James fled to France.[166] Wood calls him "One that had flattered and run with the times. False, and a man of no sincerity";[167] he appears to have sat smilingly whatever the prevailing political wind. It is further proof that doctrinal beliefs were rela-

---

Professor of Divinity there. Afterwards, when . . . he left *Oxon,* and was retir'd into the Countrey, I had the benefit of his Letters" (*Sanderson,* 1678, sig. o3ᵛ).

[163] Walton may have hoped that Barlow would reciprocate for the kindness which Bishop Morley had occasionally shown him. Among the Morley papers in the volumes which Barlow bequeathed to Queen's College, CCXVII, f. 80, bears the note, "Tractatum hunc mecum communicavit reverendiss. Wintoniensis episcopus, regiae capellae decanus et infula sacra dignissimus Geo. Morley, 1665," and CCLXXXIV, f. 147, is inscribed "Papers lent me by the right rev. G. [Morley] lord bishop of Winton, Dec. 1676."

[164] *Athenae Oxon.,* IV, 334, 336, and *Wood's Life and Times,* I, 364.
[165] *Athenae Oxon.,* IV, 335, and *Wood's Life and Times,* II, 431.
[166] *Athenae Oxon.,* IV, 335, and *Wood's Life and Times,* III, 324.
[167] *Wood's Life and Times,* II, 312.

tively unimportant as the seventeenth century aged that Barlow, for all his readiness toward accommodation, never found it necessary to modify his "thorow-pac'd" Calvinism.[168] Though Sheldon put barriers in his way toward preferment, he procured the bishopric of Lincoln through the entreaties of the secretaries of state, Sir Joseph Williamson and Henry Coventry,[169] and when Sheldon managed to avoid consecrating him at Lambeth, he had the ceremony performed at Ely House (on June 27, 1675) by Bishop Morley.[170] If his casuistry was dictated by self-ends, his episcopal aspirations were dictated by personal ambition, and Wood says that in July, 1678, Barlow had not yet visited either Buckden or Lincoln.[171] Walton's reliance upon Barlow as casuist and as Bishop of Lincoln was doomed to disappointment, and it is likely, too, that his hope that Barlow would direct him to manuscripts was also disappointed. Barlow knew how to be magnanimous without being generous: for instance, it would seem that he showered innumerable kindnesses upon Wood,[172] but Wood felt that he was not fully co-operative.[173] Barlow might have made available to Walton manuscripts which he had, but he does not seem to have done so.

Apparently his only help to Walton was the "impertinent Scrible"[174] of May 10, 1678, in which he carried out, with a minimum of inconvenience to himself, Walton's request, which he gives us in his own words: "In order to the carrying on your intended good work, you desire my assistance, that I would communicate to you such particular passages of his life, as were certainly known to me."[175] In his letter Barlow relates his own part in securing for

---

[168] *Ibid.*, I, 364. In January, 1673, Barlow rebuked William Richards, chaplain of All Souls, for preaching a sermon in which "he insisted much on the Arminian points" (*ibid.*, II, 258).

[169] *Ibid.*, I, 364–365.

[170] *DNB*, article "Thomas Barlow," and Evelyn's *Diary*, entry for June 27, 1675.

[171] *Wood's Life and Times*, II, 312.

[172] Barlow gave Wood information many times, permitted him to examine college records, gave him a letter of introduction to William Dugdale, even presented him with a reading glass "pretium 40s." for which Wood wrote in his notes, "Memento, memento, gratias." See *ibid.*, I, 50, 142, 144, 189, 435; II, 78, 80, 109, 202, 404.

[173] On three occasions, Wood went with Barlow to see the records of Queen's College. Yet he wrote, "Thus far for Qu. Coll. Much more probably might be said of it had I had the liberty given, as at some other colledges, to peruse all those writings which I thought might have advantaged me in this work" (*ibid.*, II, 78, n. 3).

[174] Barlow's own words. *Sanderson*, 1678, sig. o7ᵛ.   [175] *Ibid.*, sig. o3ᵛ.

Sanderson the kindness of Robert Boyle, and he gives Sanderson's answer to a person of quality who asked him what a young divine who wished to be a good casuist should study. His only reference to Sanderson's doctrine was of little help to Walton. He tells of Sanderson's opposition to some unorthodox books on original sin and refuses to name them "because both *the Doctrine, and the unadvis'd Abettors of it are (and shall be) to me Apocryphal.*"[176]

[176] *Ibid.*, sig. o4ʳ. The books referred to are probably Jeremy Taylor's *Unum Necessarium or, The Doctrine and Practice of Repentance* (1655), *A further Explication of The Doctrine of Original Sin* (1656), and *Deus Justificatus. Two Discourses of Original Sin* (1656).

In Sanderson, *Works*, VI, 381–389, Jacobson prints three of Sanderson's letters to Barlow about Taylor. It is easy to see why Barlow did not forward the letters to Walton. In one dated Sept. 28, 1656, Sanderson reveals that he was not happy in the chair of divinity at Oxford and that Barlow had tried to get it restored to him while the university was under parliamentary rule: "The leaving of the Chaire (had it not beene accompanied with some other sad occurrents) I should unfainedly have accounted as one of my greatest happinesses: and therefore, though I must thanke you and all other frends that endeavoured my restitution, for theyr loves; yet I must profes myselfe not at all sory, that theyr endeavours were in vaine." Although Sanderson censures Taylor's opinions, he reveals that he has not "so much as seene Dʳ Taylors booke" and that he is out of touch with its controversial subject. He advises Barlow to refute Taylor without mentioning Taylor's name, "for I could wish there might be, in these times of so much distraction, as little notice taken of differences amongst ourselves, as is possible."

In another letter, dated Sept. 17, 1657, Sanderson repeats his fear of the "Scandal that may be given to the enemies of our Church and Religion, when they shall take notice that amidst the throng of so many sects and confusions as are amongst us, those that profess themselves to be the regular and obedient sons of the Church cannot accord amongst themselves, but clash against, and fall foul upon one another, and that in points of great importance." His words censuring Taylor's refusal to conform to orthodox doctrine are wonderfully ironic, foreshadowing as they do the treatment he was himself to receive at the hands of Hammond and Pierce: "I am sorry Dr. Taylor is so peremptory and pertinacious of his error, as not to hearken to the sober advises of his grave, reverend and learned friends: if not ingenuously to retract the whole (which would best become him, but hath not been his manner hitherto in any thing) yet at least wise to qualify it by some such explications, as might tolerably reconcile it with the received opinion. Which although I confess can hardly be done, so as to give satisfaction to the judgment of a rational and considering man, (having already explained his opinion in a sense so different therefrom) yet might it be done so as to prevent some of the scandal and evil effects his former writings might have, either with the enemies of our Church, or with his admirers. Especially considering how expert he is and versute in that artifice of drawing any thing, though apparently never so distant therefrom, to a seeming compliance with his own tenents; a specimen whereof he hath given us in his endeavours to reconcile his opinion concerning Original Sin with the Articles of our Church concerning the same: between which there is as much affinity, as between light and darkness." In the letter, too, there is adequate

These words probably reveal the reason for the slightness of Barlow's note to Walton. As a thoroughgoing Calvinist, Barlow mentions only Sanderson's orthodoxy in the matter of original sin. He had no sympathy for Sanderson's shift in doctrine and he avoided writing about it. Walton's quest for doctrinal information was hindered as much by Barlow's Calvinism as by Pierce's Arminianism.

Still, Barlow owned a manuscript of *Pax Ecclesiae* and he also had a manuscript of Sanderson's "Case of the Liturgy," which was first printed by Walton in 1678 under the title *Bishop Sanderson's Judgment Concerning Submission to Usurpers*. Did Barlow, who was content to write Walton only the most superficial of letters, to indulge in such a kindness that Walton must thank him for little more than nothing, did Barlow make available to Walton these Sanderson manuscripts and the others which he had? It is more likely that Barlow's aid was limited and late and that Walton found his manuscripts elsewhere.

Walton must have had access either to the Sanderson manuscripts collected by Barlow (now at Queen's College) or to those collected by William Fulman (now at Corpus Christi) or to both. The collections have in common these Sanderson manuscripts: 1. "Pax Ecclesiae";[177] 2. "Case of the Liturgy";[178] 3. "Case of a Rash Vow";[179]

---

evidence of the very middle-of-the-road doctrine of Sanderson's which Hammond was soon to take upon himself to push in the proper direction: "And all the heat on both sides in the Arminian Controversies, which hath begotten such intricate and perplexed difficulties, as neither side can clearly acquit itself from the inconveniencies wherewith it is charged by the adverse party, had its rise from the curiosity of men, who, not content to believe those clear truths which are consented to on both sides, (viz. that of all the evil we do, and consequently of the punishment we suffer therefore, our own wills, and of all good we do, and consequently of the reward we receive thereupon, the Grace of God is the sole original cause) must needs be searching into the manner, how the Grace of God, and man's will do cooperate, and how far forth, and in what order, &c."

177 References here and below are to numbers in H. O. Coxe's *Catalogus Codicum MSS. Qui in Collegiis Aulisque Oxoniensibus Hodie Adservantur* (Oxford, 1852); Queen's College MSS are in vol. I; Corpus Christi College MSS are in vol. II. Fulman had two copies of "Pax Ecclesiae," Corpus Christi CCCVI, f. 1, and CCCXVI, f. 74 (both with the "Series Decretorum Dei"), and a separate copy of the "Series Decretorum Dei," CCCXI, f. 100; Barlow's copy is Queen's CCXVIII, f. 215.

178 Corpus Christi CCCVI, f. 26; Queen's CCXVIII, f. 183.

179 Corpus Christi CCCVI, f. 24; Queen's CCXVIII, f. 171b. Printed in 1668.

4. "Case of the Validity of a Matrimonial Contract";[180] 5. "Determinatio in disputationibus theologicis in quaestionem, An sint infideles cogendi ad fidem, habita in aede Christi, 4 Feb. 1647";[181] 6. part of Sanderson's will.[182] The Corpus Christi collection has, in addition, "Oratio in domo convocationis habita a Roberto Sanderson, Coll. Lincoln. socio, quum munus procuratorium deponeret"[183] and a fragment of a visitation sermon preached at Grantham on October 8, 1641.[184] The Queen's collection has in addition "The Case of Usury,"[185] "A Discourse concerning the Church,"[186] the "Case of the Sabbath,[187] the "Case of the Engagement,"[188] the Oxford Reasons against the Solemn League and Covenant,[189] and most of "De Obligatione Conscientiae."[190] Although the large similarity in the collections seems to indicate that one was copied from the other, their differences point to their having been made independently but to their having perhaps a common source. Of their provenance little is ascertainable. Fulman's manuscript of part of Sanderson's will bears in his hand the notation, "Transcribed out of a Copie of Mr Pullen Chaplaine to the Bishop. May 1. 1663."[191] Fulman does not tell where he got the fragment of the visitation sermon preached at Grantham; Barlow had no manuscript of this sermon, but a copy of the first printed edition (1670) in the Bodleian has prefixed a note in Barlow's hand. The note is interesting, for it shows that at least one of Sanderson's manuscripts was in the keeping of his eldest son, and it shows, too, the circuitous way in which Barlow may have come by his manuscript of Sanderson's will.

This posthumus Sermon, was printed on this occasion: Mr Roswell B. of Divinity and Fellow of C. Chr. Coll. in Oxon, meetinge with Dr.

---

[180] Corpus Christi CCCVI, f. 35; Queen's CCXVIII, f. 194. First printed in Sanderson, *Works*, V, 122–126.

[181] Corpus Christi CCCVI, f. 21; Queen's CCXVIII, f. 169. First printed in Sanderson, *Works*, VI, 391–395.

[182] Corpus Christi CCCVI, f. 39; Queen's CCXVIII, f. 197b.

[183] Corpus Christi CCCVI, f. 15, and CCCI, f. 99. First printed in Sanderson, *Works*, VI, 396–403.

[184] Corpus Christi CCCXVI, f. 72. Printed in 1670.

[185] Queen's CCXVIII, f. 200. First printed in Sanderson, *Works*, V, 127–136.

[186] Queen's CCXVIII, f. 210b. First printed in 1688.

[187] Queen's CCXVI, f. 294. Printed in 1636.

[188] Queen's CCCXL, f. 90. Printed in 1668.

[189] Queen's CCXVII, f. 177. Printed in 1647.

[190] Queen's CCXVII, f. 128; CCXVI, f. 210; CCXVIII, f. 229. Printed in 1660.

[191] I cite a photostat of Corpus Christi CCCVI, f. 40ᵛ, which differs considerably from the version in Sanderson, *Works*, VI, 344, note ‡.

Tho: Sanderson, sonne of the good Bishop, in Lincolnshire, he show'd him a Copy of this Sermon fairly writt oute with the Bishops owne hand. Mʳ Roswell read, and liked it (as he had reason) well; desired it might be printed, but Dʳ Sanderson was unwillinge, because his father forbid the printinge of any of his papers after his death. That yeare, 1669, Mʳ Reynell (Fellow of C. Christi) beinge in Lancashire, he found that a Presbyterian (Chaplain to the Lᵈ· de la mesne, Sʳ Geo. Booth) had reported, (and possess'd many in that County with the beliefe of it) that Bᵖ Sanderson before his death repented of wᵗ he had writt against the Presbyterians; and on his deathbedd would suffer noe Hier-archicall ministers to come or pray with him, but desired and had onely Presbyterians about him. Mʳ Reynell signifyes this to Mʳ Roswell, de-sires him to inquire of the truth of this, and signify to them. He con-sults Mʳ Pullen of Magd: Hall, who was my Lᵈˢ Household Chaplaine, with him in all his sickenes, and at his death: He assured him, that the good Bᵖ (as he lived, soe he) dyed a true sonne of the Church of Eng-land, that noe presbyterian ever came neare him in all his sicknes, that he had noe prayers (besides his own privately to himselfe) save those of the Church, nor any but his owne Chaplaine to read them. Be-sides, Mʳ Pullen gave him a part of the Bᵖˢ last will, wherein he gives an account of his faith, in opposition to Papists and Presbyterians: and this Sermon beinge the last wᶜʰ the Bishop writt with his owne hand, at the importunity of Mʳ Roswell, Dʳ Sanderson permitted it to be printed, to vindicate My Lᵈ his father's honor and judgement, and to confute that lyinge Presbyterian report: and soe that ly occasion'd the publishinge this truth.[192]

It is likely, then, that both Fulman and Barlow got their copies of the will from Mr. Pullen. It is likely, too, that he was their source for other manuscripts, for the publisher of Sanderson's *A Discourse concerning the Church* in 1688 wrote in a note to the reader, "about twenty years since, I received these Papers from the hands of that well-known, good man, Mr. Jo. Pullen of Magdalen Hall, his Lord-ship's domestic Chaplain. Who, upon my desire, did communicate not only these, but several other Remains of the same venerable name."[193]

Josiah Pullen (1631–1714) matriculated at Oxford in 1650 and appears to have spent all his life there except for the short time when he was Sanderson's domestic chaplain. In 1657, the year he took his Master of Arts, he became vice-principal of Magdalen Hall, and he retained this office until his death. Despite his advancement

---

[192] Sanderson, *Works,* II, 142 (note), corrected from photostat.
[193] *Ibid.,* V, 237.

during the parliamentary rule of the university, he was obviously in good favor with those who had been dispossessed. His retention of his post at Magdalen Hall and his employment by Sanderson point to this, and Wood says that when the chancellor of Oxford, Clarendon, visited the university in September, 1661, accompanied by Morley, he told Henry Wilkinson, principal of Magdalen Hall, that Wilkinson entertained a company of factious people in his house " 'and but one honest man among them,' meaning Mr Josias Pullaine."[194] Although Pullen was Sanderson's domestic chaplain, it is wrong to consider him his literary executor. Sanderson appointed none, for he forbade publication of his manuscripts not printed within his lifetime. Such manuscripts as he left were probably in the custody of his eldest son, Thomas, but Thomas was a physician, not a divine, and he probably leaned heavily for advice about the manuscripts upon his father's trusted chaplain. We may be sure that Pullen had access to the manuscripts, if, indeed, he did not possess transcripts of them, and that the collections of Barlow and Fulman stem directly or indirectly from his copies.

If we assume, contrary to the indication of limited aid evident in Barlow's letter to Walton, that Walton was permitted to use Barlow's manuscripts, we may suppose that Walton made his own copies available to Fulman, even as he had given to Fulman in 1673 the Cranmer-Sandys document sent him by Henry King. But this fails to explain why Fulman lacked many manuscripts which Barlow possessed and why he owned two which Barlow lacked; it fails to explain, too, why Fulman's manuscripts are mainly in his own hand. Or, it is possible to think that Fulman may have derived his collection from Barlow's without Walton's intervention. Fulman had long known Anthony à Wood;[195] Wood may well have known of Fulman's interest in Sanderson and have informed him of Barlow's manuscripts after he had catalogued Barlow's library in 1669.[196]

---

[194] *Wood's Life and Times,* I, 415.

[195] In September, 1665, Fulman gave Wood permission to "borrow any MS. out of the archives of the library belonging to C. C. Coll." (*ibid.,* II, 47). Wood had a file which he referred to as "Fulmaniana," where he apparently kept information received from Fulman (*ibid.,* 403). Folios 267–387 of Wood MS F. 41 contain letters from Fulman to Wood (*ibid.,* IV, 229). Fifty-seven letters from Wood to Fulman, covering the years 1672–1686, are amongst the Fulman collections at Corpus Christi (CCCX, ff. 1–63). For evidences of mutual aid, see *Wood's Life and Times,* II, 392, 432, 449, 468, 469; III, 139; and *Athenae Oxon.,* IV, 241–242.

[196] *Wood's Life and Times,* II, 174–175.

If Fulman then received Barlow's permission to copy his manuscripts, we should be able to account for his own hand, but not for
the disparity in the collections. It seems altogether more likely that
Fulman got his manuscripts directly from Pullen, some of them as
early as 1663, some of them perhaps only after his friend Walton
had sought his assistance.[197] It was Fulman, not Barlow, who probably helped Walton. The two tracts of Sanderson's first published in
1678 by Walton are closer to Fulman's manuscripts than to Barlow's.[198] Walton seems not to have known about the two unpublished manuscripts peculiar to Barlow's collection. On the other
hand, he included in the *Life* a guarded paraphrase of Sanderson's
Latin speech on his leaving his proctorship, and two copies of the
speech are in Fulman's collection. Fulman may even have done more
for Walton than provide him with manuscripts; he may have acquainted him with Pullen. The particularity of Walton's account of
Sanderson's last years shows almost certainly that Walton was told
about those years by Pullen. He probably told Walton, too, about
Sanderson's strictures on his unpublished work, for Walton refers

[197] Two manuscripts in the Fulman collection indirectly support the likelihood that Pullen was Fulman's source. Corpus Christi CCXCVIII, f. 119, is
an Appendix to Francis Godwin's *Commentarium de Praesulibus Angliae*
(1616). A note on the MS, f. 126^v, says, "Ex exemplari quod comm[isit] M.
Josiah Pullen Aul. Magd. nuper Episcopo Lincolniensi Roberto Sanderson à
Sacris. Jun. 12. 1663." Also, Fulman wrote on CCCXI, f. 90 ("Dr. Overall's
judgment concerning Mr. Williams' sermon"), "ex MS. Dr. Sanderson."
    Another copy of the first of these points also to Barlow's dependence upon
Pullen. Barlow inscribed a portion of Queen's CCXVIII, beginning with f. 169,
as follows: "Opuscula quaedem ἀνέκδοτα Domini Doctoris Roberti Sanderson
Lincolniensis Episcopi τοῦ μακαρίτου." Most of Barlow's Sanderson MSS are in
this volume, and he placed among them (f. 175) "Appendix ad Fr. Godwini
commentarium de praesulibus Angliae."

[198] Queen's CCXVIII, f. 215, is the most eccentric of the five MSS of "Pax
Ecclesiae" collated by Jacobson in Sanderson's *Works*, so eccentric that it
is hard to believe that it may have derived from the same MS as did the two
copies in Corpus Christi. Walton's text in 1678 has a number of unique
readings and a number of readings peculiar to it and only one other of the
five MSS. The Corpus Christi copies are very close to each other, and Walton's
text agrees with them on the whole far more than it does with the Queen's MS
or with Rawlinson A. 419, f. 1, and Rawlinson C. 167, f. 219 (Bodleian Library).
    The three MSS of the "Case of the Liturgy" collated by Jacobson do not
vary so greatly as do those of "Pax Ecclesiae." Walton's text in 1678 has a few
unique readings, has some readings peculiar to it and Corpus Christi CCCVI,
f. 26, and never follows Queen's CCXVIII, f. 183, when it is eccentric. It is
closer to the Corpus Christi MS than to the Queen's or to New College
CCCXXXIX, f. 119.

to them in the *Life,* though they were not contained in that part of the will which he printed from Fulman's incomplete copy.

It has seemed worth while to speculate about Sanderson's manuscripts in order to show that though Barlow was probably not among Walton's "many willing Informers," Walton did find distinguished "helps and incouragements" at Oxford in Fulman and Pullen. His willing informers were not of much help in clarifying the matter of *Pax Ecclesiae* to him; the availability of the manuscript did not prevent his misreading it, or, to put it more kindly and exactly, did not prevent him from finding in it what his betters found in it.

What use did Walton make of the other manuscripts available to him and of Sanderson's printed works? The first of the tracts which Walton had printed after the *Life* was the previously unpublished work of Sanderson's which the Fulman manuscript entitles "The Case of using or forbearing the Established Liturgy stated and resolved" and the Barlow manuscript "Dr. Sanderson's Answer to a Case of Conscience, proposed in the time of the War, 1652, about reading or omitting the forms in our Liturgy." He probably caused it to be printed because in it Sanderson justifies the departures which he made from the Book of Common Prayer in times of stress. He saw in this case Sanderson's contempt for parliamentary law and his brave attempts to outwit the enforcers of parliamentary restrictions in order to continue to serve his parish. Walton probably thought that its publication would authenticate his statements in the *Life* about Sanderson's course at Boothby Pagnol, his steadfastness to his duty, his bravery and courage in the face of persistent harrassment by the Covenanters. It is likely, though, that if he had made public *Pax Ecclesiae* partly from a hope that it might be conducive to comprehension based on Common Prayer, he saw, too, that this case might be used in 1678 by dissenters to justify their own modifications of Common Prayer. Although he condoned Sanderson's policy of accommodation during the interregnum, he did not wish Sanderson's justification to serve as a general endorsement of modification. Thus, when the case appeared after the *Life,* it did not bear the titles on the manuscripts but a unique one probably chosen by Walton: "Bishop *Sanderson's* Judgment Concerning Submission to Usurpers."[199]

---

[199] Walton works hard to show Sanderson's sufferings during the interregnum and attempts to cover up his tendency to conform to Cromwellian decrees by stressing his lack of quiet and security at Boothby Pagnol and by stressing his

When in the *Life* Walton reproduces from the case the text of
Sanderson's "Confession" in order to demonstrate the slightness of
Sanderson's variation from the Book of Common Prayer, he says
that he is setting down the very words of confession which Sanderson used "as I have it under his own hand."[200] Whether he used

---

ejection from Oxford. He had Sanderson praise God *"that he hath by his grace
prevented me from making shipwrack of a good Conscience to maintain me in
a place of great reputation and profit: and though my condition be such, that
I need the last; yet I submit, for God did not send me into this world to do my
own, but suffer his will, and I will obey it"* (*Sanderson*, 1678, sigs. g5ᵛ–g6ʳ). Although it was Walton's general purpose to show Sanderson's moderation, he
probably included the "Confession" in the *Life* and the "Case of the Liturgy"
in the appendix to counteract rumors that Sanderson had practiced and
countenanced divergence from the Book of Common Prayer. His purpose was
hardly to give a further example of Sanderson's moderation, but to demonstrate
the slightness of his concessions to usurping authority and the pressures which
caused those concessions.

The High Church was probably as embarrassed by the "Case of the Liturgy"
in 1678 as it was in 1652. Bosher shows (pp. 17–23) how crucial a document
it was and the variety of opinion it provoked. Even before its composition,
Hammond had been aware of Sanderson's stand on Common Prayer and had
written Sheldon, "When you meet him, endeavour to infuse some courage into
him, the want of which may betray his reason. His opinion expressed will betray
many." A few months after its composition, Duppa signified his agreement with
its sentiments, but added, "Only I could wish, if it were possible, the printing
of it might be prevented, (which, so many Copies being out, can hardly be
avoided,) not that it need blush to come abroad, but that I do not think it
fitting that our adversaries on every side should see the secrets of it" (Sanderson, *Works*, VI, 458). Bosher thinks it likely that the appearance of the case
may have prevented an episcopal decision against Anglican conformists to
parliamentary decrees. This was not the only occasion upon which Sanderson
embarrassed the Laudian element of the Church during the interregnum. His
"Case of the Engagement" had encouraged those Anglicans who would take
the oath of allegiance imposed by Parliament in January, 1650, when Hammond had advised the opposite (see Bosher, p. 15), and he was half-inclined
to join with some moderate Presbyterian lecturers at Grantham until he received the objections of Hammond and Sheldon. Hammond did not mince
words in writing Sheldon that Sanderson might more profitably occupy himself (see Sanderson, *Works*, VI, 377–380).

At the Restoration, Sanderson's attitude stiffened considerably. On Aug. 5,
1662, while he was engaged in a visitation of his diocese just prior to the date
scheduled for the enforcement of the Act of Uniformity, he wrote Sheldon of
the "palpable hypocrisy" of the Presbyterians who "for their worldly interest
will subscribe anything. . . . Truly, my Lord, unless the laws be executed
(and that with some severity) upon them; neither Church nor kingdom will
ever be at peace." In the same letter he made it clear that he thought that the
Church could not be settled in peace or prosperity without reviving the Court
of High Commission. Clarendon MSS 77, f. 157 (Bodleian Library), quoted by
Bosher, pp. 255–256.

[200] *Sanderson*, 1678, sig. g4ʳ.

a manuscript of the case written in Sanderson's hand or, as seems more likely, a transcript made by Fulman, is of little matter. He mentions Sanderson's own hand to authenticate the document he quotes, and we may be sure that he was himself convinced of the validity of the contents of the case. He did not alter the words of the document of confession; they are the same in the *Life*, the tract following the *Life*, and in the Corpus Christi manuscript of the case.[201] Still, notwithstanding the validity of the case for him, he did depart from the words of the case which explain why Sanderson felt obliged to make his alterations. The departures are slight, to be sure, but they reveal again that Walton interpreted facts in accord with his own purpose. In the case, Sanderson's own chronology is a little confusing. He says that so long as his congregation had no soldiers in it, or just a few, "as well after as before the Promulgation of the Ordinance of the two Houses for the abolishing of the Common Prayer" (January, 1645), he continued to use it.[202] He then says that when a whole troop was quartered in town, the soldiers were so enraged at his reading from the Book of Common Prayer the first Sunday after they had arrived "that immediately after Morning Service ended, they seiz'd upon the Book, and tore it all in pieces."[203] His account is a little contradictory, for he himself says that the soldiers arrived in the beginning of November, 1644 (that is, a couple of months before Parliament's prohibition of Common Prayer)[204] and that, for want of a Book and to prevent further outrages, he waived the use of the Book in the ordinary service. After their departure, he "took the liberty to use either the whole Liturgy, or but some part of it."[205] So he continued for some five years, until, he says, "I was advertis'd (but in a friendly manner) by a Parliament man of note in these parts, that at a publick Meeting at *Grantham,* great complaint was made by some Ministers of the Presbyterian Gang, as I afterwards found, of my refractoriness to obey the Parliaments Order in that behalf."[206] The gentleman told him that since a public complaint had been made, the magistrates who had

---

[201] The "Confession" in the *Life* varies from that in the tract appended to the *Life* only in having *"a godly, righteous, and a sober life"* (sig. g5^r) for *"a godly, righteous, and sober life"* (p. 9). It varies from the Corpus Christi MS only in having *"duties"* (sig. g4^v) for *"things"* (Sanderson, *Works,* V, 40, note ¶).

[202] *Sanderson,* 1678, p. 2.   [203] *Ibid.,* p. 3.

[204] Sanderson says that the soldiers were at Boothby Pagnol "for full six months and upwards (*viz.*) from the beginning of *November* till they were call'd away to *Naseby* Fight in *May* following" (*ibid.*).

[205] *Ibid.,* p. 4.   [206] *Ibid.,* p. 5.

formerly winked an eye at his practice would be blamed if they did
not enforce the law, and that he must either lay aside his prayer
book or be prepared to lose his living. It was at this time that he
resorted to his slight modifications, transpositions, and disguisings
of the traditional liturgy. Sanderson refers to "About two years
ago"[207] as the time of his adopting such a course, and since the Fulman and Barlow manuscripts of the case are dated November 12,
1652,[208] it is clear that he started the process which he describes
near the end of 1650.

Walton does not print the date of the case, and in his own account
of these events in the *Life* he blurs the time element. He could have
dated these events precisely had he wanted to, but they are made
to form an extension of his picture of the state of England under
parliamentary rule, a recital of Presbyterian cruelties in the country following the impressionistic history of the cruelties of the
Presbyterians at Oxford and in London. He therefore generalizes
the specific incident of the tearing of Sanderson's prayer book and
bridges the years between that event and the Parliament man's
advice with an "At this time."[209] Walton makes it appear that
Sanderson was continually disturbed by the soldiery, and he suggests that Sanderson's book was torn during the service: "For the
Soldiers would appear, and visibly disturb him in the Church when
he read Prayers."[210] If his account here seems merely a fuzzy retelling of Sanderson's story, his intention to generalize is clear soon
after in his use of the plural "In these disturbances of tearing his
Service Book,"[211] which became in 1681 "In these and other provo-
cations of tearing his Service-Book."[212] There is one further dis-
crepancy in Walton's account. In Sanderson's story, the Parliament
man tells Sanderson to abstain from reading Common Prayer or to
be prepared to leave his parish. Sanderson accepts full responsibility for his hedged readings. Walton condoned his behavior, yet
he attempts to mitigate any censure that might fall on Sanderson by
saying that "he was advis'd by a Parliament man of power and note,
that lov'd and valued him much, not to be strict in reading all the
Common Prayer, but make some little variation . . . to secure him
from taking the Covenant, or Sequestration."[213]

Walton did not print Sanderson's valedictory speech as proctor,

---

[207] *Ibid.*   [208] Sanderson, *Works,* V, 57, note ‡.
[209] *Sanderson,* 1678, sig. g4ʳ.   [210] *Ibid.,* sig. g3ᵛ.
[211] *Ibid.,* sig. g5ᵛ.   [212] *Ibid.,* 1681, p. 27.   [213] *Ibid.,* 1678, sig. g4ʳ.

though it was among Fulman's manuscripts and though he does refer to it in the *Life*. To be sure, it was in Latin, but Walton's lack of knowledge of Latin did not deter him from using other materials in the language, even if they caused him trouble.[214] For instance, when he notices Sanderson's resignation of his fellowship, his own lack of knowledge is evident in his citing *"Ego* Robertus Sanderson *per, &c."*[215] for the "perpetuus socius" of his document, but his translation is an accurate one. The words of the resignation are in Sanderson's own hand in the Register of Lincoln College, and Fulman probably transcribed and translated them for Walton.[216] Fulman may have translated, too, Sanderson's inaugural address as Regius Professor of Divinity at Oxford, which had been printed in Latin. Walton refers to Sanderson's "modesty and too mean an opinion of his great Abilities, and some other real or pretended reasons"[217] expressed in the speech to explain why Sanderson waited four years before he took his chair. His casual reference shows that he was aware of the contents of the speech but that he did not wish to list the self-deprecatory reasons which, among others, Sanderson offered: his bodily weakness, treacherous memory, stammering old age, rusty Latin, timidity, and lack of self-confidence. Fulman probably translated Sanderson's speech as proctor for Walton also, and the use Walton made of it in the *Life* explains why he did not print it among the appended tracts. He reports accurately that Sanderson did not stress in his speech the many important events of the year of his proctorship but rather presented "the Governours, and his other Hearers, with rules to keep up Discipline and Order in the University."[218] But he then characterizes Sanderson's treatment of offenders of university rules as customarily mild and kind; he says that Sanderson convinced wrongdoers "with such obligingness, and reason added to it, that they parted from him with such resolutions

---

[214] It is likely, however, that he did not even bother to look at the Latin version of *Reasons of the Present Judgment of the University of Oxford, concerning the Solemn League and Covenant.* He says that this was the original version, published so "that the Parliaments proceedings and the Universities sufferings might be manifested to all Nations," and, he continues, "these reasons were also suddenly turn'd into English by *Dr. Sanderson*" (*ibid.,* sigs. e7^r–e7^v). After the *Life*, he reprinted Sanderson's English version, which had been printed in 1647. The Latin version has "1648" on its title page.

[215] *Sanderson,* 1678, sig. c5^v.

[216] The original is reproduced in Thomas Zouch's edition of the *Lives* (York, 1796), p. 429, note f.

[217] *Sanderson,* 1678, sig. e4^v.   [218] *Ibid.,* sig. b8^r.

as the man after God's own heart was possess'd with, when he said, *There is mercy with thee, and therefore thou shalt be feared.*"[219] He says that Sanderson ended his term of office without an enemy because of his restraint and patience. There is no reason to doubt Sanderson's temperance and mildness in office, but his speech tells us that though he did not like prisons and fines he found boxing ears and using the birch effective in enforcing discipline. Walton did not care to reveal such severities, and these words, among others, remained unpublished: "Glorientur alii palam per me licet sine rivali, vel etiam clam sibi plaudant domi, quod grandem pecuniae segetem ex aliorum vitiorum semente collegerint. Id mihi potissimum laudi duxerim, quod virgas et pugnos frequentius et liberius quam multis ante annis factum meminimus distribuerim."[220]

Walton did reproduce that part of Sanderson's will for which he had a manuscript because it gave "an account of his Faith and Perswasion in point of Religion and Church Government."[221] We may be sure that only this part of the will was known to him. Sanderson had written in his will, "And here I do absolutely renounce and disown whatsoever shall be published after my decease in my name, as none of mine. . . . And that for these two reasons: First, because most of those things I wrote, which are now abroad in other men's hands, were written so hastily and sent away, that I had not time to reserve the copies of many of them for myself; and therefore doubtless would require a severe review ere they should be made public; and secondly, because I may have since changed my judgment in sundry things contained in those writings."[222] In 1665, Walton had heard of Sanderson's proviso but was not sure whether it was "a strickt charge near the time of his Death, or in his last Will."[223] In 1678, he was still not sure whether Sanderson had made his stipulation "in his Will or last Sickness," and, though he cites correctly one of Sanderson's reasons—that he might have changed his opinion since he had written—he invents the other: *"that might be said to be his, which indeed was not."*[224] He says, too, that Sanderson on his deathbed "would often with much joy and thankfulness mention, *That during his being a House-keeper (which was more than 40 years) there had not been one buried out of his Family, and*

---

[219] *Ibid.,* sig. c^r.
[221] *Sanderson,* 1678, sig. m^v.
[223] *Hooker,* 1665, p. 172.

[220] Sanderson, *Works,* VI, 401.
[222] Sanderson, *Works,* VI, 411.
[224] *Sanderson,* 1678, sig. A6^v.

that he was now like to be the first."[225] Had Walton seen all of Sanderson's will, he would have known that both Sanderson's daughters, Katherine and Mary, predeceased him. And he might well have mentioned, had he seen all the will, that Sanderson left bequests to Bishops Morley and Henchman and that he there called Sir Geoffrey Palmer, Charles II's attorney-general, and Gilbert Sheldon "the most real and constant friends I ever enjoyed in this world."[226] Walton was content to make full use of the part of the will readily available to him; he did not, however, trouble himself to search for a complete transcript.

Walton says that many of Sanderson's cases of conscience remain in private hands, and he suggests that he is aware of the contents of one on simony.[227] He may have been right, but they have not been found. He does enumerate those of Sanderson's cases which had been printed, but he shows no profound knowledge of them. In justifying his own printing of two of Sanderson's previously unpublished tracts, he says that Sanderson's prohibition ought to be regarded "as he resolves in that Case of Conscience concerning *rash Vows,* that there may appear very good second Reasons, why we may forbear to perform them."[228] This is at best a loose, general, and expedient paraphrase of Sanderson's words that "every Vow, requiring anything to be done which is repugnant to any office of piety, justice, charity, or mercy, which we owe either to God or man, is void, and bindeth not, because it findeth us under the power of a former contrary Obligation, and hath not itself power sufficient to free or discharge us from the same."[229] Nor does Walton say anything of the penalties Sanderson suggests both for the maker of the rash vow and for the person who provoked it. Again, Walton says that even after the Parliamentarians had guaranteed Sanderson's safety and privileges, he "could neither live safe, nor quietly, being several times plundered, and once wounded in three places."[230]

225 *Ibid.,* sig. m7r.

226 Sanderson, *Works,* VI, 406–408. Sanderson refers to "my daughter Mary, deceased" and to his granddaughters Katerine Holder and Ann Holder Carrington as "poor fatherless and motherless" orphans.

227 *Sanderson,* 1678, sig. iv. It is not impossible that Walton had heard of the case "Of Usury" which was among Barlow's manuscripts, that he had confused its title, and proceeded to give his own strictures on the subject of simony.

228 *Ibid.,* sig. A7r.   229 Sanderson, *Works,* V, 65.

230 *Sanderson,* 1678, sigs. h7r–h7v.

The statement works powerfully to counterbalance any idea that the reader may have about the comfort of Sanderson's position during the interregnum, but it is controverted by Sanderson's own words. In the very first paragraph of "The Case of a Military Life," published in 1666, Sanderson had written, "I have something pleased myself, perhaps too much, with my own ignorance in our home affairs, accounting it among the happinesses of my privacy and retiredness, in these unhappy times, that, amidst so much fury and bloodshed on every side, it was never my hap to be within the view of any battle or skirmish; nor did I ever see so much as a pistol discharged, or a sword drawn against any single person, since the beginning of the War."[231]

Walton tells the story of the printing of Sanderson's *Logicae Artis Compendium,* provides a definition of logic, and establishes the worth of the volume by showing its continuous popularity as a university textbook. He gives only bare mention to Sanderson's *Episcopacy . . . Not Prejudicial to Regal Power.* He praises Sanderson's Oxford lectures for their definitive content and Sanderson for his courage in uttering the truth in dangerous times. Again, he praises Sanderson for writing courageously in the prefaces to his printed sermons, but of their content he merely says that Sanderson expressed his fear of popery and his antagonism to nonconformity. Of the content of the sermons themselves he says nothing beyond praising them for their plainness, except to show a change in marginal annotation in the editions of 1632 and 1657. Walton's use of Sanderson's work in print and in manuscript shows that though he felt it his duty to acquaint himself with Sanderson's writings, he did not feel that a systematic study of Sanderson's works was necessary for an understanding of Sanderson's life. It may be that Walton tried to make such a study and that he could not cope with the subtlety of much of Sanderson's thought. It is more likely that he scanned the works for any obvious autobiographical content they might have and, beyond that, was interested only in the effect which a particular work had on Sanderson's reputation, in any visible consequence which it might have had on his career. Even here he availed himself only of such material as supported the unified and unambiguous pattern he was tracing. Even when he was dealing with a man of intellect, Walton did not think it necessary to write

[231] Sanderson, *Works,* V, 104. Jacobson conjectures from internal evidence that this case was drawn up after the Restoration (*ibid.,* I, xv).

intellectual biography, nor did he feel that intensive scrutiny of the results of that intellect might reward him with insights into the life of his subject. In the scantiness of Walton's use of Sanderson's works, in his reliance upon the judgments and skills of his helpers in the question of Sanderson's doctrine and in other matters, is further proof of Walton's real lack of confidence in dealing with the complexities of learning and scholarship, and, conversely, further indication of his predisposition to rely upon oral testimony.

Some evidence of the congeniality which Walton felt toward "willing Informers" remains in the *Life*. His conversations with Pullen have already been mentioned. He makes use of his own conversations with Sanderson. He says that John Pearson, Bishop of Chester, told him "very lately" that Sanderson had commented "with an unusual earnestness" upon the *"pertinacious confidence"* and infelicitous conversation of one of the dissenters at the Savoy Conference.[232] Sir William Dugdale, the antiquary and king at arms, showed him Sir Thomas Herbert's letter about Charles I's translation of Sanderson's *De Juramenti Promissorii Obligatione*.[233] A bookseller, Timothy Garthwaite, probably told him of a nonconformist's reaction to Sanderson's preface to his sermons (1655) and of his own offer to print any answer to Sanderson's arguments which the nonconformist might write.[234] His story of Sanderson's carefully weighed judgments, which so greatly impressed Dr. Johnson,[235] was Archbishop Sheldon's, and Walton probably did not tamper with Sheldon's words that Sanderson considered and reconsidered *"till his time was so wasted, that he was forc'd to write, not (probably) what was best, but what he thought last."*[236] Here he probably reported Sheldon's estimate accurately, for he felt obliged to add, "And yet what he did then read, appear'd to all hearers to be so useful, clear, and satisfactory, as none ever determin'd with greater applause."

He probably got from Sheldon another story, one of the most delightful in the *Lives,* but this one he touched up. Walton says that when Sheldon was admitted to Trinity College, his godfather, who was Sanderson's father, asked Sanderson to look him up. Sanderson

---

[232] *Sanderson,* 1678, sigs. l3^v–l4^r.   [233] *Ibid.,* sigs. f^v–f2^r.
[234] *Ibid.,* sigs. i2^v–i3^r.
[235] See *The Rambler,* No. 19. I am indebted for this reference to Professor M. H. Abrams.
[236] *Sanderson,* 1678, sig. k3^r.

invited Sheldon to his rooms, but the proctor's invitation caused the youthful student, who knew that he had disobeyed some university rule, to pass a sleepless night. His visit the next morning put his mind at ease. Walton uses the charming little story of the future Archbishop of Canterbury's transgressing the university statutes to show the start of a distinguished friendship. His story has, however, been doctored. Sheldon was admitted to Trinity College at the end of 1613,[237] and Sanderson was proctor for a year beginning April, 1616. If Sanderson's father was not remiss in his duty to his godson, we must assume that Sheldon and Sanderson met long before Sanderson became proctor. If, on the other hand, he did neglect to write about his godson for a couple of years, the story becomes feasible, but Sheldon's transgression becomes more serious, for conduct pardonable in a freshman not yet fifteen is not always becoming in a junior of seventeen. Walton's tale protects the elder Sanderson from negligence and Sheldon from undue lack of decorum. He was never one to let a scrupulous chronology or minor detail interfere with the effective management of a story.

Although, in gathering material for a life, Walton preferred pleasant conversation to laborious reading and tedious research, he was increasingly aware of the importance of documentary evidence. He was always ready to avail himself of such evidence if it was at hand and if he could see an immediate use for it which was not contradictory to the general intent of the life he was writing. The fullness of the documentation of Sanderson's life at Oxford shows that some university records were made available to him. He is happy to say that Sanderson was completed Master of Arts on July 11, 1608, and to authenticate his information by saying, "if I be mistaken in the time, the Colledge Records have mis-informed me: But I hope they have not."[238] Walton's account of Sanderson's career at Oxford is peculiarly detailed: he says that Sanderson matriculated on July 1, 1603, was made Bachelor of Arts before he was made a fellow of Lincoln on May 3, 1606, was completed Master of Arts on July 11, 1608, chosen reader in logic on November 7, 1608, and again on November 6, 1609, was made subrector of Lincoln in 1613, 1614, and 1616, was chosen senior proctor on April 10, 1616, was granted the degree of Bachelor of Divinity on May 29, 1617, and resigned his fellowship on May 6, 1619. His account of Sanderson's years at Oxford is far more detailed than is Wood's in 1674 in

[237] *Athenae Oxon.*, IV, 854.   [238] *Sanderson*, 1678, sig. a8ᵛ.

his *Historia et Antiquitates Universitatis Oxoniensis* (Lib. II, 167–168) and more detailed even than Wood's account of Sanderson in *Athenae Oxonienses* (where, indeed, Wood relies upon Walton) and in his entries in the *Fasti,* though Wood there lists two dates which Walton did not have: Sanderson was made Bachelor of Arts on January 23, 1604[5], and received licentiation for the Master of Arts on October 20, 1607.[239] That Walton had a special fund of Oxford material is obvious; the part of the *Life* which follows Sanderson's first Oxford period is not so precisely documented. Walton did not take the trouble to find the precise dates of the presentation of the cures of Wibberton and Boothby Pagnol to Sanderson; he is satisfied with "In the year 1618" and "about one year after."[240] It is likely that William Fulman undertook at Oxford the search for the dates which Walton reproduces, and it is likely, too, that Fulman made more than bare dates available to Walton. Fulman was a true antiquary, and his own collection of manuscripts shows that he was irresistibly drawn to whole documents rather than to piecemeal notes and little extracts. He was something of a historian, too, and he was interested in the unity and interrelationships of his materials. He had written succinct descriptions of the history of the halls and colleges at Oxford in his handbook to the university, *Academiae Oxoniensis Notitia* (1665, enlarged 1675), and one of his volumes of manuscripts contains 113 folios of "Fasti Oxonienses," from 1500 to 1685.[241] Fulman's help to Walton seems evident in Walton's account of the "many memorable accidents" of the year 1616/17.

Walton's catalogue of events for this year reads like a "Fasti," though its details were selected for their relation to Sanderson or to Walton's own interests.[242] Walton singles out Robert Abbot's being conducted in this year out of Oxford toward his diocese of Salisbury, and he tells that at Abbot's resignation of the Regius Professorship of Divinity the place was filled first by Dr. Prideaux and then by Sanderson. He mentions the advancement of Arthur Lake from the wardenship of New College to the bishopric of Bath

[239] *Athenae Oxon.,* II (*Fasti*), 301, 321.
[240] *Sanderson,* 1678, sigs. c4ᵛ–c5ʳ. Jacobson found that Sanderson had himself recorded in the parish register the date of his induction into Boothby Pagnol, Sept. 7, 1619 (Sanderson, *Works,* VI, 289, note *).
[241] Corpus Christi CCCII.
[242] The selectivity is confirmed by Walton's writing in 1681 (pp. 6–7) "many memorable accidents part of which I will relate."

and Wells, and draws an implicit parallel between Lake's attitude toward offenders deserving church censures and Sanderson's attitude toward irregular scholars.[243] He notices the resignation of Lord Ellesmere (who had figured in the *Life of Donne*) as chancellor of the university and the succession of William Herbert, Earl of Pembroke (who had figured in the *Life of Herbert*), to that office. The last two events which he mentions are the letters which King James sent to the university and the visit of the Prince of Wales to the university. In writing about Lake, Walton refers to the *Life* prefixed to his *Sermons,* and in writing about John Prideaux he has also gone beyond the information which a mere "Fasti" would likely have given him, for he mentions that Prideaux was elected Bishop of Worcester in 1642. Walton includes his "Fasti," he says, to show that though Sanderson might have discoursed about such things in his proctor's speech, he preferred to discuss matters of discipline. In this way he shows again Sanderson's modesty and integrity, but, at the same time, clearly makes the reader feel that Sanderson as proctor was connected to the glories that came to the university during his tenure in office.

Walton is right when he says that Sanderson had in his proctor's speech passed over the main events of his office "with some very short Observations." But, without question, it was these very short observations, in Fulman's manuscripts of the speech, which inspired Walton's extended annal. Sanderson had devoted only one paragraph of his speech to the important events of his tenure, but in one long sentence he had touched upon all the events which Walton elaborated, and more. Here was the seed for Walton's account, and it grew with Fulman's help. For instance, the manuscript in Corpus Christi CCCI just before one copy of Sanderson's speech contains "His majesties directions" to the university on January 18, 1616/17 (f. 97), and this provided Walton with some of the material by which he could develop Sanderson's bare reference in his speech to the King's instructions. Its seventh point reads:

That yong students in divinity be directed to study such books as be most agreable in doctrine & discipline to the church of England, & excited to bestow their time in the Fathers & Councells, Schoolmen, Histories and Controversies & not to insist too long upon compendiums & abbreviations, making them the grounds of their studie in Divinity.

[243] A parenthesis in the *Life of Herbert* vouches for Walton's interest in Lake. *Lives,* 1670 (Herbert), p. 62.

Here is the basis for Walton's statement that King James advised the young divines "they should not rely on modern Sums and Systemes, but study the Fathers and Councils, and the more Primitive Learning."[244] The document does not specify what occasioned James's strictures, but Walton suggests that James sought to control Calvinist opinion, and Fulman may have informed him of the circumstances.[245] Fulman, then, made it possible for Walton to exploit the idea which he got from Sanderson's speech of relating at length the honors which came to the university in Sanderson's year in office at the same time that he emphasized Sanderson's modesty in not doing so.

Walton may not have gone out of his way to collect documentary materials, but he recognized their worth and could use them with great effectiveness when he had them. In the *Life of Sanderson* he used documentary materials for purposes other than authenticating his facts. The Fulman papers allowed him not only to record Sanderson's career at Oxford in detail, but also to magnify Sanderson's importance and the respect accorded him. The reproduction of Pierce's letter saved him a troublesome exposition of Sanderson's doctrine. So another document saved him what would have been an equally troublesome task: the exposition of the points of view of the contending parties at the Savoy Conference. Sanderson had been present at the conference, and Walton knew that he had served as moderator during part of it. He wished to show Sanderson's patience and mildness and reason, without recounting in detail the matters upon which these had been applied. His solution was to inform the reader explicitly of Sanderson's moderation and

---

[244] *Sanderson*, 1678, sig. b7r.

[245] Also, Fulman probably furnished Walton with a document describing Prince Charles's visit to the university in August, 1616. Some of the phrases in Walton's account coincide with phrases in Wood's "Fasti" for 1616 in the *Athenae Oxon.* of 1691, but though Wood provides additional information about Charles's visit he does not list most of Walton's "memorable accidents" here or in the *Historia* of 1674. Wood and Walton follow the same document also in their accounts of those honored by degrees on Aug. 31, 1636. Walton's list of noblemen follows the order of Wood's (*Historia*, II, 436), but he errs in writing "Earl of *Hereford*" for "Hertford." The *Historia* itself was probably not Walton's source, for Wood's account does not mention the name of Meric Casaubon, and Walton's does. Wood does refer to Casaubon's degree elsewhere in the *Historia* (II, 281–282), but it is unlikely that Walton found out about it by reading casually in a Latin volume. Fulman or Wood must have shown Walton the document which Wood drew upon. Fulman's copy in Corpus Christi CCCI, f. 128 (not in Fulman's hand), oddly omits Casaubon's name.

to prove by citing a document that all the conforming party was amenable to reasonable concession and that Richard Baxter (and all the dissenters) was contentious and irrational. Such a document he had found in "The Attestation of Dr. *Gunning* and Dr. *Pearson*" at the end of Morley's *The Bishop of Worcester's Letter To a Friend For Vindication of Himself from M*^r. *Baxter's Calumny* (1662). He quotes it, with negligible change, as one of the points debated at the conference:

Concerning a Command of lawful Superiours, what was sufficient to its being a lawful Command; this Proposition was brought by the conforming Party.

That Command which commands an act in it self lawful, and no other act or circumstance unlawful, is not sinful.

Mr. *Baxter* denied it for two Reasons, which he gave in with his own hand in writing thus:

One was, *Because that may be a sin* per accidens, *which is not so in it self, and may be unlawfully commanded, though that accident be not in the command.* Another was, *That it may be commanded under an unjust penalty.*

Again, this Proposition being brought by the Conformists, *That Command which commandeth an act in it self lawful, and no other act whereby any unjust penalty is injoyned, nor any circumstance whence* per accidens *any sin is consequent which the Commander ought to provide against, is not sinful.*

Mr. *Baxter* denied it for this reason then given in with his own hand in writing, thus: *Because the first act commanded may be* per accidens *unlawful, and be commanded by an unjust penalty, though no other act or circumstance commanded be such.*

Again, this Proposition being brought by the Conformists, *That Command which commandeth an act in it self lawful, and no other Act whereby any unjust penalty is injoyned, nor any circumstance whence directly or* per accidens *any sin is consequent, which the Commander ought to provide against, hath in it all things requisite to the lawfulness of a Command, and particularly cannot be guilty of commanding an act* per accidens *unlawful, nor of commanding an act under an unjust penalty.*

Mr. *Baxter* denied it upon the same Reasons.[246]

The document serves Walton's purpose admirably. The reader is perhaps a little surprised that a conference presumably called to see what modifications were necessary in the Book of Common Prayer

[246] *Sanderson*, 1678, sigs. 12^r–13^v.

should have found itself embroiled on the question of "lawful command." Even the original proposition of the conforming party seems logical enough, but apparently that party was willing to consider Baxter's objections and to modify its definition until it seems foolproof. And then Baxter still denied its validity. He appears to be anarchistic in his stubborn resistance to the right of the magistrate or king to command his subjects. No wonder Sanderson called him bold, troublesome, and illogical.[247] The picture of Baxter harmonizes completely with Walton's picture of nonconformity in general. The conforming party, he says, amenable to change though it was, could do nothing at the conference with the dissenters; but its good faith is evident in its voluntary modification of the Book of Common Prayer at the Convocation which followed.

Walton interpreted the document exactly as Morley had in his *Vindication*. Morley insists that Baxter's assertion is "destructive of all Authority Humane and Divine, as not onely denying all power to the Church of making Canons Ecclesiastical for the better ordering and governing of the Church, but also taking away all Legislative Power from the King and Parliament, and even from God himself."[248] The "Attestation," stripped of its context at the conference, seems to deal even more with the question of temporal authority than with that of religious authority, and Morley was more than willing to interpret the propositions thus generally. Walton can hardly be condemned for not knowing that Morley is here guilty of what he himself calls "the Art of holy jugling."[249] Still, for us, the document he cites and the conclusions he draws from it seem at variance with the concepts we usually associate with Baxter.

Baxter believed that the supreme power was in the magistrate, and when, at Morley's behest, he reread Hooker and Bilson to examine what Morley believed to be orthodox opinion, he found them expressing antimonarchical principles which he considered unsound.[250] F. J. Powicke rightly says, "He was so far an Erastian as to hold that if the Magistrate's rule covers the whole nation in civil affairs it did the same in things ecclesiastical; and that, therefore, he must at least keep an eye on the church and compel obe-

---

[247] Walton has Sanderson refer to "one of the Dissenters," but Baxter is intended (*ibid.*, sig. 1₃ᵛ).

[248] *Vindication*, pp. 10–11.   [249] *Ibid.*, p. 2.

[250] *Reliq. Bax.*, II, 375 (¶250).

dience to its laws, by force if necessary."[251] He had no objection to
episcopal rule, just as long as the bishops did not invade the right
of a parish minister—*episcopus gregis*—to rule his own congregation.[252] Though he believed that "it is not Liturgies nor Ceremonies
that essentiate the Church of *England*,"[253] he told Bishop Gauden
that there was nothing in the *doctrine* of the Book of Common
Prayer which he could not assent to.[254]

If Baxter's views seem so close to those of the restored clergy, why
was he singled out for the blatantly inhospitable treatment which
he received at their hands? He himself offers seven reasons, among
them his refusal of the bishopric offered him and the general odium
which all extremists have for reconcilers, and with one of them he
ably hits the mark: "And it was not the least Cause, that my being
for Primitive Episcopacy, and not for Presbytery, and being not
so far from them in some other Points of Doctrine and Worship,
as many Nonconformists are, they thought I was the abler to under-
mine them."[255] Baxter was disliked by the Anglicans because he was
a moderate dissenter who yet wielded much influence among
Presbyterians in general. His beliefs were close to Ussher's when
Ussher saw the necessity for making concessions. The Anglicans
pointed to Ussher's beliefs as evidence of their own true liberalism,
but their restored power made them more rigid and independent
than Ussher had been. It was easy for them to show where the
zealous Presbyterians were wrong and thus to expunge them from
their ranks, but it was more difficult for them to put Baxter aside,
and still they needed to get him out of the way in order to con-
solidate moderate Presbyterianism within the Establishment and to
enforce their split with rigid Nonconformity.

The document which Morley and Walton cite provided them
with a wonderful opportunity to demolish Baxter's prestige, and
they did not lose it. But how did it come about that Baxter should
express sentiments as extreme as those which the document at-

---

[251] *Life of the Reverend Richard Baxter* (Boston and New York, n.d.), p. 267.
[252] See Frederick J. Powicke, *The Reverend Richard Baxter under the Cross*
(London, 1927), p. 212. Baxter differed from Morley, however, on the rights
and independence of the parish minister. Morley says, for instance, "it is the
Bishop of Worcester, and not Mr. *Baxter* that is Pastor of *Kidderminster*, as well
as of all other Parochial Churches in that Diocess" (*Vindication*, p. 2).
[253] *Reliq. Bax.*, app. IV, 69.   [254] *Ibid.*, II, 218 (¶80).
[255] *Ibid.*, p. 381 (¶268).

tributes to him? Walton says only, "that the debate might become more useful, it was therefore resolv'd that the day following the desires and reasons of the *Non-conformists* should be given in writing, and they in writing receive Answers from the conforming party."[256] But Sheldon had enforced petitions in writing from the beginning of the conference, which had first assembled on April 15, 1661, and though most of the Presbyterians objected, Baxter himself advocated this method.[257] The conference adjourned until May 4, when the Presbyterians presented in writing their exceptions to the Liturgy. The bishops took until June 12 to draw up their answers and read them. The first week in July, Baxter brought in his reformed liturgy, and the next week the Presbyterians had ready their replies to the bishops' answers to their exceptions.[258] But the royal commission for the conference was to expire on July 24, and the Presbyterians desired personal debates to see how much alteration the bishops would yield to. The bishops, however, insisted that they were under no obligation to treat until the Presbyterians had proved that there existed the necessity of alteration because of some element of unlawfulness in the Liturgy.[259] Baxter thought this stand destructive of the King's commission, and he saw that time would expire before the settlement of a single argument. Rather than allow the bishops to say that the nonconformists dared not dispute, that they were unable to support their accusations of the Liturgy, Baxter yielded to disputation, though he saw, too, that the conference had degenerated into a wrangle "between jeast and earnest in the Schools."[260] Unfortunately for him, he did not foresee the results of debate on this level.

Morley, in his *Vindication,* says that Baxter is guilty of falsification in pretending that the matter of the dispute was the imposition of kneeling at communion "when this very matter was expressly rejected in the very beginning of the dispute, as belonging to the *Canons,* not the Common-Prayer-Book, the lawfulness of which

---

[256] *Sanderson*, 1678, sig. 1ᵛ.   [257] *Reliq. Bax.*, II, 305–306.

[258] These dates are given in Dr. Henry Ferne's account of the conference. Ferne was not present, but was prolocutor of the Lower House of Convocation, which met on May 8, and he was in close touch with the bishops, who had to divide their time between the concurrent meetings. Ferne's account (in Add. MSS 28,053 [Danby MSS] f. 1, British Museum) is printed by Bosher, pp. 226–228.

[259] *Reliq. Bax.*, II, 335 (¶'s 188, 192).   [260] *Ibid.*, p. 336 (¶192).

Canons the Commissioners had no authority to debate, and Mr. *Baxter* knows, that his Argument was denied upon that ground."[261] Still, Morley occupies himself with the question of kneeling at communion at great length (pp. 15–32). Baxter says that he started with the imposition of kneeling

upon two Accounts, (though I took the Gesture it self as lawful) 1. Because I knew I had the fullest Evidence, and the greatest Authority of Antiquity or Church-Law and Custom against them. 2. Because the Penalty is so immediate and great (to put all that kneel not, from the Communion): And it was only the *Penalty,* and so the *Imposition* on that Penalty, which we disputed against.[262]

Morley's statement notwithstanding, the disputation from which he excerpted the propositions which he calls "The Attestation of Dr. *Gunning* and Dr. *Pearson*" starts, according to Baxter,

(Dr. *Pierson,* Dr. *Gunning,* Dr. *Sparrow* and Dr. *Pierce*) "My Assertion is, Nothing contained in the Liturgy is sinful.

"This general Assertion I am ready to make good in all Particulars, in which our Brethren shall think fit to charge the Liturgy with Sinfulness.

"And because our Brethren have as yet by way of Disputation, charged no other part of it with the Imputation of Sinfulness, but that which concerneth kneeling at the Communion, therefore my first Assertion as to that particular is this.

"The Command contained in the Liturgy concerning kneeling at the Communion is not Sinful. This Truth I am ready to prove by several Arguments."[263]

The accuracy of Baxter's account of the subject of the disputation is supported by Dr. Henry Ferne. Although Ferne thought that Baxter sometimes made "strange syllogisms and as strange answers to some of ours," he says that

it was agreed that they [the Presbyterians] should either show or prove something unlawful in the Liturgy and therefore necessary to be altered, or be concluded wilful. . . . Mr. Baxter's instance (when they came to it) was kneeling at the Communion, which he acknowledged not sinful in itself or unlawful; but the imposing of it under penalty of being denied the Sacrament was unlawful.[264]

---

261 *Vindication,* p. 16.
263 *Ibid.,* p. 358.

262 *Reliq. Bax.,* II, 346 (¶213).
264 Bosher, p. 228.

Baxter says that in a conversation Morley and Pierce told him they thought it strange that he should make such a stir for other men's liberty to forbear kneeling when he himself thought the gesture itself lawful. "I told them," he says, "that they might perceive then, that I argued not from *Interest* and *Opinion;* but from *Charity,* and for *Love* and *Peace."*[265] Baxter might have added "from pride in demonstrating my ability to engage in scholastic debate," for he divorced in his own mind the present school-argument from the function of the conference and prepared to put forth the defense of an extreme position. He says, in explanation of the bishops' displeasure that he should charge so many things in the Church as sins, that "they considered not that we were now treating what should be *imposed,* and not what should be obeyed if it were imposed: and that we would charge Sin upon their *Impositions,* in many points which might lawfully be done when *Imposed,* rather than to forsake the Churches."[266] His statement does not give the bishops credit enough. By embroiling Baxter in scholastic argument, they got him to express an extreme opinion, not what he would compromise upon or settle for.[267]

[265] *Reliq. Bax.,* II, 345 (¶212).

[266] *Ibid.,* p. 343 (¶208). Again, he writes that when the contest was over, he cast aside numerous arguments which he would have used, "foreseeing that now (when they [the conforming party] would not endure the means of Peace) my Duty would henceforth lye on the other side, to plead other Men into true and moderate Thoughts of things indifferent, and Obedience, so far as the Unity and Peace of the Church required it, and the matters imposed were not sinful to the Doers, though they might be sinful to the Imposers" (*ibid.,* p. 360 [¶235]).

[267] It was some time before Baxter was aware of the way in which he had been outwitted. In the *Mischiefs of Self-Ignorance* (1662), he tried once more to justify the logic of his position. But when he saw that Morley was using as proof of his heresy the "Attestation" in which "the Bishop never discerned (unless he dissemble it) the Reasons for our Denial, nor the Proposition denied," he permitted an account of the disputation in full to be printed: "For Bishop *Morley's* misreports with so great confidence uttered had made it of some necessity: But I added not one Syllable by way of Commentary, the words themselves being sufficient for his Confutation" (*Reliq. Bax.,* II, 377 [¶ 257], 379 [¶'s 261–262]). It is probably this account which Edward Cardwell prints in his *History of Conferences* (Oxford, 1840), pp. 364–368: "A true and perfect copy of the whole disputation at the Savoy, that was managed by the Episcopal divines as opponents, to prove that there is nothing sinful in the Liturgy. Published to make intelligible the fragment already published by the Lord Bishop of Worcester, under the hands of Dr. Pierson and Dr. Gunning; and so much of his Lordship's book against Mr. Baxter as concerneth that disputation. Printed in the year 1662."

Morley was shrewd enough to capitalize on the extreme opinion which Baxter was injudicious enough to hold even for purposes of debate. Moreover, he stripped it of its immediate context to show the utter unreasonableness of Baxter. Baxter underestimates Morley when he says that "he gathered up a scrap of an Assertion which he did not duly understand, and made it little less than Heresie."[268] Baxter had been outmaneuvered so that his assertion was little less than heretical, and Morley was quick to exploit what he could show to be not just heresy but additional evidence of Baxter's inclination to treason, sedition, and rebellion.[269] Morley made the "Attestation" demonstrate, too, the willingness and the ability of the conformists to modify and qualify their propositions to meet Baxter's objections. As Stoughton says, they had made "their logical network so fine that even Baxter, subtle as he might be, could scarcely wriggle through the meshes."[270] The conformists won an honest scholastic victory; they played the game more skillfully than Baxter. If Baxter had underestimated the stakes, they had not, and they exacted full payment.

Of the intimate details connected with the "Attestation" Walton was probably not aware. Even had he known the full context of the document, had he been able to make his way through the scholastic jungle of the debate, the weight of the opinion of Bishops Morley, Pearson, and Gunning would have been sufficient for him. For him, Baxter was another pertinacious Presbyterian, whom even the temperate Sanderson had accused of illogic and disputatiousness,[271] and the "Attestation" was abundant evidence for such an opinion. The document spared Walton the trouble of a historical account of the conference; it had Morley's sanction. Indeed, its inclusion in the *Life* recalled to readers the controversy of Morley and Baxter,[272]

---

[268] *Reliq. Bax.*, II, 377 (¶257).   [269] *Vindication*, p. 37.
[270] Stoughton, III, 184.

[271] For Baxter's account of Sanderson's calling him a "Man of Contention," see *Reliq. Bax.*, II, 357 (¶227). Baxter says that the conforming party put Sanderson into the moderator's chair "that his Learning and Gravity might put a Reputation upon his Sentence (he being a very worthy Man, but for that great Pievishness, which Injuries, Partiality, Temperature and Age had caused in him)."

[272] Morley and Baxter refrained from further controversy in print, but others kept up an exchange sufficient to impress the matter upon interested readers. Without Baxter's sanction, Edward Bagshaw ("D. E.") wrote *Letter unto a Person of Honour and Quality, containing some Animadversions upon the Bishop of Worcester's Letter* (1662). This was followed quickly by at least four

and by turning his account of the conference into a justification of Morley, Walton was paying him a pretty compliment. He was wise enough to recognize the utility of the document.

We need concern ourselves with just one document more, with *"Bishop Sanderson's Judgment in One View for the Settlement of the Church,"* which Walton included among the tracts following the *Life*. It is easy enough to see why Walton used it. Its topic was the one which was ever in Walton's mind as he wrote the *Life,* and its arguments furnished a justification for the point of view which underlies the *Life,* an explicit correlative for what, in a life, could only be a purpose implied. The first question in this case was the question which Walton sought to answer by implication in the *Life:* *"How far we may indulge good and godly men of tender Consciences dissenting from us in liberty of Conscience"* (p. 87). Sanderson's answer is an oblique one which indicates that his approach to this problem was different from that implied in the question; for him the problem is not one of indulging tender consciences but one of obedience to authority, of the imposition of lawful commands. He starts, therefore, by saying that papists, Anabaptists, Levellers, "and what not" style themselves *"The Godly"* and that "it is the easiest thing in the world, and nothing more common, than for men to pretend *conscience* when they are not minded to *obey"* (p. 88). He does not believe that the refusal of indifferent ceremonies enjoined by lawful authority is any indication of godliness, and he says that it is no very tender conscience that *"straineth at a Gnat, and swalloweth a Camel"* (p. 89). Only after these preliminaries does he suggest that tender things ought to be tenderly dealt with (p. 90).

replies: 1. S[amuel] H[olden], *D. E. defeated: or, a Reply to a late scurrilous Pamphlet vented against the Lord Bishop of Worcester's Letter, whereby he vindicated himself from Mr. Baxter's Misreports* 2. J[ohn] C[ollop], M.D., *A Letter with Animadversions upon the Animadverter On the Bishop of Worcester's Letter.* 3. [Sir Henry Yelverton,] *A Vindication Of my Lord Bishop of Worcester's Letter touching Mr. Baxter from the Animadversions of D. E.* 4. Roger L'Estrange, *A Whipp A Whipp, For the Schismaticall Animadverter Upon the Bishop of Worcester's Letter.* When Bagshaw heard that L'Estrange's reply was at press, he forestalled it with *The second Part of Animadversions, with an Answer to all that Rog. L'estrange intends to write.* L'Estrange replied with a second impression of *A Whipp* to which he appended *An Answer to a Second, and Impudent Libell From the same Hand.* He then wrote *A Memento: Directed To all Those that Truly Reverence the Memory of King Charles the Martyr . . . The First Part,* and he and Bagshaw continued to wrangle in print. See *Athenae Oxon.,* III, 948.

The emphasis on lawful authority continues in the next section, which is introduced by a long question: *"Whether good men should be suspended from the exercise of their ministry, and deprived of their livelyhood for Ceremonies, which are on all hands acknowledged indifferent: and indeed in comparison to the work of the ministry are but trifles, however some men dote on them?"* (p. 90). Sanderson's approach is implicit in the first sentence of his answer: "Let *Ceremonies* . . . be as very *trifles,* as any man can imagine them to be; yet *obedience* sure is no *trifle"* (p. 90). And, he continues, "They mis-state the *Question,* when they talk of pressing *Ceremonies.* It is *obedience* (formally) that is required."[273] For him the case is plain: *"The Bishops (under the King)* require *obedience* to the *Laws Ecclesiastical;* these men *refuse* to give it"* (pp. 92–93). The whole controversy, he says, devolves upon this point: "Whether to the *Laws Ecclesiastical* obedience be due or not? For the right determining whereof (for so much as it is confest on all hands, that *Obedience* is due to *lawful aut[h]ority* commanding *lawful* things) two other *points* are to be resolved; the one concerning the *authority* by which the Constitutions were made; the other concerning *the lawfulness* of the things therein required" (p. 93). The Presbyterians deny both; the Anglicans have chosen to affirm the second of them. Sanderson answers the question of the lawfulness of the things (especially the ceremonies) commanded by the Episcopal Church by saying, "When for *decency, order,* or *uniformities* sake any *Constitutions* are made concerning *Ceremonies,* there is the same *necessity* of obeying such *Constitutions,* as there is of obeying other *laws* made for the good of *the Commonwealth,* concerning any other *indifferent* things" (p. 94). He goes on to say that every church has the power to ordain ceremonies for the sake of order and decency (p. 97), "which being once ordained, and by publick Authority enjoyned, cease to be *indifferent* for their *use,* though they remain still so far their *nature;* and of *indifferent* become so *necessary,* that neither may a man without sin *refuse* them, where Authority requireth, nor *use* them, where Authority restraineth the use" (p. 98). And, he says, the purpose of the Episcopal Church in requiring obedience to ceremonial constitutions is to make for an orderly conformity in the outward worship of God, not to imply either the divine necessity of the constitutions or the effectual holiness of the ceremonies (p. 99). He holds that deference to the power and au-

273 Sanderson's opinion is similar to Morley's. See pp. 394–395.

thority of rules can be shown only in obedience to *indifferent* and *arbitrary* things, for people must obey things *absolutely necessary,* whether they are required by human authority or not, for these things are commanded by God (p. 100). He applies this sentiment equally in matters civil and in matters ecclesiastical (p. 109). He maintains, then, that ministers suspended by the Church are not deprived because of their refusal to follow prescribed ceremonies; they may pretend that "they are persecuted for their *consciences,* when they are indeed but justly *censured* for thier obstinate and pertinacious *contempt* of lawful authority. . . . And *contempt of authority,* though in the smallest matter, deserveth no small punishment" (p. 105). How much Christian charity would he show them? The prime consideration must always be Christian duty and obedience: in "all *indifferent things,* we ought to bear a greater regard to our *publick Governours,* than to our *private Brethren; and* be more careful to *obey* them, than to *satisfie* these, if the same course will not in some mediocrity satisfie both" (p. 111).

Sanderson makes but two concessions to dissenters in the course of this argument, and the first of these is included to justify his own behavior and that of other Episcopal churchmen during the interregnum. He says that there is *"a liberty* left for men, upon extraordinary and other just occasions, sometimes to do otherwise than the Constitution requireth" concerning ceremonies or other indifferent things, a liberty not permissible in things properly and absolutely necessary (pp. 94–95). So does he explain the right of Episcopal churchmen to forbear the use in public worship of the Liturgy, festivals, and ceremonies of the Church, established by so many former laws. (He disregards completely the question of obedience to the laws of the *de facto* government.) He also holds that all laws made concerning ceremonies or other indifferent things, civil or ecclesiastical, are mutable, and says that as these laws were first made by human authority, so they may from time to time be abrogated and repealed by human authority (p. 96).

Sanderson attacks those dissenters who must find scriptural warrant even for taking up a straw and wonders where in Scripture they find warrant for that very doctrine (pp. 114–115). He agrees that Scripture is sufficient to understand the "substantials of *Gods worship"* and the "exercises of *spiritual and supernatural graces,"* but he finds that in things which are in their nature indifferent it is necessary to rely on the law of nature and of right reason, "which is as truly *the Law* and *Word of God,* as is that which is printed *in our Bibles*" (p. 118). His dislike of Scripture-searchers is matched by his dislike of those who are scrupulous about things indifferent: because of their ignorance and partiality, they break the peace of the church by their contentions, they disturb men's consciences "by making *the narrow way to Heaven* narrower than ever God meant it," they rob Christian governors of the affection and obedience with which they ought to be honored (pp. 134, 131–132).

Two other main questions concern Sanderson. *"Whether what the* King *and* Parliament *have* determined *may be* altered *to* satisfie *private men"* (p. 138), he answers almost dogmatically. While things are in agitation, private men may make reasoned suggestions to those in authority, and those in authority ought to proceed in the prescribing of things indifferent "with all just advisedness and moderation" (pp. 138–139). But once acts are passed by public authority, private men must obey them. His answer to *"What shall a man do, that scruples in Conscience what Authority enjoyns as unlawful"* is more detailed (p. 151). Such a man is bound in conscience to do what is commanded, his doubt about its lawfulness notwithstanding. If what is commanded is unlawful, the sin is on the man who commands, not on him who obeys. Only under two circumstances does Sanderson sanction disobedience; he provides no examples or illustrations for the first and he qualifies his sanction of the second by showing that it usually stems from error and obstinacy and leads inevitably to sinfulness. The first is stated only by implication. Sanderson says that a man must obey whatever is commanded by the chief of his church, commonwealth, or family "which is not evidently contrary to *the Law* and will of God"; "God's Vicegerents must be heard and *obeyed* in all things that are not manifestly contrary to *the revealed will* of God" (pp. 153–154). We may assume, then, that Sanderson sanctions disobedience to such orders as are contrary to the revealed will of God. The second arises from the distinction which he draws between things *repugnant* to conscience and those where the conscience is merely *in doubt.* If the conscience is merely doubting, obedience is the safer way, for to disobey doubtingly may be doubly sinful: the doubt may be sinful; the lack of respect for authority is certainly sinful (pp. 158–159). However, if a man's conscience has passed a judgment upon a thing and condemned it as simply unlawful, he ought not to obey the magistrate even if his conscience has pronounced a wrong judgment. But, though Sanderson here pays respect to the sanctity of individual conscience, he goes on to say that even in such circumstances a man yet sins in disobeying the magistrate. He says too that such a situation arises by *"errour* and *obstinacy";* he has no sympathy for such a man, but says only, "And who can help it, if a man will needs cherish *an errour,* and persist in it?" (p. 157). How strongly he feels in these matters is obvious in his taking recourse in a historical interpretation of Scripture to explain away Romans 14:23, "And he that doubteth is damned if he eat, because he eateth not of faith: for whatsoever is not of faith is sin" (p. 160). He says that Paul's words were intended for a particular occasion, and ought not to be applied to different cases and times. They are meant for the *"weak ones* among *the Romans,"* a people whose liberty was not limited by any ruling authority, not for contemporary England where the authority of the magistrate has imposed laws which limit liberty. And, he goes on to say, governors may or may not (they *need not*) satisfy the doubts of private men as to the lawfulness of what they enjoin, though he is sure that "in the point of Ecclesiastical *Ceremonies* and *Constitutions* . . . this hath been abundantly done in our Church" (pp. 161–162, 164).

It has seemed worth summarizing this case for the insight we may gain in appreciating the stand of the Episcopal Church toward nonconformity. Sanderson is willing to accede the right to repeal or abrogate or change laws made about things indifferent, he grants the possibility of breaking a law upon an extraordinary occasion, he is at least aware of the possibility of a law which might be contrary to the law and will of God, and he is willing to pay homage to the sanctity of the individual conscience. But these considerations are lost in his general argument of the necessity of obedience to authority. He sees them as things possible, but he does not sympathize with them; they are remote and usually the result of error or bias. He makes no real concessions to tender conscience. The case is an eminently clear rationale of the Episcopal attitude toward nonconformity between 1640 and 1680 (and Sanderson was milder than some of his fellows). To Walton it was completely reasonable, its doctrine irrefutable. It was proof of Sanderson's logic and moderation, and these qualities were what he found lacking in Presbyterian anarchy, illogic, and extremism. No wonder he should want to print it. And we may be sure that he felt no embarrassment in printing both it and the "Case of the Liturgy" at the same time, for though in the latter Sanderson shows his circumvention of the law, Walton makes it clear by his title that the law of parliamentary government was without question a usurping law.

Where did Walton get the manuscript for this case? He had none. This is no genuine case of Sanderson's, as Anthony à Wood saw when he said of it in the *Athenae*, "The questions are form'd by the publisher. The answers are made up of scraps and parcels without any alteration taken out of the prefaces, and of several places of his sermons."[274] Wood's reference was to the publisher responsible for the original printing of the case in 1663; if, indeed, the publisher did form the questions and snip the answers, he was a skillful controversialist. The case holds together remarkably well, and except for an occasional "thirdly" where "first" and "secondly" are missing, its fragmentary character is hardly recognizable. There is no doubt that the 1663 edition was Walton's source, that the printer of the tract in 1678 set type from a corrected copy of the 1663 edition. There are occasional minor differences in capital letters, in punctuation, and in spelling, some correction of obvious errors, a few changes in paragraphing.[275] But even the casual reader of Walton's volume notes immediately that this case has a far more florid style of italics than the rest of the volume. The key words in every sentence, and many that are less important, are italicized. The printer quite obviously followed the italics of the 1663 edition, even to the extreme of frequently italicizing "the." That he had trouble in doing so is equally obvious, for he slips up occasionally and destroys the pattern or logic of italics which the original printer created.[276] But there is no question that he desperately tried to follow the 1663 text before him.

274 *Athenae Oxon.*, III, 630.

275 For example, the 1663 version has a question from which necessary but obvious words have been dropped (p. 47); the 1678 version supplies *"for Ceremonies"* (p. 90). *"An"* (1663, p. 51, l. 29) is properly changed to *"and"* (1678, p. 97, l. 22). The nonsensical *"left"* (1663, p. 82, l. 28) becomes *"self"* (1678, p. 147, l. 8). In 1678, the word *"First"* twice leads to the beginning of a new paragraph (pp. 140, 145) where in 1663 no division had been made (pp. 78, 81), and *"If"* (1678, p. 158) starts a new paragraph where the 1663 version reads continuously (pp. 88–89).

276 The printer in 1663 used *"to do . . . not to do"* (p. 53); the printer in 1678, *"to do . . . not to do"* (p. 100). "Treasons, and . . . *practises"* (1663, p. 56) becomes "Treasons, and . . . *practices"* (1678, p. 104); *"enlarge* and *illustrate"* (1663, p. 78) becomes *"enlarge* and illustrate" (1678, p. 140). Where

How important Walton felt the case to be, how badly he wanted to reprint it, is obvious in his using it though in 1663 it had been appended to a life of Sanderson, the existence of which he denied in the Preface of his own *Life*. Since, in 1663, the pagination and signatures of the case are continuous with those of the *Life*, since the case has no separate title page, since it always appears as an integral part of the pamphlet called *Reason and Judgement*, it is obvious that Walton had seen the earlier life of Sanderson. It is even possible that this life provided the seed for several details in Walton's *Life*. The borrowings (if such they are) are, to be sure, unimportant and unprecise, but there are perhaps enough of them to show that Walton had read the early *Life*. Walton had sufficiently considered the nature of the ideal country parson to have determined for himself those traits which were essential in one, and it is no surprise to find him saying that Sanderson at Boothby Pagnol did not preach high and useless notions but plain truths necessary to be known, that his parishioners complied with him in "the decent and regular service of God" and lived with him "in a religious love, and a contented quietness," and that their love for him led to their trust in his doctrine, for without love *"the most evident truths . . . either are not, or are at least the less effectual."*[277] The earlier *Life*, too, had stressed Sanderson's troubling himself to make his sermons at Boothby Pagnol "rational and just Discourses," had said that Sanderson and his parishioners had "lived up to a Religion pure and undefiled," and had vividly stated that Sanderson "understood very well how much the Applications of the Table enforced the Doctrines of the Pulpit; and how subservient the endearing of his person was to the recommending of his instructions."[278] Walton shows the King's esteem for Sanderson by quoting the King's words: *"I carry my ears to hear other Preachers, but I carry my conscience to hear Mr. Sanderson."*[279] This statement had appeared in the text of the earlier *Life* and

---

the 1663 printer slipped in balancing *"Errour* through *Ignorance"* with "Sin through *Infirmity"* (p. 46), the printer in 1678 followed his italics exactly (p. 88). Though the 1678 printer occasionally forgets to italicize where the 1663 printer does so, in at least one place he continues to italicize after the 1663 printer had stopped, and *"admit* them" (1663, p. 92) becomes *"admit them"* (1678, p. 166).

[277] *Sanderson*, 1678, sigs. c8r–c8v.
[278] *Reason and Judgement*, pp. 20, 22–23.
[279] *Sanderson*, 1678, sig. d7r.

had been repeated as a tag to fill out its last page.[280] Walton accuses the Covenanters who deprived Sanderson of his professorial chair of depriving the nation of many cases of conscience which Sanderson might otherwise have written.[281] The earlier *Life* had spent a whole paragraph elaborating this idea: "Nothing troubled him [Sanderson] more, than that he was layd aside and made useless. . . . What reason would have *suppressed* this *worth?* What people would have *deprived* this man? What Government would have laid aside so much reason, judgement and most useful Learning?"[282] In telling of Sanderson's behavior as a bishop, Walton says that he was so condescending and obliging "to the meanest of his Clergy, as to know and be known to them";[283] here, too, he may have been following the statement of the earlier *Life:* "His greatness prejudiced not his humility and diligence: the meanest Minister had free access to him."[284] It is possible, too, though verbal parallels are lacking, that Walton's description of Sanderson's attitude toward offenders when he was proctor owes something to the earlier *Life*'s description of his attitude toward nonconformists when he was bishop and that in the prayer which ends the *Life* Walton was not merely repeating what he had done in the *Life of Herbert* but was echoing the words of *Reason and Judgement.*[285]

If Walton knew *Reason and Judgement*, if, as seems possible, he received some minor aid from it, why did he not acknowledge its existence? Falconer Madan holds that "there is some fraud or mystery about this book."[286] The case which follows the early *Life* is, he says, "in some sense fraudulent, professing to be a treatise, but being in reality a cento from Sanderson's works." Madan says that the imprint "Oxford: Printed by J. W. for Will. Thorne" is fictitious, that the "London" title page with imprimatur which sometimes appears with the Oxford title page and sometimes takes its place is a cancel leaf, and that the alternative title pages were used so that "London buyers might think the book an Oxford one, and vice versa." He knows no reason for this "crooked course," nor does he know the name of the writer of the *Life*, who signs himself

---

[280] *Reason and Judgement*, pp. 33, 44.

[281] *Sanderson*, 1678, sigs. h5ʳ–h5ᵛ.   [282] *Reason and Judgement*, p. 37.

[283] *Sanderson*, 1678, sigs. l5ᵛ–l6ʳ.   [284] *Reason and Judgement*, p. 40.

[285] Compare *Sanderson*, 1678, sigs. b8ᵛ–cʳ, with *Reason and Judgement*, p. 41, and *Sanderson*, 1678, sigs. n3ʳ–n3ᵛ, with *Reason and Judgement*, pp. 43–44. See *Herbert*, 1674, p. 59.

[286] *Oxford Books* (Oxford, 1931), III, 182 (no. 2648).

"D. F." Still, it might be argued that if fraud were intended, the book is a fairly respectable fraud. It bears the imprimatur (dated February 24, 1662/3) of Dr. George Stradling, domestic chaplain to the Bishop of London, and it was duly registered with the Stationers' Company by H. Marsh (whose name appears on the London title page) on March 31, 1662/3. Madan himself is willing to call the early *Life* "an able and considered account." He is right in saying that the case after it professes to be a treatise of Sanderson's; still, on the title page, its title is qualified by the statement "In exact Resolutions Of sundry grand Cases very seasonable at This Time." There is some trickery in the book, but quite obviously not for the purpose of circumventing publishing restrictions. Indeed its being duly licensed and registered would indicate that particular care was taken to ensure the respectability of its publication. It is likely that despite the initials "D. F." with which it is signed and despite the initials of the clergyman to whom it is addressed, "*J. W.* D. D. P. L.," the trickery stems from a desire to conceal the authorship of the book. It is likely, too, that Walton was aware of these circumstances in the publication of the volume. He may even have known or guessed at the identity of D. F. But the very fact of D. F.'s reluctance to assume responsibility for his book provided an excuse for Walton; he felt no obligation to acknowledge a book which the author himself would not acknowledge.

If *Reason and Judgement* had been a detailed biography, Walton would perhaps have been forced to acknowledge it despite its anonymity. But the nature of Walton's borrowings reveals the nature of *Reason and Judgement*. It is not a life, but a character of an ideal prelate. The structure that D. F. announces he will follow cannot lead to a real biography: "1. His Education: 2. His temper of body and minde: 3. The great instances of his Life: 4. His Person and Aspect: 5. His Works or Writings: 6. His Sufferings: 7. His Rewards and Preferments: And lastly and chiefly, his Judgement and Resolution of those Cases of Conscience that concern the Discipline or Worship of our Church."[287] D. F. could not adhere even to his announced plan, but his marginal notes, which are a clue to the actual structure of *Reason and Judgement*, reveal again an approach which is impossible for real biography: "1. *His Education. 2. His Industry 3. His Temper 4. His Carriage 5. His Moderation 6. His removal from the University 7. His Preaching* [an ex-

[287] *Reason and Judgement*, p. 4.

tended sermon by D. F. on the evils of indiscriminate giving of alms]
8. *His Publike Performances* 9. *At Court and Lectures* 10. *At Con-
vocations* 11. *His Constancie and Pa*[ti]*ence.*" Indeed, although D. F.
turns his paucity of information into a compliment to Sanderson's
modesty, he reveals early in the *Life* his own awareness of its
deficiencies: "His modesty wrapped him in that privacy, and his
place kept him at that distance, that I cannot take his portraicture,
nor recount his memorials so exactly as I could wish."[288] He knows
very little about Sanderson's life. Even where his personal knowledge of Sanderson seems most precise, in his telling of Sanderson's
methods of study and of his advice to his students, he has merely
paraphrased and adapted material which he found in Sanderson's
Logicae Artis Compendium.[289] He knows four dates in Sanderson's
chronicle, all of them readily available. He admits his lack of
knowledge of Sanderson's domestic circumstances in the statement,
"He was a good, faithful, tender and loving, discreet husband, as
I take it, of one Wife, with whom he lived some years comfortably,"
though, to be sure, he mentions that Sanderson was "a good father,
prudent and indulgent to his children" (pp. 37–38). He thinks that
Sanderson's first cure of souls was at Boothby Pagnol (p. 20). He
does seem to have specific knowledge of Sanderson's eating and
sleeping habits: in his section on Sanderson's moderation he writes,
"one meal a day sufficed him, with some fruit at night: in his sleep
none more sparing, eleven or twelve at night being his usual time
of going to rest, and five, and very rarely six, the hour of his rising"
(p. 16). But these are not unconventional hagiographical details.
Despite the "he would say's" which D. F. attributes to Sanderson,
he falls back on John Fell's words about Henry Hammond in the
Life of Hammond (published two years earlier) to explain Sanderson's industry and diligence and again to show his method of
preparing sermons (pp. 12, 21). For the rest, he replaces details with
long-winded catalogues of pious generalities. At school, he says,
Sanderson was furnished with

excellent Rules of Grammar and Rhetorick, with choice pieces of History, Poetry and Oratory, with an elegancie in Latine, a good judgement
in Greek; serious in his designe, prudent in his study, industrious in his

288 *Ibid.*
289 Compare *Reason and Judgement*, p. 8 (bottom), with Sanderson, *Works*,
VI, 132 (¶3); p. 9 (bottom) with VI, 168 ff.; p. 10 with VI, 185 ff. (especially pp.
187–188).

way, clear in his apprehension, searching in his understanding; serene, orderly and methodical in his thoughts; sober and civil in his carriage: (the School having added to his great Parts that humility, meekness, modesty, obedience and civility, as, advantaged by his good disposition, rendred him to his dying day submissive to Superiours, obliging to his Equals, tender to his Inferiours, amiable and charitable to all.) [P. 6.]

Of Sanderson's temper he says:

It pleased God he had a body suited to that pains he was designed for; a faithful Assistant rather then an impediment to his great Soul; symbolizing with it in an exact temper, neither failing it through the weakness of organs, nor burthening it with the redundancy of humours, nor clogging it with sad melancholy, nor disturbing it with an active unsetledness, nor ruffling it with angry choler; neither too large for it, not too narrow, but every way proportionable [pp. 12–13].

Such a stylistic device hardly leads to sharpness of characterization even when it is used in conjunction with detailed information, but here it is unsupported. There is little biographical detail which Walton would have found necessary or helpful in writing his *Life*.

But Walton had better reasons for not acknowledging *Reason and Judgement*. As he read it, some of it must have had a very familiar ring. In two places, D. F. avoids the embarrassment of ignorance by saying that what Fell had said about Hammond is also true of Sanderson. Had he revealed the full extent of his indebtedness to Fell's book, he would have invalidated his own. Not only does he take, as he admits, Fell's words about Hammond's industry[290] and about his method of preparing his sermons,[291] but D. F.'s very words about Sanderson's just and rational discourses and the love which made those discourses acceptable to his parishioners (ideas amongst those perhaps borrowed by Walton) he took from Fell.[292] The description of Sanderson's eating and sleeping habits, so familiarly detailed that it would appear that D. F. must have watched Sanderson often at table, is taken directly from Fell.[293]

[290] Compare *Reason and Judgement*, p. 12, with Fell's *Hammond*, p. lxii.

[291] Compare *Reason and Judgement*, p. 21, with Fell's *Hammond*, p. xxii.

[292] Compare *Reason and Judgement*, p. 20, with Fell's *Hammond*, p. xxi, "a rational and just discourse"; and *Reason and Judgement*, pp. 22–23, with Fell's *Hammond*, p. xxiii, "He knew well how much the application at the table enforced the doctrines of the pulpit, and how subservient the endearing of his person was to the recommending his instructions."

[293] Compare *Reason and Judgement*, p. 16, with Fell's *Hammond*, pp. lxviii–lxix: "He seldom did eat or drink more than once in twenty-four hours, and

What he says about Sanderson's habits of study at the university,[294] his leaving the university,[295] his method of catechizing,[296] his hatred of idleness and his study even in sickness,[297] his sentiments about

---

some fruit towards night. . . . His temperance in sleep resembled that of his meats, midnight being the usual time of his going to rest, and four or five, and very rarely six, the hour of rising."

[294] *Reason and Judgement*, p. 11: "While he was in the University, he generally spent eleven hours a day in study: which industry of his, dispatched the whole course of Philosophy, and picked out in a manner all that was useful in all Classick Authors that are extant; drawing Indexes for his private use, either in his own Paper-book, or at the beginning and end of each book: which will testifie his indefatigable pains to as many as shall peruse his excellent and well-chosen Study"; Fell's *Hammond*, p. xx: "During the whole time of his abode in the University, he generally spent thirteen hours of the day in study; by which assiduity, besides an exact dispatch of the whole course of philosophy, he read over in a manner all classic authors that are extant; and upon the more considerable wrote, as he passed, scholia and critical emendations, and drew up indexes for his private use at the beginning and end of each book: all which remain at this time, and testify his indefatigable pains to as many as have perused his library." (D. F. strained at a gnat, but swallowed the camel.)

[295] *Reason and Judgement*, p. 20: "he, I say, left the University freely, making not the usual advantage of his place, which was then prudence and good husbandry, but looked upon by him as the worst Sacriledge in the *world*, as which at once betrayed the Church to the unworthy and weak, and the University to the undeserving, and the Founders Charity to those persons they never designed them for; to the shame of the present Age, and the undoing of the future"; Fell's *Hammond*, p. xxi: "he thought not fit to take that advantage of his place, which, from sacrilege, or selling of the founder's charity, was by custom grown to be prudence and good husbandry, but left the college with the same integrity that he had lived in it."

[296] *Reason and Judgement*, p. 21: "spending an hour at evening in the Church-Catechism, whereat the Parents and elder sort were wont to be present, and from whence they reaped more benefit then from his Sermons"; Fell's *Hammond*, p. xxiv: "his custom was, during the warmer season of the year, to spend an hour before evening prayer in catechising; whereat the parents and older sort were wont to be present, and from whence, as he with comfort was used to say, they reaped more benefit than from his sermons."

[297] *Reason and Judgement*, p. 11: "He disposed himself and time to perpetual industry and diligence; not only avoiding, but perfectly hating idleness, and hardly recommending any thing more then this; *Be always furnished with somewhat to do, as the best way to innocence and pleasure*"; Fell's *Hammond*, p. lxix: "His disposal of himself in the other parts of time was to perpetual industry and diligence: he not only avoided, but bore a perfect hate, and seemed to have a forcible antipathy to idleness, and scarcely recommended any thing in his advices with that concern and vigour, as 'to be furnished always with somewhat to do.' "

Reason and Judgement, p. 12: "In sicknesses, if they were not so violent as to make the recollection of his thoughts impossible, he never intermitted study, but rather re-inforced, as the best ease of his distemper, and diversion of his

friendship[298]—all these he took directly or with slight change from Fell. His digressive sermon on the evils of indiscriminate charity[299] was undoubtedly provoked by his reaction to Fell's multitudinous detail about Hammond's alms-giving.[300] D. F. had good reason to hide his name. Indeed, it is likely that the very initials he used were an invitation to his more perspicacious readers to believe that Dr. Fell had written *Reason and Judgement.*[301]

Walton would have known better. Bishop Morley's intimate acquaintance with Hammond is testified to in Hammond's will, where he is left thirty pounds and Hammond's Polyglot Bible.[302] Morley had introduced Walton to Hammond.[303] Both Walton and Morley would have read with eager eyes the distinguished *Life of Hammond* which was published a year after Hammond's death and which was so popular that another edition was printed in the following year. Its author as well as its subject was known to them, for John Fell had been made Dean of Christ Church in 1660, when Morley relinquished that place to become Bishop of Worcester. Walton's ignorance of the *Life of Hammond* cannot be proved by his attributing to Hammond in the *Life of Sanderson* a felicity for memorizing sermons[304] which is controverted by Fell's words that it was "harder with him to get one sermon by heart than to pen twenty,"[305] for Walton was never one to let a detail stand in the way of his telling a good story. Moreover, Fell's story about Hammond's refusal of tithes from a parishioner whose meadow had

---

pain"; Fell's *Hammond*, p. lxx: "In his sicknesses, if they were not so violent to make the recollection of thoughts impossible, he never intermitted study, but rather re-enforced it then as the most appropriate revulsive and diversion of pain."

[298] Compare *Reason and Judgement*, pp. 15–16, with Fell's *Hammond*, pp. lxxiii–lxxiv.

[299] *Reason and Judgement*, pp. 23–26.

[300] Fell's *Hammond*, pp. xxii–xxiii, lxxvii–lxxxv.

[301] If I am right in believing that the initials "D. F." are of no value in trying to identify the author of *Reason and Judgement,* it is probably unprofitable to put much stock in D. F.'s addressing his pamphlet to "*J. W. D. D. P. L.*" My own efforts have served only to convince me that "J. W." is the most common set of initials in the world, and that "P. L." permits plentiful latitude for guesswork. It may be worth mentioning, however, that Walton goes out of his way in the *Life of Sanderson* to say of Dr. John Wall, Morley's old tutor at Oxford, "Dr. *Wall* I knew, and will speak nothing of him, for he is *dead*" (sig. f5ᵛ).

[302] Fell's *Hammond*, p. cxix. [303] *Sanderson*, 1678, sigs. A3ᵛ–A4ʳ.

[304] *Ibid.*, sigs. g6ᵛ–g7ᵛ. [305] Fell's *Hammond*, p. lxiii.

been flooded[306] may well have been the germ for the long story
Walton tells about Sanderson's aid to a parishioner at Boothby
Pagnol whose field was in like fashion flooded.[307] Almost certainly
Walton had read Fell's *Life of Hammond* and was aware of D. F.'s
liberal borrowings from it before 1670, when he implied that a life
of Sanderson was still to be written.[308] It is impossible that he should
not have been fully informed after 1674, for in that year William
Fulman, who helped him with the *Life of Sanderson,* prefixed to
his folio edition of Hammond's works the *Life* written by Fell, with
changes and additions made by Fell or inserted by Fulman with his
permission.[309] Walton's repeated refusal in 1675 and in 1678 to grant
even the existence of D. F.'s work is a measure of his contempt for
D. F.'s accomplishment.

But our story is not finished. Why if D. F. knew next to nothing
about Sanderson's life should he have wanted to write the life?
His "remarques" and the case which follows them—for it was
probably of his contriving, not the publisher's—show that if he
knew little of Sanderson's life, he knew a great deal about Sanderson's printed works. He stresses, even overstresses, the element of
moderation in Sanderson's doctrine, much as Walton does, but
with a difference. Walton equates Sanderson's moderate behavior
with that of the High Church; D. F. is a Broad churchman anxious
to demonstrate that Sanderson is of his ilk. If we find a negative sort
of confirmation of this opinion in that his borrowings from the *Life
of Hammond* omit all references to Hammond's High Church
proclivities, there is more positive evidence in his attempt to emu-
late another life. The original plan for his structure of *Reason
and Judgement* he took directly from Bishop Gauden's *Life of
Hooker.*[310] He may even have planned originally to use Gauden's
Life as a sourcebook,[311] but have found that the eccentricities of

---

306 *Ibid.,* p. xxiii.   307 *Sanderson,* 1678, sigs. d2ʳ–d4ᵛ.
308 *Lives,* 1670, sig. A7ʳ.   309 Fell's *Hammond,* p. xiii.
310 Compare D. F.'s plan, reproduced on p. 459 above, with Gauden's: "1.
Of his Birth and Education. 2. *His genius and temper* of body and minde, with
the most critical *instances* of his *life* and *actions;* his Person also, and outward
Mine, or Aspect, which is no small indication of mens *mindes* and *manners.* 3.
Works, or κατορθώματα, as to his *Writings.* 4. His (ἀγῶνες or ἀριστεῖαι) *Sufferings*
and *Tryals.* 5. His *Rewards* and *Preferments.* 6. and *lastly,* His *Death,* and
Burial, and *Monument*" (Gauden, p. 6).
311 Compare *Reason and Judgement,* p. 4, "wherein you will observe something *admirable,* many things *imitable,* all things *commendable,*" with Gauden,
p. 1, "in whom some things were admirable, many things *imitable,* and all

Gauden's style did not lend themselves so readily to imitation and adaptation as did the less ostentatious style of Fell. Gauden's *Life* had been in print not even a year when D. F. started to write, and there is no question that his purpose in writing Sanderson's life was inspired by Gauden's achievement. Even as Gauden had pictured Hooker as a moderate Low Churchman, so D. F. tried to show that Sanderson was of that party. No member of the High Church party writing in early 1663 would have thought that testimonials by Baxter and Edward Reynolds (a reconciler turned bishop at the Restoration) added luster to Sanderson's reputation. D. F. cites their opinions along with those of Prideaux, Ussher, Hammond, Fuller, and Hall (p. [2]). No High Churchman would have thought it flattering to Sanderson to say that his attitude toward ceremonies was like Bishop Brownrigg's (p. 35).[312] D. F. is no Puritan: he has no "foolish *precisenese*" toward dice, cards, horse-matches, wine, music, and apparel (pp. 16–18). But when he implies that Sanderson feels "the best and safest way for us in all *indifferent things* is this: to be indulgent to *others,* but strict to *our selves;* in allowing them *their liberty* with the most, but taking *our own liberty* ever with the least" (p. 18), he is placing a most liberal interpretation on those words of Sanderson about things indifferent which he used in constructing the case and he is attributing to Sanderson the moderation he would like to find in him. D. F. is Baxterian in his attitude toward compliance with public authority, and he therefore cites accurately Sanderson's opinions on order and obedience (pp. 31, 38). But when he represents Sanderson's doctrine he so emphasizes its moderate characteristics that even where he is accurate the High Church of the Restoration would have preferred silence or distortion, and he is not above distortion in a different direction himself. He says that Sanderson in dealing with the points of debate between Calvinism and Arminianism "pitched upon such a mean as Bishop *Usher,* Bishop *Davenant,* Bishop *Overal* aimed

---

things *commendable.*" Also, *Reason and Judgement,* p. 6, "And now I would willingly enlarge on his minority . . . but that it is like the beginning of *Nilus,* hardly to be found," with Gauden, p. 7, "his *Originals,* like that of *Nilus,* are left obscure."

312 Ralph Brownrigg was a faithful royalist, but he opposed Laudian discipline. Although he was consecrated Bishop of Exeter in 1642, he never visited his diocese. Of his death in 1659, Hammond wrote Sheldon, "I am very sorry, though I believe the business of the Church no whit more backward for it" (Bosher, pp. 26, 99).

at, and the excellent Dr. *Hammond* approved of" (p. 34); he is right in general, but High Church orthodoxy would have preferred a slightly different emphasis. D. F. equates Sanderson's opinion on the possibility of papists being saved with Ussher's (and Hooker's) (p. 35); he is quite right, but from the time of the Restoration the High Church found it embarrassing to theorize in such matters because of more practical political considerations. But D. F. is not right when he says that Sanderson was not "such a Formalist, but that he wished an alteration of some Words, Phrases, and Method and Order, to which change of times, or Language, or the like, might *invite*" (p. 35). He has made far too positive Sanderson's thought that ceremonies are not immutable. Again, accurate as he is when he says that Sanderson felt that *"nothing was less to be stickled for or against, then Ceremonies; and yet that nothing was to be stickled for more then Obedience to Governours enjoyning even the smallest Ceremonies"* (pp. 35–36), yet he misleads by playing down Sanderson's stress on obedience and by playing up too much Sanderson's statement that he pitied and prayed for men who were tender in conscience. In like fashion, D. F. shows his Baxterian sympathies when he says that in matters of church government Sanderson "passionately inclined to any fair and fraternal accommodation, that humble, orderly and worthy Ministers might have all their, and Bishops no more than was their due by Scripture, primitive Customs, by the Laws of the Land, and by principles of order and true government among all societies of men" (p. 36). D. F. reveals his hand quite plainly when he says of Sanderson's elevation to Lincoln in 1660 that

it was thought, if his excellent temper had sooner been added as an allay to some other mens hottest spirits, possibly we had not seen things run to that disorder and ruine; his Gravity and Discretion being likely to allay and fix the Clergy to a due temperament, (guiding some mens well-meaning Zeal by such Rules of Moderation as might best preserve the Government and Constitution of this Church and Kingdome.) [P. 39.]

D. F.'s Low Church propensities explain in large part his desire to rush into print with a *Life of Sanderson* directly after Sanderson's death. He was aware of Sanderson's firm attachment after the Restoration to the High Church, but was aware too that the moderation and ambiguity of his doctrine made it possible to paint him as a Low Church divine. This he sought to do before an "official" biography appeared, but he had before him Gauden's example to show him the danger of such an undertaking. Therefore his anonymity, and therefore in "D. F." his attempt to foist off his *Life* as representative of orthodox opinion.

When Gauden's *Life of Hooker* had appeared, the High Church could not afford to be silent. As a bishop, Gauden spoke with authority about the champion of the Church, and he had found it easy to ensnare Hooker in the net of Low Church doctrine and discipline. The High Churchmen found it urgent to disentangle Hooker from the meshes in which he had been caught, to stay him in a net of their own making, and Walton had played the fisherman for them. D. F.'s pamphlet, however, was small fry; if it made a little splash, a little ripple on the sea of controversy, it soon disappeared from notice. For Walton, years later, to call attention to it, would be to remind readers unnecessarily that the Low Church had claimed Sanderson among its sons. To mention it would breed the need to argue and refute, and Walton was sufficiently insecure about Sanderson's doctrine to be silent when he might be. Even as he was sure that his *Life of Hooker* was superior to Gauden's, so he could be doubly certain that his *Life of Sanderson* far outshone D. F.'s. It will be remembered that the High Church saw no reason to suppress Hooker's last three Books; by prefixing Walton's *Life of Hooker* to Gauden's text of the *Polity,* it made certain that readers would read the last Books in their proper context. Walton must have been sure that his detailed knowledge of Sanderson's life would give conviction to what he had to say of Sanderson's doctrine. If D. F., by his painting Sanderson as an apostle of moderation, had hoped that his readers would thereby be influenced to dwell upon Sanderson's few concessions to nonconformity in the case which he appended, Walton could reprint the case because he was confident that his *Life* provided the context which showed that the case conformed admirably with his own conception of High Church moderation.

When we consider the simple clarity of Walton's beliefs about authority, ceremonies, and plain truths necessary for salvation, when we consider his limited schooling and the uncongeniality of knotty doctrine to him, when we consider Sanderson's shifting and subtle opinions, Walton's compulsion to square these opinions with High Church orthodoxy, indeed to make Sanderson fully representative of the High Church, we may well wonder that he undertook the writing of Sanderson's life. We may believe him when he says, "I found my self faint, and weary of the burthen with which I had loaden my self, and ready to lay it down."[313] Though the *Life of Sanderson* was, like the *Life of Herbert,* a loving chore, it was a far heavier one. In the *Life of Herbert,* Walton had followed his natural bent: he had written with affection about a man whose holiness was, in his eyes, uncomplicated, he had dwelt upon themes dearest to his heart, he had been able to gather without much effort an adequate store of information. The *Life of Herbert* is Walton's closest approach to "character" writing. He was sufficiently the biographer to know the value of the chronicle of a man's days, but his prime interest was always in answering "What kind of man was this?" not "What did he do?" It is his own fondness for character coupled with his love for Sanderson the man (not the bishop, not the casuist) that preserved him from the chief hazards inherent in the writing of Sanderson's life. Another biographer might well have been provoked to disputation by D. F.'s *Life,* might well have become embroiled in any one of the numerous complex issues which Sanderson dealt with. But Walton's quintessential interest in character makes him keep Sanderson the man always before his reader, except when Sanderson's suffering in bad times becomes merged with the suffering of similar men. His own inclination and probably his self-knowledge of his own deficiencies led him to meet some of the hazards upon which the *Life* might have foundered outside its structure.

The *Life of Sanderson* is a greater achievement than the *Life of Herbert.* Charming as the *Herbert* is, it suffers from the relaxation of the standards which Walton felt imposed on him as he wrote the *Life of Hooker.* Despite his recognition of the importance of authenticated fact, he was under no pressure to exert himself for materials and he used only those easily available to him. The dignity of his task in the *Sanderson* moved him to greater efforts, and, in addition, Fulman and other willing informers provided him with a mass of detail. Walton may not have cared to search records for information, but he was happy to have such information and he recognized its utility and value. He liked it not only for the tone of solid authenticity which it provided, but also for the correspondingly greater freedom which it allowed him. The stronger the

313 *Sanderson,* 1678, sig. A6ᵛ.

buttress of fact, the greater the liberty he felt he could take in matters of anecdote and opinion. In one way the exactness of his chronicle of Sanderson handicaps the *Life*, for the reader is more immediately aware of the manipulations in the structure of the *Life* than he would be if dates were not available to him. And, to be sure, there are signs in the structure of the *Sanderson* that Walton in his old age lost a little of his fine control, was more self-indulgent than he had formerly been. But the garrulity of old age, the infirmity of the hand which held the reins, are not in themselves sufficient explanation for Walton's lack of restraint in the *Life of Sanderson*. There are reasons more positive than the debilitating effects of age. His confidence in the reliability of the documents which he had, coupled with the growth of self-confidence in his position as a man of letters, led him to take liberties which add luster to his accomplishments as a biographer.

Walton had ever been inclined toward commentary and toward platitudinizing, but in the *Life of Sanderson* he is more forceful in his opinions than he had ever been before. He had ever invented conversation for his subjects; now he is not afraid to reveal his hand.[314] His seeming apology to his reader for doing in the *Sanderson* what he had always done is not the result of a sudden scrupulousness of conscience; it stems from a confidence that his reader will not be offended by his so doing and a confidence that he can do so well. His candidness here reveals that he is establishing a relationship with his reader which is different from his more modest and more remote relationship in the other lives. He is not afraid to enter into the *Life* to lead his reader from one place to another. Indeed, he is not afraid to enter into the *Life* even as a participant, to reveal his relationship and relate his conversation with his subject. Until the *Life of Sanderson*, Walton had fought his tendency to make himself known in the *Lives*. Now, surer of his facts and secure in the respect accorded him, he is not afraid to do on the stage what he had managed before from the wings. Intrusions of this kind are not new in biography, but they are normally characteristic of that life-writing which is close to the elegy and the funeral sermon, for the intrusions usually do not supplement, but replace,

[314] *Ibid.*, sig. A6ʳ: "I desire to tell the Reader, that in this Relation I have been so bold, as to paraphrase and say what I think he . . . would have said upon the same occasions; and, if I have err'd in this kind, and cannot now beg pardon of him that lov'd me; yet I do of my Reader, from whom I desire the same favour."

factual detail. Not so in the *Life of Sanderson,* where Walton gives the reader an amplitude of statistic and document. And when he himself appears on the stage, the effect is that of candor and ingenuousness, of honesty which reveals confidence to the reader. And the reader, seeing the man who writes the life, knowing the point of view from which it is written, is confident that he can read the life rightly.

The freedom which Walton allowed himself because of the wealth of his authoritative material had one further effect on the *Life of Sanderson.* Walton had always loved the intimate anecdote and had ever recognized its power to reveal character. The stronger his basis of fact, the wider the latitude he permitted himself in his use of anecdote. In the *Life of Sanderson,* he used it copiously. But he was freer in his coupling it with humor and wit. Despite the high seriousness of his subject, he had learned to humanize with comedy as well as with tragedy, he had learned to damn with wit as well as with righteousness. The story of Sheldon's youthful indiscretion makes the dour and dogmatic archbishop come to life; the King's pointing out to Sanderson, the great logician, his fallacious reasoning about the writing of cases of conscience is a fine tragi-comedy in a sentence, and Hammond's comment about Sanderson's preaching without book delightfully reveals the bonhomie which characterized their relationship. The Covenanters who presented a petition "by so many thousands, and they so arm'd, as seem'd to force an assent to what they seemed to request";[315] the common people "so happy, as every Parish might choose their own Minister, and tell him when he did, and when he did not preach true Doctrine";[316] the ministers who "ingag'd their hearers to contend furiously for truths which they understood not";[317] the dissenting brother whose conscience "slept long and quietly in a good sequestered Living"[318] —all of these are transfixed by Walton's arrows. In earlier days he would not have shafted them so cleanly and neatly.

The *Life of Sanderson* is deficient in two respects. Walton shows Sanderson's intellectual capacities only by the mechanical means of listing the titles of his works and by telling of the admiration and respect they engendered. He does not reveal the subtlety of Sanderson's mind. Here, his own lack of education prevented him from assessing the intellectual stature of Sanderson. Also, his thesis—

[315] *Ibid.,* sig. e[v].   [316] *Ibid.,* sig. f8[r].   [317] *Ibid.,* sigs. f8[r]–f8[v].
[318] *Ibid.,* sig. i2[v].

the justification of a particular bishop and, by implication, all High Churchmen—does not fit with equal success both Sanderson and the High Churchmen. In so far as he applies it only to Sanderson, it is a valid approach in its emphasis on Sanderson's learning, fortitude, and moderation. Even here we may find fault with the uniformly dark colors with which Walton paints the nonconformists in order to point up the brightness of Sanderson, and we may condemn the invention of the wounding of Sanderson, by which he elicits easy sympathy for Sanderson. But when he seeks to attribute by indirection the moderation and suffering and fortitude of Sanderson not only to Anglican divines during the interregnum but also to High Churchmen in the postwar years, he obviously applies whitewash too lavishly. Here, the extremity of his partisanship interferes with a reasonable accuracy.

Still, it is not unfair as a final measure of Walton's accomplishment in the *Life of Sanderson* to compare his work with *Reason and Judgement*. D. F.'s learning and intellect are obviously far above Walton's. He is not confused by doctrinal matters, is, indeed, able to confuse them. But learning and intellect, without genuine interest in character and proper respect for chronicle, will not make a life. On its surface, *Reason and Judgement* appears to be a modest memorial by a man who had at one time intimately known Sanderson, an "affectionate and well-meant Account," as D. F. himself calls it; "an able and considered account," as Madan terms it. But D. F. dishonestly imposed his affection and his honesty upon the reader to cloak a partisanship more extreme even than Walton's, and there is nothing so damaging to biography as the partisanship which is hidden. The voluntary self-revelation of Walton in the *Life of Sanderson,* whether or no he consciously considered it as part of the methodology of biography, is a notable forward step in his technique. D. F.'s *Reason and Judgement* is a party tract masquerading as a life. Walton's work is not free of tract material. Indeed, the course of Sanderson's life demanded the inclusion of some of this material. But it is some measure of Walton's success as a biographer that Sanderson the man is rarely lost. Walton did not confuse his book with its appendix. He wrote a life.

Walton attached a Postscript to the *Life:*

If I had had time to have review'd this Relation, as I intended, before it went to the Press, I could have contracted some, and altered other

parts of it; but 'twas hastned from me, and now too late for this impres-
sion. If there be a second (which the Printer hopes for) I shall both do
that, and, upon information, mend any mistake, or supply what may
seem wanting.[319]

Perhaps Walton knew even in 1678 that plans were being made to
prefix his *Life* to a forthcoming edition of Sanderson's sermons. At
any rate, a second impression appeared with *XXXV. Sermons* in
1681. Although Walton omitted the Postscript in 1681, contrary
to his retention of a similar stricture about the *Life of Herbert*
after twice revising it,[320] the nature of his changes in 1681 shows
that the Postscript was a mere formality, a habitual display of
modesty. The 1681 edition has several small contractions, but here
as in 1678 Walton tells his reader five times that Sheldon is the
late Archbishop of Canterbury and three times that Morley is the
Bishop of Winchester.[321] We do not expect Walton to contract in
a revision; we are not disappointed in our expectation that he will
add slightly and alter slightly. We should expect, too, in view of
Walton's preachments about the dangers of nonconformity in 1678,
that the terrible times which followed the exposures of Titus Oates
should have forced him in 1681 to state more vehemently and more
explicitly his thesis as the political situation ever more closely
justified his augury.

If the High Churchmen were shocked by the news of the Popish
Plot, they trembled at the events which followed it. They surely
frowned when the letters of Coleman, secretary to the Duchess of
York, revealed that the payment of French money to Charles was to
preface the overthrow of Protestantism in England. They must have
feared the worst when they saw an indignant Commons resolve the
impeachment of Danby, the King's unwilling pawn in intrigue with
France and their own strongest political ally. If they were mo-
mentarily relieved to see the King save Danby's head by proroguing
Parliament on December 30, 1678, they must have quavered for
their own heads when he dissolved Parliament on January 24 following. They shook when Shaftesbury's political machine, the
Green Ribbon Club, rolled into action and when, in the general
election, the Presbyterians, Independents, and Republicans swept
the polls, while their own supporters, and Danby's, shrank from 150

[319] *Ibid.,* sig. n4ʳ.   [320] *Lives,* 1675, sig. A6ᵛ.
[321] *Sanderson,* 1681, pp. 2, 9, 19, 20, 36; *ibid.,* pp. 19, 20, 22.

to 30.[322] They saw that the new Parliament wanted more than security against popery, wanted, in fact, Reformation. They listened to tales of armed Covenanters in Scotland; they saw the rabble loose in London. Early in May, 1679, they heard of the barbarous murder of James Sharp, Archbishop of St. Andrews, by fanatic Covenanters, and in June they heard that seven thousand Scottish Covenanters were in open rebellion. They knew that the Covenanters were not without supporters in England, that popular feeling against the use of troops ran high, that, indeed, the King could use troops only because he had pacified Shaftesbury by appointing Monmouth as commander-in-chief.[323] Even when the rebels were defeated on June 22 at Bothwell Bridge, they knew they must yet fear Monmouth and Shaftesbury at home.

Coleman's confession that the Duke of York knew and approved of his treasonable correspondence signaled the beginning of attempts to exclude James from the throne. But if the bishops disliked James's religion, they hated even more the disruption of law established. Shortly after the general election, Sancroft and Morley sought a conference with James and made a futile attempt to reconvert him. The King was more practical: he sent James abroad. On April 27, 1679, the Commons, accusing James of causing the Plot, voted to prevent a papist from succeeding to the throne. Charles fell back on the policy advocated by Danby and the bishops two years earlier. He promised to agree to any act which would deprive a Catholic king of the power of ecclesiastical nomination and which would prevent the appointment of a Catholic to any office of state, but he would not consent to any alteration of the lawful succession. The Parliament, however, was no more disposed to put power in the bishops' hands than in James's. Charles had his answer in the First Exclusion bill, which passed its second reading by a majority of ninety-two.[324] In order to prevent its passage, he prorogued and then dissolved Parliament, and he kept the new Parliament, full of exclusionists, prorogued until October 21, 1680. When the Second Exclusion bill received its first reading in the Commons on November 4, only three members spoke against it.[325] In the Lords, Shaftesbury, Essex, and Monmouth spoke for it; only Halifax's magnificent oratory, in speech after speech, turned the tide, and

[322] Bryant, p. 282.
[324] Bryant, p. 287.
[323] Trevelyan, *op. cit.*, p. 407.
[325] *Ibid.*, p. 306.

the bill was thrown out by a count of 63–30, with fourteen bishops voting against it.[326] Even when Charles faced still another Parliament at Oxford in March, 1681, and dissolved it as a Third Exclusion bill was being introduced, the bishops must have viewed the future darkly. They lived in constant fear that the divine right of kings would not be upheld, that the rightful heir would be set aside, that civil war would come anew, that parliamentary rule and Nonconformity would once more hold sway.

Still, the Plot made the High Churchmen again wish for the unity of the Church, again solicitous toward dissent. When at the end of November, 1678, papists were excluded from sitting in either House of Parliament and from the Councils of the Sovereign, the measure contained a strong declaration about the idolatry of Romish worship but did not mention the obligation to receive the sacrament.[327] This was no oversight by the bishops, but an omission plainly intended to benefit and conciliate dissent. Sancroft's policies, too, were milder than Sheldon's had been. But Nonconformity no longer needed to rely upon High Church concessions. It became increasingly clamorous in the Commons, and after May 26, 1679, it thundered from the presses. For, with Charles's dimissal of the first session of his first Whig Parliament, the press was emancipated by law. Free from licensing, Nonconformity roared in pamphlets which could only alarm the High Church. In the middle of 1680, even such normally liberal High Churchmen as Stillingfleet and Tillotson were sufficiently frightened that they preached against dissenters as schismatics. At the end of the year, they met with some nonconformist divines to talk again of comprehension. Yet when a measure was introduced into the Commons by the Episcopal party, the Presbyterians did not promote it, thinking it could not be carried in the House of Lords. However, another bill, which proposed to exempt dissenters "from the penalties of certain laws" was not only passed by the Commons, but was, with amendment, approved even by the Lords. The King managed to lose it, and a week after its passage in the Lords he prorogued Parliament. The enraged Commons formally resolved that the prosecution of Protestant dissenters was detrimental to Protestantism and dangerous to the kingdom. The members of the High Church party, forced to choose between showing sympathy to dissent and upholding traditional parliamentary procedure, showed again where their prime loyalties

[326] Stoughton, IV, 24.   [327] *Ibid.*, pp. 10–11.

were. They objected to the unconstitutionality of Parliament's invalidating its former acts in such a manner.[328]

So strident were the demands of the dissenters, so insecure the future of the Church, that Walton was no longer satisfied to fight with devious comment and indirect argument in his *Lives*. On the twentieth anniversary of the Restoration, he entered the pamphlet war with a tract entitled *Love and Truth: in two modest and peaceable letters, concerning the distempers of the present times. Written from a quiet and conformable Citizen of London, to two busie and factious Shopkeepers in Coventry*.[329] Even as his survey of Elizabethan nonconformity in the *Life of Hooker* was applicable to conditions in 1665 and as his recounting in the *Life of Sanderson* of the trials of the ousted clergy was applicable to conditions in 1678, so here too he effectively uses the method of historical analogy. His two "letters" concerning comprehension—the first dated *"February the 18. 1667[8],"* eight days after Parliament threw out Sir Matthew Hale's bill of comprehension, and the second *"September 12. 1679,"* not long after the country party had swept the polls a second time and just a month before the second Whig Parliament expected its summons—provide evidence for his assertion to his correspondent that "he that considers the temper of the present times, and your restless activity in it, may conclude, you are as willing to begin new Commotions, as you are senseless of the old."[330] In the first letter, Walton justifies the stand of the contemporary Church on dissent by insisting that the present age is not more severe against disturbers of settled peace and the government of Church and State than was Queen Elizabeth's. He identifies dissenters with schismatics and seditionists, and even puts the blame for the war on troublesome pretenders to conscience. He shows his real distrust of dissent in his opinions that there is no end to the desires of dissenters, that power makes them tyrannical, that they will not tolerate the tendernesses of others. In his second letter, he would show that were liberty granted to dissent, the inconveniences of *"Schism, Heresie, Rebellion,* and *Misery"* would follow. He says, as he does

[328] *Ibid.,* pp. 28–29.

[329] The case for Walton's authorship is made by H. J. Oliver in "Izaak Walton as Author of *Love and Truth* and *Thealma and Clearchus*," *RES*, XXV (1949), 24–37, and in my article, "Izaak Walton, Bishop Morley, and *Love and Truth*," *RES*, n.s. II (1951), 30–39. The date of the preliminary letter to Mr. Brome, almost certainly written by Walton, is May 29, 1680.

[330] *Compleat Walton*, p. 562.

in the *Life of Sanderson,* that the indiscreet zeal of dissenters will bring popery into England. He goes so far as to say that the Duke of York's friendliness toward dissent is expedient cajolery and flattery which will cease when dissenters have assisted him in the ruin of the English Church. He preaches at length about heresy and schism, and he justifies episcopacy, church ceremonies, and obedience to governors. Walton is willing to concede that a few members of the conforming clergy overdress and are too anxious for multiple benefices, but this is the whole of his concession. He does not see for a minute that the High Church invites schism by forcing its policy of noncomprehension. He has no faith in the ability of the Church to swallow up and control nonconformity by a policy of latitude. He sees only that the tail threatens to wag the dog.

In *Love and Truth,* Walton made explicit the main lesson which the *Life of Sanderson* implied. The violence of the times and the urgency of Walton's reaction to them are reflected in *Love and Truth.* For this reason we find in the revision of the *Life of Sanderson,* which followed it closely, only the residuum of his fury against dissent and of his belief in the integrity and kindliness of the High Church and its champions. He had given his deepest feelings direct expression in *Love and Truth;* in the *Life of Sanderson* of 1681 he was content to make slightly darker his picture of dissent, slightly brighter his picture of Sanderson.

In the speech in which the King asks Sanderson to show that episcopacy is consistent with monarchy, Walton, in 1681, has the King mention Parliament's sale of "the Cathedral Church-Land to pay those Soldiers that they had rais'd to fight against him."[331] He had said originally that the House of Commons had afforded rejoicing Covenanters the chance to buy good church lands as a reward for their assistance;[332] now he says that the Commons afforded the opportunity "both to themselves" and to their helpers.[333] He makes more vivid the picture of the havoc which Covenanters wrought throughout the nation by pointing to their "defacing Monuments" and "breaking painted Glass Windows."[334] He says for the second time that Laud's life "seem'd to be sacrific'd, to appease the popular fury of that present time," and he says that Laud at his death "did (as our blessed Saviour advis'd his Disciples,) *Pray for*

---

[331] *Sanderson,* 1681, p. 20.
[333] *Ibid.,* 1681, p. 24.
[332] *Ibid.,* 1678, sig. f8r.
[334] *Ibid.,* p. 25.

those that persecuted and dispitefully used him."[335] In 1678, he had described the reaction of nonconformists at the Restoration: "amazement and fear had seiz'd them, and their accusing Consciences gave them an inward and fearful intelligence, that the God which they had long serv'd, was now ready to pay them such wages as he does always reward *Witches* with for their obeying him";[336] in 1681, he writes, "amazement and fear had seised most of them by foreseeing, they must now not only Vomit up the Churches, and the Kings Land, but their accusing consciences did also give them an inward and fearful Intelligence, that the God of opposition, disobedience, and confusion, which they had so long and so diligently fear'd, was now ready to reward them with such wages as he always pays to *Witches* for their obeying him."[337] And he adds a new paragraph to point the lesson for the nonconformists:

At this time of the conformable Clergies deliverance, from the Presbyterian severities, the Doctor said to a Friend. "I look back on this strange and happy turn of the late times, with amazement and thankfulness; and cannot but think the *Presbyterians* ought to read their own errors, by considering that by their own rules the *Independants* have punisht, and supplanted them as they did the Conformable Clergy, who are now (*so many as still live*) restor'd to their lawful rights; and, as the Prophet *David* hath taught me, so I say with a thankful heart. *Verily, there is a God that Judgeth the earth: And, a reward for the righteous.*"[338]

Even as Walton blackens nonconformity, he compares Sanderson anew to Josiah, Daniel, Paul, and Barnabas,[339] and the sequestered clergy to the children of Israel in the days when they had hung "their neglected Harps on the Willows that grow by the Rivers of *Babylon.*"[340] He had been content to speak of Sanderson's whole life as unspotted; now he adds "so like the Primitive Christians."[341] To his picture of Sanderson on his deathbed he adds the words, "Thus as his natural Life decayed, his Spiritual Life seem'd to be more strong; and, his faith more confirm'd: still labouring to attain that holiness and purity, without which none shall see God."[342] And he adds to Sanderson's words after he had taken the sacrament for the last time:

[335] *Ibid.,* p. 30; see, too, *ibid.,* 1678, sig. f7r.
[336] *Ibid.,* 1678, sigs. k5v–k6r.   [337] *Ibid.,* 1681, p. 35.   [338] *Ibid.,* p. 36.
[339] *Ibid.,* pp. 2, 15, 28². [340] *Ibid.,* p. 35. [341] *Ibid.,* p. 33.
[342] *Ibid.,* p. 43.

I have now to the great Joy of my Soul tasted of the all-saving sacrifice of my Saviours death and passion: and with it, received a spiritual assurance that my sins past are pardon'd, and my God at peace with me: and that I shall never have a Will, or Power to do any thing that may seperate my soul from the love of my dear saviour. Lord Confirm this belief in me.[343]

In his Postscript of 1678 Walton had written that he would *"upon information, mend any mistake, or supply what may seem wanting"* in the *Life*. Except for the information that *Pax Ecclesiae* probably did not represent Sanderson's final doctrinal views, Walton had little to add. He changed the time during which Sanderson conferred with others at Laud's request in 1641 about changes in the Book of Common Prayer and in ceremonies from "3 months or more"[344] to "five months or more."[345] He had written that while the King was a prisoner on the Isle of Wight the Parliament had sent the Covenant and Negative Oath to be taken by "the *Doctor* of the *Chair,* and all Heads of Houses";[346] now he added that Parliament was "then at *Wesiminster*" and that its request was sent "to *Oxford.*"[347] He added, too, the name of the Dean of Christ Church in 1648—Dr. Fell.[348] Originally he had dated the amazement of the Covenanters prior to the Restoration "Towards the end of this year 1659" and the Restoration itself "in the beginning of the year following."[349] Now these became "Towards the beginning of the Year 1600" (a printer's error) and "the 29*th.* of *May* following."[350] In 1678, he had written correctly that Sanderson had attended the King on his progress to Oxford in 1636 and was created Doctor of Divinity on August 31.[351] In 1681, he inserted, for no evident reason, *"May* 3" as the date of Sanderson's and the King's visit, but retained August 31 as the date of the granting of the degree.[352]

Such picayune additions or changes of fact make it obvious that Walton had no radical changes to make and no important facts to add. Still, in his customary fashion, he made over two hundred slight changes in the *Life* which increase its bulk by several hundred words. He added a pretty little passage about the King's religion:

[343] *Ibid.,* p. 44.　　[344] *Ibid.,* 1678, sig. e3ᵛ.　　[345] *Ibid.,* 1681, p. 18.
[346] *Ibid.,* 1678, sig. e5ᵛ.　　[347] *Ibid.,* 1681, p. 19.　　[348] *Ibid.,* p. 23.
[349] *Ibid.,* 1678, sigs. k5ᵛ–k6ʳ.　　[350] *Ibid.,* 1681, p. 35.
[351] *Ibid.,* 1678, sig. d8ᵛ.　　[352] *Ibid.,* 1681, p. 16.

This Conscientious King was told by a faithful and private Intelligencer, *that if he assented not to the Parliaments Proposals, the Treaty 'twixt him and them would break immediately, and his Life would then be in danger; he was sure he knew it.* To which his answer was, *I have done what I can to bring my Conscience to a complyance with their Proposals and cannot, and I will not lose my Conscience to save my Life.*[353]

He has Sanderson praise the Book of Common Prayer at greater length, *"The Holy Ghost seem'd to assist the Composers: and, that the effect of a Constant use of it, would be, to melt and form the Soul, into holy thoughts and desires: and, beget habits of Devotion."*[354] In 1678, he had ended Sanderson's account of his desire to have the needful body of divinity put into fifty-two homilies or sermons with a confused sentence, *"and that this being done, it might probably abate the inordinate desire of knowing what we need not, and practising what we know, and ought to do."*[355] It was probably his attempt to make sense of this passage which led him in 1681 to expand Sanderson's reasons for his plan, to make them more forceful, and he added a pretty analogy:

And, he explain'd the reason of this his desire, by saying to me,——*All Grammer Scholers, that are often shifted, from one to another School, learn neither so much, nor their little so truly, as those that are constant to one good Master: because, by the several Rules of teaching in those several Schools, they learn less, and become more and more Confus'd; and at last, so puzled and perplext, that their learning proves useless both to themselves and others. And so do the immethodical, useless, needless Notions that are delivered in many Sermons, make the hearers: but a clear and constant rule, of teaching us, what we are to know, and do, and what not, and that taught us by an approv'd authority, might probably bring the Nation to a more Conscientious Practice of what we know, and ought to do.* Thus did this Prudent Man explain the reason of this his desire: and oh! that he had undertaken what he advis'd; for then, in all probability it wou'd have prov'd so useful, that the present Age wou'd have been blest by it: and, Posterity wou'd have blest him for it.[356]

Many of Walton's alterations were not so happy as these. The phrase "Rubbish of their Vices"[357] became "Rubbish of their Degenerousness,"[358] "a Committee for that purpose"[359] became "a select Com-

---

[353] *Ibid.*, pp. 20–21. [354] *Ibid.*, p. 30². [355] *Ibid.*, 1678, sig. i7ʳ.
[356] *Ibid.*, 1681, p. 32. [357] *Ibid.*, 1678, sig. a2ᵛ. [358] *Ibid.*, 1681, p. 2.
[359] *Ibid.*, 1678, sig. f6ᵛ.

mittee for that purpose,"[360] "affability"[361] became "an indearing affability,"[362] "namely"[363] was replaced by "that is, to note,"[364] and "men had made perjury a main part of their Religion"[365] was debilitated into ". . . a main part or at least very useful to their Religion."[366] Still, some of his changes were decided improvements. In telling of Sanderson's accompanying Dr. Kilbie on a journey, Walton had originally written that "they going together on a *Sunday* with the Doctor's Friend to that Parish Church where they then were. . . ."[367] Now he made it clear that the men did not travel on Sunday: "and they resting on a *Sunday* with the Doctor's Friend, and going together to that Parish Church. . . ."[368] Again, he had written originally that the exceptions of the Covenanters to Common Prayer and ceremonies seemed "not reasonable to the King and the learned Dr. *Laud*."[369] Now, by adding "and many others,"[370] he made sure that his reader would not see the King and Laud as a minority of two.

For every minor improvement in emphasis or clarity or accuracy, there are two changes which are pointless or redundant, which lead to tautology or unnecessary qualification. Enough changes, however, are of sufficient worth to show that Walton was still extremely sensitive in his writing, that garrulity did not come with old age. He fussed and fiddled because he had nothing more important to do with the *Life*. He had no new facts to add: his view of Sanderson had not changed. The interval between 1678 and 1681 had merely fixed a little more firmly in his mind the sentiments he had expressed in 1678, and, to a slight degree, he altered the *Life* to affirm those sentiments. Having darkened the shadows and brightened the lights, he touched up here and there. The results are unimportant, indicative of artistic conscience rather than artistic ability.

---

[360] *Ibid.*, 1681, p. 23.　　[361] *Ibid.*, 1678, sig. k^v.　　[362] *Ibid.*, 1681, p. 33.
[363] *Ibid.*, 1678, sig. h3^v.　　[364] *Ibid.*, 1681, p. 30.　　[365] *Ibid.*, 1678, sig. e5^r.
[366] *Ibid.*, 1681, p. 18.　　[367] *Ibid.*, 1678, sig. a7^r.　　[368] *Ibid.*, 1681, p. 4.
[369] *Ibid.*, 1678, sig. e3^r.　　[370] *Ibid.*, 1681, p. 18.

Conclusion

Walton, the Artist

as Biographer

THROUGHOUT his long career as a biographer, Walton insisted upon his truthfulness and belittled his artistry. At the beginning of his first venture into biography he spoke of his "artlesse Pensil" and said that it was "guided by the hand of Truth."[1] Again, in 1658, he assured his reader that his narrative was truthful. He differentiated narration from his own observation and opinion, and stated that even if he had the power to influence by means of observation and opinion, he preferred to let his reader draw his own conclusions.[2] In his note to the reader of the *Life of Hooker,* Walton expressed his confidence that the narrative part of the *Life* contained no *"Material Mistakes,"* and he said of traditional information which he had received, *"I shall not impose my Belief upon my Reader; I shall rather leave him at liberty."*[3] And, at the end of the Appendix of the *Hooker,* he reiterated that he was not an "ingaged Person," that he had merely set down the results of his inquiry, and that the reader was to be the judge.[4] When Walton wrote of his wonder that a man of his own education and mean abilities should appear in print,[5] when he confessed to his *"little Confidence"* in his performance,[6] he was deprecating not his truthfulness, but his skill in writing. When he spoke in 1675 of the possible *"mistakes"* in the *Life of Herbert,* it was clearly an afterthought, and probably he meant

[1] *Donne,* 1640, sig. A5ʳ.   [2] *Donne,* 1658, sig. A10ʳ.
[3] *Hooker,* 1665, sigs. A6ᵛ–A7ʳ.   [4] *Ibid.,* p. 173.
[5] *Lives,* 1675, sig. A4ᵛ.   [6] *Ibid.,* 1670, sig. A4ʳ.

mistakes in style,[7] for in 1670 he had referred only to improprieties and infelicities of expression.[8] In the Preface to the *Life of Sanderson,* he told his reader in his first sentence that he did not dare assure him that he had made no mistakes, but he did assure him that none of the mistakes were "either wilful, or very material." And in the last sentence of the Preface he stated his wish that posterity might have been informed of Sanderson's learning and virtue "by a better Pen." Walton not only minimized his artistry while he pointed to his truthfulness, but he ever implied what he wrote in relating Donne's vision in 1675: that he was "well pleas'd, that every Reader do injoy his own opinion."[9] But his method here is typical of his procedure throughout his career. He made the strongest possible argument for the vision, adding detail to his narrative and giving many proofs and analogies, so many that he wrote, "but I forbear, least, I that intended to be but a Relator, may be thought to be an ingag'd person for the proving what was related to me."[10]

Despite Walton's insistence on his truthfulness, he was of necessity engaged. He was more than engaged; he was wedded to his own time. In the seventeenth century, life-writing, in its diverse manifestations, groped toward a genre, but, though the need was felt shortly after the Restoration for the word "biography" and its variations,[11] there was no code and no adherence to a code. Walton, to be sure, was more aware than most of his contemporaries of the differences between a character and a life, a picture and a narrative. But the character, in its own diverse manifestations, exerted a great pull on him. He praised Donne's satires because he thought of them as characters of sins.[12] Among the topics of interest in *Reliquiae Wottonianae* which he specifically pointed out were Wotton's characters.[13] The milkmaid in the *Compleat Angler* is Overburian, and the *Angler* in its entirety is worth consideration as a discursive character of the contemplative man. Walton's fondness for the character and his belief in its usefulness are evident in the *Lives.* He included in the *Life of Donne* what he himself called "a short, but true character" of Dr. Morton,[14] and not only did he close this life in 1640 with a character of Donne, but he added substantially

---

[7] *Ibid.,* 1675, sig. A5ᵛ.   [8] *Ibid.,* 1670, sig. A6ᵛ.   [9] *Ibid.,* 1675, p. 31.
[10] *Ibid.,* p. 32.
[11] See Donald Stauffer, *English Biography before 1700,* pp. 217–219, for a correction of the statements of the Oxford *New English Dictionary.*
[12] *Poems, By J. D.,* 1633, pp. 382–383.   [13] *Reliq.,* 1651, sig. a3ʳ.
[14] *Donne,* 1658, p. 26.

to the character in 1658. In 1670, he quoted part of Donne's "The Autumnall" in the *Life of Herbert,* and he called it "a Character of the Beauties" of Magdalen Herbert's body and mind.[15] He included in the *Life of Sanderson* a long "Character of his person and temper."[16] But the extent to which Walton relied on the character is best illustrated in the *Life of Hooker.* Here, Walton interrupted the narrative of the *Life* to give his reader "a Character of the Times, and Temper of the people of this Nation,"[17] and as part of this long account quoted Sir Henry Wotton's "true Character" of Archbishop Whitgift.[18] Again, when he got Hooker to Bishopsborne, he gave a "true Character of his Person" and followed it by characterizing Hooker's disposition and behavior.[19] Although Walton used the term "character" only this once in speaking of Hooker, his *Life* contains at least four other characters of the man. The second paragraph of the *Life* is a character of the grave and scholarly child; Hooker at Oxford is made the subject of two characters— one pictures the learning and behavior of the perfect student[20] and the other the complete scholar;[21] and Hooker is charactered, too, as the prototype of the good country priest, "a pattern as may invite posterity to imitate his vertues."[22] When these characters of Hooker are viewed as a whole, Walton's picture "heightned by one shadowing" becomes immediately apparent. How deductive Walton's procedure is, he himself revealed in his character of Hooker as a youth. His picture is reconstructed "so far as Inquiry is able to look back at this distance of Time" and is based largely on an account of Hooker at the age of forty.[23] Walton shaped the child in the image of the man. Complexity and development of personality are possible only when the biographer is aware that man is shaped by his past as well as his future. The deductive approach fostered by the character led to oversimplification and one-sidedness. The diminution of light and shade in favor of a heightening by one shadow tended to produce, in biography, a too even picture because it reduced the element of struggle in a life. It made for the emphasis of a dominant trait and the adjustment of details that were consistent at every point with that trait. The spirit of the character was part of Walton's inheritance, and even as he charactered the boy

[15] *Lives,* 1670 (Herbert), p. 15.   [16] *Sanderson,* 1678, sigs. k^v–k4^r.
[17] *Hooker,* 1665, p. 48.   [18] *Ibid.,* p. 63.   [19] *Ibid.,* pp. 128–129.
[20] *Ibid.,* pp. 23–24.   [21] *Ibid.,* pp. 33–35.   [22] *Ibid.,* pp. 132–139.
[23] *Ibid.,* p. 8.

in the image of the man, so, too, he chose and shaped the detail of his narrative according to the character-image in his mind.

But every biographer has in his mind, if not a character-image, a series of character-images, a pattern, a sense of a certain unity, a sort of musical tone which explains or clarifies his subject.[24] Any adequate understanding and interpretation of a subject is based on the discovery or recognition of just such an image or pattern through psychological insight. André Maurois has wisely said that a biographer must be able to project himself into his subject in order to understand him, that all biography is associative, and, essentially, a means of self-expression.[25] The danger today in this process, according to Maurois, is that a biographer never discovers the whole of his own character in a historical character. Since he discovers in his subject only one aspect of his own character, he may distort historical truth by becoming too autobiographical; he may construct a hero according to his own needs and desires by associating other aspects of his own character with his subject.[26] Maurois assumes, of course, that the biographer is himself a person of some complexity. But Maurois himself pointed out that the seventeenth-century view of personality was simpler than our own and that the seventeenth-century man undoubtedly considered himself more of a piece than does the modern biographer.[27] The danger to the seventeenth-century biographer was the impulse to identify all of himself with one aspect of his subject; even if he found in his subject a greater complexity than in himself, he stressed only this one aspect.

Walton was not free from this impulse of his contemporaries. His revisions show his continual struggle to express himself, but his was not a struggle to articulate vague and inchoate ideas, to get them down to find for himself what he thought. He knew at the beginning exactly what he wanted to say; he struggled only to express himself more sharply and clearly. What strikes us almost immediately in Walton is the firmness and sureness of his values. The seeming simplicity, the naïveté, the innocency of Walton stems from his oneness of approach. Even among seventeenth-century men, Walton is sin-

[24] I omit, for the moment, a most important consideration: at what point in his study of his subject does the biographer make his deduction, or does he make it prior to his study?

[25] André Maurois, *Aspects of Biography* (Cambridge, 1929), ch. iv.

[26] *Ibid.*, pp. 111–117.   [27] *Ibid.*, pp. 30–31.

gularly committed to the virtues of humility, fortitude, faith in God and in God's chosen representatives. All his life he advocated a meek and contented quietness. He was aware that bluster and discontent and noise were loose in the world, but they were bad and he could not really comprehend them. His emotional range seems never to have needed to be checked by Christian virtue and middle-class propriety and respectability; it seems always to have been at home in their midst. He talked about violent emotion, but as one who had not himself experienced it or who was unwilling to reveal that he had experienced it. His education was not sufficient to lead him to that intellectual subtlety which is necessary for the weighing of alternatives. His unwavering support of Royalism and Anglicanism is an obvious manifestation of his acceptance of an inherited orthodoxy, and it is an orthodoxy which borders on dogmatism. Walton appears undogmatic in his confession that he lacks art and in his confession that he cannot grasp complicated arguments about doctrine. Still, he insists dogmatically that the pathway to heaven is a plain one and he insists dogmatically on the necessity for moderation. And, of course, he is dogmatic in his view that every High Churchman was by nature moderate and every nonconformist perverse and obdurate. Walton found and emphasized in his subjects the sureness of values and the singularity of outlook that was his own. He identified all of himself with one aspect of his subjects. The critics are right when they say that all the *Lives* reflect Walton. They are wrong, however, when they equate Walton's single-mindedness with simplicity and simple-mindedness. Certain kinds of emotional and intellectual struggle he could not comprehend, but the oppositions by others to his singleness of belief he was sharply aware of. Walton's dependence on the deductive approach is not in itself the deficiency it has been made out to be. The real deficiency in Walton as biographer is in the determined single-mindedness of outlook which limited the kind of deduction he could make or wanted to make. His character-image was, then, restricted by the narrowness of his outlook.

Walton's character-image was also influenced by other matters: the nature of his attitude toward his subject, his personal acquaintance with his subject, and the immediate purpose for which he was writing a life. Walton was neither the social nor intellectual equal of any of his subjects. His attitude toward each of them was blurred by respect, admiration, even hero worship. He regarded affection as a prerequisite for biography,[28] and when to affection was added hero worship, the result could be only panegyric. Walton's character-image was bound to be idealized. I have discussed copiously enough Walton's acquaintance with his subjects, the occasions of the various *Lives,* and how these helped determine his representation of his subjects. I have shown that the Donne whom Walton pictured was the Donne he knew personally, the powerful preacher, the devout divine. To be sure, Walton's elegy on Donne shows his acquaintance with the poetry, but the Donne of the songs and sonnets was not a living, breathing man to him. Walton consciously minimized the irregularities in Donne's life, consciously wrenched the chronology of the life to emphasize the picture of the man as he knew him. His inclination toward this procedure was strengthened by the fact that the *Life* was, after all, to be prefatory to Donne's sermons. I have indicated Walton's minute knowledge of Wotton's ambassadorial years, but his picture of Wotton was dictated by his personal acquaintance with Wotton the Provost of Eton and by his incidental desire to present in the 1650's a lesson about the evils of religious wrangling. The image of Hooker was determined by the traditional information which Walton inherited and by his desire to produce a picture more acceptable to the bishops than Gauden's. The incidental purpose of preserving Hooker as a champion of the High Church was so strong that Walton was forced into an appendix; it intruded, however, into the *Life* in many ways and dictated not only the digression on Whitgift and church property but also, in part, the picture of Hooker. Walton never knew Herbert, nor did he go to great trouble to get detailed biographical information. His *Life* is full of inaccuracies and gaps, and he made large use of Herbert's books, *The Temple* and, especially, *A Priest To the Temple, or, The Countrey Parson, his Character, and Rule of Holy Life,* to show Herbert as the prototype of the good parson. This image was reinforced by his desire to make abundantly clear what he considered the obligations and practices of the parson to be and to provide support for his belief that the Church was a worthy profession for men of the highest station, education, and abilities. The Sanderson whom Walton knew was, first, the highly respected divine who was part of the inner circle of the High Church, and then the Bishop of Lincoln, the learned acquaintance of his employer and friend, George Morley, Bishop of Worcester

[28] See pp. 191–192.

and of Winchester. But it was the experience of the staunchly meek supporter of Anglicanism with the Presbyterian peril and Walton's desire to show the dangers of nonconformity which largely determined the image which dominated the *Life of Sanderson*.

Walton not only depended, then, upon a character-image, but the image was limited by the single-mindedness of his outlook, by his disposition toward hero worship, by the extent and nature of his acquaintance with his subject, and by the purpose underlying each effort. But what of Walton's use of so many primary sources, of his scholarship and documentation? The introduction of this material largely distinguishes Walton from other biographers of his time. It is the particularity of his *Lives* which sets them apart from other life-writing of his day. And it is this particularity which highly individualizes each of his character-images.

Walton's use of documentary material was, I think, at least in the beginning, an accidental advantage. He ever preferred an oral source to a written one; he would rather indulge in discursive discussion than sift records. He preferred anecdote to fact and was more interested in elaborating a portrait by little stories than in chronicling the events of a life. But, from the start of his career, he was confronted by an embarrassing richness of document. His informants were ever-willing and overgenerous. Henry King must have deluged him with Donne's papers. Wotton's papers and letters fell to him, and the dispatches could not easily be overlooked. All the material at Lambeth and all the High Church scholarship at Oxford was made accessible to him for the *Life of Hooker*. His friends at Oxford saw that he did not lack materials for the *Life of Sanderson*. When we consider the resources he could have drawn on, the wonder is not that Walton used such material, but that he did not use more of it. Only for the *Life of Herbert* did he lack a great store of material, and there he preferred to rely on his conversations with Woodnoth and Duncon rather than to make a laborious search for documents. Walton does not seem to have done arduous research. He does not seem even to have been fully aware of the worth of what he had until in writing the *Life of Hooker* he was struck by the tremendous utility of such material in controverting the impression of Hooker created by Gauden's *Life*.

The statement that "as Walton advanced in years he grew less concerned with rendering his narrative credible in all details" is ambiguous. As Walton gained in self-confidence as a writer, he became more willing to include incidents which placed a larger burden on the credulity of his reader, but at the same time he became increasingly meticulous in controlling every detail of the incidents. The *Lives* become more imaginative and more dramatic at the same time that they become more factual and more specific. Walton became increasingly aware of the flavor of authenticity and reality that fact injected into life-writing, and, increasingly, he used fact. Still, we have seen again and again that Walton's reliance upon the character-image is nowhere more evident than in the way his predispositions and purposes shaped his facts at every point. At the same time that he included his account of Donne's vision, he buttressed the *Life of Donne* with dates. He saw that the freer his choice of incident was, the harder he must work to authenticate the *Life* in general and the incident in particular. He saw the value of the dates in furnishing an authoritative ring to the *Life*, and he used them. He saw, too, the value of a precise chronology in furnishing evidence for the validity of the incident, and he added one, though he had to invent it. Again, in the 1672 *Life of Wotton*, Walton busied himself with meticulously accurate facts. To a small degree, this was a manifestation of a desire for greater truthfulness, but it was to a larger degree a manifestation of his growing desire to render his work credible in all details. And when in this year truth of fact clashed with an impression which Walton was trying to make, Walton sacrificed the truth for the impression. In the same way, we may be tempted to assume that Walton's including Reinolds' letter in 1670 is evidence of a greater reliance on documentary truth. Walton was well aware of the value of such a document, and was glad to include it, but he included it to support his own picture. On the basis of such a letter, another biographer would have been forced to the conclusion that the youthful Hooker was independent, rebellious, Calvinist. But Walton carefully fitted the letter to conform with the Hooker he had already drawn. As Walton aged, he demanded of himself an increasing specificity of fact and detail, not for precise truthfulness, but for convincing support of increasing deviation from the truth. The greater the liberty he took with fact, the greater was his concern to authenticate with fact in order to render his narrative credible in all details.

To say that Walton's portraits are remarkably accurate, that "the apparent facts which Walton used are likely to be true only with reference to the larger picture for which he employed them" is to lose sight of the matters which narrowed Walton's character-image. But even if we were convinced that Walton had arrived at his character-image in a less stringently limited way, even if we thought he had, with breadth of outlook, tolerance for contradiction, and recognition of subtle distinctions, made an extensive examination of all the evidence and then fixed on his character-image, we must suspect the truth of his picture when we see how he customarily handled details. We may perhaps condone as biographical license Walton's treatment of the letters of Donne from which Bennett generalized; we may perhaps condone his changing of James's speech on the Venetian controversy, his combining of Paule's incidents of Whitgift dining with the Queen and then with the brothers and sisters in the almshouse. In view of the real complexity of Sanderson's doctrine, we may perhaps condone Walton's equating that doctrine with the orthodox High Church line. But what of his rather more far-fetched identification of Hooker's position on the apostolicity of bishops with that of Saravia's? What of the omission of the date of Donne's will, of the changed date of the letter Donne wrote before Christmas, of the omission of the dates in the account book? What of Walton's tailoring a councillary decree in the *Life of Wotton?* In demonstrating the glory of the Wotton family, Walton devoted a paragraph to Nicholas Wotton so that his readers would not think him negligent. What of his negligence in omitting the conversion to Catholicism of Edward and Pickering Wotton? What of his raising Fynes Moryson's mere mention of George Cranmer into a testimonial to Cranmer's worth and of his using Herbert's answer to Andrew Melville's verses as sufficient reason for the defamation of Melville's character? Was Walton using or abusing his prerogative as biographer when he read "Affliction I" as biography and cut short his reading at Herbert's reference to his fierceness and his martial desires? Does it create an adequate impression of Herbert merely to say that he struggled, or is the struggle minimized if it is not pictured so graphically as other matters are pictured? Is Walton within his rights in overriding Fell's statement that Hammond found it difficult to memorize sermons, in saying the contrary merely to make more vivid Sanderson's inability? And what of his insistence on the great suffering of Sanderson when the Presbyterians were in power? Walton's misuse of fact to create an impression which is antithetical to the truth must make us suspicious of the validity of his larger picture. His large deviation from the truth in a multitude of details must make us question the truth of the impression which any *Life* as a whole gives us.

But if such manipulations make us distrust Walton as biographer, they demonstrate, too, his acute insight into fact. We can be sure that Walton was aware of the implications of a fact if he took the trouble to manipulate it. To say that Walton had no insight into fact is to impugn his intelligence and his imagination. A man who utilizes facts to his own ends must have great sensitivity for them, regardless of his ends. Had Walton had less insight into fact, his *Lives* might have been more accurate. Had he not seen the implications of Wotton's behavior as an ambassador, his picture of Wotton the diplomat would have contradicted the emphasis on nonwrangling which he imposed on the life. Had he not seen the implications of Reinolds' letter, he might unknowingly have modified his picture of the youthful Hooker. His insight into the implications of Herbert's retention of his fellowship was probably responsible for his omitting his original reference to Herbert's resignation of his fellowship, and his insight into the implications of the statements by Ferrar and Oley that Herbert sought to resign "an Ecclesiasticall dignitie" made him suppress this fact and substitute information which led to a contrary impression. His insight into fact is seen in the care he took with even so slight a detail as the title of Sanderson's tract on the Liturgy. The limiting single-mindedness of Walton's outlook is not to be equated, then, with a lack of insight into fact on his part. It was precisely his ability to perceive so minutely the implications of a fact which, coupled with his capacity to control and manipulate fact superbly, further limited and sharpened the effect of the *Lives*.

But Walton's insight into fact and his capacity to control fact superbly have yet another result. If the desire to shape inordinately can be destructive of biographic truth, control and imagination are requisite to artistry. Much of the persuasion in the *Lives* stems from the dramatic effectiveness of the anecdote. When all else in the *Lives* is forgotten, we remember still Donne's vision, Wotton's final pilgrimage to Winchester, Hooker's tending his sheep, Herbert's music at midnight, Sheldon's youthful indiscretion, and Sanderson and Walton taking shelter from the rain and talking of liturgy over their bread, cheese, and ale. These scenes remain bright; these figures live on in the depths of the mind. Walton seems to give us "the creative fact; the fertile fact; the fact that suggests and engenders." Such special facts, Virginia Woolf has suggested, any biographer can give us if he respects facts.[29] But Walton's creative facts—and those of other biographers, too, I suspect—do not arise from mere respect for or adherence to fact. They stem from that genius for description which Carlyle thought necessary to the completion of a "light-gleam" into the significant meaning of a fact.[30] Nor is the genius for description limited to those who deal with facts alone. Walton had it, and he used it whether he was dealing with facts or not.

In this respect and in others, Walton as biographer is closest, perhaps, to Lytton Strachey. Both produce episodes which are unforgettable. Both take liberties with chronology and with the thoughts of their subjects. Both control every nuance of meaning; both depend heavily on rhetorical devices and have eccentrically beautiful styles. But there is a larger resemblance. We have seen how Walton's customary methods imposed limitations on each of the *Lives*. If we put stock in Strachey's preface to *Eminent Victorians*, we do not feel his methods as *historian* to be unduly restricting. He speaks of rowing out over the great ocean of material available to the historian of the Victorian age, of lowering his little bucket and bringing up a characteristic specimen to be examined with careful curiosity. The technique is apparently that of random selection, and we may admit its validity, though we may feel it would be safer and fairer, despite the difficulty, to haul up great bucketsful and select the representative specimen. But Strachey himself reveals that his is no random selection. His choice of subjects, he says, was determined by "simple motives of convenience and of art." When he writes that he wished "to examine and elucidate certain fragments of the truth" which took his fancy and lay to his hand, he implies that he may not have told the whole truth about the Victorian age, but that he has told the whole truth about part of that age. He insists, in other words, on the truth of the individual lives which make up his book. Again, when he speaks of himself as *biographer* rather than as historian, he says that he has excluded nothing of significance, that he has laid bare the facts dispassionately and impartially. Despite Strachey's emphasis on the twofold nature of his chore, his description of his methods as historian has frequently been read as characteristic of his methods as biographer, and with

[29] Virginia Woolf, "The Art of Biography" in *The Death of the Moth and Other Essays* (New York, 1942), p. 197.
[30] Thomas Carlyle, "Biography," *Fraser's Magazine*, V (1832), 259.

good reason. The choice of his detail is not dictated by a selection which is random or representative; it seems often dictated by convenience and by art, and he seems to have told the whole truth about part of his subject. His methods restrict his lives.

Even as Walton heightened each of the *Lives* by one shadowing based on a character-image, so Strachey imposed on each of his lives a pattern or significant form. Both thought it necessary for biography to interpret, and to interpret through structure, but neither was able or willing to *discover* the significant form in a life. Each *imposed* a form that he endowed with significance. Walton's form was conditioned in part by an idealized point of view, and the result was panegyric. Strachey's form was conditioned in part by the attitude that men were not merely human, but all too human, and the result was belittlement.

Today, Strachey's stock has sunk too low; we need to be reminded that Mrs. Woolf thought him one of the great biographers. But we are wise when we read Strachey for one aspect of the truth, not for a totally accurate account, but for a brilliant partial insight. This is easy to do with Strachey, for we are familiar with the rather more even, if less inspired, biographies of his subjects. We can temper Strachey's lives with the evenness of the "standard" lives which he so despised. We should read Walton, too, for one aspect of the truth, but this is somewhat harder to do. Walton's subjects were not, prior to his writing, commemorated in two fat volumes. Indeed, the two fat volumes now available are too frequently dependent on Walton's accounts. And since Walton's accounts are earlier in time, they have too often been viewed as the "standard" accounts. But Walton's lives and the details in the lives can no more be regarded as truthful than can Strachey's. We must read both Strachey and Walton with caution and with skepticism and be suspicious of those of their impressions and assertions which are not confirmed elsewhere.

Are we forced to conclude, then, that Walton's—and Strachey's—deficiency as biographer is in no small way due to his success as an artist? Is Mrs. Woolf right in calling biography a craft rather than an art? Her statement will lead us only to quibbling definition, for the difference is fuzzy and shifting. More important than her attempt at nominal distinction is her rightful insistence on the high place of biography. I should like to suggest here, however, that we have been led astray in evaluating biographical works because critical discussion has ever emphasized content at the expense of form, matter at the expense of manner. The opinion that biography is something apart from creative writing shows up all the more clearly today when criticism, especially of fiction, is preoccupied by considerations of form. But an examination of the biography we most admire, that of Johnson and Boswell, Carlyle and Froude, ought to convince us, I think, that biography is best when it approaches most closely the intensity of poetry, the excitement of drama, the novel's illusion of reality. We are, let us face it, only secondarily interested in the chronicle of a man's achievement. We are primarily curious about his character and personality: What sort of man is he? The best collection of facts, all of them ordered, is no substitute for our love of sharp incident, revealing anecdote, suspenseful narrative, even explicit analysis of motivation, if these are given us with insight and with style. Austin Dobson went to the heart of the matter when he wrote Gosse:

> But will you catch old Izaak's phrase
> That glows with energy of praise?
> Old Izaak's ambling unpretence
> That flames with untaught eloquence?[31]

The biographer we admire is a writer who has style. We will still find useful the biography which has only fact and document to commend it; we will still reach for the *Dictionary of National Biography;* but our impression of a man will be dominated by the account of the stylist who gets hold of him. We will ourselves modify his portrait somewhat, but the dominant impression will be his. No wonder Leslie Stephen was so furious with Walton.

The deficiency of Walton and of Strachey as biographers stems not from their being artists, but from their being limited artists, from their having narrow talents. Their deficiency as biographers is the same deficiency they would have had had they been novelists. They are the Austens, not the Tolstoys of biography. They are limited artists because they have limited outlooks. Mrs. Woolf is quite right in saying that biography enlarges its scope by hanging up looking glasses at odd corners. But she assumes that the biographer has used the odd corner only after he has scrupulously

[31] Austin Dobson, *Miscellanies (Second Series)* (New York, 1901), p. 242.

studied a full-face image. In so far as Walton and Strachey take only an angular view, we must always compensate for the distortion of their angle of vision.

But if it is difficult for a novelist, with limitations imposed only by his own capacities, to see life steadily and see it whole, to make completely credible a character of his own creation, how much more difficult is the chore of the biographer, who must do the same thing with materials which he cannot bend at will because they are subject to verification out of his context. It is almost too much to ask. We ought to be more willing to settle for biography by the limited artist. He will make his subject come to life. At the same time, he will reveal to some degree his own hand and outlook, for his style will reflect in part his prejudices and his emotions. And we will be able to temper our view of his subject by our own awareness of the sort of man he is.

Like every painstaking artist, Walton revealed, in the *Lives,* his own assumptions and predilections, his principles and his moral outlook. We have not read the *Lives* rightly because we have let the fanciful image of a naïvely honest and innocent man come between us and the image which the *Lives* themselves reveal. It is this other Walton—strenuously rectitudinous and dogmatically orthodox, at the same time that he was gentle and reserved; increasingly partisan as he became more personally involved in the day's chief issues, at the same time that he pleaded for moderation and objectivity; acutely conscious of tradition and historical parallels, at the same time that he deplored his lack of learning; unflinchingly dedicated to craftsmanship, at the same time that he belittled his artistry—it is this Walton we must picture in our minds to compensate for the angle of his vision.

Appendixes and Index

Appendix A

The Date of Walton's Notes in His Copy of *Eusebius*

SOME of Walton's books are preserved in the Cathedral library at Salisbury, where they were probably placed by his son, who was a canon of the Cathedral. The following notes in Walton's hand are on the inside of the cover of his copy of *The Ancient Ecclesiasticall Histories of the First Six Hundred Yeares after Christ, Written . . . by three learned Historiographers, Eusebius, Socrates, and Evagrius,* 1636:

[A] At his conversion take out of Jeremy the ways of man are not in his owne powr
loke doc dones letter to Tilman
& on Sr philip Sidnys salms.
on this booke folyo 28. of hims and psalms [AB] wh was his holy recreation the latter part of his life and is now his imployment in heven where he makes new ditties in the praise of that god in 3 persons to whome be glorie
[B] And his better part is now doing that in heaven which was most of his imployment on earth magnyfying the mercies and making hims and singing them to that god to whome be glory and honer and
[C] vew hookers preface: and hooker—226 & 229
vew the verses before Sands psalms [CD] and Sr Tho. Haukins his horrace. doc dons letters. and the eligies on him.
[D] in heven wher his imployment is to sing such hims as he made on erth in prase of that god to whome be grory [*sic*] and honer
[E] his deth was the prolog to joye and the end of troble
[F] vew chidlys elligies and godolpins [*sic*] on doc done where they are scracht. [F1] and vew the elligies on cartwrite
[F] vew doc cozens devotions
[G] vew the Complete woman. of a good grace. vew the penygerick on mr harvie

499

make his discription that he was 1? for his complexion. then his behaviour
then his stature. then his discourse ministerd grace to the herer
  that he was like the dove wth out gall.
  doc taylers living and dying
  doc. pridiox
  Mr Gouldsmiths poem. vossius ther[1]

Geoffrey Keynes thinks that the notes were intended for the *Life of
Donne*, 1640, and in support of that date he cites the reference to "doc
dones letter to Tilman" and Walton's use in 1640 of an image from the
poem.[2] Keynes would explain the references in the notes to works published later than 1640 by saying that not all the notes were written at
the same time. He takes specific notice of "the elligies on cartwrite,"
which were published in 1651, and asks us to believe that Walton went
to the inside cover of the *Eusebius* to write notes over a period of a
dozen years.

To be sure, the notes were written at different times, but the handwriting does not change radically. Its size varies for inserts, and probably more than one quill and more than one shade of ink were used. It
is quite likely that all the notes were written in a short interval, perhaps
over a number of days, and undoubtedly at the time when Walton was
reading *Eusebius*. His note, "on this booke folyo 28. of hims and
psalms," refers to page 28 of *Eusebius*. One of the marginal notes on
that page says "Psalmes and Hymnes," and there Eusebius quotes
Philo Judaeus on the religious men in the region of Egypt in his time:
*"They contemplate not onely divine things, but they make grave canti-
cles, and hymnes unto God in a more sacred rime, of every kind of
meeter and verse."* Although the book is dated 1636, nothing indicates
that Walton was reading it directly after its publication. Nor was he
the first owner of his copy, for erased on the fly leaf is the notation
"Francis Garrard his booke."[3]

Several notes point to a date after 1651. The volume in which the
elegies to Cartwright appear was published in 1651.[4] "Doc dons letters"
is probably a reference to *Letters to Severall Persons of Honour*, 1651.
Jeremy Taylor's *Holy Living* appeared in 1650, and *Holy Dying* in
1651. In 1651, Walton was busy with the *Life of Wotton*. In 1653, the
Compleat Angler was first published. The second edition of the *Life
of Wotton* appeared in 1654 and the second of the *Compleat Angler*
in the following year. But none of the notes in *Eusebius* refer to these
books. On the other hand, the passage which Walton referred to in

1 My transcript is based on a photograph kindly lent me by Arthur M. Coon.
2 *Compleat Walton*, p. 627.   3 Nicolas, p. cxlviii.
4 William Cartwright, *Comedies, Tragi-comedies, With other Poems* (London, 1651). Walton's elegy, the last of fifty-two, is on sig. ***10^v.

Eusebius is undoubtedly the source of a like passage in the 1658 revision of the *Life of Donne*. In this revision Walton justified Donne's divine poems by adding, "After this manner did the Disciples of our Saviour, and the best of Christians in those Ages of the Church nearest to his time, offer their praises to Almighty God." [5] He then wrote "But now oh Lord——" to show his grief at the prohibition of this manner of praise during the Commonwealth, and in the 1670 revision he added the date "1656." Although the date probably refers to the year of Cromwell's severest strictures against the Episcopal church rather than to the date of composition of the passage, it may well be that Walton's note in *Eusebius* was written at this time. Since this note and several others point specifically to additions incorporated in the 1658 version of the *Life of Donne*, it is safe to assume that Walton wrote them at some period between 1655 and 1658, and probably in 1656 or 1657.

Walton's handwriting and the subject matter of the notes both indicate that they were written in a short interval. Entry A was written first, with the revision of the *Life of Donne* in mind. B was written shortly after A. The *Life of Donne* of 1658 has a large addition about George Herbert, and B was probably written with Herbert rather than Donne in mind, though it was not immediately used for either of them. In the *Life of Herbert* (1670), however, three variations of B are found:

These *Hymns* are now lost to us; but, doubtless they were such, as they two [Donne and Magdalen Herbert] now sing in *Heaven*.[6]

A service [the singing of hymns and lauds], which is now the constant employment of that *blessed Virgin,* and *Simeon,* and all those blessed Saints that are possest of Heaven; and where they are at this time interchangeably, and constantly singing, *Holy, Holy, Holy Lord God, Glory be to God on High, and on Earth peace.*[7]

Thus he [Herbert] sung on earth such Hymns and Anthems, as the Angels and he, and Mr. *Farrer,* now sing in Heaven.[8]

AB is merely a variation of B, and that it was written shortly after B is evident not only in the subject but in its insertion in a squeezed hand. The handwriting and ink of C resemble A closely, and C was probably written soon after A. In content C is indicative of Walton's interest in Hooker. Entry D was made after C, and probably very shortly after, for it is a variation of B and AB. That CD was written after D is evident by its squeezed insertion, and it was probably written not long after C and D, since it is tacked on to C. There is greater space between D and E than between any other entries, and the quill had been newly

[5] *Donne,* 1658, pp. 78–79.   [6] *Lives,* 1670 (Herbert), p. 18.
[7] *Ibid.,* p. 52.   [8] *Ibid.,* p. 77.

dipped. E was written after D, and perhaps after F. The ink and handwriting of F resemble A and C very closely, indicating only a short lapse of time. Its content shows that it was written after CD, for the "eligies" on Donne are now specified to be those by Chudleigh and Godolphin. F1 was written at the same time as F but after its last line, for it has been inserted. Entry G was made after E or F; the small handwriting and the ink generally resemble E. The last line of G starts in the ink and hand of E, but the last three and one-half words resemble more closely in hand and ink entries A, C, and F. Here is further evidence of the shortness of the period in which the notes were written.

The many additions to the *Life of Donne* of 1658 which have their source in the *Eusebius* notes show that the notes were primarily intended for that work. The reference to "eligies" in CD and to Chudleigh and Godolphin in F help to tie together a part of the notes. The shortness of the period of their composition is better indicated, however, by the reworking of the sentence which Walton thrice used in the *Life of Herbert* and by the references to the "elligies on cartwrite" and the "penygerick on mᵣ harvie," in which Walton probably had in mind his poetic versions of the same sentiment expressed in the sentence. His elegy on William Cartwright contains the lines:

> . . . 'till we shall have
> Admission to that Kingdom, where He sings
> Harmonious Anthems to the King of Kings.

His commendatory poem to Christopher Harvey, whose volume *The Synagogue, or, The Shadow of the Temple* is written in imitation of Herbert's *The Temple* and is frequently found bound with it, contains the same sentiment. Its first stanza reads:

> *SIR.*
> I Lov'd you for your Synagogue, before
> I knew your person; but now love you more;
> > Because I finde
> It is so true a picture of your minde:
> > Which tunes your sacred lyre
> > To that eternal quire;
> > Where holy Herbert sits
> > (O shame to prophane wits)
> And sings his and your Anthems, to the praise
> Of him that is the first and last of dayes.[9]

[9] Walton's poem was first printed in 1657 with the third edition of *The Synagogue* (p. 67). If the "penygerick on mᵣ harvie" refers to the printed poem rather than to a manuscript, the notes in *Eusebius* should probably be dated 1657.

Appendix B

Walton and the Poems
about Donne's Seal

WALTON quoted from the 1650 edition of Donne's *Poems* the first two and a half lines of both Donne's and Herbert's Latin poems. He included the English version of Donne's poem in its entirety, though he combined into a single prose passage the English title prefixed to the Latin poem and the first two lines of English verse, which in the 1650 *Poems* are separated from the remaining verses and give the appearance of a motto or title.[1] The English version of Herbert's poem consists in 1650 of a set of eight lines, followed by two quatrains and a couplet. In the *Life of Donne*, 1658, Walton used as his first stanza the opening eight lines with the final couplet tacked to them, and followed this by only the first of the quatrains.[2]

In Appendix G of her *John Donne, The Divine Poems*, Miss Gardner discusses in some detail Donne's use of seals, the date of his poem, the title and setting of Donne's Latin poem and of its English version, and Herbert's poem. She shows that Walton wrongly believed that Donne had his seal of Christ upon an anchor made just prior to his death. (Donne seems to have had it made upon the occasion of his ordination in 1615.) She shows, too, that Walton erred in thinking that Donne sent Herbert both the poem and a seal ring just before he died. (Donne sent the poem to Herbert in 1615 in a letter sealed with his new seal, and he probably sent him a seal ring in 1631.) In addition, Miss Gardner demonstrates that Herbert's (English) reply printed in 1650 is not one poem, but an amalgam of a poem of eight lines, written in answer to

---

[1] *Poems, By J. D.*, 1650, p. 379. See Helen Gardner's convincing suggestion about the title and setting of Donne's poem in her *John Donne, The Divine Poems*, pp. 141–143.

[2] *Donne*, 1658, pp. 84–85.

Donne's poem, and three epigrams (two quatrains and a couplet), written after Herbert had received one of Donne's seal rings as a memorial token.

Why did Walton tack the couplet to Herbert's eight lines; why did he omit the second quatrain in 1658 and both the quatrains in 1670? Both Grierson and Hutchinson place the couplet where Walton did,[3] but Miss Gardner shows this to be wrong: the Latin equivalents of the eight lines and of the couplet are metrically distinct, though the English meters are the same. She thinks that Walton merely shuffled the lines. Hutchinson thought that Walton's omission of the first quatrain in 1658 and of both quatrains in 1670 perhaps indicated that he doubted their authenticity. Hutchinson himself apparently thought them suspect, for he pointed out that the opening lines of Herbert's poem are addressed to Donne, but the quatrains seem to have been written after Donne's death.[4] Miss Gardner's explanation is more complex. She suggests that on Donne's death Herbert wrote three Latin epigrams. Their English equivalents pose difficulties, for we have not only the two quatrains and a couplet printed in 1650, but also two English couplets which Walton first printed in the *Life of Herbert* (1670) and which, Miss Gardner says, "are plainly alternative translations of the first [Latin] triplet and the final couplet of *1650*." She suggests that either Herbert made two translations into English or that the two couplets in the *Life of Herbert* were mere drafts for the Latin which Herbert then turned into English in the two quatrains and a couplet which appear in 1650. She suggests, too, that in 1658 Walton dropped the second of the quatrains because he had no equivalent English couplet for it, and that in 1670 he dropped the first quatrain because he recognized that it had no real connection with the lines which preceded it. This is ingenious, but not, I think, correct.

Walton's treatment of Chudleigh's elegy, of Donne's "Hymn to God, my God, in my sicknesse" and "The Autumnall," and of Herbert's "Affliction" makes it clear that he frequently quoted only so much of a poem as served his purpose when he was using a poem to corroborate one of his statements.[5] In the *Life of Donne*, 1658, he was using the poems about Donne's seal as "some Testimony" that the happy friendship of Donne and Herbert was "maintained by many sacred indearments."[6] He was not interested in the "indearments" themselves, but in the holy friendship; he was interested in the poems only insofar as they were testimonies of friendship. It is quite likely that he did not particularly care for the poems as poems, for they are much too stiffly con-

[3] *Poems of John Donne*, II, 261; *Works of Herbert*, p. 439.
[4] *Works of Herbert*, pp. 599–600.
[5] See pp. 76–77, 99–100, 336–338, 333–334.   [6] *Donne*, 1658, pp. 82–83.

ceited for his taste.[7] Donne's poem and Herbert's first eight lines are so tightly conceited that Walton would have found it very difficult to give only excerpts from them. But Herbert's two quatrains and his couplet are not so difficult and close packed. These Walton could have omitted. Had he done so, however, there would have been nothing in Herbert's poem which plainly expressed his friendship for Donne. I would suggest that Walton added the couplet to Herbert's first eight lines because he grasped its meaning, liked its sentiment, and thought it a fitting and exemplary conclusion for the stanza. He used the first quatrain because it explicitly mentioned friendship and because, with his slight changes, it verified his belief that Donne was close to death when he sent his poem and his seal ring to Herbert. The first quatrain reads in 1650:

> When Love being weary made an end
> Of kinde Expressions to his friend,
> He writ; when's hand could write no more,
> He gave the Seale, and so left o're.

In the *Life of Donne* (1658), it reads:

> Love neere his death desir'd to end,
> With kind expressions to his friend;
> He writ when's hand could write no more,
> He gave his soul, and so gave o're.

In 1658, Walton omitted the second quatrain because, though it repeated the idea of friendship, the idea had been made sufficiently clear in the first quatrain; because he found it rather too clever; and because his change in the last line (*soul* for *Seale*) had made for a fine conclusion. What needed to be said after Donne had given his soul and given "o're"?

When Walton described the gift of the seal in the *Life of Herbert* (1670), he saw that it would be superfluous to quote at length from the poems. He merely cited two couplets and said that at Herbert's death they were found wrapped with the seal Donne had given him:

> *When my dear Friend, could write no more,*
> *He gave this* Seal, *and, so gave ore.*
>
> *When winds and waves rise highest, I am sure,*
> *This* Anchor *keeps my* faith, *that, me secure.*[8]

The first of these couplets is obviously based on lines three and four of the first quatrain printed in 1650, with perhaps a hint from the

[7] See pp. 76–77; also *Compleat Angler*, 1653, p. 64, where Walton expresses his preference for the "old fashioned Poetry" of Marlowe and Raleigh.

[8] *Lives*, 1670 (Herbert), p. 27.

beginning of the second quatrain, "How sweet a friend was he . . ."
Walton's second couplet is obviously based on the concluding couplet
printed in 1650, which reads:

> Let the world reel, we and all ours stand sure,
> This holy Cable's of all storms secure.

Hutchinson wisely used the word *pastiche* in referring to Walton's two
couplets. They were, I think, manufactured by Walton for the occasion.
I would suggest that he omitted the first quatrain in the *Life of Donne*,
1670, because he so closely followed its last line in the verses which he
made and inserted in the *Life of Herbert* in the same year. He let the
couplet stand at the end of Herbert's eight lines in 1670, as in 1658,
because when he used it as the basis for his own verses in the 1670
Life of Herbert he changed every word except the two which made the
rime. The relative simplicity of the couplets included in the *Life of
Herbert* is much more characteristic of Walton's verse than Herbert's.
The first is even more relaxed than that of Herbert's on which it is
based; Herbert would never, even in a draft, have been guilty of the
"*I am sure*" in the second.

Appendix C

Pages 1-136 in Hooker's Works, 1661-1662

BOOKS I–V are folios in sixes,[1] and the last page of Book V is on page 345 (sig. Rr6ʳ). Sig. Rr6ᵛ is blank, the first blank side in the text of the *Polity*. Books VI, VII, and VIII are folios in fours. To be sure, the blank side may be explained by the separate setting up of the last three Books. The first page of Book VI starts properly on sig. Ssʳ, but while the signatures between Books V and VI are consecutive, they would have to be in order for purposes of binding and the page numbers need

[1] The last two gatherings of Book IV are in fours, but it had originally been intended that they, too, would be gathered in sixes. Except for the misnumbering of p. 56, the pagination of Books I–IV is regular through p. 108. After that it is confused to the end of Book IV. Book V starts on p. 133 and is paged correctly. The following table will help clarify what happened:

1661–1662 page no.	*correct page no.*	*1661–1662 page no.*	*correct page no.*
112	109	119	117
110	110	118	118
111	111	121	119
112	112	122	120
113	113	123	121
114	114	124	122
113	115	123	123
111	116	125	124

The last page of Book IV should have been numbered 124. The gap between this page and p. 133 (the first page of Book V) represents the eight pages that would have resulted had the rest of Book IV been gathered in sixes as planned. The last two gatherings of Book IV are Xʳ–X4ᵛ, Yʳ–Y4ᵛ. The signatures of Book V start with Aa, perhaps evidence of independent composition, for we should have expected Z.

not have been made consecutive. It will be remembered that the first page of Book VI is numbered 137. On the bibliographical evidence, it is not too difficult to assume seventeen missing gatherings.

No satisfactory reason for the odd pagination has been suggested. Did Gauden find more of Book VI when he discovered additional manuscripts for Books VII and VIII, and were 136 pages suppressed after they had been printed? Sisson says:

> There can be no reasonable doubt that the Notes of Cranmer and Sandys refer to the missing first part of Book VI, which dealt with lay-elders in a historical treatment of the priesthood, as we can readily gather from their Notes. And that part of the Book has not come down to us either in print or in manuscript. It was not completed, for Sandys' concluding Note runs thus:
>> Provided that you leave not out such other points touching their new officers and consistorie as are yet unhandled.
> But what Cranmer and Sandys had before them was in an advanced state of composition. Sandys' last Note is a Note upon page 85 of the manuscript in his hands, and what he had was a fair copy written out by Benjamin Pullen and ready for the press, for one of Sandys' Notes refers to an error of the transcriber in the manuscript before him. We may readily therefore calculate the extent of this missing section of Book VI by comparison with Pullen's extant manuscript copy of Book V.[2]

This extant manuscript (Additional MS C. 165 in the Bodleian Library) has been described by Mr. Percy Simpson.[3] Its 229 numbered sheets (Pullen used both sides) became 212 pages in the 1661–1662 *Works*. If Pullen's habits did not change, the 85 "pages" which Cranmer and Sandys refer to were probably 85 sheets written on recto and verso, and would have made about 80 pages in the 1661–1662 volume; an extremely large section "yet unhandled" by Hooker would have to be predicated to account for an additional 56 pages.

It is tempting to think that the manuscript of the missing part of Book VI had been found (and found, too, with Hooker's additions), but it is unlikely, and even more unlikely that it was then printed and later excised. First, more positive evidence shows that Gauden was originally interested only in reprinting the *Polity*, that the part of Book VI which he printed was, indeed, the 1648 text. How, then, account for the printing of the entire Book VI and the excision of the previously unprinted section at a later date, when Gauden *was* interested in new manuscripts? Secondly, Houk argues convincingly that Hooker revised

---

[2] Sisson, pp. 101–102.
[3] "Proof-reading by English Authors of the Sixteenth and Seventeenth Centuries," *Oxford Bibliographical Society Proceedings & Papers*, II (pt. I, 1927), 20–24. See also Keble, II, frontis. and pp. v–vii.

his plan for Book VI; he holds that what was printed in 1648 and again in 1661–1662 was Part I of the revision, and that the original Part I (to which the Sandys and Cranmer notes refer) was in the revision to be Part II.[4]

[4] Houk, pp. 70–72.

Appendix D

The Publication of the
Life of Herbert

IN HIS bibliography of the *Lives,* John Butt refers to the collected *Lives* of 1670 as #7, and to the separate issue as #8. The separate issue is found in three forms. The title page of Type 1 (Butt #8*a*) reads, *The Life of Mr. George Herbert. Written by Izaack Walton. Wisdom of Solom. 4. 10. He pleased God, and was beloved of him: so that whereas he lived among sinners, he translated him. London, Printed by Tho: Newcomb, for Richard Marriott, sold by most Booksellers. M.DC.LXX.* The letters included in the book have a separate title page: *Letters Written by Mr. George Herbert, At his being in Cambridge: With others to his Mother, the Lady Magdalen Herbert. Written by John Donne, Afterwards Dean of St. Pauls. London, Printed by Tho: Newcomb, for Richard Marriott, Sold by most Booksellers. M.DC.LXX.* The title page of Type 2 (Butt #8*b*) reads, *The Life of Mr. George Herbert. Written by Izaack Walton. To which are added some Letters Written by Mr. George Herbert, at his being in Cambridge: with others to his Mother, the Lady Magdalen Herbert: Written by John Donne, afterwards Dean of St. Pauls. Wisdom of Solom. 4. 10. He pleased God, and was beloved of him: so that whereas he lived among sinners, he translated him. London, Printed by Tho: Newcomb, for Rich: Marriott, Sold by most Booksellers. M.DC.LXX.* Butt is undoubtedly right in saying:

Probably Type 1 is the earliest form. It seems likely that, after issuing a few copies with *a,* the publisher considered that the sub-title of the *Letters* (p. 121) would provide a good advertisement, and decided to incorporate it into his titlepage. A few copies were then issued with both titlepages (Type 3), the new one being attached as an additional leaf. Finally, *b* was introduced into the first gathering, and *a* discarded altogether.[1]

[1] John Butt, "A Bibliography of Izaak Walton's *Lives,*" *Oxford Bibliographical Society Proceedings & Papers,* II (pt. IV, 1930), 335.

1. Each *Life* in *Lives*, 1670, has its own title page, series of signatures, and pagination, and on two occasions a *Life* has been found not bound with the others, indicating that each part might be bought separately.[2] It is possible to explain #8 as a reprint only by assuming that Thomas Newcomb, the printer, distributed his type immediately after printing #7. Otherwise, he might merely have run off more copies of the *Life of Herbert* from #7.

2. The title page of the *Life of Herbert* in #7 begins gathering A. This suggests that the printer was sure that he had all his material before him and indicates that #7 is a reprint.

3. #8 has no errata; #7 has. If #7 were the original, why were only three of the ten errata corrected in #8?[3] It is more likely that #8 was the original, and that not only were its errors reproduced, but these three were added. Nor were these the only ones. "Solom." on the title page of #8 became "Salom." in #7, and Crashaw's name, which appeared with his poem on Herbert's *The Temple* in #8, was dropped in #7. Again, #8, p. 22, properly has "an *Amity*," though #7, p. 16, omits the "an" and the errata do not point out the omission. In order to explain #8 as a reprint, it would be necessary to say that here the printer voluntarily took it upon himself to make this change, though he neglected to make others which were pointed out to him. Walton wanted the "an" to parallel the "an *Amity*" which follows in the same sentence, and the 1674 revision includes it (p. 6). Also, the marginal note on the entertainment King James saw at Cambridge reads "*Albumizer. Ignoramus.*" in #7, p. 25; #8 has "*Albumazer. Ignoramus.*" (p. 37). If #7 is considered the reprint, it is easy to blame the printer for misspelling. In order to consider #8 the reprint, it would be necessary to assume that the printer improved upon Walton's spelling. In 1674, the note reads, "With the Comodies of *Albumizer, Ignoramus, &c.*" (p. 14); it is easy to imagine that Walton overlooked the inaccurate spelling of #7. If #7 is considered the original version here, Walton's spelling in 1674 would have to be interpreted as showing his conscious disapproval of the printer's more accurate spelling.

4. The Imprimatur of the *Life of Herbert*, common to both #7 and #8, is dated April 21, 1670. If #8 was hurried through the press, it probably appeared early in May. #7 was published by June 11, for on that day Walton presented a copy to Dr. Neideham.[4] #8 seems to have been printed as a promotional scheme in an attempt to sell copies of the new *Life* prior to its publication in the collected *Lives*. It is not

---

[2] See *ibid.*, p. 334.

[3] #7 improperly has "her" on p. 14, l. 4, where #8 has "his," p. 20, l. 4. #7 omits "Church" after "Parish" on p. 32, l. 22, and #8 supplies it, p. 47, l. 20. #7 lacks "it," p. 49, l. 9, and #8 includes "it," p. 72, l. 3.

[4] Butt, *op. cit.*, p. 334.

likely that the separate publication had Walton's sanction. Walton says in his epistle to the reader in #7 that he was absent from London when it was printed, and he was probably absent when #8 was printed. His apology that he had intended to look over the *Life* before it was made public is confirmed by the errata of #7. That #8 has none makes it probable that he did not see #8 through the press. Walton's words in the Introduction which accompanies both #7 and #8 show without question that he intended the Introduction to preface the *Life* published jointly with the other lives he had written. Prior to mentioning Herbert, he refers to his having written the lives of Donne and Wotton, and he writes, *"I judge it may not be unacceptable to those that knew any of them in their lives, or do now know their Writings, to see this Conjunction of them after their deaths."*[5] Moreover, there is evidence that at least one of his friends anticipated the inclusion of the *Life of Herbert* in a collected edition of the *Lives,* but not its separate publication. Samuel Woodforde's commendatory poem on the *Life of Herbert,* which appears both in #7 and in #8, is dated April 3, 1670, and its last lines have greater pertinence for the collected edition in their reference to the conjunction of the *Lives* of Donne and Herbert than for the inclusion of some references to Donne in the *Life of Herbert:*

> *Herbert,* and *Donne,* again are joyn'd,
>   Now here below, as they're above;
> These friends, are in their old embraces twin'd;
> And, since by you the Enterview's design'd,
>   Too weak, to part them, death does prove;
> For, in this book they meet again: as, in one Heav'n they love.

Woodforde, who had been ordained in 1669 by Bishop Morley and was later a prebendary of Winchester, was undoubtedly aware of Walton's plans. His writing the verses for the *Life of Herbert* less than a month after writing similar verses for the *Life of Hooker*[6] shows that he had a collected edition in mind. That #8 was a sudden attempt to capitalize on the value of the new *Life* appears feasible in the speed with which #7 followed. Probably #7 cut short the sale of #8a, and the title pages #8a + b and #8b may be explained as an attempt to dispose of unsold copies of #8 after #7 had been published.

[5] *Lives,* 1670 (Herbert), pp. 7–8.
[6] Dated "Mar. 10. 16⁶⁹/₇₀." *Lives,* 1670 (Hooker), p. 6.

Appendix E

Walton's Debt to John Ferrar and Edmund Duncon

TWO alternatives suggest themselves to Walton's dependency upon Woodnoth. The first of these is John Ferrar, who survived his younger brother Nicholas by twenty years, dying in 1657. John wrote a life of Nicholas, and it is tempting to speculate that Walton saw it. The manuscript of the life has disappeared, and it is known only through transcripts. Ferrar states that the friendship between Herbert and his brother was maintained through letters, he relates in elaborate detail the daily program at Little Gidding, and he mentions the trouble which Herbert's verses on America caused in licensing *The Temple*.[1] But Walton probably leaned on Oley's "Prefatory View" for his accounts of the friendship and the licensing,[2] and since his relation of the Little Gidding program is less specific than Ferrar's, there is no reason to doubt that he was depending on Woodnoth's oral account. That Walton does not mention Ferrar's explicit remark that Nicholas had to urge Herbert to accept the Prebend of Leighton Ecclesia and to rebuild Leighton Church does not in itself prove that Walton was unfamiliar with Ferrar's manuscript, since he disregarded, too, Oley's similar statement.[3] But there would have been no like reason for Walton to disregard Ferrar's account of Nicholas' early years, which varies sufficiently from his own so that Thomas Baker wrote in his transcript of the manuscript, "See, Mr Herbert's Life Pag: 67, 68, &c: An Account of Mr Ferrar, wch may be corrected from this MS."[4] Walton does not once mention John

[1] B. Blackstone, ed., *The Ferrar Papers*, pp. 33–59.
[2] See pp. 329–330. [3] See p. 330.
[4] Blackstone, *op. cit.*, p. 58, n. 3. Baker refers to *Lives*, 1670.

Ferrar by name in the *Life,* and he may even have thought that John died before Nicholas.[5]

Shortly before his account of Herbert's death, Walton introduced into the *Life* Mr. Edmund Duncon. Duncon was sent to Bemerton by Nicholas Ferrar to assure Herbert that Ferrar was praying for him daily and to report his condition to Little Gidding. Walton reports Herbert's condition through Duncon and gives Duncon's impression of Herbert, saying "*This* Mr. Duncon *tells me.*"[6] Walton says later that Herbert gave Duncon the manuscript of *The Temple* to deliver to Ferrar. "*Tells me*" indicates that Walton had recently seen Duncon, and, indeed, Duncon did not die until 1673. From him Walton may have received information to supplement Oley's story of the printing of *The Temple.* Duncon is never mentioned by John Ferrar in his life of his brother, and he plays a far smaller role than Woodnoth in Walton's *Life of Herbert.* Walton may have visited him at Friern Barnet in Middlesex, to which he was instituted as rector in 1652.[7] This date is interesting; Duncon, unlike his brothers Eleazar and John, was a Puritan.[8] It is doubtful that Walton would have felt congeniality toward him, nor does the *Life* indicate any. Duncon is the source of some of Walton's information, but of little compared to the many scenes viewed through Woodnoth's eyes. At one point Walton seems to fall back upon Woodnoth's information where Duncon might well have also informed him. In the *Life of Herbert,* Walton says that Woodnoth had possession of the manuscript of the *Country Parson* at Herbert's death and that he gave it to Oley, who published it. Walton refers to Oley's conscientious and excellent preface and says that he used it in his *Life.*[9] He probably knew Oley, for Oley was presented to the third prebendal stall of Worcester Cathedral on August 3, 1660, and kept it until his death in 1686.[10] Walton, it will be remembered, was Bishop Morley's steward at Worcester between 1660 and 1662. Still, there is no evidence of warmth between the men, and when Oley published the second edition of *Herbert's Remains* in 1671 with a new preface, he nowhere mentioned Walton's *Life of Herbert* except obliquely in his second paragraph where, "*To do a Piece of Right,*" he says that he was indebted to Edmund Duncon for the manuscript of the *Country Parson.* Despite this, Walton retained in 1674 and 1675 his original story that Woodnoth had given the manu-

---

[5] "Not long after his return into *England,* he [Nicholas Ferrar] had by the death of his father, or an elder brother, an Estate left him" (*Lives,* 1670 [Herbert], p. 68).

[6] *Ibid.,* pp. 66–67.

[7] Alexander B. Grosart, ed., *The Complete Works in Verse and Prose of George Herbert,* III, 259.

[8] *DNB,* article "Eleazar Duncon."　　　　[9] *Lives,* 1670 (Herbert), p. 49.

[10] *DNB,* article "Barnabas Oley."

script to Oley. It is possible that both Oley and Walton are right. Oley did not publish the *Country Parson* until 1652. Woodnoth may well have possessed the manuscript when he talked to Walton and may have thus informed him. Upon his death, the manuscript may have gone to Duncon, who gave it to Oley. It would have been strange had Duncon told Walton the story of his part in the publication of *The Temple* without mentioning his like part in the publication of the *Country Parson*. In Walton's discounting Duncon's information and in his reliance upon the older evidence of Woodnoth, there is probably a gauge of his dependency upon each.

Appendix F

Walton on Herbert's Resignation of His Fellowship

THE problem which troubled Walton—When did Herbert resign his fellowship?—has not seemed to worry Herbert's later biographers. Grosart, who reprinted Walton's first version of the *Life of Herbert* and did not cite in his textual apparatus all the changes made in 1675, does not take full notice of Walton's omitting his reference to Herbert's resignation of his fellowship and merely writes in his own Memorial-Introduction that Herbert's fragile health and the death of his mother in 1627 probably "determined his complete resignation of the Public Oratorship and retirement from the University."[1] Daniell writes, "Immediately after his mother's death, Herbert resigned both his fellowship at Trinity College, and his office of Public Orator in the University, and thus determined all connection with Cambridge."[2] Palmer does not bother with the date of Herbert's resignation of his fellowship, but in successive sentences notices the death of Herbert's mother and his resignation of the oratorship.[3] A. G. Hyde says that Herbert vacated the oratorship in 1627 and "his Fellowship soon after." [4] Hutchinson leaves the matter of the fellowship in the air as he writes, "According to Walton, Herbert retained the Oratorship as long as he did at the wish of his mother, and certainly it was only a few months after her death in June 1627 that he resigned."[5] Summers does not deal with the fellowship, but gives a

[1] *Complete Works of Herbert,* I, lvii.
[2] J. Daniell, *Life of George Herbert of Bemerton,* p. 146.
[3] G. H. Palmer, *The English Works of George Herbert,* I, 32.
[4] A. G. Hyde, *George Herbert and His Times* (New York and London, 1906), p. 150.
[5] *Works of Herbert,* p. xxx.

precise date for Herbert's official resignation of the oratorship: January 28, 1628.[6]

Whether Walton found the actual date of Herbert's resignation of his fellowship I do not know, but the reason for his omitting his reference to it is obvious. Whatever he found, he could not make the date harmonize with the sort of life he was writing. I have already suggested that Walton's emphasis on Herbert's rebuilding Leighton Church was a compensation for his inability to find the precise date that Herbert was made deacon. The date was crucial to Walton, for it would have provided definitive evidence of the exact moment that Herbert surrendered his court hopes. The diaconate did not commit its holder to the parochial life, but it did debar him from civil employment. It was for a like reason that Walton was interested in the date of Herbert's resignation of his fellowship. He knew that Herbert had become Major Fellow on March 15, 1616, and that he had been made Master of Arts in 1616. He undoubtedly knew, too, that the college statutes which governed the holding of most fellowships enforced the taking of holy orders within a prescribed period. Trinity College Statute 19 (1560) provides as follows:

Porro statuimus et ordinamus ut socii qui magistri artium sint, post septem annos in eo gradu plene confectos, presbyteri ordinentur. Quod si noluerint, intra tres menses post spatium illorum annorum penitus expletum collegio in perpetuum expellantur, exceptis illis duobus juris civilis et medicinae professoribus.[7]

According to this statute Herbert was obligated to enter holy orders in 1623 in order to retain his fellowship.

But apparently Statute 19 was not rigorously enforced. Not many years after it was promulgated, Whitgift, the master of Trinity, was thought harsh and arbitrary in depriving Cartwright of his fellowship because he had not taken holy orders after seven years. At about the same time, only two of forty fellows at All Souls', Oxford, had complied with the statutes which required them to be in priest's orders.[8] Sir Francis Nethersole, who was of Herbert's college and who was his predecessor as orator, worried lest so *"civil"* a position as the oratorship might not divert Herbert from divinity,[9] but he had evidently not worried very much about his own obligation to enter holy orders. When he

---

[6] J. H. Summers, *George Herbert, His Religion and Art,* p. 34.

[7] James Bass Mullinger, *The University of Cambridge from the Royal Injunctions of 1535 to the Accession of Charles the First* (Cambridge, 1884), p. 623.

[8] *Ibid.,* pp. 226–227.

[9] See Herbert's letter to Sir John Danvers, Oct. 6, 1619 (*Lives,* 1670 [Herbert], p. 95).

resigned his Cambridge offices in 1619, he had been Master of Arts and a Major Fellow at Trinity since 1610 without ordination. Also, though many fellowship oaths contained clauses which forbade the asking of dispensations from statutable penalties, fellows did ask for and receive dispensations. Such dispensations were repeatedly granted by the authority of the crown at Trinity.[10] It would not have been difficult for Herbert to have held his fellowship after 1623, either by dispensation or through the laxity of the enforcement of Statute 19.

Still, a man of Herbert's ambivalent inclinations may well have been troubled even by a permitted transgression of the statute. He had replied to Nethersole's warning about the secularity of the oratorship *"that this dignity, hath no such earthiness in it, but it may very well be joined with Heaven; or if it had to others, yet to me it should not, for ought I yet knew."* Nethersole was not to worry that the oratorship might divert him from divinity, *"at which, not without cause, he thinks, I aim."*[11] But if Herbert thought that the earthly dignity of the oratorship might well be joined with heaven, Statute 19 enjoined by law that the earthly dignity of his fellowship be joined with heaven, and there is reason to believe that Statute 19 weighed heavily on Herbert's mind as the period intended to prepare him for orders was drawing to a close. About ten months before the termination of the statutable period, he wrote to his sick mother:

As the Earth is but a point in respect of the heavens, so are earthly Troubles compar'd to heavenly Joyes; therefore, if either Age or Sickness lead you to those Joyes? consider what advantage you have over *Youth* and *Health,* who are now so near those true Comforts.—Your last Letter gave me Earthly preferment, and kept Heavenly for your self: but, wou'd you divide and choose too? our Colledge Customs allow not that, and I shou'd account my self most happy if I might change with you; for, I have alwaies observ'd the thred of Life to be like other threds or skenes of silk, full of snarles and incumbrances: Happy is he, whose bottom is wound up and laid ready for work in the New *Jerusalem.*[12]

"Our Colledge Customs allow" us not to divide earthly and heavenly preferment, allow us not to choose between them. Do not these words refer to the stipulations of his fellowship? The fellowship gave him earthly preferment, but adherence to its provisions made heavenly preferment inevitable. But although Herbert knows this and condones it, it is in his present condition a mixed blessing for him. He may well

[10] George Peacock, *Observations on the Statutes of the University of Cambridge* (London, 1841), pp. 96–97, 89–91

[11] Herbert tells what he has written Nethersole in the letter to Danvers cited above.

[12] *"May 29. 1622"* (*Herbert,* 1674, p. 23).

have put off the resignation of his fellowship in 1623, but he was likely sensitive to his ambiguous situation. On June 11, 1624, he obtained, according to Hutchinson, "a Grace giving him six months' leave of absence 'on account of many businesses away'; probably such leave was extended, as there is no record of his taking any further part in Cambridge business."[13] He was given the leave of absence on the condition that he appoint a sufficient deputy for the oratorship.[14] Had he by this time resigned his fellowship? According to Trinity College Statute 24 (1552) the total period of absence from college during the year by a fellow was limited to seventy days; for "justa et necessaria causa" the period could be extended another thirty days.[15] But here again enforcement was probably lax, and the grace of the university for its orator was probably deemed sufficient reason for the college to be lenient with its fellow. Herbert may have retained his fellowship despite his long absence; but, again, if he did, he must have been troubled by his knowledge that he was violating the intention of a statutory requirement.

Walton dropped his reference to Herbert's resignation of his fellowship because to allow it to stand was to reveal to his reader that Herbert did not wish to enter holy orders in 1623, that court hopes were at that time more important to him than church hopes. Because of the kind of life Walton was constructing, it made little difference to him whether Herbert had resigned his fellowship in 1623 or whether by dispensation or because of laxness in enforcing its provisions, he held it to a later date. Although Walton mentioned Herbert's love for clothes, his respect for station in college, and his being a hanger-on of the court during his oratorship, he had not properly emphasized these things because he was determined to show that Herbert was progressively more concerned with heavenly matters. His prime interest was in tracing a chain of holinesses in Herbert from the time he had entered the university. He talked about Herbert's struggle, but he did not give it adequate concrete representation to convince his reader of it, probably because he was himself convinced that an inevitable pull was exerted upon Herbert by the Church. His interest was not in Herbert's resistance to the pull, but in his surrender to it. To present the matter of the resignation of the fellowship at a time when, according to his story, the pull was gradually moving Herbert to an inevitable goal would be to disturb the pattern he was creating. Walton was prepared to leave out evidence which would

[13] *Works of Herbert,* p. xxx.

[14] Daniell, *op. cit.,* p. 88. The forty-fourth of Queen Elizabeth's Statutes for Cambridge (1570) made the obtaining of a formal grace necessary if the orator was to be absent more than three months in a year and ordered him to leave a substitute (George Dyer, *Privileges of the University of Cambridge* [London, 1824], I, 193).

[15] Mullinger, *op. cit.,* pp. 624, 626.

have disrupted his design of inevitability. Had he been completely honest about Herbert's struggle, or, perhaps, had he completely comprehended the nature of the equal attractiveness of the alternatives to him, he might have made much of the date of the resignation of the fellowship. But if Walton did not comprehend the struggle or if he did not wish to emphasize equally the elements which provoked it, he did comprehend the implications of Herbert's holding his fellowship beyond the statutory seven-year limit. He preferred not to let such implications intrude in the *Life,* and he carefully exercised his reference to Herbert's resignation.

Index